HUMAN RIGHTS' IMPACT IN INTERNATIONAL LAW

SELECTED ISSUES

Dr. ION DIACONU

Table of Contents

FORWARD 7

PART I - GENERAL ISSUES 10

CHAPTER I - IMPACT OF HUMAN RIGHTS IN SOME FIELDS OF INTERNATIONAL LAW 11
- *ABSTRACT* 11
- *INTRODUCTION* 11
- *SECTION 1 - HUMANITARIAN LAW - the PROTECTION of HUMAN RIGHTS DURING ARMED CONFLICTS* 12
- *SECTION 2 - PROTECTION of the ENVIRONMENT* 13
- *SECTION 3 - HUMAN RIGHTS and the CONCEPT of IMPERATIVE NORMS* 14
- *SECTION 4 - INTERNATIONAL RESPONSIBILITY of STATES* 16
- *SECTION 5 - HUMANISATION of the FUNCTIONING of the UN SYSTEM of INTERNATIONAL PEACE and SECURITY* 17
- *SECTION 6 - NEW APPROACHES in the JURISPRUDENCE of the INTERNATIONAL COURT of JUSTICE* ... 19

CHAPTER II - JUS COGENS - EVOLUTION IN... 22
INTERNATIONAL LAW 22
- *ABSTRACT* 22
- *INTRODUCTION* 22
- *SECTION 1 - RECOGNITION of the EXISTENCE of IMPERATIVE NORMS* 23
- *SECTION 2 - IMPERATIVE NORMS and the RESERVATIONS to TREATIES* 26
- *SECTION 3 - IMPERATIVE NORMS, UNILATERAL ACTS and CUSTOMARY NORMS* 29
- *SECTION 4 - IMPERATIVE NORMS and the IMMUNITY of JURISDICTION of STATES* 30
- *SECTION 5 - IMPERATIVE NORMS and STATE RESPONSIBILITY* 31

CHAPTER III – RESERVATIONS TO MULTILATERAL TREATIES-CONTINUING CODIFICATION 33
- *ABSTRACT* 33
- *INTRODUCTION* 33
- *SECTION 1 - NEW ELEMENTS of the GUIDELINES* 34
- *SECTION 2 - CONSEQUENCES of NON-PERMISSIBILITY of RESERVATIONS* 36
- *SECTION 3 - COMPETENCE to ASSESS the VALIDITY of RESERVATIONS* 37
- *SECTION 4 - RESERVATION to TREATIES on HUMAN RIGHTS* 38

CHAPTER IV - FUNDAMENTAL HUMAN RIGHTS-ELEMENTS OF CONTACT BETWEEN DIFFERENT LEGAL SYSTEMS 43
ABSTRACT 43
- *INTRODUCTION* 43
- *SECTION 1 - HISTORICAL OVERVIEW* 44

SECTION 2 - THE CONCEPT OF FUNDAMENTAL RIGHTS 47
SECTION 3 - FUNDAMENTAL RIGHTS AS A VECTOR OF COMMUNICATION BETWEEN DIFFERENT LEGAL SYSTEMS 48

CHAPTER V - HUMAN RIGHTS AND THE ACTIVITY OF TRANSNATIONAL CORPORATIONS 53
- *ABSTRACT* 53
- *INTRODUCTION* 53

SECTION 1- CONSIDERATION BY THE HUMAN RIGHTS TREATY BODIES 54

SECTION 2 - OBLIGATIONS OF ENTERPRISES IN THE FIELD OF HUMAN RIGHTS 58

CHAPTER VI - RESPONSIBILITY OF STATES, DIPLOMATIC PROTECTION, HUMAN RIGHTS: A CASE STUDY 62
- ABSTRACT 62
- INTRODUCTION 62

SECTION 1 - CONTENTS OF THE TWO DECISIONS OF THE COURT 63
- SECTION 2 - ANALYSIS in the LIGHT of PREVIOUS JURISPRUDENCE 64
- SECTION 3 - EVALUATION of the INJURY SUFFERED 66

PART II - INTERNATIONAL SECURITY AND HUMAN RIGHTS 69

CHAPTER VII - RESPONSIBILITY TO PROTECT 70
- ABSTRACT 70
- SECTION 1 - THE DEVELOPMENT of the CONCEPT 70
- SECTION 2 - RELATIONSHIP between the RESPONSIBILITY TO PROTECT and the PRINCIPLES of INTERNATIONAL LAW 73
- SECTION 3 - CONTENTS of the RESPONSIBILITY TO PROTECT 74
- SECTION 4 - RESPONSIBILITY to PROTECT and the INTERNATIONAL RESPONSIBILITY of STATES and of INDIVIDUALS 77

CHAPTER VIII - DEMOCRATIC SECURITY, HUMAN SECURITY 80
- ABSTRACT 80
- INTRODUCTION 80
- SECTION 1 - DEMOCRATIC SECURITY 80
- SECTION 2 - HUMAN SECURITY 86
- SECTION 3 - HUMAN SECURITY and HUMAN RIGHTS 89

CHAPTER IX - INTERNATIONAL CRIMINAL JUSTICE 92
- ABSTRACT 92
- HISTORICAL OVERVIEW 92
- SECTION 1 - INTERNATIONAL AD-HOC TRIBUNALS 93
- SECTION 2 - INTERNATIONAL CRIMINAL COURT 97

PART III – RACIAL DISCRIMINATION 104

CHAPTER X – RACIAL DISCRIMINATION - DEFINITION, APPROACHES AND TRENDS 105
- ABSTRACT 105
- INTRODUCTION 105
- SECTION 1 - GENERAL ASPECTS of the DEFINITION 105
- SECTION 2 - GROUNDS for DISCRIMINATION 108
  - A. Discrimination on Grounds of Race and Colour 108
  - B. "Descent" as a Ground of Racial Discrimination 109
  - C. Discrimination on grounds of ethnic origin 110
- SECTION 3 - SPECIAL MEASURES and the DEFINITION of RACIAL DISCRIMINATION 111

CHAPTER XI- ABOUT RACIAL STRUCTURAL DISCRIMINATION, CAUSES AND REMEDIES 113
- ABSTRACT 113
- INTRODUCTION 113
- SECTION 1 - PRACTICE of HUMAN RIGHTS TREATY BODIES 114
- SECTION 2 - The EUROPEAN COURT of HUMAN RIGHTS and the STRUCTURAL PROBLEMS 118
- SECTION 3 - CAUSES and FORMS of STRUCTURAL RACIAL DISCRIMINATION 119
- SECTION 4 - SOLUTIONS and REMEDIES 122

CHAPTER XII - SPECIAL MEASURES AS A MEANS FOR PRMOTING EQUAL RIGHTS ... 124
- ABSTRACT ...124
- SECTION 1 - SOURCES and CONCEPTS ...124
- SECTION 2 - FORMS and JUSTIFICATION of SPECIAL MEASURES ...125
- SECTION 3 - NATURE of SPECIAL MEASURES and REQUIREMENTS to APPLY THEM ...127
- SECTION 4 - POSITION of STATES ...128

CHAPTER XIII - RACIST HATE SPEECH AND FREEDOM OF EXPRESSION AND INFORMATION ... 131
- ABSTRACT ...131
- SECTION 1 - INTERNATIONAL REGULATIONS and INTERNAL LEGISLATIONS ...131
- SECTION 2 - CONTENTS OF RACIAL HATE SPEECH and its EVALUATION in CONTEXT ...135

PART IV - DIVERSITY OF CULTURES AND LANGUAGES 139

CHAPTER XIV - CULTURAL DIVERSITY AS EXPRESSION OF PROMOTING HUMAN RIGHTS ... 140
- ABSTRACT ...140
- SECTION I - PROTECTION of DIVERSITY at the INTERNATIONAL LEVEL ...140
- SECTION 2 - DIVERSITY in the CONTEXT of EUROPEAN INTEGRATION ...143
- SECTION 3 - CULTURAL DIVERSITY in TERMS of RIGHTS and OBLIGATIONS ...146

CHAPTER XV - LINGUISTIC DIVERSITY AND LANGUAGES IN DANGER 148
- ABSTRACT ...148
- INTRODUCTION ...148
- SECTION 1 - IMPORTANCE of LANGUAGES and of LINGUISTIC DIVERSITY ...149
- SECTION 2 - LANGUAGES in DANGER-EVOLUTION and CAUSES ...152
- SECTION 3 - EFFORTS for PRESERVING LESS SPOKEN LANGUAGES ...154
- SECTION 4 - LINGUISTIC DIVERSITY and the INTERNET ...157

CHAPTER XVI – MULTICULTURALISM - TRENDS AND LIMITS 160
- ABSTRACT ...160
- INTRODUCTION ...160
- SECTION 1 - CONTENTS of MULTICULTURALISM ...160
- SECTION 2 - RESPONSE to MULTICULTURALISM ...162

PART V - HUMAN RIGHTS TO A DECENT LIVELIHOOD 165

CHAPTER XVII - HUMAN RIGHTS AND THE PROTECTION OF THE ENVIRONMENT ... 166
- ABSTRACT ...166
- INTRODUCTION ...166
- SECTION 1 - NORMS of INTERNATIONAL LAW on the PROTECTION of the ENVIRONMENT ...168
- SECTION 2 - PROTECTION of the ENVIRONMENT and HUMAN RIGHTS in the ACTIVITY of JURISDICTIONAL BODIES ...170
- SECTION 3 - The PROTECTION of the ENVIRONMENT in the ACTIVITY of HUMAN RIGHTS TREATY BODIES within the UNITED NATIONS ...173
- SECTION 4 - HUMAN RIGHTS and RESPONSIBILITIES in the FIELD of ENVIRONMENT ...175

CHAPTER XVIII - CLIMATE CHANGES AND HUMAN RIGHTS 179
- ABSTRACT ...179
- INTRODUCTION ...179
- SECTION 1 - EFFECTS of CLIMATE CHANGES on HUMAN RIGHTS ...181
- SECTION 2 - EVALUATION of the SITUATION according to INTERNATIONAL LAW ...183
- SECTION 3 - INTERNATIONAL EFFORTS TO RESPOND TO CLIMATE CHANGES ...185

CHAPTER XIX - THE RIGHT TO FOOD AND THE FOOD CRISIS 189

ABSTRACT 189
SECTION 1 - The CONTENTS of the RIGHT TO FOOD 189
SECTION 2 - APPLICATION of the RIGHT to FOOD and the FOOD CRISIS 192

CHAPTER XX - THE RIGHT TO WATER AND INTERNATIONAL LAW 196
ABSTRACT 196
INTRODUCTION 196
SECTION 1 - INTERNATIONAL DOCUMENTS 197
SECTION 2 - RIGHTS and OBLIGATIONS 199

PART VI - HUMAN RIGHTS IN EUROPE 204

CHAPTER XXI - PROTECTION OF HUMAN RIGHTS ACCORDING TO THE EUROPEAN UNION'S LAW AFTER THE LISBON TREATY 205
ABSTRACT 205
INTRODUCTION 205
SECTION 1 - PREOCCUPATIONS of COMMUNITIES concerning HUMAN RIGHTS 207
SECTION 2 - NORMS on HUMAN RIGHTS APPLIED by the EUROPEAN COURT of JUSTICE 208
SECTION 3 - CITIZENSHIP of the EUROPEAN UNION 211
SECTION 4 - CHARTER of FUNDAMENTAL RIGHTS; CONTENTS, SIGNIFICANCE 213
SECTION 5 - ADHESION of the EU to the EUROPEAN CONVENTION for the PROTECTION of HUMAN RIGHTS 215

CHAPTER XXII - THE FRAMEWORK CONVENTION FOR THE PROTECTION OF MINORITIES; MINORITIES IN EUROPE 220
ABSTRACT 220
INTRODUCTION 220
SECTION 1 - UNDERTAKINGS of the STATES PARTIES ACCORDING to the CONVENTION 220
SECTION 2 - The ISSUE of NEW MINORITIES in EUROPE 224

CHAPTER XXIII - THE CHARTER FOR REGIONAL OR MINORITY LANGUAGES 230
ABSTRACT 230
INTRODUCTION 230
SECTION 1 - PROTECTION of MINORITY LANGUAGES according to the EUROPEAN CHARTER of MINORITY LANGUAGES 231
SECTION 2 - COMMITMENTS to PROTECT LANGUAGES in DIFFERENT FIELDS 236

CHAPTER XXIV - THE EUROPEAN UNION'S CITIZENSHIP - SUBJECT OF PROTECTION 243
ABSTRACT 243
INTRODUCTION 243
SECTION 1 - JURISPRUDENCE of the EUROPEAN COURT of JUSTICE 244
SECTION 2 - EVALUATION of the DECISION in the CASE ROTTMANN 246

SOMMAIRE 249

FORWARD

The purpose of this book is to bring together essays on subjects relating to human rights, written during the last ten years and updated in light of new realities and developments. They reflect the fact that human rights are a living subject, meant to respond to human needs in constant change, that the dynamics of the society determine the evolution of norms protecting human rights in different fields. They also demonstrate the impact of the evolutions in the field of human rights in different other fields and institutions of international law.

The subjects were chosen depending on the interest perceived in international organizations and other fora, among the States and the analysts and commentators. They continue to be highly topical, which is proved by the continuous and intense debate. Presenting them in the same book is intended to offer the students and other interested people the possibility to choose according to their preoccupations.

Part I studies are devoted to general issues related to the increasing significance of human rights as part of international law. It is about the impact of human rights in many fields of international law, determining important developments, such as in humanitarian law, in the protection of the environment, in the consolidation of the concept of imperative norms of international law and even in the functioning of the UN system in order to maintain international peace and security. Important norms on the protection of human rights (like the interdiction of genocide, of torture, of racial discrimination) were gradually recognized as imperative norms, including in the jurisprudence of the International Court of Justice, which contributed to the consolidation of this concept in international law.

This concept was also extended, beyond the treaties meant to derogate from these norms, to other acts expressing the will of States, like the unilateral acts and the reservations to provisions of multilateral treaties enouncing imperative norms. The trend to give more emphasis to human rights led also to the recognition of fundamental human rights, a category deserving higher protection, which becomes common to many legal systems, international and internal, and progresses as an element of contact and why not of coordination between these systems.

In the same vein, if traditionally only States were considered responsible for violations of human rights and only gradually respect for human rights was considered as not being limited to a relationship between the State and the individual, more recently guidelines and norms are developed with regard to the activities of transnational corporations, aiming to integrate respect for human rights in their activities in foreign countries, taking into account the increasing weight of these companies in the economy of different States and in the world economy.

Similarly, the codification of norms concerning State responsibility for internationally wrongful acts had to consider violations of human rights, including of imperative norms protecting such rights and, in connection with diplomatic protection, to accept new forms and means of responsibility for damages produced to foreigners as it results from the codification of these norms by the International Law Commission and from decisions of the International Court of Justice.

Part II is meant to see some aspects of the protection of human rights in connection with promoting international security and peace. We refer first to the responsibility of States and of the international community for serious violations of human rights, for preventing and responding to such violations, which became a subject of concern determined by acts of genocide, ethnic cleansing and other crimes against humanity or crimes of war which took place during the last decade of the 20th century in Africa and South-East Europe.

Taking as a starting point an extended concept of security, to include not only its political and military aspects, but also economic, societal and environmental aspects, it was felt necessary to consider practices and conceptions on democratic security and on human security, meaning that respect for democratic principles and for human rights has the potential to offer a better climate of security for States, for societies and for people.

As an expression of the same preoccupations, international fora developed the concept of responsibility to protect, stressing the primary responsibility of States to protect their populations against serious violations of human rights and the conditions under which the international community is called to support a State or to act in such cases.

In close connection with the promotion of international security and the respect for human rights, the evolution of international law conduced to the development of international criminal justice. In different parts of the world, ad-hoc tribunals and more recently the International Criminal Court prosecute and punish individuals for the most serious violations of human rights-crimes against humanity, crimes of war and genocide. Created by legal instruments of a different nature and working in different political conditions, these courts should, as a final result, do justice, prevent similar violations and offer reparation to victims.

Part III is devoted to issues concerning the interdiction of racial discrimination, first of all to the definition of racial discrimination, to approaches and trends in this field, having in view that discrimination on grounds of race in its classical terms is outdated, although it continues under new forms. As a matter of fact, discrimination on grounds of ethnic origin is the most spread around, while cultural differences are now used to justify discrimination on other grounds.

Attention is also increasingly given to structural discrimination, taking into account its historic, societal and traditional causes and consequently its pernicious effects for generations of vulnerable groups; understanding its root causes and the need to use adequate remedies are therefore of tremendous interest.

Measures which can be taken to improve the situation of vulnerable groups are called special or affirmative measures; they have to respond to precise conditions in order to be legitimate and not to become themselves discriminatory, that is to respond to circumstances regarding the situation of disadvantaged groups or individuals, to be proportional to the objective followed and to be temporary.

Racial discrimination can be promoted and incited to by racist hate speech; the examination of this issue is made in parallel with the requirements of the freedom of expression as they have to be clearly distinguished. Therefore, it is necessary to understand correctly the provisions of International Convention for the Elimination of all Forms of Racial Discrimination, the relationship between the racist hate speech and the freedom of expression, the context in which such facts should be evaluated and how the State and the society must respond to racist hate speech.

Part IV of the book presents some topical aspects concerning the diversity of cultures and languages, as cultural and linguistic rights are recognized as important within the ambit of human rights, in an increasingly diverse world. The exercise of cultural rights is important for the exercise of other human rights. Besides, there is a close connection between culture and human rights, as all human rights have a cultural dimension.

Languages spoken by different segments of the population are also very important as a vehicle to culture and education, a condition for the exercise of many human rights. This led to concerns and commitments for the protection of cultural and linguistic diversity, recognized as a value per se, as part of the protection of human rights in their entirety.

A direct consequence of this evolution is multiculturalism, the state policy which promotes cultural and linguistic diversity and by this the protection of human rights; multiculturalism is the only reasonable policy, considering that most States are multiethnic and multicultural.

Part V presents developments in connection with some economic and social rights. The evolution in these fields shows that, although the rights to water, sanitation and food are proclaimed by many documents, and many international agreements are in force for the protection of environment, human rights in these fields and the obligations of States are not directly recognized, despite some judicial decisions. They are underlined both as direct rights and as rights stemming from other human rights, such as the rights to life, to a decent life, to housing and to health.

An important debate takes place in international fora with regard to climate changes, which may adversely affect many human rights and finally human life; a wide variety of commitments are taken to avoid the adverse consequences of climate changes, under the common and differentiated responsibility of States, but the only guarantee of fulfillment is the monitoring mechanism established by the Paris Agreement of December 2015.

Efforts are also deployed with regard to the right to food and the right to water, in a more difficult context related to the lack of political will and to restrictive rules on trade.

Part VI is devoted to the protection of some human rights in Europe. It includes a chapter on the Framework Convention for the protection of national minorities, the legal document on this subject, which is based on flexibility in order to take into account the specific situation of each minority group. Accordingly, each State declares what are the national minorities it understands to protect under the Convention; the object of protection is the cultural and linguistic identity of persons belonging to these minorities.

As for the languages spoken in Europe, the Charter for regional and minority languages, concluded in 1992, is based on the same principle of flexibility, aiming at the preservation and development of languages traditionally spoken in Europe, which are not official or national. Monitoring bodies functioning within the Council of Europe examine reports of States parties on the application of these treaties and address recommendations to States parties.

A subject of interest is also the evolution of the protection of human rights in the European Union, which led from the respect of constitutional principles common to member States recognized by the European Court of Justice, to the Charter of fundamental rights adopted in 2007. The Charter enounces principles and norms covering all human rights-political, civic, economic, social and cultural. More than that, the EU Lisbon Treaty of 2007 provided that EU shall adhere to the 1950 European Convention on human rights and fundamental freedoms.

Difficulties to fulfill this undertaking after more than 6 years are related to the relationship between the system of protection of human rights of the Council of Europe, based on the protection of human rights of the individual, and that of the EU which is more related to the process of integration, and of course to the relationship between the two courts.

The protection of EU citizenship is also considered, starting from cases where measures taken by States are depriving EU citizens of rights granted by the EU law, particularly where the national citizenship is withdrawn which leads to statelessness and thus to lose the EU citizenship. To conclude, respect for human rights remains the key subject in the relationship between the EU law and international law. In this connection, the European Court of Justice proclaimed from the beginning the autonomy of the EU law and its primacy over norms of international law.

More recently, it is for the protection of some fundamental human rights that the Court reacted against resolutions of the Security Council by which sanctions were adopted against individuals and companies suspected of terrorism, without respecting the rights to defense and to a fair trial. This determined a trend to challenge internal decisions implementing such resolutions of the Security Council, if such internal decisions are not in conformity with fundamental human rights or with provisions of the 1950 European Convention on human rights.

As it was already noted, there is a trend for the adoption of specific norms of international law covering different fields of international relations; different chapters of international law are called law of treaties, law of the sea, law of space, diplomatic and consular law and others. They are not different systems of law, but chapters of international law. It is what happens also in the field of human rights. Different human rights are developed through new instruments, new specific norms are added and explicit norms are adopted concerning the protection of some vulnerable groups which extend the contents of human rights and of obligations of States.

Our analyses prove that the general features of international law - the sources, the principles, the responsibility for wrongful acts and others - are confirmed by the evolutions with regard to different human rights. Therefore, the unity of international law and the indivisibility of human rights as a chapter of international law are confirmed by this evolution.

The author.

PART I - GENERAL ISSUES

CHAPTER I - IMPACT of HUMAN RIGHTS in some FIELDS of INTERNATIONAL LAW

ABSTRACT

Although the development of norms on human rights is a new feature of international law, it has strongly influenced both the traditional and new chapters of international law. This evolution reflects increasingly, in different fields, the new standards of respect for human rights as well as the conception according to which the human person is the beneficiary of rights and freedoms, although the norms are accepted by States. Therefore, international law is adding to the relation between States the relationship between States and persons under their jurisdiction, with clear obligations to respect their rights and freedoms.

Following this idea, the study looks at the evolution of norms of humanitarian law which tend to bring the protection of victims of armed conflicts closer to the general protection of human rights, of norms on the protection of environment in connection with respect for human rights, of imperative norms of international law which include the recognition of many norms on fundamental human rights as imperative, on the State responsibility, mainly for wrongful acts violating imperative norms on human rights, and the UN system of security with regard to the responsibility of States and of the international community to protect civilian populations and even the requirement that the decisions of the Security Council asking States to apply sanctions to individual persons should be adopted and implemented with respect for human rights. The international jurisprudence, including that of the International Court of Justice, is also reflecting this evolution, giving more emphasis to norms on human rights and freedoms and to the activity of UN human rights treaty bodies.

KEY WORDS: humanization of international law, human person as beneficiary, humanitarian law, presumption of civilian nature, human rights from which States cannot derogate, protection of the environment and human rights, human right to a healthy environment, imperative norms of international law, responsibility of States, responsibility to protect, human rights and resolutions of the Security Council.

INTRODUCTION

The elaboration and adoption of most of the norms in force protecting human rights took place during the second half of the 20th century, following the adoption of the Universal Declaration of Human Rights. Interestingly enough, important developments of international law in many of its branches took place during the same period of time.

Many of the traditional branches of public international law increasingly responded to the requirements of respect for human rights; this was not only a question of coherence of public international law, but rather reflected social demands of populations that States were determined to transpose in legal norms. This is the case of instruments concerning disarmament and arms control, of norms in the field of protection of the environment, of humanitarian law, of international responsibility of States and of international organizations, of the criminal international law and even the case of norms and practices with regard to the maintenance of international peace and security. The development of norms in the field of human rights led to consolidating the concept of imperative norms of international law, to a kind of hierarchy of its norms due to the importance recognized to the values protected by each of the norms, which influences the structure of the international legal order. Human rights are also increasingly reflected in the decisions of the international jurisdictional courts.

Arguably, during this relatively short laps of time, a process of humanization of international law took place, meaning that the requirement to respect human rights penetrated all chapters of international law and became a criterion for norms adopted in different specialized fields of regulation. The comprehensive approach of international instruments concerning human rights, from the two covenants on civil and political, respectively economic, social and cultural rights, then the elimination of racial discrimination and of discrimination against women, then the rights of the child, of migrant workers and of disabled persons, to the interdiction of torture and of forced disappearances, to the documents concerning the rights of indigenous peoples, of Afro-descendent persons and of those belonging to minorities, gave such a dimension to the protection of human rights that could only influence international law in its entirety. To these, one has to add the regional instruments which, with small adaptations to the local situations, introduced at the regional level this philosophy of a universal approach of respect for human rights and created stronger mechanisms of monitoring.

It is also worthwhile to emphasize the conception on which most of these instruments on human rights are based, differently from documents on international law in general, including a few of those on human rights adopted previously, which regulate mutual relations between States, without any concern for the beneficiaries of the respective norms; the new instruments, while remaining treaties among States, provide explicitly rights of persons under the jurisdiction of those States. The human being is thus accepted as a direct beneficiary of the rights set forth; the object of these norms is no more the mutual relationship between States, which they could treat according to their interests, but to ensure the respect of the human rights provided for all beneficiaries. Every State party to the respective treaties may request that these norms be respected by any other State, with regard to every person concerned; more than that, these instruments created mechanisms to monitor their application such as courts of justice competent to consider complaints against the respective States presented by the individuals who pretend that their rights are violated, or as committees of experts which consider periodic reports of States and, when these States accept it, even individual communications from the persons concerned. A dynamic structure of application of instruments of human rights was developed this way and it is gradually followed in other fields.

SECTION 1 - HUMANITARIAN LAW - the PROTECTION of HUMAN RIGHTS DURING ARMED CONFLICTS

While the first documents on humanitarian law, the Hague Conventions of 1907 and of Geneva of 1929, referred to the protection of combatants- war prisoners, wounded, shipwrecked-, the subsequent documents extended protection to other categories of persons and to civilian goods, thus bringing the norms of humanitarian law closer to those on the protection of human rights[1].

The 1949 Conventions on the protection of victims of armed conflicts extended the protection to civilian persons, to civilian goods and to dangerous installations. They include the presumption that persons who are not taking part in hostilities are civilians and goods which are not military objectives are civilian goods and have to be protected as such. Another important clause of these Conventions is the postulate according to which the protection provided for victims of armed conflicts has to be granted without any discrimination.

The Additional Protocol I to the Geneva Conventions developed these provisions requiring that States constantly distinguish between combatants and civilian populations, which shall not be submitted to an attack; a generalized attack, including bombing of a town or village, is forbidden even if it hosts a military objective. The Protocol forbids submitting the population to hunger as a means of war, as well as the destruction of means of survival of the population and attacks on environment, on historic monuments and art works, on dangerous installations such as nuclear power plants, dams, chemical factories and others similar.

Additional Protocol II resumes many of these provisions with regard to non-international armed conflicts. According to its provisions, all persons who are not directly participating or ceased to take directly part in hostilities have the right to the respect of their person, honour and religious convictions and practices and will be treated in all circumstances humanly; acts such as violence against person, against its physical or mental integrity, torture, mutilation and any form of corporal punishment, collective punishment, taking hostages, rape, forced prostitution, slavery and traffic of slaves under any form are forbidden.

The Conventions and the two Additional Protocols provide also for judicial guarantees against arbitrary measures and give a particular attention to the protection of children and of family life, as well as to the exercise of religious freedoms. One can easily see that international instruments adopted for the protection of victims of war have taken up numerous provisions from instruments on human rights.

With regard to the instruments on human rights, we note that the International Covenant on civil and political rights, to begin with, outlines expressly those human rights from which States cannot derogate even in time of public emergency which threatens the life of the nation (danger of war according to the European and American conventions on human rights), mainly the right to life, the interdiction of torture and inhuman or degrading treatment or punishment, the interdiction of slavery, slave-trade and of servitude, the interdiction to hold somebody guilty for

---

1. Extensively on this issue Ion Diaconu, Human Rights in the Contemporary International Law, theory and practice(in Romanian), 2010, Ed. Lumina Lex, pp. 354-362.

acts which are not considered offences under national or international law at the time when they were committed, the freedom of thought, conscience and religion.

Even with regard to those rights from which States can derogate in time of war, such derogations can be adopted, according to the treaties, only to the extent they are required by the situation and provided that they are not inconsistent with other obligations under international law and do not involve discrimination solely on the grounds of race, colour, sex, language, religion or social origin.

Other instruments on human rights provide also norms which have to be applied in time of war. For instance, the Convention on the prevention and punishment of genocide is covering both times of war and peace; according to the Convention against torture, no exceptional circumstances whatsoever, a State of war or a threat of war, may be invoked to justify torture; after reaffirming the obligation of States to apply the norms of humanitarian law to children, the Convention on the rights of the child and the additional Protocol to it provide the obligation of States not to enroll in their armed forces children under 15 years and to take measures that those members of their armed forces who are under 18 years old do not take directly part in hostilities. Another Convention stipulates the imprescriptibility of crimes of war and of crimes against humanity, of genocide and apartheid.

By the same token, one has to note the conventions concluded in the field of disarmament and weapons control, such as the Convention of 1972 on the interdiction of developing, producing and stocking bacteriological (biological) and toxic weapons, the Convention of 1980 on the interdictions and restrictions with regard to the use of some conventional weapons which are supposed to be excessively harmful or to have indiscriminate effects, the Convention of 1993 on the interdiction of development, production, stocking chemical weapons and on their destruction, the Convention of 1997 on the interdiction of the use, stocking, production and transfer of anti-personnel mines and on their destruction, and successive protocols on laser weapons producing blindness and others.

Obviously, the application of these conventions aims at respecting important human rights, such as the right to life, to physical integrity and to health.

With regard to nuclear weapons, no legal international document was concluded to forbid their use. Nevertheless, in its Advisory Opinion on this issue delivered at the request of the UN General Assembly, the International Court of Justice established that, in spite of the absence of an explicit prohibition of the use of or the threat with nuclear weapons in the conventional or in the customary law, the general principles of customary international law, mainly the principles of humanitarian law, are applicable to any use of or threat to use such weapons and that „the use of nuclear weapons seems difficult to reconcile with the observance of such requirements"[2].

Indeed, the development of norms of international law on respect of human rights determined important evolutions in the field of the protection of victims of armed conflicts, leading to an increased rapprochement between the two sets of norms, to a stronger complementarity among them, which is able to define a higher standard of protection of human rights also during armed conflicts[3]. Besides, international instruments were also adopted in the field of disarmament and arms control having as a final objective to ensure the protection of the world population against the most serious violations of human rights.

SECTION 2 - PROTECTION of the ENVIRONMENT

According to international documents, environment is defined as the entirety of factors which constitute the framework, means and conditions of human life. The first document launching the issue of the protection of the environment, the Declaration adopted by the Stockholm Conference of June 1972 on the environment, refers to „global natural resources, including the air, water, soil, the flora and fauna, including representative samples of natural ecosystems". It is obvious that the deterioration of the environment has adverse effects on the benefit of human rights.

Therefore, a great number of documents of international law, some declarative, others as international treaties, have gradually enounced norms on the protection of the environment, either in its entirety or with regard to its different elements. The World Charter of Nature, adopted by the UN General Assembly in 1982, proclaimed as principles: respect for nature and its essential unaltered processes; the preservation of the population of each species,

---

[2] Advisory Opinion on the legality of the threat or use of force with nuclear weapons, Recueil CIJ, 1996, para. 104-105.

[3] On this issue, Chronique de jurisprudence internationale sous la direction de Philippe Weckel, on the decison of the European Court on Human Rights of 16/9/2014 in the case Hassan v. United Kingdom, in Revue Générale de Droit International Public nr. 4, 2014, pp. 921-933.

domestic or wild, at least at a level which ensures its survival; the administration of ecosystems and organisms, as well as of natural resources, so as to ensure their optimum and continuous productivity. The UN Framework Convention of 1992 on climate change engages States to preserve the climate system in the interest of present and future generations.

The Declaration adopted by the Rio de Janeiro Conference in 1992 on environment and development proclaims among others: the human right to a healthy and productive life in harmony with nature; the exercise of the right to development taking into account in an equitable manner the needs of development and of environment of the present and future generations; international cooperation for eradicating poverty and for promoting an economic international system able to generate economic increase and sustainable development in all countries.

The Declaration of the UN General Assembly of 2007 on the rights of indigenous peoples gives a particular attention to the right to maintain and strengthen their specific relationship, spiritual and material, with lands, territories, waters and coastal areas they traditionally detained or used, including the right to have their own laws, traditions and customs, as well as the right to preserve, restore and protect their environment.

Number of compulsory documents were adopted on the international or regional levels in sectorial fields: for the protection of maritime waters against pollution with hydrocarbons, against immersion of waste or against dumping other polluting substances; for the protection of continental waters against the pollution of rivers with chemical substances, chlorhydrates and other sells; for the protection of the air, concerning the protection of the ozone layer, the limitation and reduction of emissions of greenhouse gas, of sulphur gas and of nitrates; for the protection of wild life, of the plant and animal world, of different migrant species, of natural panoramic beauties, of the natural reservations and environment.

Other conventions refer to substances whose production, transport, distribution and use can produce adverse effects in all areas of environment, including toxic or dangerous substances, waste, ionizing radiations resulting from activities using nuclear energy. Finally, European Conventions like those of Aarhus and Espoo develop the procedural rights of the public, including n g o's, to receive information, to participate in decision-making and to challenge before the judiciary decisions concerning activities which can affect the environment, in fact human rights with regard to the protection of the environment.

The International Court of Justice and the regional courts on human rights underlined the direct relationship between respect for human rights and the protection of the environment and adopted decisions confirming the rights of individuals to a healthy environment, to health, to the benefit of a house, to private life, which can be adversely affected by the pollution of the environment.

In its several General Comments, the Committee on economic, social and cultural rights, created by the respective Covenant, underlined the intrinsic relationship between human rights to an adequate house, to sufficient food, to the highest level of health which could be attained, to water and the right to take part in cultural life, on one side, and the existence of a healthy environment, the security and the quality of the environment, on the other side.

Against this background, we may assess that nowadays the right to a healthy environment is generally recognized as a right of each individual, through a customary norm of international law, a right which is defined by the quality that all factors of the environment have to fulfill, that is water, air, soil, animal and plant world; this construction sends us to different regulations containing commitments of States and to the international practice in connection with each of these elements, which developed under the influence of the requirements of the protection of human rights.

SECTION 3 - HUMAN RIGHTS and the CONCEPT of IMPERATIVE NORMS

As it is known, the Convention on the law of treaties of 1969 defines the imperative norms (jus cogens) as norms of the general international law accepted and recognized by the international community of States as a whole as norms from which no derogation by a treaty is permitted; such a treaty would be null and void. The Convention does not offer examples of imperative norms, leaving this task to the international practice. The last report of the International Law Commission on the law of treaties presents the following examples of such norms: a) the prohibition of the use of force or the threat of force in violation of the principles of the UN Charter; b) the interdiction of any act or omission that are considered crimes under international law; c) the interdiction of any act or omission for the repression of which every State is obliged to cooperate under international law[4].

---

4. H. Waldock, The Second Report on the law of treaties, comments on art. 13, Annuaire de la Commission du Droit International, vol. II, 1963, p. 54.
5. CIJ, Recueil, 1951, p. 23.

In the Comments to the Draft articles submitted to the Conference of codification of the law of treaties (1968 and 1969) the following examples of treaties incompatible with imperative norms are cited: a) a treaty having in view an unlawful use of force in contradiction to the principles of the Charter; b) a treaty having in view the execution of any act which represents a crime under international law; c) a treaty having in view or tolerating the commission of acts such as slaves trafficking, piracy or genocide.

The International Court of Justice declared, in its Advisory Opinion of 1951 on Reservations to the Convention on the prevention and punishment of the crime of genocide, that the Contracting States have no interests of their own, but have all and each of them a common interest, that to protect the higher objectives which are the raison d'être of the Convention[5].

With the same meaning, in its Advisory Opinion on the Legal Consequences for States of the continuous presence of South Africa in Namibia, the Court outlined the obligation of States to cooperate for putting an end to the illegal presence of South Africa in the region, not to recognize this illegal situation and not to support in any way maintaining it. It is appreciated that the legal basis of this Opinion was the serious violation of the principle of self-determination of peoples, on the background of a regime of racial discrimination (apartheid) imposed by South Africa[6]. In its decision in the case Barcelona Traction, the Court included an obiter dictum according to which: an essential difference has to be made mainly among obligations of States towards the community of States in its entirety and those which arise in the relationship with another State, like in the case of diplomatic protection. Because of their nature, the first category of obligations concerns all States.

Having in view the importance of the rights protected, all States can be considered as having a legal interest that these rights are respected; those obligations are *erga omnes* obligations. These obligations result for instance, in the contemporary international law, from the out-lawing of acts of aggression or of genocide, as well as from principles and norms concerning fundamental rights of human person, including those on the protection against slavery and racial discrimination[7].

In its decision on East Timor and in its Advisory Opinion on the Legal Consequences of the building of a wall in Palestinian occupied territory, the International Court considers that respect for the right of peoples to self-determination is an erga omnes obligation. In this Advisory Opinion, the Court mentioned also obligations of humanitarian international law, without naming them[8].

Analysts submit that this evolution led to a kind of hierarchy among norms of international law: imperative norms (jus cogens); norms compulsory *erga omnes* (which would include imperative norms, but without being imperative all of them); norms *erga omnes partes* (from which some States agreed through a treaty not to derogate) and the norms of a bilateral interest, in fact the majority of norms of international law[9].

In its Comments to the Draft articles on State responsibility, the International Law Commission underlines that the notion of jus cogens is at present generally accepted in the international practice, in jurisprudence and in the doctrine[10]. The Commission recalls the examples of imperative norms previously given in its reports and adds to them the prohibition of torture, the fundamental norms of humanitarian law and the right of peoples to self-determination[11].

We note that the International Court used often in its jurisprudence the concept of erga omnes norms and later on that of imperative norms or jus cogens. Some authors held that the two notions coincide, being in both cases norms which create obligations for States towards the international community as a whole; according to other authors, the concept of norms *erga omnes* covers a larger area of norms than that of imperative norms[12].

The international law doctrine, as well as a recent decision of the International Court, uses also the concept of norms *erga omnes partes*, meaning norms set forth in regional treaties which forbid derogations from some of their clauses or from all of them. Even if we would accept this opinion, which is based on the provisions of the 1950 European Convention on fundamental human rights and freedoms and on the jurisprudence of ECHR[13], it seems

---

[6] Opinion presented by Linos-Alexandre Sicilianos, L'influence des droits de l'homme sur la structure du droit international, in Revue générale du droit international public, no. 2, 2012, p. 246-247.

[7] Case Barcelona Traction, Light and Power Company Limited(Belgium v. Spain), second phase, 1970, CIJ, Recueil, 1970, para. 33-34.

[8] Case East Timor, Recueil ICJ, 1995, para. 29; Advisory Opinion, 2004, Recueil, 2004, para. 88, respectively 156.

[9] L. A. Sicilianos, L'influence des droits de l'homme sur la structure du droit international, in RGDIP, 2012/1, p p. 8-10.

[10] Comments to article 40 of the Draft Articles, doc. A/56/10(2001), pp. 303-304.

[11] L. A. Sicilianos, art. cit., RGDIP, 2012/2, pp. 305-306.

[12] L.A. Sicilianos, art. cit, RGDIP, 2012/1, pp. 28-29.

[13] Ibidem.

obvious that such norms cannot be considered as imperative, unless they are accepted and recognized by the international community as a whole as norms from which States cannot derogate.

It results from the examples given that developments in the field of human rights contributed substantially to the consolidation of the concept of imperative norms in international law. The international practice offers mainly examples of imperative norms in the field of human rights; at the same time, different procedures created for monitoring the application of treaties on human rights found their activity on the acceptance and the recognition by the international community of the quality of these norms as imperative, allowing members of the international community, n. g. o's, even individuals, to claim the violation of the respective norms and to raise the issue of the State responsibility for such violations.

SECTION 4 - INTERNATIONAL RESPONSIBILITY of STATES

Initially, the international practice dealt with harmful acts in violation of obligations of international law only as a bilateral relationship between States, even in the case of multilateral treaties (what was called the multiple bilateral). The situation is considered different with regard to treaties on human rights; of course, when becoming a party to such treaties a State takes commitments towards each of the other States parties; nevertheless, the substance of such obligations is not a transaction between States, but a standard of respect for human rights that each State has to ensure to persons under its jurisdiction. It is still a bilateral relationship, but it contains also obligations towards individuals and each State can invoke the provisions of the treaty if another State is not respecting such rights. In terms of the international responsibility of States, the situation is the same with other multilateral treaties, with the difference resulting from the substance of the provisions and from their beneficiaries.

The situation is even more different with regard to imperative norms and to those having an *erga omnes* character. State responsibility for harmful acts of violation of obligations established by such norms is submitted to special norms, having in view the importance of the social values they are protecting. The codification of norms of international law on State responsibility for harmful acts, undertaken by the International Law Commission, takes into account this situation. The UN General Assembly took note in 2001 of the Draft Articles submitted by the Commission and recommended them to States.

To begin with, the State responsibility for harmful acts is not connected any more with causing a prejudice to the State which invokes it, which corresponds to the situation of human rights, as the violation of the norms protecting such rights does not produce a prejudice to a State, but is affecting persons under its jurisdiction. The raison d'être of the State responsibility is not a prejudice caused to a State, but the violation of an international obligation, that is a difference between the behaviour of the State and that required by its obligation. Of course, if a prejudice is also produced, the State's international responsibility includes the reparation of the damage produced.

Second, the norms set forth in the articles elaborated by the International Law Commission provide for different modalities of application of international responsibility for a violation of an imperative norm. The point of departure is the importance granted by the international community to values protected by the imperative norms, their acceptance and recognition as such by the international community of States. Consequently, articles adopted by the Commission include a separate chapter entitled „Serious violations of imperative norms of the general international law". With regard to the qualification of violations as serious, the Commission refers to their flagrant, systematic or repeated character, which aims directly at obligations accepted in the field of human rights. The document elaborated by the Commission provides also different consequences of these violations from the point of view of the State responsibility; the Commission underlines the legal interest of all States that these norms are respected and as a result, the document enounces the right of every State to invoke the responsibility of a State for a violation of an imperative norm. The document also provides the obligation of all States to cooperate for putting an end, by lawful means, to the serious violation in case, not to recognize as lawful a situation created by such a violation and not to support the maintenance of a situation created that way. Arguably, such obligations may result from the concept of fundamental interests of the international community. If as a rule a State can validate by its consent an unlawful act, excluding its harmful character, according to the codification achieved such a consent cannot refer to an act which is contrary to an obligation resulting from an imperative norm.

In its Comments, the Commission appreciates that, in case of serious violations of imperative norms concerning human rights, the State invoking the responsibility of another State may request the cessation of the harmful act and guarantees that this will not repeat, may request reparation in the interest of the State which suffered the harm or of the beneficiaries of the respective obligation, but cannot request reparation for itself, as it did not suffer a damage. The document refers also to violations of obligations due to a group of States and to the protection of a collective interest of these States; the Commission gives to the notion of collective interest a wider meaning, including the protection of the environment, the regional systems of protection of human rights, of protection of groups, of peoples and of non-state entities, as well as the security of a region.

The Commission did not adopt a clause on the right of other States to adopt counter-measures against a State which commits a serious violation of an imperative norm; nevertheless, a general clause does not exclude the possibility for other States to adopt lawful counter-measures, which means that it recognizes such a possibility.

Norms adopted in this field show that even in a decentralized international society there is the possibility to take several measures or to adopt sanctions of constraint, allowing victims to affirm their rights and to obtain at least rudimentary reparation through mechanisms of self-assistance such as the counter-measures and economic sanctions; there are also means to obtain reparation through resorting to national courts; in some cases there are mechanisms of collective constraint (those provided for in Chapter VII of the UN Charter, as well as international tribunals for the application of the criminal international law to individuals committing serious violations of human rights-criminal tribunals for former Yugoslavia and for Rwanda and the International Criminal Court [14]).

The Commission also finalized recently the codification of the norms on diplomatic protection, which offer a framework for action of States concerning the protection of the rights of their citizens against violations by other States.

These provisions give expression to the normative evolution by the adoption of an important number of treaties in the field of human rights and by the activity of monitoring bodies created by these treaties, in particular that of the regional courts on human rights. Analysts appreciate that the adoption of the concept of imperative norms and of its consequences in the field of international responsibility of States had a strategic importance for the entirety of norms elaborated by the International Law Commission on this subject[15].

In connection with the State responsibility, one has to mention also specialized systems of responsibility provided for in some multilateral treaties, particularly those on human rights, which consist of courts or expert committees competent to consider petitions from individuals against their own States alleging violations of human rights and to adopt compulsory decisions or recommendations to the respective States, or to consider periodic reports on the application of the treaties and adopt recommendations.

SECTION 5 - HUMANISATION of the FUNCTIONING of the UN SYSTEM of INTERNATIONAL PEACE and SECURITY

As it was foreseen at the adoption of the UN Charter, the system of collective security of the United Nations is based on the action of the Security Council in case of threats to or violations of international peace and security. Until recently, the problems of threat to or violation of international peace and security were considered only as a matter of conflict between States and of relations among them.

Beginning with the 1990-ties, the UN bodies started to consider also serious violations of human rights in some States and regional areas as threats to international peace and security. Even in the assessment of such situations, preoccupations concerning trans-border consequences of such violations prevailed, such as the potential intervention of other States and the danger of regional conflicts, waves of migrations and others; nevertheless, it is obvious that in such cases an extended use was given to the concept of threat to peace, including serious violations of human rights on the territory of a State. Such an assessment appears in the resolutions of the Security Council concerning the conflicts in the former Yugoslavia and Rwanda, the situation in Iraq and then related to the terrorist attacks of 2001.

Objectives of the UN action in such cases also changed from peace-making to the consolidation of peace, to measures of political reconstruction, to monitoring the elections, which means with obvious elements of respect for human rights. Resolutions of the General Assembly and of the Security Council requested States to allow humanitarian assistance to reach victims of armed conflicts and of natural disasters, not to prevent it, to create humanitarian corridors, or imposed directly the receipt and the distribution of the assistance on the territory of some States.

---

[14] Lois Fisler Damrosch, Enforcing International Law through non-forcible measures, în RCADI, 1997, tome 269, pp. 19-22.
[15] L. A. Sicilianos, art. cit, RGDIP, 2012/2, p. 254.

In some cases, the Security Council noted the persistence of flagrant and systematic violations of human rights and of the humanitarian international law and authorized the use of force (for instance in Libya) according to the Chapter VII of the Charter[16].

Still, international practice and the *opinio juris* of States does not confirm the acceptance of a right to humanitarian intervention with the use of force, in order to protect persons or groups whose rights are violated. This issue was considered by a Commission of high level international personalities; the report they submitted to the United Nations underlined „the obligation of each State to protect its own people" against serious and flagrant actions of violation of human rights, formulated some criteria of substance for resorting to armed intervention for humanitarian protection (existence of loss of human life on a large scale or extended ethnic cleansing) and conditions (a correct intention, resorting to intervention as *ultima ratio*, proportionality and reasonable prospects of success) and advanced as an absolute condition its previous authorization by the Security Council, under Chapter VII of the Charter, or by the General Assembly under the resolution Uniting for Peace (of 1950), or by a regional body with the condition of the subsequent authorization of the Security Council under Chapter VIII of the Charter[17].

The final document of the summit of 2005, called Declaration of the Millennium, adopted on the occasion of the 60th anniversary of the United Nations, underlines that each State has the obligation to protect its populations against genocide, war crimes, ethnic cleansing and crimes against humanity. The international community has the obligation, in the framework of the UN, to resort to diplomatic, humanitarian and other peaceful means in order to support the action of States for this purpose. If peaceful means prove to be inadequate and the national authorities obviously do not ensure the protection of the population against such acts, member States declared their availability to undertake a determined collective action, through the Security Council, mainly in conformity with Chapter VII of the Charter, and from case to case and when needed in cooperation with the competent regional bodies[18].

These provisions are taken up in a resolution of the Security Council which enounces also obligations of States resulting from their responsibility to protect, such as to prevent violations, to adopt legislation putting an end to impunity and punish those guilty of such violations, as well as to create efficient institutions for the application of such laws[19].

In many of its resolutions, the Security Council resumed the requirement that States respect human rights norms. In some resolutions, the Council denounced mass and systematic violations of human rights and serious violations of the Geneva Conventions on the protection of victims of armed conflicts, recalling that such acts may represent crimes under the Statute of the International Criminal Court and that those committing them should respond for their acts[20].

As a result of requirements to respect human rights, important evolutions took place also in the Council's practice with regard to the adoption of sanctions concerning some member States. The Council adopted in the 1990-ties the so called „economic global sanctions" against States like Iraq, former Yugoslavia and Haiti, among others on grounds of serious and systematic violations of human rights and of the international humanitarian law. Realities proved that such sanctions did not hurt the leaders of the respective States, but their population in its entirety.

Such sanctions proved to be inefficient and harmful, having an extremely negative impact on economic and social rights of large social segments of the population. The Council started to adopt sanctions targeting some strategic sectors or some natural and legal persons. In these cases also, the adoption of „black lists" by the Security Council and of the obligation to apply sanctions to those on the lists raised complex problems with regard to respect for human rights, because the Council does not have institutional and legal guarantees for applying sanctions which may represent violations of human rights. The European Union was confronted with such decisions; the Union's institutions adopted a regulation to implement the resolutions of the Security Council, but the legality of this regulation was challenged before the European Court of Justice on grounds of violating fundamental human rights by the adoption of both the lists and the regulation.

The Tribunal of the Court considered at the first stage that it had the competence to control whether the regulation adopted, and implicitly the resolutions of the Security Council, are in conformity with imperative

---

[16] Resolution nr.1674 (2006) of 28 April 2006 concerning Libya.

[17] Responsibility to protect, Report of the International Commission on Intervention and State Sovereignty, 2001. În this regard, Ion Diaconu, Responsability to protect versus humanitarian intervention, în Revista Română de Geopolitică și Relații Internaționale, vol. IV, nr. 1/2012, p. 45-54.

[18] Assemblée générale. Doc. A/760/L.1, Document final du Sommet mondial, adopté le 16 decembre 2005.

[19] Resolution nr. 1674(2006) of 28 April 2006.

[20] Resolution nr. 2085(2012) of 20 December 2012 on the situation in Mali.

norms of international law, but without cancelling the regulation. The decision of the Tribunal was attacked before the Court itself, which decided to cancel the regulation because the rights of persons concerned to a fair trial were not respected and underlined its right to control the observance of the fundamental human rights even by resolutions of the Security Council. This created a difficult situation for the European Union and for the Security Council[21].

As a result, the European Union asked the Security Council to establish a procedure allowing the revision of the lists on the basis of challenges by the respective persons and offering some legal guarantees; EU created its own procedure of examination of challenges with the adequate legal guarantees, for the application of the regulation. The Criminal Tribunal for former Yugoslavia also considered itself competent to control the legality of one resolution of the Security Council, even that on its establishment[22].

The application by the Security Council of some sanctions directly concerning individuals, which may violate human rights, raised also the issue of the competence of the Security Council. As a UN body, it has to respect the principles and purposes of the Charter; its competence is discretionary, but cannot be arbitrary. International, and in some cases national jurisdictions, started to examine challenges to the application of internal laws implementing resolutions of the Security Council which allegedly affect human rights of individuals.

Thus it becomes necessary for the Security Council and for its members to take into account the respect of human rights by the decisions they adopt, having in mind the prospect that these decisions can be submitted to judicial control and eventually are not implemented. Respect of human rights becomes a must also in the field where UN bodies have discretionary competences according to the Charter, and begins to determine modalities and procedures related to the exercise of such competences in order to avoid contradictions between the decisions adopted and with fundamental human rights.

Without modifying the principles of the Charter concerning cases when the use of force is permitted (individual and collective self-defense against an armed attack, a sanction established by a resolution of the Security Council and the right of peoples to self-determination), the application of the system of measures for maintaining international peace and security is submitted to an important evolution with regard to the protection of human rights and fundamental freedoms.

SECTION 6 - NEW APPROACHES in the JURISPRUDENCE of the INTERNATIONAL COURT of JUSTICE

We have seen that, in some decisions and Advisory Opinions, the International Court of Justice referred incidentally to issues concerning human rights[23]. In more recent cases, the Court dealt more directly with the substance of human rights[24]. In the Advisory Opinion on the legality of use of nuclear weapons, the Court considered whether the use of nuclear weapons would represent a violation of the right to life, provided for in the International Covenant on human civil and political rights and in the regional treaties on human rights; the Court noted that this provision is compulsory also in time of war, when norms of humanitarian law are also applied and that the use of nuclear weapons does not seem compatible with these norms[25].

In its Advisory Opinion on the Wall built by Israel in the Palestinian occupied territories, the Court noted a series of violations of treaties on human rights, including of economic and social rights of affected persons[26]. In its decision of 2007 on the Application of the Convention on the prevention and punishment of the crime of genocide, the Court retained the violation by the State Serbia and Montenegro of the obligation to prevent such a crime (without considering it an accomplice), taking as a starting point the decision of the International Criminal Tribunal for former Yugoslavia on the crime of Srebrenica, committed by persons of a Serb origin[27].

---

[21] Ion Diaconu, European Justice and Security Council Resolutions, in Journal of European Studies and International Relations,vol.I, Issue 1/2010, p. 33-42.
[22] Ibidem, p. 35-36.
[23] Ion Diaconu, art. cit., 2010, pp. 33-42.
[24] Supra, p. 5.
[25] Legality of the Threat or Use of Nuclear Weapons, Advisory Opinion, ICJ Report, 1996, p. 226.
[26] Legal Consequences of the Construction of a Wall in the Occupied Palestinian Territories, Advisory Opinion, ICJ Report 2004, p. 136.
[27] Application of the Convention on the Prevention and Punishment of the Crime of Genocide(Bosnia and Herzegovina c. Serbia and Muntenegru, Judgment of 26 February 2007, ICJ Report 2007, p. 43.

In two other cases, the Court adopted decisions which indicate new orientations in the consideration of cases of human rights violations. In the case Diallo (citizen of Guinea), that State acted on the basis of diplomatic protection for its citizen, invoking the violation of his rights in the D. R. of Congo by the arbitrary arrest and expulsion, by submitting him to humiliating and degrading treatments and by the violations of some property rights.

The Court invoked the provisions of the Covenant on civil and political rights and those of the African Charter of human rights and rights of peoples and found that their provisions on arrest, expulsion and detention were violated as a result of the arbitrary manner in which they were applied in the D. R. of Congo. The Court refers, differently from its previous practice, to the jurisprudence of the Human Rights Committee and of the African Commission of human rights and the rights of peoples on the expulsion of foreigners.

The Court refers directly, as the respective bodies, to the violation of the rights of the person concerned, without reducing it to the rights of the States which exercised diplomatic protection. The claiming State is recognized only the right to negotiate with the defending State the amount of the reparation to be granted to the person injured, which is later-on established by the Court itself, as the parties cannot arrive themselves to rich an agreement during the period of time given[28].

It is estimated that treating the case this way, the Court made an important contribution to reconcile the concept of diplomatic protection with the respect for human rights of the individual, to the difference of the Mavrommatis case where the issue was treated only as a relationship between the State exercising diplomatic protection and the defending State.

In the case Georgia v. Russian Federation, where Georgia invoked the violation of the 1965 International Convention on the elimination of all forms of racial discrimination, including ethnic discrimination, support or protection of activities of discrimination of third parties, as well as failing to ensure respect by all authorities and institutions under their control of obligations according to this Convention, the Court adopted, at the request of Georgia, an Order to both parties to refrain from committing or favouring acts of racial discrimination, to protect the rights of populations in the separatist regions according to the Convention and to permit access to humanitarian assistance[29].

The Court accepted nevertheless, at the preliminary stage, the objection of the Russian Federation according to which the requirements provided by the Convention (article 22) to resort to negotiations before submitting the case to the Court were not observed, and did not take a decision on substance. The way the Order was formulated and adopted shows clearly how the Court understands to deal with the problems raised, in conformity with the provisions of the Convention[30]. Another interesting case is that introduced by Belgium v. Senegal, concerning the punishment and the extradition of the former president of Chad Hissène Habré. Belgium requested, as a State party to the 1984 Convention against torture and on the basis of customary international law, that the former dictator of Chad, supposed guilty of acts of torture and other crimes during its violent reign of 1980-ies, who lived in Senegal for some time, be pursued under criminal law in Senegal (also a State party to the Convention) or extradited to Belgium, obligation that Senegal did not respect. Belgium informed that a petition was presented against H. Habré by Chadian citizens before Belgium courts. Belgium found its standing right in this case on the nature of the obligation resulting from the Convention, as an obligation *erga omnes* and as a State prejudiced by the violation of the obligation by Senegal.

The Court admitted the Belgium claim and retained that Senegal violated the provisions of the Convention for not undertaking immediately an inquiry on facts imputed to H. Habré and for not submitting the case for judgment to the competent authorities. The Court did not refer to the articles on State responsibility, but to the nature of the obligation provided for in the Convention against torture, as an obligation *erga omnes partes* and to the common interest of States that individuals supposed guilty are pursued and punished; accordingly, it is enough for a State to be a party to the Convention to be allowed to present such a claim to the Court[31]. It includes also an application of norms on State responsibility for harmful acts codified recently by the International Law Commission, concerning the right of a State to invoke the responsibility of another State if the violation concerns an obligation towards a group of States including the claiming State. The Court seems to

---

[28] Case concerning Ahmadou Sadi Diallo(Republic of Guinea v. Democratic Republic of the Congo), ICJ Reports, 2007.

[29] Bruno Simma, Human Rights in the International Court of Justice: are we witnessing a sea change?, in Unité et Diversité du droit international, Ecrits en l'honneur du professeur Pierre-Marie Dupuy, ed. Martinus Nijhoff, 2008, p. 718-722.

[30] Case concerning Application of the International Convention on the Elimination of All Forms of Racial Discrimination, Georgia v. Russian Federation, Order of 15 October, 2008, ICJ Reports 2008, p. 353.

[31] Questions related to the obligation to prosecute or extradite, Belgium v. Senegal, Judgment, 20 July 2012, ICJ Reports 2012, para. 96 and foll.

recognize by this a special status of treaties on human rights. The Court affirms also expressly the quality of the prohibition of torture as an imperative norm[32].

* * *

Analysts of these cases evaluate these decisions as a substantial contribution to giving a more solid basis to human rights in international law[33].

The development of norms of international law on human rights, through the series of multilateral treaties adopted during the second half of the twentieth century and the international practice, jurisdictional and diplomatic, determined important changes in the contemporary international law. In the first place, new norms of substance were adopted in many fields (called as primary norms) for regulating the conduct of States, which reflect the requirements of respect for human rights, such in the fields of disarmament and weapons control and of the environment protection; second, the concept of imperative norms was consolidated by recognizing the imperative character of an increased number of norms concerning the protection of human rights against systematic and serious violations ; third, norms of international law on State responsibility for harmful acts (the so-called secondary norms of international law) and the international practice reflect this evolution, attributing to imperative norms more important consequences in case they are violated and recognizing the increased role of the international community in the achievement of international responsibility. The jurisprudence of the International Court of Justice reflects more consistently the complex issue of protecting human rights.

Human rights take thus a place of an engine in the modern dynamics of international law[34]. The evolution of norms and the requirements for the increased respect of human rights determined significant developments concerning the substance of norms adopted in other fields of international law. The gradual recognition of some norms on human rights as imperative norms, from which States cannot derogate either in international relations, or at the internal level, led to finally accepting the existence of imperative norms and of norms *erga omnes* in the contemporary international law and consequently to a kind of hierarchy of its norms, at least of those in the field of human rights.

Procedural norms were also confirmed or adopted for the procedures applied within the criminal justice, consisting in the rights of persons accused or detained to receive information and to defense, as well as in the field of the protection of environment consisting in the rights of the public to be informed, to participate in the decision-making processes and to challenge before the judiciary decisions on activities concerning environment.

---

[32] ICJ Report 2012, para. 96.
[33] Bruno Simma, art. cit., p. 737.
[34] Emmanuel Décaux, Le vide ou le trop plein? Le droit international des droits de l'homme, vingt ans après la Conférence de Vienne, dans Unité et diversité du droit international, p. 751

CHAPTER II - JUS COGENS - EVOLUTION IN INTERNATIONAL LAW

ABSTRACT

Jus Cogens-imperative norms of the general international law- is a relatively new concept in international law, launched as part of the codification of the law of treaties, finalized substantially by the 1969 Convention on the law of treaties. Received with some coldness by the analysts in the beginning, it was gradually accepted and promoted by decisions of international and internal courts of justice, even if sometimes under other names. It was also given more substance by the examples of imperative norms enounced, particularly from the field of human rights-the interdiction of genocide, of torture, of racial discrimination, of slavery, but also from the principles of international law-the non-use of force and of threat to force, the right of peoples to self-determination.

The concept was also extended to cover unilateral acts meant to create international obligations, reservations to treaties intended to lead to derogations from imperative norms, as well as local and regional customary norms that could try to establish legal derogatory regimes. The recent codification of norms concerning State responsibility also recognized specific consequences of harmful acts violating such norms, in terms of the rights of all States to invoke responsibility and to cooperate for its application, taking into account the importance of such norms for the international community as a whole.

KEY WORDS: jus cogens, imperative norms, derogatory treaties, obligations *erga omnes*, peremptory norms, reservations to treaties, unilateral acts, customary norms, immunity of jurisdiction of States, international responsibility of States.

INTRODUCTION

The evolution of norms on human rights determined, among others, the definitive consolidation of the concept of imperative norms of the general international law. During the last years, international bodies, representatives of States and international and internal courts refer to the existence of imperative norms of international law[35], give examples of such norms and found their decisions on norms considered imperative.

As we know, the first regulation on this subject was advanced in the 1969 Convention on the law of treaties, the legal instrument elaborated by the International Law Commission (ILC) in the exercise of its mission of codification and progressive development of international law, adopted by the Diplomatic Conference convened in Vienna in 1967 and 1969.

The 1969 Convention looks at the imperative norms only from the point of view of treaties and focuses on the effect of these norms on such treaties which would be from the beginning or would become in conflict with them. Other international instruments adopted subsequently also as a result of the activity of codification of ILC refer to effects of imperative norms on unilateral acts of States, as well as in the field of international responsibility of States and of international organizations for harmful acts. In some cases considered by national courts of different States, with regard to civilian responsibility of States for damages produced to citizens of other States in the context of armed conflicts, the relationship between imperative norms of international law protecting human rights and the State immunity is also approached.

The nullity of conventional instruments in conflict with imperative norms is, consequently, not the only effect of the application of these norms. With regard to treaties in conflict with imperative norms, the concept of jus cogens is rather a preventive weapon, because situations of treaties derogating from such norms are not known in practice after the adoption of the Vienna Convention and States would rather resort to unilateral acts of violation than to conclude such derogatory agreements which would raise a strong opposition from the majority of States. The international practice shows that violations of imperative norms take place mainly through unilateral acts of some States, which are harmful acts subject to State responsibility.

---

[35] A first book on this issue was written as a doctorate thesis, on the basis of the documentation available in the 1960-ies, by a Romanian student at the Institute of High University Studies of Geneva, under the coordination of professors Paul Guggenheim, Michel Virally, Khristina Marek and Denise Bindschedler, defended in 1971 and published in Romanian in 1977 by the Editing House of the Romanian Academy. Other works on the subject were published mainly after 1990, taking into account the evolution of the international practice.

Internal and international courts of justice, as well as regional or specialized courts, have used in their decisions, initially very cautiously and using some general terms (norms of fundamental importance, norms of general interest or which create *erga omnes* obligations), then gradually with more courage the concept of imperative norms and gave examples of such norms. The issue of the competence of the courts in disputes on the application of some norms considered imperative was also raised; this was the question of extending the non-derogatory effect of imperative norms to the clauses relating to the compulsory jurisdiction in cases concerning the application of such norms submitted to courts.

SECTION 1 - RECOGNITION of the EXISTENCE of IMPERATIVE NORMS

Almost without exception, the specialized doctrine accepts the existence of imperative norms (jus cogens) in international law[36]). Even such authors who expressed doubts with regard to the concept of jus cogens itself, accepted that the prohibition of the use of force and of threat to force is an imperative norm from which States cannot derogate in their mutual relations and that jus cogens applies not only with regard to derogatory treaties, but also to unilateral acts in violation of such norms[37].

In decisions adopted prior to the Convention of 1969 and increasingly after that, the International Court of Justice recognized the existence of these norms, while using different formulations. Already in the case concerning The Corfu Strait the Court referred to obligations of the parties to take into account „elementary considerations of humanity, which are even more absolute in time of peace than in time of war"[38]. In its Advisory Opinion on „Reservations to the Convention on the prevention and punishment of the crime of genocide", the Court affirmed that „the principles at the basis of the Convention are…. recognized by the civilized nations as obligations for all States, even beyond any conventional relation"[39].

In its decision in the case Barcelona Traction, the Court gives a more precise expression to this conception; after making the distinction between obligations of a State towards another State and its obligations towards the international community as a whole(which are considered obligations *erga omnes*), the Court refers to „obligations which, in the contemporary international law, derive for example from the prohibition of acts of aggression and of genocide, as well from principles and norms concerning fundamental rights of the human person, including protection against slavery and racial discrimination"[40]. More recently, in the case „Diplomatic and consular personnel of USA in Tehran", the Court referred to the „fundamental character of the principle of inviolability" of the person of the diplomatic agent and of the premises of diplomatic missions[41].

After 1990, when regional and internal courts were increasingly placed in the situation to apply or to take into account norms of international law, these courts gave more attention to the concept of imperative norms in international law, either recognizing its consequences in their legal order or recognizing the imperative character of some norms.

Thus, the European Court on Human Rights (ECHR) examined a civilian law petition directed abroad against a State accused of acts of torture. A citizen of Kuwait, Al-Adsani, submitted a petition against the United Kingdom, as its action for damages produced by acts of torture committed by agents of Kuwait was rejected by the British courts, on the ground of immunity of jurisdiction enjoyed by the State of Kuwait in the UK. The petitioner claimed that the State immunity, recognized in this case, is contrary to the interdiction of torture which is an imperative norm of international law. The European Court recognized without ambiguity the imperative character of the prohibition of torture, as a norm of primary importance, having a jus cogens value[42], citing decisions of the Criminal Tribunal for former Yugoslavia and the decision of the Chamber of Lords in the case Pinochet. The Court admitted nevertheless the exception of immunity, appreciating that this case does not concern penal responsibility of a person for acts of

---

[36] Among the numerous studies on this issue, we note Grigore Geamanu, Jus Cogens in contemporary international law, in Romanian Revue of international studies, 1967, pp. 87 and foll; Ion Diaconu, Imperative norms in international law, 1977, Ed. House of the Romanian Academy; Antonio Gomez Robledo, Le Jus Cogens international, sa genese, sa nature, ses fonctions, in RCADI, 1981, tome 172; Lauri Hannikainen, Peremptory Norms(Jus Cogens) in International Law, Ed. L. Kustannus, Helsinki, 1988; Maurizio Ragazzi, The concept of international obligations Erga Omnes, Ed. Clarendon Oxford Press, 1997; a divergent opinion, quite isolated, Michael J. Glennon, De l'absurdité du droit impératif(jus cogens), în RGDIP, 2006, nr. 3.
[37] Olivier Deleau, La position française à la Conférence de Vienne sur le droit des traités, in AFDI, 1969, pp. 7-23.
[38] CIJ Recueil 1949, p. 22.
[39] CIJ, Recueil, 1951, p. 32.
[40] CIJ Recueil 1970, p. 32.
[41] CIJ Recueil 1980, para.86 şi 91.
[42] ECHR, decision of 21 November 2001, para. 26.

torture, but a civilian action for damages suffered due to acts of torture committed on the territory of Kuwait. In a case of 2007, ECHR retained that „according to article 1 of the Convention on genocide, the Contracting Parties are obliged *erga omnes* to prevent and to punish genocide whose prohibition is part of jus cogens" and that „for the national courts, having in mind that the purpose of the Convention…expressed mainly in this article does not exclude jurisdiction for the punishment of genocide by the States whose law provide for extraterritoriality…, (this) should be considered reasonable and convincing enough"[43].

In turn, the Inter-American Court of Human Rights, in its Advisory Opinion of 17 September 2003 on the situation of irregular migrant workers, appreciated that the principle of equality before the law, enshrined in the Covenant on civil and political rights, enounces *erga omnes* rights and obligations of States towards migrants and has the character of a norm of jus cogens. The Inter-American Court affirms that jus cogens is not limited to the law of treaties, but refers to all legal acts, to the foundations of international law[44]. According to the Opinion of this Court, the principle of equality and non-discrimination can be considered as an imperative norm of general international law, „because it is applicable to all States, regardless of being or not parties to a treaty and produces effects towards third parties, including persons". Consequently, "States… cannot act in contradiction to the principle of equality and non-discrimination so as to cause prejudice to a determined group of persons"[45].

In several decisions, the Criminal Tribunal for former Yugoslavia (created by the resolution of the Security Council nr. 827 of 5 May 1993) retained as crimes of genocide, according to the Convention of 1948 and according to its Statute, acts committed against some ethnic groups in Bosnia or in Kosovo[46]. In the case Furundzija, a chamber of this Tribunal had to decide whether acts committed against Bosnian women (threats, attacks with violence, rapes) by a paramilitary group, with the involvement of at least one public official or which acts as a de facto organ of the State (as it is provided for in the Statute of the Tribunal), represented acts of torture.

Noting the existence of the elements of the crime of torture, as in the cases Tadic and Celebic, the Tribunal condemned the accused for acts of torture and attempt to dignity, including rape, as violations of laws and customs of war. In the reasoning of the sentence, the Tribunal affirms that the prohibition of torture imposes to States *erga omnes* obligations and acquired the status of an imperative norm of international law (jus cogens)[47].

The Criminal Tribunal for Rwanda also judged crimes of violence, including sexual acts committed against Tutsi women (perceived as part of a different ethnic group, although speaking the same language and having the same culture as the majority of the population), qualified as genocide. The Tribunal condemned Akayesu for genocide, including also sexual violence, as part of the process to destroy the respective ethnic group. The Tribunal also recognized that rape and other forms of sexual violence constitute themselves crimes against humanity[48] and that many of these acts are in fact acts of torture using intimidation, degrading, humiliation, punishment, control and destruction of the person[49].

In a decision of 21 December 2005, the Tribunal of First Instance of the European Union (now the Tribunal) had to consider the legality of a regulation adopted by the Council of the Union in order to implement a resolution of the Security Council which requested States to take measures of freezing and blocking the funds of organizations and persons related to Al-Qaeda and to the movement of Taliban. The claimants, Kadi and Al Barakaat International, held that some of their fundamental human rights were violated, mainly procedural rights, the right to remedy and the right to property.

Although the Tribunal did not consider itself to be competent to control the legality of the regulation from the point of view of the general principles of the community law concerning fundamental rights, it admitted to be entitled „to control incidentally the legality of the respective resolutions of the Security Council from the point of view of jus cogens, understood as an international public order which is imperative for all subjects of international

---

[43] Case Jorgic, decision of 12 July 2007, para. 68.

[44] Advisory Opinion no. 18, 17 September 2003, para. 99.

[45] Ibidem, para. 100. We mention this Opinion having in view the position adopted with regard to the existence of imperative norms, without sharing the opinion of the Inter-American Court concerning one or the other of the norms considered imperative in this Opinion.

[46] Case Krstic(Srebrenica), decision of 19 April 2004;

[47] Case Furundzija, decision of 10 December 1998, para. 151, 153; extensively on the jurisprudence of the Tribunal for former Yugoslavia, Sean D. Murphy, Progress and Jurisprudence of the International Criminal Tribunal for the Former Yugoslavia, in AJIL, 1999, vol. 93, pp. 57-97.

[48] Akayesu, ICTR No. 96/4, decision of 13 February 1996, para. 733-736.

[49] Ibidem, para. 689; more extensively Diane Marie Amman, International Decisions, in AJIL, vol. 93, 1999, pp. 195-199.

law, including UN instances, and from which a derogation is not possible"[50]. The Tribunal exercised its control with regard to the respect for the prohibition of inhuman and degrading treatment and for the right to property and reached the conclusion that no fundamental rights relating to jus cogens were violated. The Tribunal affirms nevertheless, with reference to the provisions of the UN Charter, that „International law allows thus to consider that there is a limit to the principle of compulsory effect of the resolutions of the Security Council; they have to respect the peremptory fundamental norms of jus cogens. Otherwise, as improbable as it could be, they would not bind member States and thus neither the European Community"[51].

In its reasoning, the Tribunal outlines, as the Inter- American Court on human rights (case Caesar v. Trinidad and Tobago), the conception according to which the prohibition of inhuman and degrading treatment represents an imperative norm; this is going beyond the ECHR (case Al-Adsani) which considers as imperative norm only the prohibition of acts of torture. Although the decision of the Tribunal was appealed and cancelled by the European Court of Justice, which decided to cancel the regulation for not being in conformity with fundamental human rights recognized by the European Union (without exercising a direct control on the resolutions of the Security Council and without reference to imperative norms), this decision represents an explicit affirmation of the existence of imperative norms; together with decisions of other regional courts, it opened the way of control of internal norms which could be in conflict with norms of jus cogens or other norms protecting human rights, even if they are implementing resolutions of the Security Council.

Some internal courts also affirmed the existence of imperative norms of international law and adopted decisions in cases submitted to them requesting financial compensation for damages suffered by individuals during armed conflicts[52].

Taking into account this evolution, in the case Armed activities on the territory of Congo (R.D. of Congo v. Rwanda), where Congo tried to convince the judges that the Court has legal competence to examine disputes on the application of the Convention of 1948 on genocide (in order to reject the reservation of Rwanda to the article of the Convention concerning the jurisdiction of the Court on disputes with regard to its application), the International Court of Justice made the distinction between imperative norms of general international law (jus cogens) and those concerning its competence.

The Court affirmed that the prohibition of genocide has undoubtedly an imperative character, which both States in dispute accepted, while its competence is based on the consent of parties, which is absent due to the reservation of Rwanda[53]. Analysts appreciate that thereby the Court accepted finally and explicitly the existence of imperative norms in international law[54]. In several cases, the International Court affirmed the *erga omnes* opposability of the right of peoples to self-determination, recalling that this principle is proclaimed by the UN Charter and developed in the Covenant on civil and political rights of 1966[55].

In its Advisory Opinion on the „Legal Consequences of building a wall in the Palestinian occupied territory", the Court affirms that „This construction, which is added to measures taken previously, raises …a serious obstacle to the exercise by the Palestinian people of its right to self-determination" and by this violates the obligation of Israel to respect this right[56]. Noting that the construction of the wall violates also human rights provided for in the 1966 Covenant, the Court underlines that „ the State of Israel has to respect the obligation incumbent to it to respect the right to self-determination of the Palestinian people and obligations to which it is compelled through international humanitarian law and international law concerning human rights"[57].

It is at present generally accepted that there are imperative norms in international law, although there is no agreement on the norms which have this character, either on criteria to determine them, or on their effects in different fields and different institutions of international law. As seen above, international and internal courts recognize the existence of norms of jus cogens and give examples of such norms, most often the interdiction of genocide, of torture

---

[50] Decisions T 306/1, para. 277, 320, 339 et 344 and T 315/01, para. 226, 274, 284 and 289, reaffirmed in Ayadi and Hassan of 12 April 2006, no. T 253/02 and T 49/04.
[51] Ibidem, decision T 306, para. 281.
[52] Cases presented in the Section 4, below, pp. 92-95.
[53] CIJ Recueil, 2006, para. 64.
[54] Phillippe Weckel, Guillaume Areou, Chronique de jurisprudence internationale, Cour Internationale de Justice, in RGDIP nr. 3/2006, pp. 487-494.
[55] Advisory Opinions on Namibia and Western Sahara; decision on Western Timor (Portugal v. Australia), ICJ Report, 1995, para. 88; also supra, chapter I, p. 51.
[56] ICJ, Report 2004, para.122; extensively on this case, Phillippe Weckel, Chronique de jurisprudence internationale, in RGDIP, nr. 4/2004, pp. 1017-1036.
[57] Ibidem, para. 149.

and seldom of slavery, of racial discrimination, of the prohibition of the use of force and threat to force and the right of peoples to self-determination or of norms of humanitarian law-without justifying their choice, sometimes incidentally, without advancing the consequences of such norms or retaining different consequences.

Looking for methods to use for determining imperative norms and their effects, one author analyses the deductive approach (without resorting to international practice), the semi-deductive approach (according to which some aspects of jus cogens are proved on the basis of the international practice, while others are deducted logically) and the inductive, empiric one, based on international practice. Some authors mentioned opt for the inductive approach, considering that the imperative character of an imperative norm must be determined on the basis of the examination of international practice, of its recognition by States and by international bodies and institutions as a norm from which States cannot derogate in their relationships[58]. They extend this method also to the consequences of the imperative norms in different fields of international law[59].

Nevertheless, using this method, Carlo Focarelli concludes that there would be no difference between imperative norms and customary norms of international law, because the examination of the international practice is also the method used to establish the existence of a customary norm. It is our firm opinion that the use of the same method to establish the existence, the contents and the consequences of imperative norms and of customary norms is not a valid argument conducing to such a conclusion, because in this case we have in mind the international practice on the recognition of the imperative character of a norm which is already a customary and/or conventional norm.

According to the definition given in article 53 of the Convention on the law of treaties, such a norm has to be accepted and recognized by the international community as a whole as a norm from which States cannot derogate; the requirement of acceptation and recognition leads us directly to the international practice concerning the interdiction to derogate from the norm and to the inductive approach. The object of acceptance and recognition is different from that concerning customary norms. This does not mean that imperative norms cannot be distinguished from other customary norms, from which States can derogate in their relationships.

SECTION 2 - IMPERATIVE NORMS and the RESERVATIONS to TREATIES

Vienna Convention defines this concept in its relationship with treaties which would derogate from imperative norms, meaning that such treaties are void if they are in conflict with an imperative norm or become void when a new imperative norm emerges with which they are in conflict.

There is no reference in the Convention to the relationship between reservations to multilateral treaties and imperative norms. A reservation to a treaty is a unilateral declaration made by a State when becoming a party to a treaty, whereby it purports to exclude or to modify the legal effect of a provision of the treaty in its application to that State. On this issue, the Convention makes it explicit what reservations are not acceptable: those expressly prohibited; those implicitly prohibited (by accepting reservations only to other provisions); those which are incompatible with the object and purpose of the treaty. The Convention also provides that other States may accept the reservation formulated by a State or may object to it (articles 20 and 21); if a State accepts the reservation, the provision concerned is applied between the two States according to the reservation; if a State raises an objection to a reservation, the provision concerned by the reservation does not apply between the two States to the extent of the reservation; a State objecting to a reservation may oppose to the entry into force between itself and the reserving State of the treaty and in such a case the treaty is not applicable between them. If all States object to a reservation, the reserving State does not become a party to the treaty. A reservation is considered as accepted by a State if it does not raise an objection during a period of 12 months since the reservation was notified. The Convention does not provide a procedure to establish whether a reservation is contrary to the object and the purpose of the treaty.

From the point of view of the imperative norms, in view of their importance and of the fact that they are accepted and recognized as such by the international community, it is difficult to consider that they would not be part of the object and the purpose of the treaty enouncing them. Consequently, a reservation to a provision of a multilateral treaty giving expression to such a norm would be in conflict with the object and the purpose of the treaty. On this issue, the Human Rights Committee affirms in its General Comment nr. 24 of 1994 that „The provisions of

---

[58] This method was advanced in 1971, in the doctorate thesis submitted to the Institute of High International Studies of Geneva, then taken up in 1977 by Ion Diaconu, in the book Imperatve norms in international law, where the prohibition of the use of force and of threat to force and of slavery are examined as examples of imperative norms, on the bases of international practice of that period of time. Similarly Carlo Focarelli, art. cit., pp. 780-785.

[59] Ibidem, Carlo Focarelli.

the Covenant which represent customary international law (and *a fortiori* those who have the character of imperative norms) cannot make the object of reservations"[60].

This conclusion is perfectly valid, because the mere formulation of a reservation purports to exclude or to limit the application of the respective norm in the relationships with other States parties, and thereby to create a regime which would be contrary to the imperative norm. Accepting such a reservation expressly or by not raising objections to it leads to creating such a bilateral derogatory regime, in conflict with the imperative norm[61]. Difficulties appeared because different treaties and the general international law did not envisage procedures to determine that a reservation conflicts with an imperative norm and to declare unacceptable such a reservation. The method of objections to reservations, as noted above, is not solving the problem.

A major difficulty appeared with regard to treaties concerning human rights, because the principle of universality of human fundamental rights and freedoms opposes to reservations restraining the benefit of some rights and freedoms by the unilateral decision of a State. At the same time, the central concern was and remains to see that an increasing number of States take the commitment to respect these rights and freedoms; therefore, objections to these reservations (very numerous to some of the treaties) are not aiming at excluding the application of the treaties to reserving States, but to determine them to reconsider and withdraw the reservations.

In its General Comment, the Human Rights Committee affirms that a State cannot reserve its right to practice slavery or torture, to subject persons to cruel, inhuman or degrading treatment, to deprive them arbitrarily of life, to arrest and detain them arbitrarily, to deny their right to the freedom of thought, conscience and religion and others. Nevertheless, the Committee recognizes that there is no automatic correlation between reservations which are contrary to the object and purpose of a treaty and reservations to imperative norms, and affirms expressly that the prohibition of torture and depriving arbitrarily of life a person are imperative norms[62].

Therefore, there cannot be confusion between customary norms in their entirety and norms of jus cogens, which are much less numerous, according to the definition given by the Vienna Convention and accepted in the international practice.

Some regional courts, such as ECHR, are competent to examine the validity of reservations to treaties whose application they are monitoring and to reject those they consider unacceptable. Such competences are not recognized by other international treaties in this field. Some committees created for monitoring the application of the respective treaties (Human Rights Committee for the Covenant on civil and political rights, followed by other similar committees) considered that their attributions to examine the application of treaties by States parties include also the evaluation of the validity of reservations to the respective treaties and decided to ignore some reservations, considering that the States concerned are obliged by all the provisions of the treaties.

This conception was not accepted by some States parties and by the International Law Commission. In successive reports[63], the Commission affirmed that a reservation forms an integral part of the ratification by the reserving State of the treaty; a treaty body for human rights, created by the treaty, can appreciate whether a reservation is in conflict with the object and the purpose of the treaty, but its opinion on this issue has the same legal value as the conclusions concerning the application of the treaty by the respective State. If the treaty body has the competence to adopt binding decisions concerning the violation of the treaty by a State, that implies also the competence to declare invalid reservations to the treaty and to ignore them (the case of ECHR); if such a body can adopt only recommendations concerning the application of the treaty, its opinion on reservations will have the same legal value.

In 2011, in its final report, the Commission adopted Guidelines with regard to the Practice of Reservations to Treaties, submitted to the UN General Assembly[64], where it maintains its opinion expressed in the preliminary report. The Commission enounces the basic rule, according to which reservations in conflict with the object and the purpose of the treaty are not permitted, and explains that this means affecting an important element of the treaty which is essential in its general economy and the raison d'être of the treaty.

The Guidelines affirm that a reservation to a provision of a treaty which gives expression to an imperative norm of the general international law (jus cogens) does not affect the binding character of that provision, which will

---

[60] Human Rights Committee, General Comment no. 24/1994, doc. HRI/GEN/1/Rev. 9(vol. I), p.249.

[61] Similarly by Su Wei, Reservations to treaties and some practical issues, in Asian Yearbook of International Law, vol. 7, 1999, p. 133.

[62] General Comment 24/1994, doc. HRI/GEN/1/Rev. 9, vol. I, p. 250.

[63] A first report, Preliminary Conclusions with regard to reservations to multilateral normative treaties, including those on human rights, Ass. Gen. Doc. Fifty-second session, Suppl. No. 10(A/52/10); the last report, doc. A/CN.4/647 of 26 May 2011.

[64] Report of the Commission, submitted to the General Assembly (doc. Suppl. 10(A/66/10).

continue to apply between the reserving State and other States or international organizations. It is also stated that a reservation cannot exclude or modify the legal effect of a treaty in a manner contrary to an imperative norm.

Although it is said that reservations are allowed to customary norms provided for in the treaties, it is outlined that reservations are not allowed to provisions of a treaty concerning human rights from which derogations are not admitted in any circumstances, except the case when the reservation is compatible with the essential rights and obligations resulting from the treaty. Without underlining in particular, the place of imperative norms in the context of reservations to treaties, the Guidelines affirm with clarity the inadmissibility of reservations to those provisions of treaties which enounce imperative norms.

With regard to the admissibility of reservations to treaties, the Guidelines affirm that bodies created for monitoring the application of treaties can undertake such an evaluation, when exercising their attributions, but it has the same value as the act containing the evaluation (if this is a recommendation, the evaluation has the same value). The Commission maintained its opinion, but recommends to reserving States to give attention to such evaluations[65].

Some court decisions and some analysts launched a discussion on the validity of reservations to those provisions of treaties concerning compulsory jurisdiction of the International Court of Justice or the competence of other bodies to receive and consider individual claims on violations of human rights, mainly in cases where a violation of an imperative norm is invoked[66].

At the European level, ECHR affirmed in the case Belilos, in the name of European public order, the lack of validity of the declaration by Switzerland having the effect of a reservation, considered contrary to the 1950 Convention and in 1995, in the case Loisidou, the lack of validity of restrictions *ratione loci* and *ratione materiae* adopted by Turkey with regard to the application of the Convention to Northern Cyprus[67].

The Human Rights Committee examined the individual complaint of Kennedy v. Trinidad and Tobago, following the formulation by that State of a reservation to Protocol nr 1 to the Covenant on civil and political rights, declaring that it does not accept the examination of complaints by detainees condemned to capital punishment. The Committee declared the reservation incompatible with the object and the purpose of the Protocol and treated it separately from the act of ratification, examining the substance of the complaint[68].

Similarly, the Inter-American Court of human rights, in the case Ivcher Bronstein, did not accept the withdrawal of the acceptance of the optional clause on the jurisdiction of the Court, having in view the authority of treaties on human rights, based on the acceptance by States of higher common values, which entail also a special regime of provisions on the compulsory jurisdiction, which cannot be submitted to subsequent unilateral acts of States[69].

A different solution was given by the International Court of Justice in the case „Armed activities on the territory of Congo", where Rwanda invoked its reservation to the clause concerning the compulsory jurisdiction of the Court contained in the 1948 Convention on genocide, while D. R. Congo held that this reservation is contrary to a norm of jus cogens. The Court maintained its opinion from the Advisory Opinion on reservations to the Convention on genocide, according to which such reservations are not incompatible with the object and purpose of the respective treaty and therefore did not consider the relationship between the compulsory jurisdiction and the application of imperative norms enounced in treaties[70].

On this issue, the Guidelines on the Practice on Reservation to Treaties, adopted by the International Law Commission, states that reservations to provisions which set up mechanisms for the solution of disputes or for monitoring the application of treaties are not per se incompatible with the object and the purpose of a treaty, unless they purport to exclude or to modify the legal effect of an essential provision for the raison d'être of the treaty or to exclude the application of a means of solution of disputes or of monitoring of application, which is the mere object of the respective treaty.

---

[65] On the issue of reservations in general, sub, chapter III, pp.

[66] Extensively on this subject Gerard Cohen-Jonathan, Les réserves dans les traités institutionnels relatifs aux droits de l'homme. Nouveaux aspects européens et internationaux, în RGDIP, 1996, no. 4, pp. 915-948.

[67] Case Belilos, decision of 29 Aprilie 1988, prezented by Vincent Berger, Jurisprudence of the ECHR, fourth edition, 2002, IRDO(in Romanian), pp. 182-185; case Loisidou, decision of 23 March 1995, Serie A, no 310.

[68] Communication no. 845/1999, CCPR/C67/D/845/1999-31-12-1999.

[69] Decision of 24 September 1999 on the competence; Series C, no. 54.

[70] On this subject Ph. Weckel and G. Areou, Chronique de jurisprudence internationale, in RGDIP, 2006, no. 3, pp. 487-497.

SECTION 3 - IMPERATIVE NORMS, UNILATERAL ACTS and CUSTOMARY NORMS

The issue of unilateral acts was considered as an item by the International Law Commission since 1947. It was clear that most of the unilateral acts in international law are related to the conclusion, the application, the suspension or the termination of treaties, or for instance with regard to the length of the territorial sea till 12 marine miles; they are considered within the law of treaties, as it results from the 1969 Convention on the law of treaties. Of course, reservations to multilateral treaties are also unilateral acts and we approached in the previous section their relationship with imperative norms.

Violations of imperative norms through actions or omissions of States or of international organizations (as forms of their conduct) can also be examined within the overall subject of unilateral acts, but their relationship with imperative norms is treated as part of the issue of State responsibility for harmful acts. Other unilateral acts are the public statements of States (as expression of their will), which affirm their obligations or rights and which can be in conflict with imperative norms.

In view of the different opinions and the complexity of the issue, the Commission decided in 2004 to give priority to the consideration of unilateral acts under the form of public statements as expression of the will of States to take upon themselves obligations under international law. Consequently, in 2006 the Commission adopted Guiding Principles concerning unilateral statements of States susceptible to create international obligations, which were submitted to the UN General Assembly. The document adopted affirms from the beginning that statements made public through which a State manifests its will to assume an obligation have the effect to create legal obligations[71]. After enouncing the conditions of form to be fulfilled by such acts, the Guiding Principles affirm that a unilateral declaration which conflicts with an imperative norm of international law is void. In its decision on the case „Armed activities on the territory of Congo", the International Court of Justice did not exclude the possibility to invalidate a unilateral declaration of the State of Rwanda as conflicting with an imperative norm, but appreciated that it was not the case[72].

The specialized doctrine examines also the relationship between imperative norms and customary norms of international law. With regard to customary norms of a regional or local sphere of application, it is estimated, on the basis of analogy with the situation of treaties, that such norms are void if they are in conflict with an imperative norm of the general international law from which no derogation is permitted. Having in view the elements which lead to a customary norm, one has to admit that, if there is an imperative norm accepted and recognized as such by the international community, a practice opposed to this norm cannot be recognized as producing legal effects; accepting such legal effects would mean in fact a derogation. On the other side, in is difficult to accept that in the presence of an imperative norm recognized as such, an *opinio juris* could be formed to lead to a customary regional or local norm in conflict with the imperative norm, that is to a regime derogating from it[73]. If unilateral acts and the treaties inter se incompatible with an imperative norm are void, how could they, as elements of the international practice, lead to a valid regime derogatory from that norm.

Some authors examine also whether a customary norm of a universal application and of a dispositive character could exist (a norm from which derogations are permitted) which would be against an imperative norm and what would be the relationship between them. The author concludes that, as both norms are universal, having the same degree of generality, there would not be a problem of hierarchy between them and there would not be an issue of conflict, but one of interpretation. The conclusion of the author is that a customary norm of a universal application could exist, in spite of being in conflict with an imperative norm; as the imperative norm can be replaced only by a new imperative norm, it would for some time at least coexist with a dispositive customary norm[74].

In our opinion, it is only a school hypothesis, which leaves aside the fact that customary norms are formed on the basis of an international practice of a certain generality, accepted as a norm of law following the evolution of opinion of the subjects of law. It is difficult to foresee that such a practice could develop and could acquire a certain generality, in opposition with an imperative norm recognized and accepted as such by the international community.

One should probably examine the evolution of one of the imperative norms recognized as such and see if such an evolution could be likely to take place and could be accepted. Each norm of international law, including the

---

[71] The Commission took as a point of departure the obiter dictum of the International Court of Justice in the case Nuclear Tests of 1974, where it retained the official statement of the President of France concerning the cessation of nuclear tests in the air, as well as from the statement of Egypt in 1957 concerning the Suez Channel.

[72] R.D. Congo v. Rwanda, Jurisdiction and Admissibility, Report 2002, para. 69.

[73] Robert Kolb, Nullité, inapplicabilité ou inexistence d'une norme coutumière contraire au jus cogens universel?, dans RGDIP, no. 1, 2012, pp. 293-296.

[74] Ibidem, Robert Kolb, art. cit., pp. 284-293.

imperative norms, may present many aspects and may create multiple legal relationships; some of them can be clarified, completed, even modified by subsequent rules, without thereby changing the nature of the imperative norm. With regard to the non-use of force and of the threat with force, beyond the two circumstances where the use of armed force against another State is explicitly provided for in the UN Charter (self-defense against an armed attack and as a measure taken by the Security Council for maintaining international peace and security), a third valid ground was recognized, also on the basis of the Charter, which is the right of peoples struggling for self-determination to resort to armed force and to receive support in their struggle.

But attempts to admit exceptions form that imperative norm (in the defense of human rights, for humanitarian purposes or others) were not accepted by the majority of States; several acts of violation of the principle of non-use of force and of threat with force were rejected by other States as illegal and could not lead to new customary norms. With regard to such norms in the field of human rights, as the prohibition of genocide, of slavery or of torture, of the racial discrimination, it is difficult to foresee the development of contrary practices accepted and leading to customary norms, even local or regional.

SECTION 4 - IMPERATIVE NORMS and the IMMUNITY of JURISDICTION of STATES

Several internal and international jurisdictions had to solve cases where the violation of imperative norms was invoked in order to obtain civilian reparation for damages suffered by individuals during armed conflicts. The States accused invoked the State immunity of jurisdiction. Some judicial courts rejected this exception, as being contrary to the imperative norm affected; others accepted it, finding the case admissible, but without judging on substance.

The Greek courts were the first to invoke an imperative norm in order to adopt a restrictive conception on the State immunity of jurisdiction, denying the immunity of Germany for facts committed by the German army during the Second World War. In the case Prefecture of Voiotia v. Federal Republic of Germany of 2000[75], the Supreme Court of Justice of Greece examined a petition against the decision taken by the court district of Livadia, which granted material compensation for the atrocities committed by the German troops of occupation in the village of Distomo, in June 1944.

The Supreme Court invoked the European Convention on the immunity of States of 1972, according to which a State cannot pretend immunity in case of acts producing harm to physical integrity of persons or to private property, as well as decisions given by American courts on the basis of an amendment of 1996 to the Law on foreign State immunity of 1976, which refused to foreign States immunity in cases of claims concerning financial compensation for damages produced by acts of torture (case Letelier v. Chile and Liu v. People's Republic of China)[76]. The Greek court considered that the facts committed constituted crimes against humanity and violations of imperative norms of international law and therefore cannot be opposed the immunity of jurisdiction of States.

Similarly, the Italian Court of Cassation reaffirmed in 2008 the conclusion reached by a preliminary decision of 2004 in the case Ferrini (complaint of an Italian citizen deported in Germany, obliged to work for the weapons industry and submitted to inhuman treatment), according to which a State that committed international crimes does not have the right to State immunity and affirmed the primacy of imperative norms on other norms of international law[77].

To the opposite, in the case Al-Adsani v. United Kingdom, where the British courts rejected the request of a Kuwaiti citizen to receive damages for acts of torture committed against him in Kuwait on ground of State immunity of jurisdiction, the European Court on Human Rights recognized the imperative character of the prohibition of torture, but did not agree to remove the immunity of jurisdiction of the State in case of a civilian action before other courts than those where facts imputed took place. The Court appreciated that there is no norm of international law requesting to give up the State immunity in the case of civilian actions[78].

Similarly, in the case Jones, the Chamber of Lords did not agree to remove the immunity of the defending State as an effect of the imperative character of the prohibition of torture[79]. In the case Yeroda („Mandate of arrest" of 11 April 2000, D. R. Congo v. Belgium), where Belgium invoked the implication of the Congolese minister of foreign affairs in the commission of crimes of war and crimes against humanity, in violation of imperative norms, the

---

[75] Prefecture of Voiotia v. Federal Republic of Germany, Case no. 11/2000, decision of May 4, 2000, presented in International Decisions, AJIL, vol. 93, 2001, pp. 198-204; a critical approach by Carlo Focarelli, Immunité des Etats et Jus Cogens, in RGDIP, 2008, nr. 4, pp. 766-780 and Christian Tomuschat, L'immunité des Etats en cas de violation grave des droits de l'homme, in RGDIP, 2005, 1, pp. 51-73.
[76] Cited in AJIL, vol. 93, 2001, p. 199.
[77] Presented by Carlo Focarelli, art. cit., pp. 765-773.
[78] Analysis undertaken by Carlo Focarelli, art. cit., pp.761-793.
[79] Jones v. Ministry of Interior of the Kingdom of Saudi Arabia, presented in AJIL, vol. 100, 2006, pp. 910-908.

International Court of Justice accepted that there is full immunity of jurisdiction of the minister of foreign affairs, resulting from its mission of representation of the State. In individual opinions, some judges did not accept this solution, holding that the immunity of jurisdiction of the minister of foreign affairs is not an imperative norm[80].

The Supreme Court of the New Zeeland accepted the imperative character of the interdiction of torture, but did not admit that it would imply as an element the interdiction of refoulement[81].

One must retain that in all these cases the courts affirmed the imperative character of the norms invoked - prohibition of torture, crimes of war and crimes against humanity, but accepted the exception of State immunity of jurisdiction before courts of another State (an exception *ratione personae*, not *ratione materiae*). This is not an opposition on substance between two norms, which would diminish, replace or remove the application of an imperative norm by another customary norm of international law. The norm of State immunity of jurisdiction comes into place at the stage of the examination of the competence of jurisdiction, while recognizing the validity of the imperative norm invoked with regard to the substance of the claim.

SECTION 5 - IMPERATIVE NORMS and STATE RESPONSIBILITY

As a result of the acceptance and the recognition of imperative norms as norms from which States cannot derogate in their relationships, these norms have also different effects in the context of State responsibility for wrongful acts. This concerns also the responsibility of international organizations, as subjects of international law, when they commit wrongful acts. The wrongful act is defined similarly in case of violation of international obligations, irrespective of whether they have as a source an imperative norm or a norm having a dispositive character; it is defined as a conduct attributed to the State or to the international organization, which is not in conformity with their international obligation. Nevertheless, the codification undertaken by the International Law Commission[82] reached the conclusion according to which the consequences of the wrongful act are different in case of the violation of imperative norms, having in view the importance given to these norms by the international community when accepting and recognizing them as norms from which no derogation is permitted.

If a wrongful act is not in conformity with an imperative norm of the general international law, its wrongfulness cannot be precluded by the consent of the injured State, by invoking the self-defense, by invoking a counter-measure to the wrongful act, by invoking the force majeure, a situation of distress or of necessity. It is obvious that by precluding the wrongfulness of an act and by invoking such situations, a State could try to justify a regime which is derogatory from an imperative norm; articles adopted as codification in this field are explicit on this issue, excluding such situations.

Moreover, the document elaborated by the Commission[83] in the process of codification and progressive development of international law in this field contains a chapter on the serious breaches of obligations under peremptory norms of general international law, outlining the different consequences of such wrongful acts. Serious breaches of imperative norms are defined as involving a gross or systematic failure by the responsible State to fulfill its obligation. As particular consequences of a serious breach of such a norm, the document enounces:
- the obligation of all States to cooperate to bring an end through lawful means to any such serious violation;
- the obligation of all States not to recognize as lawful a situation created by a serious breach as defined, and not to render aid or assistance in maintaining that situation.

More than that, the responsibility of a State can be invoked by any other State for the breach of an obligation which is owed to the international community as a whole, and this is the case for imperative norms. Norms elaborated on the responsibility of international organizations are not different from those concerning the States, although they are taking into account the specificity of international organizations as subjects of international law.

As for counter-measures, as actions of response to unlawful acts, the norms adopted within this process of codification underline that such counter-measures cannot affect: the obligation of States to refrain from resorting to force or to the threat with force, the obligations on the protection of fundamental human rights, the obligation of a humanitarian character which forbid reprisals or other obligations resulting from imperative norms of international law. Without specifying the obligations concerning the protection of human rights or those under humanitarian law

---

[80] Decision of 21 November 2001, extensive and critical presentation of this decision in Chronique de jurisprudence internationale, in RGDIP, 2002, pp. 178-182; judges from the minority held that imperative norms exclude the application of the norm concerning the immunity of jurisdiction of States depriving it of any legal effect.

[81] Ibidem, p. 779.

[82] Presented in AJIL vol. 96/2002, pp. 677-684.

[83] Extensive presentation in Ion Diaconu, International Responsibility in International Law, 2013, Prouniversitaria (in Romanian).

which forbid reprisals, the document of codification excludes the counter-measures which violate them as well as other imperative norms. Wrongful acts which would violate such norms are not allowed even as counter-measures against other wrongful acts, as this would lead to derogations from imperative norms[84].

* * *

The International Law Commission started recently to consider the subject of jus cogens *per se*; a First report was presented by the Special Rapporteur, Mr. Dire Tladi, who traced the historical evolution of the concept, the acceptance in international law of its central elements, and addressed the conceptual issues of the nature and the definition of imperative norms[85]. The Special rapporteur proposed as conclusions to be adopted by the Commission in view of its future work the following: to identify the way in which jus cogens norms are to be identified and their legal consequences; to ascertain that peremptory norms may only be modified, derogated from or abrogated by norms having the same character (which adds to article 53 of the Convention on the law of treaties the concepts of derogation, which was considered only from the point of view of prohibition of any such acts, not as a result of another imperative norm, and of abrogation which has to be carefully approached, taking into account the imperative norms recognized as such at present); a statement that norms of jus cogens protect the fundamental values of the international community, are hierarchically superior to other norms of international law and are universally applicable [86].

The evolution of international practice, mainly during the last decade, led to definitively recognizing the existence of imperative norms and to the clarification of many consequences of the application of this concept in different fields of international law, beyond the law of treaties. Of course, not all consequences revealed in different documents and decisions met with the consensus or are not contested; still, this is the way to crystallize the international practice and to accept norms of international law.

It is generally recognized that treaties in conflict with imperative norms are void; a series of norms are recognized as imperative; as for other norms, some of them mentioned above, opinions vary and the international practice is not uniform. International practice is generally uniform with regard to the consequences of imperative norms in relation to derogatory treaties, but is far for being uniform with regard to other norms which in their application could come in competition with imperative norms, like those on the competence of the courts of compulsory jurisdiction or of treaty monitoring bodies, or like those concerning the immunity of jurisdiction of States which commit violations of imperative norms.

There is more clarity with regard to the consequences of imperative norms on unilateral acts of States, as statements of their will to take upon themselves international obligations, which are void if they are in conflict with imperative norms, as well as those in the field of State responsibility, under which some circumstances cannot be invoked to preclude the wrongfulness of acts violating such norms and counter-measures cannot be applied if they are themselves breaches of imperative norms; with regard to ways and means to promote State responsibility, all States have the right to invoke international responsibility for violations of imperative norms and the obligation to cooperate for eliminating the consequences of such violations and not to recognize as lawful such consequences.

Equally clear is the relationship between imperative norms and regional or local customary norms, meaning that they also cannot create legal regimes which would derogate from imperative norms. Although it is less clear, it seems difficult to accept that universal customary norms in conflict with imperative norms of general international law could be formed. International practice does not offer examples of such an evolution.

---

[84] Report of the International Law Commission on international responsibility of States doc. Suppl. No. 10(A/56/10), of which the U N General Assembly took note by the Resolution no.56/83 adopted on 12 December 2001; Report on international responsibility of international organizations, doc. Suppl. No. 10(A/66/10), of which the UN General Assembly took note by its Resolution no. 66/10 of 9 December 2011.
[85] Doc. A/CN.4/693 of 8 March 2016.

[86] Doc. A/CN.4/693, pp. 44-45.

CHAPTER III – RESERVATIONS to MULTILATERAL TREATIES-CONTINUING CODIFICATION

ABSTRACT

The problem of reservations to multilateral treaties was considered to be solved according to the provisions of the 1969 Convention on the Law of Treaties, following the Advisory Opinion of the International Court of Justice of 1951 on the reservations to the Convention on genocide and the international practice developed for some time according to these provisions. Nevertheless, the application of international treaties on human rights raised new and controversial issues, because the procedure of determining the admissibility of reservations, based on objections to reservations by other States parties, proved to be inefficient for such reservations considered to be incompatible with the object and the purpose of the respective treaties.

The new codification of rules concerning reservations to multilateral treaties, undertaken since 1993 by the International Law Commission and submitted to the UN General Assembly in 2011 as a Guide addressed to member States, summarizes some rules developed by the international practice and adds others newly proposed, based on the nature of commitments under the treaties on human rights. It will be interesting to follow how the international practice will further develop, taking into account that the system of the human rights treaties still functions according to the previous rules.

KEY WORDS: reservations, admissibility, objections, Guide, interpretative declarations, direct and indirect effect, good faith, presumption of separability, nullity, competences, legal certitude, customary norms.

INTRODUCTION

The issue of reservations to multilateral treaties is regulated in three successive conventions of codification of the norms of international law on treaties: the Convention on the law of treaties of 1969, the Convention on the succession of States to treaties of 1978 and the Convention on the law of treaties between States and international organizations or between international organizations of 1986. These conventions define reservations as unilateral statements made by States when they become parties to multilateral treaties, whereby they purport to exclude or to modify the legal effect of a certain provision of a treaty in its application to them. Reservations can be made if they are not forbidden by the treaty directly or indirectly (by admitting reservations only to some provisions) and if they are not incompatible with the object and purpose of the treaty[87].

When it appears from the limited number of States parties and the object and purpose of a treaty that its application in its entirety between all the parties is an essential condition of the consent of each of them to be bound by it, a reservation has to be accepted by all the parties. Reservations to treaties which are constituent instruments of international organizations require the acceptance of the competent organs of these organizations. With regard to reservations to other multilateral treaties, according to these conventions:
- another State party can accept a reservation; in such a case, the effect of the reservation is the modification of the treaty in the relations between that State and the reserving State, according to the reservation; this does not modify the situation of other States parties *inter se* in accordance with the treaty;
- if a State raises an objection to a reservation, the provision of the treaty concerned by the reservation does not apply between that State and the reserving State, to the extent of the reservation; the State which raises an objection can oppose the entry into force of the treaty between itself and the reserving State and then the treaty is not applicable in their relations. This does not affect the relations between other States parties *inter se*.

---

[87] With regard to the institution of reservations to treaties, in the Romanian juridical doctrine, see Ion M. Anghel, Law of Treaties, Second edition-reviewed and completed, vol. I, 2000, Ed. Lumina Lex, pp. 561-693; Ion Diaconu, Treaties of public international law, vol. I, 2002, Lumina Lex, pp. 126-130; Adrian Nastase, Bogdan Aurescu, Public international law, Synthesis, 7-th ed., C.H.Beck, 2012, pp. 264-265; E. Glaser, Reservations to international treaties, Ed.House of the Romanian Academy, 1971.

Thus, the conventions provide for a flexible regime with regard to reservations, based essentially on the Advisory Opinion of the International Court of Justice of 1951[88], having in view two principles: the State sovereignty with regard to the acceptance of a treaty (with or without reservations) and the vocation to universality of the respective treaties, so that the largest possible number of States become parties to them. That meant renouncing to the rigid conception on the need to have the consent of all States parties to the treaty regarding a reservation in order to be accepted. It is nevertheless considered that this flexible regime would leave a series of lacunae and uncertainties, mainly with regard to the evaluation of the compatibility of a reservation with the object and purpose of the treaty and to the legal effect of a reservation when it is subject to an objection[89].

It is also noted that a legal regime established by a treaty is supposed to form a unity, regardless of the fact that reservations purport to exclude or to modify a provision. With regard to this, analysts identify three categories of obligations: those of a bilateral interest, submitted to reciprocity; those whose non-application would lead to the general non-application by all States parties of their obligations under the treaty; those which pursue common objectives, whose application depends on the conduct of all States parties[90].

As it was said, „the subject of reservations to multilateral treaties is of an exceptional complexity and is even confusing (disconcerting) and it would not be useful to simplify artificially an issue complicated *per se*"[91]. Since 1993, The UN International Law Commission began to examine the subject of reservations to treaties and decided that it does not have in view an amendment to the Vienna conventions[92], and in 1996 decided to elaborate a Guide on the practice concerning reservations, which means guidelines without binding effect for States.

In 2011, the Commission presented to the Legal Commission of the UN General Assembly its Draft Guide and, by its Resolution nr. 68/111 of 16 December 2013, the General Assembly took note of the Guide and the orientations it includes and recommended to disseminate it to the widest extent possible. A close examination of the Guide shows that it reaffirms many of the norms already advanced by the conventions and confirmed by the practice; other aspects proceed rather from the progressive codification of international law, while some of them are mere recommendations.

SECTION 1 - NEW ELEMENTS of the GUIDELINES

1. With regard to the definition of a reservation, given by the Vienna conventions, the Guide extends this definition, adding to the statements which purport the exclusion or the modification of the legal effect of a provision of the treaty, those which purport the exclusion or the restriction of the application of a treaty as a whole to some situations or some categories of persons; this concerns reservations to provisions of some treaties containing norms applicable in case of armed conflicts. In the same category one should also include reservations by which some States purport to restrain the application of some treaties to the level of their legislation or of practices applied by them; it is the case of reservations to some treaties in the field of human rights.

The Guide also makes a more precise distinction between reservations and interpretative statements which multiplied and often, although called interpretative statements, aim at modifying or reducing the legal effect of some provisions of a treaty. According to the Guide, an interpretative statement is aiming to precise the meaning given by the author to a provision of the treaty, without making it a condition for its consent to become a party to the treaty;

---

[88] Cour Internationale de Justice, Réserves à la Convention pour la prévention et la répression du crime de génocide, Avis consultatif du 28 mai 1951, CIJ Recueil 1951, p. 15. In this Advisory Opinion, the Court considered that reservations to the provision on the compulsory jurisdiction of the Court concerning disputes on the application and the interpretation of the Convention are not contrary to the obiect and purpose of the Convention; the Court gave the same solution recently, in the case „Armed activities on the territory of Congo(Democratic Republic of Congo v. Rwanda, Admissibility, 2002, ICJ, Report 2006, p. 6). Separate opinions were formulated by the judges Higgins, Kooijmans, Elaraby, Owada and Sima, who maintained that the documents and the evolution of the practice on the protection of human rights makes the situation different from that existing in 1951.

[89] Sarah Cassella, Le Guide de la pratique sur les réserves aux traités: une nouvelle forme de codification?, in Annuaire Français de Droit International (AFDI), 2012, p. 33.

[90] Distinction faite among others by Bruno Sima, From bilateralism to community interest, in RCADI, 1994, vol. 250, p. 330.

[91] Situation retained already before by Hersch Lauterpacht and Paul Reuter, rapporteurs of the Comission on the law of treaties, cited by Alain Pellet, Rapport général, Société Française du Droit International, Journées de Nanterre, 2014; www.alainpellet.eu/Document/Pellet.

[92] These conventions have a different status, because that of 1996 is not in force due to the insufficient number of ratifications; the other two are not ratified by the same States. See Resolutions of the UN General Assembly nr.48/31 of 9 December 1993 and nr. 52/156 of 17 December 1997.

the proposal of the Commission is to examine the intention of the author through an objective analysis of the consequences of the statement on the application of the treaty, on the basis of the interpretation of the terms used and of other norms of interpretation of treaties and taking into account the international practice.

If such a statement is aiming at modifying or excluding the application of a provision of the treaty, it represents in fact a reservation. With regard to the withdrawal of reservations, the Guide takes into account the dominant practice, according to which the withdrawal is not submitted to the agreement of States and organizations which accepted initially the reservation, which gives priority to restoring the integrity of the treaty.

2. Regarding effects of the reservations, the Guide follows mainly the distinction between reservations accepted and those to which some States raise objections. As for the reservations accepted by one or more States, the conventions refer only to their effect of modifying the provision concerned of the treaty according to the reservation; but the conventions refer also in the definition given to reservations to their effect of excluding the application of a provision of the treaty.

The Guide underlines that a reservation of exclusion of the application of a provision excludes any rights or obligations resulting from it both for the reserving State and for all States accepting the reservation, while a reservation modifying a provision of a treaty creates an obligation of a new kind between the reserving State and States which accept the reservation.

The Guide also excludes the reciprocity in case of reservations to provisions aiming to achieve a common objective, because they are not creating obligations *inter se,* but obligations towards the entirety of States parties or they have other beneficiaries than States; this concerns treaties for the protection of human rights, the protection of the environment, treaties for disarmament or which establish uniform laws in the field of private international law.

In case of an objection to a reservation by a State which does not oppose that the treaty enter into force between itself and the reserving State, the Commission notes that the text of the conventions according to which „the provisions to which the reservation relates do not apply as between the two States to the extent of the reservation" is not clear. Of course, when a reservation aims to exclude the application of a provision of a treaty, the situation is clear: that provision is not applied in the relations between the two States, does not create for them any rights and obligations; moreover, we can note that from this point of view an objection to such a reservation has the same legal effect as its acceptance.

Even in this case, the Guide makes a distinction between the direct effect of the objection (the non-application between the two States of the provision to which the reservation relates), similar to that of accepting the reservation, and the indirect effect of the objection, meaning that the State which objects to a reservation does not accept the exclusion, which leaves open the problem of the law applicable in their relations and may lead to a dispute between them.

More complicated is the case of a reservation aiming to modify the contents of a provision; this implies separating that part of the provision subject to modification from that which is not affected; the text added „to the extent of the reservation". This means that the effect of the objection to such a reservation depends on the text of the provision targeted by the reservation and on the contents of the objection; in principle, neither the initial provision, nor that resulting from the modification is applicable between the States concerned. Nevertheless, if a significant part of the provision to which the reservation relates is not affected by the reservation, it may be useful to maintain it as an obligation between the two States[93].

It is our opinion that, even in case of reservations attempting to modify a provision of a treaty, a State which objects to the reservation may express its disagreement with the reservation, which leaves open the issue of the law to be applied between them and may lead to a dispute; the indirect effect should not be excluded in this case also.

3. On the admissibility of reservations, the Vienna conventions enounce the cases when reservations are inadmissible; nevertheless, they leave open the consequences of the situation when a State formulates a reservation which is inadmissible; it is not provided who would establish whether a reservation is admissible and on the basis of what criteria; these lacunae make it that the recognition of consequences of a reservation depends on the decision about its admissibility. One could envisage an objective evaluation of the admissibility of reservations on the basis of a method established beforehand by the respective convention, solution which seems to be foreseen by the texts of the Vienna conventions (without creating the mechanism to apply the method); an alternative is to have the

---

[93] It is the case of arbitration between France and United Kingdom concerning the delimitation of continental shelf, France formulated to the 1958 Convention in this field a reservation according to which it limited the hypothesis of delimitation of its continental shelf on the basis of the application of the principle of equidistance; UK objected to this reservation; the arbitral court gave a limited meaning to the reservation, maintaining as compulsory that part of the provision concerned which was not affected by the reservation. Cf. Délimitation du plateau continental dans la mer d'Iroise (France c.Royaume Uni), décision du 30 Juin 1977, Recueil des Sentences Arbitrales, vol. XVIII, p.130.

admissibility of the reservations determined by each of the States parties, which leads to different evaluations by States and which by and large is followed by the current international practice.

According to the Guide adopted, the Commission considers the validity of reservations as a substantial and objective issue, based on the good faith of States parties to treaties. The Commission separates the question of the validity of reservations from that of their effects; the validity of reservations precedes the establishment of their effects, through their acceptance or the objections to them. By this, the Commission moves away from the practice followed by the majority of States and international organizations, mainly with regard to the evaluation of the validity of reservations to treaties.

With regard to the substantial validity of reservations, leaving aside the reservations which are explicitly or indirectly forbidden by the treaty, the Commission gives its main attention to those reservations which are incompatible with the object and purpose of the treaty. The Guide takes as a starting point the principle enounced in the Vienna conventions, according to which those reservations incompatible with the object and purpose of the treaty are inadmissible. It includes specific orientations with regard to reservations which are vague or of a general nature, to reservations which relate to internal law in order to exclude or limit the application of a treaty provision and those which refer to human rights from which no derogation is permissible under any circumstances.

As a general method of evaluation, the Guide foresees resorting to norms of interpretation of treaties. As criteria, it refers to reservations aiming at essential elements of the treaty that are necessary to its tenure in such a way that they impair the raison d'être of the treaty. In all cases, it is obvious that it has in view a subjective evaluation of the relationship between the reservation and the treaty or one of its provisions. The international practice followed at present tends to dissociate the evaluation of the validity of reservations to treaties from the nature of the obligations they purport to exclude or to modify, taking into account also the lack of mechanisms of control on the application of treaties.

The Commission is not following this way, trying to maintain a unitary regime of reservations to treaties; at the same time, the Guide observes that the evaluation of the validity of reservations to treaties should take into account the indivisibility, the interdependence and the importance of the rights protected, a consideration which concerns mainly the treaties on human rights. The Guide refers also to the cause of the commitment of the State parties, if a reservation would be incompatible with it; this may have a meaning for those provisions of a treaty which pursue common objectives, but not for treaties and provisions which concern bilateral relations between States parties.

SECTION 2 - CONSEQUENCES of NON-PERMISSIBILITY of RESERVATIONS

The Vienna conventions contain no provisions on the consequences of reservations which are not permitted. The Guide adopted by the Commission affirms with clarity that a reservation which does not respect the substantial conditions of validity (either it is prohibited or is incompatible with the object and purpose of the treaty), as well as the formal conditions, is null and void and devoid of any legal effect. That means that the nullity of the reservation is objective, that it does not depend on the reaction of another State party and that the acceptance of such a reservation has no legal effect.

Every State could invoke any time the nullity of the reservation beyond the 12 months provided in the conventions for notifying an objection to a reservation. Such a construction is not in conformity with the majority of the practice followed at present, according to which if a State does not object to a reservation during the 12 months since the reservation was notified (which is also taken up in the Guide), the reservation is considered accepted and is applied between the two States. The Commission seems to take as a starting point the treaties in the field of human rights and that of the environment; but according to the present practice, even in the case of these treaties, the States parties are those which evaluate that reservations are contrary to the object and purpose of a treaty when they raise objections to such reservations.

Still, many States do not raise objections to reservations or not to reservations formulated by friendly States; objections to reservations are very seldom excluding that the treaty enters into force between the two States concerned, even if the State which objects to a reservation declares that it is contrary to the object and the purpose of the treaty.

Some European and Scandinavian States parties declared, when formulating objections to some reservations in the field of human rights (namely those of the USA according to which the treaty will apply in as much as it is in conformity with internal law, or those of some Islamic States which subordinate the application of the treaties to the

Sharia law), that the treaty will be applied between them and the reserving State without the benefit of the reservation[94].

The Guide elaborated by the Commission retains as a presumption the consequences of nullity and lack of any legal effect of invalid reservations. Nevertheless, this leaves many aspects not clear; that would mean that a State party could decide that a reservation formulated by another State does not produce any effect, considering the treaty fully applicable in their relations and thus ignoring the will of the reserving State. Even when a treaty monitoring body assesses the permissibility of a reservation, the Guide makes it clear that such an assessment has no greater effect than the act which contains it, that is the concluding observations or recommendations of such bodies, which have no legal compulsory effect.

Besides, some States extend the effect of their objections to other provisions of the treaty, related to those concerned by the reservation; such objections are considered counter-reservations. The Commission seems to accept this practice, if the respective provisions are sufficiently linked to those to which the reservation refers[95]. On the other side, some objections to reservations seem to give expression to a political position related to the state of relations between the respective States[96].

This is a theoretical construction which may be partially coherent, but does not correspond to the current international practice, because the international society is not equipped with competent bodies to implement it. The Guide separates the objection to a reservation from the problem of the validity of the reservation, accepting only objections to valid reservations; currently, except when some treaty bodies made an evaluation of permissibility for some reservations, States parties take it up through their objections. The approach of the Commission is going too far from the provisions of the conventions and the practice of their application, according to which consequences of reservations and objections depend of notifications made by State parties during a time frame. The Guide could be followed only where there is a competent body to take binding decisions on the validity of reservations. Otherwise, it would create disputes and uncertainties with regard to the status of States as parties to some treaties and to the application of such treaties to them.

SECTION 3 - COMPETENCE to ASSESS the VALIDITY of RESERVATIONS

According to the Guide of the Commission, the other contracting parties (States or international organizations), dispute settlement bodies and treaty monitoring bodies may assess, within their competences, the permissibility of reservations. With regard to the treaty monitoring bodies, the Commission recognizes in its comments that this concerns only treaties in the field of human rights[97]. The Commission presents as examples decisions given by the European Court of Human Rights[98], the Advisory Opinion of the Inter-American Court on human rights[99] and the General Comment of the Human rights Committee concerning reservations to the Covenant

---

[94] This opinion would be contrary to the principle of consensualism, because it accepts that by the will of a State, a reservation of another State, which is considered invalid, is separated from the expression of the consent of the reserving State to become a party to the treaty; it is the opinion of some States, expressed in the Sixth Commission of the General Assembly, doc. A/C.6/62, SR. 23, p. 12. Some authors name this practice accepting what is unacceptable; J. Klabbers, Accepting what is unacceptable? A new Nordic approach to reservations to multilateral treaties, in Nordic Journal of International Law, 2000, pp. 170-193.

[95] Reservations of some States to article 66 of the Vienna Convention on the law of treaties concerning the compulsory jurisdiction of the International Court of Justice with regard to disputes concerning articles 53 and 64 on imperative norms were met with objections of other States, which extended their objections to the application of articles of substance concerning imperative norms, thus excluding their application between them and the reserving States. It is our opinion that such a position is not reasonable, because even according to the Guide, such a reservation is not related to a provision which is essential for the raison d'être of the convention, whose purpose was not to put such a mechanism into effect.

[96] Pakistan has objected to a reservation of India for not accepting the compulsory jurisdiction of the International Court of Justice on disputes concerning the interpretation and the application of a treaty, although the reservation was expressly permitted by the treaty.

[97] One has to add also some treaties on the protection of the environment, such as the Convention concluded at Aarhus in 1998 concerning access to information, participation of the public to the decision-making and access to justice in the field of environment and the Convention of Espoo of 1991 concerning the evaluation of the impact on the environment in the transborder context. These conventions created monitoring mechanisms for their interpretation and application, which function with the support of the secretariat of the Economic Commission of the United Nations for Europe.

[98] The decision of 1988 in the case Belilos, where the Court considered without validity the declaration equating to a reservation of Switzerland to art. 6.1 of the European Convention on human rights of 1950(concerning the right to a fair and public trial, in a reasonable time frame, by an independent and impartial court); Doc. Série A, no. 132/1988.

[99] The effect of the reservations on the entry into force of the American Convention on Human Rights, Advisory Opinion, doc. OC 2/82 of 24 September 1982, Cour Interaméricaine des droits de l'homme, Séries A, Judgments and Opinions, no. 2.

on civil and political right (where the Committee holds that it has the competence to determine whether a reservation is incompatible with the object and purpose of the treaty and to consider the treaty applicable in its entirety to the respective State party[100]). We noticed the opinion of the Commission, expressed in the Guide, according to which the effect of the evaluation by treaty monitoring bodies depends upon the competence of these bodies, namely that their statement on validity of a reservation has the value of the act which contains it.

If such a body is competent to adopt decisions binding States parties to the treaty (the case of ECHR), its assessment has legal binding value, while if its competence is to adopt documents with a value of recommendations (the case of monitoring bodies created by international treaties on human rights), the assessment will have the same value. The Commission takes note of this situation, as well as of the possibility of successive evaluations by different bodies, and recommends to reserving States or international organizations to take into account such an assessment made by a monitoring body. The Commission already expressed this opinion in its Preliminary Conclusions concerning reservations to treaties, presented to the General Assembly in 1977[101]. This would be an obligation of cooperation, which the Commission seems to relate to the obligation of States to apply a treaty in good faith.

The Commission does not refer to the situation where some conventions provide expressly a modality to establish the admissibility of reservations; it is well known that the provisions of the Vienna conventions are of a subsidiary nature when a treaty contains explicit provisions. For instance, according to the International Convention on the elimination of all forms of racial discrimination a reservation shall not be permitted if it is incompatible with the object and the purpose of the Convention or if it has the effect of inhibiting the operation of any of the bodies established by the Convention.

Such a reservation is considered incompatible or inhibitive if at least two thirds of the States parties object to it (article 20.2)[102]. Such a modality was never applied, because never two thirds of the States parties raised objections to any of the reservations formulated. The Committee on the Elimination of Racial Discrimination expressed often its opinion that one or the other of the reservations do not correspond with the object and purpose of the Convention and asked the respective State to consider the possibility to withdraw the reservation made.

The Committee noted sometimes that the respective States adopted already legislation making the reservations useless and outdated. Besides, many of the reservations to this Convention are of a historic nature and cannot be considered, with some exceptions (for instance those on article 4 concerning the prohibition of racist hate speech and of racist organizations), as a major obstacle to the interpretation and application of the Convention.

SECTION 4 - RESERVATION to TREATIES on HUMAN RIGHTS

Treaties on human rights, both international and regional, are subject to a significant number of reservations, some of them throwing a serious doubt on the benefit of important human rights by those entitled. We noted already that, although the Vienna conventions proclaim the principle according to which reservations incompatible with the object and purpose of a treaty are inadmissible, these conventions do not determine how to establish that a reservation is contrary to the object and purpose of a treaty[103]. This led to an international practice which privileges the universality of treaties meant to protect human rights, but leads to accepting reservations which can be considered as incompatible with the object and purpose of the treaties, with unacceptable consequences.

To answer this situation, some of the bodies monitoring the application of these treaties adopted the „conception of separability" of reservations contrary to the object and purpose of the treaty from the consent of States to become parties, as a matter of fact refusing any effect to the respective reservations and considering States as parties to the treaty in its entirety.

First, it was the action of European Commission and the European Court of Human Rights, which decided that reservations to the 1950 European Convention on the protection of human rights which are inadmissible are

---

[100] Text in Compilation of General Comments and General Recommendations adopted by human rights treaty bodies, doc. HRI/GEN/1, Rev. 8 of 8 May 2006, pp. 200-207.

[101] Report of the International Law Commission on the work of its 49-th session, 12 May-18 July 1997, Suppl. No.A/52/10, chapter V, pp. 94-127.

[102] A more extended presentation by Bruno Simma and Gleider I. Hernandez, Legal Consequences of an Impermissible Reservation to a Human Rights Treaty: Where Do We Stand?, în The Law of Treaties Beyond the Vienna Convention, Enzo Cannizzaro (ed), pp. 60 and foll.

[103] Cases Temeltasch v. Switzerland, 1982, nr. 9116/90, în European Human Rights Reports 1982, p. 417; Belilos, cited supra, footnote 11, Chrysostomos et al v. la Turkey, nr. 15299-15300-15318/89, decision of 4 March 1991, Loizidou v. Turkey, decison of 23 March 1995, Serie A, no. 310.

separated from the consent to participate in the Convention and that States remain obliged by all its provisions[104]. The States parties to the European Convention accepted the exercise of this competence by the Court. A similar position was adopted by the Inter-American Court on human rights.

At the universal level, the Human Rights Committee, confronted with an important number of reservations to the 1966 Covenant on civil and political rights, adopted the General Comment no. 24 of 2 November 1994, where it holds that, due to the specific nature of obligations resulting from treaties on human rights, the provisions of the Vienna Convention, although applicable in principle, are inadequate. The Committee affirmed its competence to determine whether a reservation is incompatible with the object and purpose of a treaty and to consider the Covenant applicable in its entirety to the State concerned, refusing to it the benefit of the reservation[105]. The Committee also did not accept the reservation formulated by Trinidad-Tobago to the Protocol on the elimination of capital punishment (additional to the Covenant), through which the State denied the competence of the Committee to receive individual communications according to the Protocol; the Committee affirmed that it could not accept a reservation which isolates a group of persons (the detainees condemned to death) depriving them of the procedural protection enjoyed by the rest of the population and which consequently was against the object and purpose of the Protocol. The Committee concluded also that it could examine communications concerning that State according to the Protocol[106].

We noted that, in its Preliminary Conclusion of 1997 concerning reservations to multilateral treaties, the International Law Commission held that the provisions of the Vienna Convention on the law of treaties are applicable also to treaties on human rights and that the competences of bodies monitoring the application of these treaties are those granted by the treaties with regard to their application. This conception was criticized by some authors[107], who consider that the regime of the Vienna Convention on the law of treaties concerning the acceptance of reservations and objections to them, as well as the legal effect of reservations, their acceptance and objections, should not be applicable to reservations which are not permissible, mainly to reservations to treaties on human rights which are not permissible[108] and that such reservations should be separated from the consent of the State to become a party. Such a State should be held obliged by the treaty in its entirety. It is rightly affirmed that treaties in the field of human rights establish rights for human beings, do not constitute only bilateral relations between States, and that their application is not subject to the principle of reciprocity, to which the acceptance of reservations would lead.

Of course, from the legal point of view, treaties concerning human rights are adopted according, and subject, to the same principles and norms as other multilateral treaties. Still, in their case, due to the object and the purpose pursued, it is considered that the provisions of the Vienna Convention should be applied in a specific way, as they are establishing not only obligations among States parties, but also obligations for them towards human beings, which can be qualified as *erga omnes* obligations[109].

In the same vein, the Working Group on reservations, created jointly by the chairpersons of human rights treaty bodies and by the Inter-committee meeting of these bodies reached the conclusion that the specific nature of treaties on human rights is that they do not represent mere an exchange of obligations among States, but give a legal expression to essential rights that each person should be able to exercise as a human being. The Working Group agreed with the recent opinion of the Special Rapporteur of the Commission according to which a reservation which is not permissible is null and void, a State cannot prevail of it and remain party to the treaty, unless it expresses explicitly another intention[110].

In its last reports, the Special Rapporteur of the Commission, Alain Pellet, formulated the conception of the presumption of separability in case of reservations inadmissible to treaties on human rights, starting from the practice of some bodies monitoring the application of these treaties. The presumption of separability would represent, in his

---

[104] General Comment No. 24; Issues relating to reservations made upon ratification or accession to the Covenant or the Optional Protocols thereto, or in relation to declarations under article 41 of the Covenant, Compilation…, doc. HRI/GEN/1/Rev. 8, p. 200.

[105] B. Simma, Reservations to Human Rights Treaties: Some Recent Developments, in G. Hafner, G. Loibl, A. Rest, L. Sucharipa-Behrmann and K. Zemanek(eds), Liber Amicorum Professor Ignaz Seidl Hohenveldern, in Honour of his 80-th birthday, The Hague Kluwer Law International, 1998, pp. 639-680.

[106] Case extensively presented in Cases & Materials on International Law, M. Dixon, R. McCorquodale & S. Williams, 5-th edition, Oxford University Press, 2011, p. 79. Initially, Trinidad-Tobago denounced the Protocol, when several individual communications concerning detainees condemned to death in that State were submitted to the Committee; then Trinidad-Tobago adhered to the Protocol with the respective reservation. As the Committee rejected its reservation, Trinidad-Tobago again denounced the Protocol.

[107] B. Simma, G. Hernandez, art. cit., p.62.

[108] Ibidem, p. 67.

[109] Report of the Working Group on Reservations of the Sixth Inter-Committee Meeting of the Human Rights Treaty Meeting(2007), HRI/MC/2007/5, pp. 6-7.

[110] B. Simma, G. Hernandez, art. cit, p. 75.

opinion, a middle ground between the conception of the consent to the full treaty and the maximum effect of the separability of reservations[111], although he notes the inherent difficulties of such a presumption. These reservations are, of course, considered null and void, but the objections of States are not the solution for determining their inadmissibility; the Guide adopted separates the issue of validity of reservations from the effects of their invalidity.

The Comments of the Rapporteur take note of the practice of States and of the monitoring bodies according to which reservations considered incompatible with the object and purpose of the treaty do not impede upon the reserving States to become parties to such treaties.

The Rapporteur also underlines that it is up to the reserving State to take the final decision, namely not to be a party to the treaty as long as its reservation is considered inadmissible or to accept that its reservation is without effect; his starting point is the fundamental consideration of the consent of the State for any solution which could be promoted.

To summarize, a State whose reservation is considered inadmissible by other States, by a judicial body or by a body monitoring the application of the treaty has to determine whether its reservation is a sine qua non condition for its participation to the treaty and it renounces to become a party or it accepts the presumption of separability. Again, this leaves a clear uncertainty in the case where only some States consider the reservation inadmissible, while others accept it.

Even before adopting the Guide under this form, several committees on human rights extended the practice of rejecting such reservations they consider inadmissible. The Human Rights Committee adopted in 2011 a new General Comment concerning the freedom of opinion and of expression (article 19 of the Covenant), where it affirms that, having in view the relationship between the freedom of thinking and of opinion and other human rights, reservations to the respective provision are incompatible with the object and purpose of the Covenant, as well as the reservations of a general order concerning the freedom of expression[112].

In 2011, the Committee adopted a statement with regard to the reservation formulated by a State to article 40 of the Covenant, namely that it is not obliged to present periodic reports on the application of the Covenant; the Committee underlined that this reservation would impede upon the exercise of a competence which is of crucial importance for the exercise of its functions and which is essential for the raison d'être of the Covenant[113].

In the same vein, the Committee for the elimination of all forms of discrimination against women adopted the Decision nr. 47/5 of 2010, concerning the obligations of the States parties to the Convention on this subject of 1979 according to its article 2 (which enounces obligations of a general order for the elimination of discrimination against women), affirming that, because this provision enounces the essential part of the obligations taken by States through this Convention, any reservations to this article are in principle incompatible with the object and purpose of the Convention and consequently inadmissible. The Committee requested that States which formulated such reservations present in their periodic reports the effects of such reservations to the application of the Convention and measures they have taken to continue to consider these reservations in order to withdraw them as soon as possible[114].

Other committees also approached such reservations during the examination of periodic reports of States parties[115].

One may consider that the presumption of separability presents advantages, like the legal certitude, transparency, compatibility with the nature of the consent to be obliged by treaties on human rights, making easier the action of those monitoring the application of the treaty, affirming the conception of the integrality of the State's consent. Nevertheless, this does not eliminate difficulties resulting from the uncertainty of the evaluation of the validity of reservations; this refers to the moment when the treaty enters into force for a State, because a State should be considered as a party to the treaty only after establishing that the reservation is admissible; this means to respect the procedural conditions, to establish the substantial validity of the reservation and its acceptance by at least one State party.

If the evaluation of the validity of the reservation is separated from the expression of the position of other States, it remains to establish who makes the evaluation and when it is made, in order to establish when a State can

---

[111] The Special Rapporteur refers to decisions of the European Court on Himan Rights, to the General Comment of the Human Rights Committee mentioned above, as well as to the practice of several European States which objected in 2010 to reservations of USA to the Third Protocol to the Convention on some conventional weapons, First Addendum to the Fifteenth Report on Reservations to Treaties, A/CN.4/624/Add.1, 6 May 2010, pp. 23-24.

[112] Doc. CCPR/C/GC/34 din 2011.

[113] Statement reproduced in the Report of the Committee, doc. A/67/40(vol. I), pp. 9-10.

[114] Doc. A/66/38, p. 106.

[115] For instance, the Concluding Observations of CERD of 2010 concerning the report of Australia, doc. A/65/18, p. 22 and of 2011 concerning the report of Yemen, doc. A/66/18, p. 137, as well as Concluding Observations of CESC of 2010 concerning the report of Mauritius, doc. E/2011/22, p. 59.

be considered a party to the treaty; according to the current practice, the depositary of the treaty considers a State as party to a treaty as soon as its instrument of ratification, adhesion or acceptance is handled, with or without reservation or at a subsequent time provided for by the treaty. Objections to reservations can be made within 12 months from the notification of the reservation; usually, objections do not contest the quality of States parties of the reserving States, but tend to exclude the benefit of reservations, while the reserving States may consider that they cannot become parties without their reservations.

The Commission presents an intermediate solution to this problem, indicating that the position of the reserving State towards the treaty depends on its intention, on the basis of the presumption that it becomes a party to the treaty without the benefit of the reservation considered inadmissible; the State could, consequently, renounce to participate in the treaty or accept the presumption. But what if the reserving State chooses to maintain its position, rejecting or reversing the presumption? On the other side, the evaluation of a reservation may appear subsequently, at any moment, even after the 12 months allowed to making objections; what happens in the meantime? The Commission advances the idea of a reservation dialogue, taking as a model the practice followed within the Council of Europe, meaning a dialogue between the depository of the treaty and the respective State on the admissibility of the reservation before the reaction by States parties, including some warnings with regard to reservations which would be inadmissible, with the participation of States which are not yet parties to the respective treaty (but are members of the organizations which are usually the depositories of treaties on human rights).

It is known that the UN Secretary general, who is the depository of most of the multilateral treaties, including the main international treaties on human rights, registers notifications of States concerning ratification, adhesion or acceptance of treaties from the moment they are deposed within the Secretariat and considers the respective States as parties to the treaties, within the number provided for their entrance into force, without opening a discussion on the issue of admissibility of their reservations to the treaty[116]. On the other side, resorting to a dialogue of this kind is criticized because it leaves open the possibility that no State objects to an inadmissible reservation, as being contrary to the object and purpose of a treaty, and the reservation would be thus accepted[117].

* * *

According to some analysts, the Guide represents in its main aspects, mainly those on the evaluation of the admissibility of reservations, a doctrinal approach which is departing both from the provisions of the Vienna conventions and from the practice followed by the majority of States and international organizations, approach which is even not responding to the objective of the codification[118]. This would result from the fact that the central issue (that of the relationship between the modality of determining the validity of a reservation and its consequences) is taken up too late, after the adoption of the Vienna Conventions and after the development of an international practice in a different direction. It is also underlined that this Guide is treating many issues without connection with the provisions of the conventions on reservations (for instance, guidelines concerning the formulation by the States of reservations, as well as the reactions they can raise[119]).

The Guide contains also extended elaborations concerning reservations to treaties on State succession; in fact, only the Convention of 1978 on State succession to treaties contains a single provision concerning reservations with regard to the succession to treaties by newly independent States. The Commission found it necessary to take up the entirety of preoccupations concerning reservations to treaties with regard to that case and enounces orientations aiming at maintaining a balance between the principle of consensualism and a certain legal security, but recognizes to the new States the faculty to maintain or not the reservations formulated by the former State and to formulate new reservations. The Commission also deals with the situations of unification or division of States and maintains flexible rules, based on simple presumptions to preserve the treaties, while allowing the new State to express a different position. This is a field where the State practice is not very extended.

The Guide is also attempting to clarify the regime of reservations as compared to interpretative statements; it underlines that such a statement does not aim to subordinate the consent of the State to become a party to a treaty to

---

[116] United Nations, Summary of Practice of the Secretary general as Depositary of Multilateral Treaties, Ne-York, 1999, ST/LEG/7/Rev.1, para 187.

[117] With regard to reservations to this Convention, Ion Diaconu and Iurii Reshetov, Backgroung paper for the first session of the Preparatory Committee of the World Conference against Racism, Racial Discrimination, Xenophobia and Related Intolerance, doc. CERD/C/53/Misc.23 of 10 August 1998.

[118] R. Rivier, Travaux de la Commission du droit international et de la sixième Commision, in AFDI, 2009, p. 517.

[119] Sarah Cassella, art. cit., p. 55; also A. Tanzi, The resumed codification of the law of reservations to treaties, in Istituto di diritto internazionale del l'Universita di Milano, Comunicazioni e Studi, vol. 22, pp. 7-34, Ed. Giuffre, 2002.

the exclusion or modification of one of its provisions in its relations with other States, but indicates an interpretation that it intends to give to some provisions of the treaty. The Guide clarifies that those statements of interpretation, which would condition the participation to the treaty on the respective interpretation, are assimilated to reservations and subject to the same rules.

The Guide develops many recommendations applicable to these conditional statements, although the practice in this field is scarce. Some guidelines are devoted also to interpretative statements to bilateral treaties, which may not be justified, because reservations concern only multilateral treaties. Statements with regard to bilateral treaties are in fact new proposals concerning either the modification or the application of the treaty, which are of interest for the two States parties. Finally, the Guide includes also alternatives to reservations or to interpretative statements, in fact recommendations addressed to States in order to avoid them. They are, substantially, guidelines concerning negotiations between States parties, which take place before the conclusion of the treaty or before the expression of their consent to become parties, so as to avoid reservations or to make them not useful.

This a simplified vision about the way the negotiations take place, because in an international society as heterogeneous it is not always possible to obtain the consensus and negotiations are very seldom producing texts which are fully acceptable to all States; the objective followed by States during negotiations is not to avoid further reservations, but to promote some positions considered essential for their interests with the agreement of a majority. Besides, if we consider some treaties affected by reservations, we have to note that these reservations are often the result of the consideration of treaties by parliaments or other internal bodies, after the negotiations, and many States may not have become parties if they had not the possibility to make such reservations.

The Guide examines briefly the relationship between reservations and customary norms. It is rightly retained that a reservation to a provision which gives expression to a customary norm does not affect its validity as a customary norm. Probably, it was also necessary to continue the reasoning, because reservations may become an extended practice or expression of a largely followed practice, which leads to the modification or the replacement of the customary norm when it combines the two elements- a generalized practice and *opinio juris*. Indirect effects of this practice, as derogatory from the customary norm and as contribution to a new customary norm, are not examined[120].

The Commission recommended to the General Assembly to create a mechanism of assistance in the field of reservations, which could be consulted by States and international organizations; this mechanism could also ensure a more sustained reservations dialogue and could formulate proposals with a view to solving disputes concerning reservations. It also proposed to establish, within the 6th Commission of the General Assembly, an Observatory on the subject of reservations, following the model of the Ad-hoc Committee of legal counselors of public international law which exists within the Council of Europe.

The General Assembly did not give a follow-up to these recommendations; it took note of the Guide, without recommending it to State members.

This Guide offers a new model of document adopted in the context of the codification of international law; it raises, as seen above, many question signs and presents uncertainties both in relation to the three Vienna conventions on the law of treaties and in particular with regard to the practice currently followed by the majority of States and international organizations. The Commission itself qualified the Guide as a „box of tools" for the practitioners of international law and the Guide affirms that it offers an extensive area of degrees of obligations. Moreover, it is a voluminous document (680 pages of guidelines and comments, plus an annex), including many doctrine approaches, and its consultation may not always lead to practical conclusions for the State willing to follow them.

The international practice will show whether some of the recommendations contained will be followed by States when they formulate reservations or objections to them, and how will they be applied by the monitoring bodies and the depositaries of such treaties.

---

[120] For the examination of these aspects, R. Rivier, Travaux de la Comission du droit international et de la Sixième Commission, AFDI, 2010, pp. 376 and foll.

CHAPTER IV - FUNDAMENTAL HUMAN RIGHTS-ELEMENTS of CONTACT between DIFFERENT LEGAL SYSTEMS

ABSTRACT

Internal legal systems and, more recently regional and international legal systems, give a superior rank to fundamental human rights against norms or acts which would violate or restrict such rights. At the same time, one must note a variety of fundamental human rights as enshrined in different national and international instruments.

As a matter of fact, different jurisdictions have to apply the concept of fundamental rights, which may lead to the danger of different or opposed decisions on similar issues, thus endangering the juridical security and coherence. Being used in several legal systems, the concept of fundamental rights appears as a communication tool among them, when they have to evaluate acts adopted in other legal systems or to solve problems concerning fundamental rights common with other legal systems.

If ECHR avoided in general to exercise a control on decisions adopted by national jurisdictions on the basis of Security Council's resolutions imposing sanctions to individuals, the Court of Justice of the European Union decided, in similar cases, that regulations adopted by EU institutions to implement such resolutions of the Security Council were not in conformity with some fundamental rights recognized within the Union, that is with the EU law. This obliged the EU institutions to insist upon the Security Council bodies to adopt other procedures in order to respect these rights; the EU institutions also adopted their own internal procedures ensuring the respect of such rights before the adoption of compulsory documents on the basis of such resolutions.

KEY WORDS: fundamental rights, juridical pluralism, constitutional pluralism, autonomy, dualist system, juridical security, rights and principles, hierarchy of norms on human rights, communication between different legal systems, right of defense, right to fair trial.

INTRODUCTION

The increasing number of jurisdictions-international and national-and the dialogue which takes place between them, by taken up and applying common norms and concepts and by adopting solutions which can be convergent or divergent, have to be accepted as normal and positive evolutions of the extended knowledge of norms of law and of the recognition of their importance by legal existing systems. It is rightly asserted that there is a legal pluralism, which can be foreseen as an anarchic horizontality, a hegemonic verticality or as some medium way[121]. As the problems of protection of human rights are topical, we may consider that the interest for fundamental human rights proceeds also from the intensification of concerns for extending the norm of law and the democratic principles all over the world.

It has been noted that one of the privileged elements of the dialogue among jurisdictions is represented by fundamental human rights[122]; this is the field where the majority of national constitutions provide for an increased protection and request that States respect the relevant norms of international law. It is also accepted that norms enouncing these rights prevail, both at the international and at the internal levels, over other norms of law. This leads to what is called constitutional pluralism or a plurality of constitutional sources[123]. At the same time, the concept of fundamental rights is used sometimes under other names and is not given the same meaning in different legal systems, both in different States and at the international level. These legal systems are more or less autonomous institutionally, while from the normative point of view they present many common features and are interdependent and permeable.

---

[121] Edouard Dubout and Sebastien Touzé, La fonction des droits fondamentaux dans les rapports entre ordres et systèmes juridiques, in Les droits fondamentaux: charnière entre ordres et systèmes juridiques, Publications de la fondation Marangopoulos pour les droits de l'homme, Série no. 15, p. 14.
[122] Ibidem, p.12.
[123] Miguel Polares Maduro, La fonction juridictionnelle dans le contexte du pluralisme constitutionnel: l'approche du droit communautaire, in Les droits fondamentaux: charnières...., ed. E.Dubout and S. Touzé, p. 199.

SECTION 1 - HISTORICAL OVERVIEW

One can find the notion of fundamental rights used for the first time in the German Constitution of 1849, explained by German lawyers as aiming at individual rights guaranteed by norms of public law. The constitutional law of Austria of 1920, which introduced the first system of constitutional jurisdiction, gave in the competence of the new court, among others, to pronounce itself on violations of „the rights guaranteed by the Constitution". The notion of fundamental rights was taken up by the Basic law of the Federal Republic of Germany of 1949 and appears under other formulations in the Italian Constitution (rights and duties of citizens), in the Portuguese Constitution of 1976 (personal rights, freedoms and guarantees), in the Spanish Constitution of 1978 (fundamental rights and public freedoms). In France, the Constitutional Council refers, beginning with 1971, to „rights and freedoms guaranteed by the Constitution", terms used also by the Constitution in force in Austria.

The Basic German Law enounces numerous rights and freedoms: political and civil, such as dignity, equal rights, freedom to exercise an economic activity, artistic and cultural freedoms and rights related to education, as well as some social rights. A particular importance is given to the provision according to which any modification of the Basic Law which would affect the substance of fundamental rights is forbidden. Restrictions can be applied to some of these rights, but without affecting their substance.

Without containing an explicit list of fundamental rights, the Constitution of Austria refers to some political and civil rights, but also, sometimes directly or indirectly, to: the principles of non-discrimination, of equal status of women and men, of proportional representation; to the rights to health care, to freedom and to property; to the right to justice and to the independence of justice; to the abolition of death penalty; to procedural guarantees in criminal justice; to the competence of the Constitutional Court to determine whether a regulation is contrary to the Constitution. The Constitution can be revised, including with regard to these rights, only by referendum.

The Constitution of Spain also contains an extensive list of human rights considered fundamental, including equality before the law, interdiction of any discrimination on grounds of birth, race, sex, religion, opinion or any other personal circumstances or related to the social condition; the interdiction of death penalty; the freedom of ideology, religion and cult; the rights to honour, private, personal and family life; the restriction to use personal processed data; the right to literary, artistic, scientific and technical creation and production; the academic freedom; the non-retroactive application of the law; the right to education; the right to inherit; the right to create foundations of a general interest; the right to work and to choose freely the profession or the trade. These rights are compulsory for all public authorities and their exercise can be restricted only by laws which respect their essential substance.

The Constitution of Italy sets forth, under the title „Fundamental principles", the following rights: equality before the law, social equal dignity, without distinction as to race, sex, language, religion, political opinion, personal or social conditions; the right to work and to promoting conditions making it effective; equality of religious confessions before the law; development of culture, of scientific and technical research; protection of health care, of the maternity and of the child; individual criminal responsibility and numerous other political and civil rights. The Constitution provides also the competence of the Constitutional Court to decide in case of disputes concerning the constitutional legitimacy of laws and other acts having legislative value.

The Constitution of Romania, adopted in 1991, with modifications brought in 2003, enounces in its Title II numerous civil, political, economic, social and cultural rights. It is expressly provided that no revision of the Constitution will affect these rights and freedoms.

One can easily see that there are considerable differences among the constitutions evoked, both concerning criteria used and choices made, as well as the formulations given to some of the rights enounced and the nuances implied, which is true also for other constitutions the presentation of which would exceed the limits of this study.

At the international level, the UN Charter reaffirmed in 1945 faith in fundamental human rights, in the dignity and worth of the human person and the duty of States to promote and cooperate to ensure universal and effective respect of human rights and fundamental freedoms for all.

The Universal Declaration of Human Rights, adopted in 1948, proclaimed human rights as common standard of achievement for all peoples and nations. The Declaration enounced comprehensively political, civil, economic, social and cultural rights. The two Covenants adopted in 1966, one concerning the economic, social and cultural rights, the other setting forth political and civil rights, stipulated series of these rights, without declaring one or the other as fundamental.

The International Court of Justice gave, in its decisions and advisory opinions, an important place to fundamental human rights. The Court referred often to some norms as expressing „elementary considerations of humanity", as „sources of legal obligations" or to provisions „incorporating themselves norms of international law which have as a common denominator the obligation to respect the dignity of the human person"[124]. Without a direct reference to decisions of regional jurisdictional bodies, the Court takes them into account (when it refers to decisions of the Inter-American Court of human rights on the right of the individual arrested that the consular office of his country is informed and to decisions of the African Commission of human rights and rights of peoples[125]).

At the regional level, the Convention adopted by the Council of Europe in 1950 for the protection of human rights and fundamental freedoms enshrined a series of civil and political rights and created, with the changes made subsequently, a jurisdictional mechanism to examine petitions concerning violations of the rights provided. The Convention was completed by a series of additional protocols which added some more rights to those initially stipulated. Some economic and social rights are provided for in the Social European Charter adopted by the Council of Europe in 1965 and revised in 1985; this Charter is not provided with a jurisdictional body to solve disputes concerning violations of the respective rights. The European Court of Human Rights often underlined in its decisions the fundamental value of the rights and freedoms protected by the 1950 Convention. Nevertheless, one has to note that the rank recognized to norms of this Convention with regard to the internal law of States parties is different; in Austria, the convention is qualified as constitutional law, in Germany it is considered as a simple law which prevails over other laws, but is inferior to the Basic Law; similarly, in France it is considered stronger than the law, but weaker than the constitution.

The Court of Justice of the European Communities (now Court of Justice of the European Union) was confronted with the conception of fundamental rights even from the 1970s, due to the fact that some constitutional courts of member States (German and Italian) refused to accept the execution of some of its decisions, on grounds of violation of some fundamental human rights proclaimed in the national constitutions. In the case Solange I, the Federal Constitutional German Court reserved its right to proceed to a control of constitutionality of the community law, as long as the community system will not ensure to fundamental rights a protection equivalent with that of the German Basic Law[126].

Affirming the principle of autonomy of the community law, the Court of Justice accepted nevertheless the concept of fundamental rights as an integral part of the community law; consequently, the German Federal Court changed its position in the case Solange II, declaring that it will not control any more the compatibility of the community law with the fundamental rights proclaimed by the German Basic Law in as much as the protection granted by the Court of Justice is considered in general as equivalent to the guarantee offered at the national level. The Court of Justice started gradually to examine the validity of acts adopted by the community institutions from the point of view of their conformity with the fundamental principles and to consider them as part of the primary law of the Communities and then of the Union, along with the treaties.

Then the Court referred to international conventions on human rights and to the general principles accepted by the member States in this field. This created a dynamic of cooperation between the community judge and the national judges and a dynamic of development of the community law as a result of the jurisprudence resulting from cases submitted by persons[127].

The first case involved the examination of a petition alleging the violation of the right to dignity and to equal rights before the law by the application of a scheme authorized by the Commission of the European Communities concerning a programme of social assistance for which the German authorities imposed to present a coupon-sheet with the name of the person. The Court retained that the values which are common to constitutional national rights have to be respected as non-written elements of the community law, but decided that the procedure followed by the German authorities did not contain any element which could threaten fundamental rights contained in the general principles of the Community law the respect of which it has to ensure. The Court confirmed that the right to human dignity is part of the right of the Union and that nothing can be used to affect the right to dignity which is part of the substance of the rights inscribed in the Charter of fundamental rights[128].

In two other cases, Handelsgesellschaft and Nold, the Court affirmed the existence of a community concept concerning fundamental rights, mentioning as its elements the principle of proportionality, the right to property, the right to work and to commercial activities[129].

---

[124] For a study about the jurisprudence of the Court in this field, P.-M. Dupuy, Les „considérations élémentaires d'humanité" dans la jurisprudence de la Cour Internationale de Justice, in Droit et Justice-Mélanges en l'honneur de Nicolas Valticos, Pedone, Paris, 1999, p. 125.
[125] E. Dubout and S. Touzé, art. cit., pp. 25-26.
[126] Decision of the German Federal Constitutional Court of 29 May 1974.
[127] M. Case Stauder v. City of Ulm, 1979, E.C.R. 419, 1970, CMLR, pp. 112-119..
[128] P. Maduro, art. cit., p. 210
[129] Case Handelsgesellschaft, nr. 76, 1970, Rec.1125; case Nold, 14 may 1974, Rec. 45.

In subsequent decisions, the Court extended the sphere of fundamental rights and referred for these purposes mainly to the European Convention for the protection of human rights of 1950[130]. As for the determination of the substance of these rights and their application, the Court underlined the following:
- international documents on human rights to which member States cooperated or are parties may offer indications which necessarily have to be taken into account within the community law; this allowed to integrate the 1950 Convention in the community law through the general principles, as a minimum European standard (decisions in the cases Nold and Hauer);
- it will not admit measures incompatible with fundamental rights which are recognized and guaranteed by the constitutions of member States (decision in the case Nold);
- the fundamental rights should not be considered as absolute rights, but taking into account the social function of goods and activities protected, applying restrictions justified by objectives of general interest pursued by the Community (cases Nold and Hauer).

The Court invoked as sources of fundamental rights: the general principles of law, the constitutional common provisions and the international instruments on human rights to which member States cooperated or which they accepted. With regard to treaties of the Communities, some authors held that the treaties of Rome of 1957 already referred to some fundamental rights, such as: the free circulation, the right to employment, non-discrimination, the right to reparation, respect of the rule of law, democratic control and procedural guarantees[131]. The European Unitary Act of 1986 referred in its preamble to respect of the law and of human rights, on the basis of fundamental rights recognized in the constitutions and the laws of member States, in the Convention for the protection of human rights and fundamental freedoms and in the European Social Charter, in particular freedom, equality and social justice.

In its Chapter on the Union, the Maastricht Treaty of 1992 affirms that the Union respects fundamental rights guaranteed by the 1950 Convention and by constitutional national traditions. The Amsterdam Treaty underlined that the Union is based on the principles of freedom, democracy and respect for human rights and fundamental freedoms; according to this treaty, fundamental rights are taken into account also as a starting point for the competence to adopt legislation. It also attributed to institutions of the Union the competence to act for ensuring the respect of some categories of human rights (the interdiction of discrimination against women, of discrimination in general).

The Charter of fundamental rights of the Union, adopted in 2000 at Nyssa, completed in 2007 and in force since 2009, together with the Lisbon Treaty, marked a higher stage of the engagement of the EU in promoting the concept of fundamental rights, defining them in substance as well as modalities of their application in the context of the Union and in relationship with the application of the European Convention of 1950 on fundamental human rights and freedoms. The Charter enounces a series of human rights, political, civil, economic, social and cultural, grouping them in the following chapters: dignity; freedom; equality; rights of the EU citizens; solidarity; justice.

The law of the EU has to give to economic and social rights the place which they deserve within the fundamental rights, having in view the predominant economic and social nature and the overall objectives of the Union. The Charter makes a clear distinction between rights and principles, meaning that only rights can by invoked by individuals before the courts. This distinction concerns only the cases of direct petitions submitted to courts, not the compatibility of acts adopted by the EU institutions and of national laws with the provisions of the Charter.

The Court decided in a recent case that the right to health (which is formulated as a principle in the Charter and cannot be invoked directly before it) can be considered a fundamental right if it represents an objective with a constitutional value[132]. Thus, the Charter gives an integral view on the fundamental rights that the Union understands to promote and protect, which is different from the previous period when the protection of human rights was limited and accessory, as the treaties had more limited objectives.

The Charter became the main instrument setting forth the fundamental rights in the legal system of the Union. This cannot but influence, as we will try to see later-on, the application of fundamental rights within the system created by the Council of Europe, because the 28 member States of the Union are also members of the Council and took the commitment to respect the Convention of 1950. Nevertheless, the general principles of law remain a source of fundamental rights, as it is provided for in article 6 of the Charter; the Court may use general principles for the

---

[130] Case Liselotte Hauer v. Land Rheinland Pfalz, concerning the use of the right to property, where the petitioner considered this right violated by a regulation of the Community which forbade the granting of new permits to plant grape vine. Decision 13 december 1979, CMLR 1980, 3, p. 42. Similarly, in the case National Panasonic(UK) v. Commission of the European Communities, where the petitioner invoked the violation of the right to private life of the company by the search made by officials of the Commission, referring only to article 8 of the European Convention, CMLR 1980, 3, p. 169.

[131] Analysis by Manfred A. Dauses, La protevtion des droits fondamentaux dans l'ordre juridique des Communautes Europeennes, in Recvue des Affaires Europeennes n0. 4, 1992, pp. 9-21.

[132] Jean Paul Jacqué, Les droits fondamentaux dans le Traité de Lisbonne, in European Yearbook on Human Rights, no 10/2010, p. 132.

interpretation of provisions of the Charter and for clarifying the meaning of some concepts, having in view its former jurisprudence.

SECTION 2 - The CONCEPT of FUNDAMENTAL RIGHTS

Fundamental rights were defined as those expressed or guaranteed by superior norms of a legal order or which are essential for the existence and the substance of other rights of that legal order[133]. Other authors consider that a legal system contains fundamental rights if it creates normative relationships that fulfill four conditions:
- to grant rights and freedoms to the benefit of all persons within the system or to the majority of them;
- to consider unacceptable legislative acts or acts having the same contents which would render null and void these rights and freedoms or would limit them to an extent beyond a certain minimum;
- to dispose of a jurisdictional body of control, having the power to cancel unacceptable norms or to prevent that acts having such effects become norms of the system;
- to dispose of bodies having the competence to bring to the jurisdictional body of control cases of possible violations[134].

Obviously, these features cannot be found under the same form and measure in all legal systems which recognized the concept of fundamental rights. For instance, at the international level there is no jurisdictional body having the power to cancel norms contrary to fundamental rights; even the European Court of Human Rights is not deciding, in the application of the 1950 Convention, to cancel national laws or provisions which would be contrary to fundamental rights, but ascertains the violation of one or the other of articles of the Convention, leaving to the State concerned the discretion to take the necessary measures; the expert bodies created by international treaties on human rights may ascertain that a national law is contrary to an article of the treaty, that is to a fundamental human right or freedom, and may recommend to the State to cancel or to amend it; it is up to the State to take the necessary measures. Of course, the decisions of ECHR are compulsory for States, while the human rights treaty bodies adopt recommendations.

The requirement that such norms grant rights or freedoms to the benefit of all persons also does not take into account rights and freedoms granted by internal, regional or international documents to persons belonging to minorities or to other human groups. As they are similar to fundamental rights granted to all persons, they also have to be considered fundamental rights.

Thus, it is essential that such rights are protected by norms of a similar constitutional rank, by a jurisdictional or quasi-jurisdictional body competent to pronounce itself or to make recommendations with regard to the validity of norms which would attempt to cancel or to modify them substantially.

This is the conception of a hierarchy of norms of law, according to which norms which establish fundamental human rights are on a superior stage, have a constitutional or similar character, meaning that the respective rights cannot be cancelled or limited by other norms of law or other measures. Even the legislative bodies are obliged not to cancel or limit these rights; they can only establish modalities of their exercise. This led jurisdictional bodies and conventional jurisdictions to develop a control of proportionality, namely to evaluate whether the purpose of an act is justified, whether the means provided to attain it are adequate and whether these means fully respect the requirements of the fundamental right, or whether other means would be less restrictive for the substance of the right.

At the same time, this conception gives to fundamental rights a central place within the respective legal system, a superior legal value in respect to other human rights and to the norms setting forth such rights. Fundamental rights are considered to have a founding value for the respective legal system, for structuring this system, as an expression of human value of a superior rank, as well as of their universal nature, aiming at all human beings[135].

This leads also to a difference of status between the fundamental rights, protected both against cancelling them and substantial limitations and against violations, and other human rights, protected only against violations, while all of them are established and protected by legal norms.

---

[133] Laurent Marcoux Jr, Le concept de droits fondamentaux dans le droit de la Communauté Economique Européenne, in Revue internationale de droit comparé no. 4/1983, p. 695(who cites D. Perrott, The Logic of Fundamental Rights, study published in Fundamental Rights, ed. 1973 by J. Bridge and others).

[134] See Droit des libertés fondamentales, elaborated by L. Favoreu, P. Gaia, R. Ghevontian, F. Melin-Soucramanian, A. Pena- Soler, O. Pfersmann, J. Pini, A. Roux, G. Scoffoni and J. Tremeau, Précis, 5-ème ed., Dalloz, 2009, p. 90.

[135] .E. Dubout and Sebastien Touzé, art. cit., pp. 20-22; Louis Favoreu and al., op. cit., p. 97.

As seen above, national and international documents offer different lists of rights and freedoms that they consider as fundamental. Thus, fundamental rights present themselves as a concept having a variable geometry in different legal systems. They are not identical in these systems, in terms of their contents, of the means of protection, of the control bodies and the sanctions applied; nevertheless, many of fundamental rights are common to all or to several legal systems and preserve that character, even if the means and the level of protection are different.

Each of the systems can be called to pronounce itself on the validity of norms contrary to fundamental rights. Closer relationships (as among the national systems and those of the Council of Europe or of the European Union) or less structured (as those between the international system and others) are established among these systems. In their action to protect fundamental rights the legal systems can be complementary; decisions adopted within one system can be followed by others or can influence their decisions; they also can be contradictory. Such decisions can determine evolutions leading to new institutions for protecting fundamental human rights or to more uniformity of the action to protect them.

SECTION 3 - FUNDAMENTAL RIGHTS as a VECTOR of COMMUNICATION between different LEGAL SYSTEMS

This problem appeared when jurisdictional bodies had to examine, directly or indirectly, acts adopted within other legal systems or to solve cases concerning fundamental rights which are common with other legal systems. This leads to communication between legal systems with regard to fundamental rights; the need to communicate flows from the concern to ensure coherency and juridical certainty and to avoid contradictory decisions, from the need to found decisions on principles and norms making them as much as possible just and unquestionable[136].

Beyond the mere communication, the plurality of legal systems protecting fundamental human rights can lead to their mutual or unilateral alignment, meaning that competent jurisdictions give the same solution in cases submitted to them or one of them follows the solution given within another legal system. A recent example are the decisions given by the European Court of Human Rights in 2009 and 2010 with regard to the illegality of the German practice to detain for preventive purposes persons who committed serious crimes, after the execution of the punishment to which they were condemned. This was a practice followed in Germany for more than 80 years, but the number of persons in that situation increased very much during the last years. The persons concerned invoked the violation of some articles of the 1950 Convention. The Court retained that to detain a person beyond the period of time for which he was condemned represents a violation of articles 5.1.a and 7.1. On this basis, the petitioners submitted a new request to the German Constitutional Court.

Although previously that court rejected such petitions, in 2011 it accepted that the provisions of the German Basic Law have to be interpreted so as to be compatible with the 1950 Convention. The Constitutional Court also ascertained that the provisions of the German Penal Code on the preventive detention and its duration are incompatible with the fundamental right to freedom provided for in the Basic Law and fixed a dead-line for ensuring that the Penal Code is in accordance with the Basic Law[137]. It doesn't seem necessary to insist in this context on cases where national laws, and consequently national legal systems, adopted norms different from the 1950 Convention, giving increased protection to some human rights, which is generally accepted having in view the subsidiary nature of the jurisdiction of the ECHR.

The third approach of the relationship between jurisdictions in cases of fundamental rights places them into an apparent conflict, aiming either to avoid a contradiction with another system or to accept the solution imposed by the regional system. For instance, the ECHR avoided in general to exercising a European control on internal acts adopted in order to apply resolutions of the Security Council on the basis of the UN Charter. In its decision in the case Behrami v. France, the Court held that it cannot interpret the 1950 Convention for subjecting to its control acts of States covered by resolutions of the Security Council, because this would represent an interference in the fulfillment of an essential mission of the UN and because the 1950 Convention is an integral part of international law and has to be interpreted so as to be reconciled with other international law norms[138].

Nevertheless, recently the Court exercised a partial control over one of the decisions of Swiss internal bodies which applied a resolution of the Security Council concerning sanctions imposed to persons under suspicion to be involved in terrorist activities, considering that the modalities of application (interdiction of any movement of the

---

[136] E. Dubout, S. Touze, art. cit., p. 18.

[137] Presentation of this case by Christopher Michaelsen, „From Strasbourg with Love"-Preventive Detention before the German Federal Constitutional Court and the European Court of Human Rights, in Human Rights Law Review 12, 2012, pp. 148-167.

[138] E.C.H.R., decision of 31 May 2007, Behrami v. France, case no. 71412/01.

person concerned from an Italian enclave situated in Switzerland) were disproportionate with respect to the objective pursued[139].

A case where a judicial control was exercised over acts adopted to implement Security Council's resolutions, on the basis of the concept of fundamental human rights, is due to the European Court of Justice. The Court was called to pronounce itself on the legality of regulations adopted by the EU institutions in the application of resolutions of the Security Council concerning the freezing of funds and restricting the exercise of human rights of persons and organizations under suspicion of being related to Al-Qaida and the Taliban.

These are the well-known cases Kadi, where Kadi and the organization Al Baarakat contested, initially in front of the First Instance Court (now the Tribunal), the legality of the regulation of the Council of the Union nr. 881/2002 on grounds of violation of fundamental rights to defense, to the adequate judiciary protection and to property, The Tribunal excluded its competence to exercise a control of legality of the regulation on grounds of fundamental community rights, but declared itself competent to control, incidentally, the legality of the respective resolutions of the Security Council on the basis of jus cogens, understood as a public international order which is compulsory for all, including for UN bodies and from which no derogation is permitted. The violation of such norms would make it that the resolutions concerned are compulsory neither for States nor for the Community[140]. Analyzing the measures taken with respect to the human rights invoked, the Tribunal concludes that no norms of jus cogens were violated.

After examining the appeal against the decisions of the Tribunal, the European Court of Justice cancelled the two decisions of the Tribunal and the regulation of the Council with regard to the petitioners. The Court started from the principle according to which the legal order of the European Union represents an internal system which is autonomous with respect to public international law and prevails over it. The Court declares that obligations imposed by an international agreement cannot have the effect to depart from the constitutional principles of the European Community treaty, including among them the principle according to which all community acts have to respect the fundamental rights, as a condition of their legality, that the Court is obliged to control[141].

The Court ascertained the right to defense, mainly the right to be heard, as well as the right to an effective jurisdictional control, were manifestly not respected within the procedure used by the UN for including (persons and organizations) on the lists on the basis of which sanctions provided for in the resolutions of the Security Council were established (by the request of a State or of an organization). With regard to the right to property, the Court retains that, although the freezing of assets is not in itself inadequate or disproportionate, the petitioners were not offered any guarantee to present their cause. The Court rejected thus the regulation on grounds of violation of the right to defense and to an adequate jurisdictional protection, affirming nevertheless that it is not excluded that imposing such measures may be justified.

The decision of the Court placed the institutions of the Union in a difficult position, because the member States have to respect the decisions of the Security Council. The EU Commission asked the Committee on sanctions of the Security Council to convey to it the reasons for inscribing the petitioners on the lists and, after receiving the information, proposed a new regulation, maintaining the sanctions. This new regulation was again subject to an appeal at the Tribunal. In parallel, the Commission initiated within the EU a procedure in order to respect the fundamental rights of persons who were placed on the list of UN and on parallel lists of the EU.

The result of such a procedure, which would concern only member States of the EU (leading in fact to separate lists for these member States) will depend on the information submitted by the Security Council's bodies. In a similar case (the case Othman, decision of 11 June 2009), the Tribunal followed closely the solution given by the Court and cancelled the inclusion of the petitioner on the list (dressed within the EU, on the basis of that of the Security Council). The Tribunal retained that „the community judge has to be able to control the legality and foundation of measures of freezing the assets, without being opposed the secrecy or the confidentiality of some elements of proof and other information used by the Council"[142]. Similar cases were on the agenda of American jurisdictions (the District Court of the District of Columbia).

In Turkey, a first decision of the State Council of 4 July 2004 cancelled the freezing of funds of Al-Kadi (probably the same) with regard to the petitioner, because the information and the documents of the Security Council

---

[139] Case Nada v. Switzerland, presented extensively by Julie Tavernier, La ressponsabilité des Etats au regard de la Convention européenne des droits de l'homme, pour la mise en oeuvre des résolutions adoptées dans le cadre du Chapitre VII de la Charte des Nations Unies, in RGDIP, pp. 101-122.

[140] Decision of the Tribunal of 21 September 2005, Kadi v. Council and Commission, T-315/01, Rec. II-3649; similar decision Yusuf and Al Barakaat, T-305/01, Rec. II-3533.

[141] Decision of 3 September 2008, Kadi and Al Barakaat v. Council and Commission, C-402/05 P. Rec. I, p. 6351.

[142] Decision of 4 December 2008, People's Mojahedin Organization of Iran v.Council, case T-284/08.

justifying the freezing of assets were not transmitted to the Turkish jurisdiction, which thus could not control the legality of that measure. This decision was cancelled in 2007, following the appeal of the Turkish State[143].

Within the UN, the Human Rights Committee received on the 22 October 2008 a communication from the couple Sayadi and Vink v. Belgium. The petitioners claimed that, without suffering a condemnation and without being subject to a criminal prosecution, all their assets were frozen and are prevented to work, to travel and to use their funds to cover the expenses of family life. The Committee retained the violation of their rights to movement, and of their rights to intimacy and to reputation according to articles 12 and 17 of the Covenant on civil and political rights[144].

By the same token, the resolution 1597 of 23 January 2008 of the Parliamentary Assembly of the Council of Europe concerning the „Black lists of the Security Council of the United Nations and of the European Union" affirms that the respective sanctions have to respect some minimal norms of procedural protection and of legal security. The Assembly notes that the norms of procedure and of substance applied by the Security Council of the UN and by the Council of the European Union, in spite of recent improvement, do not respond to such minimal criteria and violate fundamental principles of human rights and of the primacy of law. This resolution, together with the solution given by the Court of Justice in the case Kadi, would reflect a common approach in the constitutional European tradition[145].

Similar opinions were expressed within the UN; by its resolution 60/1, the General Assembly asked the Security Council to see, with the assistance of the Secretary General, that the procedures provided for the inscription of persons and entities on the lists of those likely to be sanctioned and for deleting them from the lists, as well as for applying derogations for humanitarian purposes, are equitable and transparent[146].

According to a study commissioned by the Counsel for Legal Affairs of the UN, the Security Council is obliged by the international customary law to respect the rights of defense of persons targeted by sanctions, who should be informed about measures taken immediately after their adoption, heard by the Security Council, then advised by a counsel and could be able to launch an appeal in front of an independent body previously established[147].

It has been said that the solution of the European Court of Justice stems from the fact that the Court was confronted with a system which does not dispose of an efficient control of decisions of the Committee of sanctions of the Security Council, and which is totally incompatible with the system of guarantees that the Court has to apply with regard to decisions of the Union's institutions[148].

In substance, the Court did not accept that the terrorist threat would justify renouncing to or limiting the judicial control of acts which could be contrary to fundamental human rights. There seems to be a disparity between the European conception and that of the Security Council with regard to the relationship between fundamental rights and the measures that can be taken for the protection of security; this may have serious consequences for international cooperation in an essential field for the authority of law and for the general system of protection of human rights.

The Court affirmed the autonomy of the legal system of the Union versus international law from the point of view of fundamental rights, in a conception which is obviously dualistic concerning the relationship between the international legal order and that of the Union; according to such a conception, the validity of acts of the Union's institutions is evaluated on the basis of their conformity with norms established by the treaties of the Union, including with human fundamental rights, and not with norms or measures adopted at the international level.

This is the conception of Hans Kelsen concerning the systemic relationship among different legal orders[149]. This reminds us the position of the Constitutional German Court in the case Solange I, affirming both the requirement of the equivalent protection of fundamental rights and the autonomy of the two legal orders, thus justifying the constitutional control. The German Court changed its position in the case Solange II, noting the equivalent protection under its system and that of the European Communities.

---

[143] Sixième et septième rapports de l'Equipe d'appui analytique et de surveillance des sanctions du Conseil de Securité, doc. S/2007/132 and 677, cf. Julio Baquero Cruz, La CJCE et le système onusien; la réception de l'arrêt Kadi de la Cour de Justice des Communautés Européennes, in Les droits fondamentaux: charnière entre ordres et systèmes juridiques, ed. E. Dubout and S. Touzé, op. cit., p. 139.

[144] Communication nr. 1472/2006, Sayadi and Vinck v. Belgium, CCPR/C/94/D/1472/2006 of 22 October 2007, pp. 45-46.

[145] Julio Baquero Cruz, art. cit., p. 140.

[146] Final Document of the World Summit of 2005, 16 September 2005.

[147] Bruno Fassbender, Targeted Sanctions and Due Process: The Responsibility of the UN Security Council to Ensure that Fair and Clear Procedures are Made Available to Individuals and Entities Targeted with Sanctions under Chapter VII of the UN Charter, Study commissioned by the UN Office of Legal Affairs, 20 March 2006, pp. 8, 30-31.

[148] Bruno Fassbender, Study, p. 142.

[149] Hans Kelsen, Les rapports de système entre le droit international et le droit interne, in RCADI, 1926-IV, vol. 14, p. 231.

Serious measures have been taken within the Union for ensuring respect for the Charter of fundamental rights; even before its adoption as a document having a legal force, the European Commission decided that any proposal of a legislative act should be subject to a previous control of its compatibility with the Charter and be accompanied by a statement of compatibility[150]. The Commission adopted in 2010 a Strategy to ensure respect for the Charter, as an instrument allowing persons to enjoy the rights set forth[151].

The Strategy of the Commission includes mainly an evaluation of impact of any legislative proposal on human rights provided for in the Charter (identification of the rights potentially affected, their absolute character or restrictions possible, the positive or adverse effect of different political options on these rights, the degree of interference with the respective rights, the necessity and the proportionality of this interference with respect to the options of action and the objectives pursued). The presentation of an annual report of the Commission on the application of the Charter is also requested. The Council of the Union also adopted measures to this end, with regard to the activity of its subordinate bodies[152].

It is also interesting to see the influence of the EU Charter of fundamental rights on the jurisprudence of the ECHR and on the interpretation of the 1950 Convention. ECHR refers to provisions of the Charter in order to introduce in its jurisprudence new solutions, more adapted to circumstances and to the needs of the society[153]. As a matter of fact, each of the two courts refers to solutions given by the other and to the legal relevant documents.

Thus, according to appreciations by ECHR, the Charter of fundamental rights contributed to build a consensus of the majority of member States of the Council of Europe, which leads to common interpretations. For instance, in the case Zolotuhin v. Russian Federation, the ECHR analyzed provisions of the Charter, of international and regional instruments on civil and political rights, in order to deduce the less restrictive solution in the application of the rule *non bis in idem*, based not on the legal qualification, but on the material facts presented, meaning that it is forbidden to prosecute and judge a person for a second offense if it has its origin in identical facts or in facts similar in substance[154].

The ECHR also found the possibility to come back on one of its previous jurisprudence, on the basis of important evolutions which took place at the international level and citing among others the Charter of fundamental rights, with respect to the retroactivity of the penal law. Citing also the jurisprudence of the European Court of Justice, according to which the application of the more lenient penal law is part of the constitutional traditions common to member States, as well as the jurisprudence of the International Court of Justice, the ECHR deduces that a consensus formed at international and regional levels allows to consider that the application of the most lenient punishment, even if provided by a law which is subsequent to the moment the violation was committed, became a fundamental principle of penal law.

The Court interpreted in this way the article 7.1 of the 1950 Convention[155]. In the case Shalk and Koph v. Austria of 24 June 2010, concerning the issue of marriage between homosexuals or with transsexuals, ECHR invoked the provision of the Charter which does not refer to marriage between a man and a woman, but to the right to marriage and to build a family in general terms (that is different from the 1950 Convention), appreciating that the rights provided for in the Charter are adapted in this manner to the evolution of morals in the European society[156].

In other cases, ECHR appreciates that the provisions of the Charter led to adapting and modernizing the 1950 Convention, on the basis of a new European consensus, which justifies a different interpretation from the previous. In the case G. N. v. Italy, the ECHR based itself on article 21 of the Charter which forbids discrimination among others on grounds of genetic features or of disability, in order to interpret article 14 of the 1950 Convention as forbidding also this grounds of discrimination; in the case Peterka v. the Czeck Republic, the Court added as grounds of discrimination according to article 14 of the Convention ethnic origin, convictions, age or sexual orientation[157].

* * *

---

[150] Doc. SEC(2001), 380/3.

[151] COM(2010) 573 final, Stratégie pour la mise en oeuvre effective de la Charte des droits fondamentaux par l'Union Européenne.

[152] Conseil des Affaires Générales, 3092-ème session, Bruxelles, 23 May 2011.

[153] Analyses by Florence Benoit-Rohmer, La Charte des droits fondamentaux de l'Union Européenne dix ans après sa proclamation, in European Yearbook on Human Rights 2011, pp. 24-30.

[154] Petition nr. 14939/03, decision of 10 February 2009, para. 79; same in the case Maresti v. Croatia, petition nr. 55759/07, decision of 25 June 2009.

[155] Case Scoppoli v. Italy, decision of the Great Chamber, 10 September 2009, petition nr. 10249/o3.

[156] Cited by Florence Benoit-Rohmer, art. cit., p. 38.

[157] Petition nr. 43134/05, decision of 1 December 2009; petition nr. 21990/08, decision of 4 May 2010.

In all the cases mentioned, the fundamental human rights are the key element of contact between different legal systems, which leads to a kind of coordination, to similar solutions in similar cases, and is beneficial to legal certainty and to strengthening the importance of the rule of law, in particular that which protects human rights and freedoms.

The Charter of fundamental rights is not only a legal document on the basis of which the European Court of Justice can protect individual human rights, but it is placed at the foundation of the legislative activity of the Union, giving attention to the preventive action, to the impact study, in order to avoid adopting acts contrary to fundamental rights. As the Charter took into consideration the legal and social evolution produced in Europe and in the world, the ECHR itself uses the text of the Charter and the jurisprudence of ECJ to adapt the interpretation of the 1950 Convention and its own jurisprudence. The ECJ was also determined to control the validity of acts adopted by the EU institutions meant to implement resolutions of the Security Council in order to evaluate whether they are compatible with the EU fundamental human rights.

The ECHR also recently changed its approach, accepting to control partially internal acts adopted to implement Security Council's resolutions[158]. Internal courts also followed in the footsteps of the two courts, which gives to the fundamental rights a central place in the overall activity of jurisdictional and quasi-jurisdictional bodies for protecting human rights. The United Nations and other international bodies also must follow this evolution, in order to avoid jurisdictional control of their decisions and potential loss of effectivity.

Analysts affirm that by the adoption of the Charter a culture of fundamental human rights develops within the European Union, as a new project for the application of these rights, not only as an impediment to the adoption of acts which would be contrary to them, but also as a guide for all the activity of the Union and of member States[159].

An opinion was also expressed that the voice of the European Union, of the ECJ, that is the voice of law, would be weak in the present international context[160]. We do not share this vision of pessimism.

First, the position of the European Court of Justice is not isolated; other instances and institutions adopted similar positions, in this and in other fields; if States members of the Union will not implement measures as those contested in front of the Court, it is to be expected that other States will do the same. A constant position of the ECJ in defense of the fundamental human rights within the Union, with respect to acts adopted by other legal systems, will rather lead to finding solutions of conciliation, ensuring respect for human rights and freedoms, to the benefit of the cause of human rights in general.

Second, the promotion by the European Court of respect for the fundamental human rights cannot but influence the UN bodies in the exercise of their competences and, of course, member States of the Union, both as members of the UN and within their own legal systems, by introducing the same requirements of an impact study and in general by examining attentively any measure which could affect one or the other of the fundamental rights.

---

[158] Olivier de Schutter, The New Architecture of Fundamental Rights Policy in the EU, in European Yearbook on Human Rights, 2011, pp. 107-141.
[159] Olivier de Schutter, The New Architecture of Fundamental Rights Policy in the EU, in European Yearbook on Human Rights, 2011, pp. 107-141.
[160] Julio Baquero Cruz, art. cit., pp. 143-144.

CHAPTER V - HUMAN RIGHTS and the ACTIVITY of TRANSNATIONAL CORPORATIONS

ABSTRACT

Transnational corporations became an important factor in the economy of many States. They are working in many developing countries, carrying out economic projects which have often a negative impact on human rights. There is therefore a preoccupation to see that such activities are carried in conformity with international standards on human rights, as established by international law instruments.

The UN started looking at this issue at the beginning of the 90-ties, but a more substantial approach started within the human rights treaty bodies in their activity of considering the periodic reports of States parties (mainly the Committee on economic, social and cultural rights). The UN Human Rights Council, a newly created body under the General Assembly, started to consider this issue since 2008, on the basis of reports presented by a Special Representative of the Secretary General. After establishing a Framework entitled "Protect, Respect and Remedy", the Special Representative elaborated Guiding principles on Business and Human Rights, as well as Principles for non-jurisdictional means of enterprises and Principles for the negotiation of contracts between States and enterprises including risks for human rights.

These principles were adopted by the Council and recommended to States. A working group was also created to ensure their follow up.

KEY WORDS: transnational companies, less developed countries, vulnerable groups, restructuring with human face, globalization, impact on human rights, private actors, Guiding principles, State and enterprises' obligations, remedies, global platform of action.

INTRODUCTION

Globalization created a relationship between the transnational companies and the population of many States on the planet. Thus, foreign companies become important actors, sometimes very important, for the observation and promotion of human rights and fundamental freedoms in the world. The structure and activity of such companies have social and environmental impacts not only in the immediate communities where they operate, but sometimes also across the whole social and economic life in the respective countries.

Transnational companies operate in all countries of the world. In most of the developed countries their activity is submitted to clear rules and controls, although sometimes situations appeared also there, when their activities represented violations of human rights to health, to a sound environment and others.

The situation is different in less developed countries, as well with regard to the most vulnerable groups of people, like the indigenous people, persons belonging to ethnic groups, women and children. In such cases, either the legislation is not satisfactory to protect human rights, or is not applied, or the State accepts conditions which lead to human rights violations.

In the Report presented to the session of 2010[161] of the Human Rights Council, John Ruggie, Special Representative of the Un Secretary General for the issue of the human rights and the transnational societies and other enterprises, notes the increasing gap between the impact of economic forces and actors on human rights and the capacity of societies to manage the adverse consequences of the activity of these societies and enterprises; this leads to a permissive context where abuses are committed by enterprises without being sanctioned and without possibility to obtain reparation. He outlines also that not all States have adequate laws and regulations to manage such issues, and where laws exist, they present lacunae, their application is incoherent and the legal protection is absent, while the administration competent for the relations with enterprises works separately from institutions dealing with the protection of human rights.

It is obvious that most of the negative consequences of globalization are endangering especially economic, social and cultural human rights. It is submitted that, with the increase of unequal distribution of wealth and the exclusion of large segments of population in the world from the benefits promised by globalization, it becomes necessary to stress the need for approaching aspects of globalization on the basis of respect and promotion of human rights. International intergovernmental and non-governmental organizations are looking for ways and modalities so

---

[161] Doc. A/HRC/14/27 of 9 April 2010.

as to avoid the negative consequences of globalization and to ensure that respect of human rights is integrated in the activities of transnational companies.

SECTION 1- CONSIDERATION by the HUMAN RIGHTS TREATY BODIES

1. From the beginning of its activity, the Committee on economic, social and cultural rights (CESCR) underlined that activities of cooperation for development do not automatically contribute to the promotion of respect for economic, social and cultural rights and that an important number of activities undertaken on behalf of development appeared later-on to be ill conceived and even risky from the point of view of human rights[162]. The Committee affirmed constantly that international bodies should carefully avoid to support projects which, for instance, imply using forced labour in violation of international norms, encouraging or enhancing discrimination against individuals or groups in violation of the provisions of the Covenant, or which would lead to massif expulsions or displacement of people, without adequate measures of protection and compensation; on the contrary, they should in as much as possible support projects and methods which contribute not only to economic enhancement or to implementing larger objectives, but also to the full exercise of all human rights[163]. Even with regard to programmes and policies of restructuring related to the foreign debt, the Committee asked the States and the competent UN bodies to see that measures of protection of economic, social and cultural rights are integrated in such programmes and policies, in an approach called "restructuring with human face".

In other General Comments, the Committee asked the financial institutions, mainly the World Bank and the IMF, to give more importance to the right to education in their policy of credit and in their programmes of restructuring, and affirmed that the adoption by specialized institutions, programmes and bodies of the UN of an approach based on human rights would greatly facilitate the implementation of the right to education[164]. With regard to the right to health, the Committee underlined that all members of the society-individuals (among whom health professionals), families, local communities, intergovernmental and non-governmental organizations, including those representing the civil society and the sector of private enterprises, have a part of responsibility for the realization of this right. The Committee stressed that States should see that international instruments they negotiate and sign do not impede upon the right to health and that measures they adopt as members of international organizations take dully into account the right to health[165].

Regarding the right to water, the Committee stressed that States have the duty to take legislative and other measures which are necessary and effective to forbid third parties to refuse access under equal conditions to adequate water deliveries, or to pollute or to capture in an unjustified manner water resources, including natural resources, wells and systems of water distribution.

It was also recommended that States parties should see that third parties which manage or control services of access or distribution of water do not compromise physical access, at affordable cost and without discrimination, to drinking water of an acceptable quality and in sufficient quantity[166]. With regard to social security, the Committee considers that States should protect beyond their territory the right to social security, by preventing their nationals and enterprises under their jurisdiction to violate this right in other countries[167].

The Committee took also very firm positions with regard to the phenomena resulting from globalization. In 1998, the Committee considered the problems of globalization in the context of the Covenant which it has the mandate to monitor and to promote and stressed that international organizations and the governments which created them have a serious and continuous responsibility in this field. The Committee made an appeal to the World Bank and the IMF to officially recognize the economic, social and cultural rights and to the WTO to find methods to facilitate a systematic evaluation of the impact of some commercial and investment policies on human rights[168].

---

[162] General Comment no 2: International technical assistance measures (art.: 22 of the Covenant), Compilation of General Comments and General Recommendations adopted by human rights treaty bodies, doc. HRI/GEN/1/Rev. 8, 8 May 2006, p. 12.

[163] General Comment nr. 2, p. 12.

[164] General Comment no. 13: The right to education (art. 13 of the Covenant), Compilation…, doc. HRI/GEN/1/Rév. 8, p. 71; the same with regard to the right to health, General Comment no. 14: The right to the highest attainable standard of health (art. 12), ibidem, pp. 86-105 and the right to water, General Comment no. 15(arts. 11 and 12 of the Covenant), Compilation…., doc, HRI/GEN/1/Rev. 8, pp. 105-122.

[165] General Comment no. 14: The right to the highest attainable standard of health cited above (art.14 of the Covenant), Compilation…, doc. HRI/GEN/1/Rev. 8, pp. 86-105.

[166] General Comment no. 15: The right to water, cited above (arts. 11 et 12 of the Covenant), Compilation…, doc. HRI/GEN/1/Rev. 8, pp. 105-122.

[167] General Comment no. 19: The right to social security (art. 9 of the Covenant), Compilation…, doc. HRI/GEN/Rev. 9, vol. I, p. 187.

[168] CESCR, Statement on Globalization to the Third Ministerial Conference of WTO, 1999, doc. E/C.12/1999, para.7; among others General Comment no. 18(The right to work, art. 6 of the Covenant), Compilation…, doc. HRI/GEN/1/Rév. 8, pp. 148-161.

The Committee is also very firm with regard to the protection of the material and moral interests resulting from the intellectual property; without denying the material and moral rights of the author, the Committee underlined that intellectual property is a social good and has a social function.

Taking into account that such rights may belong to powerful corporations and be used for their own interests, the Committee underlined that States should see that excessively high prices for essential medicine, for seeds and agricultural products, for textbooks and other educational materials do not hinder the exercise of the rights to health, to food and to education for large segments of the population and that States should prevent that scientific and technical progress is used for purposes contrary to human rights and dignity, including the rights to life, to health and to private life, for instance by excluding to register brevet inventions each time that their use could compromise the full respect for these rights.

According to the Committee, States should envisage to regulating the responsibility of the private business sector, private research institutes and other non-State actors for the respect of these rights[169]. In 2001, CESCR expressed the opinion that other actors than States, including international organizations, have duties which can be monitored and that all actors have to be responsible for their obligations according to the international law of human rights[170].

The Committee on the Rights of the Child took the same position. In connection with the WTO Agreement on Intellectual Property (TRIPS), CESCR stressed that the effect of these international norms is to protect in a disproportionate manner corporatist business and interests to the detriment of human rights and to create serious concerns in many fields, mainly food security, knowledge of indigenous peoples, environmental safety and health care. The Committee on the Rights of the Child raised the same issue with regard to the bilateral and regional commercial agreements in this field (TRIPS plus) and the realization of the right to health of children and asked States to ensure that such agreements do not affect the possibility to offer the medicine necessary to children[171].

The concentration of the copy-rights in the hands of powerful enterprises is also seen as likely to restrict the circulation of cultural values and access to them. In a Recommendation of 2003 on the promotion and use of multilingualism and the universal access to the virtual space, UNESCO affirms the necessity for the States to take into account in their legislation concerning copy-right "a just balance between the interests of the author, of the owners of the intellectual rights and of related rights, and those of the public".

In the same vein, the monopoly and control over the media by powerful corporations allow to determine the contents of the information distributed and thus to undermine the exercise of many human rights, from those to participate in public life, to the right to a thorough information from different sources, to the right to health by distributing incomplete information on different medicine, food or on the situation of the environment[172].

The CESCR interpreted the Covenant so as to involve obligations for all actors acting on the territory of States parties, including the private actors, private enterprises, national or foreign and intergovernmental organizations, and consequently its right to monitor the activities of these actors from the point of view of respect for human rights under the Covenant. Other human rights treaty bodies, without having directly in their mandate the protection of economic, social and cultural rights, took also position with regard to the responsibility of the private sector for respecting human rights.

2. The Human Rights Committee (civil and political) asked the State parties to review their legislation and practices and take all necessary measures to eliminate discrimination against women in all fields, for instance forbidding any discrimination by private actors in fields such as employment, education, political activities and access to housing, goods and services[173]. The Committee also underlined that individuals are protected not only against violations of their rights by state agents, but also against acts committed by private persons, physical or moral and that States are violating these rights if they refrain from taking adequate measures or from exercising due diligence to prevent and sanction such acts committed by private persons, physical or moral[174].

3. According to the 1965 International Convention on the elimination of all forms of racial discrimination, each State party shall prohibit and bring to an end, by all appropriate means, including legislation as necessary, racial

---

[169] General Comment no 17; The right of everyone to benefit from the protection of the moral and material interests resulting from any scientific, literary or artistic production of which he or she is the author (art. 15 of the Covenant), Compilation...,doc. HRI/GEN/1/Rev. 8, pp. 122-131.

[170] CESCR, Statement on Human Rights and Intellectual Property, UN doc. E/C.12/2001/15, para. 10.

[171] CESCR, Statement to the Third Ministerial Conference of WTO, 1999, doc. E/C.12/1999/9, para. 4; cf. also M. Salomon, Global Responsibility for Human Rights, Oxford University Press, 2007, chapter 3, pp. 112 and foll.

[172] On these issues, Ion Diaconu, La Culture et les Droits de l'Homme, 2015, Edilivre, Paris, pp. 357-380.

[173] General Comment no. 28: Article 3(The equality of rights between men and women), Compilation..., doc. HRI/GEN/1/Rev. 8, pp. 218-225.

[174] General Comment no. 31: The Nature of the General Legal Obligations Imposed on States Parties to the Covenant, Compilation..., doc. HRI/GEN/1/Rev.8, pp. 233-238.

discrimination by any persons, groups or organizations. On this basis, the Committee on the Elimination of Racial Discrimination (CERD) has given a wide scope of this provision to address all kind of business and of private actors, referring to employment, labour market, private sector, transnational corporations, restaurants, housing agencies and others, as well as to different measures meant to protect victims of racial discrimination, that is legislation, but also investigation and monitoring.

Over time, the Committee increasingly has expanded the scope of ICERD to address a wide area of acts by private actors, including business, in private sphere. The Committee has not hesitated to address discriminatory acts by business enterprises in various contexts. It explicitly mentions private companies, mining companies, exploitation infrastructure projects, energy developers or other activities particularly in relation to the protection of specific groups, mainly indigenous peoples, but also some ethnic groups like Roma.

CERD has examined activities of transnational corporations in the context of extractive, forestry or other activities on the lands occupied or otherwise used by indigenous peoples. The problems considered have been mainly the removal of indigenous peoples from their land, impediments created for their use of the lands and health problems created by the exploitation of resources, environmental degradation, security issues or infringement of other rights of indigenous such as the right to freedom of movement.

Many recommendations were adopted with regard to the activities of the media, and as it is known most of them are private. States are encouraged to influence upon media to eliminate any ideas of racial superiority, or racial hatred or incitement to discrimination, to combat such expressions, to prohibit them and to encourage methods of self-monitoring by the media, through codes of conduct for media organizations. In its General Recommendations, the Committee adopted a clear position, asking States parties to protect human rights against discrimination, even if it would be the result of private activities.

In its General Recommendation 20/1996 on article 5 of the Convention which enumerates a long non-exhaustive list of human rights of all categories, the Committee states that "To the extent that private institutions influence the exercise of rights or the availability of opportunities, the State must ensure that the result has neither the purpose nor the effect of creating or perpetuating racial discrimination"[175]. In 1997 CERD adopted the General Recommendation No. 23 on the rights of indigenous peoples, which enounces the principles of protection of their rights to own, develop, control and use of their communal lands, territories and resources and prescribes indirectly measures that States have to take to protect these rights and to control activities of private companies[176].

In its General Recommendation No. 27/2000 on discrimination against Roma, the Committee recommended that States act firmly against any discriminatory practice affecting Roma, mainly by local authorities and private owners, with regard to taking up residence and access to housing[177]. In the General Recommendation No. 25/2000 on gender related dimensions of racial discrimination, the Committee asked States to take measures to ensure non-discrimination and avoid segregation in housing, including by taking action against private owners or housing agencies[178].

In its Opinions on Communications submitted under the procedure provided for in article 14 of the Convention, the Committee has examined claims regarding racial discrimination in private employment[179] and stressed that States have the obligation to monitor that private banks are not discriminating on grounds of race or ethnic origin[180].

The Committee also urged one State to take effective measures to ensure that housing agencies refrain from engaging in discriminatory practices and do not accept submissions from private landlords which would discriminate on racial grounds[181]. With regard to another communication, CERD was satisfied that the State party condemned the owner of a restaurant that refused to receive Roma, but urged it to complete its legislation in order to guarantee the right of access to public places and to sanction any refusal of access to such places for reasons of racial discrimination[182].

More recently, CERD addressed the issue of responsibility of the States of origin of such corporations for activities deployed on other territories. In its Concluding observations on Canada of 2007 the Committee noted with concern reports about adverse effects of economic activities connected with the exploitation of natural resources in

---

[175] General Recommendation nr: 15 on article 1, paragraph 1 of the Convention, Compilation…, doc. HRI/GEN/1/Rev.9, vol. II, p. 28, para.5

[176] General Recommendation nr. 23 on the rights of indigenous peoples, Compilation…, doc. HRI/GEN/1/Rev. 9, vol. II, p. 32.

[177] General Recommendation nr. 27 of 2000 on discrimination against Roma, Compilation…, doc. HRI/GEN/1/Rev.9, vol. II, p.38.

[178] General Recommendation nr. 25 on gender based racial discrimination, Compilation…, doc. HRI/GEN/1/Rev. 9, vol. II, p. 35.

[179] Communication No. 1/1994, A. Yilmaz Dogan v. The Netherlands, doc. CERD/C/36/D/1/1984.

[180] Communication No. 10/1997, Ziad Ben Ahmed Habassi v. Denmark, doc. CERD/C/54/D/10/1997.

[181] Communication No. 18/2000, F. A. v. Norway, doc. CERD/C/58/D/18/2000.

[182] Communication No. 11/1998, Miroslav Lacko v. Slovakia, CERD/C/68/D/11/1998, paragraph 11.

countries outside Canada by transnational corporations registered in the State party on the right to land, health, healthy environment and the way of life of indigenous peoples living in these regions, and encouraged the State party to take appropriate legislative or administrative measures to prevent such acts of those transnational corporations and in particular to explore ways to hold them responsible[183].

An identical recommendation was addressed to the United States of America in 2008. The Committee asked Canada and the United States to include in their next periodic reports information on the effects of activities of transnational corporations registered by them on indigenous peoples abroad and on any measures taken in this regard.

In 2009, the Committee considered, under the item "Prevention of racial discrimination, including early warning and urgent action procedure", a report about the alleged negative impact of uranium extraction activities conducted by a French State company on the traditional lands of Touareg people of Niger. The Committee requested information from the Governments of Niger and France on the matter and on measures taken to obtain prior and informed consent of the community concerned with regard to these activities. The problem was raised in March 2015, when the periodic report of France was considered; the delegation informed that a law was adopted in 2014, according to which the French enterprises have to implement risk management procedures aiming at preventing and reducing health, social and environmental damage and violations of human rights which may result from their activities in partner countries. Moreover, after the consideration of the periodic report of Niger in august 2015, CERD recommended that the State party ensures that the exploitation of uranium is not detrimental to the health of the population and to the protection of the environment[184].

More recently, after the consideration of periodic reports of Norway and The Netherlands, CERD recommended them to take appropriate legislative measures to prevent public and private national companies and transnational corporations registered by them involved in economic activities abroad from carrying out activities that negatively impact on the enjoyment of human rights of local communities, in particular the rights of indigenous peoples and minority groups and the environment in the host countries, taking into account the Guiding Principles on business and human rights adopted by the Human Rights Council in 2011[185].

4. In its General Comments, the Committee on the elimination of all forms of discrimination against women also stressed the requirement that private enterprises respect the rights of women and avoid discrimination against them. In the General Comment on the right to health care, the Committee recommends that States parties closely monitor the delivery of health services by public bodies, non-governmental organizations or private enterprises to women, so that men and women have equal access to services of the same quality[186]. In a General Comment on special measures, the Committee underlines the obligation of authorities, judicial power, organizations, enterprises and individuals to guarantee the absence of any discrimination, direct or indirect, and to protect women against any discrimination[187].

5. Similarly, the Committee on the Rights of the Child stressed the legal obligation of the States parties to the respective Convention to see that non-State providers of services (to children) respect the provisions of the Convention; the Committee reminds that the superior interest of the child should be the primary consideration in all decisions which concern children, by they taken by public or private institutions. The Committee resumes the General Comment of CESCR no. 14 cited above, stressing that all members of the society-individuals (including health professionals), families, local communities, intergovernmental and non-governmental organizations, organizations representing civil society and the sector of private enterprises-have their part of responsibility in realizing the right to health, and advises the States to use the Convention as a framework for defining international assistance to development so that the programmes of donor countries are based on respect of these rights (of the children). The Committee also asks the Group of World Bank, IMF and WTO to ensure that their activities concerning international cooperation and economic development give a primary place to the superior interest of the child and favour the full application of the Convention[188].

---

[183] Report of CERD to the General Assembly, doc. Suppl. Nr. 18(A/62/18), para. 78.
[184] Doc. CERD/C/NER/CO/R. 15-21 of 21 August 2015.
[185] CERD/C/NOR/CO/R. 21-22 of August 2015 and CERD/C/NLD/CO/R. 19-21 of August 2015.
[186] General Recommendation no.24: Article 12 of the Convention (Women and health), Compilation..., doc. HRI/GEN/1/Rev. 9, vol. II, p. 130.
[187] General Recommendation no. 25, para. 1 of article 4 of the Convention (Temporary special measures), Compilation..., doc. HRI/GEN/1/Rev. 9, vol. II, p. 132.
[188] General Comment no. 5: General measures of implementation of the Convention on the Rights of the Child(arts. 4, 42 et 44, para. 6), Compilation..., doc. HRI/GEN/1/Rev. 9, vol II, pp. 200-201, 209-211.

SECTION 2 - OBLIGATIONS of ENTERPRISES in the FIELD of HUMAN RIGHTS

According to all instruments on human rights, the State has the responsibility with regard to all persons and activities under its jurisdiction, and some precise obligations (abstention from violating itself norms on human rights, protecting these rights against violations from other persons, facilitating the exercise of these rights and ensuring the means for the exercise of some rights by those persons who are not able to do it by themselves). Observation of human rights is also an obligation for other persons, individuals or moral persons, as an expression of the horizontal effect of the norms in this field, meaning that they also have the obligation not to violate the rights of other persons, not to endanger these rights and not to oppose to their exercise. The State has to ensure the protection of human rights against these kinds of acts or omissions from these persons.

Scholars are considering also the responsibility and the obligations of the international community, of all States, mainly of the developed States, for the eradication of poverty and for promoting respect of economic and social rights in the world at large. International bodies, various conferences on development, as well as scholars, are also questioning if and to what extent other actors than States have obligations in the field of human rights, in what countries and with regard to what rights. The problem we are confronted with is whether foreign enterprises, including multinational companies, have responsibilities and obligations to respect human rights in their activities.

It is generally recognized that every person, including a legal person, is obliged to observe a number of civil and political human rights, such as the right to life, the interdiction of genocide and of torture and disappearances, the interdiction of forced labour and child labour, the interdiction of racial discrimination and of discrimination on other grounds, the interdiction to commit or to participate in war crimes and crimes against humanity and to benefit from such crimes[189].

As for the multinational companies, as a result of activities they develop on the territories of other States, many other obligations are incumbent to them, especially those related to employing individuals from those States and to the effects of their activities on local people, on the territory, on the environment. International organizations adopted some documents which go further in this direction. One can mention in this respect the document on Norms on responsibilities of transnational companies and other commercial enterprises concerning human rights, adopted by the Sub-commission for the prevention of discrimination and protection of minorities[190], the Global Compact proposed by the Secretary general of the United Nations in 1999 and reaffirmed in many documents since, the Tripartite Statement of ILO of 1977 on principles concerning multinational enterprises and social policy, the OECD Guidelines for multinational enterprises to promote a responsible conduct in business in accordance with applicable rules.

These documents have in mind not only civil and political rights as those mentioned above, but also respect for the norms of international law and the internal law concerning social rights, the right to development, rights of indigenous peoples and of local communities. These documents have a declaratory character, are not creating legal obligations and mechanisms for monitoring their implementation; their purpose is to establish principles and standards of good practices[191]. The objective followed is to create an international political environment which leads to the voluntary respect of human rights standards by multinational corporations, to their involvement in the social development of the host countries, to introducing human rights as a component of their activity.

Since 2008, the question of the relationship between business and human rights is considered by the Human Rights Council on the basis of reports of John Ruggie, the Special Representative of the UN Secretary-general on the issue of human rights and transnational corporations and other enterprises. In his report of 2008, the Special Representative proposed a Framework entitled "Protect, Respect and Remedy", which was accepted by the Council. This Framework is based on three pillars: the obligation of the State to protect against abuses of human rights by third parties, including enterprises, through adequate policies, regulations and jurisdiction; the responsibility of enterprises to respect human rights, meaning to act with due diligence to avoid the violation of other's rights and to address the adverse impacts involved; an enhanced access of the victims to effective, judiciary and non-judiciary remedies.

The Human Rights Council asked the Special Representative to operationalize this Framework, offering concrete and practical recommendations for its application. On the basis of extended consultations with States,

---

[189] Elena Pariotti, International Soft Law, Human Rights and Non-State Actors: Towards the Accountability of Transnational Corporations?, in Human Rights Review, 2009, no.10, p.148.

[190] More extensively on these norms and some of the documents mentioned, David Weissbrodt and Muria Kruger, Current Developments, Norms on the Responsibilities of Transnational Corporations and Other Business Enterprises with Regard to Human Rights, in American Journal of International Law no 97, 2003, pp.901 and following.

[191] Elena Pariotti, art cit., p. 145.

intergovernmental organizations, stakeholders and civil society, the Special Representative elaborated the Guiding Principles on Business and Human Rights, which were submitted to the Council and adopted in 2011[192]. The Report presenting these Guidelines underline from the beginning that their objective is to enhance the existing standards and practices concerning human rights in order to promote their application to the benefit of persons and communities affected by the activities of such companies and to contribute to a socially durable globalization.

The Principles recommended are the following:

A. The obligation of the State to protect human rights on its territory. It has the obligation to protect human rights against abuses by everybody, including enterprises, and for that, to take measures to prevent, investigate, punish and remedy such abuses through adequate policies, legislation, regulations and jurisdiction. States should adopt laws requiring enterprises to respect human rights, should evaluate the adequacy of such laws, should take measures to protect human rights against violations by enterprises owned or controlled by them, should ensure respect of human rights when contracting with different companies, as well as in their policies and arrangements with other States and as members of international organizations;

B. Enterprises have the duty to respect human rights, to avoid abuses and to address the adverse impact of their activities on human rights. It is underlined that their responsibility refers to human rights recognized by the Universal Declaration and the two Covenants on human rights, as well as by the ILO Declaration on fundamental principles and rights concerning work (the 8 basic conventions of ILO); depending on circumstances, other standards also have to be taken into account, mainly those deserving special attention concerning the rights of indigenous people, women, minorities, disabled people, migrants, as well as the norms of humanitarian law in situations of conflict.

Their responsibility includes: to avoid producing or contributing to adverse impact of their activities on human rights; to address such impact when it takes place, to seek to prevent or to address such impact directly related to their activities, products or services; to have an engagement adopted at the highest level to respect human rights and to make it public; to develop processes of due diligence in order to identify, prevent, address and inform how they are treating the adverse impact, as well as for its remedy; to evaluate the risks and the potential impact of their activities and integrate the result of evaluations in the functioning and the processes of the enterprise; to offer remedies and to cooperate with them (the vulnerable groups affected) in case of adverse impact.

C. States should ensure that persons and groups affected have access to efficient remedies, judiciary or non-judiciary. This means the existence of mechanisms of claims (for any injustice against a right of a person or a group, based on a law, a contract, a practice, a custom), meaning any process involving or not the State, judiciary or non-judiciary through which petitions concerning activities of business affecting human rights can be raised and remedied. Remedies include excuses, restitution, rehabilitation, compensation (financial or non-financial) and sanctions (penal or administrative), as well as prevention through injunction and non-repetition.

States are requested to ensure efficient jurisdictional mechanisms, to offer also non-jurisdictional means and to facilitate the access to the latter. Enterprises are requested to participate in such mechanisms and to establish themselves non-jurisdictional mechanisms which should be legitimate (have the confidence of those for whom they were created), accessible, predictable, equitable, transparent and compatible with human rights.

The Special Representative considers that these principles represent a global platform of action, on the basis of which progress should be achieved pursuing the development of the system on a long-term basis. With regard to the enterprises, he considers that these principles represent a general standard of their activity, which exists independently of the ability or the willingness of the States to fulfill their obligations and beyond the observance of the national laws and regulations, and that they should not undermine the ability of States to fulfill their obligations in this field.

It is obvious that these principles do not elaborate norms or obligations of international law, but enounce legal implications of the existing standards and practices followed by States and enterprises and attempt to integrate them in a coherent and comprehensive model. Moreover, they have to be applied to the specific situation of the 193 States members of UN, because there are 80 thousand transnational enterprises, ten times more subsidiaries and millions of national companies.

The document addresses the recommendation to apply these principles without discrimination and giving a special attention to the rights and needs of persons belonging to groups which may be in situations of high risk to become vulnerable or marginalized and to different risks concerning women.

The Special Representative also elaborated and submitted to the Human Rights Council Guiding Principles for the non-jurisdictional mechanisms of claims concerning human rights, created by the enterprises[193], affirming 6

---

[192] Doc. A/HRC/17/31 of 21 March 2011.
[193] Doc. A/HRC/17/31/Add.1 of 24 May 2011.

such principles, namely: legitimacy, accessibility, predictability, equitability, compatibility and the direct dialogue of the petitioner with the enterprise. Such mechanisms and respect of these principles are considered necessary in order to identify the adverse impact on human rights and to make possible the reparation of damages produced and the solution of claims.

He also elaborated Guidelines for the contracts, in order to integrate the management of risks for human rights in the negotiation of contracts between States and investors[194]. These Guidelines request partners to be prepared to manage the potential adverse impacts on human rights, to clarify the prevention of impacts and the response to them before concluding the contracts, to take as a starting point the standards applicable to the respective projects and to see that the clauses of stability do not prevent the States to adopt new laws or regulations to respond to requirements of respect for human rights; they also request that persons and communities potentially affected have access to non-jurisdictional mechanisms of claims and to other remedies ensuring as much as possible respect for human rights.

With regard to the adverse impact of different activities on human rights, the Final Document of the 1993 World Conference on human rights accepted the principle of the need of evaluating the impact on human rights of any project. UN documents requested that this impact evaluation cover three points: a) the possible negative temporary or permanent consequences of the activity proposed on the full exercise of human rights by any sector of the national society; b) the contribution of the activity proposed to the full exercise of the human rights by the population concerned; c) the participative mechanisms of monitoring and evaluation[195]. The requirement of an impact evaluation on human rights for any activity, wherever in the world, is based on the universality of human rights, which means that they have to be observed by everybody, in all activities and in the whole world.

The Agenda 2030 for sustainable development[196] includes, among the means of implementation of its goals, a call to all businesses to apply their creativity and innovation to solve sustainable development challenges. The Agenda refers to many human rights among which the rights to education, to health, to food, to water, to housing, as well as the elimination of poverty which affects the exercise of all human rights. States are engaged to foster a dynamic and well-functioning business sector, while protecting labour rights and health and environmental standards in accordance with relevant international standards and agreements and other ongoing initiatives in this regard, such as the Guiding Principles of Business and Human Rights and the labour standards of the International Labour Organization, the Convention on the Rights of the Child and key multilateral agreements, for parties to those agreements.

* * *

The human rights treaty bodies consider that the norms on the protection of human rights provided for in the respective treaties create obligations not only for States with all their authorities and agents, but also for non-state actors whose activities may endanger human rights. This concerns, of course, national enterprises, but also foreign and transnational corporations. The Principles adopted by the Human Rights Council also pointed out to a series of principles and norms that should be respected both by the host States and by the foreign companies involved in activities on their territories. There are thus standards according to which the States, international organizations and the public opinion in general can evaluate the activities of foreign companies and react to violations of human rights. They result from the universality of human rights. The problems become complicated mainly with regard to foreign and transnational companies, because they are foreign subjects, they can be protected by their national States and they are often very powerful as compared to most of the countries on whose territories they are acting.

Of course, as we noted above, the States have the right to regulate all activities on their territory and have the right and the duty to protect human rights of their inhabitants. But very often, they do not have the means to impose such rules to big transnational companies or have to make painful concessions and to accept onerous conditions (to the detriment of their population) in order to receive some investments and projects of development.

It is a reality that in many cases the protection of human rights and the interests of populations in different areas, as well as the protection of the environment, were not taken into account. There is a concern that investments and projects of development could be treated only from the point of view of economic efficiency, of competition or of maximizing the profit. Therefore, it is considered vital to work for a harmonious set of legal regimes, norms and

---

[194] Doc. A/HRC/17/31/Add.3 of 25 May 2011.

[195] Global Consultation on the Right to Development as a Human Right. Report prepared by the Secretary-general, UN Doc. E/CN.4/1990/9/Rev.1 of 26 September 1990, para.190.

[196] Adopted as a result of the Summit for the adoption of the post-2015 development agenda, resolution of the General Assembly nr. 70/1, 21 October 2015.

standards on economic development, human rights and the environment. Economic interests should not prevail over the protection of fundamental human rights and freedoms. Through their internal policies, States and other global actors have the duty to create a better environment for human economic and social rights in the world. An adequate balance has to be found through a framework of principles and practices which should not ignore, but integrate international standards on human rights into activities of investment, trade and finance, so as to balance the logic of competition with that of respect for human rights.

With regard to OECD, the Principles of corporate governance, published in 1999 and reviewed in 2003, are treating mainly the relationship with big stake-holders and the others; Guidelines for Multinational Enterprises were adopted and strengthened in 2000, and a document entitled Integrating Human Rights into Development, was published in 2006. OECD could have a fresh look at these documents, taking into account the evolution and the new concerns, and produce a new one which should place human rights in the center of any activity of such companies, at least at the same level with looking for profit, and of course the documents adopted by the Human Rights Council, mentioned above.

International organizations which are following more closely the activities of multinational corporations (like the Organization for Economic Cooperation and Development, OECD, and the United Nations Conference on Trade and Development UNCTAD) should elaborate new standards and guidelines for such corporations, including a requirement of a human rights impact study preceding any project or investment in a foreign country and of respect and promotion of human rights throughout the implementation of such projects.

The Human Rights Council and human rights treaty bodies could and should be more intrusive in the consideration of periodic reports of States parties, asking host States of such corporations and of private companies in general to take more determined measures to ensure that their activities fully respect human rights, to include in their agreements with foreign corporations clauses concerning respect and promotion of human rights, in particular the rights to life, to health, to education, to enjoy their own culture, to a healthy environment and to make any license for activities on their territories given to foreign companies conditional of an impact study of its effects upon human rights of the populations concerned and of an impact study on the effect of such activities on the environment of the area.

The Human Rights Council and human rights treaty bodies should address more actively the issue of the obligation of States where transnational companies are registered to take measures so as to prevent them to engage in activities violating human rights or endangering the environment on other territories and to hold them responsible for damages produced.

CHAPTER VI - RESPONSIBILITY of STATES, DIPLOMATIC PROTECTION, HUMAN RIGHTS: a case study

ABSTRACT

International responsibility and diplomatic protection were treated very often separately, although they are aiming at the same reality: the wrongful act of a State. The codification of norms forming the two institutions led, during the last years, to their application in close connection with respect to human rights, including by international jurisdictions. This represents an important advancement for the promotion of human rights.

Of course, each case submitted to a court presents its specific features and the court is not compelled to follow previous decisions given in cases presenting other characteristics. Nevertheless, when decisions are based on norms already recognized or promoted as a result of codification of international law, involving not only material but also moral damages for the injured persons, one has to expect that they could influence the international practice.

This presentation is proposing to evoke the main aspects of the two decisions adopted by the International Court of Justice in the dispute generated by the exercise of the diplomatic protection by the Republic of Guinea for the violations of the rights of its citizen A. S. Diallo by the Democratic Republic of Congo.

KEY WORDS: State responsibility, diplomatic protection, minimum standard, expulsion, arbitrary decisions, moral/immaterial damage, compensation, obligations *erga omnes*, common interest.

INTRODUCTION

After prolonged efforts of codification of international law in this field, the UN International Law Commission adopted in 2001 a Draft Articles on the Responsibility of States for internationally wrongful acts; the General Assembly took note of these Articles by its resolution nr. 56/83 of 12 December 2001. These Articles define the wrongful act, its relationship with the conduct of the State, the breach of the international obligation, the contents of the international responsibility of the State for the wrongful act and the modalities of promoting the implementation of State responsibility[197]. In 2007, the Commission submitted to the General Assembly a document on Diplomatic protection and the General Assembly took note of it by the resolution 62/67 of 6 December 2007; this document enounces norms concerning the protection of physical and legal persons and the conditions of the exercise of such protection. The two documents contain generally customary norms, based on the international practice of States and of international bodies, judiciary and others.

It is defined as a wrongful act the conduct of a State consisting of an action or omission which is attributable to the State under international law and which constitutes a breach of an international obligation of that State. In order to be attributable to the State, the wrongful act should be committed by persons hired by the State, by persons acting for it or under its control. The international obligation has to be in force at the moment when the wrongful act is committed. The responsibility of a State for a wrongful act consists in the cessation of the action or omission and an offer of assurances and guarantees of non-repetition and, if an injury was caused by the wrongful act, the State has to make full reparation for the injury, including any damage, whether material or moral[198].

With regard to the diplomatic protection, the norms elaborated by the International Law Commission provide for its exercise by a State in favour of its citizens by invoking the responsibility of another State for injuries suffered by its citizens or by legal persons having its nationality. Diplomatic protection can be exercised only after the exhaustion by the person concerned of all available internal remedies before jurisdictional or administrative competent bodies of the State whose responsibility is invoked. It is recommended to the State which is entitled to exercise diplomatic protection (this is a sovereign right of the State, not a right of the person, n. a.) to give due importance to exercising it particularly when a significant injury was produced, to take into account the opinion of the respective person and to transfer to that person any compensation received for the injury, except for reasonable deductions.

Two decisions of the International Court of Justice represent a crowning of the practice codified by the Commission in the two documents, an explicit application of the norms they enounce. This concerns the decisions of the Court of 30 November 2010 and 19 June 2012 in the case Ahmadou Sadi Diallo (Republic of Guinea v.

---

[197] Subject extensively treated by Ion Diaconu, International Responsibility in International Law, 2013(in Romanian), Ed. Prouniversitaria.
[198] We referred to the impact of human rights on the norms concerning State responsibility in Chapter I above, Section 5, pp. 95-97.

Democratic Republic of Congo); the first of the decisions ascertains the international responsibility of D.R. Congo for wrongful acts consisting in its behaviour against A. S. Diallo, citizen of Guinea, while the second focuses on the extension of responsibility and the amount of reparation for the injury suffered by the person concerned. In both cases, the Republic of Guinea addressed to the Court in the exercise of diplomatic protection for the violation of human rights of its citizen.

The two cases raised both issues of general international law-namely international responsibility of States for wrongful acts producing injuries to individuals and the application of the 1963 Convention on consular relations-and the issue of respect of human rights, respectively of the 1966 Covenant on civil and political rights and of the 1981 African Charter of human rights and people's rights.

SECTION 1 - CONTENTS of the TWO DECISIONS of the COURT

The Republic of Guinea, taking upon itself the claim of its citizen Diallo, a businessman, invoked its illegal detention by the authorities of Congo, inhuman treatment and the forfeiture of important investment, enterprises, movable and immovable goods and bank assets, and then his expulsion, as violations of principles of international law concerning the rights of foreigners to be treated according to the „minimum standard of civilization", to enjoy their freedom and property and to benefit from equitable procedures; it requested the Court to establish the responsibility of D. R. of Congo for such serious violations of international law. It is interesting to retain that the request by Guinea refers to several sources of law, among which a minimum standard of civilization, which was never generally accepted (and to which the Court does not give any response) and to the 1966 Covenant and the 1981 African Charter which contain norms on the rights to freedom and to the benefit from equitable procedures before the judicial bodies, but not on the right to property.

Historically, the issue of the treatment of foreigners, respectively of State responsibility for injuries produced to foreigners, was a subject matter of a conference of codification of international law convened by the League of Nations in 1930 at The Hague, which failed because of the lack of agreement on the treatment applicable to foreigners-the national treatment or an international standard. The UN International Law Commission also examined several projects on this issue from 1953 to 1961, without being able to present proposals. Since 1963, the Commission gave up on this subject and started to consider the State responsibility for any wrongful acts, including also violations of the rights of foreigners according to obligations assumed by States. The Draft Articles adopted in 2001 by the Commission, of which the UN General Assembly took note, refer to the responsibility of States for any wrongful act and make no direct reference to the violation of rights of foreigners, although they imply this aspect by the norms on the reparation for injuries[199].

Responding to preliminary objections concerning individual rights of the respective citizen and the exhaustion of internal remedies available, the Court adopted an Obiter dictum in its decision of 2007 (with regard to these exceptions), ascertaining that presently the diplomatic protection includes also the human rights guaranteed at international level[200]. The Court retains that in cases of arrest and detention on, and expulsion from, the territory of another State, a foreigner has the right not to be subject to arbitrary decisions, and considers that this right flows from the provisions of the 1966 Covenant and those of the African Charter (referring to the requirement to respect the law and to its compatibility with other provisions of these documents). The Court accepted an extended definition of the notion of arbitrary, following the position adopted by the specialized committees in the application of international documents on human rights. In this Obiter dictum the Court affirms that it has to give great consideration to the interpretation given by the Human Rights Committee, an independent body created especially for monitoring the application of the Covenant, which is important for the clarity and the coherence of international law and for the legal security of persons beneficiaries of these rights and of States which have to respect treaty obligations[201].

The Court retained a violation by D.R. of Congo of articles 9 and 13 of the Covenant (concerning the right to freedom and to security of the person and of his right, as a foreigner, not to be expelled except by decision adopted according to the law and of the right to present reasons against expulsion to a competent authority and to be

---

[199] Ion Diaconu, International responsibility, op. cit., pp. 9-11 and 31-38.

[200] CIJ, Exceptions préliminaires, arrêt du 24 mai 2007, Recueil 2007, para. 39. On this issue also M. Pinto, De la protection diplomatique à la protection des droits de l'homme, in RGDIP, 2002/3, vol. 106, pp. 513-548; S. Gribian, Vers l'émergence d'un droit individuel à la protection diplomatique?, in AFDI, 2008, pp. 119-141.

[201] Situation présented by Muriel-Ubeda Saillard, La diversité dans l'unité: l'arrêt rendu par la Cour Internationale de Justice le 30 novembre 2010 dans l'affaire Ahmadou Sadio Diallo, in RGDIP nr. 1/2011, pp. 897-923.

represented before it) and of the corresponding articles of the African Charter, as well as of obligations stemming from article 36.1.b of the Convention on consular relations of 1963, because it did not inform A. S. Diallo about his right to communicate with the consular officer of his country. Due to the lack of proof, the Court did not retain the accusation of threat to death and of inhuman treatment against Diallo; it did not retain also the violation of his right to property on social parts and as an associate, and rejected the exception presented later on for non-exhaustion of internal available remedies, as a condition of the exercise of diplomatic protection. Taking into account the fundamental character of obligations concerning human rights which were violated, the Court decided to respond favourably to the request of Guinea for granting a reparation under the form of a compensation for the injuries suffered by A. S. Diallo. The Court gave to the States in dispute a dead-line of 6 months to negotiate the amount of the compensation to be paid, deciding that the question should be again brought before the Court if the negotiations failed. Having in view the norms retained in the Articles on State responsibility, the Court decided that negotiations should take place between the two States and the compensation should be paid to Guinea, without recommending initially that it should be transferred to its citizen[202].

As the two States could not agree on the amount of the compensation, the Court proceeded itself in the second decision to establish the contents of the responsibility and the amount of the compensation. The Court considered, with regard to each of the violations retained on the side of D.R. of Congo, whether there was an injury and to what extent the injury is the consequence of a wrongful act, respectively whether there was a causal link between the wrongful act and the injury. For the first time, the Court ascertains the existence of a moral injury suffered by a physical person, noting that in this case, the wrongful behaviour of D. R. of Congo, produced "an important source of psychological sufferings which affected his reputation". With regard to the claim concerning personal goods of Diallo, the Court retained that proof brought by the claiming State is not sufficient to establish a direct damage to be repaired; the same with regard to goods lost due to expulsion and detention, with regard to bank deposits and to the remuneration due to him during the detention. With regard to loss suffered as a shareholder to some societies, the Court retained that this is not a direct loss, because it was suffered directly by the societies and only indirectly by the shareholders.

To sum up, the Court retained that the citizen of Guinea suffered a moral injury due to his illegal detention and expulsion and a material injury related to the loss of some personal goods which were in his apartment at the respective moments. The Court evaluated the compensation due at 85 thousand US dollars in order to repair the moral injury suffered by A. S. Diallo and 10 thousand US dollars for the loss of personal goods. The Court did not grant compensation for loss of profits, but fixed a dead-line for the full payment of the compensation and if this dead-line would not be respected, the State responsible had to pay damages of 6% annually. The Court recalled that the compensation due to Guinea, as a result of the exercise of diplomatic protection for its citizen is meant to repair the injury suffered by him: implicitly, Guinea was invited to restore to him the compensation received for the injury suffered[203].

SECTION 2 - ANALYSIS in the LIGHT of PREVIOUS JURISPRUDENCE

The International Court had to take a stand also previously in cases of diplomatic protection in favour of foreigners for injuries produced to them. In the case Barcelona Traction, the International Court had to distinguish between *erga omnes* obligations concerning human rights and obligations towards another State within the diplomatic protection (namely obligations corresponding to individual rights of the person resulting from commercial or other economic activities). By its two decisions in the case Diallo, the Court accepts that the area of application of diplomatic protection includes *ratione materiae* also human rights guaranteed at the international level. This raises the issue whether the State exercises its own right when it initiates the diplomatic protection, as it was retained by the Permanent Court of International Jurisdiction in the case Mavrommatis[204]; it is our opinion that in the case Diallo there is both the right of the State towards the other State to see that the rights of its citizen in the other State are respected, as well as a subjective right of the injured person whose fundamental human rights were violated. The recognition of an extended function of diplomatic protection to include all the field of human rights as guaranteed by international instruments on human rights represents an important development of the jurisprudence of the Court. It

---

[202] Decision of 30 November 2010, ICJ Report 2010, pp. 639-644.
[203] Presentation made by Arnaud Tournier, De Brunsbuttel à Kinshasa-Le droit de la réparation dans la jurisprudence des cours mondiales à l'aune de l'arrêt Diallo, in AFDI, 2012, pp. 205-221.
[204] Case Mavrommatis Concession in Palestine, decision of 30 August 1924, Serie A, no. 2, p. 12.

corresponds also to the norms retained by the International Law Commission in its activity of codification of international law concerning international responsibility of States and diplomatic protection.

With regard to the violation of obligations stemming from article 36.1 b of the Convention of 1963 on consular relations, the International Court confirmed its previous jurisprudence in the LaGrand and mainly Avena cases[205], retaining the unequivocal obligation of the State to inform without any request the person detained about his right to ask for the information of the consular officer of his State about his arrest. The Court did not accept the pleading of the D. R. Congo that the person arrested was informed orally and that the ambassador of the claiming State was informed by other means. Taking into account that A. S. Diallo was detained both in the penal and in the administrative procedure in order to be expelled, the Court refers to any form of detention or arrest, without conditioning it from a penal procedure, a conclusion which we consider very important for any subsequent cases on the application of the 1963 Vienna Convention. The Court also confirms the conception according to which the right to consular protection, including the right of the citizen to be informed about the possibility to communicate with the consular authorities of his State, becomes a subjective right, even if it is not qualified as a human right according to general international law. The Court did not retain the accusation concerning the threat to death addressed to Diallo, in the absence of beginning of proof, nor that concerning bad treatment, in the absence of convincing proof, although it confirms that „the prohibition of inhuman or degrading treatment is part of norms of international law that States are obliged to respect in all circumstances and beyond any conventional engagement"[206].

The Court recognizes the special character of human rights proclaimed in international law, according to the conception already expressed in its Advisory Opinion concerning Reservations to the Convention on the prevention and repression of genocide of 1948[207], where it noted that „in such a Convention contracting States do not have their own interests; they have only all and each of them a common interest, that to protect the ultimate objective which represents the raison d'être of the Convention". The Court was called to pronounce a judgment on the observance of the rights to freedom and to security and the right not to be expelled without a legal basis and not to be subject to inhuman treatment; the Court outlines the right of the person not to be subject to arbitrary decisions in these fields where decisions are taken by the authorities of the territorial State, attributing a larger meaning to the concept of arbitrary character, on the basis of the provisions mentioned above of the Covenant and of the African Convention. The Court affirms that everyone has to benefit of the protection against arbitrary of any decision which concerns him/her, including those for which the public authorities have a discretionary competence. This conclusion is in conformity with that formulated in similar cases by the monitoring bodies in the field of respect for human rights. The Court recognizes that it has to give due consideration to the interpretation given by the Human Rights Committee, as an independent body created for the purpose to monitor the application of the Covenant. The Court notes also that its interpretation is coherent with that given by the European and Inter-American courts of human rights.

With regard to the rights of A. S. Diallo as a shareholder to commercial societies in D. R. Congo, the Court maintained its previous conception, established in the case Barcelona Traction[208], according to which the legal situation of the society has to be considered, and rejected the conception of confusion of patrimonies and the allegations on the violation of the right of property of the citizen concerned on his social parts (reducing them to dividends and other sums resulting from the liquidation of the society) and his rights to participate in the decision-making of the society.

Recalling again the practice of human rights monitoring bodies, the Court retains that in this case the adequate form of reparation is offering a compensation for the injury suffered and affirms that A. S. Diallo suffered the damage and consequently is the real holder of the right to compensation, although it considers that this problem has to be solved by the parties in dispute according to the norms on international responsibility of States[209].

---

[205] Case Lagrand(Germany v. USA), decision of 27 June 2001, Recueil CIJ 2001, pp. 496-497; case Avena and other Mexican citizens(Mexique v. USA), decision of 31 March 2004, Recueil CIJ 2004, pp. 12 and 43.

[206] Decision in the case Diallo, para. 35.

[207] Advisory Opinion in the case Reservations to the Convention, Recueil CIJ 1948, pp. 15 and 23.

[208] Barcelona Traction, Light and Power Company, Limited, decision of 5 February 1970, Recueil CIJ, 1970, pp. 3 and 33.

[209] Solution criticized by autors like Muriel Ubeda-Saillard, art. cit., pp. 920-921, who considers that the Court pursues the objective to give full expression to special regimes of State responsiblity-in this case that of human rights-while maintaining the utility of a general regime, having in mind the risks of fragmentation of international law.

SECTION 3 - EVALUATION of the INJURY SUFFERED

In most of the cases - among which Gabcikovo-Nagymaros[210], LaGrand[211], Avena[212], Oil Platforms[213], Genocide[214], Pulp Mills[215], Jurisdictional immunity of States[216] - the Court retained the right to reparation of States injured by wrongful acts of other States, but as a modality of reparation indicated granting satisfaction to the injured State. Only in a few of its decisions the Court evaluated the damage produced as a result of one or more wrongful acts and decided the appropriate measures. The Permanent Court of International Jurisdiction examined in 1923 the case of the warship Wimbledon[217], concerning the prohibition by the German authorities of the passage through the Kiel channel of this ship which transported goods, including weapons to Poland.

The Court retained the existence of a material direct damage, resulting from the immobilization of the ship by Germany at the entrance of the channel and from taking another route, establishing the compensation on the basis of the evaluation of damages by the claiming States which was not contested by the defending State. In 1928, the Permanent Court examined the case of Chorzow Factory[218], where Germany invoked the international responsibility of Poland and claimed damages for the respective factory in favour of its citizens. The Court accepted the international responsibility of Poland, the evaluation of the damage remaining to be made later-on. It was not necessary, because in the meantime the parties agreed on a transaction on this issue.

The International Court of Justice had to solve this problem in 1949, in the case of the Corfu Strait[219]. In this case, the Court established the international responsibility of the United Kingdom for violating the sovereignty of Albania by the penetration of its military ships in the Albanian territorial waters and retained satisfaction as the form of responsibility. At the same time, the Court established the international responsibility of Albania for not informing that mines were placed in the Corfu Strait and for the damages suffered by the destruction of English ships Saumares and Volage in Albanian territorial waters and loss of human lives thereby. In order to establish the amount of compensation due by Albania, the Court took as basis the reports of experts engaged by it for this purpose.

In the case Diallo, the Court was confronted with different problems, mainly due to the evolution of norms of international law on State responsibility. According to the norms retained in the framework of codification undertaken by the Commission of International Law, the damage is not considered as an element generating international responsibility. A State engages its responsibility for a wrongful act by the violation of an international obligation in force for it, regardless of whether a prejudice is produced by that violation. Consequently, the evaluation of the damage takes place at a stage which is subsequent to the establishment of the contents of State responsibility. The Diallo case is the only one where the contents of State responsibility are established following the exercise of diplomatic protection. It is also the first case where the International Court decides upon moral damages for the injury produced by a violation of human rights.

It is worth noting that the Court starts from the recent norms of codification of international responsibility, according to which the State responsible is under the obligation to make full reparation for the injury caused, representing both material and moral damage. For that, the Court tried to identify with certitude the damage suffered by A. S. Diallo. For the first time, the Court identifies a moral damage, even if this problem was raised previously (in the cases Mavrommatis, Avena, Diplomatic and consular American personnel in Tehran)[220]. It was only in an arbitrary sentence in 1933 in the case Lusitania (concerning the wreck of this ship) that the arbitration body

---

[210] Case Project Gabcikovo-Nagymaros(Hungary v. Slovakia), decision of 25 September 1997, Recueil CIJ, 1997, pp.7-84.

[211] Case LaGrand(Germany v. USA), decision of 27 June 2001, Recueil CIJ 2001, pp. 466-517.

[212] Case Avena and other Mexican ctitzens(Mexique v. USA), decision of 31 March 2004, Recueil CIJ 2004, pp. 12-73.

[213] Case Oil Platforms(Iran v. USA), decision of 6 November 2003, Recueil CIJ 2003, pp. 161-219.

[214] Case Aplication of the Convention on the prevention and repression of the crime of genocide(Bosnia-Hertzegovina v. Serbia and Montenegro), decision of 20 February 2007, Recueil CIJ 2007, para. 463-469.

[215] Case Pulp Mills on the Uruguay river(Argentina v. Uruguay), decision of 20 April 2010, Recueil CIJ 2010, para. 269.

[216] Case Jurisdiction immunitiy of State(Germania v. Italy), decision of 3 February 2012, Recueil CIJ 2012, pp. 1-61.

[217] Case Wimbledon(United Kingdom, France, Japan and Italia v. Germany), decision of 17 August 1923, Serie A, pp. 15-34.

[218] Case Chorzow Factory(Germany v. Poland, Claim of compensation), decision of 13 September 1938, Serie A, nr. 17, pp. 30-46 and Order of 25 May 1929, Serie A, nr. 19, pp. 11-13.

[219] Case Corfou Strait(United Kingdom v. Albania, CIJ Recueil 1949, pp. 244-265.

[220] USA v. Iran, decision of 24 May 1980, Recueil CIJ 1980, pp. 3-46.

recognized that the moral injury suffered by a physical person can make the object of reparation according to international law[221].

The International Court defines the immaterial prejudice as representing „any moral suffering, attempt to the feelings of the petitioner, humiliation, shame, degradation, loss of the social position or attempt to his credit or reputation". The Court affirms also that the identification of the immaterial damage suffered by a physical person is of the sovereign competence of the judge, even if there are no elements of proof. The Court concludes that the immaterial damage suffered by Diallo results inevitably from the wrongful acts whose existence was established and that it is reasonable to retain the conclusion that the wrongful behaviour of the authorities of D. R. Congo was for this person an important source of psychological sufferings and which affected his reputation. Thus, the Court justifies its decision to establish in a discretionary and sovereign manner, according to its conviction, the existence of an immaterial damage, in the absence of any proof from the claimant.

The Court proceeds differently for establishing the material damage suffered by A. S. Diallo. For that, the Court looks for establishing the certitude of the damage on the basis of the proof submitted by parties. With regard to the loss of personal goods of the citizen, the Court reveals that the elements of proof presented by Guinea are insufficient, mainly with regard to objects of great value and to the bank deposits which would have belonged to him; the same with regard to the loss of incomes during detention and after expulsion. The Court applies the criterion of a material damage, enounced in article 31 of the Articles submitted by the International Law Commission as a result of the codification undertaken, and tries to see whether there is certitude with regard to this damage.

The Court applies the direct character of the damage with regard to personal goods, ascertaining that the wrongful expulsion of the person produced certainly a damage of this kind; without disposing of sufficient elements of proof, the Court applies the equity principle; quite to the contrary, the Court noted that there was no proof that wrongful acts committed by the D. R. Congo produced damage to the bank deposits of Diallo and to the remuneration he could receive during detention and after expulsion.

Thus, the Court established a moral damage as a result of the wrongful detention and expulsion of the person and a material damage related to the loss of some personal goods which were in his apartment at the moment of being taken into detention or arrest. The Court basis its competence to establish the amount of the compensation on equity as a principle with regard to moral damages and as a subsidiary method with regard to material damages. The Court innovates also with regard to granting penalties for delayed payment, namely by fixing a dead-line to pay the compensation and, if this is not respected, a sanction consisting in an annual rate of interest of 6% of the amount, taking into account the rate of interest in force on the international markets and the importance of a prompt execution of its decision.

To mark a difference from the previous practice, according to which the international responsibility of States and the establishment of reparation was considered a relation between the States concerned, in the case Diallo the Court never evokes direct or indirect damages suffered by Guinea; moreover, after evaluating the amount of the compensation, the Court, following the norms retained by the Commission in its draft articles on diplomatic protection, recalls that the compensation granted to Guinea following its exercise of diplomatic protection in favour of A. S. Diallo is meant to repair the damage suffered by him.

* * *

The two decisions of the Court represent an important precedent for the Court itself, but also for the regional and even national courts. At the same time, they represent a strong confirmation of the norms of codification of international law adopted by the International Law Commission and then by the General Assembly on international responsibility of States and on diplomatic protection, thus contributing to their consolidation.

As a whole, the decisions of the Court in the Diallo case are rich in clarifications and innovations concerning the contemporary international law on international responsibility and on reparation, considered in their relationships with diplomatic protection and with the protection of human rights. They reveal an important evolution of international practice with regard to State responsibility for injury produced to foreigners by the violation of international treaties on human rights.

They give expression to the unity of public international law, to the existence of principles and norms of an integrating nature, in spite of the specialization and deepening of some of its sub-branches (law of the sea, extra-atmospheric law, diplomatic and consular law, human rights, law of the environment), as a response to determined needs of the evolutions of international relations and cooperation. And here we find again human rights as a factor of

---

[221] Arbitration Sentence of 1 November 1923, Opinion in Lusitanian cases, in Recueil des Sentences Arbitrales, vol. VII, p. 40.

integration, which is present in all these fields as an expression of human needs placed increasingly in the center of preoccupations.

Finally, one cannot ignore the particular importance of the two decisions of the Court in the field of protection of human rights directly; the Court refers repeatedly to the Covenant on civil and political rights and to the African Charter on human rights and rights of peoples and founds its considerations on the provisions of these documents and on the opinions of the Human Rights Committee concerning the contents and the meaning of some provisions of the Covenant, which represents a confirmation of the increased importance of the protection of human rights in the contemporary international law.

PART II - INTERNATIONAL SECURITY AND HUMAN RIGHTS

CHAPTER VII - RESPONSIBILITY to PROTECT

ABSTRACT

Massive violations of human rights which took place during the last decade of the twentieth century in the South-East Europe and in Africa, without or with late intervention of the international community, raised again the problem of the responsibility of the States concerned and of the international community to prevent such violations and to respond to them. The main issue is to determine whether the use of force could be an answer to serious violations of human rights, like acts of genocide, of ethnic cleansing or other large scale violations and, if so, who could be entitled to intervene, taking into account that the UN Charter forbids the use of force, of threat to force and of intervention in internal affairs of States and the fact that the world's conscience asks for preventing and putting an end to such violations.

This brings again under discussion the conception of "humanitarian intervention", used in the past by great powers to impose their will and domination to weaker States, invoking different aspects of conduct with regard to their citizens. These issues were considered within and outside the United Nations, without producing significant changes to the existing legal standards and they continue to form the object of close concern.

KEY WORDS: use of armed force, humanitarian intervention, responsibility to protect, gradual approach, *ultima ratio*, protection in cases of epidemic illnesses and of natural disasters, sovereignty and state responsibility, obligations to prevent, to protect, to repair and to reconstruct, international responsibility of States and of individuals.

SECTION 1 - THE DEVELOPMENT of the CONCEPT

The concept of responsibility to protect appeared following serious and mass violations of human rights-genocide, large scale crimes against humanity, acts of ethnic cleansing-committed during the years 1990-2000, and due to the fact that authorities in States where such acts took place were involved in such acts, were promoting them or could not prevent them and the international community was not able to protect the civilian populations in danger. These were mainly the conflicts in Rwanda and in the former Yugoslavia; another element of the context was the use of armed force by States members of NATO against former Yugoslavia, in relation with the conflict in Kosovo, without the authorization of the Security Council, which provoked a strong opposition from many States and intense debate among politicians and lawyers.

In substance, the debate focused on the possibility to use armed force to bring to an end serious violations of human rights, having in view numerous and complex problems which appear: who can resort to such an action, in what conditions, under what legal regime and others. This revisited the old conception of „humanitarian intervention", often used in the past by powerful States against the small and less powerful ones and following other objectives than the protection of the populations. This issue could be treated differently before the adoption of the UN Charter (1945), when the war was not forbidden according to general norms of international law, and after the adoption of the Charter which proclaimed as a principle of international law accepted now by all States of the world to refrain from the use of force and treat to force against territorial integrity or the political independence of any other State or in any other manner in contradiction with purposes and principles of the Charter (article 2.4). The Charter provides for the possibility of resorting to armed force only in two cases: self-defense, individual or collective, against an armed attack (article 51) and the decision of the Security Council in case of a threat to international peace and security or an act of aggression (article 39). As a result of the development of the international practice, based on the UN Charter, it is also generally accepted the use of force by peoples in the exercise of their right to self-determination.

Documents adopted subsequently by consensus within the United Nations concerning principles governing relations between States confirmed that the concept of humanitarian intervention was definitively rejected. The Declaration on principles concerning friendly relations and cooperation between States (adopted by the resolution nr. 2625 of 24 October 1970) retained in clear terms that „No State or group of States has the right to intervene, directly or indirectly, for any reason whatsoever, in the internal affairs of any other State. Consequently, armed intervention and any other forms of interference or threat against the personality of a State or against its political, economic and cultural elements represent a violation of international law". Even the combination of the terms „intervention" and

„humanitarian" is considered unacceptable, because the notion of intervention reminds the old policy of force of colonial powers to defend their interests in weaker States.

Some authors held that the provisions of the Charter would leave open the possibility to resort to force, mainly in the case of protection of human rights, because such actions would not be directed against the territorial integrity and the political independence of States. This interpretation was nevertheless rejected, because it would introduce an unacceptable ambiguity in the interpretation of the Charter and the "travaux préparatoires" for the adoption of that text show with clarity that the reference to territorial integrity and political independence of States was added to complement and to strengthen the principle and not to derogate from it[222]. It is obvious that the reference to the principles and purposes of the Charter in article 2.4 has to be interpreted in the same way, as they are also clearly indicating a conduct of the member States which would not be compatible with the use of force.

Some authors also tried to demonstrate that the right to resort to humanitarian intervention would stem from a customary norm formed as a result of international practice and of the conviction of States[223]. The International Court of Justice took a stand explicitly against armed intervention on the territory of other States, rejecting arguments on such an extension of the provisions of the Charter by customary norms[224]. A review of the practice of the Security Council shows that in three cases (Somalia, Rwanda, Bosnia-Hertzegovina) the Council authorized the use of force on the territory of these States for different humanitarian purposes-for protecting operations of assistance granted to the population in Somalia, for creating a security zone for those taking refuge to avoid acts of genocide in Rwanda or for creating and protecting zones of security against bombing and armed incursions in Bosnia. In these cases, the Council ascertained the existence of a humanitarian catastrophe that it qualified as a threat to international peace and security and authorized explicitly the armed intervention.

In other two cases (interventions on the territory of Iraq in 1991 of the USA and some allies and the intervention of NATO in Kosovo, preceded by resolutions adopted with reference to Chapter VII of the Charter and to threats to international peace and security), the States concerned invoked the respective resolutions as authorizing implicitly the use of force, but there was no express authorization of the Security Council to use force against the respective States and the legality of these actions was contested by numerous other States.

It is difficult to attribute to this series of cases the character of a uniform practice or the expression of a conviction of States, which would lead to forming a customary law norm concerning the legality of the use of force against a State or on its territory for the protection of human rights against acts of genocide or other serious violations, departing from the norms of the UN Charter. Therefore, it became necessary to see whether a new political and juridical regime can be developed, having in view the interdiction to resort to force and to threat of force in international relations and on the other side the need to prevent acts of genocide, of ethnic cleansing and other serious crimes against the populations and to respond to such acts. In the speech addressed to the UN General Assembly in 1999, the Secretary General Kofi Annan invited member States to solve what he named the conflict between the principles of non-intervention and sovereignty of States and the responsibility of the international community to react to serious violations of human rights, in other words the dilemma between saving human rights by armed intervention of some States without the authorization of the Security Council and the danger that such interventions (without precise criteria for establishing who can invoke such situations and in what circumstances) may undermine the security system already imperfect, created by the UN Charter.

A process of analysis and reflection on this subject was initiated by the Government of Canada, within an International Commission on Intervention and Sovereignty of States, formed of political personalities and specialists from several States. In its Report[225] presented in 2001, the Commission proposed to replace the terms „intervention or interference" with „responsibility to protect", focusing not on the action engaged but on the objective pursued. The Commission developed a new approach of the problem; it considers that the primary responsibility for preventing a humanitarian disaster is incumbent on the State concerned and only when it cannot exercise this responsibility the international community should exercise its role.

After a thorough consideration of the issue, the Commission underlined the obligation of each State to protect its own people against serious and flagrant violations of human rights, referring precisely to genocide, crimes of war,

---

[222] Spencer Zifcak, The responsibility to protect, in International Law, fourth edition, ed. Malcolm D. Evans, Oxford University Press, 2014, p. 511.

[223] O. Corten, Human Rights and Collective Security: Is there an Emerging Right of Humanitarian Intervention ? in Alstop P. and MacDonald E.(eds), Human Rights, Intervention and Sovereignty, in The Use of Force, Oxford University Press, 2008, p. 87.

[224] Mainly the cases Military and Paramilitary Activities in and against Nicaragua (Nicaragua v. USA), ICJ decision, Reports, 1986, p. 14; Legality of the use of force (Jugoslavia v. Belgium), provisional measures, Order of 2 June 1999, ICJ Reports 1999, p. 124.

[225] The Responsibility to protect, Report of the International Commission on Intervention and State Sovereignty, December 2001, Ottawa, International Development Research Centre.

ethnic cleansing and crimes against humanity. The Commission also formulated criteria of substance for resorting to armed intervention for humanitarian protection (existence of large scale human life loss or of extensive ethnic cleansing), as well as conditions(the correct intention, the recourse to intervention as *ultima ratio*, proportionality and reasonable prospects of success) and indicated as an absolute condition its prior authorization by the Security Council according to Chapter VII of the Charter or by the General Assembly (on the basis of the resolution Uniting for Peace) or the use of force by a regional organism (arrangement or agency as named in the Charter) of security under the condition of prior or subsequent authorization by the Security Council according to Chapter VIII of the Charter[226].

The Commission developed a conceptual framework of action of the international community, following as a rule three stages: first, the responsibility to prevent, consisting in any reasonable measures to avoid the humanitarian disaster such as good governance and respect for human rights along with international support and assistance for development; then, responsibility to react, first of all by measures without the use of force, such as diplomatic negotiations and economic sanctions and only in the last instance the military intervention; then, after putting an end to the crisis, by diplomatic or military means, the responsibility to reconstruct, consisting in peace-keeping, economic and social reconstruction and other measures of development[227]. In the end, the Report draws the attention of the Security Council that, if it does not fulfill its responsibilities, interested States may not exclude other means to respond to the seriousness and the urgency of the situation. And the authors ask a rhetoric question: what is less damaging, to avoid the Security Council or to permit the killing of human beings during the Council's deliberations. Some authors appreciate that the Report has as a central idea preventing the conflicts through a series of non-military measures, including transfer of assistance, expertize and support for developing countries, that is an approach directed towards the development of these countries[228].

A High Level Panel on Threats, Challenges and the Change, created by the Secretary general in 2004, adopted the conceptual framework proposed by the Commission, including the conclusion concerning the exercise of the responsibility of the international community only on the basis of the authorization of the Security Council. In its Report, the Panel affirms that the principle of non-intervention enounced in article 2.7 of the Charter cannot be used to protect nations against the consequences of acts of genocide or other atrocities sponsored by the State and that such acts should be considered as threats to international peace and security. The Panel refers to an emergent norm on international collective responsibility to protect, which can be exercised by the Security Council by authorizing a military intervention as *ultima ratio*[229].

On this basis, the UN Secretary General proposed to accept the concept of Responsibility to protect at the Summit of the World Leaders in 2005, at the 60th anniversary of the Organization. In spite of some critics and different opinions, the Summit accepted the conception of responsibility to protect, with some qualifications and clarifications. In the Declaration of the Millennium[230], the heads of State and government of member States of the United Nations affirm, under the title „Duty to protect populations against genocide, crimes of war, ethnic cleansing and crimes against humanity", that each State has individually the responsibility to protect its populations against such acts, that it accepts this responsibility and shall act so as to conform to its requirement, while the international community should, where necessary, encourage and support States to fulfill this responsibility and support the Organization to create a mechanism of rapid alert. They committed themselves to support States to dispose of means to protect their populations against such crimes and to support States where tensions exist, before a crisis or a conflict is starting.

The Declaration continues affirming that it is the obligation of the international community to apply diplomatic, humanitarian and other peaceful adequate measures, in accordance with Chapters VI and VIII of the Charter, in order to support the protection of the populations against genocide, crimes of war, ethnic cleansing and crimes against humanity. In this context, the heads of State and government affirmed their availability to develop at the appropriate moment a determined collective action, through the Security Council in conformity with the Charter, mainly in conformity with Chapter VII, from case to case and, when needed, in cooperation with regional competent agencies, when peaceful means prove to be inadequate and when national authorities obviously do not ensure the protection of populations against such crimes. In its resolution 1674 (2006) of 28 April 2006, concerning the protection of civilian populations, the Security Council reaffirmed these provisions of the Declaration. To sum up,

---

[226] Report, pp. 31-37, 41-52.
[227] Ibidem, pp. 29-45.
[228] Spencer Zifcak, art. cit., p. 517.
[229] A More Secure World. Our Shared Responsibility, the Report of the High Level Panel on Threats, Chalenges and Change, UN Doc. A/59/565, 2004.
[230] General Assembly, doc. A760/L.1, Final Document of the World Summit of 2005, adopted on 16 December 2005.

the concept of responsibility to protect is not departing from the provisions of the UN Charter concerning the principles and purposes of the Organization.

SECTION 2 - RELATIONSHIP between the RESPONSIBILITY TO PROTECT and the PRINCIPLES of INTERNATIONAL LAW

The concept of responsibility to protect raises a number of problems. First, this concept should not be examined only or mainly in connection with the armed intervention on the territory of another State; the protection of the populations of another State can and should make necessary much more other measures preceding the use of armed force; such measures include, as indicated by the documents mentioned, offering the necessary support to the State concerned, understandably at its request, support which can be also military and can be exercised under its authority, but can be mainly economic and political. The protection by the international community through the United Nations can be achieved, according to the Charter, in the first place by diplomatic means and by sanctions without the use of armed force against the respective State, such as the severance of diplomatic relations, interruption of communications, embargo, mainly with regard to weapons. The use of armed force is only foreseen *ultima ratio*, if other means do not lead to the results pursued.

It is notable that the documents mentioned referred only to cases of armed conflict; but the civilian population may be in danger also due to other causes, when the State is not able to ensure the protection of its populations. We have in mind the responsibility to protect the health of the population in case of epidemical illnesses, which is not only the responsibility of the State where the illness erupted, but also of other States and of the international community. For instance, the International Sanitary Regulation adopted in 2005 by the World Health Organization requests that States notify to WHO any event which may represent an emergency of public health of international interest (an extraordinary event which represents a risk for public health in other countries and which makes necessary an international coordinated action). States parties committed to create and fortify national capacities of surveillance, investigation, evaluation of risks and sanitary intervention. WHO will select experts in order to create emergency committees and will ensure technical assistance to the respective State, along with other actors.

Another case is that of natural disasters. The International Commission mentioned referred in its report also to natural or ecological extraordinary catastrophes, where the State concerned is not able or is unwilling to respond to them and when important human loss takes place or is at risk, affirming that they also could justify an armed intervention on behalf of the responsibility to protect[231]. Although the situation is different from that of an internal conflict, because in case of a natural catastrophe there is no violation of international law by the State concerned, what is essential is that the population suffers loss or is in danger and that State is not responding in an adequate manner. In this field in 2005, at Hyogo (Japan), a Plan of action was adopted which provides for the necessary mechanisms to reduce substantially during the period 2005-2015 vulnerabilities and to increase resilience of nations and of communities to the impact of natural phenomena. These cases raise mainly the issue of applying the principle of international cooperation among States, where the main role belongs to the UN and to its specialized agencies to organize cooperation of other States and to ensure the necessary means for the protection of vulnerable populations in cooperation with affected States.

Having in mind that responsibility to protect can imply also the action of other States on the territory of a State if it is not able or willing to ensure the protection of its population, the problem to be solved is to conciliate such an action with respect for the sovereignty of the State which is arguably full and exclusive[232]. Nevertheless, State sovereignty is not and was never absolute, meaning an absolute freedom of action. Every State takes commitments, by virtue of exercising its sovereignty, and other States can request respect of these obligations, resorting to the institution of State responsibility for wrongful acts[233]. In the case of responsibility to protect, this is about a series of obligations stemming from customary norms sanctioning crimes of international law (the prohibition of genocide, of crimes against humanity, of some of the war crimes), from other norms concerning fundamental human rights and freedoms (the right to life, the right to health, the interdiction of torture, the interdiction of racial discrimination), some of them having an imperative character. Other obligations result from the norms of the UN Charter concerning the maintenance of international peace and security, where the Charter attributes to the Security Council the competence to apply sanctions to States violating them including by using armed force. Such obligations are consubstantial to State sovereignty, not opposed to it.

---

[231] Report, pp. 17-18

[232] Ion Diaconu, Treaties on public international law, 2002, vol. I, Ed. Lumina Lex(in Romanian, pp. 404-405.

[233] Ion Diaconu, Manual of international law, 2010, III-rd edition, Lumina Lex(in Romanian), pp. 372-381.

On the basis of such considerations, the International Commission retains in its Report that sovereignty implies the responsibility to protect, which is considered inherent to sovereignty. This means that the State cannot refuse the protection of its population and the action of the international community if it is not ensuring it, by invoking sovereignty over its territory and over persons found on this territory. This opinion is far from being accepted as the expression of a generally accepted norm; it is obvious that, with the increased importance of norms on the protection of human rights in general, on the protection of victims of armed conflicts (norms of humanitarian law) and of those of international criminal law, States are confronted, and their sovereignty also, with new requirements that nobody can ignore[234]. Sovereignty would include not only attributions of authority over the territory and the population living on it, but also attributions of protection of life, of health, of dignity and of wellbeing of this population[235]. Moreover, the action of other actors, as part of the responsibility to protect, has a subsidiary character, being expected only where the State concerned is not acting itself for the protection of its population or is not able to do it.

Responsibility to protect is not in its substance contrary to the principle of non-intervention in internal affairs of other States, because its aim is to ensure respect for important values protected by norms generally accepted by all States, many of them imperative norms from which States cannot derogate; the conceptual framework accepted by the UN documents includes aspects of cooperation with the States concerned and of support for their action to respect human rights against serious violations and only in the last instance resorting to the use of force. Affirming the exclusive competence of the Security Council to authorize such measures, the concept of responsibility to protect is not in contradiction with the principle of non-use of force and of threat to force as it is provided for in the UN Charter and generally accepted in the contemporary international law.

SECTION 3 - CONTENTS of the RESPONSIBILITY TO PROTECT

Responsibility to protect is considered as an omnibus concept; it includes the obligation to prevent actions against its own population, to react against such actions if they take place, to repair damages produced and to rebuild social or economic structures which are vital for the population affected by serious violations of human rights.

The obligation to protect aims to protect existing values against violations; it is of crucial importance in view of essential interests of humanity that it tends to protect. That makes necessary, as requested by the Security Council, to adopt legislation putting an end to impunity and to bring to justice those responsible of serious violations of international humanitarian law[236], as well as to dispose of institutions efficient to apply the respective laws, which could discourage the perpetration of such violations. The obligation to prevent can include also, as appropriate, administrative and institutional measures meant to impede the occurrence of such acts. As a form of responsibility, prevention means also the obligation of the State to refrain itself, having in view the totality of its organs, central and local, from acts of serious violation of human rights such as those incriminated (genocide, crimes of war, crimes against humanity).

The State has to protect, by its laws, its entire population against the perpetration of such violations by its own authorities, as well as by other authors, such as persons, groups, organizations, be they from its country or from outside. The obligation to protect has its source in article 1 of the Geneva Conventions on the protection of victims of armed conflicts, as well as in instruments on human rights, in particular the 1948 Convention for the prevention and punishment of the crime of genocide. This Convention stipulates not only the obligation to prevent the perpetration of a genocide within the internal order of a State, but also to see that persons under its authority do not commit such acts outside its territory, to make everything possible to impede such crimes everywhere they could be committed, which means to protect the population in general against acts of this kind. Applying this principle, in its Order for provisional measures of 13 September 1993, in the case "Application of the Convention for the prevention and the punishment of the crime of genocide", the International Court of Justice insisted on the obligation of the Federal Republic of Yugoslavia to see that its military, paramilitary units or units of an irregular army which could be under its authority, power or influence do not commit the crime of genocide[237].

---

[234] Report, p. 17

[235] Jean-Marc Thouvenin, Génèse de l'idée de responsabilité de protéger, in La responsabilité de protéger, Colloque de Nanterre, Société française pour le droit international, Ed. A. Pedone, Paris, 2008, pp.30-31.

[236] Resolution 1674, mentioned above.

[237] CIJ, Recueil, 1993, pp. 325-350, 332.

The Court underlined that an occupying power also has such obligation[238]. The State has also the obligation to cooperate with humanitarian missions acting on its territory in order to support the population affected and to prosecute and punish those responsible for committing the respective acts. Both States and international organizations, according to their mandates, have also obligations to prevent the proliferation of weapons in the conflict areas, to control and to regulate the transfer of weapons at the regional and international levels.

Arguably, the obligation to prevent implies also that to react immediately to such violations and to stop them as well as to react to imminent risks that acts of violence are committed against its civilian population. There are numerous resolutions of the Security Council by which it gave to UN peace-keeping forces the mandate to ensure the protection of civilians threatened with physical violence[239]. They included also the mandate to react to such violations and to prevent them in case of an imminent danger. The obligation to prevent implies also, for UN bodies, including the human rights monitoring bodies created by treaty, the obligation of alert when they ascertain in a State facts which demonstrate the existence of a situation likely to lead to acts of large scale violation of human rights, such as genocide or ethnic cleansing. We are reminded that before the main acts of genocide of Rwanda took place, the UN Commission on human rights and the Committee for the Elimination of Racial Discrimination drew the attention on facts of this kind on the territory of this State[240].

With regard to the obligation to repair, there is a series of possible answers and of solutions to follow. If the State concerned committed an unlawful act, violating an internal law or an obligation of international law, one should apply the norms of internal law concerning responsibility for offences or/and for the damage produced and respectively norms of international law concerning State responsibility. As for internal law, the legislation of most States provides for remedies to invoke the responsibility of the State and of its bodies; such laws are not always applied and if their violation is invoked in courts, the result depends sometimes on political factors, which could affect the independence of the judicial power. Moreover, as it is known, after some internal conflicts which implied damages for the civilian populations, „commissions of truth and/or reconciliation" were created, having as the main objective to bring to an end the conflicts, but also to inquire about the serious violations and to discover those guilty, or simply proclaimed a general amnesty for policies of violation of human rights and for the majority of acts stemming from such policies, deciding to punish only the most serious crimes which could be proved. In such cases priority was given to the interest of promoting national reconciliation, and less to the prosecution of persons guilty of violations of human rights. In its resolution 1674 (2006) mentioned above, the Security Council underlined the importance of the criminal responsibility and of commissions of truth for promoting peace, truth, reconciliation and the rights of victims.

The obligation to repair, in case of State responsibility, raises other problems. It has to be invoked by the State prejudiced by the harmful act or by any other State when defending a collective interest or in its capacity as a member of the international community. The State which committed the harmful act can be requested to cease it, to give assurances that such acts will not be repeated, granting satisfaction, as well as repairing damages in the interest of the affected State or of the beneficiaries of the obligation violated (other persons)[241]. Of course, in case of a failed State, characterized by the dissolution of all State public institutions-administration, judiciary, army and civil society-it would be difficult to apply the norms of State responsibility. In practice, a solution was tried in order to solve such a situation by the action of the international community (the case of Somalia), without resorting to the international responsibility of the State.

The activity of reconstruction is also very important as an integral part of responsibility to protect. This concerns both the State on whose territory serious violations of human rights took place and the international community, when it supports the State concerned or when it replaces the State to protect the populations in danger or victims of violations[242]. As a matter of fact, it may be necessary to rebuild the institutional, social and sometimes even the economic structure of the respective State in order to ensure the protection of the populations in danger. In the case of a failed State, the reconstruction may involve numerous state institutions and its functions, beginning with the adoption of the necessary legislation and the building of efficient institutions to apply this legislation and to ensure the security of the population, which means the reconstruction of the State. In other States, the reconstruction may concern only some of these aspects, but is not less necessary. In substance, this is about building whatever is

---

[238] CIJ, Affaire des activités armées sur le territoire du Congo, arrêt du 19 decembre 2005, para. 178.

[239] Resolutions concerning UN missions in Sierra Leone, in Burundi, in Congo, in Liberia and Sudan, cited by Pierre d'Argent, Opérations de protection et opérations de maintien de la paix, in La responsabilité de protéger, Colloque, pp. 140-141

[240] Committee for the Elimination of Racial Discrimination, doc. Suppl. no. 18(A/60/18), pp. 10-12.

[241] Marina Eudes, Les organes de protection des droits de l'homme face aux manquements à la responsabilité de protéger au Rwanda et au Darfour, in La responsabilité de protéger, Colloque de Nanterre, p. 195.

[242] Ion Diaconu, International Responsibility in International Law(in Romanian), 2013, Pro Universitaria, pp. 47-50.

necessary to ensure respect for humanitarian law and for human rights, and for the victims of violations to ensure restitution of their rights, of their properties, of their dignity. The reconstruction has in view that the State becomes able to recover the entirety of its functions and to ensure itself the protection of its population. For this purpose, the UN General Assembly created the Commission of consolidation of peace, which can be seen as a combination between the action of peace-keeping and technical cooperation and assistance. In many cases, the UN sends *in situ* teams of humanitarian assistance and specialists to support the action of State in different fields, such as the rebuilding of efficient administrative and judicial structures or of police and military forces in conformity with the requirements of respect for human rights. Responsibility to protect is thus not only a responsibility for harmful acts, but equally for the future.

Many of these obligations stem from existing norms of international law, from the UN Charter, from treaties and from customary norms. They are not created by the concept of State responsibility, which is only assembling them around the objective of protecting important human values.

Responsibility to protect includes also, for the international community, as *ultima ratio*, if the State concern cannot bring to an end the serious violations of human rights and if other conditions are reunited, to resort to measures of constraint against that State, as provided in Chapter VII of the UN Charter, namely severance of diplomatic relations, interruption of communications, embargo on commercial exchanges (for one or several products) and/or on the arms trade, blockade of coastal areas, and finally the intervention of armed forces on the territory of the State. The UN bodies can take measures of fact-finding through independent experts, special missions or rapporteurs, which prepare the adoption of adequate measures. Such measures are then decided by the Security Council if it considers that acts committed by the State concerned represent threats to or violations of the international peace and security or, when authorized by it, by regional agencies for the maintenance of security or even by some States, and eventually by the General Assembly (according to the resolution Uniting for Peace).

Obviously, the adoption of such measures by the Security Council depends of the agreement of the 5 States which have the right of veto and of the agreement of 9 member States, and of course of the qualification of the respective acts as threats to or violations of international peace and security. During the last 20 years the Council adopted a series of decisions of this kind, basing its sanctions on threats to or violations of international peace and security, although such decisions were not adopted in all cases of serious violations of human rights and sometimes were adopted late, including in cases of acts of genocide; some authors retained the double standard in the activity of the Council referring to the absence of decisions of this kind in the cases of Burma, Kenya and with a lot of delay in the case of Darfur[243].

There is not a generally accepted norm of international law which would allow resorting to such sanctions by individual States, mainly resorting to the use of armed force as a response to serious violations of human rights, which reminds what was called „humanitarian intervention". As mentioned above, the International Commission on Intervention and State sovereignty formulated conditions for justifying the use of force in such cases by the Security Council: the existence of a serious violation or a reasonable fear that such a violation or irreversible and irreparable damages could take place; a strictly humanitarian purpose of the intervention, that is to prevent damages, suffering and loss of human lives; it has to be *ultima ratio*, that is after the use of the available peaceful means; conformity with the principle of proportionality; the military means used have to be adapted to the purpose of protecting the population and to respect adequate norms of engagement; the initiation and the conduct of operations should be based on the principle of good governance, so as to avoid the failure (meaning to mobilize sufficient and rapid material and human means as a reserve). The Commission also considers, as a threshold to resort to the use of force by the Security Council, the existence of massacres, significant loss of human lives, effective or potential, as a result of the action or inaction of the State, or of acts of large scale ethnic cleansing, effective or potential, committed by killings, forced expulsion, terror or rape. The Commission explains that when it refers to „effective or potential" consequences, it means a preventive action.

As for the International Court of Justice, it adopted decisions expressing a very clear position, affirming that intervention, as well as any act of force, are not admitted under any form and under any pretext in international relations[244], reaffirming the unlawful character of armed intervention, including for humanitarian reasons[245] or affirming that the use of force in Yugoslavia raises very serious problems of international law[246]. In the same vein, the International Law Commission did not retain the humanitarian intervention as a cause for excluding the unlawful character of an action of intervention of armed forces on the territory of another State for humanitarian purposes,

---

[243] Mario Bettati, Allocution, Responsabilité de protéger, Colloque de Nanterre, p. 12.

[244] ICJ, Case of Corfou Strait, Rec. 1949, p. 35.

[245] ICJ, Military and Paramilitary Actvities in Nicaragua and against it, decision of 27 June 1986, Rec.1986, p. 134.

[246] ICJ, Case concerning the legality of the use of force, Order of 2 June 1999, para. 17.

having in view that the non-use of force and of the threat to force is generally recognized as an imperative norm of international law from which States cannot derogate[247].

Thus, it would be wrong to equate the responsibility to protect with, or to limit it to, the use of force against the State concerned.

SECTION 4 - RESPONSIBILITY to PROTECT and the INTERNATIONAL RESPONSIBILITY of STATES and of INDIVIDUALS

Responsibility to protect is a kind of responsibility of a general nature; it does not suppose always an unlawful international act. It is the case of a natural disaster, for which the State affected is not guilty and which is not giving rise to its international responsibility, while for other States and for the international community there is only the problem to assist the State's efforts for protecting the population in danger in adequate forms and with appropriate means. It is also the case of a failed State, which is not able to prevent serious violations of human rights and can be in general considered responsible for the situation created, but which has no means to prevent or to stop serious violations of human rights when they occur.

In case of a serious violation of human rights or of humanitarian law which request the responsibility to protect, the State concerned engages also its international responsibility because it violates an obligation stemming for it from a generally accepted norm of international law and commits a harmful act attributed to it, which is the cause of the violation. A State engages its international responsibility for violations taking place on its territory, on a territory occupied by it, as well as for its negligence to prevent such violations to be committed by other actors on the respective territory, including by rebel groups acting on their account[248]. According to article 41 of Articles on State responsibility for harmful acts, adopted by the UN General Assembly in 2001[249], all the other States have the duty to cooperate for the cessation of the violation and for the application of the responsibility of the State concerned in case of violations of obligations resulting from imperative norms of international law. The international community also has a responsibility to protect the population affected through adequate measures and means in the context of the situation. As a matter of fact, in this situation the State responsibility overlaps with the responsibility to protect. International organizations are in the same situation as the States; they can engage their international responsibility if peace-keeping forces under their control are committing violations of human rights; they have also obligations within the responsibility to protect, in view of their mandate and of their possibilities.

As serious violations of human rights are committed by individuals, both those who are planning and ordering them and those who commit them, the application of norms on criminal responsibility of their authors is always opened even in the case of a failed State. This is regulated in the contemporary international law mainly in the Statute of the International Criminal Court adopted in Rome in 1998, to which more than 120 States are parties. The Statute provides as crimes of international law under the jurisdiction of the Court the following: aggression, genocide, crimes against humanity and crimes of war[250]. The crime of aggression was defined as a crime committed by persons (previously it was defined as committed only by States), by the conference of revision which took place in Kampala in 2010[251]. The Rome Statute gives detailed definitions of the other categories of crimes and contains the whole of procedural norms concerning their investigation, the guarantees of a fair trial and the execution of sentences.

The Statutes of international tribunals for the prosecution of crimes committed in the former Yugoslavia and in Rwanda, created by resolutions of the Security Council[252], adopted on the basis of Chapter VII of the Charter, are also international documents which incriminate such acts; other criminal courts were created by agreement between the respective State and the UN or by internal legislative acts and function as internal courts or with international participation to prosecute crimes committed in Sierra Leone, Cambodia and Lebanon. Whatever may be the result of these courts, sometimes unsatisfactory or incomplete, they exist and they represent a modality of exercising the responsibility to protect by the international community. The prosecution and the punishment of persons guilty of serious crimes against the civilian population offer some satisfaction to the victims and to the international community and represent a warning that such acts will not remain unpunished, which is a kind of guarantee that they

---

[247] Ion Diaconu, International Responsibility, pp. 44-45
[248] ICJ, Armed activities on the territory of Congo, decision of 19 December 2005, p. 60.
[249] Resolution of the UN General Assembly, doc. A/RES.56/83 of 12 December 2001.
[250] Ion Diaconu, The International Criminal Court, A New Stage, 2oo2, IRSI, p. 96-123.
[251] Doc. Resolution RC/Res. 6 of 11 June 2010.
[252] Resolutions 827 of 25 May 1993 and 955 of 8 November 1994.

will not be repeated. International criminal responsibility of persons can be cumulated with the international responsibility of States, if they are also found guilty of condoning or promoting such unlawful acts committed by their officials.

It is obvious that the evolution of the international practice and of the concepts during the last 20-30 years led to increasingly denouncing the serious violations of human rights, such as genocide, ethnic cleansing, crimes against humanity and crimes of war. This is accompanied by a normative development, through documents of a different type, most of them of a declaratory nature, without offering a unitary and consistent conception. Humanitarian law-meaning the norms adopted for the protection of victims of armed conflicts-comes also close to the responsibility to protect, which implies also restraining the use of armed forces as *ultima ratio* and to a minimum, in order to ensure the protection of the civilian population.

On the other side, one has to note that the answer given by the international community, through sanctions or through operations on the territory of the States concerned, was not consistent. As a matter of fact, the opinion shared by the overwhelming majority considers that the decision of the Security Council is essential for involving the international community in the application of the responsibility to protect, mainly when it includes the use of armed forces. This corresponds to the UN Charter provisions. Nevertheless, the action of the Council is not certain and can come too late or be limited or insufficient, as it happened already. One has to have in mind also the selectivity of the decisions of the Council, due to the right of veto of permanent members and to the protection that some of them grant to other States or to the lack of willingness in some cases. This situation cannot, nevertheless, justify another selectivity, among the States which may act unilaterally, in group or within another organization. The present international framework called to act for the application of the responsibility to protect populations in danger, when it is necessary due to the inaction or the incapacity of the States concerned, is thus not secure and presents obvious lacunae. Nevertheless, it is a situation which is preferable to the unilateral use of force by some States, which can be even more selective and arbitrary.

* * *

It is considered that responsibility to protect, as it was developed in the documents analyzed above, did not become a norm of international law, because neither the practice of States, nor that of the Security Council is general and uniform (see the case of the action in Libya and that which did not take place in Syria), and the position of States is far from reflecting the conviction which is necessary for accepting a customary norm of international law[253].

The documents adopted, mainly the Declaration of the Millennium, retain first of all the definitive repudiation of the conception of „humanitarian intervention" by a State or a group of States in case of violations of human rights. The authorization by the UN Security Council, in the exercise of competences attributed by the UN Charter and according to the norms of the Charter (in case of threats to international peace and security or of violations of peace), remains an absolute requirement. The conception of the responsibility to protect cannot in any respect justify individual acts of use of force by States or groups of States.

Second, the recourse to armed force is *ultima ratio* and has to be preceded by compulsory efforts to solve the problems by other means-diplomatic, economic, political, including sanctions which do not involve the use of force.

Third, the cases when the application of this concept is foreseen seem to be limited to genocide, crimes of war, crimes against humanity and ethnic cleansing, considered humanitarian catastrophe; this enumeration lacks of clarity, because the sphere of crimes of war and of crimes against humanity is very wide and ethnic cleansing is among them, depending on the time when they are committed. Besides, as mentioned above, there can by other cases when the role of the State concerned and of the international community is essential for the protection of the populations affected (for instance by natural disasters).

Fourth, the State concerned has the primary responsibility to protect its population; the State is asked to adopt legislation, to create the necessary institutions and to take all measures to prevent such serious violations of human rights on the territory under its jurisdiction. This is an obligation stemming from its full and exclusive sovereignty on its territory, in a modern conception about sovereignty as a whole of rights and obligations in conformity with international law.

Fifth, the role of the international community, including other States and international organizations, is mainly to support the State concerned to fulfill its responsibility, including by economic means and assistance, to solve those problems which may have led to internal troubles and to human rights violations.

---

[253] Spencer Zifcak, art. cit, pp. 528-531.

The concept of responsibility to protect appears thus as an integratory project, which combines several existing principles and norms on human rights, international responsibility of States and the action of international organizations with the view to ensure the application of these principles and norms.

CHAPTER VIII - DEMOCRATIC SECURITY, HUMAN SECURITY

ABSTRACT

Security is no more limited to a relationship between States and to its political and military dimensions. In a thorough analysis, it includes also economic, ecologic and societal aspects. Each of these elements should be viewed from the point of view of vulnerabilities, risks and threats.

The concept of democratic security was developed mainly by the Council of Europe and is more and more related to good governance, to internal political functioning of the State, considering that a pluralist and democratic society, which is based on the rule of law and on respect for human rights, is more secure.

The concept of human security was launched by the United Nations Development Program in 1994, through its Report on Human Development. Human security would include economic, food, health care, environmental, community and political security. Another concept, launched by some States (Canada and Norway), reduces human security to protection against physical violence, that is to armed conflict and genocide, relating it to peace-keeping operations, that is to State security. Another project promoted by Japan places the emphasis on economic and social development, education, health care and social protection.

This paper is analyzing these concepts from all points of view and taking into account different vulnerable groups and the relationship between human security and human rights.

KEY WORDS: democratic security, political, economic, environmental and societal security, identity, good-governance, human security, freedom from fear and from want, human security against violence, human security through development.

INTRODUCTION

During the cold war period, due to the confrontation between the two military blocs and between the two superpowers, the conceptions about security were limited to its political and military dimensions. Nevertheless, in the 80^s a new more comprehensive approach about security was proposed; the Bruntland Report presented to the UN Conference on Disarmament and Development of 1987 launched a wider concept, accepted by many States, according to which security includes also economic, ecological and human aspects.

The new conception was initiated and developed by what is called the Copenhagen school; its exponent most well-known, Barry Buzan, developed a complex approach of security, taking into account the situation of groups of States which have interdependent interests, although sometimes common sometimes opposed, but mainly defined security by 5 elements composing it: political security, military security, economic security, societal security and environmental security[254].

Each of these elements should be analyzed in connection with every situation, from the points of view of vulnerabilities, of risks and of threats. Vulnerabilities result from the weaknesses of the system of each State, in relation to one of the dimensions of security mentioned. The risks are the result of the relationship between the vulnerabilities and the possibility that they can be used or can produce their effects. A threat means already the imminent occurrence of a situation putting in danger security, in one of its dimensions.

SECTION 1 - DEMOCRATIC SECURITY

The concept of democratic security was launched by the Council of Europe at the Summit of October 1993 of Vienna; according to the document adopted by the Summit, the heads of State and government of member States of the Council declared that they understand to contribute to democratic security, to building a democratic and secure Europe and to use the bodies of the Council for strengthening the democratic security in Europe. They expressed their conviction that building a democratic and pluralist society, which respects the equal dignity of all human beings, remains one of the main objectives of the European construction.

---

[254] Barry Buzan, People, States and Fear. The National Security Problem in International Relations, London, 1983, p.106; Barry Buzan, Ole Weaver, Jaap de Wilde, Security. A New Framework for Analysis, London, 1998.

Taking up again this theme, the Summit of Strasbourg of 1997 affirms that the significant enlargement of the Council created the grounds for a wide space of democratic security on the European continent and reaffirms the solemn commitment to the fundamental principles of the Council, namely pluralist democracy, respect for human rights and the supremacy of law. Similarly, the Summit of Warsaw of 2005 expresses the conviction that an efficient democracy and a good governance at all levels are essential for preventing conflicts, promoting stability and favouring economic and social progress.

The development of this concept represents an important theoretical and political contribution of the Council of Europe, which will have substantial consequences for the future activity of the Council, as well as for the activity of other international organizations and for the State's policies. Thus, the Council of Europe committed itself to act for building a wide space of democratic security in Europe. Member States committed themselves to apply, in their internal order and in international relations, the principles of the pluralist democratic security, of the primacy of law, of respect for human rights and of the rights of nations.

This is the expression of a human vision about the development of the society in the member States of the Council, of a conception which generates mutual confidence, stability and previsibility in international relations. This conception found its expression in the Pact of stability proposed by the European Union to States of Central and East Europe and concluded in 1995 in Paris; the States of this region committed themselves to develop democratic societies based on norms of the state of law, and among them to promote relations of friendship, of cooperation, as well as to respect the rights of persons belonging to minorities. On this occasion, some States concluded political treaties based on these principles (Hungary and Slovakia). In a recent report, the Secretary general of the Council of Europe evaluates to what extent the 47 member States of the Council are prepared to apply the 5 „pillars" of the democratic security, enumerated as follows: efficiency and independence of the judicial system; freedom of expression; freedom of assembly and association; efficient functioning of democratic institutions; inclusive societies; a democratic citizenship. Then the instruments adopted by the Council in each of these fields are presented, together with the requirements for fulfilling the criteria established, but without analyzing the situation in each member State[255].

The Strategy of Security of the European Union adopted in 2003[256] affirms that the quality of the international society depends on the quality of the governments and that "The best protection for our security is a world of States democratically governed. Spreading the good governance, supporting social and political reforms, combatting corruption and abuse, consolidating the state of law and the protection of human rights are the best means for strengthening the international order" and the document continues: „The contribution to a better governance through programmes of assistance, conditionality and commercial measures with precise objectives remains an important feature of our policy that we have to strengthen. A world which will obviously offer justice and opportunities for everybody will be more secure for the European Union and its citizens".

Within the UN, several resolutions of the General Assembly were adopted as a result of a series of conferences of new and restored democracies[257]. For instance, the Conference of Bucharest of foreign ministers of States of this category reaffirmed in 1997 „the commitment of these States to the process of democratization of (our) societies, underlining the relationship of mutual interdependence and consolidation between democracy, development and good governance"…"During the last years it is almost universally recognized that a democratic system of governance is the best model to ensure a framework of freedom for durable solutions of all political, economic and social problems confronting our societies". For this purpose, the Conference adopted recommendations in the fields of human rights, of reforming the judiciary, of eliminating corruption, combating the organized crime, managing globalization, decentralization and other fields of democratization and civil society, transparency and responsibility[258].

These resolutions underlined the close relationship between promoting institutional reforms and the maintenance of international peace and security.

Relationship between democratic security and State security. Therefore, it seems necessary to analyze the relationship between the concept of democratic security and the dimensions concerning political security and societal security, proposed in the definition analyzed by the Copenhagen school.

---

[255] Doc. F 67075 Strasbourg CEDEX, Conseil de l'Europe, 2015.
[256] A Secure Europe in a Better World, Brussels, 12 December 2003, presented extensively by Andrei Popescu, Ion Diaconu, European and Euroatlantic Organizations(in Romanian), Editing House Universul juridic, 2009, p.314.
[257] Among others resolutions 49/30 of 7 December 1994, 51/31 of 6 December 1996, 55/43 of 27 November 2000, 56/96 of 14 December 2001.
[258] Progress Review and Recommendations, adopted by the Third International Conference of the New or Restored Democracies on Democracy and Development, held in Bucharest from 2 to 4 September 1997, appendix to the doc. A/52/334 of 11 September 1997.

With regard to the political dimension of security, the premise of departure is that democracy, well understood and applied under all its aspects, creates a good security environment, a space of „democratic security". This would encompass respect for human rights and at the international level respect for the rights of all peoples and of all States.

In this spirit, the Declaration of the Millennium, adopted by the UN General Assembly in 2000[259], proclaims as a fundamental value to be promoted in international relations in the twentieth century the „freedom of men and women to live in dignity, saved from hunger and from the fear of violence, oppression or injustice" and affirms that a type of democratic governance of public affairs, based on the will and the participation of the populations, is the best to permit the guarantee of these rights.

In the same vein, the Universal Declaration of Human Rights of 1948 proclaimed that each person is entitled to a social (understood internal) and international order where rights and freedoms enounced in the Declaration can be fully respected.

Many other resolutions adopted by the UN bodies underlined that democracy, development and respect for fundamental human rights and freedoms are interdependent and that a good management of public affairs including transparency and responsibility for the fulfillment of public functions are indispensable for building peaceful, prosperous and democratic societies. Such resolutions asked States to promote pluralism, the widest participation of the public in decision-making process and to create political competent institutions, legislative bodies and an efficient and responsible public function, as well as electoral systems which would guarantee that regulate, periodic and free elections are held.

As for the societal security, the problem is to see to what extent States can be undermined or destabilized by their societies, which may feel themselves threatened or weakened in terms of societal cohesion and identity; societies are often organically related to States, but they can have direct impact on the degree of security of the States. Societies can be analyzed also separately from the States they form; they have their own values, but also vulnerabilities, and can be characterized by more or less cohesion. When this cohesion is weak or absent, there are vulnerabilities for the security of the society as well as of the State.

The starting point is that the society is a construction composed of human groups formed on different criteria, from the cultural ones to those political and social; feelings of insecurity of some important social groups may lead to increased tension in the society and consequently may affect the stability and security of the State. A society may become insecure if important social groups forming it feel insecure.

In these considerations the focus falls on the society, not on the State; part of the society may perceive real or potential threats to its existence in times of changes of different kinds, mainly threats to its existence or to its identity; it can come in conflict with other social groups or even with the State itself, which endangers the security of the society and of the State. The value which is considered to be in danger in that approach is the existence or the identity of some important social groups; societal security has in view mainly threats to the existence or to the identity of a collectivity. Some authors refer only to dangers to the identity of a collectivity, to the prohibition of the expression of its identity and of its capacity to reproduce[260], leaving aside other social dysfunctions which can seriously affect State security. With regard to dangers related to threats to identity, they affirm that they would stem from the fear of modifying the ethnic composition of the population and the fear that a culture may become dominant and that integration in a different context would leave the group in a minority situation.

Analysts consider, for instance, that the two conflicts in Transnistria and in Abhazia at the end of the twentieth century were caused by evolutions perceived as dangers to the identity of some groups of the society and by the absence of coherent strategies of the new States to respond to these preoccupations, besides the heritage of the domination of the Soviet Union and of the population of a Russian origin on the local populations, of stereotypes and emotions of a symbolic nature related mainly to the status of the language to be used in the new States and their lack of experience and of adequate structures[261]. In substance, these authors affirm that the new States were perceived as a threat to the identity of these groups, not as a source of stability and security.

Obviously, the analyze of the concept of societal security on the basis of only these two cases is reduced to the relationship majority-minority and to the fear of some groups which became minorities after being part of the majority which dominated other people and had the benefit of privileges in all fields during a period when there were no standards for the protection of minorities. It is, in our opinion, an unacceptable approach, because it tends to consider as legitimate and to justify separatist pretentions of such minorities.

---

[259] Resolution of the General Assembly nr.55/2 of 13 September 2000.
[260] Barry Buzan, op cit. 1993, p.43.
[261] A similar opinion by Ana Serafim, Societal Security in the Black Sea Region, in Democratic Security Building: Cases from the Baltic and Black Sea, (ed. Unto Vesa), Tampere Peace Research Institute Papers no.83, 2000, pp.86-87.

At the same time this approach is limited, because it does not analyze other factors which may endanger the security of a society, such as inequalities in the regional development, a social inadequate policy, inadequate allocation of resources, an intolerable activity of multinational corporations, subordination of the country to foreign interests or a foreign intervention of forces pursuing interests which are opposed to those of the local societies.

Even with regard to the two cases mentioned, an important cause was the weakness of the new States, resulting from their situation in the multinational State and the lack of preparation for a national comprehensive identity, the absence of legitimate institutions accepted by the entire population and the absence of a coherent strategy to integrate the different identities. As it was said, the new independent States were formed not following the development of a national conscience and consent, but after the sudden dissolution of the multinational State, briefly without a preparation for independence[262].

One should not ignore the influence of the external factor, the support given by institutions and organizations of the Russian Federation to separatist elements of the two regions, which contributed substantially to the separatist position adopted in the two provinces, and the subsequent evolutions confirmed it.

Beyond the issues of social and identity vulnerabilities, the concept of societal security raises also the problems of the legitimacy of the public authority, of its decisions, that is of the legitimacy of the government. To avoid such fears, the answer is a democratic evolution of the State, based of periodic and free elections and on the rule of law.

After the end of the cold war, the debate on democratization developed along with that on security and development. The discourse on the ways and means to follow in order to achieve peace and prosperity moved from economic factors and the structure of international society to the quality of State institutions[263].

In East-Europe, in the new conditions after the cold war, the problem of building security had to be solved in parallel with that of democratization. Therefore, the respective States had to solve simultaneously several problems: building democratic and stable societies, including civilian control over the army, adopting and implementing a comprehensive concept of security and their acceptance in the pan-European and Euro-Atlantic systems of cooperation and security. Democratization of society and respect for human rights, including those of persons belonging to minorities, were also criteria for being admitted in the European and Euro-Atlantic structures.

The answer to such preoccupations is to build democratic societies, to build a State based on political pluralism and on the respect for human rights, on equal rights and non-discrimination, on the principles of state of law; such a State should act and be perceived as the State of all citizens, irrespective of their ethnic origin, race, sex, political opinion and other considerations. On such a basis, the identities and groups behind them will have the guarantee that they are not threatened in their existence and can develop freely, of course living along with those of other identities as citizens with equal rights, without privileges and without discrimination. This excludes policies of assimilation, which would pursue to annihilate the different linguistic, cultural and religious identities; this excludes also separatist trends directed against territorial integrity of States and pursuing political objectives and not the respect of human rights and of identities.

Thus, democratization is foreseen as a form of government meant to create the optimum social climate for maintaining security and promoting a society without conflicts threatening its security.

Good governance. The concept of democracy and of democratic society is thus increasingly related to that of „good governance".

The concept of good governance was used by donor countries to condition the assistance to development or to select those who receive assistance, as well as by researchers trying to explain its meaning and contents and by representatives of States or of international organizations as a normative ideal.

At the beginning of the 90-ies, the World Bank defined governance as „the way in which power is exercised to manage the economic and social resources of a country for the benefit of development"; in the opinion of the Bank, good governance refers to efficiency of public services, legal norms with regard to contracts, a judiciary efficient sector, respect for human rights, free media and a pluralist institutional structure[264].

During the same period, the Programme of the United Nations for Development advanced an approach which highlights the exercise of the economic, political and administrative authority in order to manage affaires of a

---

[262] Ibidem, pp.101-105.
[263] Laura Zanotti, Governmentalizing the Post-Cold War International Regime; The UN Debate on Democratization and Good Governance, in Alternatives 30(2005), pp.461-487.
[264] World Bank, Governance and Development, Washington D.C., 1992.

country at all levels, including mechanisms, processes and institutions through which citizens and groups articulate their interests, exercise their legal rights, fulfill their obligations and mediate their disputes[265].

In turn, for the OECD governance means to use the political authority and to exercise the control in society over the management of its resources in order to achieve economic and social development[266].

That includes, according to all these opinions, both technical aspects concerning the use of resources and political ones, concerning the legitimacy, the responsibility and the ability of the governance to effectively manage the society.

The subject of good governance found its constant place on the international agenda. Different initiatives within the UN and other international organizations increasingly promote the application of the concept of good governance in the national societies in all its dimensions, not only those concerning the management of resources; critical considerations are presented with regard to a „world governance", that of transnational corporations, of criminal groups and other non-state actors, which would make it difficult to promote good governance at the national level.

The Declaration of the Millennium, adopted in 2000 by the General Assembly, enounces a wide area of values and objectives: peace, security and disarmament, protection of the environment, human rights, democracy and good governance; protection of those vulnerable; response to the special needs of Africa; strengthening of the Organization of the United Nations. It is appreciated that good governance is the main framework for transforming democratization in operational programmes which would lead to achieving these objectives.

The debate led to critics of the approach of international financial organizations which condition the granting of financial and economic assistance upon internal policies of the receiving States; it is estimated that good governance means more than multiparty elections, a judiciary and a parliament; it includes also the universal protection of human rights, non-discriminatory laws, efficient, impartial and rapid judicial procedures, transparent public agencies, responsibility of public officials for their decisions, decentralization of resources and of the decision-making process . It does not mean weakening or reducing the governance, but making it more adequate by including political aspects of democracy, but integrating also the economic and social objectives[267].

Documents adopted within the United Nations, without pretending to establish legal norms, represent rather a synthesis of good practices followed by many States in the process of governance. In substance, they refer to the existence of stable governments, truly representative for the majority of the population, transparence in government, openness and opportunities for the public participation in the examination of the most important problems, promoting economic increase and development, respect for human rights and fundamental freedoms, participation of the civil society, ensuring well-being for all sectors of the society.

Important evolutions took place at regional level in different parts of the world. It is obvious that in Europe the European Union included these principles in the Union treaties and intends to implement them in the entire set of institutions and norms which form the Union's law. States candidate to the Union must adopt legislation and measures necessary to implement the acquis communautaire and after the admission have to conform their policies to the entire Union's law. An infringement of these norms is submitted to the control by the European Commission and the European Court of Justice.

In Africa, the Summit of 2002 of Durban adopted the Declaration concerning democracy and political, economic and corporative governance. The Declaration relates the sustainable development to peace, democracy, respect for human rights and good governance; it outlines also standards of good governance: respect for a wide series of human rights, respect for the rule of law, political free, credible and democratic processes and the separation of powers, an independent judiciary and efficient parliaments[268]. The African Heads of State and government also adopted a mechanism for evaluating the progress towards achieving good governance, on the basis of a questionnaire concerning democracy and political good governance.

Many authors envisage an increased role of non-state actors; nevertheless, this can be indirectly achieved within the different aspects of good governance: representativity, transparence, openness, opportunities, participation of the civil society, in sum by the democratization of the society in its different dimensions.

From the point of view of international law, it is to be noted that many of the requirements of democracy and good governance represent the observance of compulsory norms of public international law. This category includes:

---

[265] UNDP, Governance for Sustainable Human Development, New York, 1997, pp. 2-3.

[266] OECD, Participatory Development and Good Governance, Paris,1995, p.14.

[267] Thomas G. Weiss, Governance, good governance and global governance: conceptual and actual challenges, in Third World Quarterly, Vol.21, No 5, 2000, pp.795-814.

[268] Martin Sheinin, State responsibility, Good Governance and Indivisible Human Rights, in H.O.Sano, G.Alfredsson (editors), Human Rights and Good Governance, Building Bridges, Martinus Nijhoff Publications, The Hague, 2002, p.44.

- respect for human rights and fundamental freedoms, forming the object of an important number of treaties ratified by most States of the world and of procedures of monitoring their application, including at the regional level by judiciary compulsory procedures;
- respect of political rights concerning the participation in free periodic elections, by the universal, direct and secret vote, and the participation in the conduct of public affairs (as provided for in article 25 of the Covenant of civil and political rights);
- respect for the freedom of expression, assembly and association, which are essential for a democratic society;
- the obligation to have a conduct in conformity with the rule of law;
- the existence and functioning of an independent judiciary.

Some authors are adding as standards of good governance non-discrimination, access to a court and the right to a fair trial, as well as the right of members of indigenous peoples and of minorities to enjoy their culture and their way of life[269]. Obviously, they are part of respect for human rights and fundamental freedoms.

All such norms create for States obligations of international law; for their violations, other States can invoke the international responsibility of the State concerned and exercise their rights to obtain satisfaction or reparation[270].

Other requirements, which concern democracy - the organization and the functioning of the State, the relationship between different State organs, the forms of popular participation, the role of civil society, or which concern the good governance - an adequate organization of the State apparatus, the efficient management of resources, the solution of different political or social problems - do not represent obligations under international law. Although they are not without connection with the exercise of some human rights, such as the political rights, in these fields international organizations and conferences adopted recommendations or guidelines concerning modalities of a more adequate exercise of State power. At the regional level, some States adopted such obligations in their relations, while at the universal level there are only good practices that are recommended to States and some political commitments.

The situation is different from State to State, from continent to continent; opinions as to what is good and what is less good in a governance can be different; it is accepted that almost all societies may have such good or less adequate elements of governance; therefore, it seems difficult to elaborate and to adopt norms of a general applicability on the good governance[271].

It is considered right to make a clear difference between these recommendations and respect for human rights, because in this latter field the exercise of power is submitted to the requirement of respect for obligations stemming from international norms and covered by the international responsibility of States. Good governance policies have to ensure respect for universal standards on human rights, even if such a requirement could be seen at particular moments as having adverse effects on the economic development[272]. As a matter of fact, provisions of the treaties on human rights set forth limits or conditions for the process of governance; on one side, State agents cannot act in violation of human rights, while on the other side the State has to adopt measures to obtain some results, like in the fields of health care, education, culture and social security[273]. Nevertheless, it is not always a contentious relationship; on the contrary, policies of good governance can benefit as a result of respect for human rights of the majority of the population, because this may create a climate which is favourable to implementing good policies of governance and obviously human rights can be better respected when conditions of a good governance are fulfilled[274].

Moreover, it is obvious that democracy and good governance may create a climate which is favourable to security, may avoid or diminish vulnerabilities and risks stemming from internal sources of the respective society and may diminish the possibility to be used by outside factors. They may have different contents, but have as common consequences a better cohesion of national societies, an improvement of life quality for those composing these societies[275]. They can be analyzed also from the point of view of the human security.

---

[269] Martin Sheinin, art. cit., pp.39-40.
[270] Doc. G. A. nr. 235 (XXXVIII) Annex I, art.7, cited by Michele E. Olivier, International and regional requirements for good governance and the rule of law, in South African Yearbook of International Law, 2007, 32, pp.48-49.
[271] Martin Doornbos, „Good Governance": The Metamorphosis of a Policy Metaphor, in H.O. Sano, G. Alfredsson, op. cit., p.9.
[272] Gudmundur Alfredsson, The Usefulness of Human Rights for Democracy and Good Governance, în H.O.Sano, G.Alfredsson, op. cit., p.2
[273] Mette Kjaer, Klavs Kinnerup, Good Governance, How does it relates to Human Rights, in H.O. Sano, G. Alfredsson, op. cit., p.16.
[274] Asbjorn Eide, Good Governance, Human Rights and the Rights of Minorities and Indigenous Peoples, in H.O.Sano, G.Alfredsson, op. cit., p.51.
[275] Ibidem, p.17.

In its resolution 2000/17 adopted in April 2000, the former UN Commission on human rights affirmed that good governance, including transparence and responsibility, is indispensable to build peaceful, prosperous and democratic societies. The Commission asked States to consolidate democracy by promoting pluralism and protection of human rights and fundamental freedoms.

SECTION 2 - HUMAN SECURITY

Concepts. The concept of human security was introduced on international agenda by the 1994 Human Development Report of the United Nations Development Programme. According to this Report, human security encompasses economic, food, health, environmental, personal, community and political security[276]. It is thus given a larger meaning as compared to the classical political and military security. It contains also some aspects of the contents given to security by the Copenhagen school-economic, societal and environmental. It reminds the political slogans defined as „freedom from fear and freedom from want".

A different meaning was given to human security by Canada, Norway and some other like-minded States, through the Lysoen Declaration (a small island near Bergen); Canada and Norway took a narrow approach of human security, as protection of civilians against direct physical violence, such as armed conflict and genocide, meaning State protection[277]. Although new aspects were added to this approach, it remained related to what was called a peace building agenda or a „negative peace", giving to the world community, including the civil society, an important role in compelling States to prevent and to stop actions of physical violence against their populations. It is in line with the participation of Canada and Norway in and support of peace-keeping operations, as medium-size developed States and members of NATO.

In the Report Responsibility to protect, elaborated by the Commission on Intervention and State Sovereignty in 2001, human security is defined as security of people: physical safety, economic and social well-being, respect for their dignity and worth of human beings and the protection of their human rights and fundamental freedoms. It is recognized that the concept of security concerns people as well as States. The Responsibility to protect focuses attention on the human needs of those seeking protection or assistance, thus shifting the focus from territorial security and security through armaments, to security through human development with access to food and employment and to environmental security. The Report stresses that the fundamental components of human security, the security of people against threats to life, livelihood, personal safety and human dignity, can be put at risk by external aggression, but also by factors within the country. Nevertheless, in the end, the Report focuses its response on the protection against physical violence during conflicts or caused by acts of gross violations of human rights, underlining the responsibility of the State itself and of the international community, if the State is not fulfilling its role, and stressing the function of the UN Security Council but leaving the possibility that individual States may act to stop violence in internal conflicts[278].

Although it accepts also other components of the human security, the Report follows mainly the narrow definition, aiming at the protection of people against physical violence, related to the peace-building agenda. In its Resolution 1674 on the Responsibility to protect, the Security Council notes that „the deliberate targeting of civilians and other protected persons, and the commission of systematic, flagrant and widespread violations of international humanitarian and human rights law in situations of armed conflict, may constitute a threat… to international peace and security" and reaffirms its readiness „to consider such situations and, when necessary, to adopt appropriate steps"[279].

A different approach was promoted by Japan, following more closely some aspects of the UNDP agenda, seeking to ensure human security through development, partly as a reaction to the impoverishment caused by the Asian economic crises of 1997-1999. A Commission on Human Security was established at the UN Millennium Summit in 2000, upon the proposition of the prim-minister of Japan, with the task of further developing the subject. The Commission concluded its work in 2003 and stressed the need to protect people against severe and widespread threats and situations. It defined human security as protection of the vital core of all human lives, of the fundamental freedoms of people, freedoms that are the essence of life, and stressed inter alia that human security included protection against increased impoverishment, provision of basic education and of health care and social protection[280].

---

[276] UNDP, New Dimensions of Human Security: Human Development Report, New-York, 1994.

[277] Round Table on Canada-Norway Relations: the Lysoen Declaration, 1998, Ottawa, Canadian Centre for Foreign Policy Development.

[278] The Responsibility to protect, Report of the International Commission on Intervention and State Sovereignty, December 2001, pp. 15, 47-55.

[279] Res. 1674, adopted on 28 Aprilie 2006, UN doc. S/RES/1674, 2006.

[280] Commission on Human Security, Human Security Now, 2003, pp. 6-7.

It reflects the prominent participation of Japan in development assistance programmes, in particular in the Asian region, and its constitutional restrictions to the use of force abroad. As it was noted, even in the UN there is not a singular approach on human security. Since 2005, two annual reports are published, the Human Security Report, expressing the narrow approach, and the Human Development Report by UNDP[281].

Evolution of concepts. Analysts have categorized four different approaches to human security: the basic human needs approach, which is close to the UNDP definition and incorporates all issues relevant to the freedom from fear and freedom from want; the interventionist approach, concerned mainly with the failed States that cannot provide for the security of their citizens; the social welfare related to development, which is oriented towards the attainment of sustainable development; the new security approach, related to non-traditional threats, which gives particular attention to issues such as epidemics, drugs, terrorism, cyber war and human trafficking[282].

Statistical data on human sufferings show that hundreds of millions of people suffer from hunger, from not having access to basic sanitation facilities and to drinking water or are affected by ill health and diseases, while the number of people who are victims of conflicts decreased[283]. Besides, most of the conflicts threatening human life are internal and may have multiple causes; that means that human security, if it is to be given full significance and become durable, should be approached from all these angles.

As it was noted, the peace-building approach in conflict situations was less successful in promoting welfare goals, equitable human development and inclusive democratic policies, which under this approach are considered secondary goals, left to the national authorities in the long term. Or, welfare shortcomings can jeopardize overall peace-building objectives, impede upon the consolidation of peace and can throw doubts about the legitimacy of the peace building initiatives[284]. There is also criticism showing that a peace building approach often ignores the underlying sources of conflict, emphasizing upon stability and containment, rather than conflict resolution, that it is often reduced to a technical exercise essentially value–free, and thus not conducing to durable stability[285].

It would be related to situations in weak or failed States and would be based on the belief that effective state institutions, free elections and market reforms are the solution; that would represent an externally led state building, based on the institutionalist model, neglecting the welfare needs of local populations and failing to engage with indigenous traditional institutions; it would thus alienate significant sections of the population and create the source of future conflicts[286].

Both approaches to human security-the peace building and the human development-agree that the addressee of the security policy should be the individual, but they disagree about the threats the individual should be protected against and about the means to use for this purpose. A balanced construction is nevertheless able to overcome these disagreements, because human security centered on the individual is not necessarily opposed to state security, provided that it does not ignore the requirement of human wellbeing.

A human security approach to peace building should strive to enhance not only the physical security, but also the material security of the individuals and communities, through poverty alleviation, employment creation and public service delivery to the population, thus addressing the sources of conflict, not only containing it.

The human security approach thus conceived does not rely on state institutions, democracy and markets as end goals, but as means to protect and provide for the individuals.

Therefore, many analysts present human security as a comprehensive concept, integrating the seven categories put forward by the UNDP Report, that is economic, food, health, environmental, personal, community and political security[287]. Providing for security and stability may be a priority in conflict situations or to prevent conflicts, but welfare goals such as reducing poverty, covering for immediate basic needs and service delivery and addressing other grievances is also essential in order to avoid alienation and exclusion and doubts about the legitimacy of the peace-building efforts[288].

Policies, preoccupations and studies are devoted to each of these fields from the point of view of human security. They are parts of the broad approach, which may lead to a constructive scheme in which each subject

---

[281] Nikolaos Tzifakis, Problematizing Human Security: a general/ contextual conceptual approach, South- East European and Black Sea Studies, vol. 11, No. 4, December 2011, p.362.
[282] Edward Newman, Human security and constructivism, International Studies Perspectives, no. 3, 2001, pp 243-247.
[283] Edward Newman, A Human Security Peace-Building Agenda, in Third World Quarterly, vol. 32, no. 10, 2011, p. 1737.
[284] Ibidem, p. 1741.
[285] Ibidem, p. 1745; the author gives as exemples the cases of Kosovo, East Timor, Cote d'Ivoire, Sierra Leone, Liberia and Afganistan.
[286] E. Newman, art. cit., 2011, pp. 1744-1751.
[287] Gerring 1999, pp. 379-380; Thomas 2004, p. 353; Henk 2005, p. 104; N. Tzifakis, art. cit., p. 359 and foll.
[288] E. Newman, art. cit., p. 1751.

retains its relevance and its importance. They correspond more or less to some basic human rights, which will be considered in other chapters of this book.

Most of the elements of the broad approach, relating to what was called freedom from want, can be subsumed in the general concept of development. It is generally recognized that there is no security without development and no development without security[289].

Nevertheless, there is nothing coming automatically in this relationship, and there is no guarantee that the success of efforts to ensure security (in its military and political meaning) would counteract poverty, at least on a short term basis. Human security encompasses both personal security and development, but when security is perceived as a threat to the State's existence or interests, the state perspective of security prevails over human security and the projects of development are neglected, in the internal context and as assistance to development abroad.

Of course, there is no one solution-fits-all, as the situation is different in many countries. As a study submitted to the World Bank in 2003 shows, policies and practical measures for security and development should take into account and distinguish between: States in conflict; States undergoing post-conflict reconstruction; repressive States under authoritarian rule; marginalized States[290].

Analysts note that failing States receive more attention, because they are seen as hotbeds of terrorism, than authoritarian States, although the security of the inhabitants is at risk in both of them. They note that there is an increased risk of conflict in marginalized States, that the primary challenge in such countries is to prevent conflicts and the solution is to reduce dependence on natural resources and stop the marginalization of population groups[291].

The emphasis may be different from the point of view of States and of civil society organizations. This will depend also on political interests and strategies adopted by each State, which will determine the priorities and the means applied; nevertheless, the security of States may be essential but is not sufficient to guarantee human security and wellbeing. A human perspective should lie at the basis of such policies and measures and the basic test remains to see whose security and whose development. If the answer to both is people, then the approach on human security and development could be a comprehensive and efficient one.

Other analysts are considering the concept of human security from the point of view of the protection of the vulnerable people. They refer first of all to the victims of wars and of internal conflicts and to the Convention on the regime of refugees and the Conventions of Geneva for the protection of victims of armed conflicts and the protocols thereof, as well as to the UN humanitarian agencies, but also to the difficulties to implement existing regimes and rules and to unforeseen and unintended negative effects[292].

Another category of vulnerable people to take into account is that of the victims of natural or man-made disasters. Besides some provisional ways of action in case of dramatic climate change affecting some coastal States, which are only of a recommendatory nature, there are no generally accepted plans or programmes of assistance to these people.

The third category of vulnerable people is that of those who live permanently on the edge of an economic disaster, due to the situation of underdevelopment, of chronic poverty or of economic projects pushing them into such situations. Some efforts have been made to incorporate in the aid to development some basic standards of respect for human rights. The World Bank has specified some standards to compensate certain categories of persons who are displaced or whose rights are otherwise affected by development projects, thus recognizing the need to protect them against negative effects of such projects.

It is important to mention at this point the developments which took place more recently within the Human Rights Council, concerning the responsibility of enterprises, including transnational corporations, for ensuring respect for human rights through their activities in other countries[293]. It is underlined that vulnerability may be a useful starting point for developing human security as a meaningful policy concept[294].

The concept of human security is also very differently perceived in geographic regions. In Europe, the Organization for Security and Cooperation (OSCE) considers security as comprehensive; the main documents and the activities of OSCE are devoted to humanitarian, political and military and economic/ecological issues. Human security as an approach under these three fields is presented „as a bridge which connects these three dimensions and emphasizes both their integral and indivisible character, and the ultimate end of the OSCE to increase individual

---

[289] Jan Gruiters, Security and Human Rights, 2008, no.1, p. 34.
[290] Paul Collier, Breaking the Conflict Trap: Civil war and Development Policy, Washington, World Bank, 2003.
[291] Ian Gruiters, art. cit., p. 62.
[292] Astri Suhrke, Human Security and the interests of States, Security Dialogue, vol. 30, no. 3, september 1999, p. 274.
[293] Supra, Chapter V, pp. 153-176.
[294] Astri Suhrke, art. cit., p. 275.

security in the region"[295]. In the Istanbul Declaration of 1999, the heads of State and government proclaimed that „we need the contribution of a strengthened OSCE to meet the risks and challenges facing the OSCE area, to improve human security and thereby to make a difference in the life of the individual, which is the aim of all our efforts"[296]. It is openly recognized that the challenge today is to avoid a decoupling of human rights from promoting security and stability and that thinking along the lines of human security may bring the OSCE back into innovative approach it once applied to fostering security[297].

In the Asian region, the political debate on human security has focused mainly on trans-boundary issues of mutual interest, like organized crime, drug trafficking, people trafficking and migrant smuggling, environmental degradation and humanitarian and natural disasters[298]. Human security was considered by many Asian policy elites as an extension of Western ideas related to human rights and democracy; they also considered that human centered development was not always compatible with the goals of national economic development. Besides, following the Report of the Commission on Sovereignty and Intervention on the Responsibility to Protect, human security was connected with ideas about intervention and human rights, which raised new suspicions. It is considered that the ASEAN Charter, signed in Singapore in 2007, essentially upheld the state-centered norms and traditions of ASEAN and failed to move towards a more people-centered organization. Gradually, also under the influence of the Japan's actively promoted initiatives, which are explained by the geopolitical culture in East Asia[299], Asian States tended to situate human security in the socio-economic fields.

SECTION 3 - HUMAN SECURITY and HUMAN RIGHTS

Interesting preoccupations focused on the relationship between human rights and human security; while human rights are a definite chapter of international law, well described and generally accepted in international and regional legal instruments and practice, as universal and indivisible, human security is still a concept on which there are at least two main approaches and a lot of nuances.

The main problem is to see whether the political debate on human security, including the UN documents and orientations, do not lead to limiting this concept to some categories of human rights, or to priorities conducing to neglecting the interests of vulnerable groups in different States. Reference is made to what the UNDP 1994 Report named as unchecked population growth, disparities in economic opportunities, excessive international migration, environmental degradation, drug production and trafficking and international terrorism, to which analysts added spread of diseases, instability in financial markets, as well as new threats like climate change.

It is rightfully underlined that respect for human rights is not a political choice, but a legal obligation; States cannot choose what rights to respect and to give priority to some rights ignoring others, regardless of threats from abroad or natural disasters they may be confronted with. States may derogate from some rights in case of danger for the existence of the nation, respecting a very precise procedure; even in such a case they cannot derogate from some human rights such as the right to life, the prohibition of torture and others. Every person has the right to request in internal courts or in international procedures accepted by the States that his/her rights are respected and ask for reparation when they are violated. Of course, the system is not perfect and does not always and everywhere ensure respect for human rights[300].

As for the human security, leaving aside the differences of approach and of contents attributed to, it is only a concept which is far from having a normative character and is promoted as a policy to be followed by States and international organizations. Most of the threats analyzed under the human security concept relate to some human rights which are not or may not be respected. The question is if the situation of victims of human rights abuses can be improved by resorting to the concept of human security instead of pursuing the remedies available under the national law and under the international human rights regime.

Even with regard to economic, social and cultural rights, there are clear obligations of States under the 1966 Covenant on these rights and according to national constitutions and laws; there is an important evolution in the jurisprudence of the regional courts of human rights on some economic, social and cultural rights, based on the

---

[295] Gerd Oberleitner, The OSCE and Human Security, Security and Human Rights, 2008, no. 1, pp. 68, 70.

[296] OSCE, Istanbul Summit Declaration, 1999, para. 2.

[297] Gerd Oberleitner, art. cit., pp. 71-72.

[298] Melissa Curley, Human security's future in regional cooperation and governance?, Australian Journal of International Affairs vol. 66, no. 5, 2012, pp. 527-541.

[299] Ho Satomi, Japan's human security policy : a critical review of its limits and failures, Japanese Studies, 2008, no. 28/1, p. 107(cited by Melissa Curley, p. 534).

[300] Rhoda E. Howard-Hassmann, Human Security: Undermining Human Rights?, Human Rights Quarterly, no. 34, 2012, p. 95.

principles of equal rights and non-discrimination and on the rights of indigenous peoples and minority groups; the new additional protocol of 2000 to the European Convention on human rights on non-discrimination, submitting to the Court all cases of discrimination in the exercise of human rights, and the new additional protocol to the 1966 Covenant opening the way to individual complaints for violations of economic, social and cultural rights will extend the ambit of remedies for obtaining the respect of these rights. Thus, the international regime on human rights addresses most of the threats considered under the human security concept.

As we know, international organizations, in particular the United Nations, are acting through different means for the observation of human rights treaties(presentation of national reports and consideration of the situation by the Human Rights Council, presentation and consideration of periodic reports by the human rights treaty bodies and consideration of individual complaints by such bodies if the States accept the respective procedure, reports of rapporteurs on the situation in some States, of thematic reports and the recommendations addressed to the respective States by the competent bodies), resolutions of the General Assembly and of the Security Council, including those adopting sanctions against some of them. They have a legal basis for that, they are competent under the Charter and under different applicable treaties. The responsibility for respecting the provisions of these treaties rests always with the States parties to the treaties. It is not clear on what basis, who and how should act for protecting human security if it would be separated from its human rights basis.

If for the mass and flagrant violations of human rights there is a wide agreement that the international community can react, in a first stage by diplomatic means and then by forceful measures under the authorization of the Security Council if it is considered that international peace and security are in danger, for other kinds of threats to human security foreseen under different approaches, the international community can rely only on persuasion, shaming and monitoring by the human rights treaty bodies. It is obvious that the concept of human security is not adding much to the existing mechanisms.

Analysts noted that in the human security discourse human rights appear merely as a subset of the human security, and as such as a subject deserving less attention. On the other side, the emphasis on freedom from fear or on freedom from want under the two main approaches leads to prioritizing some threats against others, which means placing some human rights over others, and may mean that some violations of human rights deserve less concern, which is unacceptable in principle and inefficient in practice. For instance, the Commission on Human Security argued that human security could make a significant contribution to defining which human rights are crucial, by identifying the importance of freedom from basic insecurities[301]. This is considered to undermine the wide body of human rights as it developed since the adoption of the UN Charter and to make easier for some States to ignore or violate some human rights in the name of human security[302].

The human rights perspective is wider and more protective than freedom from fear and freedom from want as stressed by the human security agenda. This is considered to be a minimalist view of human rights; human dignity, which lies at the basis of human rights, requires beyond freedom of fear and of want, that human beings are recognized as persons of value, are able to participate in decision-making and to freely pursue their interests. Therefore, human security cannot be a substitute for human rights and fundamental freedoms.

At the same time, there are many common elements between the concept of human security and human rights, to mention only their universality, the interdependence of their components (even in a narrow definition of human security), and the fact that they are people centered and the best way to ensure them is prevention[303]. Therefore, they should not necessarily be seen in competition. Human security can be a useful political means if it focuses on the protection of all human lives from critical threats which are not protected or are inadequately protected by the existing human rights regime. In other words, it should complement the human rights regime by new understandings, commitments and mechanisms to protect such values which do not seem adequately protected.

Even in the narrow discourse on human security, there is a search for enouncing new duties for States and international organizations and to improve international cooperation to achieve the goals proposed; this is also the preoccupation of the human rights regime through its treaties and mechanisms, for instance for increasing the protection of children, of women, of migrants and their families, of indigenous peoples and afro-descendants. That means it has to add some value to the human rights protection.

The adoption of human security policies by more and more States could be also an important tool for strengthening the human rights regime, by promoting a better implementation by States of the provisions of human rights treaties and the improvement of cooperation with human rights treaty bodies, in sum a higher level of respect for human rights and fundamental freedoms.

---

[301] Commission on Human Security, 2006, p. 9.
[302] Rhoda E. Howard-Hassmann, art. cit., p. 106.
[303] Ibidem, art. cit., p. 109.

* * *

In substance, democratic security means political pluralism, extended participation in the conduct of the public affairs, efficient, responsible and accountable State institutions. Moreover, it is considered that if a significant segment of the society feels threatened and insecure, the security of the whole society and of the State is in danger.

This means also good governance, including both the political aspects of democracy and economic and social objectives.

Some of these requirements correspond to compulsory norms of international law, such as respect for fundamental human rights and freedoms, mainly political rights, the freedoms of expression, of association and assembly, as well as norms concerning an independent and efficient justice. Others, such as the form of the government, its organization and structure, the efficient management of resources, are left to the decision of each State, and the international community adopts only recommendations concerning the best practices to be followed.

As we noted, most aspects dealt with human security are covered by norms of the protection of human rights, which are accepted by most States of the world. Human security cannot be a substitute for human rights; on the contrary it supposes their respect and promotion in all countries of the world. The approach to human security is very important: an approach limited to political and military security is linked to relations of power, to the foreign action, even intervention, and leaves aside significant risks to security, resulting from poverty and underdevelopment; an extended approach as that promoted by the UNDP reports is comprehensive and requests sustained efforts in many fields, balanced policies and a good management of resources with a permanent preoccupation for respect and promotion of human rights and fundamental freedoms for all.

CHAPTER IX - INTERNATIONAL CRIMINAL JUSTICE

ABSTRACT

Although criminal courts existed after the Second World War and others were created again more recently, one can say that this is a new institution in international relations and international law. Treaties were adopted mainly during the twentieth century by which the States parties undertook to incriminate and to prosecute through their judicial systems a series of facts directed against important values they agreed to protect. It is only for the most serious violations of such treaties that international courts were created. Most of them are ad-hoc institutions, with all disadvantages resulting from it; some of them are sui-generis courts, involving at the same time internal and international aspects. The International Criminal Court is the only permanent criminal court, but many States are not parties to its statute and it is still only at its beginnings. It is competent for crimes of genocide, crimes against humanity, crimes of war and aggression and has a subsidiary jurisdiction, when the national States do not wish or are not able to prosecute. In spite of a difficult beginning, it has already a lot of cases, has its future and has an important role to play. It became a central institution among the international organizations and may remain the only one for criminal jurisdiction.

KEY WORDS: genocide, crimes against humanity, crimes of war, aggression, international humanitarian law, jurisdiction of substitution, competence *rationae loci, ratione personae, ratione materiae*

HISTORICAL OVERVIEW

For a long time, criminal justice was exclusively a prerogative of State sovereignty, meaning that norms of criminal law were only national and only the national authorities of a State could prosecute and punish persons guilty of offences committed on its territory, while for offences committed in spaces which were not subject to national jurisdictions, each State could prosecute its citizens.

Gradually, norms of criminal international law developed, initially by custom and then by international treaties, States taking the commitment to incriminate and to punish offences committed by individuals, irrespective of their citizenship, against some social values that States considered necessary to protect. The best known example is that of the protection of the freedom of high seas; beginning with the 20th century, States accepted that piracy had to be incriminated and punished by any State which could capture the pirates.

The norm concerning the universal prohibition and repression of piracy was taken up more recently in the 1982 Montego Bay Convention on the law of the sea, according to which any State can, in the high sea or in any other place beyond the jurisdiction of another State, retain a pirate navy or aircraft, or a navy or aircraft captured by pirates or under their control, arrest the pirates and retain properties on board and the courts of the respective State could apply the appropriate punishment.

Other international conventions engaged States to sanction through their criminal laws offenses such as slavery and slave trafficking, illegal trafficking of drugs, trafficking of women and children, dissemination of pornography, counterfeiting of money, acts of terrorism against aircraft and against civilian aviation in general, or against political personalities or against UN personnel, taking of hostages, acts of torture and others. States undertook also to cooperate for the prosecution and repression of such facts.

Nevertheless, for the incrimination and punishment of such offences the territorial principle is applied, meaning that a State applies its criminal law to offences committed on its territory or on ships under its flag[304]. The Geneva Conventions of 1949 on the protection of victims of war (wounded and sick, war prisoners and the civilian population), as well as the 1948 Convention on the punishment of the crime of genocide and the 1973 Convention on the punishment of the crime of apartheid provide also the obligation of States parties to incriminate and punish such offences and to cooperate for this end[305].

In all these cases, States committed themselves to exercise their criminal jurisdiction in order to protect some values considered by the international community as deserving such a protection. In fact, States adopted norms of the criminal international law (even if in many cases they were preceded by their norms of the internal criminal law), in order to promote the widest possible application of such norms, and national courts acted also as bodies applying the norms of international criminal law.

---

[304] On this subject, Ion Diaconu, Manual of public international law, third edition, 2010, ed. Lumina Lex, pp. 389-398.
[305] More extensively, Ion Diaconu, International Criminal Court. A New Stage, 2002, IRSI, pp. 33-34.

For the first time the problem of the prosecution by international courts of persons guilty of crimes under the international criminal law was raised after the First World War. According to article 227 of the Treaty of Versailles of 28 June 1919, „The Allied and Associated Powers publicly accuse William the Second of Hohenzollern, former German Emperor, of the supreme crime against international morality and the sanctity of treaties". This article provided that a special tribunal will be created, composed of 5 judges nominated by the USA, UK, France, Italy and Japan to judge the accused. These States agreed to ask the Government of The Netherlands, where the emperor found a refuge, to surrender him in order to be prosecuted.

With regard to persons guilty of violations of norms and customs of war, the German government recognized the right of the allied and associated powers to bring them before military tribunals and undertook to surrender them at request and to offer all documents and information necessary. A Commission for the responsibility of the authors of war was created, which found that German 896 officers were responsible for war crimes. The Commission recommended to creating an international tribunal to prosecute some persons, including the former emperor for „the supreme crime against peace".

Nevertheless, many States opposed the judgment of the former emperor as being without precedent and contrary to the concept of national sovereignty[306]. The Netherlands refused to surrender him, while the prosecution of other accused was transferred to the Supreme Tribunal of Leipzig, which found the majority of them not guilty on the basis of the principle of the „superior order". Finally, only 12 of them were judged in Leipzig and only 6 of them were found guilty and were condemned to a maximum of three years imprisonment each. They were helped to escape and did not execute even a small part of the punishment. The issue of prosecuting citizens of allied and associate powers for such offences was never raised, although it is difficult to accept that only German citizens committed such offences.

In 1937, after the attempt of Marseille of 1934 against the King of Yugoslavia and the Foreign minister of France, the Convention for the prevention and the repression of terrorism was adopted, providing for the punishment of such facts and for this purpose the establishment of an international permanent tribunal. Although initially signed by 13 States, the Convention was not ratified because of events which preceded the beginning of the Second World War.

Obviously, the political willingness of States to punish authors of crimes of international law, mainly war crimes, but also acts of terrorism and others, as well as a legally articulated and generally accepted conception, were missing.

SECTION 1 - INTERNATIONAL AD-HOC TRIBUNALS

Tribunals created after the Second World War. The Second World War was characterized by atrocities without precedent against all victims of war, which determined a strong trend towards the prosecution of those guilty. The victorious allied powers decided already during the war to create two international military tribunals to judge the major war criminals, respectively German and Japanese, and to see that other persons, whose crimes could be geographically localized, are judged by the national courts of the victim countries.

The International Tribunal of Nurnberg was created by the USA, UK, USSR and France by the Agreement of London of 8 August 1945 in order to prosecute the major war criminals of the European powers of the Axes whose crimes could not be localized; at the same time the statute of the Tribunal was adopted. The Tribunal received the competence to prosecute and punish persons who, acting on behalf of the European powers of the Axes, committed crimes against peace, such as conceiving, launching and leading a war of aggression or a war in violation of international treaties, agreements or commitments, or participated in a concerted plan or a plot with the objective of achieving some of these purposes.

As objects of accusation, the Commission of investigation and prosecution included in the act of accusation the following: the concerted plan or plot against peace; the preparation and launching of the war of aggression; crimes of war; crimes against humanity. A separate law adopted by the Council of Control of allied powers established the conditions of prosecution of other war criminals. The Nurnberg Tribunal judged 22 Nazi leaders, among whom 12 were condemned to death, 7 to imprisonment and three were released. Many others were prosecuted and punished in the countries where the crimes were committed, some of them many years after the end of the war.

The International Tribunal of Tokyo was created in 1946 by the Special Proclamation of the Supreme Commander of allied forces of Asia, on the basis of the Potsdam Declaration of 26 July 1945, in order to judge the

---

[306] Reservations of USA and Japan to the Report of the Commission concerning the responsibility of authors of the war, in American Journal of International Law, vol. 14, 1925, pp. 127, 151.

major war criminals of Far East, accused mainly of planning, preparing, launching or leading a war of aggression or a war in violation of international treaties, agreements or arrangements. The tribunal condemned 7 Japanese leaders to death by hanging, 18 to imprisonment and three were released.

By a resolution of 1946, the UN General Assembly confirmed the principles recognized by the statutes of the two tribunals and by the decisions adopted. The United Nations retained thus the principles and the practice of the international criminal responsibility for the most serious crimes, mainly the aggression and crimes against peace, as well as crimes of war and crimes against humanity, including aspects of the relationship between aggression and self-defense, responsibility of political leaders and diplomatic immunity. Half a century later, the two tribunals can be seen as a preface of the present ad-hoc tribunals.

International criminal tribunals created recently. The last decade of the 20th century was confronted in Europe and Africa with particularly serious crimes, reminding some of horrors committed during the Second World War. Responding to this situation, very often too late, the UN Security Council, in charge to maintain international peace and security, adopted decisions to create ad-hoc international criminal tribunals under the Chapter VII of the Charter.

The International Criminal Tribunal for Yugoslavia (ICTY). As an answer to the large scale violations of international humanitarian law, which led to killings, detention, rape and ethnic cleansing on the territory of former Yugoslavia, the Security Council created by its resolution 827 of 25 May 1993 the Tribunal for the prosecution of persons guilty of serious violation of international humanitarian law committed on the territory of former Yugoslavia between 1 January 1991 and a date to be established by the Council when peace will be reestablished.

According to the statute of this Tribunal, set forth by the resolution, its material competence included the serious violations of the Geneva Conventions of 1949 (intentional killings, torture, serious pain or wounds to the body or to health, illegal deportation and the taking of hostages; the use of weapons which produce useless sufferings, the destruction of towns or villages, attacks upon settlements without defense, destruction of religious, cultural or educative institutions); acts of genocide, crimes against humanity.

The Tribunal judged 161 persons, among whom 80 where sanctioned by imprisonment for different periods of time, 18 were acquitted, 13 sent to be judged by the national courts, for 36 accusation were withdrawn or they died before being transferred to the Tribunal, six died in detention at the Tribunal and others were still to be judged (among them, beginning of 2016, Mladic, Karadzic, Hadzic). The Tribunal had to finalize its activity in 2016, while cases in suspension had to be transferred to the Residual Mechanism for the International Criminal Tribunals, created by the resolution of the Security Council nr. 1966 of 26 December 2010.

The International Criminal Tribunal for Rwanda (ICTR). In 1994 the Council created, by its resolution nr. 955 of 8 November 1994, the International Criminal Tribunal for Rwanda, in order to prosecute and judge persons responsible for genocide and other serious violations of international humanitarian law committed on the territory of Rwanda and Rwandan citizens guilty of acts of genocide and other serious violations committed on the territory of neighbouring States, in the time frame between 1 January and 31 December 19944.

According to the statute adopted by this resolution, the competence *ratione materiae* of the Tribunal included the crime of genocide, crimes against humanity as part of an attack committed on a large scale or systematically against a civilian population on national, political, ethnic, racial or religious grounds, as well as some violations of norms and customs of war provided for by the Geneva Conventions and the Second Protocol to them.

It prosecuted 93 accused and adopted 55 decisions of condemnation; 10 cases were referred to the national jurisdiction, for other 5 person's accusations were withdrawn or they died before being judged, 9 accused were not yet found and will be prosecuted 6 of them by Rwandese authorities and 3 by the Residual Mechanism; 6 cases are before the Appeal Chamber of the Tribunal. The planning was to close the activity of the Tribunal at the end of 2014[307].

Both tribunals were preceded by commissions of experts which collected information and made proposals. The tribunals for former Yugoslavia and Rwanda have many things in common; their mandates were similar, albeit with small differences, mainly emphasis, taking into account the facts committed; they had also in common a prosecutor and a chamber of appeal. According to their statutes, they had priority over the national tribunals, being authorized to ask at any time that a national tribunal refer to them a case. They condemned a significant number of persons found guilty of committing serious violations of human rights, more in the case of the Tribunal for Yugoslavia (in majority Serbs, but also Croats and others). They had to finalize their activity in 2008 and appeals in 2010. They prolonged their activity having new cases, among the most significant. More recently, the two tribunals

---

[307] On the activity of all criminal jurisdictions, Muriel Ubeda-Saillard and Ann-Laure Chaumette, L'activité des juridictions pénales internationales (années 2012-2013), in AFDI, 2013, pp. 359 and foll.

acquitted some high military and political officials for accusations of participating in common criminal enterprise, which was heavily criticized[308].

They were created by the Security Council on the basis of the Chapter VII of the Charter, that is as measures for maintaining international peace and security; the general prosecutor was nominated by decision of the Security Council and they functioned under the authority of the Council. All States had the obligation to cooperate for the fulfillment of the mandate of the two tribunals on the basis of the resolutions of the Council[309].

The Special Tribunal for Sierra Leone. In order to prosecute and punish persons guilty of atrocities committed in Sierra Leone, the Security Council decided in principle to create an international tribunal by its resolution 1315 of 14 August 2000. The Special Tribunal 310 was created by an agreement of 2000 between the UN, through the Secretary General and the government of this State. It was thus an institution *sui generis*, created by an international agreement, not on the basis of Chapter VII of the Charter, but with the political support from the Security Council.

It had the competence to judge serious violations of internal law and of international humanitarian law committed in Sierra Leone after 1996, including abuses against children, their enrolment as soldiers and the destruction of goods. It was composed from national and international judges, but functioned outside the national jurisdictional system. Its hybrid nature permitted to reject, on the basis of international humanitarian law and of the agreement with the United Nations, exceptions based on national law (immunity of the head of State, absence of incrimination in the national criminal law). It judged 13 cases, accusations against the leaders of some armed groups and against the former president of Liberia, Charles Taylor; 9 accused were punished, 2 died before being judged, 1 disappeared. It closed its mandate in 2013, the main achievement being the punishment of Charles Taylor, former president of Sierra Leone.

It is also interesting to note that the Court considered enslavement of persons as a crime against humanity and acts of terrorism as crimes of war. A Residual Special Tribunal was created to fulfill the obligations of the Special Tribunal (protection of witnesses, surveillance of the execution of sentences, conservation of archives).

The Extraordinary Chambers of the Tribunal of Cambodia. An agreement was concluded in 2003 between the United Nations and Cambodia on the establishment of Extraordinary Chambers within the national system of justice, in order to judge authors of crimes committed during the Pol Pot regime in violation of both Cambodian laws and international humanitarian norms. The Chambers are composed of national (the majority) and international judges, nominated by the Superior Council of Magistracy, on the basis of a list conveyed by the UN Secretary General. United Nations participate by ensuring the administrative services of the Chambers.

Their competence is limited to the serious acts committed by the high officials of the former regime[311]. One accused was judged for crimes against humanity, extermination, torture, application of a regime of slavery and crimes of war and a first sentence was pronounced in 2012 in the case Dutch; in two other cases the sanction was pronounced in 2014; other 2 leaders of the Pol Pot regime are judged for genocide, crimes against humanity, crimes of war and acts of torture.

The Special Tribunal for Lebanon. In 2007, the Security Council approved the agreement concluded by the UN with the government of Lebanon concerning the prosecution of those guilty of the attempt of February 2005, which resulted in the murder of the former prim-minister Hariri, as well as of other terrorist acts committed during the years 2004-2005, in accordance with the Lebanese law. An international tribunal was created which has priority over the national courts and is separated from the national judicial system. This is a mixt tribunal, having predominantly an international composition, formed of persons nominated by the UN Secretary General after consultation of the Lebanese government, on recommendation from a jury of selection. The acts subject to prosecution are not covered by norms of international criminal law and no threat to international peace and security was invoked.

As a matter of fact, it is a jurisdiction of substitution, chosen for political considerations. The Tribunal formulated accusations against 5 persons; only one trial started in 2014 in the case Ayyash and others in the absence of the accused and only the exception of the legality of the Tribunal was judged and rejected (the agreement on its establishment was not ratified by the Lebanese parliament, due to internal conflicts). The climate around the Tribunal is extremely tense.

---

[308] Ibidem, p. 363; they are also mentioning the case of Karadzic, to whom the agreement on Bosnia(so called agreement Hallbrooke) guaranteed immunity if he retires from public life.

[309] Jackson Maogote, The experience of the ad-hoc tribunals for the former Jugoslavia and Rwanda, in The Legal Regime of ICC: essays in honour of Professor Igor Bliscenko, 2009, pp. 63- 64; I. Diaconu, International Criminal Court, pp.53-56.

[310] Jose Doria, The Work of the Special Court for Sierra Leone through its jurisprudence, in The legal Regime of ICC..., pp. 229-254.

[311] Chambres extraordinaires au sein des tribunaux cambodgiens, Jurisprudence internationale, in RGDIP, 2010, pp. 893-901.

Preoccupations for creating a criminal court in Timor Leste. In the context of the criminal international jurisdiction, it seems necessary to evoke also the preoccupations for prosecuting and punishing those guilty of serious violations of human rights in East Timor in 1999, in connection with its fight for independence. In 2000, the Security Council authorized the creation of a UN Administration of Transition, with all legislative and executive functions and the administration of justice, and requested to bring to justice those guilty of serious violations of acts of violence in East Timor during the year 1999.

This administration gave in the competence of the Tribunal of the capital city of East Timor to create some special courts for prosecuting serious crimes of genocide, crimes of war and crimes against humanity wherever would be the persons concerned[312]. A Memorandum of Understanding was also concluded with Indonesia concerning cooperation to collect testimonies, to arrest and transfer suspects and other aspects.

In 2003, the special tribunals accused some 400 persons of committing such serious crimes, more than three quarters situated outside the territory of Timor. The general prosecutor formulated accusations against 8 high Indonesian officials. The Indonesian government declared that it will ignore them and will organize its own tribunals; the Indonesian general prosecutor named only 18 accused, most of them of an inferior rank or civilians; only 6 persons were found guilty, punished to imprisonment between 3 and 10 years; in appeal, only one remained to execute the punishment.

In 2004 the Security Council asked for the cessation of all investigations till the end of the year and of the trials in 2005, having in mind political imperatives of reconciliation with Indonesia and with the heads of the Timorese militia. In 2004, the governments of Indonesia and East Timor created a Commission of Truth and Friendship, in order to search for the truth and to promote friendship as a new and unique approach, rather than investigating the past. Thus, in the case of East Timor the preoccupations for relations between States and for national reconciliation prevailed over the criminal justice.

Other criminal courts with international involvement. In Kosovo, in 2015 the Parliament modified the constitution and approved the creation of a special tribunal to function at The Hague, for prosecuting serious crimes committed by members of the former Army of Liberation of Kosovo, many of them in key positions now. This was foreseen as a national tribunal, part of the national system of jurisdiction, but it was agreed that it will function at The Hague, in order to avoid local interference[313]. Nevertheless, the tribunal ceased its function, without pursuing any case.

In Iraq, at the USA insistence, in 2003 the government approved the statute of a Special Iraqi Tribunal for Crimes against Humanity, modified in 2005 as High Criminal Court, as part of the Iraqi system of jurisdiction. It judged Saddam Hussein and other persons guilty of serious crimes against human rights[314].

In Senegal, in 2012, at the request of the African Union, Extraordinary African Chambers of the Senegalese Courts were created by a Senegalese law, in order to prosecute crimes committed in Chad between 1982 and 1990. The Chambers are formed by African judges, nominated by the president of the Commission of the African Union under proposal by the minister of justice of Senegal. For the time being the only accused is Hissène Habré. Analysts comment that the chambers were created to solve the case of Hissène Habré who found refuge in Senegal; Chadian citizens asked the Senegalese courts to prosecute him and Belgian authorities asked Senegal to extradite him for being prosecuted in Belgium[315]. The International Court of Justice, seized by Belgium, asked Senegal to prosecute Hissène Habré or to extradite him[316]. The procedure against the former president of Chad plus other five officials began in 2015.

General comments. These are ad-hoc tribunals, created after the occurrence of the facts they were called to prosecute. Their existence was limited *ratione temporis* and *ratione materiae*. In spite of all imperfections, mainly their ad-hoc character, the difficulty to create them each time and the amount of time used for that and for establishing their mandate and the applicable law, they played an important role in promoting criminal responsibility for the most serious crimes and for crystallizing the conception and structure of institutions meant to act in such cases, and in the end to prepare the creation of the international criminal justice. Of course, being created post-factum, they lack a preventive effect and leave a doubt whether the persons who committed the facts incriminated will ever be prosecuted.

---

[312] Richard Burchill, From East Timor to Timor Leste: A demonstration of the limits of international law in the pursuit of justice, în The Legal Regime of ICC...., pp. 255-296.

[313] www.balcancaucaso.org/eng/Areas/Kosovo.

[314] Sara Williams, High Criminal Court in Irak, in Journal of International Criminal Justice, vol. 11, 2013, Issue 5, pp. 1139-1160.

[315] Anne Bodley & Sousena Kebede Tefera, The Extraordinary Role of the Exttraordinary Chambers convened to try former Chadian leader Hissene Habre, in Africa Law Today, Issue 3, 2013.

[316] Decison of the ICJ of 20 July 2012, ICJ Recueil 2012, p. 422.

They marked a real progress in the application and the development of the international criminal law, in extending its application to conflicts without an international character and in promoting the protection against the most serious violations of human rights and reducing impunity for them. Some of them proved that they can produce fair sentences. The most important innovation of these tribunals is that they instituted the criminal responsibility of heads of State (in spite of the resistance to its application in the African region), of members of government and of the administrative and military hierarchy for such crimes. It was also established that the subordination to a law or to the superior order is not creating an exception to responsibility for those who execute the crimes.

SECTION 2 - INTERNATIONAL CRIMINAL COURT

General aspects. From the beginning of its activity, the Commission of International Law had on its agenda the item concerning the creation of a permanent international criminal court. In 1950 it reached the conclusion that it is both desirable and possible to establish such a court. Several ad-hoc committees considered the issue and elaborated a draft, but its final adoption was related to the issue of the definition of aggression and to the adoption of a Code of crimes against peace and security of mankind, and thus postponed.

After the adoption of the definition of armed aggression in 1974, while the works on the Code of crimes were advanced, in 1989 the UN General Assembly asked the Commission to consider the issue of an international criminal jurisdiction, including „proposals for establishing an international criminal court or another mechanism of criminal jurisdiction". After elaborating a new project and receiving the comments of States, the Commission finalized its draft of statute of a criminal court in 1994. In 1995 a Preparatory Committee was created to finalize the draft statute for submitting it to the future Diplomatic Conference of plenipotentiaries.

The Conference was convened between 15 June and 17 July 1998 in Rome and adopted the Statute of the International Criminal Court with a majority of votes. Being ratified by more than 60 signatory States, the Statute entered into force on the 1st July 2002. This was followed by preparatory activities and the election of its members and of the General Prosecutor, as well as the formation of its office and of the Registry. The Court began its activity in 2004-2005.

The Statute of the International Criminal Court, ratified until now by more than 120 States is the result[317] of the evolution in this field, a new step towards reducing impunity for the most serious violations of humanitarian law and of human rights in the world. It takes up many of the ideas and norms developed by the preceding experiences, while adding new elements, developing and completing some norms and institutions. At the same time, it is a text of compromise adopted after long negotiations conducted with the willingness to reach a result to which as many States as possible could adhere and thus support the new court. The Court is an independent and permanent institution, open to universal participation; its jurisdiction is limited to States parties and to some offences considered the most serious.

The Court is created by a treaty, which obliges States parties. It is not a substitute for the national criminal jurisdiction and is not replacing national courts; on the contrary, it is complementary and subsidiary in relation to them. The Court is called to judge only if the national judicial system, respectively a State party, is not able to investigate and to prosecute persons guilty of committing crimes subject to the jurisdiction of the Court or if the State party refuses or fails to investigate and to prosecute such persons. The Court is thus meant to act together with the national systems of criminal jurisdiction for the punishment of some serious crimes.

The Court applies first of all its Statute, the Elements of crimes (elaborated and finalized by the Preparatory Commission in June 2000[318] and approved by the Assembly of the States parties at its first session of 3-9 September 2002), as well as the Rules of procedure and of evidence (adopted later on by the Assembly). In the second place, it applies the treaties and principles and norms of international law, including those concerning the protection of victims of armed conflicts, whenever and wherever they are applicable. If such norms are absent, the Court applies general principles of law derived by it from nationals law of legal systems of the world, including, as appropriate, the national laws of the States that would normally exercise jurisdiction over the crime. It may apply such principles and rules as interpreted in its previous decisions.

The Statute underlines that the application and interpretation of law providing from all these sources have to be consistent with human rights recognized at the international level, without any distinction found on gender, age,

---

[317] Victor Ponta, D. Coman, International Criminal Court (in Romanian), Lumina Lex, 2004.
[318] Doc. PCNICC/2000/1/Add.2, 2 November 2000.

race, colour, language, religion, ethnic origin or other criteria, that is with standards in force concerning human rights.

The Court exercises its jurisdiction on crimes committed on the territory of a State party to the Rome Statute and elsewhere by one of the citizens of a State party, or if a State which is not a party is in the same situation and accepts the jurisdiction of the Court, or when a State which is not a party surrenders to the Court a person who is not its citizen but is found on its territory (competence *ratione loci*) and is requested by the Court. Thus, the Statute combines the competence *ratione personae* with that *ratione materiae*.

The Statute provides also that the Security Council may refer to the Prosecutor a situation where one or more crimes under the jurisdiction of the Court may have been committed, in order to investigate and prosecute any person supposed guilty and whatever may be the citizenship of the person and the place where the crime may have been committed. As such, the Court becomes a partner to the Security Council by its capacity to prosecute individuals responsible of atrocities, an alternative to failing institutions of States to prosecute in such cases and a voice in combating mass crimes[319].

A person is responsible for a crime which is under the jurisdiction of the Court (competence *ratione personae*): a) if he/she committed such a crime individually or jointly with other persons; b) if he/she orders, solicits or induces the commission of such a crime; c) if he/she aids, abets or otherwise assists in the commission of the crime offering means for this purpose; d) if he/she in any way contributes intentionally to the commission or attempted commission of such a crime by a group of persons acting with a common purpose, either with the aim of furthering the criminal activity of the group or knowing its intention to commit the crime; e) if he/she directly and publicly incites others to commit the crime of genocide; f) for the attempt to commit such a crime by beginning the execution, even if the crime does not occur because of circumstances independent of the person's intentions. This is the *material element of the criminal responsibility (actus reus)*.

The other essential element of the criminal responsibility is *the intentional one (mens rea);* a person is responsible for a crime under the jurisdiction of the Court if the material element is committed with intent and knowledge, that is if the person means to engage in the respective conduct and to cause that consequence or is aware that it will occur in the normal course of events.

A first act of the Court is to establish whether a case is admissible. A case is considered inadmissible if: a) it is investigated or prosecuted by a State which has jurisdiction over it, unless the State is unwilling or unable genuinely to carry out the investigation or the prosecution; b) if the State which has jurisdiction over the case investigated it and decided not to prosecute the respective person, unless the decision results from the unwillingness or inability genuinely to prosecute; c) when the person has already been tried for the respective conduct; d) when the case is not of sufficient gravity to justify the action of the Court.

If the admissibility is contested by a State, the Prosecutor suspends the investigation until the Court makes a determination; it may ask the Court to authorize the continuation of the investigation in order to preserve important elements of evidence, to take a statement or a testimony from a witness or to prevent the absconding of a person in respect of whom he already requested a warrant of arrest. The Court decides whether a national amnesty impedes the prosecution of a case and whether a prosecution by national courts and the decision taken represent an effort in good faith in order to apply the principle *ne bis in idem*.

The Statute of the International Criminal Court enounces also the general principles of the criminal law, that the Court has to respect (*ne bis in idem, nullum crimen sine lege, nulla poena sine lege,* the principle of non-retroactivity, that of the most favourable law). The Statute offers also substantial procedural guarantees in favour of the persons prosecuted. During the investigation, they shall not be compelled to incriminate themselves or to confess guilt, shall have the right to remain silent, shall not be subject to any form of constraint, shall have the assistance of an interpreter as necessary, shall be informed about the charges against him/her and shall have legal assistance.

The Pre-Trial Chamber is competent to decide, at the request of the Prosecutor, to issue a warrant of arrest if there are reasonable grounds to believe that the person has committed a crime within the jurisdiction of the Court. Upon the surrender of a person to the Court, the Pre-Trial Chamber holds a hearing to confirm the charges in the presence of the person; nevertheless, special circumstances may justify the confirmation of the charges in the absence of the person (if the person waived his/her right to be present or fled or cannot be found and all reasonable steps have been taken to secure his/her presence in front of the Court); the person will be represented by a counsel where the Chamber considers it in the interest of justice.

During the trial, the accused has to be present and enjoys the full recognition of his/her rights: presumption of innocence, prompt information about the charges in a language he/she understands and speaks, adequate time and facilities for the preparation of defense, examination of witnesses, public and impartial hearing without delay, as well

---

[319] M. U. Saillard and A. L. Chaumette, art. cit., p. 368.

as assistance free of any cost of a competent interpreter and the necessary translations, and not to be compelled to testify or to confess guilt. The Statute also contains provisions about the protection of victims and witnesses, hearing *in camera* for the protection of children and of victims of sexual crimes.

These norms concerning the principles of criminal law and the procedural guarantees represent a combination of civil law and common law; the contradictory character of the trial is preserved, but a large competence is ensured to judges for the investigation and for questioning the witnesses.

Competence of the Court. The International Criminal Court has jurisdiction over genocide, crimes against humanity, crimes of war and aggression (competence *ratione materiae*).

Genocide, considered as a crime of international law, is defined in the Statute according to the 1948 Convention on the prevention and punishment of genocide as any acts committed with the intention to destroy, in whole or in part, a national, ethnical, racial or religious group, such as: killing members of the group; causing serious bodily or mental harm to such members; deliberately inflicting on the group conditions of life calculated to lead to its physical destruction in whole or in part; imposing measures to prevent births within the group; forcibly transferring children of the group to another group.

According to the Convention, two elements have to be reunited: the material element, consisting in one or several acts mentioned; the intentional one, the intention to destroy such a group, knowing from the beginning the consequences of the act. The existence of such a group against whom the criminal act is directed is an essential element of the definition. If such an act is directed against persons who are not members of a group of this kind, that is there is no intention to destroy a group, it cannot be qualified as genocide.

Acts of genocide were condemned, on the basis of the definition given by the 1948 Convention, by the International Tribunal for Rwanda. With regard to a provisional measure, requested in the case „Responsibility of R.F. of Yugoslavia (Serbia and Montenegro) for genocide", the International Court of Justice decided that the government of this country has „to take immediately all available measures to prevent the commission of the crime of genocide and in particular to ensure that no military, paramilitary or irregular armed unit, which may be under its direction or support, as well as any organization or person which may be subject to its control, direction or influence commit an act of genocide, conspiracy to commit or complicity to it"[320].

It is generally recognized that the prohibition of genocide is an imperative norm of international law, from which States cannot derogate in their relations[321].

Crimes against humanity are defined according to the Statute as acts committed as part of a widespread or systematic attack against any civilian population, with knowledge of the attack, such as: murder, extermination, enslavement, deportation or forcible transfer of population, torture, sexual crimes such as rape, forced prostitution, forced gravidity or others of comparable gravity, persecution against a group or collectivity for racial, ethnic or other grounds, enforced disappearance, other inhuman acts causing intentionally serious sufferings or injury to body or to mental or physical health.

This includes a conduct implying multiple acts committed against a civilian population, as systematic and on a large scale; such a conduct results from a State policy or from an organization, which should be manifestly encouraging such acts or supporting them. That concerns not only State officials, but also terrorist organizations, separatist movements or other groupings involved in such crimes. This does not concern individual isolated acts, which are not part of a plan or a policy. Crimes against humanity can be committed not only in time of war or in connection with armed conflicts, but also in time of peace. Crimes against humanity are different from genocide; their target is a population which does not constitute a racial, ethnic or religious group; they target a population, not isolated persons, as it is the case with a simple homicide. The Rome Statute is the first international treaty which codified the crimes against humanity, although most of the ad-hoc criminal courts prosecuted persons accused of crimes against humanity; in substance, it goes further than the statutes of the tribunals for former Yugoslavia and Rwanda.

War crimes come under the jurisdiction of the Court, in particular when they are committed as part of a plan or policy or as part of a large scale perpetration of such crimes. The provisions of the Statute are based on the 1949 Conventions and on the 1977 Protocols to them. They include serious violations of the Geneva Conventions as acts committed against persons protected by them, serious violations of humanitarian law provided mainly in Protocol I

---

[320] Decision on competence in the case „Application of the Genocide Convention", ICJ Reports, 1993, pp. 16, 342/343.

[321] Decisions of the International Court of Justice, case Barcelona Traction, Recueil CIJ, 1970, p. 32; case Nuclear Tests in the South Pacific, ICJ Reports, 1996, para. 104-105; cases Continental Shelf of the Northern Sea, ICJ Reports 1969, pp. 38-39; case Military activities, ICJ Reports, 1986,p p. 101-106. In the international law doctrine, Lauri Hannikainen, Peremptory Norms (Jus Cogens) in International Law, Historical Development, Criteria, Present Status, 1988; Ion Diaconu, Normele imperative în dreptul internațional(jus cogens), in Romanian, Ed. Academiei, 1977.

concerning international armed conflicts, as well as acts committed during armed conflicts without an international character, provided for in Protocol II to the Conventions, mainly against civilian populations, including the use of weapons which cause unnecessary suffering or have an indiscriminate effect on the civilian population not involved in the military operations.

It does not incriminate the use of chemical and biological weapons, although this is forbidden by international conventions, and of nuclear weapons, although it is obvious that their use would violate all norms of humanitarian law, as the International Court of Justice retained[322]. From that point of view, the Statute of the Court remains behind the international instruments on disarmament and the interdiction of the use of some types of weapons. For the first time the definition given to the crimes of war includes both norms for the protection of the victims of armed conflicts (the law of Geneva) and those concerning the means forbidden in war (the law of The Hague).

The Statute represents thus an important contribution to the codification and the promotion of the application of humanitarian law, both in international conflicts and in those without international character[323].

Aggression represents another category of crimes subject to the jurisdiction of the Court. As it is known, the definition of the aggression so as to make possible its prosecution by the Court was not adopted at the Rome Conference and was delayed for a conference to be convened 7 years after the entrance in force of the Statute, in order to consider and to adopt amendments to it on this issue. The Conference took place in Kampala (Uganda) in 2010.

The Conference of Kampala defined the crime of aggression[324] as the planning, preparing, initiating or executing, by a person in an efficient position so as to exercise control, or to direct the political or military action of a State, of an act of aggression which by its character, gravity and ampleness constitutes a manifest violation of the UN Charter. An act of aggression is understood as the use of armed force by a State against sovereignty, territorial integrity or political independence of another State or in any other manner inconsistent with the UN Charter. As acts of aggression, the amendment of Kampala enumerates those included in the definition of armed aggression given by the resolution of the General Assembly nr. 3314 of 14 December 1974.

According to the Statute, before beginning investigations with regard to a case of aggression inconsistent with the UN Charter, the Prosecutor will inquire whether the Security Council ascertained an act of aggression of the State concerned; if such a determination exists, the Prosecutor can begin investigations; if during the next 6 months such a determination is not made, the Prosecutor may proceed to investigation under prior authorization by the Pre-Trial Chamber of the Court, if there is no opposition from the Security Council.

It is obvious that both the definition of aggression as well as its application by the Court are closely related to the provisions and mechanisms of the UN Charter; this is normal, because aggression against a State is committed by another State, not by private persons acting as such, and the competence to ascertain an act of aggression belongs to the Security Council according to the Charter. The definition of aggression as committed by persons is closely related to the definition of armed aggression of 1974, which is also reaffirming the competence of the Council to determine whether acts others than those enumerated therein represent aggression, but also to determine that some acts do not have the degree of gravity to be qualified as aggression.

The adoption of this amendment is accompanied by reservations and conditions that delay for some time the exercise of the competence of the Court with regard to this crime and make it depend upon decisions taken by the Security Council. Moreover, a State party to the Statute may declare that it does not accept the jurisdiction of the Court on this crime. Analysts appreciate that these amendments are meant to favour new adhesions to the Statute of the Court, but that they will establish several regimes of the application of the Statute, a criminal justice with several speeds, at least with regard to aggression[325] and that they contributed to increased interference between political considerations and the jurisdiction of the Court.

Jurisdiction of the Court. The Court started to consider situations of violation of norms included in its Statute in 21 cases from 12 States. A number of States referred themselves to the Court such situations (D. R. of Congo, Central African Republic, Uganda and Mali). From Congo, 3 persons were judged, 3 others are in the custody of the Court and 1 has disappeared. From Uganda, only 1 person is under trial, three were not surrendered to the Court and one died. From the Central African Republic, 5 persons were set free without decisions of punishment, because they were in the custody of the Court for too long time. As for Mali, the situation was presented to a Pre-Trial Chamber of the Court by the Prosecutor of the Court and there is no decision to begin criminal prosecution in precise cases.

---

[322] Advisory Opinion of 8 July 1996, Legality of the threat or use of nuclear weapons, ICJ Reports 1996, pp. 259, 266.

[323] For an extensive presentation of the competence of the Court, Ion Diaconu, International Criminal Court..., pp. 96-123.

[324] Conférence de Kampala, Première Conférence de révision du Statut de Rome, 31 mai-11 juin 2010, in Revue générale de droit international public, 2011, Chronique des faits internationaux, sous la direction de Louis Balmond, pp. 612-615.

[325] Chronique des faits internationaux, art. cit., p. 615.

The Court also began to consider the situation in Cote d'Ivoire, at the initiative of the Prosecutor of the Court, with the agreement of the government of this State; the president of this State is judged, 2 other persons are in the custody of the Court and a third person disappeared. The Security Council referred to the Court the situations in Darfur (Soudan) and Libya. A number of 6 persons were named by the Prosecutor in connection with the situation in Sudan; 2 persons presented themselves and are judged and warrants of arrest were delivered for other 4 persons, including for the president of this country, but none of them was surrendered to the Court. As for Libya, 1 person died, a second one is prosecuted by a national court and the third one disappeared. Finally, the Court began investigating *proprio motu* the situation in Kenya for the serious crimes committed, at the initiative of the Prosecutor of the Court with regard to 4 persons; one of them was elected president of the country; the State party refused to surrender any person and the Court renounced to prosecute these cases.

The Office of the Prosecutor of the Court examines at present on a preliminary basis situations in Afghanistan, Colombia, Georgia, Guinea, Honduras, North Korea and Nigeria, which would extend the activity of the Court to other continents. Information was presented to the Prosecutor also about acts committed in Palestine and in Iraq.

The warrant of arrest of the president of Sudan was rejected by this State and by the African Union as a regional organization and the respective action was not promoted consistently by members of the Security Council. The Court also could not prosecute leaders of Libya and was not seized with a demand by the Security Council on the situation in Syria.

The International Criminal Court was confronted with difficulties from the beginning. There was and continues the opposition of the USA, which during the first years of the Court proposed in the Security Council resolutions and signed more than 60 bilateral agreements through which it pretended to except all American citizens from the jurisdiction of the Court. Those bilateral agreements also contained the commitment of the USA not to surrender to the Court citizens of the other States parties, mainly their heads of State.

Such agreements are considered by analysts not only as violations by the States parties of the Statute of the Court but also as being in contradiction with imperative norms of international law (because impeding the prosecution of persons guilty of violations of crimes of genocide, crimes against humanity, crimes of war and aggression, which are all forbidden by imperative norms)[326].

Then, the Court did not benefit of the cooperation of some States parties in the execution of its attributions. For instance, although Uganda is a State party to the Rome Statute and referred itself some cases to the Court, the government of Uganda made no efforts to surrender the respective persons and requested to withdraw the cases from the agenda of the Court, motivating that it gives priority to the national reconciliation with the rebel forces where the persons accused of crimes under the jurisdiction of the Court came from.

Although the Security Council referred to the Court the case of the president of Sudan, a State which is not a party to the Statute, African and Arab States refused to cooperate with the Court and even adopted decisions based on the immunity of heads of State in exercise, according to which they will not surrender heads of State at the request of the Court. The African Union took this position also with regard to the warrants of arrest against colonel Khadafi and against president and vice-president of Kenya. The president of Sudan continued to visit States parties to the Rome Statute and Chad and Malawi refused to apply the warrant of the Court to arrest him, invoking inviolability enjoyed by heads of State.

The Pre-Trial Chamber of the Court adopted decisions where it affirms that the immunity of heads of State (as a customary norm) cannot be opposed to measures of constraint adopted by the Court and that the two States violated their obligations under the Rome Statute[327]. The Pre-Trial Chamber did not take into consideration that this case was referred to the Court by the Security Council, which gives it another legal ground, although this does not justify the refusal of the two States to cooperate.

The International Tribunals for former Yugoslavia and for Rwanda were also confronted with such difficulties. Croatia refused for some time to arrest and surrender generals Ratko Mladic and Ante Gotovina, Serbia refused longtime to surrender several persons, accused of different crimes, beginning with the former president Slobodan Milosevic. The Tribunal for Rwanda was paralyzed in 2002 for some months by the absence of witnesses

---

[326] Telesphore Ondo, La non-cooperation avec les juridictions penales internationles, in Revue de droit international et de droit compare, no 1, 2015, pp. 97-100.

[327] For a critical evaluationn of the situation, Baptiste Tranchant, Les immunites des Etats tiers devant la Cour Penale Internationale, in RGDIP, 2013, 3, pp. 633-656. The Rome Statute itself permits that a State does not surrender from its territory persons who enjoy diplomatic privileges and immunities(art. 98.1). On the other side, the International Court of Justice retained that even adopting a warrant of arrest of a person who enjoys immunity due to its function represents a violation of its immunity(case R. D. Congo against Belgium, ICJ, decision of 14 February 2002, p. 70.

from Rwanda and the USA refused in 1996 to surrender Elisaphan Ntakirutimana, accused of genocide, for absence of sufficient evidence and of an agreement of extradition.

Within the UN also, there is not sufficient support; the Organization promoted for some time cooperation with the president of Sudan with the view to solving the conflict in Darfur, although the Security Council referred already to the Court the case of Sudan which led to the arrest warrant of the president. In other cases also (Kenya, Uganda), the UN bodies did no adopt clear cut positions for the continuation of the criminal pursuit against persons subject to warrants of arrest of the Court.

Analysts comment the situation of non-cooperation with the Court as a violation of international treaties, of the Statute of Rome, of the UN Charter and of imperative norms of international law[328]. As for the Statute, its article 86 stipulates that States parties shall fully cooperate with the Court in the investigation and prosecution of crimes within the jurisdiction of the Court; refusing to cooperate with the Court, whatever may be the reasons invoked, is certainly a violation of the Statute in conformity with the Convention on the law of treaties of 1969 (article 26, *pacta sunt servanda)*.

Moreover, the European Union included in its treaties and acts the obligation to cooperate with international criminal jurisdictions and concluded a series of treaties mainly with States of Africa, of the Caribe's and the Pacific areas, as well as with States from East-Europe under the European Policy of Neighbourliness, by which these States took the commitment to cooperate with the International Criminal Court. Of course, these commitments are part of undertakings of both sides, including some concessions from the EU, but they are obligations assumed by international treaties.

The European Union took some measure on a bilateral level in cases of non-cooperation with the Court (delaying the application of the Process of Stabilization and Association with Croatia in 2005 and Serbia in 2006 and suspending the same Process with Bosnia-Herzegovina because of its bilateral agreement on impunity with the United States).

As for customary norms, reference was made to norms of international humanitarian law, contained in the Conventions of Geneva and of The Hague for the protection of victims of war, as norms which command respect from all States, irrespective of having ratified or not international treaties giving expression to them, because they are intransgressible principles of international customary law[329]. Refusal to cooperate with the Court would represent also a violation of imperative norms of international law, like the interdiction of genocide, of torture, of slavery and others, including in application of bilateral treaties granting immunity with regard to such crimes, because that would annihilate the efforts of the Court to prosecute and punish them. Although this is not directly a derogation from the imperative norms, the result is the same and the validity of such treaties has to be refused under the norms of the Vienna Convention on the law of treaties[330]. Besides, the norms concerning State responsibility for harmful acts provide for the obligation of all States to cooperate through lawful means for bringing an end to any serious breach of such norms (article 41.1).

With regard to the cases referred to the Court by resolutions of the Security Council, refusal to cooperate with the Court represents also a violation of the UN Charter (article 25), by which member States agreed to accept and carry out decisions of the Council in accordance with the Charter.

* * *

One could maintain presently, without being wrong, that international criminal justice is still at its beginning. Important steps were made to negotiate and adopt international instruments containing primary norms incriminating acts that international and national courts have to prosecute and punish. Ad-hoc tribunals solved an important number of cases and created in the respective States a climate against impunity for serious violations of human rights, in spite of criticism about selective approaches, duration, costs and other issues.

The International Criminal Court was created as a permanent institution, numbering more than 120 member States which ratified the Rome Statute of 1998. It made its first steps, in spite of difficulties, it solved some cases and is trying to find the best ways to cooperate with States and with the United Nations bodies. There is already a positive experience, even some jurisprudence, of the ad-hoc tribunals and of the Court in solving different legal issues which confront any criminal court: jurisdiction, exoneration of responsibility, immunity, relationship with the national law and jurisdiction and others. Procedural guarantees and norms were adopted to ensure a fair trial, fully respecting international standards on human rights.

---

[328] Telesphore Ondo, art. cit., pp. 79 and foll.
[329] Advisory Opinion of the International Court of Justice, Legality of the threat or use of nuclear weapons, ICJ Recueil, 1996, p. 257.
[330] Telesphore Ondo, art. cit., p. 99-100.

The record of the International Criminal Court is far from being satisfactory. The main problem seems to be the lack of political will of States to cooperate for the fulfillment of the attributions of the Court, even from States parties to the Statute. There is the feeling that not all these States accept the principle of responsibility of political leaders for acts under the jurisdiction of the Court. On the other side, the fact that presently the Court examines only situations from the continent of Africa led to the wrong perception that it would be a European criminal court for Africa. Other reasons of criticism are the costs and the duration of some cases, the selectivity and the impact of the trials on national policies.

Nevertheless, it may be a transitory situation. It is to be expected that when the ad-hoc tribunals cease their existence and the remaining cases are transferred to the Court, other ad-hoc tribunals will not be created, if the Security Council agrees to transfer to the Court cases concerning States which are not parties to the Rome Statute. Evolutions are also expected with regard to the adhesion of other States to the Rome Statute (some 80 States, among whom three member States of the Security Council (USA, Russian Federation, China, as well as India, Arab States and others). The International Criminal Court is a new institution, which found its place with some difficulties, but started moving; it responds to real needs and will become increasingly useful in a world which wants to be more just and less violent. As a matter of fact, the activity of the Court depends substantially on the cooperation of member States to surrender the persons requested, to ensure the evidence necessary, the participation of witnesses, the execution of punishments and other moments of the criminal trial.

The establishment of a system of international criminal justice, through a permanent court and some ad-hoc tribunals, and through the relationship with the UN bodies which have the mission to maintain international peace and security, represents an important evolution in the contemporary international law. The conception that political and military leaders are responsible for serious violations of human rights is gradually generally accepted, which contributes to preventing and eliminating such violations from the world's life.

At the same time, due to the relationship of complementarity between international and national criminal justice, the principles and norms of the international criminal law penetrate the national systems of jurisdiction[331], thus creating synergies which lead to the extension of the application of these principles and norms and tend to prevent the violations. It is rightly underlined that the success of the system should be evaluated according to the extent that it leads to avoiding such serious violations[332].

---

[331] F.Jessberger and J. Geneuss, Down to Drain or Down to Earth? International Criminal Justice under Pressure, in Journal of International Criminal Justice, 11, 2013, p. 2.
[332] Payam Akhavan, The Rise and Fall and Rise of International Criminal Justice, in Journal of International Criminal Justice, 11, 2013, p. 3.

PART III – RACIAL DISCRIMINATION

CHAPTER X – RACIAL DISCRIMINATION - definition, approaches and trends

ABSTRACT

A definition of discrimination was gradually developed in several international documents, with specific elements in the respective fields. Racial discrimination was defined in the 1965 Convention on the elimination of all forms of racial discrimination. It contains different elements which are cumulative: the types of facts representing a different treatment, the grounds that qualify them as racial discrimination, the equal rights requirement and the fields of application.

Each of these problems needs clarification and marking limits, considering the scope and purpose of the Convention and all its provisions, because not any difference of treatment represents an act of discrimination. Moreover, the Committee created to survey the application of the Convention(CERD) developed a dynamic interpretation, taking into account the social needs encountered in different States parties and the overall evolution of international law in the field of human rights.

It is the purpose of this study.

KEY WORDS: discrimination, racial discrimination, distinction, restriction, preference, exclusion, race, cultural difference, descent, ethnic origin, nationality, foreigners, special measures.

INTRODUCTION

Contemporary international law presumes equal rights of all persons and prohibits any discrimination. Most international documents on human rights proclaim from the beginning the elimination of any discrimination on grounds such as race, colour, sex, language, religion, national, ethnic or social origin, political or other opinion, property, birth or any other status.

Some of these documents also defined discrimination in various areas, such as in the field of labour the Convention 111 concerning Discrimination in Respect of Employment and Occupation, adopted in 1958 by the Conference of the ILO, in the field of education the Convention against Discrimination in Education, adopted by the General Conference of UNESCO in 1960.

In its General Comment 18 (Non-discrimination), adopted in 1989, the Human Rights Committee formulates the opinion that this term, as used in the Covenant, should be understood to imply "any distinction, exclusion, restriction or preference which is based on any ground such as race, colour, sex, language, religion, political or other opinion, national or social origin, property, birth or other status, and which has the purpose or effect of nullifying or impairing the recognition, enjoyment or exercise by all persons, on an equal footing, of all rights and freedoms"[333].

SECTION 1 - GENERAL ASPECTS of the DEFINITION

1. The International Convention on the Elimination of All Forms of Racial Discrimination, adopted by the resolution 2106 A (XX) of 21 December 1965 of the UN General Assembly, brings together the main aspects of the generally-accepted standards concerning non-discrimination on racial grounds, as developed in international documents. According to the 1965 Convention, racial discrimination "shall mean any distinction, exclusion, restriction or preference based on race, colour, descent, or national or ethnic origin which has the purpose or effect of nullifying or impairing the recognition, enjoyment or exercise, on an equal footing, of human rights and fundamental freedoms in the political, economic, social, cultural or any other field of public life" (article 1 of the Convention).

---

[333] Compilation of General Comments and General Recommendations adopted by human rights treaty bodies, doc. HRI/GEN/1/Rev.8 of 8 May 2006, pp.185-188.

Obviously, this definition, which follows closely those given in preceding documents, is not limited to discrimination on ground of race *stricto sensu*, but includes also discrimination on grounds of colour, descent and national or ethnic origin. Moreover, the definition refers to a large area of actions (distinction, exclusion, restriction or preference) qualified by their consequences on human rights, in the sense that they have as purpose or effect to nullify or to impair the recognition, enjoyment or exercise on equal footing of fundamental human rights and freedoms.

As for the fields of application of the principle of non-discrimination, one should note also that the definition covers practically all spheres of public life, by reference to the political, economic, social and cultural, and any other fields. The definition of racial discrimination, as given by the Convention, is based on objective elements. It refers to acts of distinction, exclusion, restriction or preference, which means that one must identify an appropriate comparator, by reference to persons of a different race, colour, descent or national or ethnic origin. By these enumerations, the definition is able to protect all persons, as well as racial or ethnic groups.

It is notable that the definition includes all acts of discrimination, committed intentionally or otherwise, which have as purpose or, even if such purpose is not pursued, have as effect the inequality in the enjoyment or the exercise of human rights. In considering many reports presented by States parties to the Convention, CERD stressed that States must consider not only the purpose of different acts, that is those with deliberate and obvious intent to discriminate, but also the effect of discrimination such acts may entail on the exercise or the enjoyment of human rights by persons of a different race, colour, descent, national or ethnic origin. This is also confirmed by the obligation established in art.2.1 c) for States parties to adopt effective measures to amend, rescind or nullify any laws and regulations which have the effect of creating or perpetuating racial discrimination wherever it exists.

Another essential element of the definition, closely related to the exercise and the enjoyment of human rights, is the "equal footing". Having identified the comparator, one has to examine the treatment applied to persons or groups under consideration, and to check if there are distinctions, exclusions, restrictions or preferences. This again concerns both direct and indirect discrimination[334]. Nevertheless, not every difference of treatment can be considered discrimination. As CERD observed, a difference of treatment will not constitute discrimination if the criteria for such differentiation, judged against the objectives and purposes of the Convention, are legitimate or fall within the scope of its article 1.4 (as special measures).

The reference to "public life" at the end of the enumeration has already raised some difficulties of interpretation. Some States parties have given it a restrictive sense, meaning that what could be considered as "private life" would not be included in the scope of the definition of racial discrimination. In its activity, CERD relates the reference to political, economic, social and cultural fields of public life to the rights and freedoms set up in article 5 of the Convention.

In a more direct approach, in its General Recommendation no. 20 on article 5, the Committee states that "The rights and freedoms referred to in article 5 of the Convention and any similar rights shall be protected by the State. Such protection may be achieved in different ways, be it by the use of public institutions or through the activities of private institutions". CERD concludes that "To the extent that private institutions influence the exercise of rights or the availability of opportunities, the State must ensure that the result has neither the purpose nor the effect of creating or perpetuating racial discrimination"[335]. Over time, the Committee increasingly has expanded the scope of ICERD to address a wide sphere of acts by private actors, including business, in private sphere.

The Committee has not hesitated to address discriminatory acts by business enterprises in various contexts. It explicitly mentions private companies, mining companies, exploitation infrastructure projects, energy developers or other activities particularly in relation to the protection of specific groups, mainly indigenous peoples, but also some ethnic groups like Roma.

The reference to "public life" in the definition, understood in context with other provisions of the Convention, mainly those of article 5, does not mean to allow racial discrimination in private areas of human activities, which cover very important fields of human relationships, where this would infringe upon the enjoyment or the exercise on equal footing of human rights and freedoms as provided for in international documents and internal laws.

This interpretation corresponds to the express provisions of article 2 of the Convention, according to which "Each State Party shall prohibit and bring to an end, by all appropriate means, including legislation as required by circumstances, racial discrimination by any person, group or organization".

The 1965 Convention requests States parties to encourage integrationist multi-racial organizations and movements and other means of eliminating barriers between races, to adopt immediate and effective measures,

---

[334] On direct and indirect discrimination see Sandra Fredman (ed.), Discrimination and Human Rights. The Case of Racism, 2001, Oxford University Press, pp.23-29.
[335] General Recommendation no. 14 of 1993 on article 1, paragraph 1 of Convention, Compilation…, doc. HRI/GEN/1/Rev. 8, p. 247.

particularly in the fields of teaching, education, culture and information, with a view to combating prejudices which lead to racial discrimination, and to promote tolerance and friendship among nations and racial and ethnic groups. Of course, tolerance is not sufficient to ensure a normal and beneficial coexistence for the groups concerned. Nevertheless, it represents a necessary minimum, because intolerance is the step which leads from xenophobia to rejection, discrimination and exclusion.

The extremely broad scope of the grounds of racial discrimination, of the acts and areas covered by the definition of racial discrimination is confirmed by the provisions of article 5 of the Convention. In a long but not exhaustive list, article 5 enumerates human rights to equal treatment, to personal security and protection, other political, civil, economic, social and cultural rights, as well as the right of access to any places and services intended for use by the general public. States parties undertook to guarantee the right of everyone, without distinction as to race, colour, or national or ethnic origin, to equality in the enjoyment of all these rights.

2. A recurring issue when we approach most of the aspects of racial discrimination is the relationship between the individual and the group. Is it necessary to relate every person who may be a victim of acts of racial discrimination to the racial, ethnic or national group, or to a group formed on the basis of colour or descent, to which that person may belong?

The 1965 Convention protects not only persons, but also groups. According to its provisions, each State party undertakes to engage in no act or practice of racial discrimination against persons, groups of persons or institutions and to adopt specific and concrete measures to ensure the adequate development and protection of certain racial groups or individuals belonging to them. The States parties condemn all propaganda and all organizations which are based on theories of superiority of one race or group of persons of a particular colour or ethnic origin. They undertake to declare an offence punishable by law all dissemination of such ideas, as well all acts of violence against any race or group of persons of another colour or ethnic origin. These provisions obviously aim to protect persons and groups who are victims of racial discrimination.

Other provisions stipulate as a condition for taking special measures not to entail as a consequence the maintenance of unequal or separate rights for different racial groups, as well as to adopt immediate and effective measures with a view to promoting understanding, tolerance and friendship among nations and racial or ethnic groups.

The Convention thus covers not only persons, but also groups. It protects both individuals and ethnic or racial groups against racial discrimination. At the same time, States parties are obliged to take measures both against persons and against groups or organizations which commit acts of discrimination, of incitement to discrimination or of racially motivated violence.

How do we recognize such a group and its members? Is it necessary for such a group to be recognized by the respective State? How can one identify the members of such a group? The Convention is not clarifying these issues and adopted, as in other cases, the method of an extensive regulation, leaving to the practice to clarify the concepts used.

It is true that the very concept of racial discrimination implies the existence or the assumption of existence of groups. It is true that individuals are the victims of discrimination; nevertheless, they are discriminated on grounds of race, ethnicity or descent not because of their unique individuality, but because they are, or are considered to be, members of a certain more or less negatively perceived group. Therefore, the concept of discrimination is based on a pre-conceptual assumption of membership of a group[336]. But groups may not be recognized as such by some States parties and the application of the Convention for the protection of the group may thus be doubtful. A State may also contest that a certain person belongs to a racial or ethnic group, and consequently may deny him or her protection as a member of the group. That is why, racial discrimination is always a violation of some body's individual right to equal treatment; it may be also, according to the Convention, a violation of rights of the group.

Confronted with this problem, CERD adopted its General Recommendation no. 8 of 1990, expressing the opinion that the identification of an individual as belonging to a racial or ethnic group must be based on how such a person identifies himself or herself, except when there is a justification to the contrary[337]. According to an evaluation, this solution advanced by CERD reverses the burden to prove that a person does not belong to an ethnic or racial group, once that person has identified himself or herself as such, on those contesting the individual self-identification of the person[338].

---

[336] Dmitrina Petrova, Racial Discrimination and the Rights of Minority Cultures, in Sandra Fredman(ed.), Discrimination and Human Rights. The Case of Racism, 2001, p. 67
[337] Compilation…, doc. HRI/GEN/1/Rev. 8, p 244.
[338] P. Thornberry, International Law and the Rights of Minorities, 1991, p. 261-262.

The identity of a minority, and of persons composing it, includes objective elements: cultural, ethnic, linguistic features, and of course its numerical weight in a State. It also includes subjective elements: the will to preserve their identity and to act as such. It is difficult to separate the existence in time of objective features from the will to preserve them[339].

In its activity, CERD has often overcome the problem of defining whether persons belonged to a specific racial or an ethnic group or to one based on descent, because the Convention, as it results from article 1.1, relates the prohibition of discrimination against a person to grounds of race, colour, descent, national or ethnic origin[340] of that person, and not to his or her belonging to a group, which should previously be acknowledged or recognized as such. The object of protection of the prohibition of racial discrimination is, ultimately, the individual. The concept of group may be important for each person, as a criterion of reference for common cultural, linguistic and ethnic features, but the group is not *per se* the holder of the respective rights[341].

SECTION 2 - GROUNDS for DISCRIMINATION

A. Discrimination on Grounds of Race and Colour

Race and colour are the first grounds enumerated in the definition. If they are the origin of a distinction, an exclusion, a restriction or a preference, such acts represent racial discrimination if they have the purpose or the effect of nullifying or impairing the recognition, the enjoyment or the exercise on an equal footing of human rights and fundamental freedoms.

Racism is a doctrine which divides mankind in races, that is in groups formed of individuals presenting the same hereditary features, whose behaviour would be determined mainly by their belonging to such groups. From this determinism based on such features, racist doctrines establish a hierarchy of values and preferences, to justify a discriminatory treatment[342].

As a result of its scientific studies, in 1978 UNESCO adopted the Declaration on Race and Racial Prejudice according to which "all human beings belong to a single species...all individuals and groups have the right to be different...any theory which involves the claim that (some) racial or ethnic groups are inherently superior ...has no scientific foundation and is contrary to the moral and ethical principles of humanity...any form of racial discrimination practiced by a State constitutes a violation of international law".

These studies established that racism is scientifically unjustified, that all human beings are born equal in dignity and rights and form an integral part of humanity. Consequently, biological differentiation of races and racial prejudice are without foundation.

Therefore, "Racism" can be a description of attitudes (mental states of individuals or groups), of ideologies (sets of socially constructed and politically functional ideas about societies, classes, cultures, groups) or of social practices and institutions (acts of discrimination at the individual or institutional level).

As it was noted, in the contemporary world, racism seems to focus more on the differences between races than on inequality between them, more on cultural differences than on nature and biological features of the relevant persons. It is what the doctrine calls the new racism, or the racism of cultural differences. This does not eliminate the racism of inequalities, which denies equal rights to some people or human groups on grounds of race, colour or ethnic or national origin. It is rightly noted that the differentiation from the point of view of culture often integrates implicit biological features.

Although racist theories have been utterly discredited, some attitudes and behaviours persist, from ignoring people and segregating them, to racially-motivated acts of violence.

The Durban Conference of 2001 noted in the documents adopted that, despite efforts by the international community, by governments and local authorities, the scourge of racism, racial discrimination, xenophobia and related intolerance persists and continues to result in violation of human rights, suffering, disadvantage and violence[343].

---

[339] I Diaconu, Minorities..., p. 90-93.
[340] Ion Diaconu, Racial Discrimination, 2011, Eleven International Publishing, The Hague, p.48.
[341] Idem, pp. 48-49.
[342] Ion Diaconu, Racial Discrimination, pp. 51-53.
[343] World Conference against Racism, Racial Discrimination, xenophobia and Related Intolerance, Declaration and Programme of Action, Durban, 31 August-8 September 2001, doc. A/CONF. 89/12.

Racism cannot be attributed exclusively to the human mind and to psychology; nor can it be attributed to the functioning of societies, although it is a social phenomenon.

Mankind has gone through such important stages of promoting human rights and humanist universal values, that it seems unconceivable to accept the idea that we live in racist societies, which continue to foster racism. As for theories which try to justify racism by individual merit, it is artificial to combine racial prejudice with individual merit which does not need a racial justification to be recognized or to succeed. The evolution of economic and social life in many areas, especially I.T., medicine, culture and sports, shows that racial prejudice cannot relate to individual values and merit.

It is also unacceptable to reduce race and ethnicity to economic and social problems and, in order to ensure equality before the law and equality of opportunities, it is not enough to limit the struggle against racism to prohibition and penalization, or to recast differences in race or ethnic origin as mental disabilities or behavioural disorder[344].

The Committee frequently repeats the need to eliminate discrimination against people of a different race and colour, and potential discrimination against them in the judicial system. In this context, CERD considered reports on discrimination against black people, those of mixed race, indigenous people, on grounds of race, colour and ethnic origin, or against persons originating from Africa and from Europe. The Committee recommended the adoption of special measures to their benefit, including facilitation of their equal access to courts and to administrative bodies.

Realities show that we now confront a new type of racism which emphasizes cultural identity, and apparently not the racial determination of inequality. This concept tries to justify racist attitudes and practices by the axiom of cultural incompatibilities [345] or by some irreducible mental differences, maintaining that such groups are in a constant conflict on cultural grounds.

One can also observe that different cultural identities are used for racist purposes in two ways. The first affirms superiority or inferiority of some cultures over others, replacing the biological racism with a cultural one and trying to justify on that basis discrimination and exclusion. The second considers cultural differences absolute and incompatible, and the respective ethnic groups as mutually antagonistic, which leads to rejection and exclusion.

The new racism thus appears to be based on the cultural differences; the opposition of culturally different ethnic groups and the conflict of identities are replacing the classical theme of the opposition of races [346].

The answer to these preoccupations is multi-culturalism, characterized by the preservation and respect for different cultures in society, including those preceding the formation of national States and those resulting from migrations or shaped by the interaction between cultures and by free mutual access to their values.

The 1965 Convention mentions "*colour*" as a ground for which any distinction, exclusion, restriction or preference leading to inequality in the enjoyment or the exercise of human rights is defined as discrimination. However, preoccupations concerning colour are now less common, both in international documents and specialized literature, and in the activity of international bodies dealing with respect for human rights. On one side, the concepts of race and ethnic or national origin undoubtedly cover to a large extent that of colour. On the other hand, considering the mixture of populations, the nuances of skin colour are unlimited, which makes it difficult to establish categories and consequently, to analyze the situation on such a basis.

B. "Descent" as a Ground of Racial Discrimination

The Committee adopted in 2002 a General Recommendation nr. 29 of 2002 on descent-based discrimination[347] and recommended that States parties follow it when gathering information about some communities. The Committee reaffirmed that discrimination based on descent includes discrimination against members of communities based on forms of social stratification such as caste and analogous system of inherited status which nullify or impair their equal enjoyment of human rights. CERD also undertook to clarify how such communities could be defined or distinguished from others. The Committee stated from the very beginning that "their existence may be recognized on the basis of various factors, including some or all of the following: inability or restricted ability to alter inherited status; socially enforced restrictions on marriage outside the community; private and public segregation, including in housing and education, access to public spaces, places of worship and public sources of food and water; limitation of freedom to renounce inherited occupations or degrading or hazardous work;

---

[344] General Recommendation no. 32 on the meaning and scope of special measures in the International Convention on the Elimination of Racial Discrimination, doc. CERD/C/GC/32 of 29 September 2009.

[345] Ion Diaconu, La Culture et les Droits de l'Homme, 2015, Edilivre, Paris, pp. 312-313.

[346] Gil Delannoi and Pierre Taguieff, Nationalism in perspective, 2001.

[347] Compilation…, doc. HRI/GEN/1/Rev. 8, p. 267.

subjection to debt bondage; subjection to dehumanizing discourses referring to pollution or untouchability; and generalized lack of respect for their dignity and equality".

According to some scholars, the concepts of "descent" and of "national or ethnic origin" duplicate each other[348]. Realities show that even if these notions do partially duplicate each other in some countries, they have nevertheless their specific significance within the definition. There is not always duplication, and even if in some cases it may be proved that certain castes or tribes are not different from other segments of the population, by race or ethnic or national origin, there are other specific features which make it possible and necessary to consider acts of violation of the rights and freedoms of such persons as acts of racial discrimination.

The Committee did not limit its consideration to South East Asia, but found that expressions of the caste system are also present in some African States; it also considered the possibility that groups which emigrated to some western States could have brought with them aspects of discrimination based on the caste system, and recommended that such discrimination be expressly prohibited in domestic legislation as a violation of the Convention.

On that basis, the Committee recommended that States parties adopt various measures, as appropriate to their circumstances. These included: to identify communities under their jurisdiction who suffer from discrimination, especially on the basis of descent; to prohibit explicitly this type of discrimination in their national legislation; to formulate and put into action a comprehensive national strategy to eliminate it; to adopt special measures in favour of such communities; to establish statutory mechanisms in order to promote equal human rights of members of such communities; to educate the general public on the importance of such measures; to encourage dialogue between members of descent-based communities and members of other social groups; and to gather data and inform the Committee on the situation of the respective communities.

C. Discrimination on grounds of ethnic origin

The ethnic origin could be considered in the present circumstances as the most comprehensive of the grounds for which racial discrimination is forbidden, considering that biological racism is discredited, that racism on ground of colour is generally rejected and in view of the trend to justify discriminatory attitudes and treatment by the reference to cultural differences which are an important element of ethnical origins. A UNESCO Committee of experts on racial issues made a distinction between the concept of race, meaning a group or a population characterized by physical hereditary distinct features (genes) and that of ethnic origin, which refers to a cultural entity with or without physical distinct features[349].

Even if the expression "ethnic group" is the most commonly used, it is very often given a cultural context; it is admitted that the drafting of article 27 of the Covenant on civil and political rights associates "ethnic" origin with culture, referring to persons belonging to ethnic minorities and to the enjoyment of their own culture, and not to cultural minorities. They are distinct from other groups by their culture, which gives their members their specificity and identity. The concept of ethnic origin is closely related to that of national, religious and linguistic minorities, although people characterized by race, colour or descent represent very often minorities in their countries. According to many scholars, most elements forming the concept of minority are related to ethnicity, including language, religion and of course, culture[350].

One has to note that in Europe the concept used more often is that of "national minority". It follows the conception largely shared by many European States, according to which not all ethnic, linguistic or religious groups form minorities and not any ethnic, cultural, linguistic or religious differences lead to the formation of minorities. It seems also that the notion of 'national minority" is meant to put an emphasis on the importance of the group in question, with a view to distinguish it from numerically less important groups and from exclusively folkloric groups which are not recognized as minorities[351].

There is no generally accepted definition of the concept of minority. But the application of the Convention by States parties does not rely on the adoption of such a definition. As affirmed by scholars, the Convention offers protection even to migrant workers taken individually, if they are victims of racial discrimination[352]. As for the

---

[348] P. Thornberry, op. cit., p. 159.
[349] UNESCO Statement on Race, 1950, para. 4, cited by P. Thornberry, op. cit, 1991, p. 159.
[350] Ben Achour, Souveraineté étatique et protection internationale des minorités, RCADI, 1994, vol. 245(IV), p. 417.
[351] Ivan Gyurcsik, New Legal Ramifications of the Question of National Minorities, in Minorities-the New Europe's Old Issue, ed. by Ian M. Cuthbertson and Jane Leibowitz, 1995, p.29.
[352] Ian Niessen, Migrant Workers, in Economic, Social and Cultural Rights, a Textbook, ed. by A. Eide, C. Krause, A. Ross, 1995, p.323.

criterion to determine the ethnic origin of individuals, the Committee recommended that States follow what is generally accepted as a rule, that is self–identification, unless there are elements to prove the contrary[353].

SECTION 3 - SPECIAL MEASURES and the DEFINITION of RACIAL DISCRIMINATION

According to article 1.4, special measures taken for the sole purpose of securing adequate advancement of certain racial or ethnic groups or individuals requiring such protection as may be necessary in order to ensure them equal enjoyment or exercise of human rights and fundamental freedoms, shall not be deemed racial discrimination, provided, that such measures do not, as a consequence, lead to the maintenance of separate rights for different racial groups and they shall not be continued after the objectives for which they were taken are achieved. Following this provision which makes it clear that such measures shall not be deemed discriminatory, article 2.2 stipulates the obligation to adopt such special and concrete measures in social, economic, cultural and other fields, when circumstances so warrant.

The Human Rights Committee, in its General Comment on article 26 of the Covenant on Civil and Political Rights concerning non-discrimination, states that "the application of the principle of equality implies sometimes from the States parties to adopt measures in favour of disadvantaged groups, with a view to attenuate or to eliminate conditions which generate or contribute to the perpetuation of discrimination forbidden by the Covenant"[354].

According to article 1 of ICERD (which defines racial discrimination), special measures do not represent acts of discrimination and should not be considered an exception to the general norm. They represent a different treatment, in favour of disadvantaged persons or groups of persons, as compared to other persons or groups, as authorized by the respective treaties.

Considered together with the general norm on non-discrimination, special measures have the purpose of ensuring equal enjoyment and equal conditions for the exercise of human rights and fundamental freedoms by all groups and persons, irrespective of their distinctive features. In view of this experience, CERD adopted in 2009 the General Recommendation no.32 entitled "The meaning and the scope of special measures in the International Convention on the Elimination of Racial Discrimination".

* * *

Racial discrimination, as defined on the basis of definitions given to discrimination in general, is an extended concept, covering a large sphere of acts directed against persons on grounds of their race, colour, descent or ethnic or national origin, by refusing them the equal enjoyment or exercise of human rights.

Acts of racial discrimination are, according to the 1965 Convention, directed both against individuals and against groups of which they may be members. Nevertheless, the establishment of such groups or their recognition by States is not a precondition for any person to be protected against racial discrimination. The reference to groups refers to the reality that racial discrimination often affects groups of people of a particular race or ethnic origin.

As it was scientifically proved that human races do not exist and all human beings belong to the same species, the concept of "race" as a ground of discrimination as defined in the Convention, has evolved from the approach based on biology to cultural differences, which tends to establish a hierarchy of cultures and thus to justify different treatment or exclusion. The result is the same-inequality in the enjoyment and exercise of human rights.

Similarly, the concept of "descent", with or without a racial connotation, is part of the definition of racial discrimination. Acts of discrimination against persons who belong or are considered to belong to castes or other groups inheriting an analogous status are considered as racial discrimination and subject to all the provisions of the Convention.

The definition does not consider as discrimination the special measures adopted by States parties in favour of disadvantaged persons or groups, in order to ensure equal enjoyment or exercise of human rights. Such measures are subject to conditions of substance and duration, to avoid becoming discriminatory. Such special measures respecting these conditions are not exceptions to the principle of non-discrimination; they are endeavours which pursue the achievement of the same objective.

---

[353] General Recommendation nr. 14 concerning article 1 of the Convention, 1999, Compilation…, doc. HRI/GEN/1/Rev.8, p.257.
[354] Compilation…, doc. HRI/GEN.1/Rev. 8, pp. 185-187.

The definition of racial discrimination by the 1965 Convention is a broad and comprehensive one. It presents racial discrimination as a human conduct, by public authorities and institutions, by organizations and persons, which must be eliminated.

The philosophy of the definition is integrationist, in the sense of promoting the elimination of barriers between races and groups, of preventing separate rights for different racial groups, of condemning and eliminating racial segregation. At the same time, CERD often stresses the distinction which must be made between integration and assimilation.

Thus, the definition of racial discrimination given in article 1 of the 1965 Convention should be understood and interpreted in the context of other provisions of the Convention, and in the light of other international instruments on human rights, of the practice of international bodies involved in their implementation.

As it is, the definition allowed the Committee to use in a dynamic way the potential of the Convention and to draw the attention of States parties on different forms of racial discrimination, including those entrenched in the economic, social and cultural structures, in the conceptions prevailing in societies, and to deal with structural discrimination, based either on race, on descent or on ethnic or national origin.

CHAPTER XI- ABOUT RACIAL STRUCTURAL DISCRIMINATION, CAUSES and REMEDIES

ABSTRACT

It is only recently that international practice began to show interest to consider the structural racial discrimination; it refers to vulnerable groups, like indigenous peoples, Afro-descendants, some minority groups, and to causes which come from history, like cultural traditions and customs, slavery, colonialism.

In order to see how to deal with structural racial discrimination, it is necessary to reveal its causes and different forms of manifestation, as well as to consider its relationship with individual violations of the International Convention on the elimination of all forms of racial discrimination, which has established the standards applicable in this field.

As for the solutions and remedies, they have to respond to root causes and effects of structural discrimination; it is not enough to sanction individual violations; it is necessary to adopt measures affecting the social structures, in the economic, social and cultural fields.

KEY WORDS: social exclusion, indigenous peoples, Afro-descendants, Roma, descent, criminal justice, slavery, colonialism, cultural attitudes, traditions, customs, pilot-judgments, structural problems, segregation, remedies, special measures, information, education.

INTRODUCTION

Contemporary international law developed as general principles governing the whole field of human rights: non-discrimination and equality of rights of all persons. International documents on human rights proclaim from the beginning the elimination of any discrimination on grounds such as race, colour, sex, language, religion, national, ethnic or social origin, political or other opinion, property, birth or any other status. Concerns for discrimination in different fields of social life with regard to vulnerable segments of the population-women, children, disabled, aged people, or groups living in a state of poverty, as well as minority groups, indigenous, migrants, asylum seekers-led to the need to find out what are for each of these groups the causes of discrimination, those which are at its origin and those which still produce situations of discrimination, and of course how to counteract such causes.

The International Convention on the Elimination of All Forms of Racial Discrimination, adopted by the resolution 2106 A (XX) of 21 December 1965 of the UN General Assembly, brings together the main aspects of the generally-accepted standards concerning non-discrimination on racial grounds, as developed in international documents concerning non-discrimination in the fields of employment and occupation, education, non-discrimination against women, children, migrants and members of their families and disabled; such standards are developed in the general comments adopted by treaty bodies[355].

According to the 1965 Convention, racial discrimination "shall mean any distinction, exclusion, restriction or preference based on race, colour, descent, or national or ethnic origin which has the purpose or effect of nullifying or impairing the recognition, enjoyment or exercise, on an equal footing, of human rights and fundamental freedoms in the political, economic, social, cultural or any other field of public life" (article 1 of the Convention).

Obviously, this definition, which follows closely those given in preceding documents, is not limited to discrimination on ground of race *stricto sensu*, but includes also discrimination on grounds of colour, descent and national or ethnic origin. Other international instruments contain norms on non-discrimination based on sex-the 1979 Convention on the elimination of all forms of discrimination against women, establishing as a criterion equal rights of men and women, the 1990 Convention on the protection of the rights of all migrant workers and members of their families, postulating non-discrimination with regard to their rights according to the Convention on grounds of sex, race, colour, language or other statuses, the 2004 Convention on the rights of disabled persons, according to which the rights provided shall be granted to all disabled persons without discrimination on sex, race, colour or any other situation applying to the disabled person or to his or her family.

---

[355] Presentation of the Convention and of the activity of the Committee of experts in charge with monitoring its implementation in Ion Diaconu, Racial Discrimination, 2011, Eleven International Publishers, The Hague.

The two covenants on human rights, adopted in 1966, postulate that States parties undertake to respect and to ensure to all individuals within their territory and subject to their jurisdiction the rights they recognize, without distinction of any kind such as on the grounds enumerated above.

This study is limited to aspects concerning structural racial discrimination, according to the International Convention on the elimination of all forms of racial discrimination, which is covering partially discrimination against vulnerable groups for which other international documents set forth specific norms. Racial discrimination means the application of a different treatment to human beings because of their physical characteristics or of their origins. It is obvious that, as for other categories of people, violations of this principle are usually directed against individuals and are the result either of the individual conduct of State agents or of the behaviour of private persons.

The State has the following obligations: to prevent and avoid that such violations are committed by its institutions and agents; to prevent and protect against acts of violation of the interdiction of racial discrimination by private persons and if it happens, to adequately punish the perpetrators.

There are also violations which affect individuals belonging to entire categories of people and have deeper causes, related to the evolution of societies and of mentalities over longer periods of time. They lead often to social exclusion of particular groups from fully participating in economic, social and political life. Such situations have to be approached differently, without excluding the response to individual cases of violations by State agents and by private persons.

This led to the concept of structural phenomena or problems generating racial discrimination, which have continued to produce extended violations of human rights with regard to more or less important categories of population. This is no more about isolated violations concerning one or several persons, but about extended violations having deep rooted causes and concerning persons belonging to more or less numerous human groups, which are considered structural discrimination. Other concepts are sometimes used, such as systemic violations, systemic phenomena, but they have the same meaning.

Discrimination can be produced explicitly, through legislative provisions or through the activity of institutions or private persons, but can also take indirect or invisible forms, as a result of conceptions and ideas affecting the perception about excluded people, including their self-perception and their ability to claim their rights. In its General Recommendation nr. 14 on article 1, paragraph 1 of the Convention, the Committee on the Elimination of Racial Discrimination noted already that in seeking to determine whether an action has an effect contrary to the Convention, it will look to see whether that action has an unjustifiable disparate impact upon a group distinguished by race, colour, descent or national or ethnic origin[356]. This means that the Committee will go beyond the evaluation of the intention or omission of the conduct considered, but will consider also its effect on a group having such characteristics.

SECTION 1 - PRACTICE of HUMAN RIGHTS TREATY BODIES

The practice of the *Committee on the Elimination of Racial Discrimination* on this subject was not always very explicit and clear and developed mainly during the last 15-20 years, although its concerns show that the idea was present in its activity.

Without making a reference to structural discrimination or to its causes, in its General Recommendation nr. 23 (1997) on the rights of indigenous peoples, the Committee notes that "in many regions of the world indigenous peoples have been, and are still being, discriminated against and deprived of their human rights and fundamental freedoms and in particular ... they have lost their land and resources to colonists, commercial companies and State enterprises. Consequently, the preservation of their culture and their historical identity has been and still is jeopardized". The Committee especially called upon States to recognize and protect the rights of indigenous peoples to own, develop, control and use their communal lands, territories and resources and when they were deprived of …without their free and informed consent, to take steps to return those lands and resources or, when such restitution is not possible, to grant them just, fair and prompt compensation[357].

The Committee notes that certain forms of racial discrimination have a unique and specific impact on women and decided to endeavour in its work to take into account gender factors or issues which may be interlinked with racial discrimination; the Committee expresses its willingness to develop, in conjunction with member States, a more systematic and consistent approach to evaluating and monitoring racial discrimination against women, as well as the

---

[356] Compilation of General Comments and General Recommendations adopted by Human Rights Treaty Bodies, doc. HRI/GEN/1/Rev. 8 of 8 May 2006, p. 247.
[357] Compilation…, doc. HRI/GEN/1/Rev. 8, p. 255.

disadvantages, obstacles and difficulties they face in the full exercise and enjoyment of human rights on grounds of race, colour, descent, or national or ethnic origin[358].

With a more direct approach, in its general Recommendation nr. 27 (2000) on discrimination against Roma, the Committee recommended that States parties acknowledge wrongs done during the Second World War to Roma communities by deportation and extermination and consider ways of compensating for them and to endeavour, by encouraging a genuine dialogue, consultations or other appropriate means, to improve the relations between Roma communities and non-Roma communities, in particular at local levels, with a view to promoting tolerance and overcoming prejudices and stereotypes on both sides, to promoting efforts for adjustment and adaptation. The recommendation was also made to adopt and implement national strategies and programmes with a view to improving the situation of Roma[359]. Obviously, discrimination against Roma has deep rooted causes in history and in the attitudes of the population with regard to Roma groups in different countries, mainly in Europe.

Similar recommendations were addressed to the States parties concerned through the General Recommendation nr. 29 (2002) on article 1, paragraph 1, of the Convention (Descent), with regard to discrimination based on forms of social stratification such as caste and analogous systems of inherited status which nullify or impair their equal enjoyment of human rights. Such recommendations request that States take measures to protect women against multiple discrimination, to combat segregation and hate speech, or to eliminate discrimination in the administration of justice and in the exercise of civil and political rights and of economic, social and cultural rights, including the right to education[360].

The Committee refers to structural racial discrimination in its General Recommendation nr. 31(2005) on the prevention of racial discrimination in the administration and functioning of the criminal justice system. Considering that the risks of discrimination in the administration and functioning of the criminal justice system have increased in recent years, partly as a result of the rise in immigration and population movements, which have prompted prejudice and feelings of xenophobia or intolerance among certain sectors of the population and certain law enforcement officials, the Committee asks States parties to implement national strategies or plans of action aimed at the elimination of structural racial discrimination in this field[361].

The General Recommendation of the Committee nr. 34 (2011) on racial discrimination against persons of African descent includes several references to structural discrimination and a description of different elements defining its contents. It is asking States parties to acknowledge in their policies and actions the negative effects of wrongs occasioned on people of African descent in the past, chief among which are colonialism and the trans-Atlantic slave trade, the effects of which continue to disadvantage people of African descent today.

It states that racism and structural discrimination against people of African descent, rooted in the infamous regime of slavery, are evident in the situation of inequality affecting them and reflected, *inter alia*, in the following domains: their grouping among the poorest of the poor; their low rate of participation and representation in political and institutional decision-making processes; additional difficulties they face in access to and completion and quality of education, which result in transmission of poverty from generation to generation; inequality in access to labour market; limited social recognition and valuation of their ethnic and cultural diversity; and a disproportionate presence in prison population.

Underlying the importance of special measures in favour of people of African descent, in accordance with the Convention, the Committee asks the States to educate and raise awareness of the public about the importance of such measures to address the situation of victims of racial discrimination, especially discrimination as a result of historical factors. Recommendations are made with regard to measures to be taken for the protection of women and children of these communities, for their protection against hate speech and racial violence, in the administration of justice, as well as for the protection of their civil, political, economic, social and cultural rights[362].

In Concluding observations adopted after the consideration of periodic reports, the Committee also mentioned indirectly the concept of structural discrimination. In its Concluding observations adopted in 2004 concerning Brazil, the Committee refers to „structural inequalities"[363], while in those concerning Slovakia it refers to „deep-rooted discriminatory attitudes and feelings of hostility towards members of the Roma community"[364].

---

[358] Compilation..., doc. HRI/GEN/1/Rev. 8, p. 258.
[359] Compilation..., doc. HRI/GEN/1/Rev. 8, p. 259.
[360] Compilation..., doc.HRI/GEN/1/Rev.8, p. 267.
[361] Compilation..., doc. HRI/GEN/1/Rev. 8, p. 277.
[362] Doc. CERD/C/GC/34 of 3 October 2011.
[363] Report of the Committee, 2004, p. 15.
[364] Ibidem, p. 71.

Again, in 2005 the Committee referred to „invisible crypto-racism which is rooted in social relations at the inter-personal level in Barbados"[365] and to „the persistence of profound structural social and economic inequalities" in Venezuela[366], while in 2006 to „structural discrimination and institutionalized prejudice and intolerance" in Bosnia-Hertzegovina[367] and to „racism and racial discrimination entrenched" in Guatemala against some indigenous peoples, and then, under the title „Structural Discrimination" with reference to the state of poverty of the indigenous population in Guatemala, the Committee recommends that the State party adopts structural measures in order to implement fully its agrarian policy[368].

The Committee refers again to discrimination „entrenched" with regard to people discriminated on grounds of descent in India and „widespread societal discrimination against foreigners" in the Republic of Korea[369]. In its Concluding observations on Colombia, the Committee expressed its concern about „structural causes which perpetuate discrimination and exclusion from access to socio-economic rights and development of Afro-Colombians and indigenous peoples", and again its concern about the persistent structural discrimination and invisibility of Afro-Colombians, asking the State party to put an end to such structural discrimination[370]; concern was also expressed about „racism and structural discrimination in Peru"[371].

The Committee on the Elimination of Racial Discrimination refers also more recently to structural discrimination in its Concluding observations addressed to some States parties. After considering the periodic reports of Honduras, in February 2014, the Committee recommends, under the title „Measures against structural discrimination", with direct reference to indigenous peoples, to eliminate structural and historical discrimination.

Following the same pattern, in its Concluding observations concerning El Salvador of August 2014 the Committee recommends that the State party implements such policies and promote the enjoyment by indigenous peoples and the communities of African descent of economic, social and cultural rights, with a view to bring an end to structural discrimination which is embedded in the history of the State party. In its Concluding observations of August 2014 addressed to Peru, after considering its periodic report, the Committee expresses its concern that the members of indigenous peoples and Afro-Peruvians continue to be victims of structural discrimination, being confronted to the absence of economic opportunities, to poverty and social exclusion[372].

Without referring directly to structural discrimination, in its Concluding observations on Honduras adopted in 2015 the Committee noted the situation of Afro-Honduran communities and recommended that the State party continue to apply policies of social integration and development in order to reduce inequalities and poverty. In its recommendations addressed to Iraq, after considering its periodic report in August 2014, the Committee recommends that the State party acknowledge the historic discrimination perpetrated against various marginalized minority groups and study the root causes of that discrimination and its multi-faceted impact on those groups[373].

In its recommendations to Costa Rica, the Committee notes that the State party recognizes the existence of structural discrimination and asks the State party to implement its 2015-2018 Action Plan in order to eliminate structural discrimination which has historical roots in the State party[374], with reference to the Afro-descendent population. With regard to the situation in Niger, the Committee is concerned about the persistence of slavery practices within some ethnic groups, which perpetuate the discrimination on ground of descent since generations and recommends to applying the Penal Code in order to combat the persistence of the inhuman practice of slavery and to eliminate it completely[375].

After considering the periodic reports of Suriname, the Committee expressed its concern about the persistent discrimination faced by indigenous and tribal peoples and recommended that the State party take all necessary special measures to address the existing structural discrimination faced by these groups in the enjoyment of their rights[376]. In its recommendations addressed to The Netherlands, without calling it structural discrimination, the Committee stated that even a deep-rooted cultural tradition does not justify discriminatory practices and stereotypes

---

[365] Report of the Committee, 2005, p. 44.
[366] Ibidem, p. 73.
[367] Report, 2006, p. 17.
[368] Ibidem, p. 29. and doc. CERD/C/GTM/CO/14-15, May 2015, para.16.
[369] Report 2007, p.40 and 90.
[370] Report 2009, p. 39 and doc. CERD/C/COL/CO/15-16, August 2015, para.13 and 14.
[371] Report 2009, p. 75.
[372] Doc. CERD/C/HND/CO/R.1-5; CERD/C/SLV/CO/16-17;
[373] CERD/C/PER/CO/18-21 and CERD/C/IRK/CO/15-21.
[374] Doc. CERD/C/CRI/CO/19-22, August 2015, para. 11-12.
[375] Doc. CERD/C/NER/CO/R. 15-21, August 2015, para.10-11.
[376] Doc. CERD/C/SUR/CO/R. 13-15, August 2015, para. 21-22.

and recommended to the State party to actively promote the elimination of negative stereotypes which are experienced by many Afro-descendants as a vestige of slavery[377].

3. Other human rights bodies also evoked the concept of structural discrimination, in more general terms, from the point of view of their mandate, but which may have aspects of racial discrimination due to intersectionality between race and ethnicity and other grounds of discrimination. *The Committee on civil and political rights* noted, in its General Comment nr. 28 (2000) on The Equality of Rights between women and men, that „Inequality in the enjoyment of human rights by women throughout the world is deeply embedded in tradition, history and culture, including religious attitudes...States parties should ensure that traditional, historical, religious or cultural attitudes are not used to justify violations of women's right to equality before the law and to equal enjoyment of all Covenant rights...States parties should take account of the factors which impede the equal enjoyment by women and men of each right....".

In the same Comment, the Committee notes, after reviewing States parties reports, that the prevailing customs and traditions discriminate against women, particularly with regard to access to better paid employment and to equal pay for work of equal value[378].

The Committee on economic, social and cultural rights also noted, in its General Comment nr. 16 (2005)-The equal right of men and women to the enjoyment of all economic, social and cultural rights (art. 3)-that women are often denied equal enjoyment of their human rights, in particular by virtue of the lesser status ascribed to them by tradition and custom. Later on, the Comment refers to „cultural expectations and assumptions about the behaviour, attitudes, personality traits, and physical and intellectual capacities of men and women" and notes that such assumptions and expectations generally place women at a disadvantage with respect to substantive enjoyment of rights. Encouraging States parties to adopt temporary special measures to accelerate the achievement of equality between men and women, the Committee says that such measures are not to be considered discriminatory in themselves as they are grounded in the State obligation to eliminate disadvantage caused by past and current discriminatory laws, traditions and practices[379].

In two General Comments[380], on the rights to education and to the highest attainable standard of health, this Committee refers to „the formidable structural and other obstacles which impede the implementation" of the respective articles of the Covenant in many States parties. In the second of these Comments, the Committee underlines the „need to adopt effective and appropriate measures to abolish harmful traditional practices affecting the health of children, particularly girls, including early marriage, female genital mutilation, preferential feeding and care of male children" and to „ensure that harmful social or traditional practices do not interfere with access to...family planning".

The Committee on the elimination of all forms of discrimination against women also noted with grave concern, in its General Recommendation nr. 14 (1990)-Female circumcision-that there are continuing cultural, traditional and economic pressures which help to perpetuate harmful practices, such as female circumcision[381]. In a different General Recommendation, this Committee noted that traditional attitudes by which women are regarded as subordinate to men or as having stereotyped roles perpetuate widespread practices involving violence or coercion, such as family violence and abuse, forced marriage, dowry death, acid attacks and female circumcision[382]. In other General recommendations, this Committee refers to laws and customs which limit the women's right effectively to pursue or retain their equal share of property, to common law principles, religious or customary law relating to marriage which restrict women's right to equal status and responsibility within marriage, to cultural traditions and religious beliefs which have played a part in confining women to the private sphere of activity and excluding them from active participation in public life, or to societal factors that are determinative of the health status of women and to social and cultural structures and institutions maintaining such discrimination[383].

The Committee on the rights of the child also refers, in its General Comment nr. 4 (2003) - Adolescent health and development - to individual behaviours and environmental factors which increase adolescent's health vulnerability and risk, and in the General Comment nr. 7(2006)-Implementing child rights in early childhood - to

---

[377] Doc. CERD/C/NLD/CO/R. 19-21, para. 17-18.
[378] Compilation..., doc. HRI/GEN/1/Rev. 9, vol. I.
[379] Compilation..., doc. HRI/GEN/1/Rev. 8, p. 122-129.
[380] Compilation..., doc. HRI/GEN/1/Rev. 8, p. 71, 87 and 92.
[381] Compilation..., doc. HRI/GEN/1/Rev. 8, p. 297.
[382] General Recommendation nr. 19(1992)-Violence against women, doc. HRI/GEN/1/Rev. 8, p. 303.
[383] General Recommendations nr. 21(1994)-Equality in marriage and family relations, nr. 23(1997)-Political and public life, nr. 24(1999)-Article 12 of the Convention(women and health) and 25(2004)-Article 4, paragraph 1 of the Convention(temporary special measures), Compilation..., doc. HRI/GEN/1/Rev. 8, p. 3310, 320, 330, 338.

cultural expectations and treatment of children, including local customs and practices that should be respected, except where they contravene the rights of the child[384].

Giving expression to this reality, the Declaration adopted in 2001 by the World Conference Against Racism, Racial Discrimination, Xenophobia and Related Intolerance of Durban emphasized that "poverty, underdevelopment, marginalization, social exclusion and economic disparities are closely associated with racism, racial discrimination, xenophobia and related intolerance, and contribute to the persistence of racist attitudes and practices which in turn generate more poverty". Moreover, participants to this Conference recognized that colonialism has led to racism and racial discrimination and that Africans and people of African descent, people of Asian descent and indigenous peoples were victims of colonialism and continue to be victims of its consequences.

Without dealing directly with structural discrimination, the Declaration adopted in 2001 in Durban implies this concept in many of its dispositions. When referring to sources and causes of racism and racial discrimination, the Declaration expresses the regret of the States participating that the effects and persistence of structures resulting from colonialism have been among the factors contributing to lasting social and economic inequalities in many parts of the world today. The document recognizes the persistence of racism, racial discrimination, xenophobia and related intolerance that specifically affect populations of African descent, and recognizes that, in many countries, their long-standing inequality in terms of access to education, health care and housing has been a profound cause of socio-economic disparities that affect them.

SECTION 2 - The EUROPEAN COURT of HUMAN RIGHTS and the STRUCTURAL PROBLEMS

During the last decade, the European Court began also to establish the existence of structural problems in some States parties to the 1950 Convention on the protection of fundamental human rights and freedoms and to define solutions, pushed also by the escalating number of individual applications received and the danger of already unreasonable delays of their consideration[385]. In order to respond to this needs, the Court resorted first of all to pilot judgments, starting from individual cases, similar, more repetitive or to be repeated, and asked that the respective States develop a solution to be applied to all such cases. Recently, the Court moved to request States to make legislative changes, in order to solve structural problems.

The Court interpreted article 46 of the Convention (according to which member States are obliged to follow the Court's judgments on the merits) as involving two obligations: to apply individual measures, that is to eliminate the violations or compensate for damages, and to apply general measures to avoid repetition of similar violations towards other persons. In 2003 a Plenary Session of the judges of the Court emphasized the importance of applying the pilot-judgment method when a systemic or structural problem was detected in a Member State. The Resolution of the Committee of ministers of the Council of Europe of 12 May 2004 requested the Court, in its future judgments, to point out areas where a systemic problem has led to a violation of the Convention and indicate the source of the problem.

Soon after, the Court adopted the pilot-judgment in the case Broniowski v. Poland[386], where it retained that a State has a systemic problem in its legislation or administrative practice when the shortcomings of the judicial system affect a whole group of individuals, whose rights and freedoms set forth in the Convention have not been provided and if such a shortcoming of the domestic legal system or of its application by the domestic institutions can lead to many substantiated complaints to the Court. In a second judgment, the Court added for a similar case the term „structural problem"[387] and obliged the State to guarantee via suitable legislation and other measures a just balance between the lawful interests of the owners and the public interest to protect the tenants.

Another interesting case is Rumpf v. Germany, where the Court found that Germany did not have an effective domestic remedy against unreasonably lengthy proceedings; during 10 years, the Court made 40 judgments (50% of the cases concerning Germany) on merits on the same matter and other applications were to be considered. The Court affirmed that the legal system was incompatible with the principles of the Convention and gave a directive to the German government to set up within a year an effective remedy or combination of remedies to guarantee the

---

[384] Compilation..., doc. HRI/GEN/1/Rev. 8, p. 384, 483.

[385] For a general presentation, Mart Susi, The Definition of a „Structural Problem" in the Case-Law of the European Court of Human Rights Since 2010, in German Yearbook of International Law 55, 2012, pp. 385-417.

[386] In that case the Court found shortcomings in the Polish legislation due to restrictions applied to owners to increase rent, a situation which concerned some 100.000 owners and 6-900.000 tenants; judgment of 22 June 2004, RJD 2004-V, 1, para. 192.

[387] The case Hutten Czapka v. Poland, Judgment of 19 June 2006, RJD 2006-VIII, 57, para. 233.

possibility to complain about the unreasonable length of the proceedings and to receive adequate compensation. The term structural is used to evoke the probability of many individuals being victims of the same violation[388].

Other judgments followed, with reference to unclear legislation, to absence of legislation, or to administrative practices found in violation of the Convention. An analysis of the jurisprudence of the Court on this subject reveals that there are serious differences between the cases (the number of similar decisions, of potential repetitive cases) and that there is not enough clarity as to the use of terms systemic and structural problem, neither there are criteria according to which the Court gives directives to adopt new legislation, to introduce some changes, to assist the State party for developing a solution or to adopt other measures to solve the problem-numerous cases, number of potential applicants, the proportion to the total number of decisions[389].

A pilot judgment of the Court was also adopted in 2011 concerning Romania[390], in connection with a structural problem with regard to the ineffectiveness of the system of compensation or restitution of property confiscated during the communist regime. The Court requested the Government to adopt a general measure, within 18 months, to secure effective and rapid protection of the right to restitution, and adjourned the examination of the applications stemming from the same problem.

In April 2013 the Romanian Government requested the extension of the time limit by 9 months, then was given one more month. In May 2013 the Romanian Parliament adopted the Law nr. 165 of 16 May 2013 regarding measures to complete the process of compensation in kind or equivalent with respect to immovable properties unlawfully passed into the State ownership during the communist regime.

The Court is not dealing with structural racial discrimination in any of these cases. It is not referring directly to structural discrimination, but to structural or systemic problems, which of course lead to violations of human rights for a number of individuals.

The approach is different from that of human rights treaty bodies, the causes mentioned are different (the human rights treaty bodies refer to cultural traditions or customs, historical heritage, while the European Court refers to deficient legislation and administrative practices, which are not usually rooted in the respective societies). The solutions proposed are different; human rights treaty bodies recommend mainly that States adopt strategies, programmes and plans of action and the Court indicates to adopt new legislation and improve the practices in accordance with the Convention.

This does not mean that there is no structural discrimination in Europe. This concerns indigenous peoples in some European States, who were historically disadvantaged and faced exclusion from the society, as well as some ethnic minorities who have been stereotyped, degraded and discriminated against (mainly Roma) and people of a different colour or attributed race who came on the continent due to constant processes of migration and who are Afro-descendants or Asian descendants.

SECTION 3 - CAUSES and FORMS of STRUCTURAL RACIAL DISCRIMINATION

A) The international practice shows that structural discrimination is mainly the result of traditions, cultural conceptions, common manners or socially accepted behaviour, which are preventing or impeding some groups of people from enjoying their human rights[391]. They are historically rooted in the customs and behaviour transmitted from generation to generation.

Very often structural discrimination is related to the past. Racial, ethnic, gender or religious privilege and discrimination reach far back into human history. The traditional hierarchies and access to power continue to act as an important source of inequality and of restrictions on the fulfillment of basic human rights and freedoms. It leads, in some societies, for example, to the fact that for some people only dirty work at low wages is available on grounds of descent.

Being related to the past, such discrimination is more difficult to address directly because the discriminatory situation is cumulative over long periods of time, and its effects can be felt without the presence of an actual active agent. It became a trans-generational denial of access to socially valued resources, such as university degrees, high-status jobs and professions and political power for the group discriminated against as racial or ethnic group, which maintained the impoverishment and the low social status.

---

[388] Rumf v. Germany, Judgment of 2 September 2010, Application No. 46344/06; the decision of the Court is criticised for factual errors and for lack of clarity in using the terms systemic and structural problem by Mart Susi, art. cit., pp. 398-399.
[389] Mart Susi, art. cit, pp. 398-399, mainly 415.
[390] Decision of 12 October 2010, cases Maria Atanasiu and others v. Romania, requests nr. 30767/05 and 33880/06.
[391] Mirjana Najcevska, Structural Discrimination: An International Perspective, Poverty & Race, Nov/Dec 2010, vol. 19, nr. 6, p.4.

As it is known, for centuries institutions and the society defined and enforced norms, relationships and social roles that were racially distinct. For example, from the beginning, indigenous peoples and Blacks were considered inferior. Religious beliefs buttressed the conceptions of inferiority of some racial, ethnic or religious groups and justified the differential treatment and sanctions in society. Cultural customs and traditions usually continue to reinforce such thinking and continue to influence people's behaviour. When an individual or an institution acts in accordance with society's prevailing pre-conceived notions and social norms concerning specific groups (racial, ethnic, religious, gender), with negative impact on human rights of members of these groups, it is a question of structural discrimination[392].

Persons continue to behave as their previous generations did and consider it natural and normal. Part of the structural discrimination is a lack of perception of discrimination, from the side of the person who discriminates.

B) The same treatment can be applied to all peoples and groups, although their situation is different due to historic inequality of rights, violence and domination, which left behind a common behavior based on lasting stereotypes and prejudices. Persons in such a situation are in a disadvantaged position and the equal treatment could be discriminatory for them, continuing the structural discrimination. Structural discrimination can be the result of law or other measures providing for equal treatment for everybody, accompanied by specific conditions required to access some jobs or services; this could lead to discrimination against members of such groups who for different reasons (poverty, low education) are not able to fulfill the respective conditions and thus to benefit of the respective goods or services. This is discrimination in effect or indirect discrimination. It is more difficult to detect, but has the same effect of creating and maintaining inequality among people. Such laws and measures, equally intended and applied, can make it difficult for specific groups of people to enjoy their basic human rights and freedoms.

International documents on human rights define as discrimination a conduct which excludes persons or groups, on purpose or in effect, from the enjoyment of human rights on equal terms with other persons or groups, on different grounds. This means that such discrimination can be either open or indirect, and that it could occur intentionally or unintentionally.

In general, after the adoption of important treaties on human rights during the second half of the twentieth century, legislations in most countries proclaim equality of rights and non-discrimination for all.

Nevertheless, structural discrimination does not go beyond the law. It remains part of the law, but the law is applied differently to people, depending on the group they belong or are considered to belong. Structural discrimination is linked to systematic biases towards certain groups. The individuals and institutions find it more difficult, in their relations, to make judgments in cultural contexts other than their own and this leads to a situation where public policy ignores or penalizes the tradition or different culture of certain groups of people and this leads to a different treatment.

According to international documents on human rights it is generally admitted that not every difference of treatment is a discrimination, that a difference of treatment is legitimate if the criteria applied are reasonable and objective and if their aim is to achieve a legitimate purpose according to the respective treaty. States are required to adopt, when circumstances so warrant, and observing some conditions, special measures in favour of disadvantaged groups and individuals in order to achieve equality in the exercise of human rights. But applying the same treatment to persons in a different situation may lead to excluding them from the exercise of some human rights, to discrimination.

C) Structural discrimination often rejects the responsibility for the situation on the victims of discrimination. Those defending such attitudes often refer to the culture of the victims (their traditions or customs different from those of the majority), their passivity (for not using the possibilities offered by the society), their indifference (lack of interest), their personal choices (they like to live without working) or ignorance (lack of education and of knowledge). That means justifying the discrimination and considering the victim responsible for the situation. Both the society and the perpetrator of the discrimination are not required to do anything to change the situation[393].

The result is either denying the existence of discrimination, or justifying the discriminatory behaviour by the responsibility of the victim and, thus, the perpetuation of structural discrimination. This leads to the refusal to act for the elimination of such discrimination, invoking fairness or equality against allocating resources of social value and denying special measures or affirmative action in favour of the disadvantaged individuals and groups. As such,

---

[392] M. Najcevska, art. cit, p. 5.
[393] Developing ideas from M. Najcevska, art. cit., p. 4.

actual racial discrimination is supported and camouflaged by structural discrimination for instance in housing or wage policies, in the admission in universities or in the daily relations with people of a different ethnic origin[394].

According to another approach, racial discrimination and inequality would not be a matter of people's conceptions, individual intentions or behaviour, but rather a matter of the activity of public institutions and of societal practices that create or perpetuate racism; this is not entirely wrong, but leaves personal relations outside the phenomenon of racial discrimination and rejects the blame on the society as an abstract entity. Obviously, this avoids the problem, makes discrimination a collective and indefinite responsibility and is not offering a real solution to combat and eliminate discrimination. As a matter of fact, it is trying to legitimize discrimination.

Thus, structural discrimination is more than social action; in its repeated forms, it develops into a social structure. It becomes habitual and is expressed in all sorts of invisible ways: in the jobs people occupy, in their level of education and health, in the way they are treated by others, including by authorities. Historical heritage is perpetuating the circle of discrimination based on common behavior.

Structural discrimination *includes both* the individual behaviour (very often based on such traditions or cultural conceptions) and the policies of institutions, as well as the behaviour of the individuals who implement such policies, based on these traditions and cultural conceptions and which have a differential and/or harmful effect on minority groups.

This means that, without ignoring individual forms of conduct, discrimination on the grounds of people's ethnicity, religion, gender, race, culture, age, sexual orientation, etc. must be seen also from a structural perspective. Of course, individual behaviour cannot be excluded or kept apart from structural discrimination. When an individual or an institution acts in accordance with such traditions, manners and ideas of a society, promoting exclusion or discrimination, it is a question of structural discrimination.

Structural discrimination is about equal rights and about exclusion, as it raises obstacles to groups or impediments to individuals in achieving the same rights and opportunities that are available to the majority of the population. Thus, it has as result that the relationships among groups within a society exclude identified groups or individuals from the exercise of human rights and that certain groups do not enjoy an equal status in relation to other groups, being allowed different roles, rights and opportunities in the society on grounds of their race or ethnicity.

The international practice reflects also the fact that nowadays racist theories and attitudes are not placing the emphasis on biological features, but on cultural differences between groups and persons, proclaiming the superiority of some cultures over the others and considering differences between cultures (which include traditions, customs, behaviour, in general ways of life) as insurmountable and incompatible, and the respective human groups as antagonistic. Although not completely eliminated, biological racism is replaced by the differential cultural racism, which is also trying to justify discrimination and exclusion[395].

That means that, in order to combat racism and racial discrimination, there is a need to promote respect for everyone's culture and for cultural diversity, and to build a culture of multiculturalism[396]. For instance, a joint study analyzes the structural discrimination in the American penal system against the group of Sikhs for cultural differences[397].

Segregation, which is generated by official or unofficial policies or by the conditions of life of the persons themselves, is very often related to historic structural discrimination and results in further continuation of prejudices, disadvantage concerning the availability of cultural, educational and other services, worse living conditions and marginalization.

Structural discrimination is often more subtle and less intentional than open acts of discrimination. Many people believe that racism is no longer a problem, in the absence or the decrease of public displays of racism. Structural discrimination is more difficult to address when it involves behaviour that is apparently neutral, that is treating everybody equally. Only the negative effects for some groups indicate the existence of such discrimination.

---

[394] On the efforts of American lawyers to determine the State bodies and the courts to accept the existence and to act against structural discrimination in employment, using concepts like "disparate effect" and "workplace harassment", see Samuel R. Bagenstos, The Structural Turn and the Limits of Antidiscrimination Law, in California Law Review, vol. 94, January 2006, no. 1.

[395] Ion Diaconu, Racial Discrimination, 2011, Eleven Publishers, The Hague, pp. 51-56.

[396] Ion Diaconu, Cultura și drepturile omului, 2012, Ed. Prouniversitaria (in Romanian), pp. 144-159, mainly p. 151.

[397] H. Singh, J. Singh and P. Singh, A Systems Approach to Identifying Structural Discrimination Through the Lens of Hate Crimes, in LexisNexis, Asian American Law Journal, 107, 2013.

SECTION 4 - SOLUTIONS and REMEDIES

Structural discrimination has become more recently an object of interest and it is specifically addressed. Taking into account that it is based in history, in the traditions and cultural perceptions coming from the past, the structural discrimination cannot be fought by solving individual cases, by the State solely. Structural discrimination requires to review the cultural values and traditions of the society and to bring changes in the functioning of the social organization.

The situation cannot be changed by a simple reactive role of the State or by acting only when the victim of discrimination is claiming it and calls for protection. It requires acceptance from the State, but also from the private sector, of positive obligations to promote equality in public life, and to combat habits and social behaviour of discrimination.

This means that the individual-oriented approach in the elaboration of anti-discrimination legislation and the individual punishment of the perpetrator of discrimination are not sufficient to address structural discrimination, taking into account its origin and dimensions. There is a need for a systematic opposition to discrimination, involving the society as a whole, and the development of policies and institutions capable of doing this. The States have to develop policies that promote inclusion and create institutions which provide better services and promote economic and social development to the whole population.

States should at the same time undertake a thorough programme of information and education of the whole population about human rights, equality and non-discrimination, about structural discrimination and its causes. Groups who are subject to structural discrimination and their problems should be made visible, differences based on stereotypes and prejudices should be presented and the roots of discrimination should be considered. The influence of very specific issues (like past, history, tradition, religion) should be recognized and considered, both in general and in specific fields and situations. For example: the history of slavery, the transatlantic slave trade and the position of people of African descent have for centuries influenced the creation and development of a wide range of stereotypes and prejudices. Long-lasting, open discrimination has defined the starting position in life for a large number of generations. Poverty, lack of education, health problems, property differences, they all have deep roots which reach back to the days of slavery.

This means that the fight against discrimination should step also into the field of education and politics, while continuing to act against individual violations. The State should lead the way by information, cultural and educational activities against structural discrimination and should create the framework and the general atmosphere of equality. This implies the identification of structural discrimination and the promotion of a different type of behavior in all the spheres of public life, including the public and private structures and individuals. The main objective should be to remedy the systemic discrimination, to introducing positive action and be proactive, along with combating and sanctioning discrimination and to ensure an effective protection of victims of discrimination. There is a need for intensive measures to eliminate or at least seriously reduce structural discrimination.

Such measures should be based on policies of redistribution of resources according to a compensatory formula, sometimes viewed as reparations for past discrimination, or as assistance for education, training and development. That means to adopt a rights-based method to development which emphasizes non-discrimination, inclusion and empowerment, aimed particularly at vulnerable or marginalized groups.

In substance, that means States have to adopt special measures in favour of disadvantaged groups. Taking into account the objective of special measures to ensure the exercise of human rights on equal terms, the Committee for the Elimination of Racial Discrimination concluded in its General Recommendation 32 of 2009 that special measures are an integral part of the principle of non-discrimination, as it is part of the definition of racial discrimination, not an exception to the principle. According to the Convention, they are compulsory when the circumstances make them necessary in order to eliminate inequalities and as long as they are necessary for that purpose[398].

As it is, the definition allowed the Committee to use dynamically the Convention in its potential and to draw the attention of States parties on different forms of racial discrimination, including those entrenched in the economic, social and cultural structures, in the conceptions prevailing in societies, and to deal with structural discrimination, based on race, on descent or on ethnic or national origin.

Consequently, as presented above, in its Concluding Observations the Committee made recommendations to the respective States concerning the elimination of discrimination against persons and groups suffering from the structural discrimination as to their access to work and to employment, to public life in general and to education, as well as on the elimination of prejudice against racial or ethnic groups, or groups of social stratification (descent) and

---

[398] Ion Diaconu, Racial Discrimination: Using Special Measures for Promoting Equal Human Rights, in East African Journal of Peace& Human Rights, vol. 18, No. 1, 2012, pp. 1-17.

on special measures in favour of such persons and groups in order to overcome such discrimination. In many other cases, without noting the existence of structural discrimination, the Committee recommended to States parties to adopt special measures in favour of disadvantaged groups and individuals.

* * *

Although the structural discrimination is a reality for centuries, it is a new concept in the preoccupations of the world community. As it is different from the approach of treating individual complaints or petitions as they come, it has to be dealt with according to another approach; it is about discrimination embedded in the societies, in the cultures and traditions of people for generations and cannot be reduced or eliminated by sanctioning individual cases. Remedies should address the root causes of structural discrimination and its effects; they should aim at changing the social status of the respective groups, by promoting their economic and social development using as much as necessary special temporary measures and developing a thorough process of information, culture and education of the population as a whole so as to reduce and eliminate exclusion and ensuring equal rights to their members. To sum up, there is a need for policies of inclusion for the group victims of structural discrimination.

The Declaration adopted by the Durban Conference in 2001 expresses concern that in some States political and legal structures and institutions, some of which were inherited and persist today, do not correspond to the multi-ethnic, pluricultural and plurilingual characteristics of the population and, in many cases, constitute an important factor of discrimination and the exclusion of indigenous peoples. Among the remedies envisaged, the Declaration calls upon States to take appropriate and effective measures to halt and reverse the lasting consequences of practices of slavery, slave trade, apartheid, genocide and past tragedies. Many recommendations under the Declaration and the Programme of Action adopted in Durban are aiming at taking measures to overcome causes and forms of structural discrimination on grounds of race, colour and ethnic and national origin.

CHAPTER XII - SPECIAL MEASURES as a MEANS for PRMOTING EQUAL RIGHTS

ABSTRACT

International legal instruments on human rights compel States to ensure the equality of all human beings in the exercise of human rights and fundamental freedoms and, to that end, to eliminate all forms of discrimination on grounds of sex, race, ethnic origin, religion, political opinion, fortune and any other status, as well as to adopt special measures in favour of disadvantaged individuals and groups. Thus, the obligations of States are not limited to guaranteeing formal equality, which is often not sufficient to eliminate inequality and discrimination. Equal rights do not mean identical treatment all the time and for all persons, as not every difference of treatment is discrimination.

This study considers the relationship between equality, non-discrimination and the special measures; to maintain the proper balance, international law sets forth some rules and conditions for the special measures to be legitimate and to avoid becoming discrimination. For that, special measures have to be proportional to the objective pursued, to avoid creating distinct rights for different groups of persons and to be temporary, continuing as long as it is necessary to rich the objective pursued.

KEY WORDS: equal rights, different treatment, non-discrimination, special measures, affirmative measures, historical injustice, specific permanent measures, temporary duration

SECTION 1 - SOURCES and CONCEPTS

According to the 1965 International Convention for the Elimination of all Forms of Racial Discrimination (ICERD), „States parties shall, when circumstances so warrant, take, in the social, economic, cultural and other fields, special and concrete measures[399] to ensure the adequate development and protection of certain racial groups or individuals belonging to them, for the purpose of guaranteeing them the full enjoyment of human rights and fundamental freedoms". It is also added that such measures shall in no case entail as a consequence the maintenance of unequal or separate rights for different racial groups after the objectives for which they were taken have been achieved.

Similar provisions are included as an explanation to the definition of the racial discrimination, specifying that such measures shall not be deemed racial discrimination. Thus, such measures are not an exception to the principle of non-discrimination, but measures to ensure equal rights for disadvantaged groups and individuals belonging to them.

These are not isolated provisions in international documents on human rights.

Already in 1957 the International Labour Organization considered whether special measures designed to meet the particular needs of women or young workers or disabled persons, or measures taken in the interest of peoples of less-developed social or cultural status ending their integration into the national community, should not be overridden by the action against discrimination in employment.

Provisions dealing expressly with the adoption of such measures were included for the first time in the ILO Discrimination (Employment and Occupation) Convention of 1958(no.111); article 5 of this Convention permits explicitly the adoption of „special measures of protection and assistance", designed to meet the particular requirements of persons who, for reasons such as sex, age, disablement, family responsibilities or social or cultural status, are generally recognized as requiring special protection or assistance. It is also stated that such measures will not constitute discrimination.

In 1960, the Convention against discrimination in the field of education identifies as a discriminatory act the establishing or maintaining of separate educational systems. Then, the Convention determines when separate educational systems will not be considered discrimination, that is when they are set up for pupils of the two sexes on an equivalent basis, or for religious or linguistic reasons, on an optional basis and providing education according to certain standards, or when they are private educational institutions which do not exclude any group.

Members of national minorities also have the right to carry on their educational activities, such as teaching of their own language, without preventing those among them to understand the culture and the language of the community as a whole and to participate in its activities, while the States parties have to undertake all necessary

---

[399] More extensively on special measures, Ion Diaconu, Racial Discrimination, Using special measures for promoting equal human rights, in East African Journal of Peace and Human Rights, no. 1/2012, pp. 1-17.

measures to ensure the application of this right. Although it is not expressly referring to special measures, this last provision may be considered as implying this concept, taking into account the specific rights of persons belonging to minorities to use and to learn their mother tongue, stipulated in other international instruments[400]. As a matter of principle, the Convention forbids „any difference of treatment by the public authorities between nationals, except on the basis of merit or need, in the matter of school fees and the grant of scholarships or other forms of assistance to pupils....".

The two International Covenants on human rights adopted in 1966 stipulate that the States parties undertake to ensure equal rights of men and women to the enjoyment of all economic, social and cultural, civil and political rights. As it was pointed out, this text did not merely state the principle of equality, but enjoined States to ensure effective equality. In its General Comment No.18, the Human Rights Committee asserted that this text requires not only measures of protection but also affirmative action designed to ensure the positive enjoyment of rights.

The Convention on the Elimination of All Forms of Discrimination against Women of 1979 provides explicitly that the adoption of temporary special measures aimed at accelerating *de facto* equality between men and women, including those aimed at protecting maternity, shall not be considered discrimination, but shall in no way entail as a consequence the maintenance of unequal or separate standards.

Declarations adopted by international organizations also underlined the need, the legitimacy and the obligation to adopt special measures in order to ensure human equal rights. The UNESCO Declaration on Race and Racial Prejudice of 1978 requires that special measures be taken to ensure equality in dignity and rights for individuals and groups wherever necessary, while ensuring that they are not such as to appear racially discriminatory. An I.L.O. Declaration on Equality of Opportunity and Treatment for Women Workers of 1975 states that positive special treatment during a transitional period aimed at effective equality between the sexes shall not be regarded as discriminatory.

Moreover, in its General Comment on article 26 of the International Covenant on Civil and Political Rights, which enunciates the general non-discrimination principle, the Human Rights Committee states that the enjoyment of rights and freedoms on an equal footing does not mean identical treatment in every instance and that not every difference of treatment will constitute discrimination. In this General Comment, the Committee also states that a differentiation of treatment will not constitute discrimination, if the criteria for such differentiation are reasonable and objective and if the aim is to achieve a purpose which is legitimate under the Covenant. It is thus recognized that special measures are not an exception to non-discrimination, but a means to eliminate discriminatory situations and to strengthen the application of this principle[401].

In the General Comment no.13 on article 13 (right to education) of the International Covenant on Economic, Social and Cultural Rights, elaborated by the Committee for this Covenant and UNESCO in 1999, under the title „non-discrimination and equal treatment", it is indicated that „the adoption of special measures intended to bring about de facto equality for men and women and for disadvantaged groups is not a violation of the right to non-discrimination with regard to education, so long as such measures do not lead to the maintenance of unequal or separate standards for different groups, and provided they are not continued after the objectives for which they were taken have been achieved".

We note that different terms are used: affirmative action, positive action and positive discrimination. From the beginning, it seems necessary to avoid using the expression „positive discrimination", in order to avoid confusions; a discrimination is a discrimination and should be forbidden, as the term is generally used to designate „arbitrary, unjust or illegitimate" differences of treatment, and one should not convey the impression that it can be positive; affirmative action, like positive action, may be controversial, being understood as creating a favourable treatment, but without conveying the idea that it responds to a disadvantage and is meant to ensure equal rights. That is why we shall use the concept of special measures, which seems to be comprehensive, not controversial and which is used and well defined in most of the international documents on this issue.

SECTION 2 - FORMS and JUSTIFICATION of SPECIAL MEASURES

Studies of the practice in different States of applying special measures mention some basic forms of such measures, although each of them may develop into a variety of solutions:

---

[400] Ion Diaconu, Minorities-from non-discrimination to identity, 2004, Ed. Lumina Lex, pp. 150-158.
[401] Bruce Adamson, The „Special Measures" Clause in ICERD Article 1(4) is a Clarification Clause, not an Exception, submission of Center for Equal Opportunity to CERD, 4-5 August 2008.

- affirmative mobilization, consisting in encouraging and sensitizing targeted groups to apply for a social good in a field where they are disadvantaged, such as a job or a place in the educational system; this may include announcements or other recruitment efforts, the setting up of job-training programmes to enable persons belonging to such groups to acquire the necessary skills, that is making them aware of the opportunities and placing them in a condition of competitiveness;
- affirmative fairness, meaning a meticulous examination in order to make sure that members of the targeted groups are treated fairly in the attribution of the respective social goods, through a complaints procedure, review procedures and examination of practices in order to eliminate those which are discriminatory;
- affirmative preference, according to which race, gender or another feature of someone is taken into account for granting social goods; that could mean to give preference, when two equally qualified persons apply for that social good, to the person belonging to the group designated as beneficiary of the special measure; that could also mean excluding members of non-designated groups from applying for that social good, or accepting everybody but applying lower standards to members of the designated groups, or establishing informal percentages, goals, quotas or reservations in favor of the designated groups. This last form of special measures is the most controversial and is not considered favorably in many States[402].

It is underlined that, when special measures are adopted and applied, those criteria used for granting a social good should be relevant to the respective field, that is to the social good in case; States have also to take into account the specific circumstances of the society in which the measures are taken, including different historical, cultural, sociological, economic and other elements which are specific to the society in question. Obviously, such measures have to be temporary and have to be proportional to the results expected. Members of groups which were previously in a disadvantaged position may be justified to benefit of such measures as long as they are necessary to eliminate the disadvantage.

Among the justifications States give to special measures, one can find the following:
- to remedy or redress historical injustices; some disadvantaged groups have been discriminated for long periods of time, which has put their descendants in an inferior position due, for instance, to their poor education and training; in its first General Survey on Convention no. 111, the I.L.O. Committee of Experts on the Application of Conventions and Recommendations identified as a distinct type of special measures those that have the direct aim of combating discrimination to which certain categories of persons have been subjected in practice[403];
- to remedy social/structural discrimination, that is to eliminate such measures, procedures, actions or legal provisions which are neutral as regards race, sex, ethnicity, but which adversely affect disadvantaged groups without any objective justification; inequalities along racial or ethnic lines are not only a social given, but may be the result of direct and indirect discrimination;
- to create diversity or proportional group representation, which concerns mainly education and political representation;
- for social utility purposes, that is to offer better services to the disadvantaged groups and to offer them incentive and motivation to integrate and to obtain higher levels of education and qualification;
- to pre-empt social unrest, a reasoning which can be added to all the preceding;
- for a better efficiency of the socio-economic system, which is also obvious;
- as a means of nation building, another important reason, mainly for young countries, formed of different communities.

In any case, such measures should not be and should not become a label for discriminatory measures, if they would deprive other people of human rights, of freedoms or guarantees, on the basis of a criterion which is not relevant to the right or freedom in question, or if they are prolonged beyond the period of time when they respond to the disadvantage. Special measures are not an exception to the principle of non-discrimination; they are meant to ensure equal rights, meaning to avoid discrimination, and this principle establishes limits to each of the special measures.

---

[402] Report submitted by Mr. Marc Bossuyt, Special Rapporteur, to the Commission on Human Rights, doc. E/CN.4/Sub.2, 2002, 21 of 17 June 2002, pp.16-18.
[403] International Labour Conference, 47-th Session, 1963, Geneva, General Conclusions on Reports relating to the Convention no.111 and Recommendation no.111 concerning discrimination in respect of Employment and Occupation, part 3, para. 51.

SECTION 3 - NATURE of SPECIAL MEASURES and REQUIREMENTS to APPLY THEM

The whole concept and practice of special measures stems from the reality that formal equality is not sufficient to address inequality and discrimination; people and communities are aiming at substantial equality, at equality in results. International instruments on human rights promote the substantive model of equality, which should include equality of opportunity, equality of access and equality of result. If opportunity is by and large created for everybody, different forms of racial discrimination preclude or limit the access to opportunities of members of particular groups. As racial discrimination is not a natural principle of human behaviour, but is socially constructed, there is a need for a concerted action against inequality and such mechanisms and factors that perpetuate it. Therefore, special measures have to be considered as one of the tools for the elimination of all forms of racial discrimination.

Special measures target members of disadvantaged groups, such as women or racial or ethnic minorities or people with disabilities and seek to overcome such institutional and societal obstacles preventing members of these groups to avail of existing opportunities on equal footing with other members of the society. The adoption of such measures does not imply that the beneficiaries are somehow undeserving or should change, but seeks to address the failure of the society to provide equal opportunities for all. So, the problem does not lie with these persons, but with the society and its institutions[404].

Special measures can be isolated measures, with regard to one right or freedom or to one aspect of their exercise, or more often a coherent package of measures, taking into account the close relationship between different human rights and different fields of social life. Such measures are aiming specifically at correcting the position of the groups or individuals benefitting from, in one or more aspects of social life in order to obtain effective equality.

In each of the fields, special measures are to be taken in favour of the groups and individuals who are disadvantaged. According to the International Convention for the Elimination of All Forms of Racial Discrimination, special measures can be adopted to the benefit of „certain racial or ethnic groups or individuals requiring such protection". The ILO Convention no.111 on discrimination in the fields of employment and occupation refers to „persons who, for reasons such as sex, age, disablement, family responsibilities or social or cultural status, are generally recognized as requiring special protection or assistance". In its General Comment on article 26, the Human Rights Committee refers to „the general conditions of a certain part of the population" which „prevent or impair their enjoyment of human rights". In its first General Comment, the Committee for Economic, Social and Cultural Rights refers to „the disadvantaged sectors of the population", which should be the focus of the State's positive action aimed at securing the full realization of their rights.

Each State has thus to determine those groups and individuals who should be the beneficiaries of special measures. While this is a sovereign right of the State, it has to be exercised on the basis of objective criteria, not in an arbitrary manner. It has to be based on the existence of a disadvantage and it has to be applied to the respective group; second, it has to be proportional to the elimination of the disadvantage; and, of course, it has to be temporary.

That is why human rights treaty bodies and other bodies called to monitor the implementation of international instruments on human rights need data on the economic, social and political situation of different groups living on the territory of a State, in order to be able to evaluate the level of implementation and to engage in a dialogue with the State on this issue. But the States themselves need such data in order to define good policies in favor of their citizens and to adopt measures when necessary for ensuring equality in the exercise of human rights and for avoiding social unrest. This is for every government a question of good governance.

The monitoring bodies have the right to evaluate if a State has taken special measures where they are necessary, to ask questions and to make recommendations. They also have the right to evaluate if such special measures taken are justified and proportional.

First of all, States can adopt new legislative acts, instituting those special measures in favour of the group or the groups concerned. Sometimes such measures are meant to correct past or societal discrimination, to redress past inequalities and disadvantage; they could be justified if such inequality or disadvantage persist; otherwise, if the present situation does not require such measures, they will create discrimination instead of eliminating it; they have to be well explained and promoted, in order to be understood and accepted by the population. It is very important to avoid and to combat structural discrimination, which may be created by laws and measures apparently neutral as to race, colour or ethnic origin, but which may have an adverse effect on some groups; such laws and measures have to make the necessary exceptions for groups who are or may become disadvantaged.

---

[404] Manuela Tomei, Affirmative Action for Racial Equality: Features, impact and challenges, I.L.O., 2005, p.9.

Special measures may be adopted in various fields. The ICERD refers, in its article 2.2, to the social, economic, cultural and other fields, which leaves open the extent *ratione materiae* of possible special measures. In the economic field, they may consist of programmes or projects of development concerning disadvantaged groups or areas where they live, as well as different kinds of subsidies or contributions granted by the State.

In the social field, they may include contributions, grants or other facilities meant to improve the situation of disadvantaged groups with regard to social security, health and access to public services. In the political field, a State can institute such systems of representation in local and central legislative and administrative bodies which could ensure the presence of members of the respective groups and thus their representation in the exercise of the State power; another possible measure can be the creation of such bodies representing minorities or other disadvantaged groups and establishing the obligation for the State organs to consult with such bodies before taking decisions on matters of direct concern to the respective groups.

It is obvious that special measures can be taken in the linguistic and cultural fields, in order to improve the situation of disadvantaged groups, to give them the possibility to study and to use their mother tongue and to enjoy their culture, in the different forms this may take.

Special measures can be important means to attack causes of de facto inequality affecting racial or ethnic groups, such as poverty, poor education, malnutrition or geographic isolation.

SECTION 4 - POSITION of STATES

Some States parties to the ICERD denied that they would have under this Convention the obligation to adopt special measures; others denied the need to adopt at present such measures for some groups of their population; others gave a very restrictive interpretation to the texts of articles 1.4 and 2.2 of the Convention. The Committee for the Elimination of Racial Discrimination recommended many times to the States parties to consult the communities concerned, both to find out when it is necessary to adopt special measures and on the nature and the extent of such measures.

The first question to be answered is whether it is compulsory to adopt special measures in favour of disadvantaged groups. The text of article 2.2 is not leaving any doubt on this issue, postulating that "States parties shall, when the circumstances so warrant, take…special and concrete measures to ensure the adequate development of certain racial groups or individuals belonging to them….". According to this provision, the adoption of such measures is compulsory.

Of course, there has to be established that the circumstances, meaning the situation of the group, the timing, the place and other practical elements warrant such measures. The State is called to make such an evaluation, also on the basis of objective criteria, and take the necessary decisions. But the monitoring bodies, the international community in general, can also evaluate the situation and appreciate the need for special measures in a State, in favour of a racial or an ethnic group, and can address recommendations to the State.

The second question concerns the relationship between special measures and non-discrimination; as we have seen, special measures are not an exception to the principle and they are not to be deemed discriminatory. Their starting point is the postulate that equality does not mean always an equal treatment, that a different treatment is sometimes necessary and justified to ensure equal exercise of human rights. At the same time, special measures also do not have to lead to discrimination. Their purpose is to ensure to such groups or individuals equal enjoyment or exercise of human rights and fundamental freedoms. This means that they should be carefully designed so as to meet the particular needs of the group to be protected; there has to be a good choice of the type of measures, of the timing and the location of their application; they have to be based on objective and reasonable criteria. Otherwise, they may create a different treatment which does not correspond to the equal enjoyment and exercise of human rights, which is not justified and which is discriminatory.

The third requirement concerns their duration; such measures "shall not be continued after the objectives for which they were taken have been achieved" (article 2.1 of ICERD). They should not have as a consequence the maintenance of unequal or separate rights for different racial groups. That means that the different treatment has to discontinue as soon as the objective of equality in the exercise of human rights is achieved; after that, it becomes racial discrimination, which is forbidden by the Convention.

This results from a logical interpretation of all the provisions of the Convention, beginning with its purpose and objective to eliminate all forms of racial discrimination (the same purpose is affirmed by the Convention on the Elimination of all Forms of Discrimination against Women) and with its preamble, according to which "there is no justification for racial discrimination, in theory or in practice, anywhere"[405]. According to the International Covenant on the Civil and Political Rights, even in a case of "public emergency that threatens the life of the nation", a State cannot derogate from this principle, by taking measures which would discriminate on the ground of race.

Within the I.L.O., the Committee of Experts on the Application of Conventions and Recommendations underlined in its report of 1963 that special measures are subject to periodic re-examination of their continued justification[406]. The Committee of Experts developed a test according to which special measures in this field must genuinely pursue the objective of offering protection or assistance, must be proportional to the nature and scope of the protection needed or of the existing discrimination and should be re-examined periodically in order to ascertain whether they are still needed and remain effective. Within UNESCO, a consultation of member States on measures taken for the implementation of the 1960 Convention (covering the period 2000-2005) elaborated guidelines asking States parties to show in their periodic reports what affirmative action and positive measures are being taken for enabling children who are victims of social exclusion and poverty to have access to education.

Special measures, having such a temporary character, should not be confused with permanent measures States have to take in favour of minority groups in order to protect their identity. Such measures are, for instance, those meant to protect the rights of indigenous peoples with regard to the land they occupy or use and those meant to ensure that ethnic, linguistic and religious minorities may preserve and use their language, enjoy their culture and profess and practice their religion. For instance, schools and classes in or teaching mother tongue can be permanent, as long as there are requests and there is a minority living in the area.

In its General Recommendation on art.4.1 of the International Convention for the Elimination of All Forms of Discrimination against Women, the Committee created by this Convention makes the distinction between "special temporary measures" aimed at improving the position of women to achieve their *de facto* equality with men, and measures meant to ensure a justified non-identical treatment of men and women due to their biological differences, as well as policies adopted to improve the situation of the woman and the girl child.

Such permanent measures respond to specific rights of persons belonging to minorities and are not related to a disadvantage or past discrimination (although it may have taken place, but is not a condition for permanent measures related to the exercise of specific rights). Some of them may imply different aspects as compared to the general picture of human rights, but this derives from the contents of the specific right to be exercised.

Special measures are also not a substitute for anti-poverty measures which concern the society as a whole or segments of it, on a non-discriminatory basis; they are not a substitute for laws and measures against discrimination. At the same time, some measures, for instance in the field of combating poverty, may be general in scope, but may be targeting a group of persons of a certain race, ethnic or national origin; they are special measures, in spite of their general character.

As examples of special measures one can mention in the field of education scholarships offered to students belonging to an ethnic group, a *numerus clausus* provision to be admitted in some secondary schools or in universities, or bussing to school districts for students from some communities in order to avoid segregation; in the field of employment, programmes of training can be initiated in favor of members of some communities and for some occupations.

Adopting special measures in favour of disadvantaged racial or ethnic groups is not a question of resources; a government cannot justify the absence of such measures by the lack of resources, because this is about disadvantaged groups in the society and refusing such measures means giving a preference to the majority and to other purposes. Special measures are dealing with the condition of those who are discriminated as against those who are not. They are about protecting vulnerable ethnic, racial or other groups. Therefore, special measures have to be granted, when they are necessary, within the amount of resources available, because the State should find ways and means aiming at equality in the enjoyment of human rights for all its citizens.

The scope of special measures should be determined after consultation with all relevant beneficiaries, as well as with representatives of the majority, so as to have a clear picture of the perceptions, preoccupations and expectations of such groups and of course of the wider society. This is important for the implementation of such measures and for the social cohesion in the respective State.

One problem may arise for federal States, when competences are shared between the federal government and the local authorities and the latter are competent in most of the fields in which special measures can be adopted. According to international law and to the constitutions of the federal States, they are the only subjects of international law; the federal State is responsible to implement the provisions of international treaties to which it is a party.

---

[405] Bruce Adamson, art. cit., p.11.
[406] I.L.O. Special Survey on Equality in Employment and Occupation, 1996, paragraphs 135 and 136.

Therefore, the federal State has to adopt special measures, when circumstances so warrant, or to design conditions and criteria to be applied by the federate competent authorities in order to adopt such measures. The federal States should prevent the local governments to maintain or to establish such situations or distinctions which may create or perpetuate a disadvantage for some racial or ethnic groups. Moreover, the federal State cannot justify the lack of special measures, when they are necessary, by referring to the competences granted to federate authorities by the Constitution; according to article 26 of the Vienna Convention on the law of treaties of 1969, a State cannot invoke a provision of internal law to justify the non-application of an international treaty.

* * *

Experience shows that discrimination cannot be eliminated overnight and that the social structures and attitudes, which perpetuate disadvantage and inequalities, are very much alive, in spite of the laws forbidding discrimination. Both anti-discrimination legislation and special measures are necessary to reduce and combat the different forms of discrimination in the various fields where it takes place.

Special measures have to be carefully defined, proportional to the objective followed and their beneficiaries should be established according to clear objective criteria, to fair and transparent procedures. They have to be temporary, and the same objective and transparent procedure has to be followed to discontinue them. Moreover, States have to ensure the widest possible support for the special measures adopted, through consultations with all interested groups and forces, in order to avoid the stigmatization of the potential beneficiaries and the opposition of important groups in the society.

CHAPTER XIII - RACIST HATE SPEECH and FREEDOM of EXPRESSION and INFORMATION

ABSTRACT

International norms on human rights are protecting both the freedom of expression and the freedom from incitement of hate, from discrimination or violence on grounds of race, ethnic origin or religion. But they may come into conflict, when freedom of expression is used to incite to racial hate, to discrimination or violence. A balance has therefore to be observed so that freedom of expression, which is indispensable in a democratic society, be exercised without becoming a call for racial hate, violence or discrimination.

Definitions of the hate speech and criteria for distinguishing it from the legitimate exercise of the freedom of expression were proposed by international organizations and by human rights bodies, including the European Court of Human Rights; but the proper evaluation and conclusion have to be adopted for each specific case, because numerous aspects involved in each case can make the situations different from others.

Some parameters can be drawn from the international practice, but they will have only guiding functions; it remains for each State and international body called to take a decision to evaluate the different aspects of each case: the author of the speech, the addressee, the purpose followed, the potential impact, essentially the context of the exercise.

KEY WORDS: freedom of expression, racist speech, restrictions, war propaganda, xenophobia, publicity, denial, genocide, race, colour, descent, ethnic origin, insult, defamation, prejudice.

One of the most controversial issues in human rights theory and practice is, even among States and scholars who agree on universal values, like tolerance, equal rights, mutual respect, human dignity and equal worth of human beings, how to distinguish between freedom of information and expression and inciting to national, racial or religious hate.

The consideration of this issue is strongly influenced, in recent years, by the measures adopted in Europe on equality and non- discrimination, especially by the adoption of EC Directive 2000-43 on the application of equal treatment irrespective of racial or ethnic origin. This led to reviewing anti-discrimination legislation and policies in Member States through the adoption of juridical definitions and criteria and to reforming and strengthening legal bodies dealing with issues of equality and discrimination. Another important step in this direction is the adoption by the EU Council of the Framework Decision 2008/913/JHA on fight against certain forms and manifestations of racism and xenophobia by means of criminal law.

As a result, preoccupations about hate speech and racist speech have taken a new impetus[407]. It becomes also possible, in light of international practice, to set parameters for establishing a balance between freedom of speech and racist speech, although the application of these rules requires a rigorous and sensitive assessment, which should be decided by the judiciary for each case.

SECTION 1 - INTERNATIONAL REGULATIONS and INTERNAL LEGISLATIONS

1. Freedom of opinion and expression is a fundamental right in any democratic society, a prerequisite for achieving the principles of transparency and accountability, including the promotion and protection of human rights. At the same time, everyone is entitled to be treated with equality and dignity and to be protected against expressions of hatred based on race, ethnicity, religion or other aspects of his/her personality. Racist discourse, promoting hatred based on race, ethnicity or religion is a serious threat to society. It offends the dignity and self-evaluation of individuals or human groups and leads to strained relations, even to conflict.

Therefore, international documents make a clear distinction between freedom of opinion (*forum internum*), which raises no problem, and freedom of expression (*forum externum*), which involves duties and responsibilities and is subject to restrictions.

In any democratic society an appropriate balance must be set between these rights, for freedom of expression is not a license to hatred, a right to offend others. No human right is absolute; according to the modern concept of

---

[407] For an overview, Anne Weber, "*Manuel sur le discours de la haine*" (Discourse on the hate speech), Publishing Editions, Conseil de l'Europe, 2010.

human rights, different rights and freedoms must support each other to build a strong and durable system. Without directly referring to this problem, the Declaration adopted by the UN Human Rights Conference in Vienna in 1993 states that "All human rights are universal, indivisible, interdependent and related to each other. The international community must treat human rights globally, correctly, on an equal footing and with the same emphasis ". Universal Declaration of Human Rights stated, in 1948, that the exercise of any human right should be done in a way that is consistent with other rights.

2. The International Covenant on Civil and Political Rights of 1966 provides, in art. 19, that everyone shall have the right to hold opinions without interference; the right to hold opinions cannot be subject to restrictions.

The Covenant also provides for the freedom of expression, including the right to seek, receive and impart information and ideas of all kinds regardless of frontiers. According to the opinions adopted by the Human Rights Committee when examining individual communications received under the Additional Protocol to the Covenant, freedom of expression concerns the political speech, comment on public issues, discussions on human rights, journalism, cultural and artistic expression, commercial advertising and religious speech. The Covenant provides for the protection of all forms of expression and means of dissemination of information (oral, written, by signs, art, audio-visual and through any other media chosen).

At the same time, the Covenant stipulates that the exercise of the freedom of expression carries with it special duties and responsibilities. Consequently, two types of restrictions are allowed to the exercise of this freedom:
- for respecting the rights or reputation of others;
- for protecting the national security, public order or public health or morals.

The European Convention of 1950 on the protection of fundamental human rights and freedoms, adopted within the frameworks of the Council of Europe, also provides for the prohibition of discrimination on grounds of race, religion, ethnic origin or any other status and the right to freedom of expression, subject to restrictions to protect the same values.

Such restrictions cannot endanger the very freedom of expression (the restrictions may not become the norm); moreover, the application of restrictions is subject to strict conditions: to be provided by law and applied only for the reasons set out, to be necessary and proportionate to the objective followed (according to a constant jurisprudence of the European Court of Human Rights).

Also, according to art.20 of the Covenant any State shall prohibit by law propaganda for war, and any advocacy of national, racial or religious hatred that constitutes incitement to discrimination, hostility or violence. This article is considered *lex specialis* to art. 19.

Likewise, according to the International Convention on the Elimination of All Forms of Racial Discrimination of 1965 (art. 4), the States parties are obliged to declare an offense punishable by law all dissemination of ideas based on racial superiority or hatred, incitement to racial discrimination, as well as all acts of violence or incitement to such acts against any race or any group of persons of another color or ethnic origin. The Convention provides for the prohibition of discrimination on grounds of race or ethnic origin in the exercise of the freedom of opinion and expression (art. 5).

The Covenant of 1966 also prohibits incitement to religious hatred, while the 1965 Convention deals only with issues of discrimination on grounds of racial or ethnic origin. We must not ignore the intersection that often occurs for some individuals between race, ethnicity and religion, which apparently makes discrimination on religious grounds to sometimes disguise racial or ethnic-based discrimination.

We note also the Protocol relative to the criminalization of racist and xenophobic acts, supplementing the Convention of 2004 on combating crime in cyberspace, adopted by the Council of Europe, which extends these norms to the Internet.

3. At the European level, apart from the Convention of 1950, we note Decision 2008/913/JHA adopted by the European Union (in fact, a directive), with the purpose of fighting against some forms and manifestations of racism and xenophobia through criminal law[408]. This decision was adopted in application of Art. 29 of the Treaty of Union, which sets as its objective to provide citizens with a high level of protection in an area of freedom, security and justice, through a joint police and judicial cooperation in criminal matters, to prevent racism and xenophobia and to combat these phenomena. The Decision aims to deepen the legal instruments to combat racism within the Union and of course to harmonize national laws of Member States in this field.

The Decision specifies at the outset that it does not alter the obligations to respect the fundamental rights and principles, including freedom of expression and association, and does not require that States adopt measures contrary to these rights, especially freedom of the press and freedom of expression by other means; it also does not alter the

---

[408] Extended presentation by Bernadette Renauld, The Framework Decision 2008/913/JHA of the European Union Council: again on the fight against racism (*du nouveau en matière de lutte contre le racisme!*), in Review of human rights, no. 81/2010, pp. 119-140.

responsibilities of the press and other medias and the appropriate procedural safeguards. Setting legal limits to the exercise of these freedoms, the Decision is based on generally accepted concepts in international law that such limitations, aiming at the suppression of racism and incitement to racial hatred, are compatible with conventional and constitutional provisions guaranteeing freedom of expression.

According to the Decision, Member States must sanction in criminal law public incitement to violence or hatred, targeting a group or one of its members on grounds of race, color, religion, descent or national or ethnic origin, including when incitement is committed through dissemination or distribution of tracts, images or other media. It also provides for the punishment of complicity to commit such acts. Moreover, it states that such acts can be punished only if they are intentional. The decision offers an alternative to Member States, adding that they may choose to punish only such behaviour that is likely to disturb public order (taking into account the conditions and the context in which it takes place), or if it is threatening, abusive or insulting.

Advertising is, according to the Decision, a constituent of the offense, just like the intention. Advertising is made by press, television, broadcast or any work distributed, and by the Internet, but also through oral speech. It is considered that the use of German Nazi symbols or reference to them is an indication of the willingness to incite racial hatred, while dissemination of historical documents for scientific or educational purposes shall not be interpreted as such.

The Decision requires Member States to punish condoning, denying or grossly trivializing in public the genocide, crimes against humanity and war crimes as defined in the Statute of the International Criminal Court, targeting a group of persons or one of its members defined with reference to race, color, religion, descent or national or ethnic origin, when this behaviour is exercised in a way that incites hatred or violence against such a group or such persons, and condoning, denying or trivializing in public crimes defined in the Charter of the Nurnberg Military Tribunals annexed to the London Agreement of 1945, targeting such groups or individuals. It also provides for punishment of incitement to commit such acts. States may declare that they will punish denial, apology or trivializing of crimes of this kind only if they were punished by the final decisions of international or national courts.

Holocaust denial is thus equated with inciting to racism by referring to the same categories of group victims and to the same behaviour that incites to violence or hatred against such a group or such a person. It is estimated that the objective pursued by punishing denial is not to restore the historical truth in court, nor to suppress historical errors, but to fight against racism, because condoning, denying or trivializing crimes are disguised forms of incitement to hatred, to violence or to racial discrimination. The European Court of Human Rights said that the denial of established historical facts, as the existence of the Holocaust, "calls into question the values underlying the fight against racism and anti-Semitism and are likely to seriously disturb public order"[409]. What is criminalized is not simply a presentation of the history departing from the facts proven by decisions of courts, but the use of history, by deforming and denial, in order to incite racial hatred.

In connection with other crimes, the Decision requires Member States to take the necessary measures so that the racist or xenophobic motivations are considered aggravating circumstance or that the courts are taking into account the racist motivation in determining the sentence. In many European countries, criminal law provides for the taking into account the racial motivation as an aggravating circumstance.

It also provides that legal persons may be criminally liable for acts of racist incitement committed by their organs or any person acting on their behalf, without removing the individual responsibility of the individual concerned. Penalties range from fines to the prohibition of certain activities and even dissolution. For individuals, the maximum penalty is of one to three years' imprisonment.

It is important to note that, under this Decision, at least for the most serious facts, the prosecution does not depend on the victim's complaint, but should be followed automatically.

4. Freedom of expression is not absolute; its exercise should take place with respect for other human rights and for other values protected by the rules of law.

Thus, the international treaties provide for the protection of both values: freedom of expression and freedom from racist acts. Committees which oversee their implementation by States parties stressed the compatibility of the two sets of provisions and adopted clear positions on this matter.

In its General Recommendation no. 15 of 1993, the Committee on the Elimination of Racial Discrimination stated that the prohibition of dissemination of ideas based on racial superiority or hatred is compatible with the freedom of opinion and expression. In its General Comment on Art.20 of the Covenant, the Human Rights Committee states that the obligation to prohibit by law any advocacy of national, racial or religious hatred that constitutes incitement to discrimination or violence is fully compatible with the exercise of freedom of expression which implies special duties and responsibilities.

---

[409] Case Garaudy v. France, decision of 24 June 2003.

It is therefore absolutely necessary to reconcile the two values, both protected by rules of law, and to establish a balance between the prohibition of dissemination of racist acts, of calls to hatred and racial discrimination, and freedom of expression, within the general framework of human rights and fundamental freedoms.[410]

5. Ideas and words are powerful; their power may be used for positive or negative purposes; they can undermine the freedom and equal rights as well as the democracy and stability. Expressions of hatred have the power to cause damage, to isolate and marginalize some people only for their personal characteristics as ethnicity, race and religion; in fact, hate is directed generally against vulnerable people or groups, but sometimes against majority populations in different countries, following a history of intolerance, prejudice and discrimination.

Most national laws criminalize hate speech with significant differences. In Europe, for example, national regulations range from the ban of Holocaust and genocide denial, the prohibition of insults on grounds of belonging to a racial or religious group, to punishing attacks directed to religious feelings or to national unity[411].

Some laws associate the inciting to hatred with the one to violence or discrimination, or to hostility and sometimes discord (Bosnia-Herzegovina, Montenegro, Romania, Serbia, and Turkey). According to other legislations, only the incitement to violence is incriminated, without mentioning the incitement to hatred (Austria, Cyprus, Greece, Italy, and Portugal). Other legislations follow closely the Convention of 1965 on the elimination of all forms of racial discrimination, punishing incitement to hatred, discrimination or violence (Belgium). Many States criminalize racist speech as an affirmation of inferiority or superiority of races, extending it to the nationality or religion (Azerbaijan, Croatia, Denmark, Switzerland, Liechtenstein, Poland, Russia, and Slovenia). Some add qualifications such as "challenge" (France), "propagation' (Bulgaria), "ill will" (Cyprus), "promotion of division" (Montenegro, Romania, Serbia, Turkey), "creation of an atmosphere of intimidation, hostility, humiliation" (Romania); other States are incriminating individual support to a group aimed at inciting to hatred (Belgium, Italy, Luxembourg, Russia) or even a support containing an incitement (Luxembourg, UK). Many laws prohibit symbols related to Nazi associations or which deny the holocaust or genocide. Some legislations limit the prohibition to the situation where the incitement to racial hatred involves a danger to public order (Germany, Austria), or affects the human dignity (Germany, Austria, Liechtenstein). Others add the use of violence as an aggravating circumstance of the incitement to hatred (Armenia, Bosnia, Latvia, Montenegro, Serbia, Slovenia and Ukraine).

The laws of most European States resumed the provisions of Art. 20 of the Covenant on Civil and Political Rights. Many States are incriminating in the same provision incitement to hatred or discrimination for other reasons (religious, political, on the grounds of class, sexual preference etc).

Several legislations add the requirement that incitement be public. For some, the public nature of incitement to hatred is an aggravating circumstance (Armenia, France). Other laws make it an aggravating circumstance, if the call to hatred is made through mass media (Armenia, Azerbaijan, Malta, Czech Republic and Romania). The trend in the majority of legislations is not to limit to incitement involving a clear and present danger, but to include both direct incitement and that which is only implied.

Some laws require that the intentional element is met (Cyprus, Portugal, Ukraine), while others recognize that this offense can be committed through negligence (Ireland, Malta, Netherlands, Norway and United Kingdom). Penalties provided range from 1 year (Belgium, France, Netherlands), up to 10 years (Albania).

We can also note that often the advocacy or incitement to racial hatred is incriminated along with hatred on religious grounds; they can be, of course, distinguished if the object of the call is clear. The result may be different because in some States the call for religious hatred is punishable only if accompanied by a threat (United Kingdom) and the Venice Commission recommended not to incriminating criticism of a religion or religious insult[412]. Often, however, the call for hatred is directed at persons or groups for both racial and ethnic origin and their religion, given the frequent cases of intersection between race, ethnicity and religion.

Of course, these provisions of prohibiting the call or incitement to hatred are part of more global policies or legal instruments aimed at combating discrimination; the application of aggravating circumstances was gradually added when the common-law crimes were racially motivated and therefore are more severely punished; they remain distinct from hate speech advocacy or incitement, but are supplementing them in the combat against discrimination.

---

[410] A brief analysis by Ion Diaconu, (*Liberté d'expression et les discours d'incitation à la haine*), Freedom of expression and the discourse of incitement to hatred, in Tangram 27, Bulletin of the CFR, June 2011, pp. 53-54.
[411] Exhaustive presentation by Louis-Leon Christians, (*Atelier d'experts au sujet de l'interdiction de l'incitation à la haine nationale, raciale et religieuse, Etude pour l'atelier sur l'Europe)*, Workshop of experts on the interdiction of incitement to national racial and religious hatred, 9-10 February 2011, Vienne, pp. 5-8.
[412] CDL- AD (2008) 026.

SECTION 2 - CONTENTS OF RACIAL HATE SPEECH and its EVALUATION in CONTEXT

1. Offenses inspired by racism are different from other criminal behavior in that they are aimed at groups of people or their members defined by reference to race, color, descent, national or ethnic origin and, according to some international documents, by religion.

The term of race is mentioned, because it is used by those who have circulated racist theories, although it was proved that it has no scientific basis; to show that it is not accepted, some legislations refer to "alleged or presumed race".

The EU Council Decision of 2008 states that religion is used as a term of reference, because criticism against religion may in fact be motivated by racist or xenophobic intent, to the extent that religious elements are used against an ethnic group; reference to religion is envisaged to cover conduct which constitutes a pretext used to act in reality against groups or persons defined by reference to race, color, descent or national or ethnic origin. It is the expression of the concern to distinguish a critique of a religion motivated by hate that can be equated with racism from the one that belongs to the debate of ideas and of philosophical concepts, which has to be protected under the freedom of expression.

2. Of course it is sometimes difficult to distinguish between the racist speech and the expression of views; as stated by the European Court of Human Rights, freedom of expression includes even the most unacceptable views that may embarrass or shock the conscience of others[413].

In its Recommendation 20 (1997), the Committee of Ministers of the Council of Europe defined "hate speech" as "covering every form of expression that spreads, incites racial hatred, promotes or justifies racial hatred, xenophobia, anti-Semitism and other forms of hatred based on intolerance, including intolerance which is manifested in the form of aggressive nationalism and ethnocentrism, discrimination and hostility against minorities, immigrants and those resulting from emigration".

In turn, the European Commission against Racism and Intolerance (ECRI) adopted in 2002 the Recommendation no.7 on national legislation against racism, demanding that "the law should punish the following conduct as criminal offence, if it is performed intentionally: a) public incitement to violence, hatred or discrimination; b) public insults or defamation; c) threats against a person or a group of persons on grounds of their race, color, language, religion, nationality or ethnic origin or national; d) the public expression, with a racist purpose, of an ideology which claims the superiority of a group of people on grounds of race, color, language, religion, nationality or ethnic origin or national, or which slander or denigrate a group of people; e) public denial, gross minimization, justification or apology, with a racist purpose, of crimes of genocide, crimes against humanity or war crimes".

The Parliamentary Assembly of the Council of Europe proposed, in its Recommendation no.1805 (2007), as definition of hate speech "a statement that calls for subjecting a person or group of persons to hatred, discrimination or violence on account of their religion or any other reason." The Parliamentary Assembly made a new appeal in its Resolution 1754 of 2010 by inviting States to apply criminal penalties according to their law against public inciting to violence, to racial discrimination and intolerance, including Islamophobia, and if no such legislation exists, to introduce in their criminal law provisions of this kind and implement the recommendation of the Committee of Ministers 20/1997.

After 2003, in several decisions, the European Court of Human Rights has addressed the issue of incitement to hatred, understanding by the speech of hate "any form of expression which propagates, incites, promotes or justifies hatred based on intolerance (including religious intolerance)"[414]. In one of the cases, the Court took into account the nature of artistic expression and did not find a violation of the Convention of 1950, showing that even if some passages of certain poems seem to be calls for the use of violence, their artistic nature and their very little impact allow them to be considered less as a call to rebellion and more as an expression of disappointment with the difficult political situation[415].

We note that, in its decisions, the Court takes into consideration: the purpose aimed at by the one who is expressing, the context in which it occurs, people who are expressing and those to whom it is addressed, and the potential impact of the expression.

---

[413] Handyside v. United Kingdom, Vincent Berger, The Jurisprudence of the European Court of Human Rights, 6-th ed., Dalloz, 1998, pp. 1117-1122.

[414] . Among other cases Garaudy v. France, decision of 24 June 2003; Norwood v. United Kingdom, decision of 16 November 2004; Alinak v. Turkey, decision of 29 March 2005; Leroy v. France, decision of 2 October 2008; Feret v. Belgium, decision of 16 July 2009.

[415] Case Karatas v. Turkey, decision of 8 July 1999, p. 52.

In its General Recommendation no. 30 of 2005 (discrimination against non-citizens), the Committee on the Elimination of Racial Discrimination recommended the States parties to the Convention of 1965 to consider especially hate speech and racial violence and to take decisive measures to counter any tendency to target, stigmatizing, make the subject of a stereotype or profile, on the basis of race, color, descent or national or ethnic origin, members of non-citizens groups, especially by politicians, officials, educators and media, the Internet or other communication networks.

We retain as common elements of these definitions and descriptions: all forms of expression or statements, which propagate, incite to hatred or discrimination against a person or a group, or justify it, that defame or threaten, or give expression to an ideology of superiority of a group of people against others, on grounds of race, ethnic origin or religion, or intolerance justified racially, ethnically or religiously. It is necessary to separate the appeal to hatred of the one to violence, in order to comply with the Covenant on Civil and Political Rights, considering them two separate offenses. In European countries, on the basis of the intention and the message behind the denial of Holocaust or of genocide, it is estimated that they amount to an indirect incitement to hatred.

We must distinguish between the debate of ideas, opinions, even the most controversial ones, that aim to transform society, its institutions and its way of life, and the discourse with racist content, which does not concern a debate with speakers and arguments, but aims to propagate, incite, promote or justify hatred or superiority over another group on account of race or ethnicity, or that contains a public appeal to discriminatory behavior or violence against persons belonging to such groups, aimed at triggering a hostile reflex[416]. These types of action involve the intention to produce such consequences, although the hypothesis of imprudence of the author cannot be excluded, without making excusable such a speech. We note that sometimes even a rhetoric debate of ideas can skid to assign a person or a group features, of course negative, thus making them subject to incitement to hatred or discrimination.

To qualify a speech as a racist one requires to consider its context, as well as to evaluate the effect pursued, its impact on those to whom it is addressed, especially the context in which it was issued, which means evaluating each case depending on its specific elements. In this respect, the European Court of Human Rights adopted a meticulous analysis of the facts alleged, considering for example that the mere fact of defending Sharia during a TV show, without calling for violence to impose it, does not constitute a hate speech[417]; the Court unequivocally condemned incitement to racial hatred, considering that the offensive and disparaging remarks made at immigrants and ethnic groups established in Denmark by a group of young members of the extremist supporters of the Ku Klux Klan was more than an insult to members of targeted groups[418]. In this case, the Court has given a different treatment to the journalist who broadcast these remarks, bearing in mind that it has exercised its freedom of expression for public information, without a racist purpose. The Committee on the Elimination of Racial Discrimination held, after examining a communication on the Supreme Court of Norway's decision of acquittal for a march and speeches in honor of Nazi Rudolf Hess and expressing hate against Jews, that it was a violation of the Convention of 1965 on the Elimination of All Forms of Racial Discrimination[419].

In another case, the European Court considered a complaint of a Belgian citizen, president of the National Front, convicted by his country's courts for incitement to discrimination, segregation or hatred towards the immigrant community in Belgium in leaflets, which relied on freedom of expression. In its decision, the Court states that "acts committed against persons by insults, ridicule or slander or against parts of specific groups of its population, or incitement to discrimination, as was done in this particular case, are sufficient for the authorities to privilege the fight against racist discourse against irresponsible freedom of expression that harms the dignity, or even the security of these parties or these population groups. Political speeches inciting to hatred based on racial, ethnic or cultural prejudice are a threat to social peace and political stability in democratic states". The Court added that "it is of paramount importance that politicians, in their speeches to the public, avoid broadcasting such words that promote intolerance"[420].

The Program of Action adopted in 2001 by the World Conference against racism, racial discrimination, xenophobia and related intolerance highlighted the role of politicians and political parties in the fight against racism and encouraged such parties to take concrete measures to promote equality, solidarity and non-discrimination in society, especially through the adoption of internal codes of conduct so that their members refrain from public statements and actions that would invite or induce discrimination and racism.

---

[416] Louis-Leon Christians, art. cit., pp. 8-10.

[417] Case Gunduz v. Turkey, decision of 4 December 2003, application no. *35071/97*, para. 51.

[418] Case Jersild v. Denmark, decision of 23 September 1994, application no. 15890/89, para. 34 and 35.

[419] Communication no. 3o/2003, CERD/C/67/D/30/2003, para. 9.4.

[420] Case Feret v. Belgium, decision of 16 July 2009, para. 73 and 75.

It is estimated that "incitement" to hatred or racial discrimination goes beyond information, ideas or criticism, pamphlets, jokes, cartoons, opinions, which are not characterized by the desire to incite to discrimination, segregation and violence[421]. We also believe that the application of the concept "clear and present danger" (that incitement should actually be followed by violence) would unacceptably limit the scope of criminal acts and would open even more the way to arbitrary interpretations, which is already not excluded by the existing provisions.

At the same time, it is accepted that critical expression of ideas in the context of public debate of ideas, as well as the expression of shocking opinions is not a violation of human rights. Thus, in the case of Klein v. Slovakia, the European Court held as violation of the Convention the conviction of a journalist for the harsh criticism of an archbishop that proposed a ban on a movie channel[422]. The Court also accepted that some expressions, as shocking as that of attributing religious significance to an earthquake and assigning the blame for this to a religious community, do not incite to hatred and violence against the community[423].

3. Taking into account the role of the hate racist speech in processes leading to mass violations of human rights and genocide, and on the basis of its own experience and that of other human rights treaty bodies, CERD adopted the General Recommendation No. 35 on Combating racist hate speech, after substantial consultations with the States parties and non-governmental organizations. The Committee mentions members of the groups usually affected by the racist speech-indigenous peoples, minorities, descent based groups, immigrants and non-citizens, migrant domestic workers, refugees and asylum seekers, and on the basis of inter-sectionality women members of such groups and person of a different religion.

The Committee regards as of particular concern statements attributed to high ranking officials, to parliamentarians and political parties, in view of their impact on the public opinion and on the state authorities as such.

Resuming previous recommendations, CERD reminded that as article 4 of the Convention is not self-executing, States are required to adopt legislation to combat racist speech declaring as offences and effectively sanction:

- all dissemination of ideas based on racial or ethnic superiority or hatred, by whatever means;
- incitement to hatred, contempt or discrimination against members of a group on grounds of race, colour, descent, or national or ethnic origin;
- threats or incitement to violence against persons or groups on the grounds mentioned;
- expression of insults, ridicule or slander of persons or groups or justification of hatred, contempt or discrimination on the said grounds, when it clearly amounts to incitement to hatred or discrimination;
- participation in organizations and activities which promote and incite racial discrimination.

The Committee also recommended that denials or attempts to justify crimes of genocide or crimes against humanity, as defined by international law, should be declared as offences punishable by law, if they clearly constitute incitement to racial violence or hatred.

At the same time, CERD recommended to consider offences only serious cases of racist expression, to be proven beyond reasonable doubt, while less serious cases should be addressed by means other than criminal law, taking into account, *inter alia*, the impact on the targeted persons and groups.

For the qualification of dissemination and incitement as offences, the Committee considers that contextual factors should be considered, such as: the content and form of the speech; the economic, social and political climate prevalent in the society at the moment of the speech; the position or status of the speaker; the reach of the speech, respectively the audience to which it is directed; the objective of the speech. As for the incitement, CERD adds that it seeks to influence others to engage in certain forms of conduct, including the commission of crime, through advocacy or threats.

The Committee notes also the danger that banning racist speech may be used for other purposes, especially to restrict unacceptably the freedom of speech and criticism of government policy, thus making it an instrument of political struggle, while the reason of its interdiction is the protection of human rights. In this respect, the Venice Commission of the Council of Europe for Democracy through Law stated that "The application of legislation regarding hatred must be assessed to evaluate the results (of it) so that the potential restrictions to protect minorities against abuses, extremism and racism should not have the perverse effect of reducing to silence the opposition and

---

[421] Bernadette Renauld, art. cit., p. 130.
[422] Case Klein v. Slovakia, no. 72208/01, decision of 31 October 2006, para. 28.
[423] Case Nur Radyo Ve Televizyon Yaynciligi AC v. Turkey, no. 6587/03, decision of 27 November 2007, para. 84.

the dissenting voices of minorities and of strengthening of political discourse and the dominant social and moral ideology"[424].

In its General Recommendation, CERD also underlined the importance of respecting the freedom of opinion and expression of everybody without discrimination, while considering that the expression of ideas and opinions made in the context of academic debates, political engagement or similar activity, and without incitement to hatred, contempt, violence or discrimination, should be regarded as legitimate exercise of the right to freedom of expression, even when such ideas are controversial. The Committee also underlines that the protection of persons from racist hate speech is not simply one of opposition between the right to freedom of expression and its restriction for the benefit of protected groups, because the persons and groups entitled to protection under the Convention also enjoy the right to freedom of expression and freedom from racial discrimination in the exercise of that right.

The Committee also stressed the importance of effective measures taken by States in the fields of teaching, education, culture and information, with a view to combating prejudices which lead to racial discrimination and to promoting understanding, tolerance and friendship among nations and racial or ethnic groups, the importance of intercultural education, based on equality, respect and esteem and genuine mutuality, including knowledge of the history, culture and traditions of "racial or ethnical" groups present in the State party, inter alia indigenous peoples and persons of African descent.

The Committee also recalled the essential role of the media in promoting responsibility in the dissemination of ideas and opinions, in representing ethnic, indigenous and other groups based on principles of respect, fairness and the avoidance of stereotyping. States should encourage the public and private media to adopt codes of professional ethics and press codes based on respect for the principles of respect for the fundamental human rights, including the interdiction of racial discrimination under all its forms.

* * *

The difficulties and dangers to evaluate hate speech and to distinguish it for legitimate exercise of the freedom of expression should not be considered as an obstacle to the enforcement of international law and national laws that prohibit hate speech. This is often preceding acts of discrimination, intolerance and even violence against people from different ethnic groups, immigrants, refugees or asylum seekers. Despite the difficulties it involves, this dilemma must be solved, so as to protect both human values, freedom of expression and freedom from incitement to hatred or to discrimination based on race, ethnicity or religion, all of them human rights enshrined in the documents generally accepted in international law.

The relationship between the interdiction of racist hate speech and the exercise of the freedom of expression should not be seen as a zero-sum game, where the promotion of one means diminution of the other, but as complementary contributions to the promotion of equally important human values.

There are certainly some guidelines, practices, examples, but the solution should be given in each case taking into account the specific elements: the purpose of the person who delivers the speech, her/his place in society, to whom it is addressed, the context in which it takes place and the impact which its expressing can generate.

Beyond the decision which may be adopted in one or other of cases, the problem must be addressed in a broader framework, including the education of the entire population and creating the climate to exclude such acts or to produce the reaction to reject them in a democratic society that respects and promotes human values.

---

[424] CDL-AD (2008) 026, para. 58.

PART IV - DIVERSITY of CULTURES and LANGUAGES

CHAPTER XIV - CULTURAL DIVERSITY as EXPRESSION of PROMOTING HUMAN RIGHTS

ABSTRACT

International law gradually recognized diversity as a human value whose protection is necessary as an element of respect for human rights and fundamental freedoms. Numerous instruments on human rights and in other fields postulate respect for human rights irrespective of their sex, race, ethnic origin, political and other opinion, fortune and any other status.

UNESCO underlined in many documents the importance of cultural diversity and its close relationship with the protection of human rights; international and regional documents insist on the protection of the identity of minorities and of indigenous peoples, on the need of respect and dialogue among different civilizations.

In Europe, important documents were adopted for this purpose, such as the Framework Convention for the protection of minorities, the Charter for regional or minority languages and some OSCE documents. It is of particular interest to consider the documents adopted by the European Union within the process of European integration, mainly the Charter of fundamental rights and the Lisbon Treaty of 2007, containing important provisions on respect for the richness of cultures and languages of Europe and for the identity of member States, including within the functioning of the Union.

This paper enounces also rights and obligations regarding the protection of diversity, both for the States and for international organizations and underlines the importance of a correct management and treatment of diversity for maintaining stability and coherence of societies, for respecting human rights for all.

KEY WORDS: human diversity, interdiction of genocide, tolerance, cultural diversity, cultural expressions, European integration and diversity, principle of subsidiarity, Charter of fundamental rights, EU functioning, official languages, diversity in terms of rights and obligations.

SECTION I - PROTECTION of DIVERSITY at the INTERNATIONAL LEVEL

The recognition of human diversity and the requirement to respect it are expressed already in the Charter of the United Nations adopted at San Francisco in 1945. According to the Charter, „determined to reaffirm faith in the fundamental human rights, in the dignity and the worth of the human person", the United Nations set as their purpose to achieve international cooperation in promoting and encouraging respect for human rights and for fundamental freedoms for all, without distinction as to race, sex, language or religion; they also committed themselves to promote universal respect for these rights and freedoms.

Numerous documents developed this conception. The Universal Declaration of Human Rights, adopted in 1948, recognizes from the beginning the inherent dignity and the equal and inalienable rights of all members of the human family, as the foundation of freedom, justice and peace in the world. According to the provisions of substance of the Declaration, all human beings are born free and equal in dignity and rights; they are entitled to enjoy all rights and freedoms, without distinction of any kind, such as race, colour, sex, language, religion, political or other opinion, national or social origin, property, birth or other status.

The Declaration proclaims among others the right to freedom of thought, conscience and religion, the right to freedom of opinion and expression, the right to peaceful assembly and association, as well as the right freely to participate in the cultural life of the community, to enjoy the arts and to share in scientific advancement. According to the Declaration, everyone has duties to the community in which alone the free and full development of his personality is possible.

According to the two human rights Covenants adopted in 1966, all people have the right to self-determination, by virtue of which they freely determine their political status and freely pursue their economic, cultural and social development. The Covenant on economic, social and cultural rights takes up the provisions of the Universal Declaration on cultural rights and adds the request that States take the necessary measures for the conservation, development and dissemination of science and culture and encourage international contacts and cooperation in these fields. The Covenant on civil and political rights takes up the provisions of the Declaration concerning dignity and equal rights and develops the texts on the public freedoms mentioned. With regard to States in which ethnic, religious or linguistic minorities exist, the Covenant provides that persons belonging to such minorities shall not be denied the right, in community with other members of their group, to enjoy their own culture, to profess and practice their own religion, or to use their own language[425].

In light of the objectives they pursue, other international instruments also contribute to the protection of human diversity of peoples, communities and persons. The 1948 Convention on the prevention and punishment of genocide stipulates the interdiction and the punishment as crimes of a series of acts committed with the intention to destroy some human groups on grounds of nationality, race, ethnic origin or religion. The International Convention of 1965 on the elimination of all forms of racial discrimination provides for the interdiction and the elimination of any distinction, exclusion, restriction or preference based on race, colour, descent or national or ethnic origin which has the purpose or effect to create inequalities in the exercise of human fundamental rights and freedoms. The right to freedom of thought, conscience and religion, the right to freedom of opinion and expression and the right to equal participation in cultural activities are enounced in this Convention among other human rights in a non-exhaustive list[426].

As for the right of colonial peoples to self-determination, the Declaration 1514(XV) of 1960, without an explicit reference to the respect of the diversity of those peoples, implies such an obligation for the colonial powers, by reaffirming the right of all peoples to self-determination and to promote freely their economic, social and cultural development, and proclaiming the need to bring an end unconditionally to colonialism under all its forms. This conception was reaffirmed and developed by the Declaration on principles of international law concerning friendly relations and cooperation among States according to the UN Charter, adopted by the resolution 2625(XXV) of 1970.

The evolution of the international community and of preoccupations of member States led, after the period of the cold war, to new approaches and developments in this direction. The Declaration adopted by the General Assembly in 1992 on the rights of persons belonging to ethnic, linguistic or religious minorities focuses on respect for and protection of the identity of minorities and of persons forming them under all aspects of their culture, language and religion.

The Declaration on the rights of indigenous people, adopted by the General Assembly in 2007 (resolution 61/295) proclaims the right of these people to preserve and strengthen their distinct political, economic, social and cultural institutions; they have the right to belong to an indigenous community or nation, according to the traditions and customs of the respective community or nation, as well as the right to respect and revive their cultural traditions and customs, to practice and promote their religious and spiritual traditions, to use and to transmit to future generations their history, language and traditions.

More recently, the Declaration and the Programme of Action adopted by the World Conference of Durban in 2001 against racism, racial discrimination, xenophobia and related intolerance affirm from the beginning that all peoples and individuals constitute one unique human family, rich in diversity; they have contributed to the progress of civilizations and cultures; their cultural traditions and customs represent a common heritage of humanity. It recognized at the same time that members of certain groups with a distinct cultural identity face barriers arising from a complex interplay of ethnic, religious and other factors, as well as their traditions and customs. States are requested to ensure that their political and legal systems reflect the multicultural diversity of their societies, to adopt measures for educating the population in the spirit of respect for the diversity and for the identity of different groups.

Following the evolution of the world due to interdependences and globalization, the need appeared at the end of the 20th century and the crossing into the new millennium to recognize the existence of different cultures, to develop the exchanges and cooperation between them, to promote the conceptions of interculturalism and multiculturalism of the modern societies as well as the dialogue among civilizations. The Declaration of the Millennium, adopted by the resolution of the UN General Assembly nr. 55/2 of 8 September 2000 includes, among the fundamental values which should lie at the basis of international relations in the twentieth century, „tolerance", affirming that „People have to mutually respect each other in all the diversity of their beliefs, cultures and languages. The differences which exist among societies and within societies should not produce fear neither repression, but should be venerated as precious goods of mankind. It is necessary to actively promote a culture of peace and dialogue among all the civilizations".

The heads of State and government engaged to promote more harmony and tolerance among all societies. In 2001, the General Assembly proclaimed, by its resolution 56/6, the Global Agenda for the dialogue among civilizations, where the objectives of this dialogue were established(to promote mutual understanding and respect, to inform, to make known and to appreciate mutually the richness and the wisdom of each civilization, to identify and

---

[425] For an extensive presentation of these documents, Ion Diaconu, Human Rights in contemporary international law, Ed. Liumina Lex(in Romanian), 2001, pp. 26-48.
[426] Extensively on the contents and the application of this Convention, Ion Diaconu, Racial Discrimination, 2011, Eleven International Publishing, The Hague.

promote the common values), the principles which should be respected (among which the recognition of cultural diversity as a fundamental feature of human society, the right of each person to preserve and develop its cultural heritage), as well as a programme of action to be followed by the governments.

International documents underline constantly the close relationship between respect for human rights and the cultural diversity and the need to see that globalization does not lead to cultural homogeneity and ensures to all respect of diversity; at the same time, international community should respond to the challenges of globalization and exploit its opportunities so as to guarantee the respect of cultural diversity.

Within the UN, documents underlined mainly the diversity of minorities and of indigenous peoples[427], as well as the need to respect the different civilizations and to increase the dialogue among them.

On the basis of its Constitution, which refers in its first article to the „ fertile diversity of cultures", and of its object of activity, UNESCO proclaimed repeatedly cultural diversity as a universal value which should be protected and as a principle of its activity and of the policies of member States. Provisions with these contents can be found in the 1966 Declaration on the principles of international cultural cooperation, in the 1970 Convention on means to forbid and to prevent import, export and transfer of illicit ownership on cultural goods, in the 1972 Convention for the protection of the cultural and natural heritage of mankind, in the 1978 Declaration on race and racial prejudice, in the 1989 Recommendation concerning the protection of traditional and popular cultures and others.

The General Conference of UNESCO adopted in 2003 the Universal Declaration on cultural diversity. The Declaration affirms from the beginning that culture is understood as a set of distinct spiritual, material, intellectual and emotional features of the society or of a social group, which, along with arts and literature, includes lifestyles, ways of living in collectivity, systems of values, traditions and beliefs. The Declaration proclaims diversity as a common heritage of humanity, as an integral part of the unique feature and plurality of the identities of groups and societies forming the world, and which should be recognized and affirmed to the benefit of present and future generations.

The Declaration affirms the importance of cultural pluralism and interaction as a factor of development and of respect for human rights, mainly of cultural rights, and of guaranteeing cultural diversity. It asks States to encourage linguistic diversity and support the expression, the creation and the dissemination of culture in several languages, to respect and protect the traditional knowledge, in particular that of indigenous peoples, and to develop cultural policies meant to implement these principles.

In 2005 the General Conference of UNESCO adopted the Convention on the protection of the diversity of cultural expressions. The Convention takes up and develops principles of the 2003 Declaration and insists on the rights and obligations of States for respecting them. Among the principles formulated one has to mention: recognition of equal dignity and respect for all cultures, including those of minorities and of indigenous peoples; complementarity between economic and cultural aspects of development; equitable access to a large and rich sphere of cultural expressions of the entire world; openness to other cultures[428].

Reaffirming the sovereignty of States to formulate and apply cultural policies and measures meant to promote cultural diversity, the Convention enounces a series of measures that States can take, as well as obligations, such as: to create an environment which encourages persons and social groups to create and disseminate their own cultural expressions; to protect and to preserve cultural expressions from their territories; to educate the public with regard to the importance of protecting and promoting the diversity of cultural expressions; to promote international cooperation in this field.

At the European level, diversity found its expression first of all in documents of the Council of Europe and of the Organization for Security and Cooperation in Europe concerning minorities. The Framework Convention for the protection of national minorities, adopted by the Council of Europe in 1995 takes as a starting point the postulate that a pluralist and democratic society has to respect the ethnic, cultural, linguistic and religious identity of each person belonging to a national minority, but also to create conditions which allow such persons to express, to preserve and to develop their identity; the Convention places its emphasis on the respect and development of the identity of persons belonging to minorities. For this purpose, it provides that States parties will encourage the spirit of tolerance and of the intercultural dialogue, will recognize the rights on the use of mother tongues, on learning and education in mother tongue, will take measures to encourage the knowledge of culture, history, language and religion of national minorities and of the majority[429].

---

[427] Dieter Kugelmann, The Protection of Minorities and Indigenous Peoples; Respecting Cultural Diversity, în Max Planck Yearbook of United Nations Law, vol.11, 2007, pp.233-263.

[428] About this Convention, Ion Diaconu, 10 years from the entering into force of the Framework Convention for the protection of national minorities. Th experience of Romania, in Romanian Journal of International Law nr. 6, (in Romanian), January-June 2008.

[429] On this Convention, Ion Diaconu, La Culture et les Droits de l'Homme, 2015, Edilivre-Paris, pp. 230-232.

The European Charter on regional or minority languages adopted by the Council of Europe in 1992 refers to the cultural diversity as an essential element for Europe, contains provisions for the preservation of the diversity of languages as vehicles of cultures and underlines that national sovereignty offers the framework for this diversity.

Within OSCE, the Document adopted in Copenhagen in 1990 sets forth, *inter alia*, that persons belonging to minorities have the right to express, to preserve and to develop their ethnic, cultural, linguistic and religious identity and to maintain and develop their culture under all its aspects, free from any trend to assimilation against their will. The States participating committed to protect the ethnic, cultural, linguistic and religious identity of national minorities living on their territory and to create conditions for promoting this identity[430].

SECTION 2 - DIVERSITY in the CONTEXT of EUROPEAN INTEGRATION

The evolution of conceptions and practices of the European integration bodies with regard to cultural diversity is of a special interest.

At the beginning of the 1950th, the European communities were created as organizations having as objective the economic integration; they gradually planned and achieved the customs union, the common market, the economic and monetary union, the foreign and security common policy, all of them facets of integration, which increased with each treaty and with each normative and institutional evolution.

Nevertheless, the process of integration did not lead to the loss of identity and of specificities of European peoples and States. The European peoples are bearers of a common culture and civilization, having deep roots in the Greek and Roman cultures, but with strong inputs from the cultures of the Vikings, of Slavic, Germanic and Tcheltish peoples and others. Europe is and remains from many points of view diverse, in terms of cultures, of languages spoken, of traditions, which all represent contributions to the European and universal culture.

States members of the Communities, and since 1993 of the European Union, as well as those which became members later-on, have been diverse including from the point of view of state structures and of institutional organization, although a process of rapprochement and harmonization has taken place; more than that, the European Union values, promotes and protects the diversity of member States and of cultures they are hosting.

One has to note the increase within the European Union of preoccupations for the protection of fundamental human rights and freedoms which has taken place in parallel with the affirmation of diversity as a value and with preoccupations for preserving and protecting it.

Equal rights and non-discrimination, fundamental values and principles of the European construction, stem in particular from the existence of diversity and from the need that individuals, in their diversity, enjoy fundamental rights and freedoms under equal conditions and are not discriminated in their exercise on grounds of their diversity.

The way the process of European integration was initiated and developed led to a more comprehensive concept of promoting identities and diversity. It includes both the identity and diversity of persons and communities within each member State and preoccupations concerning even the identity and diversity of the participating States, covering both norms of the Union's law and the composition, competences and functioning of institutions. Identity and diversity as values find their expression also at the institutional level of the functioning of the Union[431].

The European Communities were foreseen as associations of States, while respecting their national identities. Elements of integration developed in their evolution, in the beginning in the economic and social fields, then in the political field, but the preoccupation for preserving their identities and diversity remained constant.

Although the process of integration included gradually the principles of direct and immediate application of norms of community law, the member States maintained their institutional autonomy and the right to adapt some norms (those established by directives) to their own conditions.

The principle of subsidiarity was adopted, according to which in such fields where the Union has not exclusive competences (that is besides the customs policy, common commercial policy, monetary policy in the Euro zone, the norms of competition and the protection of fish resources in the maritime areas), the Union acts only if and in as much as the objective of the action proposed cannot be realized in a satisfactory measure by member States at the central, regional or local levels and, due to the dimensions and the effects of the action proposed, this objective can be achieved better at the level of the Union.

---

[430] Texts in Valentin Lipatti, Ion Diaconu, Security and Cooperation in Europe, Documents, 1989-1992(in Romanian), pp.24-40, Ed. Academiei.

[431] On the institional evolution of European Union, Jean Paul Jacqué, Droit institutionnel de l'Union Européenne, deuxième ed., 2003; Augustin Fuerea, European Community Law. General Part, 2003(in Romanian), Ed. All Beck; Dan Vataman, Institutions of the European Union, 2011(in Romanian), Ed. Universul Juridic; Andrei Popescu, Ion Diaconu, European and Euroatlantic Organisations, 2009(in Romanian), Ed. Universul Juridic.

Moreover, there is the requirement that the measure proposed is proportional to the objective pursued. The national parliaments have the right to take a stand in the application of this principle with regard to any legislative project and if one third of them consider inadequate the measure proposed, the European Commission has to reconsider it[432].

Norms of the Union with regard to respect for cultural diversity, for European cultures, for the European culture in its entirety, were gradually adopted, in parallel with the adoption of norms and documents concerning respect for human rights and fundamental freedoms.

The Maastricht Treaty of 1992 which established the European Union enounced in its preamble the willingness of member States to deepen the solidarity among their peoples, while respecting their history, culture and traditions. According to the Treaty, the Union will respect the national identities of member States, whose systems of government are based on principles of democracy, and will respect human fundamental rights as they are guaranteed by the European Convention of 1950 for the protection of fundamental human rights and freedoms and as they result from the constitutional common traditions of member States.

According to changes brought by the Amsterdam Treaty of 1997, the Treaty on the European Union provides that the Union is based on the principles of freedom, democracy, respect for human rights and fundamental freedoms and of the state of law, as principles common to member States.

The summits of the European Council of Amsterdam and Nyssa introduced also important changes in the treaty concerning the European Community. According to these new provisions, the European Community shall contribute to the flourishing of cultures of member States while respecting their national and regional diversity and at the same time promoting their common cultural heritage.

The action of the Community shall aim to encourage the cooperation between member States and when necessary to support their action towards the amelioration of knowledge and dissemination of culture and history of European peoples and towards the preservation and protection of cultural heritage with European significance. It is also indicated that, in its activity according to other provisions of the Treaty, the Community will take into consideration the cultural aspects, in particular with the purpose to respect and promote the diversity of cultures.

The Charter of fundamental rights of the European Union adopted in 2000 at the Nice summit and finalized in Strasbourg in 2007 proclaims in its preamble that „ The Union contributes to the preservation and development of these common values (the indivisible and universal values of human dignity, freedom, equality and solidarity, enounced in the preceding paragraph), respecting the diversity of cultures and traditions of European peoples, as well as the national identity of member States and the organization of their public authorities at the national, regional and local levels…".

The Charter provides for the respect of equal rights, the interdiction of any discrimination based *inter alia* on race or ethnic origin, as well as respect of cultural, linguistic and religious diversity of persons.

The Lisbon Treaty of 2007 takes up in substance and sometimes *expressis verbis* these provisions. According to this Treaty, the Union respects the richness of its cultural and linguistic diversity and sees that the European cultural heritage is protected and developed; the Union respects the equality of member States with respect to treaties, as well as their national identity, inherent to their fundamental political and constitutional structures.

The Union recognized by this Treaty the rights, freedoms and principles provided for in the Charter of fundamental rights as it was adopted in 2007 and granted it legal value equal to that of the treaties.

It is interesting to note the provision of the Treaty on the functioning of the Union, according to which the Council decides in unanimity on negotiation and conclusion of agreements in the field of trade with cultural and audio-visual services, in case where such agreements risk to endanger the cultural and linguistic diversity of the Union.

The Treaty confirms that the Union has 23 (presently 24) official languages.

The European Union law contains, thus, precise norms on the protection of cultural, linguistic and religious diversity, even in the Treaties of the Union. These norms aim both at the preservation and respect of the existing diversity and at extending the awareness and the promotion of diversity. This may have important legal and political consequences, meaning that member States as well as the institutions of the Union have to take measures to fulfill this objective.

As this is a field in which the Union has only competences of coordination and support for the member States, it can adopt compulsory regulations for member States only if they agree; the Union's institutions are obliged by the treaties, when they adopt regulations in other fields (including those concerning the internal market) to ensure respect

---

[432] Important clarifications on this aspects were made by the Lisbon Treaty of 2007; see Andrei Popescu, The Lisbon Treaty-changes and reform of the European Union, in Romanian Journal of Community Law nr. 2/2008, pp. 105-120; Diana Trascu, Marcela Monica Stoica, Lisbon Treaty-the engin necessary for the good functioning of the EU vehicle, ibidem, pp. 97-106.

for the European cultural diversity. If such a requirement would not be respected, such regulations can be challenged before the European Court of Justice.

Nevertheless, the Union's law may develop; as a result of the mobility of persons and of the new technologies, the need may appear to take stronger measures at the level of the Union in order to protect cultural values, the identity and diversity of cultures. The Lisbon Treaty, adopted by the heads of State and government in December 2007 does not exclude the adoption by the Union of compulsory regulations in the fields of culture, education, youth and the professional training, but excludes expressly the adoption of measures of legislative harmonization in these fields.

The cultural diversity exists also within the States; this concerns cultures which are specific to ethnic groups, to minorities and to indigenous peoples, meaning multiple cultural, linguistic and religious diversities. The norms of the Union's law contain the obligation for member States to take the necessary measures to protect diversity on their territory. Adopting measures which would endanger cultural diversity or which would tolerate acts against it may constitute a violation of the Union's law and open the way to an injunction of the European competent institutions.

It is also provided, as already mentioned, that for concluding international agreements in the field of trade of cultural or audio-visual services which could endanger the cultural diversity of the Union, the Council has to act in unanimity. These cultural goods and services have, as it was amply proved, a double significance: they can enter the civil circuit as commercial goods, but they are at the same time „vectors of identity, of values and feelings" and should not be treated as mere commodities or consumption goods[433]. Therefore, their preservation and protection in the patrimony of the respective peoples and access to them as part of the universal cultural heritage should be ensured.

The conception of respect for and preservation of identities and diversity can be observed within the European Union also in many aspects of its organization and functioning. The Union respects its multilingualism, having 24 official languages and ensuring translation of all documents in these languages. The presidency of the Council of the Union is ensured by rotation for 6 months by all member States; in the European Parliament (as in the consultative bodies-the Economic and Social Committee and the Committee of Regions) all member States are represented proportionally to the size of their population; the European Commission is formed of commissioners from all the member States, and in future they will be elected by rotation from all these States; the European Court of Justice and the Tribunal are formed of judges from all member States.

The Union respects the institutional autonomy of member States, at central, regional and local levels; although state bodies have to apply the Union's law which is of direct, immediate and exclusive application, and member States are responsible if the Union's law is not respected, each State organizes its system of institutions and bodies as it sees adequate; it is obvious that the constitutional structures of all 28 member States are different; the relationship between the head of State and the government is not the same; some States are federal, others are unitary; although the Union's law is applied everywhere, common law remains different from the continental law of roman inspiration; the judicial systems present many specificities. The Union is not proposing to eliminate these differences; on the contrary, it has for principle to respect the identity of member States and their institutional autonomy.

As we noted, the Maastricht Treaty created the institution of European citizenship; but the Union does not grant this citizenship; a European citizen is the person who has the citizenship of a member State, obtained according to its legislative system. The Amsterdam Treaty made it explicitly clear that European citizenship does not replace the national one, but complements it.

European citizens have the right to freely circulate and participate in economic activities in other member States, to take part in elections for the European Parliament, to take part in the local elections in the country where they have their residence, to submit petitions to European institutions and receive an answer in their language, to benefit of the diplomatic and consular protection from embassies of other member States in third States where their country is not represented at this level. Some rights related to the political system and to the identity of each State are nevertheless reserved to national citizens: participation to elections for the national parliament, occupation of functions which suppose the exercise of public authority and others[434].

The preoccupations for respecting the political diversity and national options are also reflected in the field of foreign policy and common security, which remains essentially a field of intergovernmental cooperation; decisions

---

[433] On the issue of the double significance of the cultural values and goods, see: UNESCO Universal Declaration on Cultural Diversity, adopted by the General Conference of UNESCO in 2003; UNESCO Convention on the protection and promotion of the diversity of cultural expressions, adopted by the General Conference on 20 October 2005.

[434] On this issue, Dumitru Mazilu, Relationship between the European citizenship and the national citizenship and the European identity in an integrated Europe, in Romanian Journal of Community Law nr. 2/2008, pp. 45-52.

are adopted as a rule by unanimity or on the basis of strategies adopted themselves by unanimity; the principle of constructive abstention , according to which a State may not participate in the adoption of a decision, is not opposing to its adoption, but is not obliged by it, follows the same orientation.

It is the same with the institution of strengthened cooperation, to which some member States may resort depending on their interests and possibilities, while respecting some conditions so as to avoid affecting the interests of other member States, which is also meant to maintain and respect some diversity of forms of integration and cooperation. The Monetary Union, the Schengen System, evolutions of some modalities in the field of the common defense are the expression of a „Europe with several speeds", which remains topical, in spite of the criticism it faced.

SECTION 3 - CULTURAL DIVERSITY in TERMS of RIGHTS and OBLIGATIONS

The conception of diversity is generally accepted as a principle of law at the international and European levels. It generates rights for communities and persons and obligations for States and international bodies.

First of all, this is about rights and obligations in the field of human rights and fundamental freedoms. States are obliged to respect those human values and rights which give the meaning and substance to diversity: equal rights and non-discrimination on grounds of race, colour, ethnic or national origin, language or religion; rights of persons directly related to the preservation and development of their identity (the benefit and the development of their own culture, the use of mother tongue in public and in private, the professing and practicing of their own religion, the preservation and the practice of their traditions and customs); the preservation of the identity of communities living on their territory; the expression and the development of different cultures, their interaction; wide access to all cultures and the international cooperation in this field.

Respect of these rights and values imposes to States several types of conduct: respect by themselves, involving all state bodies, of these rights and values, which supposes abstaining from any obstacles, discrimination or other violations; protection of these rights and values against violations from any other persons, legal or moral, which means the adoption of legislative, administrative and other measures for their protection and the application of sanctions to those guilty of such violations; ensuring the exercise of some rights and the protection of some values in such cases where States have to create material conditions for their exercise and protection (preservation and development of minority or regional cultures, teaching of less spoken languages, maintaining and foster some traditions which may imply efforts and expenses that the State has to contribute with, as obligations towards their own citizens, their own peoples).

International organizations also have obligations according to their constituent treaties: to promote and sometimes to monitor the application by member States of commitments taken concerning respect for human rights; to initiate and to promote international regulations which may become necessary for that purpose; to react mainly when massive violations of human rights take place often directed against minority groups, putting in danger their identity and survival, in order to bring an end to such violations.

Organizations of integration, like the European Union, are bearers of more comprehensive obligations in this field; they have to ensure themselves respect for human rights and the diversity of persons and communities, of the identity of member States, through their activity of regulation in the fields of their competence; they also have to monitor how member States are respecting these rights and values, according to the commitments taken within the organization, using means of constraint, including their judiciary system.

At the international level, these organizations have to promote in their relations with other organizations and States, such activities and regulations which would not endanger their own cultural diversity and identities, as well as in other parts of the world.

It is of particular importance to promote an adequate management of cultural diversity and of the preservation and development of identities, both at the national level and by international organizations. Because the preservation of diversity and of identities supposes measures of States in favour of minority groups and cultures, it is necessary to ensure an appropriate balance at the level of the society in its entirety, so as to avoid discontent and trouble which may be source of conflict.

Special measures which have to be taken in favour of disadvantaged groups, in order to ensure the exercise of human rights in conditions of equality, have to be temporary and avoid to creating distinct rights for different groups. Permanent measures in order to ensure the exercise of some specific rights of minority groups to enjoy their own culture, to use their mother tongue and to practice their religion have to concord with the general situation of the respective country and avoid creating privileges. These are requirements which have to be followed also by international organizations both in their activity of monitoring and of elaboration of new standards. It is thus necessary to ensure a correct management of diversity.

* * *

It is necessary to understand that diversity and identities are not static and rigid; on the contrary, cultures evoluate as a result of social needs and mainly of the interaction and exchanges with other cultures, while identities tend to acquire new facets as a result of interdependence. The trends to uniformization, generated by globalization, are confronted with the reaction of identities and of cultures which feel threatened. History proves that a series of cultures disappeared and the monuments which they left behind show how advanced they were for their time.

The problem the States and their different forms of cooperation, mainly the international organizations, have to solve is not only to preserve diversity, different cultures and identities, as vestiges of the past, but mainly to ensure the development of the existing cultures in a climate of tolerance, of coexistence and mutual interaction. Policies of interculturalism and multiculturalism are thus necessary for promoting the development of each culture and identity but also fertile exchanges, a wider and an unlimited access to all cultures, to the universal culture. To achieve such an objective makes it necessary to adopt measures of a legislative and administrative nature, as well as an extended process of education of the entire population in the spirit of openness, understanding and tolerance towards other cultures and identities.

The world will continue to be diverse and the identities will continue to exist, without being static. States and international organizations have to act so that diversity is not a ground of intolerance, of rejection and conflict, both at the individual and at the collective levels, that it is treated correctly, with understanding and respect, as an opportunity for mutual spiritual enrichment. Therefore, particular attention should be given to the evolution of cultural diversity and of identities in the world, in each country.

CHAPTER XV - LINGUISTIC DIVERSITY and LANGUAGES in DANGER

ABSTRACT

Some 6-8 thousand languages are spoken in the world; most of them are in danger to become extinct, due to demographic natural or societal changes. Some of them are official or national, but many of them have no alphabet and are only oral; they are mostly in danger.

Still, a language is important for the persons and communities using it as a vehicle for communication, for access to culture and knowledge and for the transmission of cultures and traditions to future generations. The extinction of a language means a loss of an element of identity of persons and groups, a first step for cultures and traditions to disappear. Besides being an essential element of culture, the language opens the way to participate in social and political life. That is why minority groups are often trying to preserve and develop their mother tongue. In many parts of the world efforts are made to revival some languages at risk to disappear.

UNESCO is encouraging and supporting such efforts. Of crucial importance are efforts deployed by UNESCO for developing the means allowing the use of internet in many languages, taking into account the increasing place it takes in disseminating information and as a means of communication, in particular in the fields of education, science and culture.

KEY WORDS: human diversity, language diversity, linguistic policy, public good, dialect, vulnerable, at risk, in danger, extinct languages, society of knowledge, technologies of information, unique code, code with multilingual characters, multilingualism.

INTRODUCTION

According to the UN Charter, determined to affirm their confidence in fundamental human rights, in the dignity and value of human beings, the United Nations fixed as their objective to achieve international cooperation in the promotion and respect of human rights and fundamental freedoms for all, without distinction as to race, sex, language or religion, and undertook to promote the universal respect of these rights and freedoms. This is giving expression to the conception of human diversity and clearly affirming that it cannot be a ground for not respecting human rights or for inequality.

Number of international documents developed this conception, promoting among others, the diversity of languages and linguistic rights. The Universal Declaration of Human Rights, adopted in 1948, recognizes from the beginning the inherent dignity and equal and inalienable rights to all members of human family, as a basis of justice, freedom and peace in the world. According to substantial provisions of the Declaration, all human beings are born free and equal in dignity and rights; they are entitled to enjoy all rights and freedoms without any distinction, namely on grounds of race, colour, sex, language, religion, public or other opinion, national or social origin, fortune, descent or other status.

The Covenant on civil and political rights resumes the provisions of the Universal Declaration on dignity and human rights and develops the provisions about the political freedoms mentioned. As already mentioned, according to the Covenant, in such States where there are ethnic, religious and linguistic minorities, persons belonging to these minorities have the rights, in community with other members of their group, to enjoy their own culture, to profess and practice their own religion and to use their own language.

Other international conventions follow also objectives which aim at the protection of human diversity of peoples, communities and persons[435]. The Convention of 1948 on the prevention and repression of the crime of genocide has the purpose to protect the existence of human groups who are different from others, providing for the interdiction and the punishment of crimes of a series of acts pursuing the destruction of human groups on grounds of race, ethnic origin or religion, that is to protect human diversity.

The 1965 Convention for the elimination of all forms of racial discrimination provides for the interdiction and the elimination of any distinction, restriction, exclusion or preference on grounds of race, colour, decent, or ethnic or national origin, which have as purpose or effect inequalities in the exercise of human rights and fundamental freedoms. Among the human rights mentioned in this Convention there are the freedom of thought, of conscience

---

[435] Extensive presentation of these documents by Ion Diaconu, Human Rights in Contemporary International Law, theory and practice (in Romanian), Ed. Lumina Lex, 2010, pp. 24-26.

and religion, the freedom of opinion and expression and the right of equal participation in cultural activities. That means, essentially, to protect human diversity against acts of discrimination based particularly on elements of diversity.

It became necessary, in the conditions of development of interdependences and globalization, at the end of the twentieth century and the beginning of the new millennium, to recognize the existence of different cultures and languages, to develop exchanges and cooperation among human communities behind them and to promote conceptions about inter-culturalism and multiculturalism of the modern societies as well as the dialogue between civilizations.

According to the Declaration of the Millennium, adopted by the Resolution of the UN General Assembly nr. 55/2 of 8 September 2000, heads of State and government placed "Tolerance" among the fundamental values which should lie at the basis of international relations in the twentieth century, affirming the following: "People have to respect themselves mutually in all diversity of their beliefs, cultures and languages. Differences which exist within societies and among them should not produce fear or repression, but should be venerated as priceless goods of humanity. It is necessary to actively promote a culture of peace and dialogue among all civilizations". The heads of State and government undertook to promote more harmony and tolerance in all societies.

In 2003, the General Conference of UNESCO adopted the Universal Declaration on cultural diversity which asks States, among others, to encourage linguistic diversity and to support the expression, creation and dissemination of culture in as many languages as possible, to respect and to protect traditional knowledge, mainly that of indigenous peoples. In order to ensure cultural diversity, the Declaration underlines the importance of the realization of the cultural rights provided(the right to expression, creation and dissemination of works in mother tongue, the right to participate in cultural life and the right to exercise one's own cultural practices). The Declaration insists that "all cultures should be expressed and make themselves known" and adds that "The freedom of expression, pluralism of the media, plurality of languages, equal access to artistic expression, to scientific and technologic knowledge, including in numeric form, as well as the possibility for all cultures to be present in the means of expression and dissemination, are the guarantees of cultural diversity".

In 2005, after laborious preparation and negotiations, the General Conference of UNESCO adopted the Convention on the protection and promotion of the diversity of cultural expressions. The Convention resumes and develops the principles of the Declaration of 2003 and insists on rights and obligations of States to respect them. The Convention defines the cultural expressions as the ensemble of forms of expression and transmission of culture, including through diverse means of artistic creation, of production, dissemination and distribution of cultural expression and of benefiting of them, irrespective of the means and technologies used, that is in a more extended meaning than the traditional concept of cultural goods and services.

The cultural diversity is presented as a fact deriving from the originality and diversity characterizing groups, communities and societies which form the world. Without mentioning explicitly linguistic diversity, it is obvious that the diversity of cultural expressions implies mainly the cultural expressions through the national language, mother tongue or another language freely chosen.

SECTION 1 - IMPORTANCE of LANGUAGES and of LINGUISTIC DIVERSITY

Some schools of thought, giving expression to clear objectives and reflecting obvious social practices, presented majority languages as vehicles of modernity and mobility, having an instrumental value, and the minority ones as carriers of culture and traditions, having a sentimental value[436]. This conception is much too simplified and incorrect; minority languages can also be vehicles of modernity and mobility, if they are studied and used adequately; majority languages also have an instrumental value, and undoubtedly carry cultures and traditions, as well as the feelings of the majority populations.

In reality, for the groups who are using them, languages represent essential goods, having an intrinsic value, because: each language is the expression of a culture, with all this entails (richness of ideas, of creation, of traditions and customs); each language is a treasure of knowledge about nature, about environment and human relations, about means of production and others, perceiving and presenting reality in their specific way; each language is itself a human creation , with its specific script, sound, grammar structure and syntax; it offers persons and groups the

---

[436] Stephen May, Misconceived Minority Language Rights; Implications for Liberal Political Theory, in Language Rights and Political Theory, ed. W. Kymlicka, A. Patten, Oxford University Press 2003, pp. 123-152.

understanding about their place in society and the way towards social solidarity with those using it; it is unique for its speakers, as the central element of their identity[437].

That is why the extinction of a language means a loss of a paramount element of identity of persons and groups, while at the international level it means the disappearance of forms of the immaterial cultural heritage, consisting in social practices, rituals and events, oral traditions and expressions of the respective community. Mother tongue is, thus, one of the fundamental human resources; nevertheless, it is an extremely fragile resource, as well as the diversity of species of plants and animals[438].

Therefore, the loss of a language represents an impoverishment of humanity from many points of view, as it means the loss of knowledge and achievements of human spirit, of ways of organizing life, with their discoveries and progress, which may still be important for people. This is true, of course, for all languages, be they spoken by the majority or by a minority; one cannot say that some of them are more valuable than others. A commercial approach, based on the costs implied by the preservation or the revitalization of a language, is not acceptable in this field, being in contradiction with respect for human rights. Of course, this does not mean to maintain artificially some languages, if there is no human and social basis to use them or against the individual will of persons, against their rights to freely choose their cultural and linguistic references. A just linguistic policy has to start from fundamental human rights and freedoms and from the principles of a democratic society.

The loss of a language has also adverse effects for the communication with other persons, for transmitting and receiving opinions and information, experience and knowledge, in the last instance on the exercise of many human rights. The loss or the restriction of the use of minority languages impedes also upon biological diversity, because the traditional knowledge about animal and vegetable nature expressed by languages spoken by diverse communities represents also methods of sustainable exploitation of natural resources, of respect for ecosystems and of their judicious management. As it is well known, these resources and ecosystems are endangered by intensive and destructive exploitation and by the climate changes it produces. Consequently, it should be accepted that it is in the interest of all to preserve the languages in danger.

Cultures and languages are social phenomena evolving and responding to a great number of challenges from the environment in which they operate; if this environment is radically changed, their space of action may reduce until disappearing. Thus, there is the danger to lose the languages which are not supported by strong communities determined to preserve their linguistic identity; this threat becomes a problem when it is the result of discrimination or of exclusion from the State or from other communities.

Of course, the extinction of mother tongues did not start in our century; this is a lengthy process, extending to the duration of several generations. Nevertheless, it is a foreseeable process for any language, if it is not transmitted to new generations. In many cases, historic injustices, colonization and imperial policies lie at the origin of the loss of some languages. Still, researchers are concerned nowadays by the dramatic pace of extinction of spoken languages; they present as causes of this evolution the national State, migrations, the phenomena of industrialization and modernity and globalization. According to some scholars, the causes of losing a language could be: present discrimination against it; past discrimination based on the linguistic status; refusal to grant an official status to the language in the political field; unequal advantages resulting from the status of minority languages[439].

The process of disappearance of languages is viewed as evolving at five levels: a vulnerable language is that which is studied by a decreasing number of children; a language in danger is that which is spoken only by adults; a language in serious danger is that which is spoken only by aged people; a language in critical situation is that which is spoken by a few aged speakers; a language is extinct if it is not spoken any more[440]. As this is a process, one can imagine also other stages, as much as the revival in the existence of a language which cannot be excluded as a result of the evolution of communities of speakers.

Almost all languages which have no alphabet, are not written and are only oral, although they are still used by the respective communities and transmitted to new generations, are vulnerable and are exposed to becoming obsolete. Many languages have an alphabet, which creates the condition and premise for written use, for the creation and for the transmission to future generations in that form; still, this is not an absolute guarantee, as there are languages having an alphabet and a well-established literary form, but they are in danger due to the phenomena of modernity, mainly due to the dramatic reduction of the number of persons speaking them.

---

[437] Denise Réaume, Beyond Personnality: the Territorial and Personal Principles of Language policy Reconsidered, in Language Rights and Political Theory, W. Kymlicka, A. Patten(eds.), Oxford University Press, New-York, 2003, p. 283.
[438] Atlas des langues en péril dans le monde, 1996, UNESCO, p. 8, 17.
[439] Michael Blake, Language Death and Liberal Politics, in Language Rights and Political Theory, p. 220.
[440] Atlas des langues en danger, p. 11.

Researchers tried first to elaborate criteria to establish what languages are in danger, because the situation of languages spoken in the world is extremely different: from the official to those spoken by small communities or by a limited number of aged persons, from those spoken by communities living concentrated in a territory to those spoken by people dispersed in one or several States; some languages are only oral, without alphabet; moreover, languages which are national or spoken by the majority in some States may be in danger to disappear in other States. The simpler criterion which defines the situation of a language in danger is considered to be the fact that it is not transmitted to young generations. This may be caused either by policies or measures of impeding the transmission, by the lack of institutions and means of transmission or by the loss of interest in mother tongue due to the integration of speakers in communities speaking a language which is official, majority or of a wider circulation[441]. Some languages evolve by the modification of syntax and vocabulary, suffering limited or substantial changes; others evolve by a rapprochement to the languages spoken by the majority of the population, until the assimilation with them.

Linguistic diversity is, in turn, considered a public good with its own value and benefiting to all, which has to be protected as the expression of a more dynamic world, of different cultures, as an expression of human differences, as well as a set of collective human achievements and manifestations of creativity and originality, adding a positive value to human life at the universal level[442]. At the same time, the languages of indigenous peoples are considered to have also a scientific value, taking into account the experience and knowledge they can transmit[443].

The restriction of the linguistic diversity is a general phenomenon, concerning all continents and almost all countries in the world. The Atlas of languages in danger, published by UNESCO in 1996[444], signaled this evolution provoking the reaction of linguistic communities and specialists, of the media and civil society. The third edition of the Atlas, published in 2009[445], points out to the serious and urgent situation of languages which are vulnerable, in danger or on the way to disappear; moreover, it makes a thorough analysis in order to better understand the causes of this phenomenon and to define a set of ways and means to counter such an evolution.

The message of UNESCO is clear: to act as quickly as possible to stop the destruction of cultural values through the extinction of languages which give expression to these values, to reverse this evolution by resuming, reviving and extending the use of those languages which are now vulnerable or in a critical situation. If the attachment of speakers to their mother tongue is the decisive factor for the survival of languages in danger, it has to be promoted and supported by policies and measures in various fields of public life, beginning with education in mother tongue and its intergeneration transmission.

The Resolution 61/266 of 2007 of the UN General Assembly proclaimed 2008 as the International Year of Languages and invited UNESCO to serve as the leading agency in this field. UNESCO analyzed in particular the application of policies concerning national languages and their impact in 2009, 2010 ad 2011; then it published the Atlas concerning languages which are in danger or disappearing in the world. UNESCO concentrated mainly on "facilitating the development of activities meant to respect, to promote and protect all languages, in particular those in danger, as well as linguistic diversity and multilingualism".

According to this message, languages are essential not only for the identity of groups and persons and for their peaceful coexistence, but are also a strategic factor of progress towards sustainable development and to attain those objectives contained in the Programme of action concerning "Education for all; let's implement our collective commitments", adopted by the Education Forum of Dakar in April 2000 and in the Objectives of Development of the Millennium.

Reports of UNESCO enumerate activities in different States in this field in 2008 and 2009, mainly activities in the fields of education and of languages in danger. Many of these activities referred to languages of indigenous peoples, but also to languages in China and Vietnam. Other activities mentioned are aimed at cultural exchanges and translations, activities of the civil society and the use of languages in the cyberspace, projects on indigenous languages and the role of languages in socializing and integrating people.

The conception about linguistic diversity includes also the attitude towards dialects of official languages or of other languages spoken on the territory of a State or even on the territory of other States. As practice shows, it is difficult to distinguish languages from their dialects; objective criteria can be applied sometimes and measured in

---

[441] Atlas des langues en danger..., p. 11-12.

[442] Daniel Nettle, Suzanne Romaine, Vanishing Voices: the Extinction of the World's Languages, New-York, Oxford University Press, 2000, p. 43; Idil Boran, Global Linguistic Diversity, Public Goods and the Principle of Fairness, in Language Rights And Political Theory, p. 198.

[443] Nettle, Romaine, p. 60.

[444] Atlas des langues en péril dans le monde, 1996, Ed. UNESCO, dir. S. Wurm.

[445] Atlas des langues en danger dans le monde, 2009, Ed. UNESCO, ed. Christofer Moseley; other works on this subject Ethnologue: Languages of the World, 2009, SIL International and Encyclopedia of the world endangered languages, Ch. Moseley, 2007.

percentage-common vocabulary, mutual intelligibility, morphological and syntactic analysis; nevertheless, such criteria do not respond to all situations; very often, the differentiation is difficult and can be contested and sometimes is based on political considerations and leads to restraining the use of some linguistic varieties. Speakers are sometimes writing in the literary language and use dialectal expression in their oral communication.

Therefore, in its studies UNESCO adopts an elastic approach and hesitates to make the difference between languages and dialects, treating them alike and emphasizing only the number of speakers and if the language is standardized or only oral. In a study elaborated within the United Nations on this issue, no distinction is made between language and dialect; it take as a starting point the history of languages, which shows that different dialects, far from being imperfect versions of languages, developed almost independently, are not less systematized than the languages, have their rules concerning grammar structures, pronunciation and vocabulary and are not less adequate for the needs of communication in the social context where they are spoken[446].

One has to take into account also that some varieties, practically new languages, developed at the contact between some local languages and the colonial powers; it is evaluated for instance that 77 Creole languages were created by the colonization, at the contact of local languages with French, Dutch, Portuguese, Russian, Spanish, as well as many others created on the basis of English[447].

SECTION 2 - LANGUAGES in DANGER-EVOLUTION and CAUSES

The number of mother tongues spoken in the world is evaluated at 6000-9000[448]. Many of them are vulnerable or in danger, and more than 2000 are spoken by less than 1000 persons. There are notable differences from continent to continent and in the same continent from area to area. Some 90% of the population of the world would speak 100 of the more diffused languages, while some 6000 languages would be spoken by 10% of the world population. More than 300 languages have an official status in different States. The text of the Universal Declaration on Human Rights is published in more than 320 different languages, including Chinese (with more than 1 billion speakers), followed by English, Russian, Arab, French, Spanish and others. The greatest linguistic diversity is in Africa (2390 languages), followed by Oceania (1322) and South-East Asia (1317)[449].

The international and regional diversity is not static, but suffers the influence of social-historic events, such as massive migration, colonization, wars, endemic diseases and others. Languages become more and more territorial, due to the concentration in larger communities as a result of urbanization, which leads to their loss in the areas of traditional use; some languages are used also increasingly only in private and family life, while in other fields the official or the common language is used for communication. The extension of the use of English in fields of the modern economy (banks, telecommunications, scientific research, tourism), determines the introduction of English in school and the reduction of the use of less spoken languages. The most languages in danger are those of the indigenous peoples; this loss is viewed as a symbol of the more general crisis of biodiversity, as a huge loss of knowledge, because indigenous languages contain a great richness of ecological information, which is lost with them[450]. If this pace is maintained, it is estimated that more than half of the languages spoken in the world will disappear till 2050[451].

Therefore, linguistic diversity is in danger; this is seen not only in the extinction of less spoken languages, but also by the spreading in the world of goods with general cultural contents in the form of advertising of other types of consumption goods, of socio-political models of society, which represent the expression of other cultures and languages. Consequently, because ethnic, cultural and linguistic diversity is threatened, it cannot be left to the free evolution and it is considered that it has to be the subject of a political intervention in modern societies[452].

In Africa[453], the most frequent phenomenon which leads to the extinction of some mother tongues is their evolution in contact with languages spoken by more important communities; the latter gain ground, being used also as languages of communication, as for instance Swahili in Eastern Africa, Hawsa in Western Africa, Wolof in some

---

[446] Cicle d'études consacré aux sociétés multinationales, doc. ST/TAO/HR/23, 1999.

[447] Ethnologue: Languages of the World, 2009.

[448] Victor Ginsburgh, Shlome Weber, How many Languages Do We Need?, 2011, p. 32, Princeton University Press.

[449] Data contained in the UNESCO publication Mesurer la diversité linguistique sur Internet, UNESCO 2005, p. 52.

[450] Alan Patten, Will Kymlicka, Introduction, Language Rights and Political Theory: Context, Issues and Approaches in Language Rights and Political Theory, p. 10.

[451] Ibidem, p. 54.

[452] François Grinn, Diversity as Paradigm, Analytical Device and Policy Goal, in Language Rights and Political Theory, p. 179.

[453] Data presented in the following pages are based on the Atlas des langues en danger dans le monde, ed. Christofer Moseley, UNESCO 2009, p. 21 and following.

States on the Atlantic shore, mainly in Senegal, Amharic in Ethiopia, or languages developed on the basis of English or French, to the expense of other languages which reduce their use. This derives also from the orientation of the population towards systems of value of other African communities, with a more modern economic occupation (cattle breeding instead of hunting/collecting), from the changes in the environment and displacement of the population in other areas where another language is used. As a whole, the small African communities should have sufficient economic and cultural conditions in order to maintain mother tongues as a means of communication.

In the Middle East, armed conflicts had serious consequences on minority languages, the respective communities being decimated or obliged to emigrate (in Iraq the Assyrian group, as well as speakers of Aramean and Mandean languages, in Syria the speakers of the Syriac language, everywhere the speakers of Iudeo-arabic languages).

In Europe, some languages in danger are closely related to national languages, being considered dialects from the socio-linguistic point of view; from the Uralian family for instance Latvian languages such as Voro-seto, Carelian and Olonetian; Slavic languages such as Torlak, spoken in the South of Serbia, closer to Bulgarian; Kachoube, language considered a dialect of Polish; the Polesian language spoken in the border area between Poland, Belarus and Ukraine; Germanic languages such as Frisian in Holland and Germany; Scanian and Gutniska, dialects of the Swedish; and Jute, distinct from Danish; among the Celtic languages, Breton in France, Gaelic in United Kingdom, Norman language in Anglo-Norman islands; as Romanic languages, Corsican, Languedoc, Provencal, Limousin and Auvergnat in France; Piemontan, Ligurian and Venetian in Italy; Aromanian in Romania and in Balkan States; the language spoken by so-called Vlachs in Serbia and in other Balkan States, a variety of Romanian; Megleno-Romanian in Greece; in Spain, Asturian, Leonese and Galician in different provinces; among the languages of the Indo-European group, Romani with its varieties (Carpathian, Balkanic, Kalo-Finish, Sinte and Gaelic), Tat and Juhuri spoken in the Caucasus and Zazaki spoken in Turkey and others.

Some of these languages are in danger as a result of processes of economic and social integration, others due to migrations and to the reduction of number of speakers, and others due to restrictive linguistic policies. In spite of efforts made in some Nordic States, there are also in danger the languages Sami, spoken by indigenous peoples in Norway, Sweden and Finland, different among those States and sometimes within the same country; in the Russian Federation in the European area Carelian, Olonetian and Lude languages, and in Siberia, Buriat, Nenets, Mansi, Even, Ciulim and other languages.

In Asia, which hosts very many languages spoken, but also most of the languages in danger, the situations are very diverse. The area of Central Asian mountains Pamir and Karakorum hosts many languages of the family of Iranian Oriental languages (Whaki, Ishkashimi, Yaghnobi), Occidental Iranian (Parachi, Ormuri, Ashtiani), Turkish (Bukhari, Dungana, Parya), Nuristan (Prasun, Waigali, Ashkun), and Dard (Kunar, Chitrali, Gowro); these languages have no official status, are spoken by communities in continuous numerical diminishing and many of them without a written form.

Some of them lost ground in favour of other local languages spoken by stronger communities-Pachtu, Dari, Tajik and Uzbek. In Manchuria languages such Bargu, Buriat, Eleut-Manchou, Evenki are in danger; they can be found on both sides of borders, many without written form and spoken by less numerous communities. In Central Asia, dominated by Turkish, Mongol and Chinese Mandarin, there are in danger to disappear languages such as Oara, Ordos, oriental and occidental Yougur, some Tibetan dialects, as well as Manchou and Tunguza.

In India and the area of Himalaya there is a true mosaic of languages, dominated by the languages Hindi, Urdu, Benghali and Nepalese; some 300 languages are in danger, among them Darai, Darma, Kudmali in Nepal, all Tibetan-Burmese languages in Bhutan, Manipuri, Meitei, Bodo, Mizo, Garo Khazi and many others in India, Sak and Mru in Bangladesh, Vedda in Sri-Lanka.

In South-East Asia, Austro-Asiatic languages are spoken, mainly those of Khmer origin, Sino-Tibetan and Austro- Thai. There are in danger: in Cambodia languages such as Cham de West, Jarai, Thai-Khadai; in Laos Idu, Arem, Bana and some of Thai languages; in Malaysia Orang, Seletar, Urak, Lawoi, Temuan; in Myanmar Chawte, Mru and Sak; in the Philippines all Austronesien languages, such as Agta, Alta, Atta; in Singapore some languages from India or Malaysia, as well as varieties of Chinese which are different from the Mandarin; in Thailand Mon, Mlabri, Thavung; in Vietnam O'du, Thai Kaddao and three languages Gelao are in critical situation; in the South of China languages from the Sino-Tibetan, Austro Thai, Hmong Mien, Mon-Khmer, as well as varieties of Chinese different from Mandarin are in danger. In Indonesia, a quarter of the 600 languages spoken are considered vulnerable or in danger; in Papua New Guinea, Solomon, Vanuatu, New Caledonia, Micronesia and Polynesia many local languages are in danger.

Some of these languages are spoken in several countries in the area and are in different situations in these States; from those official or spoken by important communities in some States to those in a process of extinction. Among the most important causes there are: the increase of the place occupied by official languages, such as

Russian, Tajik, Uzbek in the respective States, Pachtou and Urdu in Pakistan, Hindi in India, Mandarin in China, Nepalese in Nepal, Lao in Laos, Malaysian in Malaysia, Philippino in Philippines, Indonesian in Indonesia, to the expenses of languages spoken by smaller communities; the reduction of the number of speakers, as a result of internal and international migration; economic and social situation of many minority groups; dispersion and location at large distances of the small communities speaking some of these languages; conflicts in Iraq, Afghanistan and in other places in the area; linguistic policies of States which either promote official languages or recognize and support only some minority languages, or adopt an indifferent position on this issue, which means that they give no support to languages in danger; lack of vocabulary and of the written form; the expansion of English in States as Bhutan and Singapore, in insular States of Pacific area, and in some parts of India.

As a result, many of these languages are not studied in school, which means that their intergenerational transmission is difficult. It is mainly in continental Asia that some languages are spoken in several neighbouring States, in some of them vigorous, spoken even by majorities, in others in danger; in some States these languages have their alphabet, are literary languages, while in other countries they are only oral. In other countries there is a common written language, while oral languages are completely different. The linguistic diversity in the Asiatic area is also characterized by the multitude of symbols used: Chinese, Japanese, Indian, Thai, Lao, Cambodian (khmer), Myanmar and others.

In Australia, the majority of Aboriginal languages are in danger due to policies of integration adopted for centuries. It is only in 2004 that a plan was officially launched for Aboriginal languages in one of the component States. An effort of revitalization of some of these languages is made since several decades in different areas inhabited by Aborigines, beginning with the process of education of children in their mother tongues; it is still difficult to evaluate the effects of these efforts and how many of the several hundred Aboriginal languages will resist.

In South America, in spite of the recognition of indigenous languages through constitutions and laws and of intensified research on these languages, many of the 400 indigenous languages are in danger due to the reduction of the number of speakers, to a lack of motivation to transmit them to young generations and to the massive adoption of dominant European languages (Spanish and Portuguese). In Columbia the prolonged conflicts led to displacement of populations, which affected indigenous languages; in Brazil, where the indigenous most spoken language is Tikuna, with some 30 thousand speakers, the small number of speakers of other languages leads to their gradual extinction; in Venezuela languages spoken by relatively isolated populations (Awake, Kaliana) are in danger; even in Paraguay, where Guarani is the majority language, other indigenous languages are in danger; in Argentina, languages which are strong in neighbouring States are still spoken, such as Guarani and Checiua; other indigenous languages are on the way to extinction; in Chili, the language spoken by the population Mapuche maintains itself in spite of difficulties, but other indigenous languages are in danger; in the Andin countries(Ecuador, Peru, Bolivia) Checiua and Aymara are generally spoken, but other languages are in danger as a result of displacements of populations and attraction of cities, due to the conditions of life.

In Mexico, more than 100 indigenous languages are in danger or in a critical situation, as a result of internal migration and of frequent recourse to the lingua franca, Spanish; in countries of Central America languages as Maya, Garifuna and Miskito are still spoken, but many others are in danger.

What is characteristic for the majority of Latin-American States is the official recognition of indigenous languages, in some of them as official languages at national or regional levels, as well as efforts for their study in school, often in education of a bilingual kind and academic research on these languages.

In the United States, due to the small number of speakers and to the opposition to bilingualism and the pressure of the dominant English culture, in spite of efforts of linguistic indigenous communities (Karuk in California, Navajo in Arizona) without any support from the authorities, few of the indigenous languages which survived are still learned by children. More chances seem to have Spanish, due to the large number of immigrants which is increasing. In Canada Inukticut is still spoken by Inuits, Ojibway is spoken by the First Nations and a series of mixed languages are spoken by Matis. Other languages are in danger due to the geographic distance where speakers live. In general, all indigenous languages are in danger due to migration, to the mixing of populations, to the dominant influence of English and French and because the indigenous population of Canada suffers a process of aging, which makes difficult the intergenerational transmission of mother tongues.

SECTION 3 - EFFORTS for PRESERVING LESS SPOKEN LANGUAGES

In spite of the difficult situations mentioned in all continents, in different parts of the world there are initiatives, programmes and measures for preserving, sometimes for revitalizing some of the languages in danger to disappear. It is admitted that an indispensable condition for preserving and developing a language is to transmit it to young generations. For this purpose, there are efforts to reintroduce some languages in education, even if only in private schools, while some languages are promoted at the level of intellectual circles through studies, publications and broadcasts; in some regions or States institutional efforts are made through international treaties and institutions for promoting regional or minority languages.

It was also proved in many regions that the extension of cultural activities contributes to revitalizing minority languages and that a dynamic relationship operates between linguistic policies, the attitude towards the local cultures and revitalization of local languages[454]. The three factors sustaining the preservation, the development and revitalization of languages are the family, the community and the education in school.

In Europe, many of the languages spoken in the nation States are in competition with the language spoken by the majorities, which makes necessary efforts for their preservation. It was also noted that many languages in danger are related to the official language, with its literary form and are considered dialects; consequently, there are no preoccupations for their protection. In other States, political preoccupations, very often related to their history, are retaining States to recognize and to protect some local languages, although spoken by relatively many speakers (Silesian language in Poland, Latgalian in Latvia)[455].

In some States there are efforts for revitalizing traditional languages in parallel with political evolutions towards the establishment of regimes of autonomy. For instance, in the United Kingdom, while Celtic languages suffered important losses throughout centuries, in the Wales the Cornik language (spoken in the area of Cornuailles) was institutionalized in partially bilingual system. The system of education in Gaelic is well established and knows a positive evolution; more than 50 thousand students in primary school use this language as a medium of education in 600 schools (1/3 of the total), as well as in 200 secondary schools. In 1981 the Law on television was adopted and a TV channel was created in this language. In Scotland, a simplified system of education was established, consisting in subventions granted by the Scottish ministry of education for the education in mother tongue and the dissemination of educational material in this language in primary schools; to respond to the request of parents, a programme of tertiary education was created and administrative measures were taken to pursue and to develop the education in that language.

Efforts are made to establish and to disseminate TV programmes in the local language. In Northern Ireland, the use of the Irish language suffered as a result of the political situation and of the conflict between the protestant and catholic churches; the authorities of Northern Ireland adopted beginning with the 1990 a more favourable policy for the education in Irish. In Spain, the Catalan, Basque and Galician languages are recognized as national languages and are the object of linguistic policies of the respective provinces. In Italy, the French in the area of Vale d'a Osta and German in the province of Bolzano are at the basis of the regime of autonomy applied to these areas.

As presented above, in the European region the Council of Europe adopted in 1992 a legal instrument and created a mechanism for promoting and protecting traditional languages spoken on the continent, the European Charter for regional or minority languages, to which 25 States are parties. The application of the Charter is monitored by a committee of experts from the States parties, which makes visits and has discussions with the authorities and the representatives of speakers of these languages and then considers periodic reports of States parties and makes recommendations to States parties which are submitted to the Committee of ministers of the Council. Obviously, this regulation and mechanism cover most of the languages in danger, because they are usually the traditional, regional or minority languages, including those spoken by indigenous peoples in the Nordic States.

At the same time, leaving aside that only 25 States of the continent are parties to the Charter (bigger States as Russian Federation, France, Turkey, Italy are not parties), the scheme of ratification allows States to choose only some languages, to place them in one or the other category of protection and to accept commitments à la carte, which limits from the beginning the level of protection of languages in danger. In spite of these limits, the Committee of experts deploys a complex and substantial activity, considering the periodic reports, pursuing the promotion of the respective languages through repeated recommendations and insisting for their application. Other provisions concerning the protection of minority languages are adopted in the Framework Convention for the protection of national minorities of 1995; its application is also followed by a committee of experts.

In Africa, efforts in favour of promoting languages concern mainly African languages spoken by majorities, taking in view that the formation of African States is still an unfinished process and that a unitary language is considered as an essential element for achieving state unity; therefore, majority languages gain ground to the expense of other African languages. Exceptions makes the Tamazight language, for which there is an increased mobilization

---

[454] Birger Winsa, Cultural Development in Minority Regions: The Influences of Language policies on Social Capital in Multilingual Regions, in Rights, Promotion and Integration Issues..., pp. 170-179.
[455] Tomasz Wicherkiewicz, Welcome and Unwelcome Minority languages in Multilingual Regions, in Rights, Promotion and Integration Issues..., pp. 181-188.

in Algeria and Morocco, where it is recognized officially, is studied in school and is the object of scientific research. A movement in favour of this language develops also in Mali and Niger.

In Latin America, during the last decades all States recognized through constitutions and laws indigenous languages, sometimes as official, or as regional but in official use. In some of these States mother tongues of indigenous peoples are considered as symbols of their continuity on the respective territories, of their resistance to policies of assimilation. Many of them adopted programmes of intercultural bilingual education and ensure instruction in some indigenous languages or their learning in a bilingual model, while the media are increasingly used for these purposes.

In Chili there is a revival of the study of languages spoken by indigenous peoples; academies were created for promoting the study of Rapa Nui, Aymara and Mapuche languages[456]. In Venezuela, the study of mother tongues of the majority of indigenous communities in a bilingual system is extended[457]. National bodies were also created for the problems of indigenous peoples, while institutes of research or documentation, authentic linguistic centers, study the indigenous languages and form the documentary basis for their preservation and study. The recognition and research of indigenous languages offer the basis for acting for their teaching in school and for their use in the public space, although the results are still modest.

In Canada, the wish of young indigenous to learn the traditional language as the second language is noted and the Canadian government finances programmes, such as linguistic nests, the formation of educators, documentation and archives, communication and media, including the elaboration of dictionaries and the rectification of the orthography of different languages.

In the *United States of America,* such initiatives are taken by linguistic communities, such as the Karuk community in California, which opted for the learning of the language on the basis of communication, or the community Navajo of Arizona, which organized a programme of scholar immersion implying the use of the indigenous language during the first years of preschool and of the preparatory course; other types of programmes of revival and education of a wide diversity, including modern methods like the Internet and distance learning, concern indigenous languages such as Cherokee, Cheyenne, Sioux, Mohawk, Shoshone and others.

In *Mexico*, since 2006 the law on education gives to speakers of indigenous languages the right to benefit of bilingual education, in mother tongues and Spanish.

In *Australia,* efforts deployed since two decades started reversing the trend, as the languages in danger reappear, their decline was interrupted and a process of revitalization takes place, many of them having now speakers of all ages, including children. An important support for maintaining those languages is the recourse to media that is to radio and TV in Aboriginal languages. In some component States, linguistic community centers were created and a solid documentary basis about the Aboriginal culture and language is ensured. In *New Zeeland*, where the Maori language is in danger, linguistic nests were created at preschool and primary levels, in which education is offered in Maori, which ensures its preservation as a functional language.

In some of the *Pacific Islands (New Caledonia, Polynesia, Vanuatu)*, some indigenous languages were revitalized and are now part of school curricula. In many of the territories in the Pacific area, confronted with the phenomena of globalization, a strong sensitivity towards the regional cultural and linguistic richness and attachment to preserving cultural identities are noted. There are also linguistic centers of research and academies which pursue the study and the preservation of languages in danger.

The area of *Asia* presents a variety of situations, resulting from the policies followed by the respective States. In *South-East Asia*, many of the States recognized the rights of minority indigenous groups and some of them made an official classification of these groups, even if this does not fully reflect the linguistic situation in these countries. In *Thailand*, promising efforts are deployed at the level of diverse communities for preserving their languages, while in *Vietnam* smaller ethnic groups are recognized officially and supported and governmental initiatives in the field of learning indigenous languages in school are notable. In *China*, indigenous languages are studied thoroughly, but this is limited to the 55 national minorities recognized. On the *Indian sub-continent,* the majority of children learns in school mother tongues and uses them in the family, but learns also the majority language and English, in a bilingual or trilingual model, which ensures the survival of mother tongues, but in a marginal position.

The area of *Central Asia and Siberia* is characterized by the policies of China and the Russian Federation; China recognized national minorities and granted them regimes of autonomy, which includes also the use of regional languages in school and in administration, along with the Chinese (Mandarin), but made no effort for developing them as written literary languages. The Russian Federation, continuing the policy of Soviet Union, granted a status of

---

[456] Reports of Chili to the Committee for the Elimination of All Forms of Discrimination, doc. CERD/C/CHL/19-21 of 19 May 2013, p. 27.
[457] Reports of Venezuela to CERD, doc. CERD/C/VEN/19-21 of 16 January 2013, pp. 73-76.

cultural autonomy to its subjects of the area (republics, regions, districts), but in general Russian is used in administration and in education, while mother tongues are learned in many places as one of the subjects.

A series of activities organized under the auspices of UNESCO during the International Year of Languages (2008) in different parts of the world, in favour of languages in danger or on the way to disappear, are presented in the Final Report submitted to United Nations in this regard[458].

SECTION 4 - LINGUISTIC DIVERSITY and the INTERNET

The problem of linguistic diversity on the Internet is in the center of the debate on the society of information[459]. UNESCO launched, in this field, the concept of "a society of knowledge", which places its accent on plurality and diversity in the field of the cyber-space. This concept is the answer to the preoccupation according to which in the process of informatics hundreds of local languages will be ignored, which will speed up the reduction in the number of those that use them, and therefore their extinction.

The situation of different languages on the Internet shows important disparities. Thus, English, which has twice and a half less speakers than the Latin languages, has twice and half more pages on the Web than all Latin languages together. The most important international data basis shows that only 1/10 of the scientific and technical publications produced in English would be published in Latin languages. With regard to literature, the Latin editions would produce more than 19% from the world production. In spite of this, French takes the second place on the Web and Spanish the third place. Nevertheless, as for access to Internet, one notes the increase of the number of Chinese and of Indians, which makes it possible to foresee an interesting evolution.

There would be three causes of disparities in the use of the Internet: a) pre-existent, when a government or an industry refuses to make available to persons using another language the information, technologies or products available; b) technical, consisting in the difference between a code in Latin letters and that in another alphabet; a more recent Unicode would need two-three times more space; c) emergent, consisting in the use of the information system for other purposes than those initially in view[460].

In order to have access to technologies of information on the Internet it is necessary to reunite: an infrastructure-a network of telecommunications of such dimensions which would offer services to a number of users in the languages chosen; economical access to that infrastructure, at prices in conformity with the economic level of the respective population; users should be literate and the language spoken by them should have an alphabet allowing its treatment on the Internet. A study on the Greek language proved that its alphabet cannot be used on Internet and therefore a form of this alphabet adapted to the Romanic languages was preferred.

Internet is not an open and democratic institution. It is dominated by monopolies of telecommunications in different regions of the world, which detain the infrastructure permitting the access to Internet and links with other users, most of them in the USA, which makes it necessary to use English in commercial contacts. Second, companies which produce informatics materials and the necessary soft have the same influence, producing keyboards, screens and the systems of exploitation favouring some languages, mainly European, considering also the needs to cover their costs. Other bodies ensure regulations, for instance of names and numbers, and the regional centers take decisions on connections to Internet. The American body (Internet Corporation for Assigned Names and Numbers-ICANN), which administers the system of names in the field, accepted with difficulties a variety of Unicode which allows multilingual names of fields.

The development of a unique code represents an important element for the multilingual use of the Internet. The initial Code was elaborated in the 50-60-th by the American National Institute of Standards, containing 128 characters, which was convenient for the English spoken in the USA. It was then developed by International Organization of Standardization with 256 characters, with the purpose to offer comparable codes for all languages. Accepting this form of Unicode is seen as the best hope for an infrastructure of the Internet of international use. Despite this, for technical, economic and organizational reasons, the international use of Internet favoured languages based on the Latin alphabet and in particular English, which took profit of the standard code established initially. In order to eliminate these disadvantages, the Unicode should be more disseminated[461].

---

[458] Doc. A/63/752 of 10 March 2009.
[459] Presentation extended in Mesurer la diversité linguistique sur Internet, UNESCO, 2005.
[460] Mesurer la diversité linguistique sur Internet, p. 46
[461] Mesurer la diversité linguistique sur Internet, pp. 74-75.

As it is foreseen, in a decade from now on, the products of the technology of information and communications can accomplish multiple tasks. As a result of the development of norms of code with multilingual characters, used also by Unicode, the linguistic coverage in the recent version of Windows increased at 123 languages; most of them are nevertheless European languages and only a few Asian and African[462].

Under the auspices of UNESCO, a conception of ethics of information is promoted. It is obvious that technologies of information and communication (TIC) are not neutral from the cultural point of view; as they have their origin in western cultures, mainly in the North American culture, they transmit and promote their cultural values and their preferences. These values and in particular these preferences come in conflict with those of the countries which receive the technologies, which may lead either to limiting the trade with the respective technologies or to affecting the local values and cultures[463].

According to the conception of ethics of information, if it is accepted that the numeric education is essential to pass to an inclusive informational society, this education should respond to the fundamental ethic criterion of respect for the cultural and linguistic diversity and avoid ethnocentrism and the implied colonization through technologies. The informational society supposes a public field of knowledge, which was accumulated for centuries and proceeds from all peoples of the world, and consequently should not make the object of market rules. In fact, elementary resources on which lie the programmes on the Internet proceed most often from research financed by public funds and the benefit of these programmes often belongs to some commercial companies for which neither the language in which they were produced or their source are used or known.

The liberalization of linguistic resources produced from public funds, as well as a system of scientific editions, based on open notions and leading to free logic applications, is considered necessary, as well as another linguistic policy of States, which should promote multilingualism in the field of information.

In view of this situation, UNESCO launched in 2005 the Plan of action of the World Meeting on the society of information, which promotes the cultural and linguistic diversity and recommends " the elaboration of policies which should encourage the respect, preservation, promotion and strengthening of cultural and linguistic diversity and of the cultural heritage in the context of the informational society...". As it was said above in a different context, the Universal Declaration on cultural diversity 2001 affirms that the freedom of expression, the pluralism of media, multilingualism, equal access to artistic expressions, to scientific and technological knowledge, including under numeric form, as well as the possibility for all cultures to be present in the means of expression and dissemination, are all guarantees of cultural diversity.

For this purpose, UNESCO favours equal access to numerical information, both regarding the production and the use, for all cultural and linguistic groups. For that, it underlines: the need to encourage the numeric alphabet and to master the new technologies of information and communication; the need to promote linguistic diversity in the numeric space, encouraging through world networks access to information belonging to the public space; the need for policies favouring access of developing countries to the new technologies, in parallel with facilitating the numeric circulation of cultural internal products and access of these countries to numeric resources available at the world level in the fields of education, culture and science[464].

*   *   *

In numerous places on the planet important efforts are deployed to revitalize mother tongues in danger, as languages spoken along with the official ones, or even for their recognition as official or national languages. The problem of the extinction of some mother tongues is related to numerous factors affecting the evolution of different communities. One of these factors is the territory on which a language is spoken; it can suffer modifications, and the inhabitants speaking a mother tongue may leave it for different reasons; they can move to urban agglomerations, where they must speak another language in order to integrate socially and to survive; as a rule, these persons are constraint to speak one or several majority languages to communicate with more important groups. Analysts of this phenomenon note that languages in danger are concentrated in particular in the Indian Sub-continent, in the Pacific Islands (mainly New Guinea), in the area of indigenous peoples in Australia, in American continents, in Siberia and the Scandinavian peninsula, as well as among the peoples of Sub-Saharan Africa and in South-East Asia,

---

[462] Ibidem, p. 96.
[463] On effects of the use of Internet in the field of human rights, Ion Diaconu, Human Rights in International Law, theory and practice, 2010, pp. 373-378.
[464] Mesurer la diversité linguistique...pp. 96-97.

respectively in the poorest areas of the world[465]. These are the effects of the historic injustice, of poverty and inheriting a difficult economic situation. Some regions remain still isolated from the modernity, but many of them are exposed to migrations, to displacement to the peripheries of towns, to the aggression of multinational companies and of modern communications, all factors which accelerate the reduction of the use of mother tongues and finally lead to their extinction.

The linguistic geography of the world offers an immense variety and different situations, both due to historic evolutions and to the preoccupation of communities to preserve their languages or to linguistic policies followed by different States. The repartition and evolution of languages are closely related to topography, to the climate, soil and other numerous factors which allow and affect human settlements; disappearance or the modification of these factors may lead to diminishing the number of speakers and endanger the maintaining of their mother tongues.

The main factor for the survival and preservation of mother tongues is considered to be their intergenerational transmission, and the main factor of decline of the use of minority languages would be the permanent contact with majority languages and the need to use them in the day to day life. This shows the need to organize from the youngest age education in mother tongue or at least its learning. As for the contact with majorities, in modern and multinational societies this cannot be avoided; therefore, the solution is to ensure learning minority languages and the majority language and, depending on the factual situation, to ensure the largest possible use of mother tongues in public life, so that the preservation of minority culture and language is not a problem. Other requirements refer to ensuring access to modern technologies in as many languages as possible, in order to avoid the reduction of the use of the languages in this field and of the access to cultural values of other communities and peoples.

---

[465] Stephen May, Language and Minority Rights: ethnicity, nationalism and the politics of language, Harlow, U.K., Pearson Education, 2001, p. 4.

CHAPTER XVI – MULTICULTURALISM - TRENDS and LIMITS

ABSTRACT

Most of the existing human societies are multiethnic and multicultural. Different cultures coexist on the same territories and more or less important segments of population are behind them. This situation can develop into intolerance, rejection and conflict or into mutual respect, interrelationship and cooperation.

International law, as it evolved during the second half of the twentieth century, is recognizing and protecting cultural diversity and identity of peoples and communities, as well as cultural rights for everybody, and specific rights for persons belonging to minorities and for indigenous peoples.

The post-industrial societies, mostly in West Europe and North America, are hosting millions of people of a different culture, many of them already at the third generation and citizens of the respective States. The only standard applicable to them in this field should be multiculturalism, well understood and implemented. This is what we are trying to demonstrate.

KEY WORDS: segregation, assimilation, pluralism, diversity, indigenous peoples, traditional and local cultures, modernity.

INTRODUCTION

Most of the existing state societies are, nowadays, ethnically and culturally heterogeneous, that is are multiethnic and multicultural; one may say without being wrong that evolution of mankind tends towards cultural pluralism in each country, towards multiculturalism in the world.

This raises the problem of the relationship between cultures, more precisely between the social groups who are bearers of different cultures. In each country, this concerns the majority culture and the minority cultures. Of course, the size of the group behind a culture is important for the preservation and the development of the respective culture, but the willingness of the members of the group to preserve it and to resist pressures which can endanger it is equally important.

This concerns at present particularly post-industrial societies in Western Europe and North America, where significant numbers of migrants established; they are at the third generation, many of them acquired the citizenship of the host States and there is no prospect that they return in the countries of origin. It concerns also, may be to a different degree, developed countries on other continents, like Australia, Japan, Republic of Korea, which receive and may receive more migrants.

SECTION 1 - CONTENTS of MULTICULTURALISM

The concept of multiculturalism is not enounced in the multilateral or regional treaties on human rights. It is submitted that it is implied in the provisions of these documents on cultural rights, on the right to the use of mother tongue and the religious freedoms, because the respect for these rights conduces to multiculturalism in each State, as much as the principle of non-discrimination on grounds of language, culture or religion[466]. In several opinions on individual communications examined, the Human Rights Committee retained that granting rights only to some religions, financing exclusively some schools or imposing the use of the official language only, without following reasonable and objective criteria, represent violations of the Covenant on civil and political rights[467].

Considering this situation, States and the majority groups concerned may adopt several attitudes towards minority cultures:
- Segregation, meaning maintaining or placing the cultural minority groups in a state of separation and isolation and ignoring them. It is only apparent that this behavior is meant to protect the cultural identity of

---

[466] Fernand De Varennes, Multiculturalisme et discrimination positive dans l'ordre juridique international, in Le Multiculturalisme, L'Observateur des Nations Unies, 2007-2, pp.143-144.
[467] Cases Ballantine, Davidson, McIntyre v. Canada, CCPR/C/47D/359/1989 and 385/1989/Rev.1, Waldman v. Canada, CCPR/C/67/D/694/1996 and Feu J.G.A.Diergaardt and consort v. Namibia, CCPR/C/69/D/760/1997(2000).

minority groups; through isolation, it impedes the development of the respective cultures, while in social life it leads to inequalities and discrimination, even to the deterioration of the existence of the minority group.
- Assimilation is the policy meant to determine a minority group, through intolerance, constraint or other means, to abandon its culture, traditions and mother tongue and to adopt those of the majority or of another group, that is to renounce to its identity.
- Cultural pluralism, which supposes by definition the coexistence in the same geographic space of different cultures, which entails the preservation of different cultural identities and of specific institutions of culture, education and religion, the acceptance and recognition of cultural values and unimpeded interaction and exchanges between cultures.

Such a conception is not opposed to objective trends towards economic and social integration in a context which allows to each person an extensive participation in social life, without losing its specific features. As a matter of fact, democracy cannot be limited to political and economic life, because of the indissoluble links between politics, economics and cultural life.

Per international law, segregation is forbidden. States parties to the 1965 International Convention on the elimination of all forms of racial discrimination, numbering now 177, condemned racial segregation and apartheid and committed themselves to prevent, forbid and eliminate from the territories under their jurisdiction any practice of this nature. As culture is an essential element of ethnicity[468] and distinct cultural groups are usually also ethnic groups, the concept of racial integration includes also segregation on cultural grounds.

The interdiction of racial discrimination is recognized as an imperative norm of international law, from which States cannot derogate even in case of exceptional danger for the existence of a nation[469]; therefore, segregation as a form of racial discrimination is also forbidden by this imperative norm.

It is also forbidden to States to apply policies and practices of assimilation of minority groups against their will. This obligation is expressly included in European documents mentioned (the Framework Convention of 1995 and the Copenhagen document of 1990) and is implicit in the UN Declaration of 1992 on the rights of persons belonging to national or ethnic, religious and linguistic minorities, according to which States shall protect the existence and the identity of these minorities on their territory.

If these obligations are respected, cultural pluralism remains the only peaceful, viable and constructive solution. This raises the problem of the relationship between different cultures which may exist on the territory of a State, which is characteristic for the situation of most States of the world.

Several concepts are used in order to define this situation, like "multiculturalism" or "pluriculturalism", which mean accepting the legitimate existence of several cultures; other authors prefer the formula of "interculturalism", which would underline better the interaction between cultures[470]. Even the concept of multiculturalism is differently understood; in the United States it is treated from the point of view of races, while in Europe it is considered in connection with ethnic minorities and with foreigners.

In this context, a clear distinction must be made between cultural assimilation and economic and social integration. Cultural assimilation means the process through which a group of persons starts losing its language, traditions, customs and other cultural features and embracing the culture and the values of the majority of the society where it lives. Economic and social integration supposes the coexistence of majority and minority groups within a country and their participation in social and economic life, while respecting and maintaining their identity, their customs, languages and other aspects of their culture.

If during the decades 1960-1990 the migrants sought to integrate in the national communities in developed States of reception, mainly of Western Europe, analysts note that presently important communities of migrants are also preoccupied to preserve their cultural identity and that the models applied during the twentieth century are not adequate any more. Therefore, they seek a new approach which would recognize multiculturalism as a fundamental specificity of western societies of today[471]. As there is also the concern to avoid the fragmentation of societies, the

---

[468] On this subject Ion Diaconu, Minorities in the contemporary international law, 2009, Ed. C.H.Beck (in Romanian), pp.140-142.

[469] Opinion held by I. Brownlie, Principles of International Law, 1979, p.513; Ion Diaconu, Imperative norms of international law (jus cogens), Ed. Academiei (in Romanian), 1977, p.161; the International Court of Justice took this position in the case Barcelona Traction Light and Power Co. Ltd, Reports 1970, p.3.

[470] For a presentation of the debate on these issues in Canada, see Yasmeen Abu-laban and Daiva Stasiulis, Ethnic Pluralism under Siege; Popular and Partisan Opposition to Multiculturalism, in Canadian Public Policy, February 1993, pp.365-379.

[471] Roger Cotterrell and Andre-Jean Arnaud, Comment penser le multiculturalisme en droit ?, in Le multiculturalsme, L'Observateur des Nations Unies, 2007-2, vol.23, pp.8-9.

question is whether the norms of law can ensure the social unity and cohesion and at the same time respond to the requirements of the cultural pluralism.

In substance, it is necessary to build a "culture of multiculturalism"[472], where cultural diversity and identity are recognized and accepted as important values of mankind, as legitimate ways of expression of human personality. It seems to be the only way to ensure the preservation and the optimum development of the cultural and linguistic richness of the world in conditions of a peaceful evolution, of avoiding ethnic or other conflicts, which vary often destroyed or endangered cultural values, secular cultures and did not solve any problem.

SECTION 2 - RESPONSE to MULTICULTURALISM

Some authors submit that for a legal approach of the cultural phenomenon in its diversity it is necessary to decompose its elements, which would allow a different treatment.

They refer to the protection in the economic field, against discrimination in working places, to access to employment and to public services, to the protection of supreme values or beliefs (those religious, with all what they entail for human life), to traditions and the family way of life (including the use of mother tongues, the preservation of the common memory and history) and to emotional inclinations (attachment to the country of origin, prejudices and feelings of hostility towards other racial or religious groups or communities)[473].

From the beginning, we think we must exclude from the concept of cultural interaction such issues like discrimination in employment and in society, which represent of course a reality, but constitute a different subject; such issues are treated from the point of view of other norms concerning human rights, those postulating equal rights and non-discrimination. As for emotional inclinations, they may have a historic and temporary character, are the result of social evolutions and of a certain level of culture, but cannot be considered elements of human culture in general (mainly prejudices and feelings of hostility towards other groups), even with regard to more restraint groups.

Therefore, we prefer to consider the essential elements of culture-the cultural creation and access to it, the preservation and the development of mother tongues, religious freedoms and traditions-from which international law derives rights for individuals and obligations for States and other social actors, and to see the way different segments of the population living on a territory enjoy such rights and perceive their mutual relations.

The situation should not be examined as an inevitable hurt between cultures, as a confrontation which should be solved in favour of one or the other of the trends and in which the rule of law would be called only to ensure peace through constraint. Quite to the contrary, the rule of law has a subtler task, that to regulate different types of relations among people, among groups, in the exercise by all human rights in the different fields of culture.

Multiculturalism should also not be seen as a sign or a ferment of social fragmentation, in view of the fact that different cultures have behind them human communities, larger or more restraint, which may legitimately pretend the preservation of their cultural systems[474]. To sum up, the fear is expressed that accepting national minorities and indigenous peoples as bearers of different cultures, and consequently obligations to respect and preserve their cultures (in a wider meaning, ways of life, systems of values, traditions) would mean to accept factors of des-aggregation of national unity or that multiculturalism would mean to affirm the differences instead of equality.

In substance, the authors of such fears do not accept the concept of cultural identity, considering that it would lead to the idea of social groups which would preserve the same cultural features and would pretend some special rights. They repeat the conceptions according to which minorities would be only those formed as a result of territorial changes, excluding those formed through massive migrations of populations[475], which reduces the discussion to arbitrary criteria, without connection with the substance of the problem, with the existence of different cultural features of these people and the need to respect their human rights.

Multiculturalism is based on respect of human rights, of the rights of persons of another language, culture or religion (different from those of the majority population) to use their own language, to enjoy their culture and to profess and practice their religion, of the rights of each person to opinion, to expression, to assembly and association in community with other persons sharing the same culture, language or religion, as well as with other persons.

---

[472] Cf. Jose Bengoa, Report on "Education and Minorities", presented to the Sub-commission for the prevention of discrimination and the protection of minorities, doc. E/CN.4/Sub2/AC.5/1996, W.P.3/22 March 1996, p.3.
[473] Roger Cotterrell and Andre-Jean Arnaud, art.cit., pp.11-12.
[474] Geneviève Koubi, Multiculturalisme et fractionnements des référents culturels : la dérive vers la question de l'origine, in Le multilatéralisme, p.31.
[475] G. Koubi, art. cit., pp. 32-47.

Understood and applied with this meaning, multiculturalism is not a threat to State's unity and integrity and should not lead to fragmentation. Of course, nobody can legitimately pretend on behalf of multiculturalism a State organization which would create separate administrative structures, would destroy the unity of States or create factors of dissolution, or pretend territorial arrangements of the type of secession or autonomy on ethnic grounds against the will of peoples.

In view of the situation of plurality of cultures on their territories, which is now common to most of the States, their obligations are numerous. The first norm to be respected is to guarantee the freedom of choice for each person to maintain the different elements of its culture, to practice them individually or in community with others or not to practice them. Another obligation is to respect the free choice made by a person and to avoid any interference with it. The State also has the obligation to protect the exercise of cultural rights against actions by other actors, persons, associations or communities which would try to impede a person to exercise them freely. Finally, as for other economic, social and cultural rights, States have the obligation to support and to ensure the exercise of some rights of this category by groups and persons who need such support.

In this context, analysts consider that States have to ensure equal opportunities of access to cultural knowledge and to the necessary abilities in the fields of education and culture, and that the absence of such knowledge and abilities may affect even the freedom of choice, the effective protection of human rights in general[476].

These rights and obligations can find their expression in internal laws and in institutional relationships established by law; nevertheless, the law cannot regulate all relations among persons within a community, in the exercise in common of some of the respective rights and freedoms, mainly of religious freedoms and of traditions. Such freedoms can be exercised, even if they are not expressly regulated; however, their exercise is subject to respect for fundamental human rights and freedoms of members of the community, as well as those of other persons, and to fool respect of the free choice of everybody.

That means that, beyond the individual freedoms, exercised individually or in common with others, and respect for fundamental human rights, there are a series of internal norms of the community or of the religious association which are not regulated by law and should be accepted by other groups. Rules of law can intervene, of course, to ensure even in such cases respect for human rights and in particular to prevent and forbid manifestations of intolerance, of incitement to racial hatred or to violence.

A positive approach to multiculturalism supposes to overcome such fears towards the existence of several cultures in the same geographic space and to treat them as subsystems in a constructive perspective, along with common values, in view of the willingness to live together. This supposes negotiation, research of a consensus and ultimately responsibility from all those concerned, both for the diversity of the cultures in presence and for the common values, so as to allow beneficial exchanges which bring together on a long run the respective social groups, building bridges of convergence.

Multiculturalism is considered to be one of the basic features of future societies; each society will have to adopt the common most adequate project, which ensures to each community its place and its role, and ensure to all, on the basis of their willingness to live together, peace in conditions of respect for their cultures[477].

This means, in terms of social education, to form a culture of diversity, of respect of the rights of each person, of fundamental rights and freedoms for all.

Another problem which concerns both the contents of each culture and their diversity and identity, is that of *the impact of the scientific and technologic development on* culture. As a matter of fact, access to the achievements of science and technology and to their benefits is part of the extended concept of culture, as well as the material civilization, as an integral part of the way of life. Nevertheless, the scientific and technologic progress is not neutral regarding the cultural development[478] of persons and groups; it determines orientations, allows access to new values and knowledge, but also may lead to the loss of some traditional knowledge and values.

« *The dilemma of modernity* » which confronts traditional cultures is treated differently by representatives of different approaches[479]. The partisans of community cultures maintain that modernity has as a consequence the disappearance of small communities, because of anomy and alienation, of losing the links with communities of origin. The most frequent example offered is that of indigenous peoples, presented as "victims of the progress".

Other authors note that modernity brings not only losses, but also gains; it would facilitate a more comprehensive integration of the world as such, a wider access to cultural values of other peoples, and on a personal

---

[476] J.Almqvist, op. cit., pp.79-80.
[477] Roger Cotterrell, Andre-Jean Arnaud, art. cit., p.25.
[478] Ben Achour, Souveraineté étatique et protection internationale des minorités, in Recueil des Cours de l'Academie de Droit International, vol. 245, 1994, p.427.
[479] For a wider presentation, see Marlies Galenkamp, art, cit., pp.164-167.

level would allow more freedom from the relations within the smaller groups. The discovery of the free person, with its identity as a human being, whatever may be his ethnic or social identification, would be one of the greatest achievements of modernity. This is, in fact, in full conformity with international standards in force on human rights, which place the human being as such, in its dignity and freedom, in the center of any evolution.

Of course, « modernization » produces important consequences, first of all regarding the freedom of choice, the right of option to maintain and develop his/her original traditions and culture or to depart from them. According to the same principle of the personal freedom of choice, to which one cannot oppose traditions or requirements to preserve cultural identity, modernity cannot be stopped or limited. A "nativist movement", which would affirm the superiority of old traditions[480] and would oblige persons to preserve their culture and customs, in spite of their will to abandon them, would represent in fact forced assimilation which, as seen above, is forbidden in international law.

Modernity *per se* does not produce adverse consequences for a culture, for an identity; it may affect all cultures, all cultural identities, perhaps some more than others; it depends on their capacity to adapt to the progress. It remains nevertheless an objective process, which cannot be stopped or limited. The single criterion which can and should be applied is respect for human rights.

As a matter of principle, the new technologies and developments –in the fields of energy, biotechnology, informatics- are not contrary to human rights; it is obvious that they affected the universal culture and the cultures of different peoples and groups; nevertheless, it is necessary that States consider constantly and ensure that these new technologies and developments are used to the benefit of the human being and prevent that human rights are endangered by new research or practices based on the new technologies.

They can have as effects a wider access to the culture of other peoples, to the universal culture and a free choice of persons; that may produce changes in the contents and the expression of different cultures, but this is an objective process which can be ignored only with the price of isolation and backwardness, with serious social consequences[481].

* * *

Culture means communication, exchange, mutual enrichment, fertile meeting with other cultures; the exercise of cultural rights supposes communication with other cultures and access to them; cultural identity does not mean cultural isolation.

The history of universal culture, the history of different cultures demonstrates the mutual interaction and influence among cultures of different peoples, of minorities and majorities, whatever may have been the political relations of force between them.

According to the Declaration on the principles of international cultural cooperation, adopted by UNESCO in 1966, all cultures are part of the common heritage of the world, in their rich variety and diversity and with the mutual influences they exercise on each other. The Declaration proclaims, among the objectives of the international cultural cooperation, to ensure for everybody access to knowledge, the benefit of arts and literature of all peoples, the benefit of the progress of science in all parts of the world and of their results, as well as the requirement to contribute to enriching the cultural life.

The process of globalization takes place along with the revival of cultural specificities and the realities of multiculturalism. An increasing intercultural communication takes place, as well as a pregnant manifestation of cultural identities and diversity. This corresponds to the modern conception and standards on the respect for human rights and fundamental freedoms, including the rights of persons belonging to minorities. Considering these conception and e standards, one should reject trends or claims for linguistic, spiritual and cultural homogeneity, which consider cultural diversity as an error, a sin or an expression of chaos, as well as any kind of fundamentalism which promotes the closing of the borders, the isolation of the world and refuge in the old myths and customs.

---

[480] Ibidem, p.167.
[481] Extended presentation Ion Diaconu, Human Rights in the contemporary international law, 2010, Ed. Lumina Lex (in Romanian), pp.366-369.

PART V - HUMAN RIGHTS to a DECENT LIVELIHOOD

CHAPTER XVII - HUMAN RIGHTS and the PROTECTION of the ENVIRONMENT

ABSTRACT

There is a close relationship between the protection of the environment and the state of human rights. If one accepts the definition of the environment as the entirety of factors which constitute the framework, the means and the conditions of human life, it is obvious that the modification of this framework can affect the enjoyment of human rights.

There are of course some developments in this field; international documents are adopted, as well as decisions taken by international courts and human rights bodies. Nevertheless, humanity is far from having learned and undertaken to protect its environment. The study underlines those human rights that are mostly affected by the changing situation of the environment and the phenomena which are producing such effects, their causes, in particular those resulting from human activities. More recent documents focus on what is called the democracy of the protection of the environment, meaning the information of the public, its participation in the decision-making process on activities affecting the environment and the right to judicial remedies in order to protect a safe and healthy environment.

This should lead to the development of applicable principles and norms, rights and obligations of people, of communities, of States and of the international community, for such a global issue.

KEY WORDS: safe and healthy environment, natural phenomena, emission of green-house gas, protection of maritime waters, of continental waters, of the air and of wild life, toxic and dangerous waste, human rights and responsibilities, procedural rights.

INTRODUCTION

The relationship of interconnection between respect for human rights and the protection of the environment is increasingly recognized and becomes a topical issue of national and international policies, in as much as changes of the environment have a more adverse impact on life on the planet. Several studies and reports have been elaborated within the United Nations in this field and it is difficult to say that some conclusions and practical orientations resulted from them[482].

The environment is defined as the entirety of factors which constitute the framework, the means and the conditions of life of human being. The Declaration adopted by the Stockholm Conference in June 1972 on environment refers to „natural global resources, including air, water, land, flora and fauna", including representative samples of natural ecosystems. The 1992 Convention of the Council of Europe on civilian responsibility for damages resulting from activities dangerous for the environment offers the following definition: „Environment includes: natural resources, both biological and non-biological, such as the air, water, land, fauna and flora and the interaction between these factors, the property which is part of the cultural heritage and such aspects which are characteristic for the landscape"[483].

It is obvious that the deterioration of the environment has a negative impact, direct and indirect, on the enjoyment of human rights. It affects, at different degrees, the entire population, all peoples and States, but mainly the most disadvantaged groups in all countries and the entire population of developing States. The human rights which are particularly affected are the rights to life, to health, to housing, to food, but also other economic, social and cultural rights. The concept of „environmental security" is increasingly taken into account as an important element of any strategy of security, along with political, military, economic and societal elements[484].

If it is relatively easy to accept that there is a relationship between the state of the environment and respect for human rights, a legal analysis of this complex issue raises a number of theoretical and practical questions: what evolutions of the environment affect human rights and if and to what extent they are the result of human activities or of natural phenomena; if there is a human right, or if there are human rights, to a healthy environment; if this is the

---

[482] The first study on this theme was presented by the expert to the Sub-Commission for the prevention of discrimination and protection of minorities, Ms. Fatima Zora Ksentini, Rapport sur les droits de l'homme et l'environnement, 1994. doc.(E/CN.4/Sub.2/1994/9 et Corr.1).
[483] International Legal Materials, 32(1993), p. 1228.
[484] Conception launched by the Copenhagen school, represented by Barry Buzan and others, presented extensively by Ion Diaconu, Democratic Security, in The Annuary of University Spiru Haret, Series Juridical Sciences, An VII, 2009(in Romanian).

case, who are the holders of such rights and who has the obligations corresponding to them; if these rights and obligations are regulated by norms of internal or international law or by both; in view of the fact that phenomena affecting environment have effects beyond borders, what are the norms concerning their trans- boundary effects.

1. It is taken as a truth that a healthy environment is a precondition for the exercise of human rights, that human life and dignity are protected when individuals have access to an environment which responds to some basic qualities[485]. To evaluate the state of environment makes it necessary to analyze the situation of its composing factors, including air, water, land and biodiversity.

The environment of the atmosphere is subject to deterioration as a result of human activities generating emissions of polluting gases, industrial powders or others, as well as due to the increase of the population and of the industrial production, which led to the pollution of the air, to climate changes and to the reduction of the ozone layer of protection.

The aquatic internal environment is affected by the immersion of polluting substances, mainly chemical, by the irrational use of water resources and the reduction of sources of drinkable water; the marine environment is deteriorated by the immersion of polluting substances, mainly hydrocarbons and other waste materials, by the pressure on marine life because of irrational fishing and the destruction of marine fauna and flora.

The land environment is seriously affected by deterioration, deforestation and desertification; even if they may have a rather regional impact, some of these factors have also global effects (deforestation, desertification). The loss suffered by biodiversity, by the disappearance of some species of animals and plants, has adverse effects on human life in general, but mainly on communities whose way of life depends on the existence of these forms of life.

No doubt, the elements of the human environment can be affected by natural phenomena such as hurricanes, typhoons, tropical cyclones, tsunamis, volcanic eruptions, floods, drought, sliding muds and earthquakes; in connection with such phenomena it is also necessary to see what are the human rights and the obligations of States and of the international community. According to statistics, after the year 2000 more than 2500 such natural disasters took place, affecting billions of people and causing 1,5 million deaths. Some of them are the result of geologic processes, but others are aggravated by human activities, such as the emissions of greenhouse gases in the atmosphere which, as it was proved, led to reducing the ozone layer of protection and to melting the icebergs, to the warming of water, to the increased intensity of cyclones, to drought, desertification and floods[486].

These phenomena affect to the highest degree human rights and it is necessary to see what people, communities, States and the international community can do to avoid them, to prevent them as much as possible and to be better prepared to face them.

After the adoption of the Stockholm Declaration, till the 1990-ies, some States included in their constitutions provisions on the protection of the environment; till 2010 some 140 States adopted similar provisions in their legislations. Many of these internal documents proclaim the right of each person to a healthy environment. For instance, the Constitution of Romania of 2001, with amendments adopted in 2003, provides in article 35 that "The State recognizes the right of every person to a healthy and balanced environment".

The constitutional provisions were certainly developed in legislative norms in different fields, according to the concerns and the interests of each State. The norms of internal law are important in order to create in each State a regime of protection of the environment, to grant eventually rights to physical and legal persons in this field, including the right to a remedy in front of the courts and to apply sanctions for activities which produce significant damage to environment and, of course, as the main instrument to implement the obligations undertaken at the international level.

The internal legislation of different States, together with the international practice, is also an important factor in the process of forming customary rules of international law. This offers to lawyers the area of analysis to see whether new norms of customary law are accepted concerning human rights in the field of environment.

This chapter is meant to present briefly the international practice of States and international bodies in this field, having in mind the two approaches offered by relevant international documents: the approach based on human rights and the requirements to respect them in the field of the protection of the environment, which is called also the anthropocentric approach (that is the protection of the environment as one of the requirements for respecting human rights), and the approach starting from the international law on the protection of the environment (that is from norms

---

[485] Report of the High Comissioner of the United Nations for Human Rights, Analytical Study on the relationship between human rights and the environment, doc. A/HRC/19/34 of 16 December 2011.
[486] Ion Diaconu, Climate changes and human rights, in The Annuary of the University Spiru Haret, Series Juridical Sciences, 2011(in Romanian), An XII, pp. 179-187.

on the protection of nature and of different elements of the environment, and inferring from them consequences on the enjoyment of human rights), called also bio or eco-centric[487].

SECTION 1 - NORMS of INTERNATIONAL LAW on the PROTECTION of the ENVIRONMENT

Most of the norms on the protection of environment concern elements of the environment wherever they are, that is on the territory of States and beyond it. They refer to activities of States on their territory and abroad; this means that the protection of the environment should be treated as a set of norms both of internal and of international law.

The Declaration of the Stockholm Conference of the United Nations on environment of 1972 proclaims that „The human being has a fundamental right to freedom, to equality and to satisfactory conditions of life, in an environment of a quality allowing him to live in dignity and welfare" (Principle I).

International documents on human rights contain no reference to the protection of the environment or to human rights in the field of environment. Exceptions are the African Charter of human rights and the rights of peoples of 1981, according to which „all peoples have the right to an environment generally satisfactory and favorable to their development" and the San Salvador Protocol of 1988 to the Inter-American Charter of human rights of 1969 according to which „everybody has the right to live in a healthy environment and to have access to basic public services" and „ States parties will promote the protection, the preservation and the improvement of the environment".

After the Stockholm Declaration, other documents of a general bearing were adopted, among which:
- The World Charter of Nature, adopted by the UN General Assembly at 28 October 1982. The Charter proclaims as principles: respect of the nature and of its essential processes unaltered, respect of the genetic viability of earth; maintain the population of each species, domestic or wild, at least at a level sufficient to ensure its survival; grant a special protection to some parts of the planet surface, of land or water; management of ecosystems and living organisms, as well as of natural resources, so as to maintain their optimal and continuing productivity.
- The UN Framework Convention on climate changes, adopted in New-York at 9 May 1992, by which States parties committed themselves to preserve the climatic system in the interest of present and future generations, on an equitable basis and depending on their common but differentiated responsibilities and their respective capacities. It also provides that States should take precautionary measures to foresee, to prevent and to attenuate climate changes and to limit their adverse effects.
- The Declaration adopted by the Rio de Janeiro Conference at 13 June 1992 on environment and development, which proclaims, among others, the following principles: the human right to a healthy and productive life in harmony with nature, right which is in the center of preoccupations on sustainable development; the rights of States to exploit their resources in accordance with their own policies in the fields of environment and of development and their obligation to ensure that activities under their competence or control do not endanger the environment in other States or in areas beyond their jurisdiction; the exercise of the right to development taking into account in an equitable manner the needs of development and of environment of present and future generations; the protection of the environment as an integral part of development; the international cooperation for eradicating poverty, for preserving and protecting the environment and for promoting an international economic system which generates economic increase and sustainable development in all countries.
- The UN Declaration for the Millennium, adopted by the General Assembly at 8 September 2000, which called States to adopt a new ethics of conservation and management of the environment, to put in force, respectively to apply a series of international treaties in this field and to ensure the sustainable exploitation and management of forests and waters.
- The Declaration of the UN General Assembly of 2007 on the rights of indigenous peoples, which gives attention to their spiritual and material relationship with lands, territories, waters and coastal areas they

---

[487] Approaches prezented by Alexander Fluckiger, Droits de l'homme et environnement, in Introduction aux droits de l'homme, Chapitre 2, Maya Hertig Randall et Michel Hottelier (dir.), Schulthess Média Juridiques, S.A. Genève, Zurich, Bâle, 2014, pp. 606-607.

traditionally detained or used, including their right to have their own laws, traditions and customs, their systems to detain land, as well as their right recognized to the preservation, the restoration and the protection of environment.

Many of them are documents of a declaratory nature, which are not creating rights and obligations, but can be considered as contributions to forming customary norms in the field of environment.

However, numerous instruments with a legal nature have been adopted in the sectorial fields of the protection of environment. They are:

- *for the protection of maritime waters*: the Convention of 1954 on the pollution of maritime waters with hydrocarbons, whose areas of application and interdictions were extended in 1962 and 1969; the conventions of 1969 on the civilian responsibility for damages caused by the pollution with hydrocarbons and on intervention in high seas against ships under foreign flag in case of accident which generates or may generate pollution with hydrocarbons; the Convention of 1972 of London for the prevention of the pollution of seas by the immersion of waste; the conventions for the codification of the law of sea of 1958 and respectively of 1982 which confirmed the obligations of States in these fields; several legal instruments were concluded by States at the regional level for the protection of the Nordic, Baltic, Black and Mediterranean seas, of waters of the Golf, of the Red Sea, of the South and South-East Pacific and of the Caribbean Zone[488].

- *for the protection of rivers and inland waters:* the Convention of 1976 for preventing the pollution of the Rhine with chemical substances, chlorates and other salts; the Convention of 1994 on the cooperation for the protection and sustainable use of Danube; the Convention of the Economic Commission for Europe on the protection and use of trans-border waters and international lakes; tenth of treaties on rivers of North and South America, of Africa and of Asia, which take up provisions concerning the prohibition of pollution with substances which produce significant damage to other riparian States, along with arrangements on sharing the water resources; we note also the Convention on the use of international water courses for other purposes than navigation, adopted by the UN General Assembly in 1997, which contains number of norms on the protection of sweet waters against pollution[489].

- *many conventions were adopted for the air protection,* such as: the 1985 Convention on the protection of the ozone layer, completed by the Montreal Protocol of 1987 on substances which contribute to diminishing the ozone layer, with amendments brought in 1990 and 1992; the Kyoto Protocol of 1998 on the limitation and the reduction of green gas emissions and the Protocol of Sofia of 1988 concerning the freezing of emissions of nitrogen oxides at the level of the preceding year[490].

- *for the protection of wild life*, among the instruments adopted, there are: the Convention of Canberra of 1980 for the protection of marine flora and fauna of Antarctica; the Convention of Washington of 1973 on the trade with wild species of fauna and flora threatened to disappear; the Convention of 1979 on the preservation of migrant species belonging to the wild fauna; the Agreement on tropical wood of 1983; the Code of conduct on the responsible fishing of 1995 and others. Several regional or sub-regional conventions were also concluded: in the area of Americas, the Convention of 1940 on the protection of flora and fauna and of natural panoramic beauties; in Africa, the Convention of Algiers of 1968 on the conservation of nature and of natural reservations; in Europe, the Convention of Berne of 1979 on the conservation of wild life and of the natural environment[491].

Other *international instruments* are *of a transversal character*, regulating the distribution and the use of substances which can produce adverse effects in all elements of the environment. This category includes among others:

- documents of a declaratory nature on toxic or dangerous substances, adopted within OMS, UNEP or OCDE, as well as at the regional level (those adopted by the European Union are compulsory);

---

[488] Presentation and analysis of these documents in Ion Diaconu, Treaties of International Law, vol. III, 2005(in Romanian), Ed. Lumina Lex, pp.130-142.
[489] Ion Diaconu, Treaties, pp. 143-148.
[490] Ibidem, pp. 148-149.
[491] Ibidem, pp. 151-162.

- instruments concerning toxic or dangerous waste (pharmaceutics, fito-sanitary products, those containing dangerous metals such as arsenics, mercury and others, mainly the Basel Convention of 1989 on the control over the trafficking of dangerous wastes and their elimination);
- the protection against ionizing radiations, resulting from activities of the production and the use of nuclear energy. This includes first of all documents in the field of disarmament-the treaties on the prohibition of nuclear tests, in 1963 in the atmosphere, in the outer space and under the water, then in 1996 in all environments; in 1979 the Agreement on the prohibition to depose on the Moon and install on the orbit objects carrying nuclear weapons; the conventions of Vienna of 1960 and 1963 concerning the civilian responsibility for nuclear damage and those of 1986 concerning the rapid notification of a nuclear accident and assistance in case of nuclear accident or of radiologic emergencies; the 1997 Convention on the safety of the management of the used fuel and of radioactive waste[492].

Regarding procedural rights in connection with the protection of the environment, according to Principle 10 of the Rio Declaration on biologic diversity „Problems of the environment are at the best treated with the participation of all those interested, at the adequate level. At the national level, each person shall have appropriate access to the information detained by public authorities, including on dangerous materials and activities in their communities, as well as the opportunity to take part in the decision-making process. States shall facilitate and encourage the knowledge and the participation, and ensure that the information is largely available, as well as an effective access to the judiciary and administrative procedures, including for obtaining sanction and reparation".

For the application of this Principle, a Convention concerning access to information, the right of participation of the public in the decision-making process and access to justice on issues concerning the protection of the environment (the Aarhus Convention) was concluded in 1998, under the auspices of the Economic Commission for Europe.

According to this Convention, „In order to contribute to the protection of the right of every person of present and future generations to live in an environment adequate for his or her health and wellbeing, each Party shall guarantee the rights of access to information, to public participation in decision-making, and access to justice in environmental matters in accordance with the provisions of this Convention".

The Aarhus Convention is considered an important extension of the rights in the field of environment as well as of human rights; although the emphasis is placed on the respective procedural rights, the Convention contains also important provisions on the protection of the environment, such as the Annex I which enumerates the dangerous activities to which the Convention is applicable.

Similar provisions were included in the 1993 North-American Agreement on the cooperation in the field of environment, which recognizes the legitimate interest of persons and non-governmental organizations to initiate procedures for the application of internal law in the field of environment. Procedural rights of the same type are provided for in other conventions concluded within the UN Economic Convention for Europe (the 1991Convention on the evaluation of impact on environment in the trans- boundary context, the 1992 Convention on the protection and the use of waters, the 2003 Protocol on the strategic evaluation of environment).

SECTION 2 - PROTECTION of the ENVIRONMENT and HUMAN RIGHTS in the ACTIVITY of JURISDICTIONAL BODIES

International jurisdictions also approached aspects of the protection of the environment in connection with human rights. In the jurisprudence of the International Court of Justice, there is its Advisory Opinion of 1966 concerning „The lawfulness of the threat with nuclear weapons and of their use", where the Court admits indirectly that the use of nuclear weapons would represent a violation of legal principles and norms applicable to armed conflicts, while with regard to self-defense, it affirms that the respect of the environment constitutes a criterion of the necessity and the proportionality of the use of nuclear weapons.

The Court interpreted the provisions of the Protocol I to the 1949 Geneva Conventions for the protection of victims of armed conflicts with the meaning that „they postulate a general obligation to protect the natural environment against extended, durable and serious damage…; it postulates the interdiction of methods and means of

---

[492] I. Diaconu, op. cit., pp. 162-166.

war which would pursue …to cause such damage, as well as the prohibition of attacks against the environment through a war of reprisals"[493].

In the case Gabcikovo-Nagymaros, between Hungary and the Slovak Republic, the Court stressed the fundamental principle which forbids producing damages to the environment of another State, affirming „the general obligation that States have to see that activities exercised within their jurisdictional limits or under their control respect the environment in other States or in areas beyond the national jurisdiction is now part of the corpus of norms of the international law of environment". The Court also affirmed as general principles of international law in the field of the environment: prevention, precaution and the evaluation of the impact, underlying the …" continuous, and necessarily in evolution obligation…to maintain the quality of Danube waters and to protect nature[494].

The jurisprudence developed on issues of environment by European, African and Inter-American jurisdictional bodies of human rights has contributed to clarifying some aspects of the impact of the deterioration of environment on the enjoyment of human rights. The three bodies took note of the direct relationship which exists between a healthy environment and respect of human rights, taking as a basis the provisions of the treaties they are called to monitor. In decisions, they adopted as an answer to individual or collective petitions concerning violations of human rights, they stressed the environmental dimension of human rights such as the right to life, the right to private and family life, the right to property and the right to development.

Although the 1950 European Convention on the protection of fundamental human rights and freedoms contains no provision concerning the environment, issues on environment were dealt with by the Court in connection with some of the rights provided for in the Convention. The Court contributed to confirming the relationship between human rights and the environment in decisions given in some cases submitted to it concerning the pollution of the environment. The Court retained that the pollution of the environment can endanger several human rights, in particular the right to life and the right to family life and private life. Moreover, it retained that the State is obliged to protect persons against the environmental risk and clarified the responsibilities of the State, such as the adoption of adequate legislation, monitoring its application and disseminating information to the public about environmental risks.

In order to analyzing the relationship between environment and human rights, the Court started from the conception of democracy in the field of environment. Thus, it estimated that the obligation to protect individual rights should be balanced against the collective interests of the society. Moreover, it stressed that a State has a certain margin of appreciation in the elaboration of its environmental policy, but this discretion is not absolute and has to be restricted by the proportionality between the impact foreseen and the individual rights affected. The Court underlined the importance of the national procedural guarantees allowing the dialogue on the environmental policy, including the information of the public, the capacity to take part in decision-making process and to request a jurisdictional control over the decisions of the public authorities[495].

In the case Fredin v. Sweden, in connection with the cancellation of a permit because the respective exploitation made too much noise, without taking a direct position on this issue, the Court affirmed that „in the society of today the protection of the environment is a consideration of increasing importance"[496]. A direct relationship between the protection of the environment and respect for human rights was established by the Court in the case Lopez-Ostra; a family living at a distance of 12 m from a waste-treatment factory complained that their physical and mental health was affected. The European Commission on human rights established a causal connection between the gas and fume emissions and the illness of the daughter of the claimant. Then the Court decided that a serious pollution of the environment, even without seriously endangering health, may have as consequences to affect the wellbeing of persons and impede the enjoyment of their houses, thus affecting their private and family life[497].

In other cases, the Court rejected the petition of 10 Swiss citizens for not proving that the functioning of a nuclear plant exposes them to a personal serious and imminent danger[498], while when other claimants invoked the fact that the Italian government did not offer information about the danger of pollution, the Court decided that not

---

[493] ICJ, Recueil, 1996, para. 29.

[494] CIJ, Recueil 1997, para. 53-140; Decion of the Court presented extensively by Sandrine Maljean Dubois, L'arrêt rendu par la Cour Internationale de Justice le 25 septembre 1997 en l'affaire relative au projet Gabcikovo-Nagymaros(Hongrie/Slovaquie, in Annuaire Français de Droit International, 1997, p. 331 and following and by Jochen Sohnle, L'irruption du droit de l'environnement dans la jurisprudence de la CIJ: affaire Gabcikovo-Nagymaros, in Revue Générale de Droit International Public, 1998, p. 92 and foll..

[495] Doc.A/HRC/19/34, para. 37-38; cases *Ömeryildiz v . Turkey*, petition nr. 48939/99 (2004), *Fadeyva v. Russia*, petition nr. 55723/00 (2005) and others.

[496] European Court of Human Rights, nr. 12033/86, decision of 18 February 1991, Serie A, nr. 192, para. 48.

[497] Ibidem, case Lopez-Ostra v. Spaniei, nr. 16798/90, decision of 9 December 1994, Serie A, nr. 303-C, p. 277.

[498] Case Balmer-Shafroth and others v. Switzerland, ECHR, decision of 3 August 1996, Rec. 1996..

informing the local population about the risk factor related to the chemical factory and how to proceed in case of accident represented a violation of the Convention[499]. The Court affirmed that it was ready to deduce the existence of a right to environment from the catalogue of the existing rights.

More recently, the Court ascertained the violation of the right to life in case of a flow of mud[500] and of a flood[501], in case of waste in front of the door and under the windows[502], of non-collecting urban waste[503] and others.

The Court enounced the obligation of States to adopt practical measures for an effective protection of their citizens whose life can be threatened by dangerous economic activities[504].

The Court also affirmed rights of a procedural character in the field of environment, in connection with human rights to life and to private life, and the corresponding obligations of States to proceed to a study of impact on environment and to inform citizens at request when these human rights are threatened[505]. The Court applied, in cases concerning the relationship between rights provided for in the Convention and the protection of environment, the right to a fair trial and the right to have access to a court of law, but did not accept the right of organizations involved in the protection of environment, except for protecting material interests of their members, and not for the general public interest[506].

At the European level, also, the European Committee for social rights, a monitoring body created by the European Social Charter, indicated the environmental dimensions of the right to health. The Committee interpreted the provision on the elimination of causes of a deficient health (article 11 of the European Social Charter) as guaranteeing the right to a healthy environment, ascertained that Greece did not fulfill its obligations to eliminate such causes, did not adopt measures neither developed a strategy to combat threats to public health and established that air pollution resulting from the exploitation of lignite mines in order to produce electricity in Greece represented a violation of the right to health[507]. The Committee underlined that the protection of the environment is a key element of the right to health and indissolubly linked to the right to life. The Committee also indicated that States must take all possible measures in order to protect the right to health, which includes the adequate implementation of international agreements on the environment[508]. The European Court, together with the European Social Committee, gives primary attention to the protection of human rights, per their mandate under the relevant conventions, and indirectly to a healthy environment, in as much as its pollution could endanger human rights.

The African Commission of human rights and rights of peoples (which exercised temporarily jurisdictional functions, until the formation of the African Court on human rights), dealt in particular with the rights of indigenous and tribal peoples, affected by the deterioration of the environment in the region, because of extractive activities and of forced displacement of populations from their ancestral lands. The Commission underlined the importance of the right to a healthy environment, stipulated in the 1981 Charter, and insisted upon the importance of the impact environment study and upon the scientific independent evaluation before beginning such activities. It also affirmed the right of the respective populations to benefit of their natural resources and their right to development, stressing the importance of their free, previous and well informed consent for such activities[509].

In the case Ogoniland, the African Commission held that article 24 of the African Charter imposes upon States the obligation to adopt reasonable measures to prevent pollution and ecologic deterioration, to promote conservation, sustainable development and the ecological use of natural resources. The Commission asked the respective State[510] to fully clean the land and waters prejudiced by operations with crude oil, to prepare an environmental and social impact, to ensure information on health and environmental risk and effective access to regulatory bodies and to the decision- making process.

---

[499] Case Guerra and others v. Italy, ECHR nr. 116/1996/735/932, decision of 19 February 1998, Rec. 1998 I..

[500] ECHR, Boudaieva v. Russia, no. 15339/02, decision of 20 March 2008, Rec. 2008.

[501] ECHR, Omeryldiz v. Turquie, no. 48939/99, decision of 30 November 2004, Rec. 2004 XII.

[502] ECHR, Kolyadenko v. Russia, no. 17423/05, decision of 28 February 2012.

[503] ECHR, Surugiu v. Romania, no. 48995/99, decision of 20 April 2004.

[504] ECHR, Di Sarno v. Italy, no. 30765/08. decision of 10 January 2012.

[505] ECHR, case Budayeva and Omeryldiz, cited above.

[506] ECHR, Tatar v. Romania, no. 67021/01, decision of 27 January 2009; Grimkovskaia v. Ukraine, no.38182/03, decision of 21 July 2011; Guerra and others v. Italy, cited above.

[507] CEDS, Fondation Marangopoulos pour les droits de l'homme v. Greece, no. 30/2005, 6 December 2006.

[508] Case Fondation Marangopoulos v. Greece..

[509] General presentation in doc.A/HRC/19/34, para 39.

[510] Case SERAC and CESR v. Nigéria, communication no. 155/96, 27 May 2002 ; also the case *Centre pour le développement des droits des minorités (Kenya) et Minority Rights Group International pour Endorois Welfare Council v. Kenya*, communication no. 276/2003, 4 February 2010.

The Inter-American Court on human rights contributed to the elaboration of important norms in the field of environment concerning the protection of indigenous populations. It affirmed with clarity that indigenous and tribal peoples have a right of property over the lands and territories they occupied traditionally. For this purpose, the Court interpreted the American Convention on human rights in the light of the international Covenants on human rights, mainly based on the right of peoples to self-determination, and considering the 169 Convention of International Labour Organization concerning indigenous and tribal peoples, which expressly provides these rights.

The Inter-American Court also elaborated a system of guarantees to be applied when a State has in view to approve projects of development or investments which are likely to compromise the exercise of the rights of indigenous peoples (such as independent environment and social evaluations, adequate schemes of sharing the advantages, adequate and efficient consultations, as well as obtaining the free, previous and well informed consent[511].

A particular interest in this context presents the decision of the Inter-American Commission on human rights, which considered in 1985 a petition versus Brazil concerning activities of developers and companies engaged in the exploitation of minerals and wood in the area of Amazons, inhabited by the Indians Yanomani. The Commission ascertained that interference of these developers and companies, which included also the construction of a high-way on the land inhabited by Yanomani, produced trouble in their social life and brought illnesses which decimated the population. The Commission concluded that Brazil violated the provisions of the American Declaration on human rights and freedoms, in particular the rights to life and to the protection of health[512].

Substantial interest raised also the conclusions of the Inter-American Commission in the case Maya Indigenous Community of Toledo; according to the Commission, the concessions to build on the territories used by that community threaten on a long term basis to bring irreversible damage to the natural environment on which the agricultural system of subsistence of this population depends. The Commission underlined that activities of development should be accompanied by adequate and effective measures to ensure that they do not take place to the expense of the fundamental rights of persons who can be adversely affected, including the indigenous communities and the environment on which they depend regarding their physical, cultural and spiritual wellbeing. The Commission asked the State of Belize to repair the damage produced to the environment and to take measures for the demarcation and the protection of the land of the community in consultation with it[513].

To summarize, although they had in view different human rights, the European, African and American bodies on human rights underlined the environmental dimension of human rights that they must protect according to their legal instruments. Their decisions in cases concerning the pollution of the environment, the extraction of minerals or other exploitations in areas traditionally inhabited by indigenous people or in case of forced displacements of populations allowed them to affirm the responsibility of States with regard to the protection of individual rights and to the decision-making processes in the field of environment.

Nevertheless, this is not guaranteeing the right to a healthy and satisfactory environment, in cases which are not based on claims related to violation of a right provided for in the respective treaty. On the other side, we note that the jurisprudence does not consider cases concerning climate changes and the irrational use of natural resources, which represent the most serious challenges to a healthy environment on our planet[514].

SECTION 3 - The PROTECTION of the ENVIRONMENT in the ACTIVITY of HUMAN RIGHTS TREATY BODIES within the UNITED NATIONS

Human rights treaty bodies within the UN also approached issues related to the protection of the environment. The Committee on economic, social and cultural rights (CESC) and the Committee of Human Rights (on the civil and political rights- HRC) appreciated that the realization of the rights under their mandate depends largely on a healthy environment[515]. In its General Comment no.4(1991) on the right to adequate housing, CESC

---

[511] Presentation in doc. A/HRC/19/34, para. 32. ; decisions concerning some aspects, for example *Moiwana Community v. Suriname*, 15 June 2005; *Claude-Reyerand consortsvc. Chili*, 19 September 2006; Indigenous *Community sawhoyamaxavc. Paraguay*, 29 March 2006.
[512] Yanomani Indians v. Bresil, decision 7615, Annual Report of the Inter-American Commission on Human Rights, 1984-1985.
[513] Case 12053, Report no. 40/04, IACHR, OEA, Ser.I/V/II, Doc. 5, Rev. 1, p. 727, 2004.
[514] P. Birnie, A. Boyle and C. Redgwell, op. cit., p. 302.
[515] Doc. A/HRC/19/34, para. 56- 61.

interpreted this right as including access to employment options, health-care services, schools and other facilities and should not be built on polluted sites nor in immediate proximity of pollution sources[516].

In its General Comment nr. 12(1999) on the right to adequate food, CESC affirmed that this right is inseparable from social justice and requires the adoption of appropriate economic, environmental and social policies and that these policies are crucial in order to guarantee that food does not contain dangerous substances resulting from the contamination due to a bad environmental hygiene. The General Comment also mentions the productivity of land and other natural resources as closely related to a healthy environment, meaning of the soil and of water[517].

In its General Comment nr. 14(2000) on the right to the highest attainable standard of health, the Committee stressed the elements of the right to health and its determining factors, among which the existence of a healthy environment, affirming that the safety of the environment helps to combat and to prevent endemic illnesses. The Committee also invited States parties to elaborate and implement national policies meant to reduce and eliminate the pollution of air, water and soil, including pollution with heavy metals such as lead resulting from gasoline[518].

The Committee appreciates that article 12.2 b of the Covenant (which provides for the adoption of measures to improve all aspects of environmental and industrial hygiene) postulates "the right to a natural and professional healthy environment".

CESC recognized the existence of a fundamental right to water, which is vital for human dignity and for realizing other human rights, in particular the right to a sufficient standard of living, enounced in article 11 of the Covenant. For this purpose, in its General Comment nr. 15 (2002) on the right to water, the Committee explicitly linked the right to water with environmental hygiene, observing that an adequate delivery of water should be free from micro-organisms, chemical substances and radiological hazards and that water should be of an acceptable colour, odor and a taste for each personal or domestic use, that the benefit of the right to water depends of its quality from the point of view of the environment[519].

Considering the relationship existing between numerous human rights and the access to cultural goods and services related to environment, the Committee indicated in its General Comment nr. 21(2009) on the right of each person to participate in cultural life, that the availability of cultural goods is necessary to enjoy this right. Among the numerous cultural goods and services, the Committee includes "the benefits of nature", that States are obliged to protect from deterioration and from destruction, in order to respect the right to cultural life.

The indigenous peoples have also the right "to act collectively for the observance of their right to preserve, protect and develop their cultural heritage", which includes their knowledge on plants and animals as well as on genetic resources". In view of this right, States parties are obliged to respect the principle of the "previous consent of indigenous peoples, given freely and in full knowledge of the situation"[520].

Although it starts with human rights, CESC deals very often with the protection of different elements of the environment as a value *per se,* affirming the obligations of States in the context of a progressive approach indicated by the Covenant on economic, social and cultural rights.

The Human Rights Committee also contributed to clarifying some aspects of the relationship between human rights and the environment. For instance, its jurisprudence on the rights of indigenous peoples, mainly the right to benefit of their own culture, played an essential role in the elaboration of norms concerning the effective participation of vulnerable groups to consultations concerning activities which can affect them. In its General Comment nr. 34(2011) concerning article 19 of the Covenant on civil and political rights (on the freedom of expression and information), the Committee recognizes explicitly the right of access to information, which is essential to have knowledge about the environmental risks to which human beings and communities are exposed, in order to adopt the necessary preventive measures[521]. The Committee had to solve also some communications concerning human rights in connection with environment.

In the case Hope Environmental Group v. Canada, the Committee accepted the position of the petitioners according to which deposits of nuclear waste raise a serious problem for the right to life of local residents and for the future generations, in accordance with article 6 of the Covenant, but declared the communication inadmissible because the internal available remedies were not exhausted[522]. The case Bordes v. France, concerning a

---

[516] Compilation of general comments and general recommendations adopted by human rights treaty bodies, doc. HRI/GEN/1/Rev. 9, 27 May 2008, vol. I, p. 18.
[517] Ibidem, p.67.
[518] Ibidem, p. 93.
[519] Compilation..., Rev. 9, vol. I, p. 115.
[520] Doc. E/C.12/GC/21 of 21 December 2009.
[521] Doc. CCPR/C/GC/34 of 21 July 2011.
[522] Communication nr. 67/1980, 2 Selected Decisions of the UN Human Rights Committee, 1990, p. 20.

communication about nuclear tests in the Pacific Ocean, was rejected because the Committee considered that there was no proof of a serious danger for human life[523].

In its General Comment nr. 15 (2013), the Committee on the Rights of the Child draws the attention on the importance of the environment for the health of children. The Committee affirms that climate changes represent one of the biggest threats for the health of children, and requests that States place the children's health in the center of strategies in this field. The Comment recalls the obligation of States to take into account the risks of pollution of the natural environment for the health of children, to ensure them an adequate house, a framework which ensures good ventilation, without fumes, the absence of toxic substances and a family hygiene which is at the basis of growth[524].

In its General Recommendation nr. 23 of 1997 on the rights of indigenous peoples, the Committee for the Elimination of Racial Discrimination (CERD) asked States in particular to recognize and protect the right of indigenous peoples to own, develop, control and use their communal lands, territories and resources and, where they have been deprived of this right without their free and informed consent, to take steps to return those lands and territories.

The Committee also included, among the criteria adopted in 2007 to initiate the early warning and urgent action procedure, "the pollution or dangerous activities which reflect a type of racial discrimination conducing to substantial damages to specific groups". In its observations and recommendations addressed to States following the consideration of their periodic reports as States parties to the 1965 Convention on the elimination of all forms of racial discrimination, the Committee expressed its concern about activities of deforestation and other destructions of the environment and asked that States take urgent measures to combat the "ecological racism" and the deterioration of the environment in the areas inhabited by minorities or by indigenous peoples, to ensure the environment control, to develop specific policies of environmental impact for projects which could affect them and to ensure the consultation and participation of their members on issues of environment[525].

To sum up, the committees created by treaties on human rights also contributed to clarify some aspects of the environmental dimension of human rights. Continuing this evolution, the Human Rights Council, a specialized body created by the General Assembly in 2006, declared that the illegal circulation and disposal of dangerous substances and waste threaten the human rights to life and to health and that climate changes have an adverse impact on the rights to life, to health, to food, to housing and on the right to self-determination of peoples[526].

SECTION 4 - HUMAN RIGHTS and RESPONSIBILITIES in the FIELD of ENVIRONMENT

Both international documents and decisions of some courts, as well as constitutions and national laws, affirmed the right of each person, some of them also the right of peoples, to a healthy environment. This right is defined by reference to the quality of factors of environment, concerning all its elements, that is air, water, soil, flora and fauna. This construction is sending us to different regulations concerning each of these elements, to commitments taken by States to protect environment against factors of pollution.

This right, which may be recognized now by a customary norm of international law, has for correspondent several obligations of States resulting from a series of international conventions in different fields. The sphere of obligations incumbent to various States is different, but all States undertook obligations towards persons living on their territory and towards other States, that is indirectly towards their populations.

The right to a healthy environment is related to numerous human rights, which present important environmental dimensions, meaning that their enjoyment and exercise can be affected by the deterioration of elements of the environment. In this respect, international documents and practice refer to:
- the right to life, which can be endangered by numerous polluting human activities and by natural disasters;
- the right to health, which depends to a large extent on the quality of the environment, of air, water, soil, of flora and fauna;
- the right of private and family life, which can be affected by modifications of the living environment produced by polluting activities;

---

[523] Communication nr. 645/1995, Report of the Committee, GAOR A/51/40, vol. II.
[524] Observation générale nr. 15/2013 sur le droit de l'enfant de jouir du meilleur état de santé possible (art . 24), doc. CRC/C/GC/ du 17 avril 2013.
[525] Cases presented extensively by Ion Diaconu, Racial Discrimination, 2011, Eleven Publishers, The Hague, pp.92, 115, 116-117, 230, 349.
[526] Numerous resolutions of the Council, for example nr. 7/14, 7/23, 9/1, 10/12, 13/4 and others.

- the right to housing, which depends of maintaining environmental conditions allowing the constant and optimum use of the house;
- the right to sufficient food, which can be affected by conditions of environment which are not adequate for acceding to food or which destroy food reserves, which pollute food or sources producing it;
- the right to water of quality, meaning both drinkable water and water used for other uses necessary for a decent life;
- the right to enjoy one's own culture, of access to culture under its different forms, which can be seriously affected by the pollution of the environment, by the destruction of cultural objects and values or by impeding access to them;
- the right to development of persons, communities and peoples, because serious deterioration of elements of environment reduces on a long-term basis the possibilities of development and can destroy the resources necessary to a sustainable development.

To these universal rights, which belong to each person, one has to add the right of indigenous peoples to preserve, restore and protect their way of life, including their natural environment, consisting of the land and natural resources used by them traditionally, which are closely related to their identity and culture. International documents and the constitutions of many States also recognize the right of these peoples, as well as the right of other minority groups, to be consulted and to give their free, previous and well informed consent with regard to activities which could take place in the areas where they live.

In terms of procedures, some documents and judicial decisions, mainly in Europe, affirm the obligation of States to undertake activities of evaluation and impact studies before authorizing activities which can affect the environment and to respect the principles of prevention (meaning to avoid any activity which could produce pollution of the environment, taking into account proportionally the benefit achieved as against the potential damage) and of precaution (to refrain from any activity which could produce serious damage to environment even if impact studies and scientific research are not conclusive in this respect) in connection with such activities.

Some international documents and documents of the European Union provide, as obligations of States under different forms of monitoring and as corresponding rights of the public concerned (persons and non-governmental organizations), the information of the public about such activities, the participation of the public to the decision-making process on such activities and access to justice in case of refusal to inform and to allow the public participation, and even access to justice to challenge the validity of decisions to authorize activities which could have adverse effects on environment.

These are aspects of human rights generally recognized in international law, which aim at the practical application of these rights in a specific field of human life, that is the relationship between the human being and the nature surrounding him/her, considering that activities of people, organized in States and communities, can produce serious damage to environment which would endanger the exercise of many human rights. A process of "greening human rights" is recommended to States as one of the ways to protect the environment[527].

Political and civil rights offer a large basis for protection of the individual against such activities affecting elements of the environment which would endanger the exercise of one or the other of these rights. They also offer the basis for the action of persons, individually or associated in different forms, for the protection of the environment, exercising their rights to information, to expression, to participate in public activities and to the public process in modalities provided for by the law, as well as the right to address to a court of law. The jurisprudence of regional courts and of human rights treaty bodies recognized the protection of environment as a legitimate objective, both in the policy of States and in the petitions presented by persons with regard to violations of their rights.

The approach of the protection of the environment starting from human rights is of course important to protect the human being from activities affecting him/her by the pollution of the environment; analysts consider nevertheless that this approach is limited, because it protects the environment by ricochet, does not protect nature as a value per se and leaves aside the animal and vegetal world, the landscape, the biological diversity[528]. It also supposes traditionally the existence of an individual interest to resort to justice with a view to protecting these rights, excluding action for the general interest, mainly that of non-governmental organizations which promote the protection of the environment[529].

---

[527] Patricia Birnie, Alan Boyle and Catherine Redgwell, art. cit., pp. 282-283.
[528] Alexander Fluckiger, art. cit., pp. 613-614.
[529] Ibidem, pp. 616-617.

The other approach tends to grant to nature itself some rights that States, communities and persons commit themselves to respect; it would be reflected by documents such as the World Charter of Nature, adopted by the UN General Assembly in 1982, the treaties on Antarctica, the 1979 Berne Convention on the protection of wild life and of the natural habitat, the 1992 Convention on biologic diversity, the Convention on climate changes and others mentioned above.

Analysts of these evolutions ascertain that the legal system develops in the way of reconciling the two approaches, gradually promoting a fundamental human right to an environment qualified as healthy, sometimes as salubrious, safe and adequate for ensuring the wellbeing of people, for ensuring a viable, sustainable and ecologically balanced development.

One may appreciate that the documents adopted based on the Framework Convention on climate change, mainly the Paris Agreement of December 2015, reflect this conception, because the entirety of its provisions aim both at the protection of human rights, closely related to sustainable development and to interests of vulnerable groups, and at the protection of elements of nature which are indispensable for the respect of human rights and for sustainable development.

It is considered necessary to overcome the classic approach of individual rights in order to ensure effectively the preservation of biodiversity, of the climate, of landscape, of the soil fertility, of natural resources and of the genetic animal and vegetable heritage, at present and for the future generations, in substance a right which would protect both the individual and the general interest. The concept proposed is that of a fundamental right to a healthy and ecological harmonious environment[530].

* * *

We note that the protection of the rights of elements of nature *per se,* of the environment and the adoption of obligations of States and of people to protect biodiversity, the climate and natural resources, represent an approach which is already present in the sectorial instruments mentioned above concerning the reduction and the elimination of the pollution of air and water, as well as those on different substances which can produce serious damage to the environment. To this, one has to add commitments taken sometimes individually by States, otherwise within international organizations, concerning ecologically protected areas.

These regulations prove the increasing trend to protect different elements of the environment, through substantial obligations taken by States, in view of the collective interests of humanity. It is to be expected that international law progresses by the adoption of such regulations containing stronger obligations concerning elements of the environment and thus extending its protection.

The Agenda 2030 for sustainable development, adopted by the UN General Assembly (resolution A/70/1 of 21 October 2015) as a result of the Summit concerning post 2015 agenda, includes among the objectives of that period to protect, restore and promote sustainable use of terrestrial ecosystems, sustainable manage forests, combat desertification, halt and reverse land degradation and halt diversity loss. It provides time - frame for each of these objectives, while States are asked to integrate ecosystems and biodiversity values into national and local planning, in the development processes and in the strategies for reducing poverty. With regard to the right to health, the Agenda provides for the access to affordable essential medicines and vaccines, in accordance with the Doha Declaration on Agreements concerning intellectual property (TRIPS) and public health, according to which developing countries have the right to fully use the provisions of this Agreement with regard to flexibilities to protect public health, and in particular provide access to medicine for all.

Human rights to a healthy environment are closely related to the exercise of the majority of rights considered economic, social and cultural, because to ensure a decent standard of living (food, housing, health conditions) depends on the quality of the environment; this in turn depends on the level of development, on the participation of the entire society in the economic and social development and on the cultural level of education of the society.

The quality and the protection of the environment represent also a right of solidarity, because the communities and peoples are those affected by the environment and thus have the right to act by legal and political means for an environment adequate to health and to the normal life and activity of the human being[531]. One can appreciate that this is also a collective right[532], if we refer to the rights of indigenous peoples to preserve and protect

---

[530] Supra, pp. 4-5.
[531] Patricia Birnie, Alan Boyle Catherine Redgwell, International Law & the Environment, Oxford New-York, 2009, pp. 271-272.
[532] Ion Diaconu, Human Rights in the Contemporary International Law, theory and practice, second edition, 2010, pp. 246-250, Ed. Lumina Lex (in Romanian).

their special relationship with the lands and resources they own or traditionally use, as a crucial element for preserving and developing their culture and identity.

As in other fields of the social life-economic, political, cultural - human rights present specific aspects in connection with each of the elements of environment and are confronted with some of the most various violations.

The answer to them should be environmental policies and measures aiming at the full respect of human rights, as well as instruments allowing the democratic management of elements of the environment, by the extended information and participation of the public in the elaboration and the application of policies in this field. Underlying these specific aspects of the application of human rights in connection with each of the elements of environment, as well as the corresponding responsibilities of States in international documents which the UN proposes to undertake by the last studies, is particularly important for enhancing and deepening the action of the international community in this field, for mobilizing the public opinion in favour of preserving a healthy environment on our planet.

CHAPTER XVIII - CLIMATE CHANGES and HUMAN RIGHTS

ABSTRACT

It is a fact that climate phenomena such as hurricanes, earthquakes, drought and floods are nowadays more destructive, more frequent and adversely affect larger areas of the Earth. Researchers proved that the cause of this situation is the warming of the Planet produced by the greenhouse gas emissions.

The increase of the global average temperature of Earth produces the melting of icebergs, the raising of the level and of the temperature of waters of the oceans, the prolongation of periods of extreme temperature and of waves of heat, the increased intensity of tropical cyclones, the abundance of rain or snowfall in some areas and the extension of areas affected by drought in others. These factors produce serious violations of human rights, such as the right to life, to health care, to clean water, to a decent standard of living, many rights of indigenous peoples, in the areas affected, as well as of the right to self-determination of island people and other peoples living on low lands.

Who is responsible for such violations? What have mankind, peoples, States to do to protect themselves against such effects? What is the state of international law in this field? One may note that there are no determined efforts of the States to respond to these developments which are dangerous for the future of mankind.

KEY WORDS: climate change, greenhouse gas emissions, warming of the Planet, violations of human rights, mitigation, adaptation, precaution.

INTRODUCTION

Our planet has always known climate changes, some more destructive than others, which led to changes in human life, sometimes abrupt, often unexpected, through the accumulation of substances, through the reduction or even disappearance of some elements of nature.

However, mankind is confronted nowadays with climate phenomena which are extremely destructive, repeated and affecting extended areas of the globe. It seems that never hurricanes, earthquakes, drought and floods had the intensity and the frequency of today.

The question we should ask ourselves is to what extent the human being is, and in whatever way, at the origin of some of these phenomena and how could States, the human society act in order to prevent them, to protect themselves and to diminish their effects, to eliminate their consequences, briefly to protect people and all which is related to life on earth. Therefore, climate changes became an important subject on the international political agenda. Technical studies were elaborated, but it is obvious that such problems cannot be solved by scientists; they need substantial and determined measures which imply political decisions by States.

Technical studies show that if drastic measures are not taken to reduce the volume of greenhouse gases, dramatic changes in the living conditions on the planet will take place: extinction of 20-30% of the species of existing plants and animals, destruction of some ecosystems, erosion of coasts, extreme climate phenomena, reduction of water and food sources, starvation and increased frequency of some illnesses. At the regional level, effects will be different; the most affected will be Africa (the lack of water resources), the coastal and delta areas of Asia subject to floods, Australia (an important loss of biodiversity), in Europe (the melting of glaciers and the lack of water in the South of the continent), in Latin America (the loss of tropical woods and of biodiversity), in Northern America (restrictions of water and strong waves), in the polar areas changes in the ecosystems, and in the area of small island storms and floods[533].

Successive reports of the Intergovernmental Group on Climate Changes (IPCC), created in 1988 to study these issues, reveal a clear scientific consensus, with more than 90% certainty that the essential of the warming of the planet observed during the last 50 years is due to emissions of gases having a greenhouse effect because of human activities[534]. The present level of concentration of gas with greenhouse effect is by far higher than the pre-industrial levels registered in the ice polar areas, the main cause being the burning of fossil fuels.

---

[533] Extensively presented by Paul C. Harris, Introduction: glacial politics of climate change, in The Politics of Climate Change; Environmenta Dynamics in Internatiuonal Affairs, New-York, 2009, p. 2.
[534] Climate change 2007-Synthesis Report, adopted by IPCC Plenary XXVII, Valencia, 12-17 November 2007(IPCC AR4 Synthesis Report), p. 72; more recently, Conseil des Droits de l'Homme, Rapport du Haut-Commissariat des Nations Unies sur les liens entre les changements

The main variations of the climate observed in relation with the warming of the planet are:
- reduction of the areas covered by snow and the reduction of the icebergs;
- raise of the level of sea waters and of their temperature;
- increased frequency of the moments of extreme temperature and of waves of heat;
- abundance of rains in some areas and extension of areas affected by drought;
- increased intensity of tropical cyclones (typhoons, hurricanes).

Studies show that this evolution affects human live in six important fields: ecosystems; food production; water; health; maritime coasts; industry, human settlements and society. The legal framework in this field is the Framework Convention of the United Nations of 1992 concerning climate changes. According to this Convention, climate changes taken into account are those attributed directly or indirectly to human activities which change the composition of the atmosphere and are added to the natural variability of the climate. By this Convention, States parties set up as their objective to stabilize the concentration of greenhouse gases in the atmosphere at a level which prevents negative effects on the climate, and to attain such a level in a period of time which is sufficient for the ecosystems to adapt to changes, for the food production not to be threatened and to allow sustainable economic development.

For that purpose, the States parties committed themselves among others: to set up, to keep updated and to publish national inventories of greenhouse gases; to set up and to publish national and as needed regional programmes containing measures meant to alleviate climate changes, taking into account these gas emissions; to encourage and support cooperation for applying technologies, practices and methods allowing the control, the reduction and the prevention of such emissions; to prepare the adaptation to the impact of climate changes and to set up integrated plans and ensure their management; to encourage scientific and technological research, the exchange of data and the education of the population with regard to climate changes.

As the studies show that industrialized countries contributed more to the emissions of greenhouse gases, while the consequences of climate changes are unequally distributed and affect more poor countries and regions, the 1992 Convention provided for the obligation of States parties to preserve the climatic system „on an equitable basis and taking into account their common but differentiated responsibilities and their capacities"; it is specified that developed countries should be in the forefront of struggle against climate changes and their adverse effects, and that needs of the developing countries , mainly those particularly vulnerable to adverse effects of climate changes, should be taken into account.

According to this Convention, developed countries shall reduce emissions of greenhouse gases till 2000 at the level of 1990. In the meantime, some emergent countries developed much more their industrial production (China, India) and increased significantly their share of greenhouse gas emissions; this raises the issue of the level of their commitments in this field.

The Convention asks the Conference of parties to periodically examine the obligations of the parties and the international arrangements under the Convention in the light of its objectives, of the experience gained in its implementation and the evolution of scientific and technological knowledge.

On this basis, States parties concluded in 1998 the Kyoto Protocol, in force since 2005, containing their quantitative commitments to reduce until 2012 emissions of greenhouse gas by 5,2% below the level of 1990. Nevertheless, this Protocol was not accepted by the United States of America, which at the end of the twentieth century released the biggest quantity of such gases, and encountered difficulties in its application. Subsequent negotiations started from this Protocol, without changing the commitments of States. During that period, a scheme of selling licenses of emissions developed, according to which States which produce greenhouse gas emissions below the level of 1990 may sell on the market such shares to States which continue to produce such emissions above the level of those of 1990. Although this does not contribute *per se* to the reduction of the volume of greenhouse gases and offers mainly to the developed States the possibility to continue the same way, it is a fact that due to the costs implied a trend made its way in the States concerned to develop sources of energy which are not producing emissions of greenhouse gases (such as the energy of winds, of waves, as well as solar energy)[535]. Successive reviews did not lead to any new commitments for States parties. The review of 2008 ended without a clear outcome or a plan for a follow-up.

---

climatiques et les droits de l'homme, A/HRC/10/61 of 15 January 2009; World Bank Report 2010, Development and Climate Change, November 2010; more extensively Anaid Panossian and Christophe Colette, A propos de la 15-e Conférence des Nations Unies sur les changements climatiques et de l'Accord de Copenhague, in Revue Générale de Droit International Public, no. 1, 2010, p. 129 and following.

[535] Subject developed by Richard Benwell, Linking as leverage: emissions trading and the politics of climate change, in The Politics of Climate Change, pp. 90 and following.

According to Agenda 2030 for sustainable development, adopted by the UN General Assembly resolution nr. 70/1 of 25 September 2015 as a result of the Summit for adopting the development agenda after 2015, this Convention is considered the primary intergovernmental forum for negotiating the global answer to climate changes. The Agenda notes with grave concern the significant gap between the effect of pledges taken concerning annual emissions of greenhouse gases by 2020 and the emissions pathways consistent with holding the increase of global temperature below 2 degrees Celsius.

The Agenda sets up as objective of the durable development the adoption of urgent measures to combat climate changes and their impact and, in this context, to implement the commitment taken by the developed countries to mobilize 100 billion USA dollars annually until 2020 in order to respond to the needs of developing countries related to the action against climate change.

The Paris Conference of State parties of November-December 2015 adopted an Agreement which contains new commitments of the States parties to the 1992 Convention, including to maintain the level of the global increase of temperature to the maximum 2 degrees Celsius and a system of communication of the gradual reductions of carbon emissions and of examination of these reductions by the States parties (which is referred to below).

As a result of these evolutions, the main strategies of struggle against climate changes are presently attenuation and adaptation. *Attenuation* has in view the diminution of the degree of warming of the planet, by the reduction of the level of emissions and the holding of the concentration of greenhouse gases in the atmosphere. Adopting such measures is the main objective of international negotiations on climate changes.

Scientific studies and the political and economic preoccupations in this field show that the level of danger compared with the pre-industrial period, from the point of view of climate variations, would correspond to a maximum increase of the temperature of the globe of 2%. If the increase of the temperature of the planet remains below 2%, the negative consequences on human life would be sensibly reduced.

This supposes that the total emissions of greenhouse gases, after attaining the highest level in this decade, should be reduced below 50% until 2050 and the reduction of emissions should begin in the following 15 years. Even this scenario would lead to an increase of the average temperature of the planet with 2-2,4% compared to the pre-industrial level.

Adaptation supposes measures to face the climate changes, because even if measures foreseen to reduce emissions are taken, the warming of the planet and climate changes will continue as a result of the long-term effects of the previous emissions of greenhouse gases. It includes a series of measures and strategies, from building works of defense against sea waters to the displacement of populations from areas subject to floods, management of water, combating drought, to systems of early warning and of intervention.

SECTION 1 - EFFECTS of CLIMATE CHANGES on HUMAN RIGHTS

The increase of global temperature has already negative effects on human environment; climate changes contribute to the modification of ecosystems, to the pollution of the environment and to the increase of the level of tropospheric ozone in urban areas.

International documents proclaim the fundamental human rights to freedom, equality and satisfactory conditions of life, in an environment allowing him/her to live in dignity and wellbeing (1972 Declaration of the United Nations Conference on environment of Stockholm). The contemporary international law postulates an inherent relationship between the environment and several fundamental human rights, among which the rights to life, to health, to food, to water and to housing.

The warming of the planet has negative effects on the entirety of human rights; however, some of them are more directly affected by climate changes.

The right to life is explicitly guaranteed by the treaties concluded in the field of human rights; no derogation is allowed from this right even in case of danger for the existence of a State. The committees created by such treaties specified that States have the obligation to take positive measures for the protection of the right to life by reducing the infant mortality, eliminating malnutrition and epidemics and ensuring a healthy environment[536]. The Report of evaluation of effects of climate changes refers to the increase of the number of deaths, of illnesses and wounds because of waves of heat, of hurricanes, fires and periods of drought. They will have also as effects the aggravation

---

[536] Human Rights Committee, General Comment no. 6, para. 5; Compilation of General Comments and General Recommendations adopted by Human Rights Treaty Bodies, doc. HRI/GEN/1/Rev. 8, 8 May 2006, pp. 166-167; Committee on the Rights of the Child, General Comment no. 7(2006) on implementing rights in early childhood, para. 10, ibidem, pp. 432-451.

of hunger, of malnutrition and of other factors which affect the growth of children, as well as to multiply the cardio-respiratory diseases and the mortality due to tropospheric ozone.

Climate changes have also for effect the amplification of natural disasters, which endanger human life, mainly in developing countries. The United Nations Programme for Development estimated at 262 million each year the number of persons victims of climate disasters between 2000 and 2014, more that 98% of them in developing countries[537]. The right to life is also closely related to the exercise of some economic and social rights which are enounced below.

The right to sufficient food. Several international instruments on human rights provide for this right and the obligation of States to take measures to ensure its exercise, as we will see in one of the following chapters. As a result of climate changes, it is estimated that at lower altitudes the output of the agricultural production will reduce, resulting in the increase of famine and of food insecurity in the poorest areas of the world; it is estimated that more than 600 million of people will suffer of malnutrition as a result of climate changes[538]. A report submitted to the UN Human Rights Council on the right to food shows that extreme climatic phenomena increasingly endanger the means of subsistence and food security[539].

Consequently, it is considered that the exercise of the right to sufficient food requires to give particular attention to vulnerable groups, mainly to persons living in areas exposed to natural disasters and to indigenous peoples, whose means of subsistence are at risk to be destroyed[540].

The right to water will be extensively presented in one of the following chapters. Studies show that the melting of glaciers and the reduction of the layer of snow will have negative consequences for one sixth of the population of the planet concerning the supply of water. At the same time, floods and prolonged periods of drought have also consequences on the supply of water. Climate changes interact with other factors which aggravate the supply of water, such as the increase of population, the deterioration of the environment, an inadequate management of water reserves, poverty and inequalities.

Climate changes amplify the difficulties of supplying water and of access to drinkable water, while more than 1 billion people are presently deprived of it. These negative effects can be mitigated by adequate measures and policies.

The right to health. This right supposes ensuring under equal conditions a benefit of health care, of access to goods, services and conditions for this purpose. Climate changes have an impact on the state of health of millions of people, due to malnutrition, to the increase of the number of illnesses and accidents produced by extreme meteorological phenomena. In some regions of the world the warming of the planet may lead to the spreading of paludisme and other epidemic illnesses. Negative effects of the climate changes will be more strongly felt in Sub-Saharan Africa, in South Asia and in the Middle East. The most exposed will be persons and communities having reduced capacities and conditions of adaptation.

The right to a suitable house. Climate changes affect also this right in many ways. In the coastal areas, the increase of the level of sea waters and the waves of hurricanes have a direct impact on inhabitants, producing the destruction of houses. In the Arctic areas and in the areas of low islands these phenomena already produced displacement of some populations and communities. The low areas of deltas are exposed to floods which already affected millions of persons and houses. Poverty due partly to climate changes will increase the rural exodus to the periphery of the towns or on the shore of rivers where they will be even more vulnerable.

In conditions of climate changes, respect of this right would include: the adequate protection of houses from the climate phenomena; access to housing in areas which are not in danger; access to shelter and to measures of management of disasters if the displacement cannot be avoided; protection of communities evacuated from dangerous areas.

The right of peoples to self-determination. The increase of the level of sea waters and extreme meteorological phenomena related to climate changes threaten even the territorial existence of many insular States formed of low islands. These changes can also deprive indigenous peoples of their natural territories and resources. This affects dramatically the right of these peoples to self-determination. The flooding of some islands would lead to the disappearance of some States. This would raise numerous legal issues concerning the status of their populations, their future, their cultural identity and others.

---

[537] United Nations Development Programme(UNDP), Human Development Report 2007/2008, Fighting climate change: Human solidarity in a divided world, p. 8.
[538] UNDP Human Development Report, 2006, Beyond scarcity: Power, poverty and the global water crisis.
[539] Doc. A/HRC/7/5, para. 51.
[540] CESCR General Comment no. 12(1999) on the right to food(art. 11), para. 28; Compilation..., pp. 63-70.

More vulnerable groups. It is estimated that women are particularly exposed to climate changes, due to the rolls they are attributed, mainly in less developed societies, as a result of a more reduced degree of preparation and of discrimination. Children also are particularly exposed to risks of mortality and illness and may have difficulties to continue their scholarship.

Climate changes, associated with pollution and degradation of environment, constitute a serious danger for indigenous peoples, who are often living on marginal lands and in natural fragile ecosystems, particularly sensitive to climate changes. For instance, the traditional income resources of Inuit communities from polar regions were already affected, which led to their transfer in other areas. The indigenous peoples from the areas of low islands are in similar difficult situations.

These peoples have their traditional experiences and knowledge concerning adaptation and reaction to natural phenomena; therefore, they should participate in the setting up of strategies to respond to such phenomena in their areas. It is notable that in 2005 a group of Inuits from the Arctic areas of Canada and the USA (Alaska) presented to the Inter-American Commission of human rights a request of compensations from USA for what they considered a violation of their fundamental rights by the climate changes caused by emissions of greenhouse gases released by USA. Although it considered the request inadmissible, the Inter-American Commission drew the attention of the international community on threats to indigenous peoples produced by climate changes[541].

Climate changes may also have as effect strong human migrations. It is estimated that until 2050 some 150 million people will be displaced because of desertification, lack of water, hurricanes and floods, mainly within poor countries and areas. Those persons have the right, in their countries, to the entirety of guarantees concerning human rights, and when they cross the border in another State they also have some basic human rights. A possible scenario is that of complete submersion of small insular States; in this situation, there are States such as Kiribati, Maldives and Tuvalu, which already consider schemes of displacement to higher areas.

According to some studies, climate changes, in interaction with economic, social and political problems, can generate an increased risk of violent conflicts in 46 States where 2,7 billion people live, situated mainly in Sub-Saharan Africa, Asia and Latin America[542]. Such conflicts would have a direct impact on the guarantee and the exercise of human rights. The Special UN Rapporteur on the right to food notes that some conflicts in Africa, including in the area of Darfur, Sudan (now an independent State), are related to the degradation of soil and to the struggle for resources[543].

SECTION 2 - EVALUATION of the SITUATION according to INTERNATIONAL LAW

Rights and obligations. It is thus generally recognized that climate changes have negative effects on the exercise of human rights. One must consider to what extent those causes which produce such phenomena, in particular the emissions of greenhouse gases, can be qualified as violations of human rights, according to the existing norms of international law.

First of all, one should establish a causal link between the emissions of greenhouse gases which took place in one State, or produced by certain industries or enterprises, and their effect on the exercise of human rights in the respective State and in other States. However, the respective emissions may have their origin in several States and from several industries, which is the case in real terms; they cannot be identified by country and based on origin. Second, the effects of the warming of the planet on human rights are only hypothesis on which one cannot found cases of violation of human rights. They may serve only as a basis for strategies meant to attenuate or avoid the warming of the planet.

At the national level, each State has the obligation to protect persons under its jurisdiction against any violation of human rights. However, to what extent a State can be hold responsible for violations of human rights caused by climate changes? Of course, States have to take measures of protection in case of threats to human rights which are foreseen, such as floods in some areas, imminent hurricanes and others. The European Court of Human Rights retained that not adopting measures against foreseen risks can be eventually assimilated to a violation of human rights; the Court retained as violation of the right to life in a case where the authorities of the respective State

---

[541] Cited in the Rapport du Haut Commissariat des Nations Unies aux droits de l'homme sur les liens entre les changements climatiques et les droits de l'homme, doc. A/HRC/10/61 of 15 January 2009, p. 20.
[542] International Alert and Swedish International Development Cooperation Agency, A Climate of Conflict, 2008, p. 7.
[543] Doc. A/HRC/7/5, para. 51.

did not implement a policy of territorial accommodation and of emergency support, although they were informed that an important flow of mud had to take place[544].

Second, States have obligations regarding the exercise of economic, social and cultural rights, irrespective of events which may happen. It is recognized that some aspects of these rights can be realized only progressively, in as much as the resources necessary are available. However, States have the obligation to take some measures of an immediate nature, using at the maximum the resources available to ensure the exercise of some rights, such as the right to health care. Irrespective of the level of available resources, the State has also to guarantee non-discrimination as to the access to these resources, as well as the minimum obligation to ensure the exercise of the essential part of each of the rights provided for in the Covenant.

The information of the public and the access of the public to information on climate changes are also essential to face such events. The lack of information of the public about a risk which is known represents another violation of the obligations of a State, as it can be considered as a cause of violations which otherwise could have been avoided[545]. International documents refer to the duty of States to inform about and to facilitate the access of the public to information on climate changes; the European and Inter-American courts on human rights insisted on the importance of access to information on the risks of the climate changes. At the same time, it is considered that participation in decision-making is an important aspect in the efforts to face the climate changes. Several international documents provide for the right of persons and peoples concerned by decisions concerning areas where they live to be consulted and the obligation to obtain their previous, free and well informed consent with regard to such decisions[546].

Third, the struggle against effects of the climate change needs the cooperation of all members of the international community; as it is a global phenomenon, with global effects, the struggle against it needs the efforts of all of them.

In its comments on the Covenant the application of which it is charged to monitor, the Committee on economic, social and cultural rights affirmed that States have legal obligations: to refrain from impeding the exercise of human rights in other countries; to take measures to impede third parties, for instance private companies on which they have control or influence, to interfere with the exercise of human rights in other States; depending on available resources, to act in order to facilitate the full exercise of human rights in other States, including by offering support in case of disaster and assistance to refugees and to displaced persons; to see that international agreements give due attention to human rights and avoid endangering them[547]. That means that respect for human rights is considered as a general principle applied to all activities at the national and international levels, as human being is the central subject of development.

The 1992 Framework Convention, as well as other documents on international cooperation in the field of environment, established the principle of common but differentiated responsibility; according to this principle, as provided in the 1992 Convention, the developed countries committed themselves to assist developing countries to face the cost of their adaptation to the negative effects of climate changes and to take into account the special needs of the less advanced countries with regard to financing and transfer of technology.

The Framework Convention also affirms some of the most important principles to be applied in the context of climate changes, mainly those of equity and of inter-generational justice and that of precaution, thus reaffirming the close relationship between the law of environment and human rights.

UN and UNESCO documents underlined the duty of the present generations to preserve the environment, its cultural and natural values, in general the conditions of life, and to transmit them in a good state to future generations. It is obvious that climate changes, produced because of human activities, may endanger natural and cultural values of the planet and substantially modify the conditions of life on the planet. Therefore, acting to avoid and to reduce the negative consequences of climate changes responds also to this objective.

The Convention enounces also the precautionary principle, according to which the absence of absolute scientific certitude should not be used as a pretext to delay the adoption of measures with a view to foresee, to prevent and to attenuate the causes of climate changes and to reduce their negative effects. This approach corresponds to the human rights philosophy and practice, as it draws the attention on the risks of not taking in time measures for the protection of these rights.

---

[544] Budayeva and others v. Russia, ECHR, case nr. 15399/02.

[545] Case Guerra and others v. Italy, ECHR nr. 116/1996, decision of 18 February 1998, Rec. 1998 I, cited in Chapter XVII above on Human Rights and the Protection of Environment. .

[546] The Framework Convention of 1992, art. 6; The UN Declaration on the rights of indigenous peoples, art. 19.

[547] General Comments nr. 12(1999) on the right to adequate food, nr. 13(1999) on the right to education, nr. 14(2000) on the right to the highest attainable standard of health and nr. 15 on the right to water.

SECTION 3 - INTERNATIONAL EFFORTS TO RESPOND TO CLIMATE CHANGES

It is obvious that the action of States and of the international community for reducing the emissions of greenhouse gases, by reducing the use of fossil fuels, is essential. A series of efforts were launched by the Kyoto Protocol of 1998 and an additional Protocol to it of 2004. The United States of America, which represented some ¼ of the volume of greenhouse gases thrown out in the atmosphere did not accept the Kyoto Protocol and did not adopt such measures. The European Union announced, at its level, the intention to adopt even unilaterally such measures. Big countries, such as China and India, economic powers and important consumers of energy produced from fossil fuels, but from other points of view still developing countries, still hesitate to engage themselves in this direction.

The meeting of States parties to the UN Convention on climate changes, which took place in Copenhagen in December 2009, demonstrated the difficulty to achieve significant progress in this field. Although it was preceded by a mobilization without precedent of the public opinion and many heads of State participated in, the meeting closed with a so-called Agreement, negotiated in the last resort by the delegations of the USA and China (with the participation of delegations of India, Brazil and South Africa), and the Conference took note without approving it.

According to this Agreement, States set up as objective to limit the increase of the average global temperature to less than 2 degrees C above the pre-industrial level, beyond which the Intergovernmental Group of experts on the climate evolution considers that climate changes would have major consequences. This commitment was already advanced by the G8 at the high-level meeting of Aquila (Italy) in 2009; no commitments were taken concerning quantified reductions or time rames for realization, although other previous meetings announced such commitments[548]. The only progress noted was the acceptance by the States which did not take any obligation until then (developing countries) of the commitment to present each second-year reports about their action to limit emissions of greenhouse gases, without submitting this to an international mechanism of monitoring.

The Copenhagen Agreement stressed also the crucial role of forests in stabilizing the climate; however, applying an agreement to maintain the level of forests is difficult due to the lack of institutional and technical capacities; moreover, from the point of view of its efficiency, it is not established what would be its consequences and it is obvious that maintaining the level of forests *per se* does not lead to the reduction of emissions of greenhouse gases. The setting up of a Green Fund for Climate, meant to support the most vulnerable countries to adapt and to attenuate effects of climate changes was also discussed, without providing individual specific obligations or commitments.

To sum up, it is considered that the Copenhagen Agreement represents a letter of intention[549]. It retained attention the fact that it was established outside of the UN, among a number of States including the USA and China which are not among the partisans of the reduction of greenhouse gases emissions and without the participation of the European Union, which was usually the proponent of practical results in this field.

The High-Level Meeting convened by the UN in Paris, between 3o November and 12 December 2015, with the participation of 196 States, adopted by consensus the Agreement of Paris which is viewed as a moment of crossroads in this field. Participating States engaged to maintain the global increase of temperature above the pre-industrial level at less than 2 degrees Celsius and to make efforts to reduce it at 1,5 degrees C, to increase the capacity of adaptation to the negative impact of climate changes, to promote the reduction of emissions of greenhouse gases, so as not to affect the food production and to ensure financial flows consistent to these efforts. It is recognized that efforts to reduce emissions of greenhouse gases will be more limited for developing countries.

Each State party commits itself to adopt programmes of its efforts and to communicate them; their application will be followed by a mechanism created by this Agreement. The meeting was confronted as previously with the different opinions of developed and developing countries. Differently from the previous situation, it was recognized that presently the biggest quantity of emissions of greenhouse gases is produced by China, while India also produces increasing quantities. Nevertheless, developed countries remain responsible for the quantity of greenhouse gases accumulated in the atmosphere in the preceding period.

The document adopted gives also great importance to the increase of the capacity of the societies to adapt to climate changes at local, sub-national, national, regional and international levels and to the need to contribute to the protection of peoples, communities and ecosystems, considering immediate and urgent needs of those of the developing States which are the most vulnerable to the negative effects of climate changes. It provides also the

---

[548] Extensively, Anaid Panossian and Christophe Colette, art. cit, pp. 137 and foll.
[549] A. Panossian, Chr. Colette, art. cit., p. 142.

allocation of resources by developed States to support developing countries to respond to their obligations and to adapt to climate changes.

The commitments taken do not contain explicit obligations, but promises of conduct; the mechanism of control will have rules of functioning only after the first conference of evaluation. The Agreement will enter into force when it will be ratified by 55% of the participating States which represent at least 55% of the emissions of greenhouse gases. The application of these commitments depends thus on the attitude of the parties, mainly those which contribute more to the emissions of greenhouse gases.

Environmental security. The political and legal debate on issues of environment, mainly of climate changes, included gradually the problem of security, taking in view that some climate changes can seriously affect the security of some States and peoples. The Report published in 1987 by the World Commission for Environment and Development, entitled Our Common Future, used for the first time the concept of environmental security. As we presented in a previous chapter, the Copenhagen School included environmental security among other aspects of a more comprehensive concept of security of States, along with the military, political, economic and societal[550]. One of the leaders of this school affirmed that „environmental security aims at maintaining the local and planetary biosphere as an essential system of support on which all other human activities depend"[551].

Other authors opposed this linkage, affirming that it could lead to increased competences for the military and would lead more to the „militarization" of the environment than to the „greening of security"[552]. In April 2007 the implications of climate changes on security were discussed in the UN Security Council; opinions of the participants in the debate were different regarding the opportunity to consider climate changes and the degradation of the environment as a problem of security.

It is estimated that a relationship between the climate changes and security would lead to unacceptable consequences, as the protection of security is traditionally related to an enemy, to a conflict and induces the idea of measures against those who are guilty[553]. The analysts of the Copenhagen school tried to eliminate such an understanding of their conception, stating that they have in mind environmental security as part of a public debate on a potential reality, which needs political decisions and allocation of resources[554]. The debate continued within the UN, more and more voices after the cold war period taking the stand that the degradation of biosphere represents one of the most serious dangers which threatens life on the planet.

Other opinions tried to explain some of the conflicts (Darfur, Somalia) by problems of the environment, neglecting the social and political causes of these conflicts.

At the same time, the debate on human security removed the emphasis from the State security to the legitimate concerns of the individual, to his/her security of each day, including also the environment. The Report of the UN Programme for Development of 1994 identified environmental security as a relevant element of human security, along with economic, political, food, health and personal security, together with that of the community, as an integrated and comprehensive concept[555]. The need for a sustainable development and for the protection of diversity and of local resilience to factors of degradation of the environment was stressed. However, the debate centered mainly on threats in the field of environment as threats for the global order and stability, leaving aside problems related to effects on human health, to over-consumption of non-renewable resources, that is not on aspects related to economic development and to respect for human rights.

It became obvious that usual practices of protection of security, measures of a military nature and others of constraint, are not adequate to respond to threats resulting from climate changes and from other environment dangers. In the UN debates also appeared the concept of the „security of the climate", with the meaning to maintain the existing conditions of climate; this includes a paradox, because the existing conditions are those which lead to the deterioration of the climate and to insecurity from this point of view.

Nevertheless, the debate developed as we have seen by the adoption of the need to reduce the emissions of greenhouse gases in the atmosphere as a strategic priority, able to promote the security of the climate through a rapid transition to a sustainable economy based on the reduced use of coal and petroleum[556]. This approach presents positive aspects, because it gives up the relationship between regional conflicts and the environmental security and

---

[550] Supra, p. 229, footnote 1.

[551] Barry Buzan, Peoples, States and Fear: an agenda for international security studies in the post-cold war era, New-York Harvester Wheatsheaf, 1991, pp. 19-20.

[552] Jyrki Kakonen (ed.), Green Security or Militarized Environment, Aldershot, UK, 1994.

[553] Maria Iulia Trombetta, Environmental Security and Climate Change, in The Politics of Climate Change, pp. 132-133.

[554] B. Buzan, Ole Waver and Jaap de Wilde, Security: a new framework for analysis, 1998(Boulder, Colorado), pp. 23-24.

[555] Report UNDP 1994, pp. 22-24.

[556] Trombetta, art. cit., p. 139.

recognizes the need to take measures in particular by those States which are heavy consumers of fossil fuels; nevertheless, it reduces the problems faced by the environment and the climate to the field of energy, ignoring other causes like the over-consumption, economic projects and other measures taken by States which affect the environment, as well as the necessity of sustainable development, of the increase of resilience of vulnerable populations and of ensuring public services to local populations. Limiting the debate to energetic security may lead again to an approach in terms of military security, because energy is related to economic security and finally to security in its wider sense.

The UN Charter offers no basis for including threats resulting from the degradation of the environment on the planet as a result of human activities among those concerning the threats to international peace and security, which would open the way for the action by the UN bodies, mainly by the Security Council. These threats have as causes human activities over long periods of time, the activity of industries and exploitation of resources related to important economic processes in different world States. The solution is not of a political or military character, but an economic one, meaning the change of the production structures, the consistent application of the concept of sustainable development, that is ensuring a development which takes into account the requirements of the protection of the climate and the environment and those of respect for human rights.

* * *

The Convention on climate changes creates a regime which is based on flexibility, with regard both to substantial commitments and to the mechanism of compliance[557]. It allows to having in view the different situations and levels of development, but it proved to be difficult to function efficiently. There is nevertheless increased awareness that measures have to be taken because populations in different countries demand it increasingly. Therefore, analysts raised the issue of improving the balance between flexibility and stability in the design of this regime[558].

Of course, the reduction of emissions of greenhouse gases may determine a reduction or a slackening of the industrial production, in as much as some big industries are still using solid or liquid fuels which produce such gases: petroleum and coal. Many economies do not seem to be ready to use for these industries other energy resources, which may not exist in sufficient quantities or are still more expensive than coal and petroleum. But these are not renewable and the moment is foreseen when they will be exhausted; however, it may be too late if in the meantime climate changes produce irreparable damages and make life impossible for large segments of the world population. Already the damages produced by climate changes seem to overcome the advantages of the use in excess of such fuels.

Even in the USA we can note evolutions to understand the necessity to treat in a responsible manner the issue of reducing emissions of greenhouse gases, taking into account the mere interests of USA. A study entitled „The US economic impacts of climate change and the costs of inaction", published in 2007, draws the attention on climate phenomena which hit the USA during the recent years and on their consequences, including those in the economic field, that is on the increasing costs supported by the American society as a result of climate changes and of inaction in this field.

The issues concerning threats resulting from climate changes cannot be treated as threats against international peace and security traditionally dealt with within the United Nations, because their causes are dispersed, uncertain, difficult to quantify and to attribute to one or the other of international actors, that is are difficult to use in a confrontational context. In this field, preventive, non-confrontational measures, on a medium and long term basis are the way to follow, with an emphasis on economic and social aspects and measures of restructuring.

The international community is far from acting in a coherent and determined manner in this field. The solution seem to be an international agreement which would establish specific obligations for all States but differentiated, on medium and long term basis, pursuing the realization of agreed objectives in order to halt the warming of the planet, but also others with regard to the protection of biodiversity and the reduction of consumption of non-renewable resources. Moreover, a process of sustainable development on the entire planet should be ensured, because peoples left outside such a process will not feel obliged to respect commitments in the field of the protection of environment. Such an agreement should be accompanied by sanctions and an efficient mechanism of monitoring and of the solution of disputes similar to that of the World Trade Organization.

---

[557] Harro van Asselt, Between the Devil and the Deep Blue Sea: Enhancing Fkexibility in International Climate Change Law, in Netherlands Yearbook of International Law, 2014.
[558] Ibidem, p. 282.

The public opinion of all States should react firmly in the present situation so as to determine the governments to engage resolutely in this direction. The ecologic political parties have the responsibility to make of this subject their electoral objective and to attract larger interests for such a political orientation. Organizations promoting the protection of the environment have the mission to promote a more determined action of governments and international organizations in the struggle against negative effects of climate changes on human being. Such an activity should be based on a comparison between the damages caused by climate changes, supported by many States in the world and mainly by the vulnerable groups, and the income resulted from the use of the fuels producing greenhouse gases and by other activities affecting the environment, which would show that the situation becomes increasingly difficult to support by the mankind.

CHAPTER XIX - THE RIGHT to FOOD and the FOOD CRISIS

ABSTRACT

The right to food is generally recognized, although not explicitly, as a fundamental human right; nevertheless, millions of people suffer from hunger and the world is confronted, with different intensity from year to year, to a food crisis in some continents, mainly in Africa, due to conflicts, to droughts or other factors. Besides, there are areas of poverty in all States where people suffer from hunger and other shortages.

International instruments on human rights contain some provisions on this issue and the human rights treaty bodies considered the situation in different States and made recommendations, including by general comments, clarifying different aspects of this right and the obligations of States and of the international community. Some of these rights and obligations are considered to be of immediate application, others are obligations of a medium or long term. This raises issues concerning the production of food, and in this connection access to land and to water, the use of the land for agriculture not for industrial products, and the trade of agricultural products.

Different crisis-economic, financial and environmental-should be dealt with in a way to protect the right to food for all. International community, all States have important responsibilities in this field for increasing the agricultural production and encouraging the producers, for ensuring access to land, to water and to genetic resources and for improving the conditions of the trade of agricultural products.

KEY WORDS: right to food, access to land, access to water, availability, accessibility, acceptability, obligations to respect, to protect and to give effect, non-discrimination, food crises, distribution of resources, genetically modified products, sanctions affecting the right to food.

The right to food is recognized as one of the human fundamental rights. Nevertheless, for many years mankind is confronted with a food crisis. It is obvious that this food crisis seriously affects the human right to sufficient nutrition, which is the right to food.

What are the contents of this fundamental right and why is it not respected everywhere? What is the meaning of the food crisis and what are its causes? Who has obligations to ensure the observance of this right and what could be the remedies?

SECTION 1 - The CONTENTS of the RIGHT TO FOOD

The Universal Declaration of Human Rights of 1948 proclaims in its article 25 the right of everyone to a standard of living adequate for the health and wellbeing of himself and of his family, including food, clothing, housing and medical care. Taking up and developing these provisions, the International Covenant on economic, social and cultural rights of 1966, to which more than 150 States are parties, requests States to recognize the right of each person to such an adequate standard of living, as well as to the continuous improvement of living conditions. States parties committed themselves to adopt appropriate measures for the realization of this right, while recognizing the essential importance of the international cooperation.

According to the Covenant, recognizing the fundamental right of each person to be free from hunger, States parties shall take, individually and through international cooperation, measures and specific programmes necessary for: a) improving the methods of production, conservation and distribution of food products by fully using technical and scientific knowledge, by disseminating the principles of nutritional education and by developing or reforming agrarian systems, so as to achieve the most efficient development and utilization of natural resources; b) ensuring an equitable distribution of world food supplies in relation to the needs and taking into account the problems of both food-importing and food-exporting countries (article 11).

In its General Comment nr. 12 on article 11 of the Covenant, the Committee on economic, social and cultural rights affirmed that „the right to adequate food is realized when every man, woman and child, alone or in community with others, has physical and economic access at all times to adequate food or means for its procurement"[559]. Starting from this definition, the UN Special Rapporteur on the right to food defined this right as that „ to have access regularly, permanently and freely, either directly or through monetary means to buy it, to food of a quantity and quality adequate and sufficient, corresponding to the cultural traditions of the people from which the consumer

---
[559] United Nations, Committee on economic, social and cultural, rights, General Comment nr.12: The right to adequate food(art. 11), doc. E/C.12/1999/5,12 May 1999, para. 6.

originates, and which ensures psychological and physical, individual and collective, free of fear, satisfactory and dignified livelihood"[560].

International instruments having vocation to universality stipulate the right to adequate food and to be free from hunger. This implies for any State the obligation to take all necessary measures so that its population has access to sufficient and healthy food. It is estimated that this right includes also the right of each person to have his/her food needs covered with dignity. Although this aspect was proclaimed in documents of the Food and Agricultural Organization and in resolutions of the UN General Assembly[561], there are reservations to its recognition in this more extended meaning from financial institutions (the Monetary Fund and the World Bank) and from the World Trade Organization, as well as from some States.

Some authors maintain that the right to food has two essential elements, which are the right of access to land and the right of access to water[562]. The right of access to land would be the first essential element of the right of each person to food and would have a direct impact on food subsistence and security of the populations. States should ensure that the financial resources for food production are accessible in efficient, equitable conditions and without discrimination. Water would represent also a primary element necessary for a dignified and healthy existence. Access to water is essential for the entire food production cycle, for the realization of agricultural productions on which depends the exercise of the right to food.

It is also estimated that the right to food supposes that, in order to consider satisfied the minimal requirements of food in conformity with human dignity, different types of aliments should fulfill several criteria:
- to be available in quantity, meaning that each person disposes of food in sufficient quantity to be free of hunger; this is determined by the volume of the internal production, by the capacity to import, the existence of some stocks and the food assistance;
- to be of quality, meaning to respond to the requirements of taste, to be nutritionally rich, to correspond to the physiological human needs and to be free from adverse substances;
- to be physically accessible, that is to be found in the proximity of the person, in order to be easily procured, and accessible economically, that is at prices permitting to be procured irrespective of the financial situation of the person;
- to be acceptable, that is to be tolerable for each person and compatible with the physiological situation and with cultural and religious values of the person[563].

Corresponding to the right to food, there are obligations of the States and of other persons. Of course, it is the obligation of each State to ensure the right to food for its population. According to the 1966 Covenant, the main obligation of States is to take measures for the progressive realization of the right to adequate food. Every State has a margin of discretion with regard to the approach followed, but the Covenant requests that each State takes the necessary measures so that nobody suffers from hunger and that everybody could enjoy as soon as possible the right to adequate food. This means, according to the Comment of the Committee mentioned above, the obligation to ensure for each person under its jurisdiction an access to a minimum essential of sufficient food, nutritionally adequate and safe (paragraph 14). This supposes the adoption of a national strategy to ensure the security of food for all, identifying available resources and the most efficient ways of their utilization.

States have first of all the obligations of a general nature concerning equal rights and non-discrimination, as well as international assistance and cooperation, with a view to ensure respect for this right. They have also important specific obligations corresponding to this right, such as:
- the obligation to respect the right to food of each person, meaning to respect the possibilities each person has of access to adequate food, to refrain from any measure which would deprive a person from his/her means of subsistence, from resources he/she can use for this purpose, and refrain from endangering his/her food resources (by contamination or in any other way);
- the obligation to protect the right to food, that is to prevent, forbid, prosecute and sanction any attempt by third parties-persons or enterprises, respectively private activities- against the exercise of the right to food

---

[560] United Nations, General Assembly, doc. E/CN.4/2001/53, 7 February 2001, para.14.

[561] FAO, Rapport du Conseil, vingt-septième session, Rome, 22-27 novembre 2004, CL 127, REP; resolutions A/RES/62/164 of 18 December 2009 of the General Assembly on the right to food and A/HRC/7/L.6/Rev.1 of 26 March 2008 of the Human Rights Council.

[562] Abdoulaye Soma, Le droit à l'alimentation, Chapitre 4, in Introduction aux droits de l'homme, ed. Maya Hertig Randall and Michel Hottelier, 2014, pp. 772-773.

[563] CESC, General Comment nr.12, cited above, Compilation of General Comments and General Recommendations adopted by human rights treaty bodies, doc: HRI/GEN/1/Rev: 9, 27 May 2008, pp. 67-75.

by other persons, taking care that the private sector is not depriving persons from having access to adequate food;
- the obligation to give effect to the right to food (to fulfill), that is to ensure to every person under its jurisdiction access to the minimum of food necessary, sufficient from the nutritional point of view and healthy, so that all persons are free from hunger, first of all by proactively engaging in activities intended to strengthen people's access to and utilization of resources and means. In case of food crisis, when persons and groups are not able to ensure what is necessary for their livelihood, the State should assume at least the fundamental obligation to ensure directly the vital minimum. For that purpose, it should use the necessary means and resources for the food subsistence and security of the population[564]. This applies also to persons who are victims of natural or other disasters.

The Committee considers that some of these obligations are of an immediate application, while others are more of a long-term character, aiming to achieve progressively the full realization of the right to food. A State violates its immediate obligation if it fails to ensure the satisfaction of at least the minimum essential level of food required to protect people against hunger. Considering the provisions of article 2.1 of the Covenant, according to which States have to take the necessary measures using at the maximum the resources available to fulfill their obligations, if a State would invoke the lack of material resources to ensure this minimum, it has to demonstrate that it uses all the resources available to satisfy this minimum as a priority.

Even when a State would be in the situation of severe economic constraints, caused by economic recession, by climate conditions or by economic structural adjustment, the Committee considers that it must take measures to ensure the right to adequate food in particular for vulnerable groups and persons.

Any discrimination with regard to the access to food or to means to procure food, on grounds of race, colour, sex, language, age, religion, political or other opinion, national or social origin, fortune, descent or other status represents also a violation of the Covenant. The Committee estimates that the adoption of legislation or policies which are manifestly incompatible with legal pre-existent obligations concerning the right to food, as well as failing to give effect to international obligations on the right to food when concluding agreements with other States or with international organizations, represent also violations of these obligations under the Covenant.

As for other economic, social and cultural human rights, some States and numerous analysts consider that the right to food is not justiciable, meaning that it does not belong to those human rights which can be invoked by any person in front of a court, in petitions against the State or against other persons. They maintain that this right would be different from other human rights, and would belong rather to the field of principles or objectives, that even the provisions of the Covenant do not confer subjective rights to individuals, being not precise and subordinated to the general clause of art. 2 concerning the progressive application[565].

However, other authors consider that, with regard to economic, social and cultural rights, including the right to food, each human right and its specific situation have to be taken into account. Thus, they consider that the prohibition of discrimination and of regressive measures in the exercise of the right to food represent obvious cases which should be justiciable; the obligation to respect, which requires the mere refraining from the State, should also be submitted to justice. As for the obligation to protect, its observance by the States should be submitted to the judiciary or to a kind of quasi-judiciary control, as this concerns measures of the State with regard to other persons[566].

On this issue, the Committee on economic, social and cultural rights asked States to establish national mechanisms to look after the observance of this right, as well as the procedural remedies available, specifying that each person or group victim of a violation of the right to adequate food should have access to effective resources, judiciary or others, at the national or international levels; victims have also the right to an adequate reparation, compensation, satisfaction or guarantee that it will not be repeated[567].

---

[564] General Comment nr. 12, para. 15.
[565] Among other autors, Fréderic Sudre, Droit européen et droit international des droits de l'homme, 7-ème éd., Paris, 2005, pp. 24 and foll.
[566] Opinions held by Giorgio Malinverni, former member of CESC and of the European Court of Human Rights, cited by A. Soma, art. cit., p. 778.
[567] General Comment nr. 12.

SECTION 2 - APPLICATION of the RIGHT to FOOD and the FOOD CRISIS

Despite the general recognition of the right to food, mankind is confronted nowadays with a serious food crisis. A Report of the Food and Agricultural Organization (FAO) of 2005 noted that almost 1 billion of people suffer from hunger and from the lack of drinkable water, more than 62 million, including 6 million children, die each year for causes related to hunger, which is the main lethal agent[568].

It is estimated that the causes of the food crisis are the unequal repartition of food products, as well as the reduction of offer and the high prices of these products. According to studies of FAO, the price of food products raised during one year (2007) by 50%, and within it of cereals with 90%. In such conditions, many developing countries continue to be threatened by the specter of hunger, which is the case also for larger or more restraint strata of population in countries considered in transition or even in developed countries.

As a matter of fact, the demand of food products increases constantly, because of the process of urbanization and of economic increase in some States, while food stocks are regressing. A combination of factors represents the cause of this situation, such as: climate phenomena which reduced exports from big producers like Australia and Ukraine; conflicts which led to the destruction of crops and of land leaving without food large groups of people; problems affecting the environment, like the degradation of soil, an inadequate management of water or the reduction of arable land. One has to add the priority given to cultivating products for export intended for industrial consumption, to the expense of products for food consumption, which is called agriculture for non-food purposes, including the production of agro-carbons, as well as the competition of products imported from and subsidized by developed countries, which led to the reduction of the production of cereals and other food products in less developed countries. At the level of the world economy, the increase of the price of petroleum resulted in the increase of the cost of agricultural exploitations and of the transport of food products, while the speculative movements of capital on the market of cereals led to the increase of prices without connection to the production.

The food crisis affects human health, many other human rights, and even the right to life, as the situation in countries from the Horn of Africa (Ethiopia, Somalia) and the Sudan and of other African States show for some years. Moreover, it affects their development in general, their social progress and stability of some States and of entire geographic areas, in the last instance international security, because of massive migratory flows and conflicts generated. It was recognized within the UN that food security represents an element of preventing conflicts[569].

The Summit on Food, organized in 1996, took up the definition mentioned above of food security and underlined that it includes both the quantitative and the qualitative aspects. Several international meetings organized on this subject during 2007-2009 led to some commitments been taken, mainly within the High-Level Conference on food security, challenges of climate changes and of bio-energies, organized by FAO in Rome, in June 2008. The 180 participating States, the European Union and organizations of civil society committed to contribute to the creation of funds in order to respond to the needs of countries affected by the crisis, as well as to increase investments in agriculture, to deal with obstacles to access to food and to use in a more sustainable way the resources of the planet[570].

Possible solutions. There is the obligation of each State to ensure the exercise of this right by its population. According to the Covenant, each State party undertakes to take steps, individually and through international assistance and cooperation, especially economic and technical, to the maximum of its available resources, with a view to achieving progressively the full realization of the rights provided for (among them the right to food). According to the Committee on economic, social and cultural rights, this general provision obliges States to respect, protect and ensure these rights[571].

The realization of the right to food raises a series of complex issues, amongst which the repartition of food resources, access to land for the production of these resources, the problem of agro-carbons and of genetically modified organisms. The situation of the repartition of food resources in the world shows the disparity which exists between the quantity of food resources available and their accessibility, and the causes are: inequalities of level of development and with regard to the social situation, the market control in favour of big producers, exclusion and discrimination.

One has to add the phenomenon of monopolizing the land intended for agricultural production by private companies or persons in developing countries, which leads to the dispossession of peasants, to the impoverishment

---

[568] FAO, L'état de l'insécurité alimentaire dans le monde, 2005, p. 18.
[569] Report of the Secretary General „The Prevention of Conflits", doc. A/55/985-S/2001/547, 7 June 2001, para. 113-118.
[570] FAO Declaration on World Food Security, 2008.
[571] General Comment nr. 12, cited above.

of small producers and to the use of land for other purposes than producing food products; this reduces the quantity of food products and very often reduces access of persons to water.

In many countries, mainly those which are important producers of food products, with a view to face the energetic crisis and to protect the environment, the areas cultivated with cereals were reduced while extending the cultivation of plants which are sources of biological energy or of carbons; a series of food products are also extensively used to produce carbons(maize, corn, sugar beet, sugar cane, soya, sun flower), which removes these aliments from the food market, while millions of people suffer from hunger. With regard to genetically modified products, the developing countries importing them in order to satisfy the food needs of their populations face the problem of sanitary risks resulting from the use of such products; this does not facilitate their acceptance, while another obstacle is to obtain the means necessary for satisfying the food needs.

Several possible solutions were advanced in the juridical, commercial and institutional fields. One of the ideas launched refers to the strengthening of the application of the Rio Convention on climate changes by the struggle against desertification, by the protection of biodiversity, by including in the protocol subsequent to that of Kyoto provisions intended to combat effects of climate changes on the availability of food products. Another proposal, presented by Jean Ziegler, Special Rapporteur on the right to food of the UN Human Commission of human rights and then of the Human Rights Council, refers to a moratorium of 5 years on the cultivation of agro-carbons, motivating his proposal by the fact that the increase of arable areas cultivated with plants dedicated to bioenergy leads to the reduction of areas intended for cultivating cereals.

In the field of trade and assistance for development, suggestions were presented to reduce the service of foreign debt and to increase the part of assistance granted to agriculture taking into account its constant reduction (3% in 2006 compared with 17% in 1980) and to survey the speculations on the market of food products. A series of States also request the elimination of tariff obstacles to their products and of subsidies granted by developed countries to agriculture.

In the institutional field, the debate centered on the functioning and efficiency of FAO, which has increasingly less means of action; such means are in the hands of other fora, such as the World Food Programme, the financial international institutions, the regional banks and others. As the majority of agricultural markets do not have a world dimension, a solution would be the development of regional cooperation. The financial institutions also could give priority to investments in the agriculture of subsistence in countries affected by the crisis and to the transfer of technologies for this purpose.

The international community is confronted with a financial and economic crisis, a food one, an energetic one and that of the environment. There are obvious links among these crises and the solutions adopted in any one could worsen the situation in other fields and each of them has an impact on human rights.

It is estimated that the world agricultural production can cover the needs of the world population[572]. The problem is of a political nature, that is whether the developed States, in particular the main producers of cereals and other agricultural products, are ready to adopt a series of measures of an economic and commercial character and whether international financial institutions are ready to adopt measures in the field of investments, both to favour the agricultural production in developing countries and to ensure covering for the food needs where it is necessary. International effective cooperation is thus necessary to deal with these problems, taking into account the needs of the population in different States and the concerns for the protection of environment and for the sustainable development.

The role of the international community. With regard to the international level, the General Comment of the Committee emphasizes the role of the international cooperation and the commitment of States to act separately and in common for the realization of the right to adequate food. For this purpose, they have to respect the exercise of this right in other States, that is to refrain from acts which could endanger it, to protect the exercise of this right by taking care that physical persons and enterprises under their jurisdiction do not impede the building of conditions for the realization of this right in other States, as well as to offer support when asked. They also must take care that international agreements to which they become parties do not endanger the exercise of the right to adequate food in other countries.

As it is known, one of the objectives established by the Declaration of 2000 for the Third Millennium was to reduce to half the number of persons who suffer from hunger. The Agenda 2030 for sustainable development also proclaims as objectives the elimination of hunger, the achievement of food security and the promotion of sustainable agriculture till 2030; for this purpose, the Agenda asks to eliminate any form of malnutrition, mainly for children, and to double the productivity in agriculture and the income of small-scale food producers, in particular women, indigenous peoples, families of farmers, pastoralists and fishers, including by ensuring equal access to land, to other

---

[572] Rapport du Secretaire general sur l'agriculture, doc. E/CN.17/2008/3 du 22 fevrier 2008.

productive resources and inputs; other objectives, with time frame till 2020, are to maintain the genetic diversity of seeds, cultivated plants and farmed and domesticated animals, including through seed and plant banks and to promote fair and equitable access to genetic resources and to traditional knowledge.

With regard to trade of food products, the Agenda asks to correct and prevent trade restrictions and distortions in world agricultural markets, including through the elimination of all forms of export subsidies and all export measures with equivalent effect, in accordance with commitments taken previously at the Doha Development Round.

The Paris Agreement adopted in December 2015 by the Conference of States parties to the UN Framework Convention on Climate Change of 1992 recognizes from the beginning as a fundamental priority the safeguarding of food security and ending hunger, and the particular vulnerabilities of food production systems to the adverse impacts of climate changes. One of the main objectives of the Agreement is to increase the ability to adapt to the adverse impact of climate changes and foster climate resilience and low gas emissions development, in a manner that does not threaten food production. Many of its provisions refer to the protection of people, livelihoods and ecosystems.

A serious problem was raised by the application of sanctions against some States; this concerns sanctions applied according to the UN Charter, under the authority of the Security Council, which are legitimate, but also measures applied individually by some States which represent often violations of international law; such sanctions and measures can affect the right to adequate food of the population of States subject to them.

The Committee on economic, social and cultural rights considers that States should refrain from adopting measures of embargo concerning food or similar measures which endanger the production of food and the access to food in other States. In substance, it is underlined that food should never be used as an instrument of political or economic pressure.

In its General Comment nr. 8 of 1997 (The relationship between economic sanctions and the protection of economic, social and cultural rights), the Committee analyzed situations occurred as a result of sanctions imposed by the Security Council with regard to South Africa, Iraq, parts of former Yugoslavia, Somalia, Libya, Liberia, Haiti, Angola, Rwanda and the Sudan, and reached the conclusion that they almost always had a dramatic impact on the rights provided for in the Covenant, leading often to the disruption in the distribution of food and in supplies of pharmaceuticals, jeopardized the quality of food and the availability of clean drinking water and severely interfered with the functioning of basic health and education systems.

The Committee considers that when such sanctions are adopted, their nefarious consequences on human rights must be taken into account and that deliberations on this subject should have as a dimension respect for human rights. The Committee also underlined that when some of the sanctions inhibit the capacity of States to fulfill their obligations under the Covenant, the terms of such sanctions and the manner in which they are applied become a matter for its concerns.

If the State subject to sanctions remains obliged, according to the Covenant, to ensure the largest possible exercise of the right to adequate food, using at the maximum its available resources, the Committee considers that the party or parties which impose sanctions, be it a State, a group of States or an international body, has the following obligations: to take fully into account economic, social and cultural rights when establishing sanctions by impact studies, by a wider range of exempt goods and services and greater overall flexibility; to ensure effective monitoring of the application of sanctions, so as to protect economic, social and cultural rights of the population affected; to adopt measures of assistance and cooperation, mainly economic and technical, in order to respond to any disproportionate suffering experienced by vulnerable groups of population.

In the end it is underlined that inhabitants of a given country should not suffer because the leaders of that country have violated norms related to international peace and security and that the legitimacy of the collective action should be based on respect for human fundamental rights[573].

Analysts place high hopes in the Additional Protocol to the Covenant, adopted in 2004 and in force since 2013, giving to the Committee the competence to examine individual petitions for violations of the provisions of the Covenant against States which accept this procedure. It is estimated that this quasi-judicial procedure of monitoring the application of the Covenant, including with regard to the right to food, may strengthen the activity of the Committee for the application of the Covenant and determine new developments also with respect to the observance of the right to food under all its aspects.

* * *

The right to food is thus generally recognized, but its application is insufficient in many States of the world. This depends on the general difficulties encountered by the process of development in the world, but also on the

---

[573] General Comment nr. 8, Compilation..., doc. HRI/GEN/1/Rev. 9, vol. II, pp. 53-56.

specificities of the food crisis which confronts mankind. It is the obligation of each State to ensure the exercise of the right to food and for this purpose to use all available resources. The international community is able to act both with regard to the world crisis at the global level, which affects to the highest degree the right to adequate food, and with regard to the observance of this right by each State. This situation makes it that agriculture and the need to feed the population are placed in the center of the international debate. However, it is a complex and multidimensional problem and the answer to the right of people to adequate food needs a global and coordinated strategy. UN initiated such efforts in 2008, with the participation of specialized institutions, including the financial ones. A High-Level Conference was organized in Rome in June 2008. At the end of the Conference, the European Union committed itself to contribute with other 6 billion EURO (along with the 6 billion promised previously) and a final Declaration was adopted. The Declaration insists on the need to urgently respond to requests of assistance from countries needing it in order to strengthen their systems of feeding the population and create conditions to increase the productivity.

Although no practical engagements were adopted, the participants engaged to stimulate investments in agriculture, to deal with impediments to access to food and to use in a sustainable manner the resources of the planet for future generations. The Committee of the World Food Programme adopted a plan of action which stresses the need to support local markets in order to eliminate malnutrition and to set up systems of warning and of analysis in order to attenuate effects of natural disasters[574].

The meetings of the UN General Assembly devoted to this issue revealed that limited efforts were accomplished for this purpose; the economic and financial crisis which occurred in the meantime blocked such efforts, while the crisis of massive migration to Europe of 2015 created other difficulties which did not favour new developments. The commitments retained in Agenda 2030 for sustainable development contain other important objectives for eliminating hunger and ensuring access to food for all; the realization of such objectives could produce significant evolutions also in this field.

---

[574] Chronique des faits internationaux, Revue Generale de Droit International, no.3, 2008, p. 651-657.

CHAPTER XX - THE RIGHT to WATER and INTERNATIONAL LAW

ABSTRACT

The right to water is not directly provided for in the international instruments of human rights. It is nevertheless recognized in regional instruments on human rights, adopted on all continents, and is considered as closely related to other human rights, adding to it the right to sanitation. The Committee on economic, social and cultural rights considers it as an autonomous human right. An important debate on the contents of the right to water and to sanitation takes place nowadays in the UN Human Rights Council.

It is of great interest to clarify the rights and obligations related to access to water, from the point of view of economy, including the trade of goods and services, from the point of view of human rights or as a public good, as well as the conditions that supplies of water must fulfill: to be adequate in terms of quality, to be available and accessible. The main obligations are to respect, to protect and to ensure access to water, as well as those resulting from the principles of equal rights and non-discrimination.

It is also estimated that States have some obligations in the international arena, such as: to respect the exercise of the right to water in other countries, to refrain from depriving other States of the capacity to respect this right, to refrain from using water as a means of political pressure, to prevent violations of the right to water in other countries by its citizens and companies, to support other States and to cooperate in this field.

KEY WORDS: right to water, right to sanitation, right to health, right to drinking water, right to a decent standard of living, humanitarian law, use of international water courses, water as a public good, minimal obligation.

INTRODUCTION

Until recently, water was treated in international law only as way of international navigation or of marking limits between State's borders, within what was called the law of international watercourses. Access to water resources also was treated only as a problem of management and of economic efficiency, in the context of the increased consumption and of the reduction of resources in some parts of the world, in a strict logic of the market economy. It was only around the end of the twentieth century and the beginning of the twenty first that international documents and analysts started to refer to the right to water of persons and communities[575]. There is now in the world a water crisis; approximately 884 million of people have no access to safe drinking water, more than 2,6 billion do not have the benefit of basic sanitation, approximately 1,5 million children under 5 years of age die and 443 million school days are lost each year because of water and sanitation- related diseases[576]. This crisis is not due to the lack of availability of water, but to social and development inequalities[577].

Considering the social evolutions in the world, this crisis tends to aggravate, as a result of social and economic disparities, of the growth of the world population and of migrations, affecting mainly the poor areas of the world. It is obvious that one of the objectives of the Millennium for Development, to reduce at half the world population which has no sustainable access to drinking water and to elementary sanitary installations (objective 7.10), was not attained till the end of 2015 as established[578].

The Committee on economic, social and cultural rights adopted in 2002 the General Comment nr. 15 on the Right to water, affirming without any doubt the existence of this right[579], which is the object of an extensive debate at the international level during the last 10 years[580].The Committee states that:" Water is a limited natural resource and a public good; it is essential for life and for health. It is a previous condition for realizing the other

---

[575] Pierre-Marie Dupuy, Le droit à l'eau, un droit international, in European University Institute, EUI Working Papers nr.6/2006; L. Mehta, Problems of publicness and access rights: perspectives from the water domain, in Producing Global Public Goods, ed. Inge Paul, Oxford 2001.
[576] The Human Rights to Water and Sanitation, doc. UNGA, 64-the session, A/64/L.63/Rev. 1, 2010.
[577] Rapport mondial sur le développement humain, PNUD, 2006, p. 2.
[578] Declaration of the World Summit of Millennium, 8 September 2000.
[579] Compilation of General Comments and General Recommendations adopted by human rights treaty bodies, doc. HRI/GEN/1/Rev. 8, 8 May 2006, pp. 105-122.
[580] On this subject, Mélanie Dubuy, Le droit à l'eau potable et à l'assainissement et le droit international, in Revue générale de Droit International Public no. 2, 2012, pp. 275 and foll.

human rights"; then, it presents the right to water as consisting of sufficient supply, physically accessible and at an affordable cost of safe water of an acceptable quality for personal and domestic uses of everybody[581].

The Committee considers also, as an element of this right, the access to adequate sanitation, defined as a system of collecting, transporting, evacuating or re-using of human dejections, to which related installations of hygiene are associated[582]. The right to drinking water and to sanitation is defined in similar terms by the London Protocol of 1999 concerning water and health, which is additional to the 1992 Helsinki European Convention on the protection and use of trans-boundary water courses and of international lakes; the Protocol refers also to the collection and transport of domestic used waters through collective systems or through installations deserving one household or enterprise.

Water is necessary for many other human needs: for some industrial production processes and mainly in agriculture, as well as in the exercise of some professions and of some cultural practices. The right to water includes also the right to sanitary installations, which are of particular importance for human life and health.

The Committee on economic, social and cultural rights holds that the right to water for personal and domestic needs should have priority with regard to the allocation of resources of water, in particular for preventing hunger and illnesses[583].

SECTION 1 - INTERNATIONAL DOCUMENTS

The two Covenants on human rights adopted in 1966 contain no direct reference to the right to water. They refer to the right to life, interpreted by the Human Rights Committee as including also economic and social rights on which the right to life depends, and to the highest attainable standard of health, the right to housing and to adequate food, interpreted by the Committee on economic, social and cultural rights as including the right to water. However international instruments adopted later on explicitly provide this right. According to the Convention on the elimination of all forms of discrimination against women adopted in 1979, States parties shall ensure to women the right to benefit of adequate conditions of life, in particular with regard to supply of water (article 14.2). Similarly, the 1989 Convention on the rights of the child requests States parties to combat illnesses and malnutrition which affect children by supplying adequate food and drinking water (article 24.2).

Some international instruments on the right to water were also adopted at the regional level. In 1968 already, the African Convention on the conservation of nature and of natural resources requested States to make efforts to guarantee to their populations continuous and sufficient supply of adequate water. This obligation was reaffirmed in several documents: the Protocol to the 1981 African Charter on human rights and the rights of peoples, on the rights of women, adopted in Maputo in 2003, according to which African States should take the necessary measures to ensure to women access to drinking water; the African Charter on the rights and well-being of children of 1990; the Declaration of Abuja of 2006 of the first high level meeting Africa-South America. The right to water was also affirmed in documents adopted by the non-aligned movement (Havana 2006, Sharm El Sheik 2009).

In Latin America, the Additional Protocol to the Inter-American Convention on human rights, adopted in San Salvador in 1988(concerning economic, social and cultural rights) provides for the right to live in a healthy environment and to have access to basic public services. The Declaration adopted in Santa Cruz in 2006 enounces the commitment of States to implement a plan of action of sustainable development and to ensure equitable and effective access to minimum health care, to a high level of food security, to a satisfactory level of food, to work, to housing and access to drinking water. Following the same conception, the Inter-American Court of human rights interpreted the Inter-American Convention on human rights (its provisions concerning the right to life and to personal integrity) as including the right to have a life project which includes essential elements such as the rights to education, to a convenient house, and in particular to water and to sanitation[584].

In the Pacific-Asian area, numerous States accepted the Declaration of Beppu of 2007 by which the participating States recognized the human right to have access to drinking clean water and to minimum sanitation as a basic human right and as a fundamental aspect of human security. At the Conference of New-Delhi of 2008 a

---

[581] General Comment nr. 15, Compilation…, doc. HRI/GEN/1/Rev.8, p. 106.

[582] C. de Albuquerque, Promotion et protection de tous les droits de l'homme, civils, politiques, économiques, sociaux et culturels, y compris le droit au développement, Report presented to the Human Rights Council in 2009, doc. A/HRC/12/24, 1 July 2009, para. 63.

[583] The Convention of 1997 on the law concerning the uses of international water courses for other purposes than navigation, adopted by the resolution of the UN General Assembly nr. 51/229 of 21 May 1997.

[584] Inter-American Court of human rights, Comunidad Indigena Yakye Axa c. Paraguay, decision of 13 June 2005(where the Court upheld the right to water of indigenous populations), Serie C, no. 125.

number of 8 States of the area recognized access to drinking safe water and to sanitation as a fundamental human right.

As for Europe, the right of access to drinking water and to sanitation was provided for in the Protocol on water and health, additional to the 1992 Convention on the protection and the use of trans-boundary water courses and international lakes; States parties committed themselves to take all adequate measures to ensure an adequate supply of drinking water, safe and without microorganisms and to allow sanitary conditions in order to ensure human and environment health. The Committee of ministers of the Council of Europe made in 2001 a recommendation to States parties to the European Convention of 2001 on water resources, affirming that everyone has the right to dispose of a quantity of water sufficient to satisfy his/her essential needs.

In a Report on the Evaluation of the world situation of water supplies and of sanitation in 2000, the World Health Organization and UNICEF considered that a quantity of 20 liters of water by person daily should be necessary[585]; analysts expressed doubts whether this could cover all needs in terms of consumption and hygiene[586].

Although the 1950 European Convention of fundamental human rights and freedoms contains no reference to rights concerning water, the European Court on Human Rights related such rights to some of the fundamental rights set forth in the Convention and adopted relevant decisions. Among the decisions adopted by the Court, a relationship was retained between the prohibition of inhuman and degrading treatment and the lack of drinking water in a detention house (case Viorel Burzo v. Romania, 2009), between the right to property and the pollution of a source of water by cyanide (case against Sweden), or between the right to family and private life and pollution by a station of cleaning of water (case Lopez Ostra v. Spain); other cases referred to the pollution of underground and surface waters produced by a gold mine (case Tatar v. Romania), even in connection with the right to a fair trial (cases Fischer v. Austria, 1995, Buian and Dragomir v. Romania, 2008)[587].

The European Union's institutions also affirmed rights related to water and to its quality. The Directive 2000/60 CE established a framework for a community policy in the field of water. The European Parliament adopted in 2009 a resolution which presents the access to water as „a vital and fundamental right of the human being, and not only as an economic good submitted exclusively to the rules of market". The Council of the Union also adopted a Declaration in 2010, where it related obligations of States concerning the rights to water and to sanitation, to human rights to housing, to food and to health. The European Commission challenged to the European Court of Justice several States for violating a directive on the treatment of urban waters (Italy, Spain) and because their water treatment stations were not in conformity with the directive (Belgium, Luxemburg).

At the international level, besides the interpretation given by the two committees on human rights to some provisions of the Covenants, numerous declaratory documents were adopted concerning the rights related to water. The 1977 Conference on water of Mar del Plata adopted the Declaration which proclaims the right to water for entire peoples, as follows: „All peoples, irrespective of their level of development and of their economic and social situation, have the right to have access to drinking water of a quantity and quality corresponding to their essential needs".

Another Declaration adopted in New Delhi in 1990 insisted on the necessity to deliver in a sustainable manner a sufficient supply of drinking water and of sanitary services convenient to all, while the Declaration of Dublin of 1992 encouraged States to recognize the fundamental human right to drinking safe water and to an adequate hygiene at an affordable price. The Cairo Conference of 1994 on the population and development also affirmed a series of principles which state the right of human beings to supplies of water and to adequate sanitation.

Beginning with 1999, the Organization of United Nations adopted resolutions which qualify the right to water as a fundamental human right. The Objectives of the Millennium, established by the General Assembly in 2000, refer not only to access to water, but also to an economic access, meaning one which is accessible also to those without resources. The 1995 Conference of Johannesburg set up the objective to reduce to half till 2015 the number of persons deprived of physical access to drinking water, as well of those deprived of access to basic sanitation[588].

The Agenda 2030 for sustainable development, adopted during the Summit of September 2015, contained in the resolution of the General Assembly nr. 70/1 of 21 October 2015 proclaims, among the objectives proposed for that period, to ensure the availability and the sustainable management of water and of sanitation for all persons, and

---

[585] Presented by J. Bartram and G. Howard, Domestic water quantity, service level and health; what should be the goal for water and health sectors, OMS, 2002.

[586] Milja Trilsch, Quelles perspectives pour la procédure de communication individuelles devant le Comité des droits économiques, sociaux et culturels?, in Revue de droit international et de droit comparé, 2015, no. 1, p. 76.

[587] Cases cited above, in Chapter XVII, Human Rights and the Protection of the Environment, p. 9.

[588] Declaration of the Millennium, doc. A/RES/55/2 din 2000; Declaration of Johannesburg on durable development, 4 September 2002, doc. A/CONF. 199/20, Chapter 1, Resolution 1.

for that purpose, to ensure universal and equitable access to drinking water, available and safe for all till 2030, the improvement of the water quality, the reduction of the pollution of water sources, the integrated management of resources of water and the restoration of ecosystems related to water.

Reports and resolutions of UN bodies on human rights affirm consistently that the right to drinking water is a human right, both individual and collective, and closely related to other rights explicitly provided for in legal instruments. An independent expert was nominated in 2008 for the right to water and presented reports to the Human Rights Council. In its resolution nr. A/64/292 of 20 July 2010, the General Assembly qualified for the first time the access to water as a fundamental human right, as a right to drinking safe water, which is essential for the full exercise of the right to life and of all human rights.

In its resolution of September 2010, presented by Germany and Spain and openly supported by France, the Human Rights Council refers to the fundamental right to drinking water and to sanitation as closely related to other rights, such as the right to a satisfactory standard of life, the right to the highest attainable standard of physical and mental health and the rights to life and to dignity. In the opinion of the expert, Mme. C. de Albuquerque, these resolutions confirm that the human right to water and to sanitation is now part of international law and demonstrate the political will of the international community to respond to the world crisis existing in this field[589]. In its resolution of 2010, the Human Rights Council requests that States create adequate mechanisms (plans, programmes, strategies) which should be adopted and implemented with active, free and effective participation of the local communities concerned[590].

Other norms for the protection of water resources are part of the humanitarian international law for the protection of victims of armed conflicts. They forbid attacks against installations (including those related to water) which are indispensable to the survival of the civilian population and any action of poisoning the resources of water. Number of other provisions concerning the protection of resources of water are contained in the Geneva Conventions of 1949 concerning the prisoners of war and the protection of the civilian population and in the two additional protocols of 1977, having in mind the direct relationship between water and human life, water and human environment.

Some significance presents also the 1997 Convention on the use of international water courses for other purposes than navigation (convention resulting from the activity of codification of international law in this field, undertaken by the International Law Commission), according to which, having in mind the multiple uses of water, a special attention has to be given to satisfying essential needs of the human being (article 10.2).

In spite of this evolution, analysts hold that there is no right to water established in international law; they speak about legitimacy to have access to water and sanitation as opposed to the legality of a right to water[591].

SECTION 2 - RIGHTS and OBLIGATIONS

Considering these evolutions, the question is whether there are in the contemporary international law norms concerning the right to drinking water and to sanitation, whether they are autonomous rights or rights derived from other human rights expressly recognized and what are the contents of such rights, respectively what are the rights of the individual and the corresponding obligations of the State and eventually of other actors.

1. The questions concerning rights and obligations related to water can be examined from the economic point of view, that is as a good (according to the GATT Agreement) or as a service (according to the Agreement on the trade of services), or from the point of view of human rights, that is of the right of each person to have access to water in quantity and of a quality necessary for his/her life. If we consider water as an object of trade, within GATT, the export of water in large quantities (by pipe-lines, channels or other means) would be submitted to the most favoured nation clause and to norms on the prohibition of quantitative restrictions.

The possibility is provided to apply exemptions which are necessary for the protection of health and of the life of human beings or animals, for the preservation of plants or the protection of exhaustible resources within the sustainable development concept. It seems easier to apply such norms to the trade with water in bottles. As for the trade with water as a service, this is about a product which is incorporated in the activity of a supplier in order to respond to a consumer; States can accept, according to the respective Agreement, obligations resulting from the lists

---

[589] Report cited above, C Abuquerque, para. 59.
[590] Doc. A/HRC/L. 14, 24 September 2010.
[591] Bas de Gaay Fortman & Michela Marcatelli, Between Soft Legality and Strong Legitimacy: A Political Economy Approach to the Struggle for Basic Entitlements to Seif Water and Sanitation, in Human Rights Quarterly, vol. 37, 2015, p. 941-976.

established concerning the access to the market and the application of the national treatment. During the negotiations on this subject, many States did not accept that services of supplying of water are submitted to the rules of the market and insisted on the need to ensure drinking safe water to all by the most appropriate means of management of water resources, essentially to maintain their options to adopt the adequate public policies for that purpose[592].

The so-called „Consensus of Washington" is known, according to which the common goods become merchandise within the market economy, that is a model of the management of water that some authors deplore as being based on the conception that everything is to be sold, considering water as a good or service on the market, including social services and natural resources[593]. To summarize, the norms applicable in the field of trade create several obligations which, if applied *ad literam*, can have as a consequence to limit the possibilities of States to offer drinking water to all, in particular to disadvantaged persons and groups.

Although it recognizes the economic character of water, as a good which is the object of trade, the Declaration of Dublin mentioned of 1992 affirms that the concept of economic good has limits compared to the logic of human rights, which includes an equitable distribution of resources.

Some authors analyze however the right to water on the basis of the consideration that water represents a public good, related to the fields of health and food security[594]. What would qualify a public good would be its non-exclusive character, meaning that nobody can be excluded from its use/consumption and that its use/consumption by somebody does not impede its use by others. This category would include the air and water[595]. This concept would come closer to that of common heritage of mankind. The European Charter of water of 2001, adopted by the Council of Europe affirms that „Water is a common heritage whose values should be recognized by all. Everybody has the duty to economize it and use it with care". Going further, the Charter of the water in the Lemanic area affirms that „Water is a common good of humanity; water is a vital element and a factor of development of societies. Water is not a merchandise as others and nobody has the right to appropriate it". We note however that there is no consensus in this respect at the international level and among authors; although it is considered a common resource, in many parts of the world water divides peoples and communities and the access to this resource reflects relations of power and notorious inequalities[596].

2. It is obvious that this right is more closely related to some of the rights provided for in the Covenant on economic, social and cultural rights (the rights to health, to housing, to a living decent standard); it is nevertheless difficult to deny its close relationship with the right to life. The conception according to which the right to life would have as counterpart only negative obligations, to refrain from actions which would endanger human life, is not acceptable.

The Human Rights Committee already took a stand on this matter, stating in its General Comment nr. 6 of 1982 that the right to life cannot be understood in a restricted meaning and that the protection of this right requests that States adopt positive measures. The Committee referred to measures to reduce infant mortality and to increase the life hope, in particular by adopting measures to eliminate malnutrition and epidemics[597]. This includes undoubtedly the duty to ensure drinking water, because life is not possible without it, in particular at the age which is meant by the Committee.

The recognition of the fundamental character of the right to water is based on the real importance of water as an element of life and has in view the world crisis resulting from the lack of drinking water for numerous populations in many parts of the world. If the interdependence and indivisibility of human rights is recognized, the order of priority given to their guarantee can be different from State to State and from area to area, depending on the situation. With regard to the right to water, there is no such question, because it is closely related to several other human rights.

Following the conception of human rights about the right to water and to sanitation, States have the primary responsibility to take the necessary measures to make possible for all persons under their jurisdiction the exercise of this right. While setting up this obligation, international documents leave to States full freedom to organize the supply of water and its distribution.

---

[592] Cf. Melanie Dubuy, art. cit., p. 304.
[593] M. Barlow, T. Clarke, L'or bleu, le grand enjeu du XXI-ème siècle, ed. Pluriel 2002, p. 12.
[594] S. Paquerot, Eau douce: la nécessaire refondation du droit international, Presse de l'Université du Quebec, 2005, p. 17.
[595] M. Desai, Public goods: historical perspective, in Inge Kaul a. o(ed.), Fournir des biens publics mondiaux: gérer la mondialisation ?, N.Y. PNUD.
[596] S. Mehta, art. cit., p. 556.
[597] Compilation..., doc. HRI/GEN/1/Rev. 8, p. 167.

The contents of the right to water and to sanitation were elaborated by the Committee on economic, social and cultural rights in its General Comment nr. 15 adopted in 2002[598]. According to this Comment, the right to water includes first the right of each person to have access to the existing sources of water, without impediments or interference from the State or from other persons, free from arbitrary disconnections and without being contaminated.

Water offered should be adequate in quantity and quality and should be considered as a social and cultural good, not primarily as an economic good, and its supply should be sustainably ensured, taking into account present and future generations. Water should be available, that is sufficient and continuous for the personal and domestic needs. This includes: drinking water, water for sanitary installations, for washing, for preparing food and for the personal and household hygiene. It must be of quality, which means without microorganisms, chemical substances and radiological risks which would represent a danger for personal health.

Water and water facilities and services should be accessible for all without discrimination, that is should be physically accessible for all segments of the population, should be of a good quality and culturally adequate, economically accessible for all and non-discriminatory, including for the most disadvantaged segments of the society and information about access to water should be accessible to all.

As general applicable principles, the Committee refers to non-discrimination and equal rights. States are requested to adopt measures to eliminate *de facto* discrimination through investment and allocation of resources for services and facilities for the benefit of large segments of their population, to give attention mainly to those persons and groups who had traditionally difficulties to exercise the rights related to water, that is women, children, minority groups, indigenous peoples, refugees, asylum seekers, internally displaced persons, migrant workers and detained persons. States should take measures for the progressive realization of this right, in the limit of available resources.

There is the presumption that regressive measures (those taken to limit existing conditions of access to water) are forbidden by the Covenant. If however such measures are adopted, they have to be justified with reference to the entirety of the rights provided by the Covenant and in the context of the maximum use of available resources[599].

As specific obligations, similar to other economic and social rights, the right to water contains:

- the *obligation to respect*, that is the obligation of States: to refrain from interfering directly or indirectly with the enjoyment of the right to water; to refrain from engaging in any practice or activity that denies or limits equal access to adequate water; to refrain from arbitrarily interfering with customary or traditional arrangements for water allocation; to refrain from unlawfully diminishing the quantity or polluting water; to refrain from limiting access to water services and infrastructure during armed conflicts, as well as to ensure the protection of water installations and supplies during armed conflicts;
- the *obligation to protect*, that is to prevent third parties (individuals, groups, corporations and other entities) from interfering in any way with the enjoyment of the right to water; this includes: adopting effective legislative and other measures to restrain third parties from denying equal access to water, from polluting and inequitably extracting from water resources; where water services are operated or controlled by third parties, to prevent them from compromising equal, affordable and physical access to sufficient, safe and acceptable water; for this purpose, to establish an effective regulatory system and independent monitoring, public participation and imposition of penalties for non-compliance;
- the *obligation to fulfill*, which includes the *obligation to facilitate*, that is to adopt special measures in order to assist persons and communities to enjoy this right; the *obligation to promote*, that is to adopt measures for the protection of water resources and for using methods to reduce the water wastages, as well as measures of education of the population concerning the hygienic use of water; the *obligation to fulfill*, that is to adopt the necessary measures towards the full realization of the right to water, by the recognition of this right within the national political and legal systems, by national strategies and plans of action to ensure that water is affordable to everybody and by ensuring sustainable access to water for all, in particular in rural and deprived urban areas; to provide the necessary quantities of water when individuals or groups are unable, for reasons beyond their control, to exercise this right by the means at their disposal.

The Committee underlines that access to adequate sanitation is fundamental for human dignity and for private life, as well as one of the important means for protecting the quality of resources and supplies of water[600]. It also

---

[598] Compilation..., doc. HRI/GEN/1/Rev. 8, pp. 105-121.
[599] General Comments of the Committee nr. 4/1991 and 14/2000, cited above, in connection with the right to health and the right to housing.
[600] General Comment of the Committee on th right to water, Compilation..., doc. HRI/GEN/1/Rev. 9, vol I, p. 122.

insists on the obligation of States to progressively extend adequate sanitation services, in particular to rural and deprived urban areas, taking into account the needs of women and children.

With regard to obligations at the international level, the Committee affirms that States should respect the exercise of this right in other States, that is: to refrain from actions that would impede, directly or indirectly, the enjoyment of this right in other countries; to refrain from activities which would deprive another State of the ability to realize the right to water for persons under its jurisdiction; not to impose embargoes or similar measures with regard to supplies of water or services and goods related to it (not to use water as an instrument of political or economic pressure); to prevent the violation of the right to water in other States by its citizens or companies; to support and facilitate the exercise of this right by supplies of water, technical and financial assistance to other States, mainly those developing; to give due attention in international agreements to the right to adequate water and to promote it in international organizations they are members of[601].

As core obligations, the Comment adopted by the Committee enumerates: to ensure access to the minimum essential quantity of water that is sufficient and safe for personal and domestic uses; to ensure the right of access to water, to water facilities and services without discrimination, in particular for disadvantaged or marginalized groups; to ensure physical access to water facilities or services that provide sufficient, safe and regular water without prohibitive waiting times and at reasonable distance from the household; to ensure equitable distribution of all available water facilities and services; to adopt and implement a national water strategy and plan of action addressing the whole population, elaborated on the basis of a participatory process, with precise indicators and benchmarks and giving a particular attention to disadvantaged or marginalized groups; to monitor the extent of realization of the right to water; to adopt programmes of low-cost supply of water in order to protect vulnerable and marginalized groups; to adopt measures to prevent, treat and control diseases linked to water, in particular by ensuring access to adequate sanitation[602].

Some authors think that the problem of access to water should be solved in the framework of economic and social development; they take as a starting point the data used by the UNDP, according to which two out of three persons lacking access to safe drinking water survive on less than 2 US dollars a day and one in three on less than 1 dollar a day[603]. They deny the right to water *per se* and accept access to water only as a condition for giving effect to other human rights. They make access to water depending on economic factors like property rights, costs and the context of its realization and maintain that economic, political and social structures are necessary behind situations where rights are not realized[604]. It is true, but the economic and social development is a process which takes some time and is facing itself many difficulties, while access to water is an urgent necessity for millions of people.

Examples are given when collective action of citizens and n g o's led to court decisions respecting the right to water of groups of citizens. In 2007, in the case Santa Casa de Misericordia de Santa Rosa do Viterbio Hospital v. Basic Sanitation Company of Sao Paulo State (Brazil), the hospital was disconnected of water because of non-payment; the Supreme Court of Brazil found that, although it was legitimate to interrupt water services due to non-payment, this did not apply to all circumstances, such as when public schools, nurseries, universities or hospitals were involved, because that would threaten human life. The Court ordered the company to re-establish the water connection of the hospital. The legal basis for this judgment was the Act to protect and defend consumers, which compels public utilities and their concessionaries to deliver continuous services, which means public services.

Similarly, in 1996, in the case Vellore Citizens Welfare Forum v. Union of India, applicants stated that tanneries were discharging untreated effluent in the Palar river, which is the main source of water supply to the residents of the area. The Supreme Court of India found that the tanners have absolutely no regard for the healthy environment in and around the tanneries, that in spite of the importance of the tanneries for the country, they have no right to destroy the ecology, degrade the environment and pose a health hazard. The Court also ruled that tanneries pay compensations to affected persons and restore the damaged ecology. It based the judgment on legal principles under the sustainable development, as well as on precautionary principle and the polluter pays principle, as well as on the constitutional and statutory provisions on person's rights to fresh air, clean water and a pollution free environment.

In 1995, in a case of privatization, a local company of Argentina, subsidiary of the transnational water company Vivendi, obtained a contract to provide water services to the province of Tucuman (North of the country). The company raised the tariffs and the water was contaminated by manganese. Associations of consumers contested the concessions contracts and asked for participation in the reform of the water sector and the prohibition of

---

[601] General Comment on the right to water, Compilation..., pp. 122-123.
[602] General Comment on the right to water, pp. 123-124.
[603] UNDP, Human Development Report 2006, Beyond Scarcity: Power, Poverty and the Global Water Crisis, 84, 2006.
[604] B. G. Fortman & M. Mercatelli, art. cit., mainly pp. 950-958.

disconnections. They obtained a law which prohibits water cut-off to those who consume less than the basic amount. It is also a case when the solution found is based on the conception that water is a public service. This conception is also the basis of movements in South Africa for the right of everyone to have access to sufficient food and water as an answer to privatization of such resources[605].

These cases are illustrative for evolutions in legislation and international practice in this field; they should not be discarded because coming from some developing countries, but emergent and having increasing influence on international arena. As presented above, in Europe, Latin America and Africa also courts adopted decisions in favour of the protection of environment, which includes respect of the right of access to water in sufficient quantity and quality[606].

While maintaining their doubts as to the recognition of the right to water, authors recognize that „the recent attention towards water and sanitation within the international community (particularly the UN General Assembly and the Human Rights Council) may be interpreted as an overdue acknowledgement that the deprivation suffered by people lacking essential services is severe enough to demand immediate judicial and political intervention"[607].

* * *

The majority of States accept, through legal instruments, mainly regional, and through declaratory documents the existence of the right to water, in some instances as an autonomous right, in others as deriving from other human rights. Some States contest even the existence of such a right (Australia), others contest its character as a fundamental right which would prevail over other rights, accepting that it would be only an economic and social right (USA), while others contest its autonomous character (United Kingdom) or invoke the lack of sufficient and conclusive international practice (United Kingdom, Canada). It is estimated that States which oppose to recognize explicitly this right as a fundamental human right are afraid that this would affect economic interests and would create for them direct obligations and have financial implications, including from rich countries to the developing ones. Considering the situation, some analysts consider that the moment has come to elaborate an international convention on the right to water[608] and that there is a trend to recognize it as an autonomous right[609].

Even if it is not generally recognized as an autonomous and fundamental human right by all States, but only as a right derived from other important human rights, the right to adequate water and to sanitation becomes increasingly an integral part of the whole of human rights, the exercise of which is indispensable for respecting most of other human rights. The evolution of international documents and practice, which responds to social needs, will tend to a stronger and more explicit expression of the norms applicable in this field.

---

[605] B. G Fortman & M. Mercatelli, art. cit., pp. 959-963.
[606] Firtman & Mercatelli, art. cit., pp. 975-976.
[607] Chapter XVII above, pp. 8-12.
[608] S. Mehta, art. cit., p. 554.
[609] M. Dubuy, p. 300.

PART VI - HUMAN RIGHTS in EUROPE

CHAPTER XXI - PROTECTION of HUMAN RIGHTS ACCORDING to the EUROPEAN UNION's LAW after the LISBON TREATY

ABSTRACT

After the entry into force of the Lisbon Treaty of 2007, which granted legal force to the Charter of Fundamental Rights, the issue of human rights in the European Union has gained a new momentum. For the first time, the Union has to implement a very complex document on human rights in all fields-political, civil, economic, social and cultural- which creates obligations for the institutions and for the member States, either to respect and protect immediately some human rights, or to adopt legislation and take measures to implement some principles in this field.

The European Court of Justice is competent to consider cases concerning the observation of the Charter provisions by EU institutions and by member States. The Charter becomes the criterion of validity of acts adopted by the EU institutions and of laws and other measures adopted by member States when they apply the Union's law.

More than that, the Lisbon Treaty commits EU to adhere to the 1950 Convention for the protection of human rights and fundamental freedoms, which would submit it to the jurisdiction of the European Court of Human Rights of Strasbourg, a longtime debated question within the Communities.

Romania, as a member of the Union and party to the European Convention of 1950, is interested to see a coherent and clear system of protection of human rights in Europe.

KEY WORDS: Charter of fundamental rights, legal validity, proportionality, juridical certitude, retroactivity, non-discrimination, European citizenship, powers and tasks.

INTRODUCTION

The initial treaties which created the European Communities contained no provisions on the protection of fundamental human rights, having strictly economic objectives. Now, when the Union evaluated from an economic community to a political, economic and social entity and has more extended powers, the requirement to respect human rights has to be dealt with in other terms.

1. After the entry in force of the Treaty of Lisbon, on the 1st December 2009, the issue of human rights received another dimension within the European Union. First, the Treaty provided for the entry in force of the Charter of fundamental rights of the Union[610]; for the first time, the Union disposes of a comprehensive document on human rights having a legal value, of a catalogue of human rights which is compulsory for its institutions and for member States. Thus, the European Court of Justice will be able to consider complaints about the observance of the provisions of the Charter by institutions in their activity and by member States when they apply the Union's law.

Thus, the Charter of fundamental rights became the criterion of examination of the validity of acts adopted by institutions of the Union; it can be invoked for this purpose by an institution or by a member State, as privileged parties, and less easily by physical and legal persons if they prove to have a direct interest; it can also be invoked by any person as an exception to the application of an act of the Union, and the Court will have to take a decision.

The Charter has become also a criterion of validity for acts adopted by member States in the application of Union's law; any person, citizen of the Union, can challenge before national jurisdictions an act of a member State as being in contradiction with a provision of the Charter; it is expected that the national courts ask for a preliminary opinion of the European Court of Justice.

The Charter is grouping human rights around some basic concepts (dignity, equality, freedom, solidarity, justice), which may allow the European Court, according to its constant practice, to go beyond the explicit provisions and to apply a kind of pretorian justice.

Second, the Lisbon Treaty provides that the Union shall adhere to the European Convention for the protection of human rights of 1950 with subsequent modifications and thus will become a party to this Convention as any

---

[610] Andrei Popescu, The Lisbon Treaty-change and reform in the European Union, in Romanian Journal of Community Law, nr. 2/2008(in Romanian), pp. 105-120 ; Diana Trașcă, Marcela Monica Stoica, The Lisbon Treaty-engine necessary for the good functioning of the EU vehicle, ibidem, pp. 97-106.

member State; its acts can be challenged by any person at the European Court of Human Rights for violating civil and political rights enounced in the Convention and in the additional Protocols to which the Union will adhere. The Lisbon Treaty established this as an obligation for the Union, while adding that this will not modify the powers of the Union. The participation of EU to the 1950 Convention was considered necessary because: in Europe there are now two legal instruments on human rights (the 1950 Convention and the Charter of fundamental rights), between them there are some differences and 28 States members of the EU are parties to both instruments; the system of protection established by the 1950 Convention is the most elaborated; there is a need to ensure a uniform application of norms on human rights throughout Europe, and for that to strengthen the protection of human rights in the Union by an external control on its acts by the European Court of Human Rights; as the Union presents itself as a legal order based on the state of law and on respect of human rights, it is also a question of public image for the Union.

Already in 1994 the Council of the Union asked for the advisory opinion of the European Court of Justice about the quality of the European Community (the Union did not yet have the quality of subject of international law) to become a party to the 1950 Convention, on the basis of a proposition of the European Commission which presented this idea in 1979. The European Court of Justice gave a negative opinion, invoking the lack of competence of the Community to adhere to the Convention and advanced that the only solution would be to adopt an express provision in the treaties. The Court also declared that it cannot decide on compatibility of the acceptance of the 1950 Convention with the EC Treaty in the absence of sufficient information on institutional arrangements required by such an acceptance[611].

Beginning with 2009, preparations started for the adhesion of the Union to the 1950 Convention. On the basis of a mandate given by the Council, negotiations took place between the European Commission and the Council of Europe and a draft agreement of compromise was established, but in December 2014 the European Court of Justice gave again a negative opinion[612] with regard to this draft agreement. The problem remains open. This evolution may have consequences which are yet difficult to ascertain.

2. According to article 20 of the Constitution of Romania of 1991, with the modifications adopted in 2003, "The constitutional provisions concerning rights and freedoms of citizens shall be interpreted and applied in conformity with the Universal Declaration of Human Rights, with the Covenants and other treaties to which Romania is a party. If there is non-conformity between the Covenants and the treaties on fundamental rights to which Romania is a party and the internal laws, international regulations shall have priority, except for the case where the Constitution or internal laws contain more favourable provisions".

Romania is a party to the European Convention of 1950 for the protection of human fundamental rights and freedoms. Romania also accepted the legal validity of the Charter of fundamental rights of the European Union by the ratification of the Lisbon Treaty; the Charter has now the value of a treaty for member States.

As a State party to the 1950 Convention, Romania does not have an easy situation, being among the States parties with the highest number of cases submitted to the European Court of Human Rights and being the object of a significant number of decisions which ascertain violations of provisions of the Convention, that is of human rights. Such decisions are often accompanied by the obligation to pay to the Romanian citizens victims of such violations important amounts of money as compensation.

Therefore, the negotiations mentioned and the evolution of regulations within the European Union in the field of human rights, as well as potential changes that may result for the activity of the two European courts, present a major interest for our country, because the 1950 European Convention, the Charter of fundamental rights and the regulations of the European Union are part of the Romanian legal system as a result of the application of the Constitution of Romania, and any arrangement which may be adopted with regard to the activity of the two courts may have consequences for the application of the two legal documents to our country.

This evaluation should be based on what is the interest of Romania: to have in Europe in the field of human rights two systems of reference and of jurisdiction, with different structures and competences and with the possibility to give different solutions (with all the consequences resulting from this for the citizens and authorities), or a system as harmonious as possible, even if there are two courts of justice, where the conception of protection of individual rights of the person prevail over the economic and commercial interests, conception which is better reflected in the 1950 European Convention and in the activity of the European Court of Human Rights.

3. As it is known, member States of the Communities hesitated initially to give more significance to human rights within the community law, on one side in order to avoid that the Court uses it to extend the application of community law in fields they considered of their competence, to advance the commercial objectives of the common

---

[611] Opinion of the European Court of Justice nr. 2/94 of 28 March 1996 (Rec.1996, I-1759).
[612] Opinion 2/13, Accession of the European Union to the European Convention for the Protection of Human Rights and Fundamental Freedoms(2014), ECLI, EU, C/2014, 2454.

market stressing "market rights" to the expense of human fundamental rights, and to act as a second European court on human rights, and on the other side being concerned that community institutions could be submitted to the system of Strasbourg and to the jurisdiction of the European Court of Human Rights.

However, fundamental human rights were inscribed in the constitutions of member States, on the basis of the Universal Declaration of Human Rights and of the 1950 Convention for the protection of fundamental human rights and freedoms. Thus, there was a disparity between the constitutions of States and the community law; as the acts of the Communities were more often affecting rights and interests of persons, such a disparity could not continue for long time, with the risk of raising questions about the democratic legitimacy of Communities. Cases appeared where national constitutional courts refused the application of decisions of the European Court of Justice, motivating that they violated a fundamental human right established in the internal constitutional law[613].

Taking into account this situation, although it continued to underline the autonomy of the general principles of community law in relation with the principles established in the constitutions of member States, the Court admitted that the general principles and the rights protected within the community law are not independent from the juridical culture and traditions of member States[614]. The Court referred, as a source of inspiration, to the common traditions of these States, affirming that it will not support measures incompatible with fundamental rights recognized and protected by the constitutions of member States[615], as well as to the international treaties in this field accepted by member States.

SECTION 1 - PREOCCUPATIONS of COMMUNITIES[616] concerning HUMAN RIGHTS

Political institutions of the Communities expressed also with clarity their position on this issue. In a common Declaration of the Council, the Parliament and the Commission of 1977 on fundamental rights, the three institutions underlined the importance they give to fundamental human rights, as they derive mainly from the constitutions of member States and from the 1950 European Convention, and stated that, in the exercise of their powers and in the pursuit of the objectives of the Communities, they respect and will continue to respect these rights.

The European Court of Justice gradually referred to international conventions and to general principles accepted by member States in this field.

With regard to the contents of these principles, the Court stressed the following:
- it will not admit measures incompatible with the fundamental rights recognized and guaranteed by the constitutions of member States;
- international documents on human rights with which member States cooperated or to which they adhered can offer indications to take into account within the community law, which allows to integrate the 1950 Convention in the community law, through the general principles, as a European minimum standard;
- fundamental rights should not be considered as absolute, but taking into account the social function of goods and activities protected by them and applying limitations justified by objectives of a general interest pursued by the Community[617].

In other cases, the Court requested member States to apply the provisions of the community law based on the protection of human rights, affirming that they reflect a general principle of law, based on common constitutional traditions of member States[618].

---

[613] Presentation of the position adopted in this respect by the constitutional courts of the Federal Republic of Germany and of Italy by Ion Gâlea, Adhesion of the European Union to the European Convention of human rights, Critical Analysis, 2012, Ed. C.H. Beck (in Romanian), pp. 20-26.

[614] Among others, case Nold, nr. 4/73, Nold v. Commission (1974), Repertory of ECJ, 491.

[615] Case Rutili, nr. 36/75, Rutili v. Ministry of Interior(1975), Repertory of ECJ, 1219, with direct reference to the provisions of the European Convention of 1950; case Hauer, nr 44/79, Hauer v. Land Rheinland-Pfalz(1979), Rep. ECJ, 3727, with reference to the Protocol 1 to the European Convention on the right to property.

[616] It is only after 1993 that we can speak about the European Union and until 2007 it is still a community law, although the Union adopted some decisions which were included in the treaties.

[617] Case Nold, supra, note 5.

[618] With this meaning, decisions of the Court of Justice in the case Schmidberger, C-112/00 Rep. ECJUE I-000(where it accepted that the freedom of expression and of association, both recognized by the European Convention and in the constitutional traditions of member States of the Union, may represent restrictions to the principle of free circulation of goods, in connection with the closing of the tunnel Brenner between Austria and Italy by an authorized manifestation); the case Omega, nr. C-36/02, decision of 2004, Rep. ECJEU I-9609, where the Court retained as an injury to human dignity the offer of a game with laser which feigned the killing of some persons, as an exception from the free circulation of goods and services ; the Court referred to the common constitutional traditions of member States on human

Institutions of the Communities continued to adopt documents in this field, such as a new Common Declaration of the three institutions in 1986, other declarations and resolutions on racism and xenophobia (adopted by the Council), a Declaration of the Parliament concerning fundamental human rights and freedoms adopted in 1989, the Community Charter on fundamental social rights, signed by 11 member States in 1989[619].

The Maastricht Treaty of 1992 included several clauses on respect of human rights; it provides that the policy in the field of cooperation for development (that is in the relations with countries which received assistance) should contribute to the general objective of development and consolidation of democracy and of state of law, as well as to the respect of human rights and fundamental freedoms. In the chapter about the Union, it affirms that the Union will respect human rights guaranteed by the 1950 Convention and the national constitutional traditions; the requirement to respect human rights is mentioned also in the pillars II (European Common Foreign and Security Policy) and III (Justice and Internal Affairs).

According to the Amsterdam Treaty of 1997, the Union is based on the principles of freedom, democracy and respect for human rights. This provision became justiciable, which means that the jurisdiction of the European Court of Justice extended from the community pillar to other issues where the communities received powers (those concerning asylum, immigration and civil law). The Treaty also empowered the Council to suspend some rights to those member States found responsible of serious and persistent violations of these rights. The requirement to respect these rights was also considered as a condition to ask to become a member and to adhere to the Union.

The Amsterdam Treaty integrated, in a distinct chapter, the Agreement on the social policy (which was previously an intergovernmental agreement among States which ratified it, due to the opposition of the United Kingdom) and added articles on education, culture, public health, as well as chapters on economic and social cohesion and on the policy of employment, with the objective of promoting full employment. Other provisions refer to the European Social Fund, created to give financial assistance in order to achieve some of the social objectives of the Community, such as support for the professional training and the promotion of employment, in particular for disadvantaged groups like the long term unemployed, migrant workers or women who resume their activity after interruption.

The social provisions of the Treaty created the basis for the legislative action of the Community in view of ameliorating the working and living conditions of workers, including equality between men and women on the labour market.

Fundamental rights are also taken into consideration as a point of departure for the power to legislate. The Treaty provides, in this respect, the power of the community institutions, within their attributions, to take adequate measures in order to combat discrimination on grounds of sex, racial or ethnic origin, religion or belief, disability, age or sexual orientation.

The Court admitted however that there are limits to take human rights as a basis for the legislative activity of the Community. It affirmed that specific measures of the Community for the protection of human rights can be adopted, under the condition not to bring changes to the treaties through the modification of the objectives of the Community[620].

In parallel with negotiations for the Lisbon Treaty, the Charter of fundamental rights was elaborated in a wider framework, with the participation of members of the European Parliament and of the civil society, and then was adopted in a solemn manner but without receiving legal character. It was then introduced as a distinct title in the draft of the Treaty of a Constitution for Europe, but that treaty was not ratified by some member States and was abandoned.

The Lisbon Treaty adopted in 2007 (when some changes were brought also to the Charter) confirms the adoption of the Charter and gives it compulsory legal force.

SECTION 2 - NORMS on HUMAN RIGHTS APPLIED by the EUROPEAN COURT of JUSTICE

As noted above, the Court considered respect for human rights as a condition of the legality of Community acts and accepted that specific measures can be adopted by acts of the Community in this field, but without the modification of treaties and of the objectives of the Community.

---

[619] With regard to documents adopted by institutions of the Communities and of the Union on human rights, Andrei Popescu, Ion Diaconu, European and Euroatlantic Organizations, 2009, Ed. Universul Juridic, pp. 267-269(in Romanian).

[620] Exhaustive presentation by Octavian Manolache, Treatise of community law, 5-th edition, 2006, Ed. C.H. Beck (in Romanian), pp. 26 and foll.

On the basis of some provisions of treaties and also of principles applied by the national laws of member States, the Court defined a series of principles for the evaluation of the activity of the Community and of acts of institutions, which are relevant for the protection of human rights even if they do not affirm directly such rights[621].

1. Proportionality is considered as a general principle of community law. Its substance consists in ensuring a balance between the objective pursued and the means used; this supposes to evaluate whether the means used correspond to the objective, if they are necessary for that and if they do not impose excessive obligations to persons or too important restrictions as compared to the benefits and costs of the measure adopted.

To evaluate proportionality, interests concerned are identified and their importance is determined, then alternative ways are considered and it is established whether the decision or the measure taken is proportional to the objective pursued, including its conformity with the existing norms of community law.

As for the actions of member States, the Court evaluated more severely the conditions of proportionality mainly when they concerned the freedom of circulation of persons, of goods or services, but accepted restrictive measures when there were authentic preoccupations for public health.

2. Legal certainty (non-retroactivity) refers mainly to community norms which may have in reality a retroactive effect; this concerns cases when the norm is enforced before its publication or when it applies to events produced before its adoption.

Both the Court and national tribunals are very reluctant to accept a retroactive application of norms. In a case where the Commission adopted a regulation granting compensatory damages, then by two other regulations modified the amount of compensations and provided their application 14 days before their publication, the Court affirmed that there was a fundamental principle of the community legal order, according to which a measure should not be applied to those concerned before they had the possibility to have knowledge about it.

The Court affirmed that a regulation may have effects before its publication only exceptionally, when the objective pursued requires it and if the legitimate expectations of those concerned are respected.

Based on these requirements, there is a normal presumption against the validity of measures of a retroactive application; the Court accepted the validity of such measures only in the field of agriculture, in connection with ensuring the stability of the market.

3. Apparent retroactivity or legitimate expectation concerns the situation where legislative acts apply to events already produced, but which are not finally closed. This means that administration should modify its policy because of the new legislative act, even if this may have effects on the conduct of persons, as provided for in the previous acts. In the case of the adoption of new regulations, without providing for transitory measures for the contracts still to be executed, the Court decided as a rule in favour of petitioners, sometimes granting even compensation for the damage suffered.

4. Non-discrimination is a general principle which obliges Communities and member States when they apply community law; the treaties mention non-discrimination on grounds of citizenship, in the context of the free movement of persons, of the equal treatment of women and men, between producers and consumers, in the field of agriculture and others.

As noted above, the Amsterdam Treaty provided the power of the Community to act against discrimination and more directly, that of the Council to take measures, at the proposal of the Commission and after consulting the European Parliament, in order to combat discrimination on grounds of sex, social or ethnic origin, religion or belief, disability, age or sexual orientation, that means from the point of view of human rights.

The European Court of Justice applied non-discrimination as a general principle, aiming at any unequal, arbitrary or unjustified treatment in the fields of the power of the Community. It was thus accepted that the Community could take measures against discrimination based on criteria applied in the field of human rights, without conditioning them on the realization of economic objectives. At the same time, not every different treatment was considered discriminatory.

As for reasons for which a different treatment can be justified, it is obvious that direct discrimination or deliberately disguised on grounds of sex or citizenship could not be easily justified. Indirect or non-intentional different treatment could be justified if it is proportional to a workplace requirement and derives from it (for instance, a higher payment for the full programme of work as compared to the partial one, even if it is indirectly discriminating women, can be justified by the needs of the working process; similarly, the knowledge of the language, even if indirectly it may discriminate non-citizens).

As a general principle, discrimination can be invoked as a reason for challenging community acts, for invalidating them or in requests for their interpretation, as well as for obtaining compensation, and similarly against acts of member States.

---

[621] Presentation of these principles and of the decisions of the Court on which they are based by Octavian Manolache, op. cit., pp. 33-49.

5. Transparency tends to be recognized as a general principle; initially, the Community acted within closed bodies, with limited access of the public. After the Maastricht Treaty, the issue of transparency gained more interest. In 1993 the Council and the Commission adopted a Code of conduct in this regard. The Intergovernmental Conference which prepared the Amsterdam Treaty insisted to improve the access of public and transparency of the activities of the Union institutions.

Nevertheless, transparency was not recognized as a general principle having legal effects; the Court did not ask for the adoption of secondary legislation in this field, declaring that decisions of the Council on access to documents can be based on the rules of procedure.

Other fundamental principles applied by the Court in its decisions are:
- the principle of legal certainty, which finds its expression in time limits and foreclosure for the exercise of powers and of remedies by the Community institutions, in the non-opposability of an act which was not adequately publicized, as well as in the clarity and precision of the rule of law;
- the principle of the protection against arbitrary or disproportionate interventions of public authorities;
- the principle of subsidiarity;
- the principle of legitimate expectation.

In some of its decisions, the Court referred to the following human rights:
- the right to property, guaranteed in the community order according to common principles of the constitutions of member States;
- the right to free exercise of economic and professional activities, which is protected in the Community, with legitimate restrictions concerning activities protected for social reasons;
- respect for the private and family life, for the inviolability of domicile and correspondence, with the exception of the interference of organs of public order according to the law and of the power of inquiry of the European Commission in the field of competition;
- *non bis in idem*, meaning not to cumulate two sanctions for the same violation; it concerns two sanctions of the same nature, as well as the situation where the same case is submitted to the jurisdictions of several member States;
- the right to movement and to residence for citizens of member States;
- the right to have adequately motivated the decisions which challenge a right conferred by a community norm;
- procedural rights, such as the right to an efficient judicial remedy, non-retroactivity of criminal decisions and others;
- the contradictory procedure for adopting most of the decisions concerning violations of community law or other acts of institutions with regard to rights of persons[622].

Nevertheless, the Court also adopted decisions on the basis not of economic and "market rights", but on the respect for human dignity and equality, as a fundamental right. A first case concerned a petition according to which the application of a community scheme would violate the right to dignity. The Court decided that any discrimination should be avoided (between the beneficiaries of subsidized food), as well as any violation of the right to dignity, in the interpretation of the respective measures. It referred to "fundamental human rights contained in the general principles of community law" and protected by the Court. The Court confirmed that the fundamental right to human dignity is part of the Union's law and that none of the fundamental rights can be used to injure the right to dignity, which belongs to the substance of the rights inscribed in the Charter of fundamental rights.

The Court also confirmed that the fundamental right to the integrity of the person is part of the Union's law and includes, in the fields of medicine and biology, the free and well informed consent of the donor and receiver of parts of human body[623].

Of course, cases where the Court invalidated acts of community institutions for injuring human rights are not frequent. It is more often that the Court decided in favour of persons contesting specific administrative acts.

---

[622] Enumeration presented with small differences by Octavian Manolache, op. cit., pp. 26-33; the same by Ovidiu Ținca, General Community law, III-rd ed., 2005, Ed. Lumina Lex (in Romanian), pp. 275-276.

[623] With regard to decisions of the Court concerning such rights, Cornelia Toader, Constitutionalizing community law. The roll of the Court of Justice of the European Communities, in Romanian Journal of Community Law, nr. 2/2008(in Romanian), p. 21.

In cases where treaties allow that States derogate from the community law, the Court considered that it was competent to exercise its jurisdiction to consider the conformity of measures taken by States as derogations from fundamental rights, if the respective problems are related to the application of community law.

Equal rights between men and women. A special attention was given within the Community and then the Union to the elimination of discrimination against women and to ensuring equal rights with men. The Maastricht Treaty imposed to the Community the obligation to adopt legislative measures in the field of equal opportunities and treatment of women and men on the labour market.

The Court decided that the general principle of equal treatment between men and women is a fundamental principle of the legal community order and that the elimination of discrimination on grounds of sex is one of the fundamental human rights, which has to be protected by the community law.

This principle was extended by legislative acts and by decisions of the Court; although according to the treaties it refers to the entirety of economic and social problems, in fact it is limited to the fields related to work.

The community law contains three areas of application of this principle: equal pay, equal treatment and social security. Equal pay for equal work was initially provided as a problem within the power of the Community. The Court added, by its decisions, the equal pay for work of an equal value.

Equal treatment was provided for in the Amsterdam Treaty, with the objective of ensuring equal conditions of competition in different member States; it proclaimed the equal treatment concerning conditions of work.

The Court stated that the principle of equal treatment of men and women is a fundamental principle of community law.

In a Directive of the Council concerning equality of treatment in three fields (access to employment and promotion, professional training and conditions of work), it is defined as the elimination of any discrimination on grounds of sex, direct or indirect, mainly in connection with the marital or the family status. In another Directive, States were asked to provide a minimum protection at work for pregnant women, for women who breastfeed or who recently gave birth.

The Amsterdam Treaty provides also for the possibility of positive action in order to ensure *de facto* equal rights of women and men, with regard to the professional training and compensation for some disadvantages in the career. However, the Court did not admit other measures of protection for women except those related to pregnancy and to maternity.

If initially the right of husbands to parental holidays was not accepted, later on a Directive of 1996, following a Framework Agreement concluded by the main organizations of employers and employees, decided that a minimal individual right to parental holiday will be granted both to men and women for the purpose to take care of a child or to adopt a child for that purpose. It is left to member States to establish specific conditions of granting these holidays.

In order to ensure equal treatment in the field of social security, after the ratification of the Amsterdam Treaty directives were adopted in unanimity by the Council. The basic norm is equality of treatment and absence of any discrimination based on sex, be it direct or indirect; as examples given of forms of discrimination prohibited there are: different conditions of access or restrictive schemes, discriminatory obligations to contribute or contributions; differences in the calculation of benefits; conditions about duration; discriminatory deductions. Exceptions are admitted regarding age criteria, to taking care of children and to the situation of dependent wives.

The field of struggle against sexual discrimination, although accepted as a fundamental principle of community law, remains one complex and which suffers continuous modifications both at the community level through directives and through decisions of the Court and at the national level. Its application has inherent limits, being related to work problems, to the evolution of the economy and to social relationships[624].

The Court is now controlling respect of fundamental rights both with respect to community acts and with regard to acts of member States when they apply community law. The criterion used by the Court regarding acts of States is whether their subject matter falls within the field of application of community law.

SECTION 3 - CITIZENSHIP of the EUROPEAN UNION

The Maastricht Treaty introduced this new conception in the Union's law and the Amsterdam Treaty added some clarifications.

---

[624] With regard to the elimination of discrimination based on sex, decision of the European Court of Justice, case Defrenne, aff. 149/77, Rep. 1365.

The law of the European Union does not have its own system of granting European citizenship; according to the treaties it derives automatically from the citizenship given by a member State; it is not replacing the national citizenship, but complements it.

The treaties of the Union grant some rights to European citizens, one of the most important being non-discrimination between citizens of different member States. The rights corresponding to European citizenship form a limited set of rights, those which are specific to this institution; the European citizens continue to enjoy all human rights granted in accordance with their national law and in accordance with international instruments on human rights.

Moreover, these rights have a progressive character, as they can be supplemented by the Council acting in unanimity at the proposal of the Commission and after consulting the Parliament. The decision of the Council has to be approved after words by member States according to their constitutional procedures.

The following rights are provided for by the treaties:
- the freedom of movement and of residence within the territory of member States, of course within the limits and conditions provided;
- the right to vote and to stand as a candidate at municipal elections and at elections to the European Parliament in the State of residence under the same conditions as nationals of that State; a Directive of the Council of 1993 sets forth the principles of the exercise of the right to participate in the elections to the European Parliament: the freedom to choose between the country of residence and the State of which they are nationals. A derogation is admitted in case where the proportion of citizens of the Union with right to vote represents more than 20% from the national citizens with the right to vote; the respective State can impose for non-nationals the condition to have a duration of residence of 5 years to vote and of 10 years to stand as a candidate; this derogation applies only for Luxembourg. A Directive of 1994 extends the same principles and possible derogation for the participation in municipal elections; at the same time, it allows that member States reserve to their citizens some functions in the municipal executives and to limit to citizens the participation in the election of electors or in the elections for one of the parliamentary assemblies (for States with bicameral parliaments).
- the right to petition to the European Parliament and the right to refer to the European Ombudsman cases of maladministration in the activity of institutions, bodies, offices or agencies of the Union, when they consider that such acts affected their rights;
- the right of access to documents of the institutions, bodies, offices and agencies of the Union and for this purpose to address to any organ of the Union and to receive an answer in an official language;
- the right to protection by the diplomatic and consular authorities of any member State of the Union in the territory of a third country in which the member State of which he or she is a national is not represented; a decision on this issue was adopted by member States reunited in the Council in 1995. The diplomatic or consular protection is granted in cases of death, illness, arrest or loss of documents, with the agreement of the State of the national, which covers also the expenses occasioned[625].

According to a norm of general international law, the granting of assistance by an embassy or a consular office to a citizen of another State supposes the agreement of the State of residence of the person. This problem should be solved by agreements of the Union with third States. There is no information about such negotiations until now.

The European Court of Justice took a stand recently with regard to the right of movement of a head of State on the territory of another State member. Hungary asked the Court, in a petition of non-action against Slovakia, to decide that the latter violated the right of the president Solyom to circulate freely on the territory of Slovakia, as a citizen of the Union. Slovakia contested this right referring to norms of diplomatic law according to which the visits of heads of State are submitted to some norms of international law. The Court accepted that diplomatic and good neighbourly relations between member States are not in the competence of the Union. It also accepted that the head of State cannot be considered as an ordinary citizen and that his visits in other States are submitted to norms of public international law. The Court recognized in this case the priority of international law over the rule of freedom of movement, based on the specific status of the head of State as it is recognized in international law[626].

---

[625] With regard to European citizenship, Andrei Popescu, Ion Diaconu, op. cit., pp. 277-279.
[626] ECJEU, case C-364/10, decision of 16 October 2012; case presented and analyzed by Niki Aloupi, Les rapports entre droit international et droit de l'Union Européenne, in RGDIP nr. 2-13, I, p. 35.

The Charter enounces also, under the title "Citizens' rights", the right to good administration, including the rights to be heard before a measure affecting them is taken, to have access to their file, to write to the institutions of the Union in one of the official languages and to receive an answer in the same language, which concern obviously all persons residing on the territory of a State, including its nationals.

SECTION 4 - CHARTER of FUNDAMENTAL RIGHTS; CONTENTS, SIGNIFICANCE

In 2000, the Intergovernmental Conference of Nice adopted the Charter of fundamental human rights of the European Union, as a declaratory document. It was then included as a chapter in the draft constitutional Treaty for Europe which was not ratified by some member States and was abandoned. The reform Treaty adopted in Lisbon contains a transversal reference to the Charter, as its text was agreed at the Intergovernmental Conference of 2004 with a few changes in 2007, recognizing its legal compulsory value, but without including it in the text of the Treaty itself.

The Charter of fundamental rights[627] is now a legal compulsory document, in the category of treaties, which obliges the EU institutions and member States (only when they are implementing EU law) and, in so far as it refers to individual conduct of persons, also creates rights for EU citizens.

While reserving the powers and the tasks of the Union and the principle of subsidiarity, the Charter reaffirms human rights as they result, in particular, from the constitutional traditions and international obligations common to the member States, from the European Convention for the protection of human rights and fundamental freedoms, the Social Charters adopted by the Union and by the Council of Europe, as well as from the case-law of the Court of Justice of the European Union (CJEU) and of the European Court of Human Rights (ECHR). It is expressly indicated that the enjoyment of these rights entails responsibilities and duties with regard to other persons, to the human community and to future generations.

The Charter stresses that, in order to promote a balanced and sustainable development and ensure the free movement of persons, services, goods and capital, as well as the freedom of establishment, that it seeks to promote, it is necessary to strengthen the protection of fundamental rights.

It is of particular interest to see the significance of the provisions of the Charter as it results from its preamble:
- for the first time the judicial institutions of the Union and the national tribunals will have the competence to solve disputes concerning violations of fundamental rights enounced in the Charter, as part of the EU law;
- the Charter reaffirms rights; it does not create them; the text points out that the Union recognizes the rights, freedoms and principles enounced, a formulation which seems restrictive;
- respect for the powers and tasks of the Union is enounced as a previous condition for recognizing the respective rights; this could conduce in some cases to consider in opposition the two sets of objectives and values, which would generate difficulties of interpretation and application;
- the sources of these rights are the constitutional traditions and international obligations of member States and the jurisprudence of the two courts; for the first time the jurisprudence of the European Court of Human Rights is placed on equal footing with that of the European Court of Justice.

It is an extremely complex combination of sources, reservations and considerations where the European Court of Justice, its Tribunal and specialized tribunals provided for in the Lisbon Treaty, as well as the national tribunals will have to find the grounds for interpreting the Charter and for motivating their decisions.

Fundamental rights are structured within titles, as follows:
- dignity (human dignity, the right to life, the right to the integrity of the person, the prohibition of torture and inhuman or degrading treatment or punishment, the prohibition of slavery and of forced labour);
- freedoms (the right to liberty and security, respect for private and family live, the protection of personal data, the right to marry and to found a family, the freedom of thought, conscience and religion, the freedom of expression and information, the freedom of assembly and of association, the freedom of arts and sciences, the right to education, the freedom to choose an occupation and the right to engage in work, the freedom to conduct a business, the right to property, the right to asylum, the protection in case of removal, expulsion or extradition);

---

[627] Extended presentation and analyzes of the provisions of the Charter, Andrei Popeascu, Ion Diaconu, op. cit., pp. 279-283.

- equality (equality before the law, non-discrimination, cultural, religious and linguistic diversity, equality between women and men, the rights of the child, the rights of the elderly, the integration of persons with disabilities);
- solidarity (the right of workers to information and to consultation within the enterprise, the right to collective bargaining and action, the right of access to placement services, protection in case of unjustified dismissal, fair and just working conditions, prohibition of child labour and protection of young people at work, the right to family and professional life, social security and social assistance, health care, access to services of a general economic interest, environmental protection, consumer protection);
- citizens' rights (the right to vote and to stand as a candidate for elections to the European Parliament, the right to vote and to stand as a candidate at municipal elections, the right to good administration, the right of access to documents, the right to address to the European Ombudsman, the right to petition, the freedom of movement and of residence, the diplomatic and consular protection);
- justice (the right to an efficient remedy and to a fair trial, the presumption of innocence and the right to defense, the principles of legality and of proportionality of criminal offences and penalties, the right not to be tried or punished twice in criminal proceedings for the same criminal offence).

It is obvious that the Charter includes both civil and political rights (which are stipulated in the European Convention of 1950 and some of its additional protocols and are protected under the jurisdiction of the European Court of Human Rights), and economic, social and cultural rights, which under the system of the Council of Europe are set forth in other documents, are protected by committees of experts under a non-jurisdictional procedure and are only seldom submitted to the jurisdiction of the ECHR, when they are closely related to a civil or political right or when a discrimination is alleged. Thus, the Charter enounces a large sphere of human rights; for the first time, economic, social and cultural rights (some of them enounced in imperative terms as compared to other documents, including to Covenants on human rights, affirming for instance that every person has the right) will be the object of jurisdictional protection at this regional level.

At the same time, some fundamental rights are formulated in more general terms than in other international instruments; this will make it necessary, in case of dispute, to resort to explanations elaborated and updated under the authority of the Presidium of the European Convention which drafted the Charter (in its previous form) and of course to conventions adopted within the Union or within the Council of Europe and to the respective jurisprudence.

Some of the fundamental rights concern criminal law, meaning the judgment and punishment for criminal acts, which are incriminated as such in the national laws of member States, not in acts of the Union.

The text reflects also evolutions produced after the adoption of the 1950 European Convention, including rights in fields like biotechnology, data protection, access to documents, etc.

The Charter makes the distinction between its provisions enouncing rights and freedoms and those setting forth principles. Only those of the first category can be directly invoked in justice, in case of violation. It is clearly provided for that it is admitted to bring to justice cases concerning principles only for the interpretation and control of the legality of acts adopted for their implementation.

The dispositions of the Charter are compulsory for institutions, organs and agencies of the Union, while respecting the principle of subsidiarity, without extending the scope of application of the Union's law beyond its powers, without modifying its powers and tasks and without creating new powers and tasks. They are applied also to member States, when they implement the Union's law.

It is understood that these reservations and clarifications have in view the protection of powers which remain in the hands of member States in the field of human rights, as well as to prevent the extension of powers of Union's bodies in these matters using the provisions of the Charter.

The Charter provides for the possibility of applying restrictions to the exercise of fundamental rights, which must be provided for by law and respect the essence of the respective rights and freedoms. Such restrictions are subject to the principle of proportionality and may be made only if they are necessary and genuinely meet objectives of general interest recognized by the Union or respond to the need to protect the rights and freedoms of others.

In order to ensure the necessary coherence between the Charter of fundamental rights and the European Convention of 1950, it is stipulated that, in so far as some of the rights correspond to those guaranteed by the European Convention, their meaning and scope shall be the same as those laid down by the European Convention. In particular, it is provided that nothing in the Charter should be interpreted as restricting or adversely affecting human rights and fundamental freedoms as recognized by Union's law, by international law, by agreements to which the Union or all member States are parties, including the European Convention of 1950. It is affirmed explicitly that the level of protection ensured by the Charter shall never be inferior to that guaranteed by the European Convention.

The objective pursued by repeated references to the European Convention for the protection of human rights and by indicating its provisions as a source of fundamental rights is to ensure a substantial rapprochement of the two documents, a uniform interpretation and application of the Charter of fundamental rights and of the European Convention.

Of course, number of problems concerning the application of the Charter of fundamental rights remain to be solved by the practice, like the interpretation of its provisions in conformity with the European Convention (and with what additional protocols, having in view that not all member States are parties to the same protocols), the coherence of the two systems of protection of human rights, how to avoid and solve eventual conflicts of competence between the two courts and others.

SECTION 5 - ADHESION of the EU to the EUROPEAN CONVENTION for the PROTECTION of HUMAN RIGHTS

According to the Lisbon Treaty, in force since 2009, the European Union shall adhere to the 1950 European Convention. After a few years of technical discussions between the EU Commission and an ad-hoc group of the Council of Europe, a draft agreement on the adhesion of EU to the European Convention was finalized in 2013. The draft agreement has in view that EU adheres to the European Convention (with modifications made by the Additional Protocols 11 and 14 concerning the functioning of the Court) and to Protocols 1 and 6 concerning the rights to property, to education, to free elections and respectively on the abolishment of death penalty. The Commission asked for the opinion of the Court whether the draft agreement is compatible with the treaties of the Union.

In its advice, the Court retained several possible consequences of adhering to the 1950 Convention[628], as follows:
- external control by the institutions created by the 1950 Convention over the institutions of EU, in particular over the decisions of the CJEU, on the basis of compulsory interpretations given to the provisions of the Convention by the ECHR; there is no provision on taking into account the interpretation given by CJEU to the Convention and to the Charter of fundamental rights; the control of ECHR would extend also to acts adopted within the Common Foreign and Security Policy, a field where CJEU has no competences in all its aspects, which according to CJEU is incompatible with the autonomy of the EU law;
- the Court also considers that ascertaining the responsibility for violations of the European Convention, as resting upon EU or member States or both as appropriate, would lead to the intervention of ECHR in the sharing of competences within the Union, which is of strict power of EU; the agreement negotiated proposes a mechanism of common responsibility of EU and member States, which is not considered fully adequate; another concern refers to the possibility for ECHR to adopt decisions which would interpret and evaluate the EU law;
- the coordination of the application of the 1950 Convention and the application of the Charter is not ensured, because the Convention gives to States parties the possibility to adopt standards of protection of human rights higher than those enounced in its provisions, while the EU treaties do not allow this; the Court considers that where the rights recognized by the Charter correspond with those provided for in the Convention, this possibility given to States parties to the Convention should be limited (for EU member States) to ensuring the level of protection provided for by the Charter, in order not to compromise the primacy, the unity and efficiency of Union's law;
- treating EU as any State party, from all points of view, would ignore the specificity and the intrinsic nature of EU; the 1950 Convention requests each State party to check whether other States parties respect human rights, while according to EU law there is the obligation of mutual trust among the member States within the common space of freedom, security and justice; adhering in such conditions would destroy the EU balance and would undermine the autonomy of the EU law;
- the Protocol nr. 16 of 2013 to the 1950 Convention allows tribunals of States parties to ask from ECHR advisory opinions on the interpretation and application of the provisions of the Convention; if EU member States would request such opinions, this could affect the autonomy and efficiency of the procedure of preliminary decisions of CJEU provided for by EU treaties for the uniform application of

---

[628] Extensively presented by Alisa Vekeman, The Impact of Accession to the ECHR on the autonomy of the EU Legal Order, Universiteit Gent, Academiejaar 2014-2015.

the EU law, mainly in cases where the rights guaranteed by the European Convention correspond to those guaranteed by the Charter.

Considering these consequences, the Court considers that the adhesion of EU to the 1950 Convention is not compatible with the treaties of the Union.

These issues were considered by several authors, well informed on these matters, before and after receiving the advice of the European Court of Justice[629]. A brief analysis of the opinion of the Court shows that this aims in substance to preserve untouched the autonomy of the Union as an order of law, independent both with regard to internal order of member States and to international legal order.

Thus, with regard to the external control by ECHR on acts of EU institutions and the possibility to decide on their validity, although ECHR has no competence to declare null a national law (that means equally not a EU act), its decisions having a declaratory character as to the observance or violation of provisions of the Convention, the draft agreement included a preliminary procedure by which CJEU could be invited to take a stand on the compatibility of the EU law with the European Convention before a case is examined by ECHR. This procedure was agreed by the presidents in office of the two courts in 2011. In its advice, CJEU considers that this solution is not satisfactory, because it refers only to the compatibility of the respective provision, not to its interpretation, mainly with regard to provisions of the secondary law adopted by EU; also the invitation of CJEU to take a stand in such cases should not be left to the appreciation of ECHR; finally, the interpretation given by CJEU to a provision of the European Convention is not accepted as compulsory.

As this is about another legal order, the question is whether this last preoccupation is well founded. As some authors show, if decisions of the EU or of CJEU would be compulsory in all these cases, even the participation of the Union to the European Convention would be without any object. The purpose of adhering is just to submit acts of EU to the control of ECHR with regard to respect of the provisions of the European Convention, which is the essence of adhering to the Convention. If ECHR would have to follow the decisions of EU on the compatibility of EU acts with the European Convention, that would mean that EU takes the decisions on the observance or non-observance of the Convention. If the interpretation given to EU law by EU should be taken into consideration by ECHR, it is not normal that the interpretation of the European Convention should be made by CJEU and be compulsory.

With regard to the affirmation that submitting acts adopted within Common Foreign and Security Policy to the control of ECHR would undermine the EU autonomy, because CJEU has no exclusive competence on these acts, it seems obvious that the jurisdiction of ECHR in matters where ECJ has no competences is not attempting at the autonomy of the EU law; if such acts would represent violations of human rights, they have to be submitted to a jurisdictional control; if EU adheres to the Convention, such acts are submitted to the same regime even if CJEU would be competent.

With regard to the issue of responsibility for violations of the Convention, in order to avoid that ECHR takes decisions on the sharing of competences between EU and member States, the draft agreement advanced a complex solution, including even an amendment to the European Convention taking into account the specificity of EU, according to which there can be common responsibility of EU and member States; in spite of this, the Court considers that it still contains elements incompatible with the EU treaties (the possibility that ECHR decides whether a party is admitted as jointly responsible in a case, the possibility that only one party is found responsible by ECHR and the possibility that a State is considered responsible for a provision to which it made a reservation). These hypotheses would lead to the exercise by ECHR of an evaluation of the sharing of competences within EU, respectively on the responsibility of the EU and member States separate or in common. However, other legal bodies have also such competences, like for instance the mechanism of settlement of disputes within the World Trade Organization which can decide whether the EU is the sole responsible in a case or jointly with member States; it is not possible to exclude completely the roll of an external organisms each time when the interpretation of the EU law is necessary[630]. If the ECHR would not be able to establish who is responsible for a violation of human rights, when responsibility seems to be common (the decision was taken by a EU institution and its execution is made by a

---

[629] In the Romanian legal specialized literature, Ion Gâlea, Adhesion of the European Union to the European Convention on human rights, a Critical Analysis, Ed. C. H. Beck, 2012; other opinions by Jean Claude Piris, The Lisbon Treaty, A Legal and Political Analysis, Cambridge University Press, 2010 ; Lock Tobias, Walking on a tightrope: the draft accession agreement and the autonomy of the EU legal order, Law and governance in Europe Working Paper Series, 12/2011, Center for Law and Governance in Europe, London; Lemmens P., The Relationship between the Charter of Fundamental Rights and the ECHR, Maastricht Journal of European and Comparative Law, no. 8/2001.

[630] Adam Lazowski and Ramses A. Wessel, When Caveats turn into Locks: Opinion 2/13 on Accession of European Union to ECHR, German Law Journal no. 1, 2015, pp. 12-13

member State), a situation may occur where although the violation is ascertained, the party responsible is not designated, which would affect the mere substance of the participation of EU to the Convention[631].

As for the primacy, unity and efficiency of the Union's law, the opinion of the Court expresses the concern that article 53 of the European Convention, which allows States parties to adopt standards of protection higher than those stipulated by its provisions, could be used by member States of the Union to adopt standards higher than those adopted within the Union, which would affect the unity and primacy of the Union's law[632]. Explicitly, the Court considers that the power offered to EU member States should be limited with regard to the rights common to the Charter and to the European Convention, so as to ensure that unity and primacy of the Union's law are not compromised. Or, in accordance with a generally accepted conception, in the field of human rights provisions which guarantee a higher level of protection should prevail over those offering a lower level of protection[633].

As this is about the protection of human rights, it is difficult to accept that the Union and member States should not have the right to accept higher standards of protection. It is even more difficult to accept such a restrictive approach, taking into account that the Charter of fundamental rights itself provides that the Union ensures the protection of human rights at least at the level ensured according to the European Convention. Besides, it is appreciated that it is unacceptable to oppose the primacy of a source of law which ensures a superior level of protection and that invoking the primacy of the EU law over respect for human rights is alien to the field of human rights and fundamental freedoms[634]. It may be worthwhile to emphasize that, despite the EU commitments to respect human rights, in several similar cases the solutions given by the ECHR and CJEU were different, the European Court of Justice applying a lower level of protection[635]. It is also important to note that the system of jurisdiction of EU contains limits with regard to the access of physical persons to petitions against acts of the EU institutions[636], which is not the case for the European Convention.

There are thus serious arguments to ensure that the application of the highest standard of protection of human rights prevails in both systems of norms and in both courts. Of course, it is to be expected that the Union adopts some rules based on interests related to the process of economic integration and of internal market, while the European Convention guarantees individual rights very often of strict interpretation; on some of these issues there are already different appreciations between them, like in the fields of non-discrimination, of the policy of immigration, of private life, protection of property or procedural guarantees. The Union and the 28 member States cannot however justify the application of reduced standards of protection of human rights for reasons related to objectives of internal markets or of integration.

With regard to the right of each State party to the European Convention to check whether other States parties respect the provisions of the Convention, a norm which is applied for many years by ECHR, the European Court of Justice takes as a starting point the principle of mutual trust between the States members of EU which forms the basis of the area of freedom, security and justice and the presumption that member States respect the fundamental rights in concrete cases. Following this concern, if according to the European Convention an EU member State would check the application of the provisions of the Convention (which are identical to those of the Charter) by another EU member, this would undermine the application of the Union's law.

This argument ignores the fact that in very few cases States parties to the European Convention initiated procedures against other States parties (Cyprus v. Turkey, Ireland v. United Kingdom, Georgia v. Russia). The bulk of the petitions examined by ECHR are submitted by persons who consider that their rights were violated, including by citizens of EU members against their States, and the petitions may concern human rights which are guaranteed also by the Charter of fundamental rights. ECHR cannot avoid to taking decisions in such cases, only because the rights are similar to those inscribed in the Charter. This preoccupation of CJEU does not respond to a real situation or requirement.

Another concern expressed by ECJ derives from the adoption of Protocol 16 to the European Convention, according to which national tribunals of States parties can ask for a preliminary opinion of ECHR on the interpretation and application of the Convention, and refers to the case where tribunals of EU member States would

---

[631] Ion Gâlea, op. cit., pp. 119-125.

[632] In the case Melloni the European Court of Justice retained that States can adopt the national standard on the protection of human rights, provided that this does not compromise the primacy, unity and efficiency of the Union's law (CJEU, Grand Chamber, case C-399/11).

[633] In the same vein Evert A. Alkema, Rob van der Hulle and Rick van der Hulle, Safeguard Rules in the European Legal Order: the Relationship Between Article 53 of the European Convention on Human Rights and Article 53 of the Charter of Fundamental Rights of the European Union, in Human Rights Law Journal, vol. 35, no. 1-8, August, 2015, p. 8.

[634] E. Alkema, Rob and Rick van der Hulle, art. cit., p. 18.

[635] Ion Gâlea, op. cit., p. 37-39.

[636] Ibidem, p. 50-51.

ask for such opinions with regard to human rights which are guaranteed also by the Charter of fundamental rights. In the approach of CJEU, such opinions of ECHR could be in contradiction to preliminary decisions of CJEU in similar cases or could be an alternative to them.

As a matter of fact, the Protocol 16 is not yet in force and there is no proposal that EU adheres to it. CJEU seems to take already precautionary measures for the case when the Protocol will be in force. Rightly so, the CJEU underlines the importance of its preliminary decisions for ensuring the uniform application of Union's law. What CJEU wishes is to forbid that national courts of EU member States ask for opinions of ECHR on legal issues, which would create a regime of inequality with other States parties to the Convention. Efforts should be continued to find a solution respecting both the preliminary opinions of ECHR and the preliminary decisions of CJEU, both having clear and useful social functions.

A robust analysis of the issues concerning the adhesion of the European Union to the 1950 European Convention considers that it can have some incidences on the EU legal order, as it is the case for all States parties to the Convention; it is also appreciated that there is no reason for EU to pretend more than States parties the protection of its juridical autonomy with regard to human rights issues[637].

It is also maintained that the interpretation by ECHR of some provisions of the Convention would not have *prima facie* as effect to endanger the autonomy of the EU legal order, because: ECHR considers that it bestows to national authorities to be the first to interpret internal law and treaties to which a State is a party, that is that ECHR would not have vocation to interpret the EU law; as for any jurisdiction, ECHR will take into account the EU law as a fact in the interpretation given by EU[638].

A reading of the Opinion of the European Court of Justice of 18 December 2014 shows that much more importance is given to the problem of autonomy of institutions and structure of EU, including to the powers of CJEU, than to the observance of human rights guaranteed by the Charter of fundamental rights[639]. No analysis is made on differences of contents existing between human rights as they are stipulated in the Charter and in the European Convention, in order to derive consequences for the application of the Charter to be considered by ECHR.

Very often, the Opinion of ECJ emphasizes respect for human rights not as an objective *per se,* which is the purpose of the EU adhesion to the European Convention, but because of respecting the autonomy of the EU law, which is a different issue.

Many of the concerns of CJEU are related rather to the way member States and EU institutions will interpret and apply the agreement on adhesion within the institutions of the European Convention. Some authors advance also the argument that one of the purposes followed by CJEU would be to delay the participation in the European Convention in order to build enough jurisprudence of its own on the application of the Charter of fundamental rights and avoid being influenced too much by the jurisprudence of ECHR[640].

In precedent cases also CJEU opposed to accepting competences of other jurisdictions in case of disputes involving either member States or their citizens, concerning issues for which these other instances were competent according to treaties concluded by the Union, in order to protect its exclusive jurisdiction[641]. As some authors described the situation, the European Court of Justice places itself, similar with regard to norms of general international law, in the position of the court which in any situation has to be on top of any system of jurisdiction[642].

As a result of the advice of the European Court of Justice of December 2014, the Union cannot for the time being become a party to the European Convention of 1950, meaning that it cannot implement an important provision of the Lisbon Treaty. The strange situation remains where 28 States members of the Union are parties at the same time to the system of protection of human rights within the EU and to that within the Council of Europe, set forth by the 1950 Convention. EU member States form also the majority of States members of the Council of Europe and of the States parties to the 1950 Convention (28 out of 47). The situation seems to be similar with regard to the European Social Charter adopted by the Council of Europe in 1961 and revised in 1996, to which many States members of the Union are parties. There are obvious differences between this Charter and the norms applied by the

---

[637] Ph. Manin, L'adhésion de l'Union Européenne à la Convention de sauvegarde des droits de l'homme et des libertés fondamentales, in L. S. Rossi, dir., Vers une nouvelle architecture de l'Union Européenne, Bruxelles, Bruylant, 2004, pp. 261-262.

[638] O. de Schutter, Adhésion de l'Union Européenne à la Convention européenne des droits de l'homme, feuille de route de la négociation, in Revue trimestrielle des droits de l'homme, 2010, p. 535, as well as Aymeric Potteau, Quelle adhésion de l'Union Européenne à la CEDH ; pour quel niveau de protection des droits et de l'autonomie de l'ordre juridique de l'UE, in RGDIP, 2011-1, p. 102.

[639] For instance, S. Peers, The CJEU and the EU's accession to the ECHR; a clear and present danger to human rights protection, in EU Law Analysis, 18 December 2014.

[640] Adam Lazowski & Ramses A. Wessel, art. cit., pp. 12-13.

[641] Case of the court created by the Treaty concerning the Economic European Space and that of the Community Court of Patents, presented by Alisa Vekeman, op. cit., pp. 17-18.

[642] Ion Gâlea, op. cit., pp. 62-69.

European Union; this issue is examined by an expert in the field of economic, social and cultural rights who is also advancing the idea of the adhesion of the Union to the European Social Charter[643].

The solution is thus to come back to the table of negotiations and to continue the process of mutual conviction in order to find the compromise accepted also by the European Court of Justice. Ideas are advanced with regard to the modification of the Lisbon Treaty or of its annexes concerning adhesion to the European Convention. This would of course depend on political evaluations and evolutions.

* * *

European Union develops its own system, rather substantial, of protection of human rights. The Charter of fundamental rights is a result of a gradual evolution, from rights related to the freedoms resulting from economic integration to fundamental principles and to the European citizenship; it includes both political and civil rights and economic, social and cultural rights, some formulated in more general terms as principles, others more explicitly as rights; the Union and member States have the obligation to implement this document with a value of a treaty, while the Court is competent to solve disputes on alleged violations.

However, few cases were submitted to the Court by now; it can be said that the application of the Charter of fundamental rights is still at the beginning. European States, including those which are members of the Union, have their problems with regard to respecting human rights, may be less serious and of a different type than on other continents. As respect of human rights is a question of permanent concern for all States, efforts should continue in Europe also.

The Charter of fundamental rights stipulates that it has to be applied by the institutions and organs of the EU and by member States, when they apply the Union's law. But the Charter is now part of the Union's law and provides for numerous human rights that persons have to be able to claim at the national level as well as within the Union; consequently, the sphere of application of the Charter has to be and progressively will be extended.

The European Union decided to adhere to the European Convention of 1950 for the protection of human rights and fundamental freedoms. The opinion of the European Court of Justice stopped this process for the time being; there is a debate whether the motives invoked are justified, but it is obvious that solutions can be found to a situation where 28 States members of the European Union are parties to both the EU and the Council of Europe systems for the protection of human rights which developed separately and with some differences. The Union will certainly have to find a rapprochement with the European Convention for the protection of fundamental human rights and freedoms, so as to realize a uniform regime of protection of human rights on the continent.

---

[643] Olivier de Schutter, L'adhésion de l'Union Européenne a la Charte sociale européenne, in Revue trimestrielle des droits de l'homme, no. 102, 2015, pp.260-316.

CHAPTER XXII - THE FRAMEWORK CONVENTION for the PROTECTION of MINORITIES; MINORITIES in EUROPE

ABSTRACT

This study is a presentation of the Framework Convention, adopted by the Council of Europe in 1994. It is also looking at the interpretation and the application of the Convention since its adoption, taking into account that there is no definition of the concept of national minority and that each State declares what are the minority groups on its territory qualified as such and covered by the protection of the Framework Convention.

The Advisory Committee, a body created by the Committee of ministers of the Council of Europe to monitor the implementation of the Convention, is thus limited to the examination of periodic reports of the States parties, limited to what these States consider to be the personal scope of the Convention and expressing only wishes if it considers that other minority groups should also be covered by the Convention.

A section is devoted to the situation of minority groups in Europe, in a mirror with the provisions of the Convention and with general standards on human rights; many of these groups are ignored, even if their members are citizens of the respective States; their cultural rights are not protected. It becomes a political issue of importance for the stability and security on the continent.

KEY WORDS: national minorities, good-faith, self-identification, in community, equal rights, self-determination, special measures, freedom of expression, culture, language, religion.

INTRODUCTION

On the 10th of November 1994, the Committee of ministers of the Council of Europe adopted the text of the Framework Convention for the protection of national minorities. 35 States members of the Council are presently parties to the Convention[644].

It is the first multilateral legally binding instrument devoted to the protection of the rights of persons belonging to minorities. It was preceded only by some articles in instruments concerning categories of human rights: article 27 of the 1966 International Covenant on civil and political human rights, article 14 in the 1950 European Convention concerning fundamental human rights and freedoms and article 2 of the 1960 UNESCO Convention on the elimination of discrimination in education, containing specific provisions concerning persons belonging to minorities. One has to add also the Declaration adopted by the UN General Assembly in 1992 on the rights of persons belonging to national or ethnic, religious and linguistic minorities, which is a recommendation.

It is a framework Convention, which results from its title, but mainly from its preamble, which enounces the resolve of the States parties „to define the principles to be respected and the obligations which flow from them, in order to ensure ...the effective protection of national minorities" and their determination to "apply the principles set out in this Framework Convention through national legislation and appropriate governmental policies". In the same spirit, the Explanatory Report to the Convention, adopted at the same time, affirms that the Convention contains „mostly programme-type provisions setting out objectives which the Parties undertake to pursue "and which are „not directly applicable"[645].

As it was noted, many of the provisions of international instruments on human rights have this character of enouncing principles; some provisions of the Convention are nevertheless directly applicable, taking into account the way they are drafted; their interpretation, according to a general norm of the interpretation of treaties, has to be made in conformity with the principle of effectivity, so as to ensure the achievement of their objective[646].

SECTION 1 - UNDERTAKINGS of the STATES PARTIES ACCORDING to the CONVENTION

---

[644] The Convention was signed by 42 States, from among the 45 members of the Council of Europe; 35 States members of the Council are parties to it; the Convention was not signed by Andorra, France and Turquie; seven other States signed, but did not ratify it.
[645] Doc. CM(94) 161 of 9 November 1994, p. 14.
[646] Patrick Thornberry, Maria Amor Martin Estebanez, Minority Rights in Europe. A review of the work and standards of the Council of Europe, 2003, pp. 91-92.

The Convention postulates a series of general principles which are also common to other legal instruments on human rights, as undertakings of States parties.

In the first place, the Convention clarifies some problems of principle, which represent a synthesis of other international documents on human rights, adding the specific dimension of minority issues. The following provisions are of particular interest in this context:
- placing the issues concerning the protection of the rights of persons belonging to minorities and of national minorities as an integral part of the international protection of human rights, and as such within the scope of international cooperation;
- the application of the respective principles in good faith, in a spirit of understanding and tolerance and in conformity with the principles of good-neighbourliness, friendly relations and cooperation between States;
- the principle of self-identification, meaning that every person shall have the right freely to choose to be treated or not as a member of a national minority and that no disadvantage shall result from the exercise of the rights which are connected to that choice.

This principle is also connected with the absence of a generally accepted definition of the concept of minority; although the Framework Convention does not contain a definition, it refers in its different provisions to mother tongue, culture, own traditions, own religion and access to information in mother tongue, which are among the main elements defining a minority group. Nevertheless, the principle of self-identification is not of an absolute nature; according to the comments contained in the Explanatory Report to the Convention, not every ethnic, cultural or linguistic difference leads to forming a minority and the text adopted (article 3.1 of the Convention) does not imply for a person the right to choose arbitrarily to belong to any national minority. This subjective choice is inseparably linked to objective criteria relevant to the person's identity;
- the rights and freedoms of persons belonging to minorities may be exercised individually or in community with others; although the Convention is called "for the protection of national minorities", it results from its provisions that this objective has to be achieved by respecting and implementing the rights and freedoms of persons belonging to minorities[647]; as a matter of fact, these are rights and freedoms which may be exercised individually, but are usually exercised in community with other persons. These rights have naturally a social dimension, without thus becoming collective rights; that means that, although the respective rights are usually exercised in community, the Convention does not recognize to minority communities a legal status implying the exercise of the rights and freedoms granted on behalf, above or against their members[648];
- equal rights and non-discrimination; at the same time, the Convention contains the commitment of the State parties to adopt, where necessary, adequate measures in order to promote effective equality between persons belonging to minorities and those belonging to the majority in all areas of economic, social and cultural life and, in this respect, to take due account of specific conditions of the persons belonging to minorities. It is expressly provided for that such measures will not be considered as discriminatory. This is the concept of „special measures" or of „positive action" in favour of persons belonging to minorities[649];
- refraining from policies or practices aimed at assimilation of persons belonging to minorities against their will; States are obliged to protect these persons against any action aiming at their assimilation; this is without prejudice to measures taken for implementing a general policy of integration;
- respect for the legislation of the respective State and for the rights of other persons. The Convention states expressly that, in the exercise of the rights and freedoms set forth, any person belonging to a national minority shall respect the national legislation and the rights of others, in particular those of persons belonging to the majority or to other national minorities;
- the relationship between the Framework Convention and other international documents in the field of human rights; it means in particular the relationship with the European Convention and its protocols, as this is considered the basic document of the Council of Europe in this field, that is the need to ensure a coherent application of the two documents taking into account the first principle mentioned above, according to which the protection of minorities is an integral part of human rights.

---

[647] P. Thornberry, M. A. E. Esteban, op. cit., p. 98.

[648] On special measures, Ion Diaconu,.Racial Discrimination: using Special Measures for Promoting Equal Human Rights, in East African Journal of Peace & Human Rights, vol. 18, n0. 1, 2012, pp. 1-17.

[649] For a presentation on special measures, IonDiaconu, Minorities-from non-discrimination to identity, 2004, Lumina Lex, Bucharest, pp.75-88(published with financial support of UNESCO, and distributed by the Organization).

The Convention accepts moreover, in favour of more extended rights of persons belonging to minorities, that its provisions shall not be construed as limiting or derogating from any of the rights and fundamental freedoms which may be granted to these persons by the law of a State party or in conformity with international agreements to which it is a party.

As for *the main specific obligations undertaken by the State parties*, two kinds of provisions have to be noted. Some of them ask States parties to recognize certain rights or freedoms to persons belonging to minorities or to take measures to ensure the respect or protection of such rights and freedoms, as well as to refrain from some activities which would interfere with or hinder the exercise of such rights, . Other provisions though have pro-active character, containing the commitment of the State parties to create the necessary conditions, to promote equal opportunities or even to ensure, within some limits, the benefit of some rights and freedoms.

In *the field of culture*, the States parties undertook first of all to promote the conditions necessary for those persons to maintain and develop their culture, and to preserve the essential elements of their identity, namely their religion, language, traditions and cultural heritage. It is a thorough formulation, which evokes both the extended definition of culture and the elements that constitute the identity of a person belonging to a minority group[650].

Many provisions of the Convention refer to the *use of mother tongue*, reflecting the fact that mother tongue is the vehicle of communication, of preservation, of transmission, as well as of development of the culture of all persons. States parties undertook to recognize to any person belonging to a minority the right to the freedom of expression, including the freedom to have opinions and to receive and impart information and ideas in the minority language, without interference by public authorities and irrespective of borders, and to ensure that these persons are not discriminated against in their access to the media.

For this purpose, the States parties shall not hinder the creation and the use of printed media by such persons, and shall ensure licenses for their own radio and television broadcasting or cinema enterprises, which can be submitted to licensing without discrimination and based on objective criteria. In the same context, States committed to adopt adequate measures in order to facilitate the access of the respective persons to the media and to permit cultural pluralism.

More detailed provisions are aiming at the use of mother tongue by persons belonging to minorities, not only in a general formulation concerning the right to use freely and without interference mother tongue, in private and in public, orally and in writing, but also in more precise fields as follows:
- States shall endeavour to ensure conditions making possible the use of the minority language in relations with the administrative authorities in the areas inhabited by such persons traditionally or in substantial numbers, if those persons so request and where such a request corresponds to a real need;
- States committed themselves to guarantee to each person the right to be informed promptly, in a language which he or she understands, of the reasons for his and her arrest, of the nature and cause of any accusation and of the right to defend him or herself in this language, if necessary with the free assistance of an interpreter; this is an absolute and unconditional right, as the person is deprived of freedom and is subject to criminal accusations;
- States shall recognize the right of each person to use his or her own name in the minority language and the right to its official recognition, according to modalities provided for by the law, as well as the right to display in that language signs, inscriptions and other information of a private nature visible to the public;
- States shall endeavour to display also in minority language traditional local names, names of streets and other topographic indications intended for the public, in areas traditionally inhabited by substantial numbers of persons belonging to a national minority, in the framework of their legal system or, where appropriate, per agreements with other States and taking into account their specific conditions.

In close connection with cultural rights should be considered also the religious rights. Per the Convention, States parties shall ensure respect for the right of every person to freedom of thought, conscience and religion and shall recognize the right to manifest his or her religion or belief and to establish religious institutions, organizations and associations.

In the field of education and research, similarly to the field of culture, according to a provision of a general nature, States are engaged, in as much as it is necessary, to act for promoting the knowledge of culture, history, language and religion of minorities, as well as those of the majority. More specific provisions refer to:
- the obligation of States parties to offer, among others, adequate opportunities for teacher training and access to textbooks, and to facilitate contacts among students and teachers of different communities;

---

[650] Doc. ACFC/OP/II/(2005)007, Strasbourg, 23 February 2006, p. 7, also doc. ACFC/OP/III(2012)001, Strasbourg, 4 June 2013.

- the undertaking to promote equal opportunities for access to education at all levels for persons belonging to national minorities;
- the recognition of the right of these persons, within the framework of the State's national system of education, to set up and to manage their own private establishments of education and training, without entailing any financial obligation for the State;
- the undertaking to recognize the right of every person belonging to a national minority to learn his or her minority language;
- the commitment of States to endeavour to ensure that persons belonging to national minorities have adequate opportunities for being taught the minority language or for receiving instruction in this language, in areas inhabited by them traditionally or in substantial numbers, if there is sufficient demand, as far as possible and within their education systems, and without prejudice for the learning of the official language or the teaching of this language.

The Convention affirms also that States parties shall create the conditions necessary for the effective participation of persons belonging to minorities in cultural, social and economic life, and in public affairs, in particular those affecting them. In close connection to this, States parties are obliged to ensure respect of the right of these persons to freedom of peaceful assembly and freedom of association.

States parties also committed themselves not to interfere with the right of persons belonging to minorities to establish and maintain free and peaceful contacts across frontiers with persons lawfully staying in other States, in particular those with whom they share an ethnic, cultural, linguistic or religious identity or a common cultural heritage, as well as with the right of those persons to participate in the activities of non-governmental organizations, both at the national and international levels.

Giving expression to the close link between the rights provided for in the Convention and human rights in general, the Convention stipulates that these rights and freedoms can be subject only to those limitations, restrictions or derogations which are provided for in international legal instruments, in particular in the 1950 Convention, in so far as they are relevant to these rights and freedoms.

The majority of the provisions of the Convention refer to the relationship between States parties and persons belonging to national minorities living on their territories. Nevertheless, as shown in the beginning, States parties affirm that the respective rights and freedoms fall under international cooperation, as an integral part of the international protection of human rights. Even the conclusion of the Framework Convention within the Committee of ministers of the Council of Europe, and the fact that this Committee of ministers received the main task of monitoring the application of the Convention, mean that the issues concerning the rights of minorities are part of the cooperation among the member States of the Council.

Of course, they are also a subject of the bilateral cooperation between States. According to the Convention, States parties shall endeavour to conclude, where necessary, bilateral and multilateral agreements with other States, in particular neighbouring States, in order to ensure the protection of persons belonging to minorities (it should be understood to protect the rights and freedoms recognized by the Convention) and shall take measures to encourage trans- frontier cooperation, where relevant.

The Convention affirms in its preamble that the realization of a tolerant and prosperous Europe does not depend solely on cooperation between States, but requires also transfrontier cooperation between local and regional authorities, without prejudice to the Constitution and territorial integrity of each State. As it is known, Romania included detailed provisions on the rights of persons belonging to minorities in its political treaties with Hungary and Ukraine and concluded a bilateral agreement in this field with Serbia. These treaties created also bilateral mechanisms for promoting their application.

The relationships between States, as parties to this Convention, are governed also by the general clause according to which no provision of the Convention will be interpreted as implying the right to engage in activities or to perform any act contrary to the fundamental principles of international law, and in particular of the sovereign equality, territorial integrity and political independence of States.

The Convention provides the monitoring by the Committee of ministers of the Council of Europe concerning its application by the States parties. For this purpose, the Committee created an Advisory Committee, formed of 18 experts, which examines the periodic reports of States parties, makes visits and has discussions with authorities and representatives of minority groups in these States and then presents its reports to the Committee of ministers.

In Romania, the Convention is applied presently to 20 minorities: Albanian, Bulgarian, Croatian, German, Greek, Hungarian, Italian, Macedonian, Polish, Roma, Russian-Lipovenian, Ruthenian, Serbian, Slovak and Czech (represented by one organization), Tatar, Turkish, Ukrainian and Yiddish[651]. Along with Serbia, Croatia and Bosnia-Hertzegovina, Romania is among the States parties that recognized the highest number of national minorities. Other States declared a small number of minorities, sometimes not the most important minority groups living on their territories.

It appears from the considerations and findings of the Consultative Committee, although not explicitly said, that in Romania attention is given to the big minorities and the smaller ones are neglected, mainly in the fields of education, culture and media. Many recommendations refer to the situation of Roma, in many fields of economic and social life.

SECTION 2 - The ISSUE of NEW MINORITIES in EUROPE

In connection with the application of this Convention, and in general in connection with the protection of the rights of persons belonging to minorities, the problem was raised whether this concerns all minorities, irrespective of the period when they formed themselves, respectively if it takes into account only the „old minorities" as opposed to the „new minorities". According to the data conveyed by the States parties to the Convention, more than 200 minorities would exist in Europe, more ancient or recently formed on the territories of the States parties. Many of them are not recognized as such within the scope of the Framework Convention.

The problem of new minorities covers presently two situations: that of minority groups in the new States, formed after the dissolution of the federal States - Soviet Union, Federal Republic of Yugoslavia and Czechoslovakia -, where the tracing of the new borders left groups which were formerly part of ethnic majorities as minorities in the new States; and that of States where, in the second half of the twentieth century, as a result of migration of labour within the continent and from outside, in the first period of time encouraged, then curbed but never stopped, numerous groups of persons of a different ethnic origin, culture, language, sometimes another religion established mainly in the European and North American States.

If the new States, formed on the territories of the former federal States, recognized the new minorities living on their territories and, in principle, apply to them the Framework Convention, one cannot say the same about minority groups formed on the territories of other States as a result of the process of migration.

This concerns communities formed of migrants who settled in the majority of West-European States after the second world war (Turks in Germany, The Netherlands and other States, Serbs, Croats and other South Slavs in Germany, Austria and other States, Algerians, Moroccans and other Arabs in France, Belgium, Italy, Spain and other Western States, Pakistani and Indians in United Kingdom and some Nordic States, Surinamese and Guyanese in The Netherlands, but also Portuguese, Spaniards and Italians in other States members of the European Union).

The Framework Convention makes no difference between the new and the old minorities and contains no conditions or clarifications leading to such a classification, but is not giving a definition to the concept of minority; the Council of Europe renounced to such a definition because of divergences among State members[652]. We note that some provisions of the Convention refer to persons belonging to minorities which "live traditionally" in some areas of the States (articles 10.2, 11.3, 14.2); this would send to old minorities; but the text adds immediately „or in substantial numbers", which is obviously aiming at another situation characterized by the criteria of numbers and of living concentrated in a geographic area on the territory of a State. The text is similarly explained in the Explanatory Report which accompanies the Convention, affirming that the term „inhabited...traditionally" does not refer to historical minorities, but only to those still living in the same geographical area[653]. Even interpreted in a restrictive manner, the formulation „inhabited traditionally" is used only in three texts concerning the use of a minority language: in public administration, for the public signage and for the education in mother tongue. All other provisions refer to all persons who could be in a minority situation.

The Preamble of the Convention also leads to an extensive interpretation, when it refers to promoting stability, democracy and peace, to the objective of a pluralist and democratic society and to „creating a climate of tolerance and dialogue, which is necessary to make cultural diversity a source and a vector of enrichment of each

---

[651] Explanatory Report, Doc. CM(94) 161, p. 14.

[652] Explanatory Report, para. 66, p. 73.

[653] According to information at the disposal of the Committee, some 7.4 million of non-citizens would live presently in Germany, among them 1,85 million citizens of other member States of the EU, including 291 thousand Poles, 214 thousand Croats, more than 2 million Turks, 737 thousand coming from Serbia and Montenegro, and other smaller groups. Some of them have obtained the German citizenship, being there at the third generation. In Austria would live, according to official statistics, 761 thousand foreigners, including more than 341.000 from the former Jugoslavia and 134 thousand Turks. Spain would host 1,3 million foreigners and Switzerland 1,2 million. These information is certainly outdated, taking into account the last waves of migration.

society and not one of division". Because of the absence of a definition of the notion of minority, States Parties must decide themselves to what groups of population on their territory they will apply the Convention.

Some States made statements as to the scope of the application *ratione personae* of the Convention when they ratified it. Most States did not make such statements and had to precise the scope of the application of the Convention in their periodic reports. Other States clarified, during the first series of reports examined by the Advisory Committee, to what ethnic groups they understand to apply the Convention or completed the statements made previously.

Among those which made such statements, some States parties give their own definition of the concept of minorities, others enumerate the groups to whom they understand to apply the Convention (some of them in a geographic area of the State, while others combine the definition with the enumeration). The majority of those which gave a definition of the concept of minority included the requirement of citizenship as compulsory. Other States parties added conditions such as „those who live and have their traditional residence" or „ those who have long time, strong and durable relations" with the country or who are „established there for numerous generations".

Following the consideration of the reports, the Advisory Committee noted that some States did not recognize some ethnic groups as deserving the protection of the Convention (the Polish community in Austria, recently formed in this country; the populations of Faroe islands and Greenland which are part of the Kingdom of Denmark, as well as Roma in that country; in Romania, the groups of Hungarian Csangos and Aromanians; in Spain, the Jews and the Berbere population of autonomous cities of Ceuta and Melilla; in the United Kingdom, the inhabitants of Cornwall.

The Committee expressed clearly in favour of the application of the Convention to indigenous populations, regardless of whether they are called minorities or do not accept to be named as such (the Sami, the Crimean Tatars, the populations of Faroe and Greenland). The Committee made no reference to the numerous communities of migrants, settled in many Western countries, a good number of them having already the citizenship of these States.

The Committee accepted that, in the absence of a definition of the concept of national minority in the Convention, States Parties should examine the scope of its application *ratione personae* which they should ensure in their countries. While accepting that States have in this regard a margin of discretion, in order to take into account the specific situation of their countries, the Committee notes at the same time that this margin of appreciation has to be exercised in conformity with the general principles of international law and with the principles set forth in article 3 of the Convention (mentioned above).

The Committee underlined mainly that the application of the Convention should not be a source of arbitrary decisions or of unjustified distinctions. On this basis, the Committee considered that it was its duty to verify the correct application of the principles set forth in article 3 and to examine the scope of personal application given to the Convention by each State, in order to check if arbitrary or unjustified distinctions were made.

With regard to the different names used in the legislation of States parties, the Committee adopted the opinion according to which the applicability of the Convention does not necessarily depend on the use by the authorities of the term „national minority" to describe the respective group. With regard to indigenous peoples, the Committee considers, for instance, that the protection under the Convention remains available if persons belonging to them wish to benefit from.

Noting that other ethnic or linguistic groups also exist in some States parties which do not consider them at this moment as being covered by the Convention, the Committee appreciates that it would be possible for the States Parties to have in view to include persons belonging to such groups, including as appropriate those without their citizenship, in the application of the Convention article by article. The Committee adopted the opinion that States parties have to examine this problem in consultation with those concerned, members of the respective groups[654].

Thus, the Advisory Committee accepts the position of many States that became parties to the Framework Convention, according to which persons who are not their citizens are not members of minorities and do not enjoy the protection of the Convention. The Committee adopts thus a position which is different from that of the Human Rights Committee created by the International Covenant on civil and political rights. Similarly, the Committee continues not to take into account the situation of ethnic groups formed on the territory of States parties from migrants and their descendants of many generations who obtained the citizenship of the respective States, and makes no recommendation to them. That means that the Committee accepts also the long-term presence on the territory of a State as a criterion for considering the existence of national minorities.

---

[654] In some UN documents it is also appreciated that, when on the territory of a State there are stable minorities of certain importance, whose members are in substantial numbers non- citizens, States should find the means to have their representatives participating, at least on a consultative basis, in the decision-making on issues which concern them as a group. With this meaning, the working document „Citizenship and the applicability of minority rights to non-citizens", presented by Mr. Asbjorn Eide, doc. E/CN.4/Sub.2/AC.5/1999/WP.3 of 15 April 1999, p.13.

Without adopting a clear position, the Committee appeals to States Parties to apply the provisions of some articles of the Convention, from case to case, to those groups and persons who are not their citizens, while ignoring those who are already citizens, but do not respond to the long-term presence criterion.

As a matter of fact, many of the provisions of the Convention refer to fundamental human rights and freedoms, to which every person is entitled, irrespective of whether he or she is part of a minority, or whether the respective group is recognized as a minority (equal rights-article 4, maintaining of the cultural identity - article 5, protection against acts of discrimination, hostility or violence-article 6, the right to peaceful assembly, to association, to belief, conscience and religion-article 7, freedom of expression - article 9 and others).

The Committee takes note of the appearance of new minorities in the States newly formed on the territories of the former Soviet Union, Yugoslavia and Czechoslovakia and even asks the new States to apply to them the Convention under equal terms with the minorities previously recognized. The Committee remains nevertheless silent with regard to new groups formed in many European States during the second half of the 20th century, as a result of the massive process of migration. These groups, much more numerous than the national minorities recognized by the respective States, have undoubtedly a distinct identity from the majority of the population - by their language, culture, religion, traditions -that they obviously want to preserve; they are firmly settled on the territories of these States and are not expected to migrate again.

Moreover, it is only in one of its articles that the Convention refers to creating the conditions for the participation of persons belonging to minorities in public affairs, mainly those affecting their cultural, social and economic life (which is quite normal for all public affairs, if they are citizens, under the conception generally accepted, but it is normal also for non-citizens, except for political life). The Explanatory Report mentions *exempli gratia*, as measures which can be promoted in the context of the constitutional systems of the States Parties, the following:

- consultations with these persons through adequate procedures, through their representative institutions, when legislative or administrative measures which would affect them are intended by the States Parties;
- involving these persons in the preparation, implementation and assessment of national and regional plans and programme of development likely to affect them directly;
- undertaking studies, in cooperation with these persons, to assess the possible impact on them of the projected development activities;
- effective participation of persons belonging to national minorities in the decision- making processes and in elected bodies, both at national and local levels;
- decentralized or local forms of government[655].

It is obvious that this text and the measures indicated have in view minority groups formed of citizens for the exercise of some rights (participation in elected bodies) and can cover all other minority groups for other measures, irrespective of the citizenship of their members. The text is not implying the possibility for the States to treat differently minority groups living on their territories. Other texts refer to human rights, with their specificity for persons belonging to minorities in connection to their cultural, linguistic and religious identity, which should not imply any different treatment for their beneficiaries.

One must note also that both the Committee and some States parties argue that persons belonging to some minority groups did not request to enjoy the protection offered by the Convention or communicated that they do not wish it; on the other side, some States are requested to reconsider their position with regard to some ethnic groups that wish to enjoy this protection and to include them in the scope of application of the Convention.

But the Convention refers to „requests" from persons belonging to minorities only with regard to the use of mother tongue in relations with State authorities, to displaying topographic indications in mother tongue and to ensuring opportunities for educating them in mother tongue, and in the last two cases, to „sufficient requests" in order to endeavour to take such measures.

One must note, that introducing a preliminary procedure of requests in order to establish whether some human rights are recognized and protected for some persons, is unusual in the field of human rights; no other international legal instrument of human rights was interpreted and applied as such.

It is our firm opinion that to propose as a criterion the requests from groups to apply the Convention offers an easy way for some States to exclude some groups from the scope of the Convention and for the Advisory Committee to avoid a difficult dialogue with the respective States. Moreover, this leads to a double standard, as it results also from the opinions and recommendations of the Committee, and reduces substantively the scope of the application of the Convention, with long term unacceptable consequences within the Council of Europe.

---

[655] Doc. CM (94)161, p. 25.

It is necessary that the determination of those groups which are considered national minorities be done based on objective criteria and with the purpose of respecting human rights. The instruments and practices applied within the United Nations recommend an open approach, based on objective criteria, in the assessment of the situation in different States and with regard to different human groups; this approach seems to be implied in the requirement of good-faith to which article 2 of the Framework Convention refers. The Explanatory Report refers several times to objective criteria (with regard to the assessment of the need to use mother tongue in relation with authorities, to the individual choice of a person concerning its identity). Objective criteria should be used also for determining the minority groups to which the Convention has to be applied.

It is a reality that the groups of migrants, older or more recently formed, are presently a constant feature of the process of globalization and an important issue in the whole area of OSCE-both in East[656] and West. Analysts appreciate that the policy of full integration of these communities failed (having in mind cultural integration, which was a wrong expectation from the beginning). The attitude of the majorities toward these groups was often negative and characterized by xenophobic reactions and by discrimination.

On the other side, the presence and the enlargement of such communities led to changes in the image of many towns and created several practical problems to the host States concerning education, health care, housing, the exercise of religious rights, the right to association, access to culture and others. The situation was not thoroughly considered in Europe, where it is of much topicality. It is obvious that there is no European policy or approach regarding the „new minorities".

From the point of view of international law, the solution in conformity with the entirety of norms concerning human rights would be to extend to these communities, following objective criteria, the standards applied to national, ethnic, linguistic or religious minorities. If it is accepted, for the time being only theoretically, that human rights to education, culture and religion cannot be refused to them, and they are partially recognized and exercised in many countries by the communities of migrants, the issue to be solved is whether regarding the rights to political participation the same approach can be followed[657].

But the institution of citizenship has the potential to respond at least partially to this issue, because these rights belong to citizens, irrespective of their ethnic origin, and not to communities as such. Communities can participate in political life in accordance with the constitutional system of the country; this problem is usually regulated by the law which can establish the place of such communities and the possibility of non-citizens to participate in political life. Obviously, communities of migrants can be implied and consulted locally, regarding the solution of practical problems, without conferring them an exaggerated political role.

In the opinion of the High Commissioner of OSCE for National Minorities, an adequate solution of the issue of new minorities is essential to ensure the democratic government in open societies, where the diversity is extended as a result of migration; it is not a technical issue, but one of values. There are at the same time alarming signs that discrimination, racism, intolerance and xenophobia get ground; majorities manifest intolerance being afraid of losing their identity and way of life; many immigrants, mainly young people, are disproportionately hurt by unemployment, feel discriminated and organize themselves in groups based on ethnic or racial criteria, as a means of defense; as a reaction, extremist movements appear within the majorities, around nationalist-chauvinist and xenophobic ideas. He appreciates that inter-ethnic problems will not disappear in an extended Europe and that the risk of tension and even of conflict remains; it is only by encouraging the „new minorities" to take part in the economic, social, cultural and political life of their new States that they can be integrated in the new societies.

Of course, the members of these communities have to respect the laws and, for reasons of public order, security, health and moral, to change some aspects of their behaviour, but have to be allowed to maintain their religion, language and other key elements of their identity, which have to be protected. This does not concern those elements of culture which would violate human rights as established in international and European instruments.

Integration must be economic, social and political; it does not concern culture; States should not pretend that people give up their culture, except those aspects which violate human rights. If such integration is not realized, this would lead to ghettos, to mutual suspicions and to condemning a group to under-development, practically to difficulties for the State. This may have serious effects, including for the internal and international security, mainly in such States where there are numerous and strong minority groups, fostering sources of conflict.

It seems that Europe has still many things to do in this field, mainly in connection with the new minorities, because respect for diversity, inclusive approaches and integration are in its interest. Considering the substance of the rights granted to persons belonging to minorities-preservation of their ethnic, linguistic and religious identity, the

---

[656] In the Russian Federation there is also a clear trend to form ethnic communities from persons having their origins in the States formerly part of the Soviet Union (Moldovans, Ukrainians, Azeris, Tadjiks and others) who are living and working mainly in Moscow and other towns.
[657] H. van Roijen, A. Bloed, E. Bakker, Round Table on „New Minorities", The Hague 2003, p. 2.

right to use their minority language, the right to their own culture, practicing and professing their own religion-they cannot be restrained to citizens and neither to old minorities and refused to the new ones.

The problems related to the new minorities are one of the dimensions of human rights and fundamental freedoms at the beginning of the twenty first century. The majority of the East-European States members of the Council of Europe consider that the provisions of the Framework Convention are applicable to a great number of minorities living on their territory, although in its opinions the Advisory Committee recommended to recognize also others.

In the European Union, minorities have been formed because of the freedom of circulation and of establishment of the citizens of member States wherever in the Union. These persons, sometimes in substantial numbers, are also citizens of the European Union. Analysts refer to two additional groups which may also possess features of minorities in the EU: citizens of third countries and of the EU who moved to another member State and share similar features with members of existing minorities, and others who form themselves such minority groups different from others; they may be considered as members of existing minorities or new minorities[658]. The groups of migrants from non-EU countries are not included in these analyses.

The Law of the European Union, beginning with the EU Treaties, sets forth obligations for the Union and the member States concerning the protection of and respect for the cultural and linguistic diversity; that implies the obligation to adopt, in cooperation with the respective communities, measures to ensure the preservation of the cultural, linguistic and religious identity of persons forming those communities. It is obvious that European Union did not yet take measures to deal with this issue.

One should have in mind also that what constitutes a national minority is a dynamic reality, depending of demographic developments and cannot be considered as immobile. As the report presented by Ireland to the Committee affirms, the number and the composition of national minorities in a State can change and develop in time.

It is thus necessary to have a more balanced and consistent international approach on issues concerning the new minorities. Such an approach may have found its expression in the Treaty of Lisbon of 2007, in force since 2009, according to which „The Union is based on values of respect for the dignity, freedom, democracy, equality, rule of law and respect for human rights, including the rights of persons belonging to national minorities. These values are common to member States in a society where pluralism, non-discrimination, tolerance, justice, solidarity and equality between women and men prevail".

* * *

Persons belonging to minorities, as well as groups as such, formed on the basis of race, colour, descent, national or ethnic origin, regardless whether such groups are recognized or not, fall under the protection of the 1965 International Convention on the elimination of all forms of racial discrimination. This is not depending on a definition of the concept of minority being generally accepted or on a classification of minority groups, which have to be solved by each State function of the situation and circumstances in each country. The provisions of this Convention apply to persons belonging to minorities, even if some States do not recognize their existence as groups. In their capacity as citizens, along with other persons under the jurisdiction of States parties to several international instruments on human rights, they are entitled to all human rights and to the regime of non-discrimination provided for by that Convention. The non-recognition of minorities affects some rights concerning the participation in political life, the dialogue with the authorities and the representation of minority groups, and not such human rights that each person may exercise individually.

The activity of the Advisory Committee under the Framework Convention for the protection of national minorities, within the parameters it applies presently, is limited and restrictive; it pretends to some States, those of East-Europe, to treat all minority groups as national minorities and to offer them the benefit of the Convention; as for the Western States of Europe, the conditions of citizenship, of long-duration settlement in the country and, more recently, that of the express request of the respective minority groups, severely limit the scope of the Convention.

Generally speaking, except for Roma, many States declared as national minorities less numerous minority groups and ignored others formed of millions of persons of an ethnic origin which is different from that of the majority of the population; this makes it that the application of the Convention is artificially limited and responds only partially to the situation on the continent.

The fact that the activity of the Advisory Committee is timid and reserved is the result of the mandate given to it by the Committee of ministers; the result is the limitation of the capacity of the Council of Europe to deal with

---

[658] Tawhida Ahmed, The Treaty of Lisbon and Beyond: The Evolution of EU Minority Protection?, in European Law Review, Vol. 38, No 1, February 2013, p. 36.

the issues of human rights in Europe as a whole and at the level of all the continent. Analysts consider that a more firm point of view of the Advisory Committee as to what represents a minority in different member States would strengthen the efficiency of the application of the Framework Convention[659].

Those dramatic evolutions which took place in some States with well consolidated democracies in Western Europe at the end of 2005 show that the time has come to reconsider the situation of groups formed of immigrants and refugees, citizens and non-citizens, established on the territories of the respective States, in the light of the entirety of norms of human rights and specific rights of persons belonging to minority groups, to seek solutions consulting those groups and to involve them in public life, mainly in the areas where they live more compactly.

This becomes more and more a problem of a political, economic and social order, of good governance in democratic societies, in a final analysis of stability, security and prosperity.

---

[659] P. Thornberry, M. A. M. Estebanez, op. cit., pp. 115-116.

CHAPTER XXIII - The CHARTER for REGIONAL or MINORITY LANGUAGES

ABSTRACT

All European States are plurilingual; this raises the issue of using several languages on the territory of each State, both in private and public life. If the use of any language in private life is usually not a problem, the situation is different in public life, as no State is able to ensure the use of all languages on its territory on grounds of administrative coherence and of economic efficiency (leaving aside discriminatory policies).

As a result of migrations and of the freedom of movement, but also of the policies followed by States, some less spoken languages are in danger to disappear. For the protection of such languages, the Council of Europe adopted in 1992 the European Charter for Regional or Minority Languages. This study presents briefly the system imagined by the authors of the Charter for promoting and protecting these languages. It is a system of a minimum standard for all languages recognized as regional or minority and of a flexible sliding scale of commitments for some of these languages in the fields of education, culture, media, justice, administration and public services and trans-frontier exchanges.

KEY WORDS: linguistic diversity, regional or minority languages, languages of migrants, dialects, special measures, substantial numbers, territorial concentration, numeric threshold, multilingualism.

INTRODUCTION

The problems generated by the diversity of languages, religions and cultures are not completely new in Europe. The coexistence of different religions within the same political entity was preceded and often followed by the well-known religious wars. The movement of nationalities, which led to the formation of many national States in Europe during the 19th century, was founded on the idea of the existence of cultural communities and of languages spoken in common by members of these communities, different from languages and cultures of other peoples. The national States represented an efficient model of social integration, created new relations of solidarity and the framework for the development of the modern democracy, but also united around the concept of citizenship other populations who very often preserved their language and traditional way of life.

Nevertheless, the formation of national modern States did not make the linguistic and cultural heterogeneity disappear in Europe; it was maintained by human groups who formed specific entities with their own names and who remained in constant exchanges and contacts with communities from other parts of Europe to which they are related by the feelings of belonging to the same culture; they continued to speak their language and to transmit to new generations their language and culture. Other distinct communities appeared through the retracing of borders after the two world wars and by the more recent dissolution of some multinational States. Irrespective of the origin of these groups, their recognition as such and the policy towards them depended on many factors, like: their demographic size compared with the majority of the population of the respective State and the degree of their geographic concentration, including whether in some places they formed the majority of the population; their economic power (natural resources, level of the economic development, their geopolitical position); history, whether they have been submitted to cultural and linguistic repression or isolation, mainly the democratic deficit which has to be corrected; the status of their linguistic variety and the degree of its acceptance by the majority.

A considerable number of linguistic varieties are still spoken in Europe, different from the point of view of the area they are spoken, of the number of speakers and of course of their structure, of written symbols and of phonetics. According to an encyclopedic study, some 267 native languages would be spoken in Europe, some official or national, others minority languages, spoken by larger or more restraint groups[660], some of the latter considered in a "minority situation" or dialects. Due to different factors, many of the minority languages are in danger to disappear. The distinction which is made between minority languages and those "in minority situation" does not seem to be justified and is not based on realities.

Taking into account this situation, in close connection with the efforts for the protection of human rights on the continent, a system of norms and institutions was developed for the protection and promotion of minority languages, which offers elements of real interest, although it presents obvious lacunae and is not accepted by all European States.

---

[660] R.G. Gordon, Ethnologues: Languages of the World, 2005.

SECTION 1 - PROTECTION of MINORITY LANGUAGES according to the EUROPEAN CHARTER of MINORITY LANGUAGES

During the period 1980-1990, European societies became aware of the fact that they were increasingly diverse, as a result of the mixture of populations generated by internal and mainly external migration, but also because the ancient cultural and linguistic regional communities continued to exist and claimed more intensely respect for their identities.

In 1988, the Permanent Conference of Local and Regional Authorities of the Council of Europe (CLRAE) adopted a resolution suggesting the adoption of a convention having as objective to protect languages spoken by minority groups in different parts of the European States, thereby preserving the cultural richness of the continent. In the Declaration and the Programme of education for democratic citizenship, adopted on 7 May 1989, the Committee of ministers of the Council of Europe stressed that „the preservation of linguistic diversity in Europe is not an aim in itself, but is of equal importance for the edification of a society which is more free, more tolerant, based on solidarity, on common values and on a cultural heritage enriched by its diversity"[661].

At their summits, heads of State and government of Europe considered education for a democratic citizenship as a priority for the Council of Europe and gave languages a central place in the exercise of democratic citizenship, taking into account the need of an active participation of these citizens in political decision-making and in social life; they also stressed that plurilingual knowledge, that is the ability to effectively and adequately interact with other European citizens, is implied in the need for an active participation in political and public life of Europe and of their own country.

The answer to these preoccupations was the European Charter for regional or minority languages[662], to which 25 States members of the Council are parties; other 8 States signed the Charter, but did not ratify yet. It is the only international legal instrument devoted to the protection of less spoken languages, which exist on all continents.

The definitions; critical approach. The European Charter defines as regional or minority languages the languages traditionally used within a given territory of a State by its citizens who form a group numerically smaller than the rest of the State's population, which are different from the official language or languages, without including the dialects of official languages or the languages of migrants. The Charter defines also non-territorial languages as languages used by nationals of the State which differ from the language or languages used by the rest of the State's population, but which, although traditionally used on the territory of the State, cannot be identified with an area thereof. The latter are languages spoken by persons who do not live concentrated in an area of the State. The Charter does not offer criteria to explain or to clarify these concepts.

No distinction is made between regional and minority languages, and it is obvious that the definition includes both of them in the same category, referring to a given territory of a State and to a group numerically inferior to the rest of the population of the State. In their reports, States parties use both notions or one of them, without giving them different legal consequences[663]. The criterion of traditional use sends us to the duration of the presence of speakers on the territory, which practically leaves its application to the will of the States and may lead to restrictive approaches; many States are guided by an average duration of a century, which may raise problems of the evaluation of the presence of some human groups on a territory; nevertheless, this approach is accepted by the Committee of experts in the process of consideration of State's reports.

Many territorial changes, including the formation of some national States, took place by the end of the First World War, and since then one century did not yet elapsed. It is obvious that, at least regarding some languages, this criterion can prove to be arbitrary.

The criterion of the use of a language by citizens of the State, correlated with that of traditional use and the exclusion of the languages of migrants, raises even more difficulties in establishing the scope of application of the Charter in a State, because the concept of migrant is often determined by the place of origin of a person, ignoring his/her quality of citizen of the State. This leads to considering significant categories of persons as migrants, although they are citizens of the respective States and are at the third generation on their territory; consequently, in

---

[661] CM(99), p. 76.
[662] For a historic presentation, J. M. Woehrling, The European Charter for Regional or Minority Languages : a critical commentary, 2005, Strasbourg, Council of Europe.
[663] To make it shorter, this may lead to excluding some languages from the protection of the Charter.

the context of the Charter, this leads to excluding the languages spoken by the respective minority group from the regime of promotion applied to other languages.

This is a limitation which runs contrary to the principle of promoting linguistic diversity on the continent, which is the objective of the Charter; time going on, languages spoken by these persons become territorial, if not traditional, and are spoken by increasingly more citizens and by persons who are joining the respective groups through migration. As it is pointed out in a book which presents the Charter and the mechanism of its application, it is possible that in some years several languages which are not European historically may be considered regional or minority languages spoken by citizens of States parties with sufficient traditional presence (for instance of several decades or more than a generation).

It is appreciated that, considering the philosophy of the Charter, it cannot become an instrument of the preservation of the linguistic European ecosystem of the end of the 19th century, but must have the capacity to evolve, since the social changes taking place will make it necessary to reconsider these concepts within a reasonable period of time[664].

The Committee of experts already noted that some languages traditionally spoken on the territory of some States are consolidated by the influx of migrants speaking the same language (Russian language in Finland through the immigration from Russia, Croatian languages in Austria through immigration from Croatia, as well as Italian immigration in Switzerland, Serbian in Slovenia and others). In 2001 in Finland there were some 500 local Russian speaking and 15-25 thousand Russian immigrants[665], in Switzerland 279.273 Italian speaking lived outside the traditional Italian area and 85% of them were immigrants[666]. The Committee decided to promote the protection of the respective languages without making a distinction between the new and the traditional speakers. Therefore, if they are identical with one of the languages traditionally spoken in one of the States parties, such languages enjoy the protection offered by the Charter, even if the number of new comers may exceed that of those traditionally speaking the language.

Another element of the definition is the territorial one; according to the Charter, the respective languages must be spoken on the territory of the State, in a geographic area where it represents the mode of expression of several people that justifies the adoption of measures of protection provided for. According to the Explanatory Report to the Charter, it is the area where the language is spoken to the largest extent, even if only by a minority, and has its historical basis. The application of this criterion leads to establishing the character of territorial or non-territorial language, which entails different obligations of substance. According to the Report, determining the territory where a language is spoken is a matter within the competence of each State; however, it is not a discretionary power, because States have to respect the geographic area where a language is spoken and this obligation is monitored by the Committee of experts. For instance, in the case of Hungary, the Committee considered that Polish is a territorial language, because the majority of speakers are concentrated in a few places. It also considered Romani languages as territorial in Croatia, because they have a traditional presence in identified areas, where they should enjoy certain degree of protection[667].

With regard to statements of some States which referred to internal laws establishing a threshold of the number of speakers of a language to be considered territorial, the Committee adopted a different position, stressing that it will not be led by the restrictive internal laws, but will evaluate the application of the Charter regarding different languages taking into account the situation on the ground. The Committee interprets the territory of a language with some flexibility and is concerned that traditional territories of such languages are not excluded from the application of the Charter[668].

A problem raised in connection with the territorial element was whether the provisions of the Charter concerning historical languages of Europe are also applicable in the non-European territories of some States parties. On this issue, when they ratified the Charter, United Kingdom and The Netherlands made statements according to which their external territories are not the object of the Charter. The Committee took in consideration these statements and did not discuss this issue on the occasion of the examination of their periodic reports. Spain and

---

[664] Shaping language rights; Commentary on the European Charter for Regional or Minority Languages in light of the Committee of Experts evaluations, in Regional and Minority Languages, No. 9, 2012 ed. A. N. Lopez, E. J. R. Vieytez, I. U. Libarona, p. 64-65, Publishing Editions of the Council of Europe.
[665] Application of the Charter in Finland, 2001, para. 14 and in Austria, 2009, para. 16.
[666] According to Shaping language rights, p. 109-110.
[667] Application of the Charter in Slovakia, 2009, para. 12-13; in Hungary, 2009, para. 12; in Romania, 2011; in Austria, 2009, para. 15; in Sweden, 2009, para. 11-14.
[668] J. M. Woehrling, The European Charter for Regional or Minority Languages: a critical commentary, Strasbourg, Council of Europe, 2005, p. 59.

Denmark did not make such statements. According to a scholar who presented the Charter[669], languages spoken within the non-European territories under the sovereignty of European States may also be the object of the application of the Charter. The Committee of experts considered the situation of languages spoken in Ceuta and Melilla, territories belonging to Spain in Northern Africa, as being subject to the provisions of the Charter. Similarly, the Committee asked the Danish authorities to include languages spoken in the Faroe Islands and in Greenland under the protection of the Charter and considered irrelevant that authorities of these islands showed lack of interest or less interest to the application of the Charter, stressing that the objective is to protect the cultural heritage of Europe[670].

Another issue concerns the status of the languages to which the Charter is applicable; according to the definitions, regional or minority languages to which the Charter is applied cannot be official languages of States. Yet, the legislation of States contains many notions which cover sometimes different realities, like for instance languages of indigenous populations, languages of interethnic communication; such languages cannot be considered official languages and can be protected according to the Charter, if they correspond to other criteria. Are excluded only official languages spoken on the entire territory of a State; languages like Galician in Spain, Gagauz in the Republic of Moldova or Scottish in United Kingdom are not excluded and can be placed under the application of the Charter, even if they have an official status in the respective areas.

Nevertheless, the Committee took in consideration the *de facto* situation of some languages, even those declared official languages of States parties. For example, in the case of Cyprus, although Turkish is declared official on the entire territory, the Committee considered the fact that this language is not official any more on the territory under the control of the government of Cyprus and consequently it should be applied the treatment offered to other regional or minority languages[671].

As for the non-territorial languages, these are languages which are spoken by persons who are not living concentrated in some areas of the State's territory and which are protected according to the provisions of Part II of the Charter. Only three States mentioned non-territorial languages with the occasion of ratification (Cyprus, Poland and Sweden), while others referred to them in their reports and the Committee of experts brought into discussion other situations during the consideration of reports. Romania declared that it will apply the provisions of Part II of the Charter to ten languages and those of Part III to ten others, without naming some of them as non-territorial.

In many States Romani and Yiddish languages are considered non-territorial. As for Romani languages, it is appreciated that to the extent that this population becomes sedentary, they should be considered territorial regional or minority languages[672]. States parties undertook to apply to non-territorial languages the provisions of Part II of the Charter, but measures to be taken for this purpose shall be determined in a flexible manner, bearing in mind the needs and wishes of the groups using them, as well as the traditions and characteristics of these groups (article 7, paragraph 5 of the Charter). In the opinion of the Committee of experts, languages considered non-territorial do not have to be notified on ratification, because they benefit from the regime of minimum protection provided for by the provisions of Part II which are applicable to all minority languages spoken on the territory of a State.

The Committee of experts, based on a recommendation approved by the Committee of ministers of the Council of Europe, proceeded to establish *ex officio* those languages and, on the occasion of the examination of periodic reports of States parties, asked them to extend the official recognition to those languages which were not mentioned in the instruments of ratification[673].

Languages which are official, but are less spoken, are in a different situation; they have an official status, but their situation is comparable with that of minority languages. According to article 3 par.2, a State party may notify that it accepts undertakings under Part III of the Charter regarding such languages. This is the situation of some official languages in Finland, Switzerland, Croatia or Spain, as well as of other official languages which, in some parts of State's territory, are in difficulty. In their instruments of ratification, Switzerland declared that it will apply this provision with regard to Italian and Romanche languages[674], while Finland mentioned the Swedish.

---

[669] Application of the Charter in Denmark, 2004, para. 26 and 2007, para. 24.
[670] Explanatory Report to the Charter, Council of Europe, 1995, p. 14. 12.Shaping language rights, p. 73.
[671] Application of the Charter to Cyprus, 2006, para. 40 and 2009, para. 25; note also many recommendations addressed to Croatia for the Slovene language, to Switzerland for German in some cantons, to Slovenia for Croatian, Serbian and German, to Spain for Portuguese, Galician and Tamazight in some provinces, to Cyprus for Arab Maronite, to Denmark for the languages spoken in Faroe Islands and Greenland; cited in Shaping language rights, p. 128.
[672] Application of the Charter to Switzerland, 2008, para. 15 and 2010, para. 11.
[673] Cases presented by Woerhling, op. cit., p. 65.
[674] Application of the Charter to Switzerland, 2008.

These provisions were extended also by Norway to Nynorsk, a variety of the Norwegian, although it is not mentioned in the instrument of ratification of Norway[675].That means that the provisions of Part III of the Charter will be applied to these languages in areas where they are in this situation.

Objectives and the nature of commitments. The objectives placed at the basis of the Charter are: to recognize these languages as an expression of the cultural richness; to respect their geographic area; to take resolute action to promote, facilitate and encourage their use in speech and writing, in public and private life; to maintain and develop links between groups using such languages and others in the country and in other States; to provide for appropriate forms and means for the teaching and study of these languages; to provide facilities enabling non-speakers of a regional or minority language living in the area where it is used to learn it if they so desire; to promote studies and research on these languages; to promote transnational exchanges of appropriate types in connection with languages used in identical or similar form in two or several States.

For fulfilling these objectives, the Charter provides obligations that States parties commit themselves to respect in several fields (education, culture, media, justice, administration and public services, economic and social activities, transfrontier exchanges), in a gradual manner and on a sliding scale, offering to States parties several possibilities depending on their specific situation concerning each minority language spoken in the country[676].

The most important feature of the solution adopted by the Charter of 1992 is its great flexibility, with the purpose to allow States parties to adopt such measures which are most appropriate to their situation, in substance a commitment à la carte, meant to ensure a minimum standard of protection to minority languages.

All minority languages spoken on the territory of a State party and which correspond to the definition given enjoy a minimum level of protection provided for in the Part II of the Charter, which enounces rather principles and objectives (recognition of these languages, respect for their geographic area, preserving the relationship between groups who speak these languages in the country and abroad, elimination of discrimination, the possibility to study these languages in adequate forms taking into account the needs and the wishes expressed by the speakers and others).

At the same time, when a State ratifies the Charter, it has to specify to what languages it will apply the provisions of Part III of the Charter, which contain more precise commitments. For these languages, the State party has to accept at least 35 paragraphs or sub-paragraphs concerning the fields of application, including at least three paragraphs or sub-paragraphs from articles concerning respectively education and cultural activities and at least two from articles concerning the other fields of application mentioned.

Thus, from the beginning the Charter has a limited scope of application, excluding the languages of migrants, which are nowadays millions, many of them having already the citizenship of the host States, and dialects, which very often become autonomous languages; moreover, the scope of application of the Charter, that is the level of protection of different minority languages depends upon the commitments taken by each State at the moment of ratification. Many States parties declared to what languages they will apply the Charter when they presented the first report.

That is why, the commitments taken by States parties to the Charter offer a great variety, including some times linguistic smaller groups and ignoring languages spoken on a larger scale; differences appear also with regard to the Framework Convention of 1995 for the protection of national minorities[677], which is difficult to justify because a national minority has first of all as specific feature the language spoken.

One must note also that the provisions of the Charter refer to the protection of minority languages, enouncing alternative obligations at the choice of the States, without any reference to the rights of persons belonging to minorities, although they are obviously the beneficiaries of the use of minority languages. Thus, to the difference from international instruments on human rights, the commitments taken by the States parties according to the Charter generate interstate obligations concerning the use of some languages and only indirectly human rights for those speaking them. Though, it is undeniable that promoting the use of minority languages represents a substantial contribution to the respect of some fundamental human rights.

On the other side, the Charter gives expression to a multilingual conception of the respective countries, to a spirit of linguistic tolerance, providing for modalities of use of minority languages along with the official language. The Charter is not opposing the minority languages to official languages, but is promoting multilingual societies. At the same time, the Charter is not limited to the recognition of or granting some rights in favour of such languages,

---

[675] According to Woerhling, they are also regional or minority languages; op. cit., pp. 68-71.

[676] A more recent study, Commentary on the Charter in the light of the Committee of Experts' evaluation, by A. N. Lopez, E. J. R. Vieytez and I. U. Libarona, Shaping language rights, Council of Europe Publishing, 2012.

[677] Ion Diaconu, Ten years from the entry into force of the Framework Convention for the protection of national minorities and the situation of minorities in Europe. Experience of Romania, Revista Română de Drept Internațional, no.6, 2008(in Romanian).

but requests States to effectively support the use of these languages by their active policies, including special measures. This is not about a kind of passive multilingualism, or merely accepting the existing situation; for some languages, there is the need to revive or to restore them (languages spoken by Roma in different States, Sami languages and others).

Both the Charter for regional and minority languages and the Framework Convention of 1995 for the protection of national minorities reflect a practice accepted increasingly by numerous States, including in international documents such as the Declaration of UN General Assembly of 1992 concerning the rights of persons belonging to national or ethnic, religious and linguistic minorities and the OSCE Document of Copenhagen of 1990, all of them having as a starting point article 27 of the Covenant on civil and political rights. The mechanisms created to follow and promote their observance ensured some coherence and contributed to increasing the preoccupations for their application within the Council of Europe. The Charter also recognizes the communitarian aspect of the use of these languages, asking that States respect their geographic area and apply measures in their favour in the respective areas.

It is obvious that both the provisions of the Charter and those of the Framework Convention offer an extremely large area of commitments taken by States regarding the protection of minority languages, respectively of the rights of persons belonging to minorities. Thus, the free use of mother tongue in private and in public, the information of each person in a language he/she understands about the reasons for his/her detention and the accusations against, as well as the right of defense and resorting to an interpreter, contacts with persons from other countries who speak the same language, the freedom of expression, access to information and dissemination of information in mother tongue and the use of the name and first name in this language-all of them are rights which imply strict obligation of States. As for other aspects, such as the use of the minority language in the relations between these persons and State authorities, displaying the place-names also in that language and education in mother tongue, the commitment of States parties is to make efforts to fulfill them, depending on the local conditions, on the situation of the respective language and on requests, and of course within their legislative system.

According to the European Charter, States can realize these objectives under different degrees of complexity and of integrality, according to commitments they take individually when ratifying the Charter. Similarly, the Explanatory Report to the Framework Convention of 1995 on the protection of national minorities, adopted at the same time with the Convention, which represents thus an authentic interpretation of its provisions, refers repeatedly to possible difficulties, administrative and financial, to implement such provisions and to the need to adopt flexible solutions allowing States a margin of discretion in order to apply them taking into account specific circumstances[678].

According to international documents, an important element used very often by States, in order to justify their policy when they apply a different treatment among the languages spoken, is the number of those speaking a language different from the official one. Different terms are used by these documents: substantial numbers, the situation of each language, a language largely spread in the territory, or where it is possible, or adequate measures, the idea being the same: wherever there is a relatively important number of persons speaking a language different from the official one it would not be reasonable for the respective State not to offer certain services in their language. This may depend also on the resources available to the State. Of course, it may happen that some speakers of minority languages feel disadvantaged, because no State is capable to offer services and activities in all languages spoken by persons living on its territory. This is a problem of balance between different interests and preoccupations.

In connection with the number of persons, another criterion considered is the geographic concentration of inhabitants speaking a minority language. If an important number of persons live compactly in an area of the State, it would be not reasonable not to offer them services and activities in mother tongue. It is expected that these persons use more their language in their day to day relations and are less fluent in the official language.

Of course, each State has a linguistic policy, because language is essential for accomplishing many State functions; though, a State cannot use in an equal manner all languages spoken on its territory when accomplishing its functions. Therefore, the different situations of languages spoken on the territory of a State lead to different undertakings from the States. Respecting this reality, the Charter is nevertheless proposing to obtain the highest possible degree of use of minority languages in the States parties.

Another important factor which may determine whether a State would favour the use of several languages along with the official one is the amount of resources- human, financial or material, at its disposal. For less spoken languages, it may be too expensive to translate official acts, to hire qualified personnel in all districts and fields of activity, that is to offer all services and in all geographic areas. The choice of commitments according to the Charter allows that States take into account such preoccupations. Therefore, the possibility to differentiate among these

---

[678] Doc.CM (94)161, 1994, pp. 22-24.

languages corresponds to their different specific situations, and States have to combine the territorial and personal criteria.

SECTION 2 - COMMITMENTS to PROTECT LANGUAGES in DIFFERENT FIELDS

In the field of education[679], the Charter provides for each State party the possibility to take, with regard to pre-school, primary school, secondary school, technical and professional education, higher education and education of adults, gradual commitments from: making available education fully in minority language; or a substantial part of it; or its teaching for children whose families so request and in sufficient number; or to encouraging and favouring the application of such measures if the States have no direct competence in these fields. States also may commit themselves to ensure the study of the history and culture reflected by the respective language and the basic and further training of teachers for the commitments undertaken and to set up a supervisory body to monitor the measures taken in these fields.

Again, States must take in consideration the number of persons concerned, their geographic location, the possibilities of transport and other factors such as the lack of education materials in a language, of trained teachers, of financial resources, as well as the prevailing of a lingua franca or a popular opposition to the use of a mother tongue as a medium for education in the area.

One cannot seriously deny the advantages of using mother tongues in education. The situation of each language should lead to establishing the educational offer, if there is sufficient demand and the wish of the beneficiaries, or only a kind of policy of support, according to the case. It is explicitly provided for that none of the commitments accepted is impairing upon the teaching of the official language of the State, because responding to the need to balance different rights and interests implied and to rich the final objective to ensure *de facto* and *de jure* equality, should not lead to depriving the children of the benefits of studying the official or the majority language spoken in the State where they live.

The interdiction of discrimination cannot be invoked to eliminate the study of the official language, which is necessary so that persons speaking minority languages are not excluded for participating in public life, in the social life as a whole, and in order to avoid creating inequalities. Moreover, adopting educative policies in conformity with the principle of non-discrimination in the field of the use of languages should not lead to isolating minorities in linguistic ghetto's which would exclude them from many benefits in their capacity as citizens.

The Charter gives primary importance to education for the promotion of these languages. According to the Charter, it is appreciated that this is the way preferred, the key factor for promoting linguistic diversity[680], because it ensures the transmission of a language to future generations. The Committee of experts underlined the need to adopt an active position, through positive measures, in order to apply the provisions concerning education. The Committee also pointed out that speakers should not have upon themselves the burden to request the respect of the obligations of the Charter, which belongs to State's authorities. It also did not accept the argument that the respective tasks are in the power of local authorities.

The Committee insists that undertakings accepted are respected, so that if one State committed itself to offer education in a minority language, it will not be considered sufficient to ensure the teaching of 50% of the topics in mother tongue; there can be also more flexible models, if there is one which offers full education in mother tongue and speakers have the possibility to choose. As for the commitment to offer substantial education in mother tongue, the Committee did not accept that teaching only the language for a number of hours a week or also of religion and history are sufficient to consider the undertaking fulfilled. If a State committed itself to ensure only the teaching of the minority language as part of the curricula, the Committee insists to see it respected and does not accept only the learning of songs, poems or stories in the regional language. The lowest undertaking is to teach the minority language if there are sufficient demands; this raises the problems of informing persons concerned about the existence of such a possibility and of the number of demands considered sufficient. The Committee considers that asking for a number too high of demands would be contrary to the spirit of the Charter and that families concerned have the right to demand and to dispose of a right to recourse[681].

---

[679] A. N. Lopez and A. Previtali, Article 8.1 and article 8.2 of the Charter, in Shaping language rights, pp. 247-300.
[680] Shaping language rights, p. 250; also ECRML, the Committee of experts' interpretation and evaluation practice concerning the interpretation of articles on education of the European Charter for Regional and Minority Languages, Strasbourg, 3 June 2006, doc. MIN-LANG, 2006, 3, p. 2.
[681] Application of the Charter in Ukraine, 2010, para. 57-60.

With regard to the commitment to teach history and culture related to the minority language, it is very important to combat prejudice, to cultivate confidence and a climate of understanding; the problems which appear are related to the absence of a systematic approach concerning history and culture of minority groups. The training of didactic personnel is considered a necessity for fulfilling other commitments in this field; some problems derive from the lack of recognizing diplomas of study obtained in other countries, from the limited number of personnel needed, which imposes difficult conditions of work in order to cover the requested norms of teaching, and from the lack of incentives to interest the personnel which is needed. As for the commitment concerning setting bodies to survey and evaluate the education in regional languages, in most of the cases States are reporting that such activities are fulfilled by the existing authorities, although reports on the results are not dressed and not published.

According to another commitment, States are requested to encourage or to offer education in regional languages outside the areas where they are traditionally used, if the number of speakers justifies that. The State may authorize the learning of these languages, encourage it or even offer the conditions necessary. Different models can be imagined, as for instance optional education, distance learning, including the use of modern means.

A general problem retained by the Committee of experts is the lack of continuity, meaning that an adequate offer of education in or of the respective minority languages is not ensured from the lower levels to the higher ones; other problems would be the restrictive commitments for preschool and primary education, which are essential for transmitting the language, or commitments which are too restrictive or too ambitious in view of the situation of some languages, or prejudice existing with regard to some languages, or drastic demographic reductions due to emigration, or long distances from the school and of course the high cost of education in regional languages.

In the field of the use of media[682], States parties to the Charter committed themselves to ensure, at their choice, for persons using minority languages in the respective areas, taking into account the situation of each language, to the extent public authorities are competent or have a role to play in this field and respecting the independence and the autonomy of the media: the creation of at least one radio station and one television channel in the minority language; to encourage or facilitate their creation by private actors; or to make adequate provision so that broadcasters offer programmes in these languages (if the radio and TV carry out a public service function); to encourage or facilitate the production and distribution of audio and audiovisual works in this language; to encourage or facilitate the creation and/or maintenance of at least one newspaper in that language or the regular publication of articles in that language; to grant financial assistance to the media in minority languages similarly to media in other languages; to support the training of journalists and other media personnel; and finally to guarantee the freedom of direct reception of radio and TV broadcasts from countries where the minority language is spoken.

The provisions of the European Charter offer in this field also the possibility to engage on a sliding scale, considering the number of speakers and their geographic concentration. A State can require, when it grants a license, the fulfillment of some conditions concerning certain contents of emissions, provided that such requirements are reasonable and necessary in a democratic society, that they respect the rights and interests of the persons concerned and the interests of the State, and are not discriminatory. Restrictions to the freedom of expression and free circulation of information in the written press are submitted to requirements in terms similar to those provided for in the European Convention for the protection of human rights. As it is known, at the level of the European Union, a State has the right to fix quotas with regard to the linguistic contents of broadcasts, but it has to do it in a non-discriminatory manner. The EEC Directive on television across borders accepted that a State can impose the obligation to use the national language for a certain quantity of programmes in that language.

A State can grant financial assistance to private media using an unofficial or minority language, which is not granted to the media in the official language. Such measures are legitimate if they pursue a reasonable objective, because non-discrimination does not mean always an equal treatment.

The Committee of experts was confronted with the phenomenon of the privatization of media, which takes place in many countries and can lead to excluding minority languages; the Committee recommended that States adopt measures of regulation of this issue, so that private radio and TV continue to broadcast in these languages[683] and insisted on the duration and the timing of broadcasts, without enouncing clear standards.

After underlining the importance of the television for the protection and promotion of minority languages in the modern society, the Committee insisted for an effective presence of these languages, for the regularity of broadcasts and their dissemination at hours of enhanced audience and did not accept the application of non-significant quota for broadcasting in these languages[684]. In other cases, the Committee recommended the application

---

[682] Robert Dunbar, Article 11. Media, in Shaping language rights, pp. 373-424.
[683] Shaping language rights, p. 382.
[684] Shaping language rights, p. 382.

of special measures in favour of some minority languages[685]. Similarly, with regard to audio and audiovisual productions, it recommended to support the creation of private posts and the production and dissemination of such productions in minority languages, including through special measures, such as (for the radio) granting licenses to function without strictly taking into account the rules of competition[686]. As for news- papers, the Committee retained that a publication is considered a journal if it appears at least weekly, which is not ensured for many minority languages, and addressed the recommendations necessary, including regarding subventions for additional costs of publications in these languages.

With regard to cultural activities and facilities[687], mainly libraries, cultural centers, museums, archives, academies, theater and film, the States parties commit themselves, in the territories where minority languages are used and in as much as the public authorities are competent, have attributions or play a role in this field: to encourage different types of expression and initiatives specific to minority languages; to promote access to works in these languages or in other languages by supporting translations, dubbing, post- synchronization and subtitling activities; to ensure that State bodies responsible for organizing or supporting cultural activities of various kinds include in their activities the knowledge and the use of minority languages, and have at their disposal staff who have a full command of the minority language; to encourage the direct participation of the representatives of speakers in providing facilities and planning cultural activities; to encourage or facilitate the creation of a body or bodies responsible for collecting, preserving and publishing works produced in these languages; and if necessary create or promote and finance translations and services of terminological research in the minority language.

As for the territories others than those where the minority languages are traditionally used, the State parties may undertake to allow, encourage or provide adequate cultural activities, if the number of users of a minority language justifies it. States must choose among these commitments at least three among the 35 needed to ratify the Charter.

It is thus recognized that the language spoken is the vehicle of an active cultural life. Although confronted with a lack of information from States parties, the Committee of experts gave importance to the allocation of funds for encouraging the cultural expression and for promoting access to culture; it insisted that persons speaking the minority languages be hired by the bodies dealing with cultural activities[688] and for including culture in these languages in cultural activities abroad[689].

With regard to the administration of justice[690], there may be situations when the use of a unique language in courts may have serious effects for persons who do not speak and do not understand the language of the court, even if in practice only the official language is used in most countries due to the small number of speakers of other languages and to some practical difficulties. According to international instruments on civil and political rights, when a person is accused of a crime, he/she has to be informed about the nature of the charges against him/her in a language that he/she understands and has the right to an interpreter free of charge if he/she does not understand or speak the language of the court. In many States these rights are related to the right to a fair trial. They can be also examined as an application of the principles of equal rights and non-discrimination. If these rights are not recognized or not respected, this may have serious consequences on human rights, in particular on the right to freedom of the respective person. This is a minimal guarantee, which is not dependent upon the number of speakers living in a geographic area.

The judicial procedures, as well as activities taking place in the relationship between administrative bodies and citizens, can be considered as a "public service" of the State, as they are conducted as part of the activities of State structures. Therefore, to the extent this is reasonable and possible, the need to use mother tongues of those involved should be taken into account.

The Charter provides for alternative commitments concerning the use of minority languages in criminal, civilian and administrative justice, as well as the acceptance of documents drafted in these languages, of legal documents between parties in such languages and with third parties, as well as concerning the publication in minority languages of the most important statutory texts and of those which refer especially to those speaking these languages. The application of these commitments is subject to three conditions: they can be applied only in the judiciary respective districts; the situation of each language has to be taken into account; if the judge does not consider that such a facility hampers the proper administration of justice.

---

[685] Application of the Charter in Ukraine, 2007, para. 486-487.,
[686] Application of the Charter in The Netherlands for Frisian, 2001, para. 59; in Finland for Swedish, 2001, para. 1005.
[687] Elizabeth Craig, Article 12. Cultural activities and facilities, in Shaping language rights, pp. 425-443.
[688] Application of the Charter in Germany, 2006, para. 526-527.
[689] Application of the Charter in Slovenia, 2004, para 151; in Germany, 2008, para. 103-106.
[690] Anna Pla Bois, Article 9. Judicial authorities, in Shaping language rights, pp. 301-336.

As for the judiciary districts, it is accepted to exclude those situated outside of the area of traditional use of the minority languages; therefore, States are requested to define those judiciary districts where the number of speakers justifies taking organizational measures for applying these provisions. With regard to the situation of each language, a number of factors have to be taken into consideration: the number of parties in proceedings, of judges, prosecutors, counsels, other officials of the courts, of witnesses who speak this language; if the respective language developed the adequate legal terminology; if the speakers of the regional language are fluent in another language used by the courts; the social and political place of the respective language in the State.

With regard to the decision of the judge, according to the Explanatory Report such a decision (denying the use of the language) has to be motivated and to take into account the nature of the proceedings and the circumstances of the case and should intervene only when it is strictly necessary, in exceptional cases and should be open to appeal or review[691].

The Charter contains more strict provisions than other treaties, providing for the right to the use of the minority language even if the person concerned speaks the language of the proceedings. It was considered that these persons may feel the need to express themselves in a language which is emotionally closer to them or in which they are more fluent. At the request of one of the parties in the proceedings, they have to be conducted in the minority language. Documents connected to the case should also, at request, be translated in that language. Alternatives with regard to these commitments are offered to the choice of States, and their application is limited to judiciary districts.

As for the civilian and administrative justice, States may commit themselves alternatively to ensure, at the request of one of the parties, that the proceedings are conducted in the minority language, to allow the oral use of the language without additional expenses for the parties and to admit written documents and evidence in that language, at the request of the party concerned. Separately, States can accept to support the expenses for interpreters. The terms civilian and administrative courts include any institution which judges such cases. The Committee found that in some States the effective application of provisions of article 9 is not ensured due to difficulties related to translation and interpretation[692].

Regarding admission in courts of legal documents, the Charter refers only to documents drafted in a minority language, without mentioning any condition of validity; of course, such conditions may be established by the law. The Committee of experts considers whether the laws of States restrain the validity of documents with regard to the languages in which they are drafted.

The provision concerning the translation in minority language of the most important statutory texts has in mind such texts adopted at the national level, but also legislative texts referring especially to those speaking the respective languages. The Committee of experts insisted for the translation of such texts and noted that such translations are not ensured in a sufficient measure and that access to them should be improved[693].

The Committee of experts found that in many States the application of article 9 is only formally guaranteed, that the judicial personnel and citizens are not aware of this possibility, that in some languages the legal terminology is not developed, there are no legal dictionaries and there is a lack of interpreters and translators, or that persons hesitate to ask for the use of a regional language in order not to appear as producing difficulties. Recommendations were consequently addressed to the States concerned.

In the field of administrative authorities and public services[694], the 1992 Charter stipulates that in the administrative districts where the number of speakers using minority languages justifies such measures, if this is reasonable possible, States parties undertake to ensure either the use of the respective language in administration, or that some officials can use it, or that oral and written requests are admitted and answer is given in that language, or only the reception of such requests or only of documents in this language. They can accept also to make available for the population texts and forms widely used in mother tongues and to allow that authorities elaborate documents in these languages.

In other areas, taking into account the number of speakers of such languages, States may commit themselves only to encourage or to allow such measures; other commitments refer to the publication of official documents of local and regional authorities also in minority languages and to the use of these languages by local authorities in their assemblies, without excluding the use of the official language, as well as to the use of traditional place-names in minority languages.

With regard to public services (transports, health care, social assistance, waste collection, water supplies, electricity and gas), the Charter enounces as alternative commitments: to ensure the use of the minority language, or

---

[691] Explanatory Report, p. 94.
[692] Application of the Charter in Finland, 2007, para. 210; in Slovakia, 2009, para. 84.
[693] Application of the Charter in Spain, 2005, para 234; in Norway, 2010, para. 168.
[694] Jutta Engbers, Article 10. Administrative authorities and public services, in Shaping language rights, pp. 337-371.

to receive requests and give answers in that language or only to receive such requests. For this purpose, States undertake to ensure translation or interpretation, to organize the recruitment and training of public servants or to designate in these functions persons who know the language. The Charter contains also the commitment to allow the use or the adoption of family names in minority languages at the request of those concerned.

The criteria for accepting such commitments would be the number of speakers, but also the frequency of the use of the regional language, the situations when it is used and as appropriate its vocabulary; as for what is reasonable as a commitment, the real need, the ability to use the language and the burden it may create for the State are to be taken into consideration[695]. The Charter leaves to States some discretion in establishing what is reasonable, taking into account the different situations. In Europe, various solutions are applied. In Estonia, the Law on languages provides for a threshold of 50%; in the Basque community of Spain the threshold for other languages is 20%, in Finland 8%, in Slovakia 20%, in Romania 20%. It is appreciated that States should tend to a balance considering the nature of the service offered, the frequency of contacts with the public, the linguistic composition of the area and the impact on individuals.

The Committee considers that a threshold of 20% is too high and limits dramatically the application of the Charter and, therefore, recommended to the States concerned to reconsider the situation and to reduce the threshold[696], without indicating a solution. The Committee asks that such commitments should be specified in internal laws and regulations, and asks for a proactive attitude of States in their application; as for federal States or those practicing a wide decentralization, it underlines the obligation to give the necessary instruction for the application of these undertakings.

As for the public services, the Committee of experts pointed out that States should ensure that enterprises offering such services use the regional languages, according to the commitments taken by the State.

In the field of economic and social activities[697], States parties can commit themselves: to eliminate any legislative provisions which would forbid or prevent the use of the minority language in documents without a reasonable justification, including in contracts of employment and in the instructions concerning the use of products or installations; to forbid the introduction of clauses excluding or limiting the use of this language in internal regulations of companies or in private documents, at least among those using the language; to oppose to practices intended to discourage the use of the minority language; to facilitate and to encourage the use of this language through other means. In so far as they are competent, and as far as this is reasonable possible, within the territory where the minority language is used, they can commit: to adopt financial or banking regulations which would allow the use of the minority language in documents of payment or in other financial documents; to organize in the public economic and social sectors activities for promoting the use of the minority language; to ensure that services of social care, such as hospitals, retirement homes and hostels offer the possibility of receiving and treating in their own language persons using the minority language who are in need of care; to ensure that safety instructions, as well as information on the rights of consumers offered by public authorities, are also drawn up and available in the minority language.

The starting point is the freedom of information of the public; this would not be compatible with the exclusive use of the official language. Of course, the possibility of the State to interfere with social and economic life depends on the type of activity, on the State's competences in the respective field and on the rapid changes which take place.

The Committee underlined that these commitments are not limited to an exclusively passive attitude of the State, but need a proactive role. The Committee insisted mainly on ensuring the use of regional languages in the sector of health services.

The text of the Charter combines non-discrimination with the adoption of a proactive attitude in particular in the field of health and social care services. The Committee also underlined that integration according to the conception of the Charter should allow full participation in economic, social and political life and the opportunity to preserve the linguistic and cultural identity[698].

The Committee notes that the undertakings are fulfilled if there are no prohibitive clauses concerning the use of regional languages; as for the companies, the Committee considered sufficient a general legislative clause forbidding such exclusions[699]. With regard to the opposition to practices preventing the use of regional languages in

---

[695] Application of the Charter in Germany, 2007, recommendation of the Committee of ministers, para. 1.

[696] In connection with the threshold of 20% of speakers of a minority language in order to apply the provisions of the Charter in the field of administration, see application in Slovakia, 2009, para. 13; Montenegro, 2010, para. 2010; Czeck Republic, 2009, para. 46; Serbia, 2009, para. 29; Romania, 2011; as for the territorial delimitations, Sweden, 2006, para. 16; Spain, 2005, para. 64.

[697] I. U. Libarona, Article 13. Economic and social life, in Shaping language rights, pp. 445-484.

[698] Application of the Charter in Slovenia, 2004, para. 88.

[699] Application of the Charter in Croatia, 2005, para. 105.

this field, the Committee considered sufficient legislative instruments providing for sanctions for discrimination or other similar laws[700]. The Committee considers such measures from the point of view of their efficiency. With regard to economic and social sectors detained by the State or under its control, it is considered that they include transports of all kind, postal services, the banks under the State control, the waste collection, services of infrastructure of a general interest (gas, electricity, telephone, telecommunications, areas of habitation publicly detained). In these fields, the Committee pretends effective action of the State, programmes and planning of activities in order to fulfill the commitment.

The Committee of experts and the Committee of ministers addressed most of the recommendations with regard to social services. It is considered that commitments in this field require results, meaning a practical available offer of these services with the use of the minority language through a structural policy[701]. A bilingual policy of human resources should be a component of this approach; translations are not considered to be a good solution[702]. The same position seems to be adopted with regard to the safety instructions. As for the information on the consumer rights, the Committee considers the undertaking fulfilled if the legislation on the protection of consumers is available in the minority language. This field is important for the survival of minority languages, but the use of the language has also a direct purpose, being directly related to the exercise of other human rights.

Transfrontier exchanges (article 14 of the Charter) represent another field concerning the use of minority languages. Commitments that States may take refer to: the application of existing agreements or the conclusion of agreements with States where such a language or a close one is used, as a means of promoting contacts among speakers in the fields of culture, education, information, training of personnel and permanent education; favouring or promoting cooperation between regions and local authorities of territories where such languages are used.

Such exchanges increase the number of speakers, contribute to maintain and promoting minority languages and to the development of the cultures they express. This article of the Charter can be regarded in connection with articles 7.1, 11.2, 12.3. The Committee of experts evaluated both the existence of the respective agreements and that of exchanges and of their intensity. It also underlined the shared responsibility of the central and local authorities to favour such cooperation and encouraged them to create joint bodies of cooperation.

* * *

The European Charter of regional or minority languages represents a legal status of protection and promotion of less spoken languages on the European continent. The Charter gives expression to a multilingual conception of countries of Europe, to a spirit of linguistic tolerance. It is the main reference with regard to policies to follow in Europe concerning minority languages and for the evaluation of the action of States in this field. The Charter created a dynamic mechanism to monitor and promote its application which, with all its limits, started to produce results. Some languages spoken by few persons begin to come to life and are revived as a result of adequate policies of States; many States adopted new laws in this field or modified the existing ones in order to respond to the recommendations received. For the States parties to the Charter, the commitments accepted and the recommendations of the Committee of experts become the

criteria of evaluation of the legislation and of the policy of each State in the linguistic field[703]. Several States have a federal structure or a regime of decentralization, recognizing extended competences for regional or local administrations, which may create complications in the fulfillment of the undertakings taken; the Committee repeatedly underlined that the responsibility for the fulfillment of the commitments taken and the application of the Charter is incumbent to the federal State which has to take the measures necessary so that authorities of the component units respect these commitments. Moreover, this issue is brought, through the Charter and the activity of the Committee of experts, within the framework of political democracy of States members of the Council of Europe, which gives it other dimensions.

The Charter was elaborated in its present form at the end of the 1980s. During the more than 20 years which elapsed, demographic changes which affected the situation of minority languages have taken place in the European States. An important change is determined by the influx of immigrants, internal and external to Europe; many of

---

[700] Application of the Charter in Spain, 2008, para. 324.
[701] Application of the Charter in Slovakia, 2007, para. 181; in The Netherlands, 2004, para. 186; in Germany, 2008, para. 595.
[702] Application of the Charter in Spain, 2008, para. 535.
[703] The situation in the United Kingdom is examined, for instance, by Wilson McLeod, A New Multilingual United Kingdom? The Impact of the European Charter for regional or Minority Languages, in S. Pertot, T. Priestly and C. Williams, Rights, Promotion and Integration Issues for Minority Languages in Europe, Palgrave, London, 2009, pp. 44-59.

them are already citizens of the States parties, live in some areas of these States and continue to use their language, be it only in private life. Their number is increasing because of the circulation of persons in modern times; in some States mother tongues of these groups are studied, following models of bilingual education. Second, even as compared with the moment when some States ratified the Charter, they find now that some commitments taken by them are either too ambitious or too restrictive with regard to the situation of the respective languages, which makes it difficult to fulfill them.

The demographic situation in the States parties continues to change; groups of speakers increase or diminish depending on internal and external migration and the commitments taken by States do not correspond any more to the situation of languages spoken. This makes it necessary to elaborate, at the level of the Committee of experts and of the Committee of ministers of the Council of Europe, a scheme which should allow a periodic adaptation of the undertakings under the Charter to the evolution of the situation of regional languages and consider the entire population residing in the States parties.

The developments which take place in Europe at present, although incomplete, have as a starting point respect for individual rights and for the specificities of persons and groups, meaning their languages and cultures. This is not limited to tolerance towards these specificities, but implies their promotion taking into account the situation of each language and culture; this is the expression of common values of democracy and the state of law, of respect for human rights, including rights of persons belonging to minorities.

CHAPTER XXIV - The EUROPEAN UNION's CITIZENSHIP - subject of protection

ABSTRACT

Treaties of the European Union established the EU citizenship; is an EU citizen a citizen of a member State; the EU citizenship is not replacing the national citizenship; it is complementing it. The EU citizenship entails some rights which are related to the presence of citizens of member States on the territory of other member States.

EU recognizes, thus, the citizenship granted by member States, that is also the norms applicable to granting and withdrawing the national citizenship.

In some cases considered, the Court of Justice of the EU did not question the law applied by the receiving State to refuse or to withdraw the citizenship, or the law of the departing State according to which a person loses automatically its citizenship when obtaining that of another State. Nevertheless, the Court decided that the situation was not acceptable because the respective persons became stateless and lost the European citizenship or were not recognized this citizenship.

This raises a lot of questions: can one dissociate the EU citizenship from the citizenship of a member State? If so, what is the source of the EU citizenship? can one accept the application of the national laws on citizenship, except when their application would lead to the loss of the EU citizenship or to a refusal to recognize it? is the EU citizenship prevailing over the national laws on granting and withdrawing citizenship?

KEY WORDS: European citizenship, admissibility, control of proportionality, abuse of right, equality of treatment, fundamental status, principle of non-discrimination, naturalization, statelessness, political space, autonomy.

INTRODUCTION

The 500 million citizens of the member States of the European Union are at the same time citizens of the Union. The relationship between the two citizenships gave rise to many debates and reflections, some more optimistic, others more skeptical, some limiting themselves to the terms of the treaties, others looking with more courage to the future. The treaties, beginning with that of Maastricht of 1993, foresaw the European citizenship as deriving from the national citizenship of a member State, as indivisibly linked to the national one, but with different contents given by the documents of the Union. No possibility was foreseen concerning the evolution of the European citizenship to have an existence which would become independent from the national citizenship.

Nevertheless, the Decision of the European Court of Justice reunited in the Grand Chamber on the 2nd of March 2010, in the case Rottmann, with regard to the existence of the European citizenship in relation to the granting or withdrawing of the national citizenship of a member State points out to such a situation. Other decisions of the Court regarding effects of the European citizenship followed and offer new subjects of reflection.

As it is well known, The Treaty of Maastricht instituted the citizenship of the European Union, with the following specific rights for the Union's citizens: the freedom of movement on the territories of member States, including for exercising a lucrative activity, the freedom of residence and of establishment; the right to take part and to stand as a candidate in elections for the European Parliament in the State where they have their residence; the right to take part and to stand as a candidate in local elections in the State where they have the residence; the right to diplomatic and consular protection in countries where their State has no diplomatic mission or consular office (by the missions of other States parties); the right to petition and the right to request and receive information[704]. These rights are presented more explicitly in the Lisbon Treaty and in particular in the Charter of fundamental rights of the Union, adopted in 2007 and in force since 2009 together with the Lisbon Treaty. The Charter added the rights to the protection of personal data, to a good administration and to access to documents, which are obviously not specific to the European citizenship, being granted by Union's acts to all persons having their residence on the territory of member States.

The Decision of the 2nd March 2010 in the case Rottmann[705] was the answer of the European Court to the reference for a preliminary ruling submitted by the German Federal Administrative Court. According to the facts

---

[704] For a more extensive presentation,, Andrei Popescu and Ion Diaconu, European and Euro-Atlantic Organizations, , Ed. Universul Juridic, 2009(in Romanian), pp. 277-279; see also the chapter nr. above, pp.
[705] Case C-135/08, ECR 2010 I-01449.

exposed, an Austrian citizen, Mr. Rottmann, asked for the German citizenship and received it in 1999. He hid that he was pursued in Austria in a criminal case and that a warrant was launched in 1997 against him by the Austrian authorities, which informed about this the authorities of the land of Bavaria in 1999, after the granting of the German citizenship. Following that, the authorities of the land of Bavaria withdrew the citizenship granted to Mr. Rottmann. According to the Austrian legislation, a person who obtains, at request, the citizenship of another State, automatically loses the Austrian citizenship. By the withdrawal of the German citizenship, Mr. Rottmann became a stateless person. The decision of the land authorities of Bavaria was confirmed by the Federal Administrative Court in 2005. The same year, Mr. Rottmann requested before the Federal Administrative Court the revision of the decision of withdrawal of citizenship; that means that the decision of the land authorities had no immediate effect and that the withdrawal of citizenship did not have legal effect until 2005.

Because the German Federal Court had doubts whether the loss of citizenship and consequently becoming stateless was in conformity with the Community law, it submitted to the European Court a preliminary question. In substance, the German Federal Court asked the European Court: whether the law of the Union is opposed to the loss of the European citizenship as a result of the decision taken in conformity with the national law to withdraw the national citizenship obtained fraudulently; if the answer is affirmative, does the State which granted the citizenship obtained fraudulently have to refrain from withdrawing it, as long as it leads to the loss of the European citizenship, or the State of origin has to interpret, apply or adapt its law in order to avoid such a consequence?.

The Court had to decide first on the admissibility of the preliminary question, in particular in view of the opinion of the States concerned, Austria and Germany, of the European Commission, as well as of other States, according to whom the problem raised belongs to internal law and not to community law. The decision in this regard was also the answer to the first question asked by the German Federal Court. But the European Court of Justice followed another way, looking for solutions to protect the European citizenship without denying the right of member States to grant and to withdraw citizenship, and to relate the exercise of this right to requirements of the Union's law.

SECTION 1 - JURISPRUDENCE of the EUROPEAN COURT of JUSTICE

The European Court of Justice took also previously decisions on questions concerning European citizenship. In the well-known case Micheletti, it was about the rights of a citizen of a member State on the territory of another member State. The problem raised was whether Spain could, in a case of double citizenship, on the basis of its civil code, consider that Argentinian citizenship corresponding to the residence of the person before arriving in Spain prevails over the Italian citizenship obtained by birth, and thus refuse the right of residence to that person as a European citizen. It is appreciated that, by this decision, the Court expressed already a „reservation", affirming that a member State does not have the right ..."to restrain the effects attributed to citizenship by another member State, setting up an additional condition for recognizing this citizenship in order to exercise the fundamental freedoms provided for in the treaty" (of the Union). The Court affirmed that obtaining and losing the national citizenship belong, according to international law, to the competence of each member State, but also that, in the exercise of their competences in this field they have to respect the community law[706].

In another case, the Court was confronted with the refusal of Belgian authorities to accept the changing of the name of two children having double nationality, Belgian and Spanish, in order to bear not only the name of the father (according to the Belgian law), but also that of the mother (according to Spanish law). The Court did not accept the argument of the Belgian authorities that changing the name of the two children, Belgian citizens having their residence in that States from birth, belonged to the competence of internal bodies, and founded its decision by reference to the status of the European citizen. The Court applied the control of proportionality, considering the refusal of Belgian authorities as disproportionate in view of the status of European citizen[707].

The Court also referred to the status of European citizen when it rejected the exception of inadmissibility raised by United Kingdom in the case of a child who obtained the Irish citizenship by birth on the territory of Northern Ireland (according to the Irish law) and who claimed the right to residence in the United Kingdom (in Wales); the United Kingdom held that there was no movement on the territory of another State[708].

UK held also that the movement to Northern Ireland of this Chinese citizen, in order to obtain the Irish citizenship of her child, was an abuse of right. The Court reaffirmed that even if that was the purpose followed by the

---

[706] Case Micheletti, nr.C-179/98, decision of 11 November, 1999, Rec., p.1, 7955.
[707] Case Garcia Avello, nr. C-148/02, decision of 2 October 2003, Rec., p.1, 11613.
[708] Case Zhu and Chen, nr. 200/02, decision of 19 October 2004, Rec., p.1, 9925.

person concerned, a member State cannot restrain the effects of the citizenship granted by another member State through an additional condition for the exercise of fundamental freedoms granted by a treaty.

In other cases, the Court referred to the status of European citizen with a view to give a wider interpretation to the principle of equal treatment between citizens of a member State and Union's citizens, with regard to some social benefits: for instance, granting an allocation of education to the child of a woman who lost the status of migrant worker; granting the minimum income to a student; granting a credit for education to a student; equality in the field of fiscal law; the right to a name[709].

The Court also interpreted provisions of the secondary law[710] concerning the rights of Union's citizens and of members of their families to freely circulate and take residence on the territory of member States so that these rights produce useful effects. Thus, the Court considered that a regulation of a member State requesting that a citizen of a third State, husband of a citizen of the Union and residing in a member State, had a legal right of residence in another member State before arrival, in order to benefit of the provisions of the Directive 2004/38/CE of the Parliament and the Council of the Union of 29 April 2004, was contrary to the Directive. The Court decided that the right to residence was granted according to the Directive irrespective of the way that person arrived in the respective State[711].

In another case, concerning the right to leave the territory of a member State by one of its nationals, which was refused to him because he was subject to expulsion and to readmission in accordance with a bilateral agreement, the Court affirmed that the status of a European citizen is the „fundamental status" of citizens of member States and their right to free movement excludes limitation on the basis of internal reasons only[712]. The Court also gave preference to the law of the State of residence over that of the State of citizenship, with reference to the Union's citizenship, thus recognizing what could be called as a kind of citizenship of residence, moving away from the traditional conception of the personal status which follows a citizen wherever he could find himself[713].

The European Court was called recently to take a stand in a series of new cases, concerning mainly effects of the status of the European Union's citizen, which marked new developments with regard to the scope of effects of the European citizenship, repeatedly considered by the Court as the „fundamental status" of citizens of a member State.

The best known of these decisions concerns the case Zambrano[714] and was adopted in 2011 by the Grand Chamber. In this case, two children of a couple of Columbian citizens, established in Belgium, obtained the Belgian citizenship as an effect of the Belgian law in force when they were born (because otherwise they would have become stateless). Their father, Ruiz Zambrano, contested the repeated refusal of Belgian authorities to grant him unemployment assistance, motivated by his situation of illegal residence. The Court had to consider whether the petitioner was entitled to avail himself of the Belgian citizenship of his children, taking into account that he lived on the territory of the respective State and never exercised the right to free circulation on the territory of a member State, in order to exercise rights deriving from it (the right to take residence, to a work permit and others). The Court ascertained that the two children were citizens of the Union, which represented their fundamental status and that, consequently, article 20 of the Treaty on the functioning of the Union (which enounces the rights of European citizens) „opposes to national measures which would have as effect to deprive European citizens of essential rights granted by their status of citizens of the Union". Consequently, the refusal of the right to residence of the parents Zambrano would have as effect to constrain the two children, Belgian citizens, to leave the territory of the Union with their parents, thus depriving them of the rights deriving from their status as Union's citizens.

In a rather different case, the Court refused to a citizen of Jamaica the right to residence on grounds of family reunification, availing himself of the British citizenship of his wife, Shirley McCarthy. The Court considered the fact that the person concerned, S. McCarthy, resided constantly in the member State she is a citizen thereof and did not exercise the right to circulate, retaining that the elements of this case have no connection with the situations provided in the law of the Union. As a difference with the Zambrano case, the Court notes that the rights of the Union's citizen, S. McCarthy, are in no way affected, as she is not obliged to leave the territory of the State she is the citizen thereof. She cannot avail herself of her rights to request a right of residence for her husband who is a citizen of a State who is not a member of the Union[715].

---

[709] Case Forster, nr C-158/08, decision of 18 November 2008; other cases cited by Jean-Denis Mouton, Reflexions sur la nature de l'Union Européenne à partir de l'affaire Rottmann, Revue Générale de Droit International Public, tome CXIV, 2010, p. 268.
[710] Taking into account the Directive 2004/38/CE of 29 April 2004, JOCE nr. L 158 of 30 April 2004.
[711] Case Metock and others, nr. C-127/08, decision of 25 July 2008.
[712] Case Jipa, nr. C-33/07, decision of 10 July 2008.
[713] Case Grunkin, nr. C-353/06, decision of 14 October 2008.
[714] Decision of 8 March 2011, case Gerardo Ruiz Zambrano, C-34/09.
[715] Decision of 5 May 2011, case Shirley MacCarthy, C-434/09.

In a similar case, where persons of Turkish, Nigerian, Sri Lankan, Kosovar and Serbian citizenships availed themselves of the right to remain with the Austrian husband/wife or to take residence in Austria as descendants of parents who became Austrian citizens, the Court tried to clarify its decisions in the cases Zambrano and McCarthy. The Court pointed out the criterion applied, namely the fact that a citizen of the Union was obliged to leave not only the territory of the State of origin, but the entire territory of the Union. At the same time, the Court affirmed that petitioners can found their pretentions on fundamental rights provided for in article 7 of the Charter of fundamental rights (concerning the right to respect for private and family life)[716], that is not on rights related to European citizenship. It is maintained that by this the Court pursued to close the door open by the decision given in the Zambrano case[717].

In other decisions, the Court derived some effects of the European citizenship in the field of occupational activities or of the application of other internal regulations, including with reference to the public order, which could affect the freedom of circulation of European citizens. For instance, in the case of an activity of air transport of passengers by a dirigible with hot air performed by a German operator over the territory of Austria, the Court resorted to the conception of fundamental rights, in particular to the principle of non-discrimination with regard to citizens of the Union. The Court retained that article 18 of the Treaty on the functioning of the Union opposes to a regulation of a member State, which would pretend that a resident in another member State having a license for such activity, has also a residence or a social central office in a second State, that is that such a regulation would be contrary to the norms of the Union[718].

In a similar case, the Court retained that a fiscal exemption for real estate business in favour of Greek citizens, of persons of Greek origin and of those having their permanent residence on the territory of Greece, when purchasing their first residences on the territory of this State, was contrary to the norms of free circulation of workers which exercise a professional activity, as well as to the norms on European citizenship[719].

The Court also applied the norms on European citizenship regarding attempts to justify restrictions to the freedom of circulation based on public order of a member State, regarding the right of a citizen to leave the territory of a State in the exercise of this right. In a first case, the Court considered that the Union's law does not oppose that an internal law gives to an authority the right to forbid to a citizen the right to leave the country, because he did not pay off a debt to a society he is the manager thereof, under a double condition: to respond to a real threat for an important interest of the society and to ensure that the objective pursued is only of an economic order. The Court found that the measure adopted had an automatic character and the two conditions were not respected, but the evaluation was of the competence of the national judge[720].

In a second case, the Court specified that the status of a European citizen of a person resident in Bulgaria, who was condemned in Serbia for drug trafficking and executed the punishment, gave him the right to leave the Bulgarian territory and that restrictions imposed by the Bulgarian law to the right of citizens to leave the country were contrary to EU norms. The Court relied on the provisions of the Directive 2004/38/CE of the Parliament and the Council concerning the right of citizens of the Union and of members of their families to freely circulate and take residence on the territory of member States and on article 21 of the Treaty on the functioning of the Union concerning the European citizenship[721].

Therefore, there is consistent jurisprudence of the European Court of Justice regarding European citizenship, in the sense of protecting the rights entailed to it in relation to any national competences with regard to the rights of national citizens or of other citizens of the Union.

SECTION 2 - EVALUATION of the DECISION in the CASE ROTTMANN

Regarding the case Rottmann, member States held that a control by the Court on the right to withdraw a citizenship obtained fraudulently would affect the sovereignty of member States as it results from article 17.1 of TEC, which became article 20.1 of TFEU, according to which is citizen of the Union every person who has the nationality (term used to designate national citizenship) of a member State; this text takes up that of article 9 of the Treaty of the Union.

---

[716] Decision of 15 November 2011, cases Murat Dereci and others reunited, C-256/11.
[717] Denis Simon, Cour de Justice et Tribunaux de l'Union Européenne, in AFDI, 2011, p. 694.
[718] Decision of 25 January 2011, case Michael Neukirchinger, C-382/08).
[719] Decision of 20 January 2011, case Commission v. Greece, C-155/09.
[720] Decision of 17 November 2011, case Petar Aladzhov v. Bulgaria, C-434/10.
[721] Decision of 17 November 2011, case Hristo Gaydarov v. Bulgaria, C-430-10.

Other documents were also invoked, among which the Declaration nr. 2 concerning the citizenship of a member State, annexed to the Treaty instituting the European Union of 1993, according to which..." the problem to know whether a person has the citizenship of one or the other of member States is regulated only with reference to the national law of the State concerned" and the repeated declarations of the United Kingdom concerning persons who will be considered as having the quality of its citizens under the community law[722].

In spite of this, while accepting that the granting and the withdrawal of citizenship are not regulated by the Union's law, but by the national law of member States, the Advocate-general of the Court maintained that the entirety of rights and obligations related to European citizenship cannot be limited in an unjustified manner by national citizenship, and that the conditions of granting and of withdrawing the citizenship have to be compatible with the law of the Union, that is that the exercise of the rights deriving from the citizenship of the Union are under the control of the law of the Union.

Accepting that the withdrawal of a citizenship obtained by fraudulent maneuvers corresponds to a general interest and is in conformity with international law, but ascertaining that the measure taken leads not only to the loss of the national citizenship, but also to losing the citizenship of the Union, the Court proceeded to a control of the proportionality of adopting this measure in view of its consequences on the situation of the person concerned from the point of view of the Union's law.

With regard to the State which granted the citizenship by naturalization, the Court considered necessary to check whether the loss of the rights of a citizen of the Union is justified, taking into account the seriousness of the offence, the time elapsed between the granting of citizenship and the decision of withdrawal and the possibility to re-acquire the citizenship of origin. If the respective State is not obliged to refrain from withdrawing the citizenship, the principle of proportionality compels it to give to the respective person reasonable time to re-acquire the citizenship of the State of origin. For the State of origin, the principle of proportionality would imply an obligation to interpret its national regulation to avoid the loss of the citizenship of the Union.

In substance, the Court affirms, through the application of the principle of proportionality, the right of the Union to control the application of the laws on granting and loosing citizenship, to avoid cases of statelessness, which lead to the loss of the European citizenship. Moreover, resorting sometimes also to invoke the principle of non-discrimination, the Court affirmed that by laws and other internal measures (concerning either the conditioning of the exercise of some professions by persons residing in another member State, or by expelling a parent, which would lead to a situation where children who are European citizens have to leave the territory of a member State, or by restraining the right to circulate in another member State relying on internal grounds concerning the public order, or by granting fiscal facilities only to persons of a certain ethnic origin), member States cannot apply restrictions to rights provided for by the Union's law, deriving from the right of every European citizen to free circulation and residence on the territory of each member State.

Some authors qualified European citizenship as an interstate citizenship, because the most important of its specific rights are exercised by citizens of a member State on the territories of other member States, giving expression to the trend to ensure equal treatment with their own citizens[723]. In its conclusions in the case Rottmann, the Advocate-general advanced the theses of emancipation of the European citizenship from the national one, as a legal and political status which manifests itself beyond the national community, in another geographic and political space and which forms the basis of a new political space.

The Advocate - general uses two notions as being completely different-citizenship for the relationships within the European Union and nationality for the legal and political relationship with a member State - in order to create the impression that the European citizenship would be independent and separate from the national one. As it is known, the two notions are used in some East-European States to designate two different realities: the citizenship as the legal and political relationship with the State, and the nationality to designate a different ethnic or minority group, which has its origin in the movement of nationalities of the 19th century.

The Treaty of the functioning of the Union (article 18 and the following) uses the notion of citizenship always with regard to the Union, while regarding member States that of nationality is mostly used, although there are also references to the „national citizenship" when it is placed in parallel with the European citizenship (article 20, former 17). It is our opinion that the two notions should not be used for the purpose of separating the European citizenship artificially from the national one and present them as independent and separate, which is against the explicit provisions of treaties, while of course underlining the specificity of the European citizenship and protecting the rights and freedoms it entails.

---

[722] Documents annexed to Treaties of the Union, mentioned by J. D. Mouton, art. cit., pp. 266-267.

[723] Christoph Schoenberger, European Citizenship as Federal Citizenship. Citizenship Lessons of Comparative Federalism, in Revue Européenne de Droit Public, vol. 19, nr. 1, p. 61.

In the conclusion of its Decision, the European Court of Justice is not declaring that the national norms on granting and withdrawing citizenship would become in a way part of the law of the Union, but submits the decisions of application of such norms to its control of proportionality. It is rightly estimated that this decision of the Court represents in fact more than a control of the application of the national law in this field[724].

The Decision of the Court should be analyzed first in the light of the provisions of the Union's treaties. According to these treaties, the Union respects the national identity of member States, inherent to their fundamental political and constitutional structures (article 4.2 of the Treaty of the Union); obviously, granting the status of a member of the national community represents an essential element of that identity. The Court itself reaffirmed this principle in several decisions (case United Kingdom v. Eurojust, case UGT-Rioja and case UTECA[725]). In the case Rottmann the Court reaffirms the competence of member States in the field of citizenship, but confirms its previous jurisprudence concerning the exercise of this competence with the observance of the Union's law. It is a Decision which tries to conciliate the two trends: to protect all the consequences of the status of European citizenship and at the same time to respect the national identity of member States.

Nevertheless, significant differences have to be noted between this case and the previous and subsequent ones: if in those other cases the concern was to protect some rights deriving from the status of European citizen (the rights to circulation, to residence), in this case the issue was the mere granting and withdrawing the national citizenship, which calls in question the exercise of the right of the State member to decide in this field. Considering this decision of the Court, if in future a member State would be in the situation to withdraw the citizenship granted to a person, for reasons provided for in its law, it should be sure that the person does not become stateless and thus loses the European citizenship.

Moreover, a State which examines a request of naturalization of a person coming from a State which does not accept double citizenship should ensure that by its refusal to grant citizenship a case of statelessness is not created. In cases concerning children and adoptions one can have in mind much more other hypothesis which could lead to statelessness. Such differences result from differences between national laws of different States on accepting or forbidding double citizenship, which is a field where the Union is not yet proposing to achieve legislative uniformization.

Consequently, if a person becomes a citizen of the Union because he/she is or becomes a citizen of a member State, this person cannot lose the European citizenship (becoming stateless) and its effects under the law of the Union; member States cannot take measures which would affect this status, although their laws on the subject matter are accepted as expression of their national identity. The European citizenship would this way acquire a certain autonomy from the national citizenship, although it has its origin in decisions taken within the national legal system of a member State.

* * *

Obviously, the debate on this issue will go on; it is probably necessary to adopt common rules at the EU level which consider different specific situations, in order to avoid cases of statelessness and to protect the status of European citizen once obtained, and without affecting competences of member States in the field of citizenship.

International existing instruments - the 1961 Convention on the reduction of cases of statelessness, concluded within the United Nations and the European Convention on citizenship of 1967 concluded within the Council of Europe - do not entirely respond to these preoccupations. The reaction of constitutional courts of member States is also expected. A law was adopted recently in Germany according to which modifications in the field of family law, established by secondary acts of the EU institutions, will be in force only after their ratification by the German Parliament.

As several analysts affirm, the European citizenship is a new institution which is certainly open to developments; the European Court and national institutions were confronted with some practical aspects; others will obviously appear, because European citizenship is closely related to the reality of European integration through the freedoms of movement and of residence and it has effects on other human rights and fundamental freedoms and on other institutions of the Union's law.

---

[724] J. D. Mouton, art. cit., pp. 273-274.
[725] Cases mentioned by J. D. Mouton, art. cit., p. 277

SOMMAIRE

Le but de ce livre est de rassembler des essais sur des thèmes relevant des droits de l'homme, écrits pendant les dix dernières années, revus et mis à jour, à la lumière des évolutions et des plus récents documents internationaux. Ils reflètent le fait que les droits de l'homme sont un sujet vivant, qui reflète les besoins humains en évolution constante, le dynamisme de la société qui détermine le développement des normes du droit international sur la protection des droits de l'homme dans divers domaines.

L'examen de l'évolution des normes du droit international dans ses divers chapitres soulève le problème de l'unité du droit international: est-ce que cette unité est préservée? N'y a-t-il pas le danger de fragmentation du droit international, avec tous les risques pour sa cohérence et sa continuité?

On a déjà noté la tendance à adopter des normes spécifiques de droit international dans divers domaines des relations internationales; divers chapitres du droit international sont appelés droit des traités, droit de la mer, droit diplomatique et consulaire et autres.

Notre analyse prouve que les traits généraux du droit international-les sources, les principes, la responsabilité pour des actes illicites-sont confirmés par l'évolution du droit international dans le domaine des droits de l'homme; les chapitres que nous présentons démontrent aussi l'unité et l'indivisibilité des droits de l'homme en tant que chapitre du droit international public.

La première partie est dédiée à des questions d'ordre général concernant l'impact des droits de l'homme dans l'évolution d'importants domaines du droit international: le droit humanitaire, la protection de l'environnement, la responsabilité des Etats, les normes impératives. Un certain nombre de normes fondamentales des droits de l'homme ont été graduellement reconnues comme normes impératives, y compris par la Cour Internationale de Justice, ce qui a consolidé cette institution dans le tableau général du droit international. Reconnu à l'origine uniquement par rapport aux traités qui se proposeraient de déroger aux normes impératives, le concept de jus cogens s'est étendu aux actes unilatéraux destinés à produire des effets juridiques, ainsi qu'aux réserves aux traités multilatéraux visant des normes impératives et aux coutumes locales qui se voudraient dérogatoires.

Un chapitre est consacré aux normes impératives et à leur impact sur d'autres institutions du droit international. L'institution des réserves aux traités multilatéraux, qui a fait l'objet d'une nouvelle codification de la part de la Commission du droit international, a également subie l'impact des droits de l'homme conduisant à une présomption de séparabilité des réserves contraires à des dispositions concernant l'objet et le but des traités sur les droits de l'homme; un chapitre essaie d'analyser cette proposition à la lumière de la pratique courante en la matière.

Dans le même ordre d'idées, on a noté avec beaucoup d'intérêt le développement du concept des droits fondamentaux de l'homme, qui est de plus en plus accepté et appliqué dans divers ordres juridiques-international, régionaux et nationaux-et qui devient l'élément de contact, pour quoi pas de convergence et de coordination entre ces systèmes; un chapitre est dédié à ce problème, compte tenu des développements dans l'Union Européenne et dans la jurisprudence internationale. Si traditionnellement on estimait que la responsabilité pour le respect des droits de l'homme revenait uniquement aux Etats, graduellement on a reconnu que le respect des droits de l'homme n'était pas exclusivement un rapport entre l'individu et l'Etat et que d'autres acteurs peuvent y être impliqués. Il s'agit d'autres individus et surtout de compagnies multinationales, ayant la nationalité d'autres Etats, ce qui soulève des questions plus complexes. On a examiné récemment la responsabilité des compagnies multinationales pour le respect des droits de l'homme et le Conseil des Droits de l'Homme des Nations Unies a adopté des principes et des orientations pour les Etats et les compagnies, afin d'assurer que le respect des droits de l'homme soit intégré dans leurs projets économiques dans d'autres pays.

Toujours au sujet de la responsabilité des Etats pour des actes illicites, la codification des normes dans ce domaine entreprise par la Commission du Droit International reflète aussi l'évolution des normes concernant le respect des droits de l'homme, consacrant l'interdiction d'invoquer de faits visant à exclure la responsabilité et d'appliquer des contre-mesures en violation des droits de l'homme, des normes du droit humanitaire ou des normes impératives.

De même, la codification des normes sur la protection diplomatique a conduit à reconsidérer la responsabilité internationale des Etats pour les dommages causés aux étrangers. Une décision récente de la Cour Internationale de Justice, qui est examinée dans ce contexte, fonde cette responsabilité sur les instruments internationaux et régionaux concernant les droits de l'homme et accorde à l'individu victime des violations une compensation matérielle et immatérielle.

Dans *la deuxième partie*, l'objectif poursuivi est d'examiner certains aspects concernant la protection des droits de l'homme dans leur connexion avec les problèmes de la sécurité internationale. Tout d'abord, il s'agit des responsabilités des Etats et de la communauté internationale pour prévenir et sanctionner les violations graves des droits de l'homme, préoccupation internationale déterminée par les crimes graves de génocide, d'épuration ethnique et autres perpétrés pendant la dernière décennie du vingtième siècle en Afrique et en Europe du Sud-Est. Dans un premier chapitre on analyse le concept de la responsabilité de protéger, avec ce qu'on lui assigne comme contenu dans le cadre des Nations Unies, au sujet des responsabilités des Etats et de la communauté internationale.

A partir d'une conception étendue sur la sécurité, comprenant non seulement les aspects militaires et politiques, mais aussi les composantes économique, sociétale et écologique, on examine ensuite les conceptions et la pratique concernant la sécurité démocratique et la sécurité humaine selon lesquelles le respect des principes démocratiques et la sécurité de l'homme fondée sur le respect des droits et libertés fondamentaux pour tous sont de nature à offrir un meilleur climat pour la sécurité des Etats et la sécurité internationale.

En étroite connexion avec la promotion de la sécurité et le respect des droits de l'homme, nous envisageons aussi l'activité dans le domaine de la justice pénale internationale qui, dans certaines régions du monde, s'est attachée à juger les plus graves violations des droits de l'homme-les crimes contre l'humanité, les crimes de guerre, le génocide. Il s'agit de tribunaux de type différent, crées pour régler des situations différentes et par des instruments juridiques divers, mais qui ont tous pour finalité de rendre justice et de donner une réparation aux victimes de ces violations, ainsi que de prévenir des violations similaires.

La troisième partie est dédiée à des questions concernant l'interdiction de la discrimination raciale, tout d'abord la définition, puis les approches et les tendances, compte tenu du fait que la discrimination raciale dans ses formes classiques est dépassée, car il est établi que les hommes appartiennent tous à la même espèce, tout en continuant sous d'autres formes et que la discrimination fondée sur l'origine ethnique est la plus répandue, alors que les différences culturelles sont à présent la nouvelle justification pour ce type de discrimination.

L'attention est ensuite portée sur la discrimination structurelle, ayant en vue ses causes historiques, sociétales et traditionnelles, et ses effets pernicieux sur des générations de groupes vulnérables (les femmes, les groupes auxquels on attribue une autre race, les peuples autochtones) ; il est important de comprendre les causes profondes et les remèdes appropriés de cette discrimination, car la sanction des faits individuels de discrimination ne suffit pas ; des mesures d'ordre économique et sociale sont nécessaires.

Ceci nous conduit vers un autre chapitre, qui concerne les mesures spéciales en tant que moyens pour promouvoir l'égalité des droits; de telles mesures, appelées aussi action affirmative, sont destinées à améliorer la situation des groups et des personnes désavantagés; la nature et la justification de telles mesures et leur relation avec la définition de la discrimination sont examinées, de même que les normes qui exigent qu'elles soient adoptées et les conditions à remplir. De telles mesures doivent répondre aux circonstances concernant la situation des individus et des groupes concernés, doivent être proportionnelles à l'objectif poursuivi et être temporaires pour qu'elles ne créent des différences de traitement inacceptables et ne deviennent elles-mêmes discriminatoires.

Un dernier chapitre dans cette partie se réfère au discours de haine raciale en rapport avec la liberté d'expression et d'information, question controversée dans la doctrine juridique et dans la pratique. La liberté d'expression et la liberté d'être à l'abri de la haine raciale sont les deux des valeurs protégées par les droits de l'homme; encore faut-il définir correctement le discours de haine raciale et l'évaluer dans le contexte social, afin de protéger les personnes et les groupes qui en sont souvent les victimes, sans porter atteinte à la liberté d'expression et d'information qui est indispensable dans une société démocratique.

La quatrième partie traite de la diversité des cultures et des langues dans le monde, vu l'attention qui est portée à la protection de la diversité devant le processus de la mondialisation. Le premier chapitre est dédié à la diversité culturelle en tant que valeur protégée et en tant qu'expression de la promotion des droits de l'homme, car la culture est un élément essentiel de l'identité des personnes, des communautés et des peuples. La culture est définie dans son sens le plus large, comprenant la création humaine sous toutes ses formes, les traditions et le mode de vie des personnes et des groupes.

Le droit de l'homme de jouir de sa culture, individuellement ou en communauté avec les membres du groupe dont il fait partie, ainsi que d'avoir accès à la culture, sont reconnus; il y a un lien étroit entre la culture et les droits de l'homme, entre les droits culturels et les autres droits de l'homme, car ils ont tous une dimension culturelle; le respect de la diversité culturelle s'impose en tant que conséquence de l'exercice de ces droits. Enfin, la protection de la diversité culturelle est examinée en termes de droits et d'obligations pour les Etats, les individus et les communautés. Il ne s'agit pas de droits collectifs et la norme principale qui s'impose est la liberté de choix de chaque personne en ce qui concerne la culture qu'elle pratique et la communauté culturelle à laquelle elle adhère.

Le chapitre suivant se réfère à la diversité linguistique dans le monde et aux langues en danger de disparaître. Les langues parlées par différent parties de la population sont très importantes en tant que véhicule de la culture et de l'éducation, une condition-même pour l'exercice de beaucoup de droits politiques. Les droits linguistiques font partie intégrante des droits de l'homme; ils incluent le droits d'utiliser la langue maternelle en privé et en public, ainsi que dans la société, compte tenu de la situation du groupe des locuteurs. Cependant, la plupart des langues encore parlées sont vulnérables ou en danger d'extinction, à cause de l'émigration des locuteurs, de la pression des langues majoritaires ou dominantes et bien sur des politiques discriminatoires. Sur la base des rapports de l'UNESCO on présente la situation de ces langues ainsi que les efforts qui sont entrepris dans diverses parties du monde pour protéger et pour revigorer certaines de ces langues.

Une conséquence directe de ces évolutions est le multiculturalisme, qui définit à la fois la situation de la plupart des Etats du monde et une politique d'Etat qui promeut la diversité culturelle et linguistique. Puisque la culture représente le trait fondamental de l'identité et de la personnalité des individus et des communautés qu'ils forment, le multiculturalisme apparaît comme la seule politique raisonnable car la plupart des Etats sont multiethniques et multiculturels.

La cinquième partie présente des évolutions survenues au sujet de la protection de certains droits économiques et sociaux, sous le générique des droits à une vie décente. Deux chapitres sont consacrés à la relation entre la protection de l'environnement et les changements climatiques d'une part et le respect des droits de l'homme de l'autre. Beaucoup de documents internationaux continent des normes sur la protection de l'environnement dans ses composantes et proclame le droit de l'homme à un environnement sain.

Une pratique internationale consistante s'est établie au niveau des juridictions internationales et des organes de surveillance créés par des traités sur les droits de l'homme sur la protection de certains droits de l'homme (surtout les droits à la vie, à la santé, au logement, à la vie privée et de famille) à la suite de dommages graves causés à l'environnement. Sur la base de cette évolution on peut essayer d'envisager les responsabilités dans le domaine de l'environnement afin d'assurer la protection des droits de l'homme.

Un important débat a lieu dans divers forums internationaux sur les changements climatiques qui peuvent affecter les droits de l'homme, la vie sur la planète. On essaye de voir quelles en sont les causes profondes, comment les prévenir et atténuer leurs effets, comment s'y adapter et quelles mesures doit-on prendre pour renverser la tendance au réchauffement de la planète. Des engagements ont été pris concernant la réduction de l'utilisation des combustibles fossiles et d'autres sont envisagés à la suite de la conférence de Paris de décembre 2015. Il s'agit en somme du droit de l'homme à un climat qui ne porte pas atteinte à ses droits fondamentaux à la vie, à la santé, au logement et autres.

Deux autres chapitres sont dédiés au droit à la nourriture et au droit à l'eau et aux installations sanitaires. Si le droit à la nourriture adéquate est consacré dans les traités internationaux en tant que droit économique et social, son respect n'est pas assuré dans beaucoup de pays et il y a en permanence une crise alimentaire qui frappe les pays sous-développés à cause des phénomènes climatiques, du manque d'investissements et de l'évolution des marchés internationaux des produits agricoles. La quantité de la nourriture produite dans le monde est suffisante pour couvrir tous les besoins du monde, mais elle est répartie d'une manière inégale; de plus, des terres fertiles sont de plus en plus détournées de la production agricole vers des plantes utilisées dans les industries. Là-aussi il faut voir quelles sont les responsabilités des Etats et de la communauté internationale et les mesures à prendre pour que ce droit soit respecté partout dans le monde.

Quant au droit à l'eau et aux installations sanitaires, qui est prévu dans certains traités régionaux et internationaux sur les droits de l'homme, mais est souvent déduit des droits à la vie et à la santé, il faut l'examiner surtout dans ses liens indivisibles avec d'autres droits de l'homme. On s'attache à voir quelles sont les responsabilités des Etats et de la communauté internationale, les droits et les obligations liés à la mise en œuvre de ce droit dans le monde.

La dernière partie se réfère à la protection des droits de l'homme en Europe, dans le but de présenter certaines particularités des évolutions dans ce domaine sur le continent. Un premier chapitre est dédié à la protection des droits de l'homme selon le droit de l'Union Européenne après le Traité de Lisbonne de 2007 en vigueur depuis 2009 (qui prévoit la ratification par l'Union de la Convention européenne des droits de l'homme de 1950). L'évolution de la protection des droits de l'homme dans les communautés européennes et puis dans l'Union, d'abord marquée par la jurisprudence de la Cour Européenne de Justice puis graduellement par des actes et des déclarations des institutions, a conduit depuis les principes constitutionnels reconnus par la Cour Européenne de Justice jusqu'à la Charte des droits fondamentaux de l'Union.

La Charte énonce des normes et des principes concernant tous les droits de l'homme-politiques, économiques, sociaux et culturels. De plus, le Traité de Lisbonne prévoit que l'Union adhère à la Convention européenne de 1950 concernant la protection des droits et libertés fondamentaux de l'homme. Les difficultés de respecter cet engagement plus de 6 ans après avoir été pris sont liées à la relation qui devrait s'établir entre le système de protection des droits de l'homme du Conseil de l'Europe, basé sur la protection des droits individuels et celui de l'Union Européenne, lié plutôt au processus d'intégration économique, et aux rapports futures entre les deux cours de justice.

Les arguments pour et contre sont examinés d'une manière critique, car il reste un problème délicat pour les 28 Etats membres de l'Union qui sont également membres du Conseil de l'Europe et parties à la Convention européenne, donc participants aux deux systèmes de protection entre lesquels il y a des différences.

Un autre chapitre est dédié à la Convention cadre sur la protection des minorités nationales, conclue en 1995, le premier document juridique à ce sujet sur le plan international. Afin de tenir compte de la situation spécifique de chaque groupe minoritaire, l'application de la Convention est fondée sur la flexibilité; chaque Etat partie déclare quels sont les minorités nationales sur son territoire qu'il entend protéger selon la Convention. L'objet de la protection est l'identité culturelle et linguistique des personnes appartenant à ces minorités.

Au sujet des langues parlées en Europe, qui fait l'objet d'un autre chapitre, la Charte pour la protection des langues régionales ou minoritaires, conclue en 1992, vise à la préservation et au développement des langues non-officielles traditionnellement parlées dans les Etats parties, qui sont moins répandues et sont en danger. La mise en œuvre de la Charte est fondée sur le même principe de flexibilité, chaque Etat parties déclarant les engagements qu'il prend à l'égard de chaque langue (énoncés par la Charte sur une échelle descendante, depuis les plus forts jusqu'aux plus faibles), à condition d'accepter 35 engagements dont au moins trois dans chacun des domaines sur l'éducation et la culture et un dans chacun des domaines concernant la justice, les autorités administratives, les média, les activités économiques et sociaux et les échanges transfrontaliers. La surveillance de la mise en œuvre des deux Conventions est assurée par des comités d'experts qui examinent les rapports périodiques des Etats parties, adressent des recommandations aux Etats et font rapport au Comité des ministres.

La tendance à protéger la citoyenneté de l'Union contre des actes des Etats membres qui pourraient y porter atteinte, reflétée dans les décisions de la Cour Européenne de Justice, soulève des problèmes qui sont examinés dans le dernier chapitre. Puisque la citoyenneté européenne découle de la citoyenneté accordée par un Etat membre selon sa législation, il faut voir si la relation entre les deux peut subir des changements à la suite de décisions adoptées par les Etats membres et surtout si les systèmes juridiques des Etats membres ne doivent rien faire qui pourrait porter atteinte à la citoyenneté européenne. En d'autres termes, il faut voir si la citoyenneté européenne peut être découplée de celle nationale et revêtir un caractère autonome, et quelles en seraient les conséquences pour les Etats membres.

www.ingramcontent.com/pod-product-compliance
Lightning Source LLC
Chambersburg PA
CBHW081143180526
45170CB00006B/1906